Mathematical Studies
Standard level
for the IB Diploma

**Caroline Meyrick
and Kwame Dwamena**

CAMBRIDGE
UNIVERSITY PRESS

CAMBRIDGE
UNIVERSITY PRESS

University Printing House, Cambridge CB2 8BS, United Kingdom

One Liberty Plaza, 20th Floor, New York, NY 10006, USA

477 Williamstown Road, Port Melbourne, VIC 3207, Australia

4843/24, 2nd Floor, Ansari Road, Daryaganj, Delhi – 110002, India

79 Anson Road, #06–04/06, Singapore 079906

Cambridge University Press is part of the University of Cambridge.

It furthers the University's mission by disseminating knowledge in the pursuit of education, learning and research at the highest international levels of excellence.

Information on this title: education.cambridge.org

First published 2013
20 19 18 17 16 15 14 13 12 11 10 9 8 7 6 5

Printed in the United Kingdom by Latimer Trend

A catalogue record for this publication is available from the British Library

ISBN 978-1-107-69140-7 Paperback

Cover image: © sharon zilberczvig / Alamy

Contents

Topic 3: Logic, sets and probability   232

Topic 4: Statistical applications   333

Topic 5: Geometry and trigonometry

Topic 6: Mathematical models

Sample examination papers

Two example examination papers written by the authors to support revision of this course are available online:
visit **education.cambridge.org/mathsstudiespaper1** and **education.cambridge.org/mathsstudiespaper2**

Introduction

This book has been written for students and teachers taking the Mathematical Studies SL course of the International Baccalaureate®. The syllabus is divided into seven topics and the book follows this structure, with each topic divided into chapters within that theme. The syllabus is designed to emphasise the practical mathematics that will enable students to continue to use their learning at university, in training courses, or when working, and the book encourages this. Explanations, worked examples and exercises are all firmly rooted in ideas that might be met in the course of normal experience.

As this book will be used by students from widely differing mathematical backgrounds, we have included fast forward and rewind indicators that mean it is not necessary to follow the order of the book exactly as it has been written; teachers will be able to integrate appropriate sections of the book with their own schemes of work:

 The rewind indicators will refer the reader back to another section in the book if any prerequisite information is required to complete a section.

 The fast forward indicators inform the reader where topics will be covered in more detail later in the book.

The concepts in Topic 6, Mathematical models, have been extended throughout the text. Problem solving is a vital skill, and confidence with this is achieved by students who realise that they can approach solutions from different perspectives. Worked examples aim to show that there might be several ways to find an answer: through drawing diagrams, working from first principles, through algebra or the use of technology.

It is important to understand that the Graphical Display Calculator (GDC) is fundamental to the course, and is allowed not only in both examinations, but also when students are working on their project. Where appropriate, all examples requiring the use of the GDC are illustrated by screen shots, and if students need additional support, the GDC chapter at the end of the book gives more detailed instruction of how to use their GDC. The calculators used in the writing of this book are the Casio *fx-9750G11* and the Texas TI-84 Plus Silver Edition. While many students might find they need to use slightly different key strokes from those that are given, the examples are close to those in the authors' experience of the many different versions of GDC that students have shown them.

How to use this book

Book structure

Each topic begins with an introduction that emphasises the place of that topic within mathematical history, practical experience, or with some information about internationally recognised mathematical people. It also lists any prior knowledge that is required, and any previous chapter that needs to be completed before this topic is started.

Each chapter of the book follows a pattern designed to be helpful to students from different national educational programmes, and familiar with different mathematical traditions. Like the topics, each chapter starts with an introduction that gives some context to the chapter content in terms of mathematical history, practical experience, or a historical person. There are also 'In this chapter you will learn' panels that list the learning objectives of the chapter.

The chapters contain numerous worked examples throughout. These are arranged with the formal written mathematics on the right-hand side (in blue font), and the thought processes or hints on the left-hand side in speech bubbles. Initially the worked examples can be followed using the ideas in the speech bubbles. For revision, the hints can be covered up, and the student can concentrate on the formal written mathematics that they will need in their examinations.

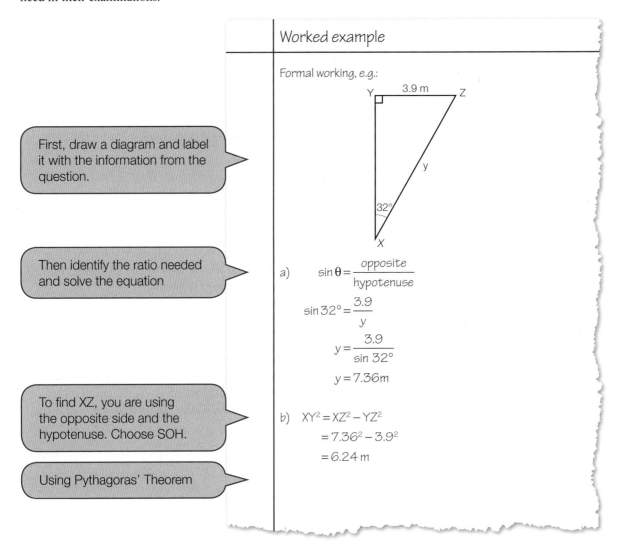

Worked example

Formal working, e.g.:

First, draw a diagram and label it with the information from the question.

Then identify the ratio needed and solve the equation

a) $\sin \theta = \dfrac{\text{opposite}}{\text{hypotenuse}}$

$\sin 32° = \dfrac{3.9}{y}$

$y = \dfrac{3.9}{\sin 32°}$

$y = 7.36\text{m}$

To find XZ, you are using the opposite side and the hypotenuse. Choose SOH.

b) $XY^2 = XZ^2 - YZ^2$

$= 7.36^2 - 3.9^2$

$= 6.24\text{ m}$

Using Pythagoras' Theorem

At the end of each sub-section of a chapter is an exercise. This allows the student to check their knowledge and understanding of the chapter and the methods learned so far. These are in the format of drill-like questions that act as a quick self-assessment of progress.

Each chapter finishes with summary list of what the student should know once they have completed the chapter. This can be tested using the Mixed Examination practice questions that follow. These include a selection of exam-style questions written by the authors in the style of IB examination questions, and some real exam questions taken from past IB Mathematical Studies papers.

The questions are designed to make sure that students understand the mathematics studied in that chapter and how to use it. For some questions, particularly in the latter half of the book, students might be expected to use concepts from more than one topic, which is a common theme for IB questions. It is very important that students have practised combining ideas and techniques before they attempt any past examination papers.

Supporting panels and icons

Within each chapter there are various support panels and icons to guide the student, or encourage them to look beyond their immediate studies.

Learning links

These are designed to link the course with more formal mathematical processes that might have been learned in the past. They **do not** have to be used because they are not on the syllabus. However, if the student wishes to see the connections between this syllabus and previous learning, the link is easy to follow.

Help with using the text

These are integrated throughout the book, often recalling the student's attention to a particular point in the text or a worked example, or reminding them of a general point of good mathematical practice.

These points allow students to easily go backwards or forwards to any section if they need reminders.

This book is based on a specific syllabus, but should not be seen solely as a guide to the final examinations. However, for all students it is reassuring to have common mistakes and misunderstandings pointed out, so that their examinations can be approached with confidence.

Icons linking in the wider IB Diploma ethos

The Theory of Knowledge is central to the IB Diploma. These panels aim to link questions met in the TOK course with ideas explored in the Mathematical Studies SL course.

These panels link to other subject areas providing cross-curricular support as well as links to wider applications of mathematics in the practical world.

Critical thinking is part of mathematics as it is a tool that can be used in many contexts and cultures. These panels highlight issues about the application of mathematics in the real world and to other subject areas. It also includes links to mathematical history, which places today's mathematics in context and shows the breadth and spread of mathematical ideas.

 The internal assessment

All Mathematical Studies students complete a project as part of their diploma course. It is worth 20% of their final mark, and needs to be given approximately 20% of the time allowed for an SL subject.

Throughout the book, some comments are made about ideas and techniques that may be useful in projects. There is also a chapter at the end of the book giving advice in more depth, concentrating in particular on the different assessment criteria, giving advice about how to make sure that these are understood and correctly interpreted.

Use of technology

The use of technology is encouraged on this course. This does not need to be restricted to the use of the GDC. Personal computers (PCs, Mac, Laptop, tablets etc.) can also reinforce and encourage understanding; this can be through using commercial geometric or statistical packages, as well as programmes that students already know, such as spreadsheets. There are also many websites and videos online that can be very helpful; though students should be cautious about trusting the site before using them.

Online material

There are two practice examination papers available online at

education.cambridge.org/mathsstudiespaper1

education.cambridge.org/mathsstudiespaper2

Paper 1 has fifteen questions, and each question is marked out of six. The paper takes 90 minutes, so students should aim to gain one mark a minute.

Paper 2 has six questions, and the mark for each question can vary depending on its length and complexity. The total time for the paper is 90 minutes, and the total marks are also 90, as in Paper 1. In paper 2, if a question is marked out of 15, the student should aim to complete it in fifteen minutes.

We hope you find the Mathematical Studies SL course both interesting and accessible. Mathematics is a unique combination of understanding and practice, and we have written the text and exercises to help you with both sides of the subject. If you can build on the knowledge you already have, you should be able to move forward with a useful background in mathematics that will be relevant in future studies and your workplace.

Kwame Dwamena

Caroline Meyrick

Acknowledgements

The authors and publishes are grateful for the permissions granted to reproduce materials in either the original or adapted form. While every effort has been made, it has not always been possible to identify the sources of all the materials used, or to trace all copyright holders. If any omissions are brought to our notice, we will be happy to include the appropriate acknowledgements on reprinting.

IB exam questions © International Baccalaureate Organization. We gratefully acknowledge permission to reproduce International Baccalaureate Organization intellectual property. This work has been developed independently from and is not endorsed by the International Baccalaureate (IB).

TI-83/TI-84 font material reproduced with permission of Texas Instruments Incorporated.

TI makes no warranty regarding the accuracy of the information presented in the respective materials, including the fitness for use for your intended purpose. Also, TI is under no obligation to update the information presented in these materials.

Casio fonts are reproduced with permission of Casio Electronics Company Ltd (to access downloadable Casio resources go to http://edu.casio.com/dl/).

Text

p2 Ada Lovelace quotation: 'Note G' from Ada Lovelace's translation and commentary of a 1842 document called Sketch of the Analytical Engine by L.F. Menabrea (information sourced from www.allonrobots .com/ada-lovelace.html); p194 Data: the consumption of softwood throughout the UK for 2000-2009 www.forestry.gov.uk/forestry, p195 Data: average pump price of fuel per litre in 194 countries in 2010 www.data.worldbank.org; p277 U.S. field production of crude oil between 1920 and 2010 U.S. Energy Information Administration (2012); p592 Extract from Simon Singh's book *Fermat's Last Theorem* Simon Singh, *Fermat's Last Theorem* (London: Fourth Estate, 1997); p592 Quote of a saying of mathematician Hugo Rossi Hugo Rossi, *Notices of the American Mathematical Society*, (Vol 43, Number 10, 1996); p613 Quote from Ian Stewart's book *Seventeen Equations that Changed the World* Ian Stewart, *Seventeen Equations that Changed the World (*Profile Books,2012); p232 1899 'Everything that can be invented has been invented' A misquote attributed to Charles Holland Duell, Commissioner of the US Patent Office, 1899; p232 1943 'only be a world market for maybe five computers' Commonly attributed to Thomas J. Watson, Chairman of International Business Machines (IBM), 1943; p232 Quote from Richard Brealey and Stewart Myers, *Principles of Corporate Finance* 1988 Richard Brealey and Stewart Myers, *Principles of Corporate Finance* (McGraw Hill,1988).

Images

We would like to thank the following for permission to reproduce images:

Cover: © sharonzilberczvig / Alamy

p1 mbortolino / iStock; p2 Tim Jenner / Shutterstock; p9 Wejp-Olsen, Werner /CartoonStock;p20 London Community Gospel Choir; p37 maggio07 / iStock;p46 GeorgiasKollidas / Shutterstock; p50 carterdayne / iStock;p54 PinkBadger / iStock;p65 Phillip Lange / Shutterstock; p88 Nicku / Shutterstock;p98 vblinov / Shutterstock; p110 ene / Shutterstock;p110 Bjorn Hoglund / Shutterstock;p112 X-rates.com; p116 Aaron Bacall /CartoonStock; p128 courtesy of Nissan Motors GB Ltd; p141 DamirK / iStock; p182 Marty Bucella / Cartoonstock; p183 http://hdl.loc.gov/loc.pnp/cph.3b11632 /Library of Congress; p206 bikeriderlondon / Shutterstock; p220 jennyt /Shutterstock; p222 visuelldesign / Shutterstock; p232 Brocreative / Shutterstock;

p233 © INTERFOTO / Alamy ; p233 mathisworks / iStock; p256 Nelson Minar /Sydney Powerhouse Museum; p265 S Harris / CartoonStock; p288 mikhailshiyanov / Shutterstock; p290 Arno van Dulmen /Shutterstock; p318 Pgiam / iStock; p333tLledo / Shutterstock; p333bhttp://commons.wikimedia.org/wiki/File:Cancer_smoking_ lung_cancer_correlation_from_NIH.png; p334 Bill Greenhead-Stik / CartoonStock; p335 bilwissedition Ltd. & Co. KG / Alamy; p371 SPL; p380 Christoff / Shutterstock; p395 dumayne /iStock; p409 Chinese Pythagorean theorem, from Joseph Needham's *Science and Civilization in China: Volume 3, Mathematics and the Sciences of the Heavens and the Earth*; p410 Pavila / Shutterstock; p440 Robert F Balazik /Shutterstock; p467 S Harris / CartoonStock; p477 Kotse /Shutterstock; p492 ardaguldogan /iStock; p524 Redshinestudio / Shutterstock; p536 s_oleg/Shutterstock; p539 sumak77 / iStock; p552 AKTS; p571 EpicStockMedia / iStock; p571 kolb_art / iStock; p572 Grafissimo / iStock; p572 Photos 12 / Alamy; p590 ZigaCamernik / Shutterstock; p596 McKevin / iStock; p613 The CAPN navigation software (www.thecapn.com); p626 RASimon / iStock.

1 Number and algebra

What have you done today? Did you:

- solve a puzzle?
- look at something on the internet?
- take some medication?
- use your cell phone?

What might you be doing in ten years' time? Do you think that you will be:

- working in a design office?
- using spreadsheets to analyse large amounts of data?
- involved in making financial or investment decisions?
- looking into the global logistics of moving goods and materials?

In all of the above activities, algorithms are used to calculate the most efficient way of solving a problem. An **algorithm** can be defined as *a detailed set of instructions that leads to a predictable result or a set of instructions that helps you to finish a task as efficiently as possible.*

The mathematical skills of manipulating numbers and using algebra provide a powerful tool in devising, understanding and applying algorithms.

Prior learning topics

It will be easier to study this topic if you:

- are comfortable with the four operations of arithmetic (addition, subtraction, multiplication, division)
- understand the **BIDMAS** order of operations (**B**rackets, **I**ndices, **D**ivision, **M**ultiplication, **A**ddition, **S**ubtraction)
- can use integers, decimals and fractions in calculations
- can recognise prime numbers, factors and multiples
- know some simple applications of ratio, percentage and proportion
- can identify intervals on the real number line
- are able to evaluate simple algebraic expressions by substitution
- are comfortable with basic manipulations of algebraic expressions such as factorisation, expansion and rearranging formulae
- understand how to use the inequalities $<, \leq, >, \geq$
- are familiar with commonly accepted world currencies such as the euro, United States dollar and Japanese yen.

Chapter 1 Number

In this chapter you will learn:

- about the different types of numbers
- how to make approximations
- about estimating and how to check solutions using your GDC
- how to express very small and very large numbers and perform operations with them
- about SI (Système International) units.

An Analytical Engine

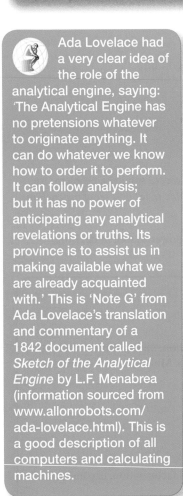

Ada Lovelace had a very clear idea of the role of the analytical engine, saying: 'The Analytical Engine has no pretensions whatever to originate anything. It can do whatever we know how to order it to perform. It can follow analysis; but it has no power of anticipating any analytical revelations or truths. Its province is to assist us in making available what we are already acquainted with.' This is 'Note G' from Ada Lovelace's translation and commentary of a 1842 document called *Sketch of the Analytical Engine* by L.F. Menabrea (information sourced from www.allonrobots.com/ada-lovelace.html). This is a good description of all computers and calculating machines.

Charles Babbage (1791–1871) is described in some histories as 'the father of computing'. A mathematician and inventor, he was looking for a method to improve the accuracy of mathematical tables. These lists of numbers included squares and square roots, logarithms and trigonometric ratios, and were used by engineers, navigators and anyone who needed to perform complex arithmetical calculations. The tables were notorious for their inaccuracy, so Babbage designed a machine to re-calculate the numbers mechanically. In 1822, the Royal Society approved his design, and the first 'difference engine' was built at the inventor's home in London.

Babbage went on to develop an improved machine, called an 'Analytical Engine', which is now seen as the first step towards modern computers. He worked on this machine with Ada Lovelace (1815–1852), who invented the punched cards that were used to 'programme' the machine. Lovelace is considered to be the first computer programmer.

1.1 Different types of numbers

The natural numbers, ℕ

The **natural numbers** (ℕ) are the counting numbers, the first numbers that people learn and use.

1, 2, 3, 4, 5, … are all counting numbers.

−1, −2, −3, … are negative numbers and therefore are **not** natural numbers.

1.5, 2.3, 6.7 are not whole numbers and therefore are **not** natural numbers.

When small children learn to count, they soon realise that '3' will always mean the same quantity, three, whether they are counting apples, sheep or chairs.

Natural numbers are also the numbers typically used for comparison. For example, you might say, 'I have read all seven Harry Potter books; the second and the seventh were my favourites.'

Natural numbers can be shown on a **number line**:

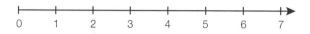

We can also write the natural numbers as follows:

$\mathbb{N} = \{0, 1, 2, 3, 4, 5, \ldots\}$, where $\mathbb{N}$ is the symbol for natural numbers.

The curly brackets { } enclose all the numbers represented by the symbol $\mathbb{N}$. These brackets signify that the natural numbers form a **set** (or collection).

 Sets and set notation are explained in Chapter 8.

The integers, $\mathbb{Z}$

Natural numbers can only be used for counting in one direction: left to right along the number line, starting from zero. It is often useful to be able to count down to below zero. This is where a larger set of numbers, called the 'integers', comes in.

The **integers** are defined as all whole numbers: positive, negative and zero.

-79, -2 and 10001 are all integers.

-9.99, $1\frac{1}{4}$ and 10001.4 have decimal or fractional parts and are therefore **not** integers.

Integers can also be shown on a number line:

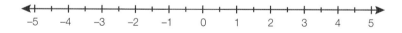

We can use set notation to write the integers, as we did for natural numbers:

$\mathbb{Z} = \{\ldots -3, -2, -1, 0, 1, 2, 3, 4, \ldots\}$, where $\mathbb{Z}$ is the symbol for integers.

$\mathbb{Z}^+$ is defined as the set of all positive whole numbers, or integers greater than zero.

$\mathbb{Z}^-$ is defined as the set of all negative whole numbers, or integers less than zero.

The place of zero among the natural numbers is a point of debate. Not all definitions of the natural numbers include zero. In this IB course, the natural numbers do include the number zero.

The number line is infinitely long and extends from negative infinity to positive infinity. The concept of **infinity** is very important to mathematicians, but it is difficult to define. Imagine a line, divide it in half, then divide in half again, and continue in this way. No matter how many times you divide the line in half, you can always divide it again. So you can do an 'infinite' number of divisions. The symbol for infinity is ∞.

The symbol $\mathbb{Z}$ comes from 'Zahlen', the German word for numbers.

The rational numbers, $\mathbb{Q}$

A **rational number** is a number that results when one integer is divided by another. Dividing one integer by another creates a **ratio**, which is where the term 'rational numbers' comes from.

If q is a rational number, then $q = \frac{a}{b}$, where a and b are both integers, with $b \neq 0$ (a is called the **numerator** and b is called the **denominator**).

$$-\frac{7}{2}, \frac{1}{5}, \frac{28}{9}, 5\frac{3}{4} \text{ are all rational numbers.}$$

hint

$\mathbb{Q}$ stands for **quotient**. A quotient is the result of a division.

Note that mixed numbers such as $5\frac{3}{4}$ are also rational numbers. This is true because you can rewrite them as **improper fractions**, e.g. $5\frac{3}{4} = \frac{23}{4}$.

Rational numbers are often written as decimals, which can make it less obvious that they are rational numbers. For example:

$$-3.5, 0.2, 3.111111111\ldots\text{are all rational numbers.}$$

hint

Remember that a mixed number is made up of a whole number and a fraction, e.g. $1\frac{2}{3}$. An improper fraction is a fraction where the numerator is larger than the denominator, e.g. $\frac{5}{4}$.

You can check by writing each as a fraction:

$-3.5 = -\frac{7}{2}$, so -3.5 is a rational number.

$0.2 = \frac{2}{10} = \frac{1}{5}$, so 0.2 is a rational number.

$3.111111111\ldots = \frac{28}{9}$, so $3.111111111\ldots$ is a rational number.

Numbers like $3.111111111\ldots$, where a digit (or group of digits) repeats forever, are called 'recurring decimals' and are often written with a dot above the number that repeats, e.g. $3.\dot{1}$. All recurring decimals are rational numbers.

hint

All integers are rational numbers too, e.g. $5 = \frac{5}{1}$ is a fraction with denominator 1.

Rational numbers can also be shown on a number line:

Worked example 1.1

There are an infinite number of fractions to choose from. A number line can help you make a correct choice.

Q. | Find a rational number between $\dfrac{1}{4}$ and $\dfrac{5}{8}$.

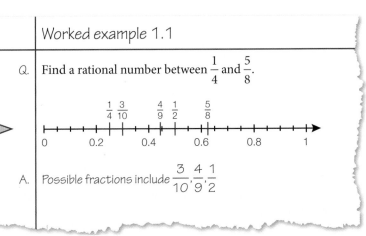

A. | Possible fractions include $\dfrac{3}{10}, \dfrac{4}{9}, \dfrac{1}{2}$

The irrational numbers

An **irrational number** is a number that **cannot** be written as a fraction. The decimal part of an irrational number has no limit to the number of digits it contains and does not show a repeating pattern.

A well-known example of an irrational number is π (pi). You know this as the ratio of the circumference of a circle to its diameter:
$\pi = 3.14159265\ldots$

Modern computers enable mathematicians to calculate the value of π to many millions of digits, and no repeats of groups of digits have been found!

Other irrational numbers include ϕ (the 'golden ratio') and the square roots of **prime numbers**:

$$\phi = 1.61803398874989484820\ldots$$

$$\sqrt{2} = 1.414213562373\ldots$$

$$\sqrt{7} = 2.6457513110645\ldots$$

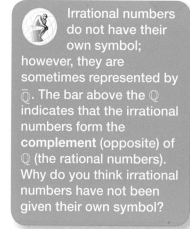
Irrational numbers do not have their own symbol; however, they are sometimes represented by $\bar{\mathbb{Q}}$. The bar above the $\mathbb{Q}$ indicates that the irrational numbers form the **complement** (opposite) of $\mathbb{Q}$ (the rational numbers). Why do you think irrational numbers have not been given their own symbol?

The real numbers, ℝ

The **real numbers** are all the numbers that can be represented on a number line.

They include the natural numbers, integers, rational numbers and irrational numbers.

It may be easier to think of the various types of real numbers in the form of a **Venn diagram**.

A Venn diagram uses shapes (usually circles) to illustrate mathematical ideas. Circles may overlap or lie inside each other. In the example below, ℕ is inside ℤ because all natural numbers are integers.

 You will learn about Venn diagrams in Chapter 8.

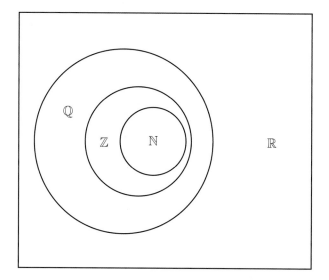

It can be proved that there are an infinite number of real numbers. Georg Cantor constructed the proof in 1874. It is a powerful proof, surprisingly simple, and worth reading about and understanding. The ideas behind the proof are very profound and have had an important influence on the work of mathematicians following Cantor.

exam tip

In this course, all the numbers you will encounter are real numbers.

Irrational numbers are included in the definition of real numbers. In the Venn diagram they are represented by the region **outside** the natural numbers, integers and rational numbers.

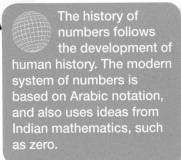

The history of numbers follows the development of human history. The modern system of numbers is based on Arabic notation, and also uses ideas from Indian mathematics, such as zero.

The cells have been filled in to show that:

- −2 is an integer, a rational number and a real number
- $\frac{3}{7}$ is a rational number and a real number
- $\sqrt{13}$ is an irrational number and a real number
- 3π is an irrational number and a real number
- 10 000 is a natural number, an integer, a rational number and a real number.

Do you think that numbers have always been in existence, waiting to be discovered, or are they an invention of mathematicians?

These are all integers; note that $2^3 = 8$.

Remember that −5 is also a rational number $\left(-\frac{5}{1}\right)$.

Worked example 1.2

Q. Mark each cell to indicate which number set(s) the number belongs to.

	−2	$\frac{3}{7}$	$\sqrt{13}$	3π	10 000
Irrational					
$\mathbb{N}$					
$\mathbb{Z}$					
$\mathbb{Q}$					
$\mathbb{R}$					

A.

	−2	$\frac{3}{7}$	$\sqrt{13}$	3π	10 000
Irrational			×	×	
$\mathbb{N}$					×
$\mathbb{Z}$	×				×
$\mathbb{Q}$	×	×			×
$\mathbb{R}$	×	×	×	×	×

Worked example 1.3

Q. Look at the list of numbers:

$$\sqrt{5}, -\frac{3}{7}, \pi, -5, 7, 2^3.$$

(a) Which numbers are integers?

(b) Which numbers are both rational and negative?

(c) Which numbers are not rational?

(d) Which numbers are not natural?

A. (a) $-5, 7, 2^3$

(b) $-\frac{3}{7}$ and -5

$\sqrt{5}$ cannot be written as a fraction, and as a decimal it does not have a limit or a recurring pattern; the same is true for π.

These are not counting numbers, so they are not natural.

continued . . .

(c) $\sqrt{5}$ and π

(d) $\sqrt{5}, -\dfrac{3}{7}, \pi, -5$

Exercise 1.1

1. Look at each of the following statements and decide whether it is true or false. If it is false, give the correct statement.

   (a) 2.4 is a rational number.

   (b) $6 + (-2)$ gives an answer that is a natural number.

   (c) $\sqrt{17}$ is a rational number.

   (d) 1.51 is an irrational number.

   (e) 5π is a real number.

   (f) An irrational number is never a real number.

   (g) If you add two integers, the answer will not be an integer.

   (h) If you divide one integer by another, the answer is a real number.

   Srinivasa Ramanujan was a mathematical genius. Born in 1887 near Madras in India, he was fascinated by numbers and made many significant contributions to the theory of numbers. He is also well known for his collaboration with the famous mathematician G. H. Hardy of the University of Cambridge.

2. Write down a number that is:

   (a) a real number and an integer

   (b) a rational number, but not an integer

   (c) a real number and an irrational number

   (d) a natural number that is also rational.

3. Copy the number line below, and put these numbers in the correct place on the number line:

   $$\dfrac{12}{13}, -\sqrt{3}, 3.1, -1 + \pi, -4.2, -4.25, \sqrt{13}$$

   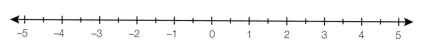

4. (a) Put the following numbers in ascending order:

   $$12, -5.\mathrm{i}, \sqrt{3}, \sqrt{2}, -2, 0, \dfrac{6}{7}, -2.5$$

   (b) Write down the natural numbers in the list.

(c) Write down the integers in the list.

(d) Write down the rational numbers in the list.

(e) Which numbers have you not written down? Why?

5. Look at each of the following statements, and use the given words to fill in the blanks, making a correct sentence.

rational, irrational, real, negative, natural, integer

(a) If you add two natural numbers, the answer is a(n) .... number.

(b) If you add two rational numbers, the answer can be a(n) .... number, a(n) .... (number) or a(n) .... number

(c) If you add a negative integer to another negative integer, the answer is a(n) ………………….. ………………

(d) If you add a natural number to an irrational number, the answer is a(n) ………………… number.

(e) If you add a natural number that is greater than 12 to an integer between −10 and zero, the answer is a(n) ………………..

6. (a) Find a rational number between $\dfrac{4}{5}$ and $1\dfrac{3}{4}$.

(b) Find a rational number between $2\dfrac{2}{3}$ and $3\dfrac{3}{4}$.

7. Look at the list of numbers below, and use it to answer the following questions:

43, 2, 21, 15, −6, 17, 6, −4, 13

(a) Write down the prime numbers.

(b) Write down the multiples of three.

(c) Write down the even numbers.

(d) Which number have you written for both (a) and (c)?

1.2 Approximation and estimation

Modern calculators and computers allow us to calculate with great precision. However, in everyday life most people use estimates and few people are comfortable with very large, very small, or very long numbers.

With the increasing use of calculators and computers, it has become more important to know how to estimate a rough answer and to 'round' the results obtained by technology so that we can use them sensibly.

There is a well-known saying about modern technologies: 'Garbage **in**, garbage **out**'. This means that you need to put sensible input into your calculator or computer, in order to be able to make sense of what you get as an output.

We also need to agree upon our methods of **rounding**; for example, if one shopkeeper always rounds her prices **down** to the nearest cent, while her rival always rounds his prices **up** to the nearest cent, what will be the result?

Your graphical display calculator (GDC) is a piece of modern technology that is fundamental to this course. You cannot achieve a good understanding of the material without it! It is important that you are able to:

• estimate a rough answer before using your GDC

• put information into the GDC accurately

• sensibly use the GDC's ability to work to nine decimal places.

It is very easy to accidentally press the wrong key on your GDC, which could lead to an incorrect answer. If you already have an estimate of what you think the answer will be, this can help you to identify if the answer your GDC gives you looks about right; if it is completely different to what you expected, perhaps you pressed a wrong key and need to enter the calculation again.

Approximation by rounding

Rounding is an idea that many people apply instinctively.

When someone asks you 'how long was that phone call?', you would usually not reply 'nine minutes and thirty-six seconds'. You would probably say 'about ten minutes', rounding your answer to the nearest minute. The 'nearest minute' is a **degree of accuracy**.

When asked to round a number, you will normally be given the degree of accuracy that you need. Some examples are:

• to the nearest yen

• to the nearest 10 cm

• to the nearest millimetre

• to the nearest hundred

• to one decimal place

• to three significant figures.

To round numbers you can use either a number line or the following rule:

- If the digit to the right of the digit you are rounding is less than five (<5), then the digit being rounded stays the same.

- If the digit to the right of the digit you are rounding is five or more (≥5), then the digit being rounded increases by one.

Remember the meaning of the following symbols:
< 'less than'
≥ 'greater than or equal to'
≈ 'approximately equal to'

Worked example 1.4

Q. Use the rule above to round the following numbers:

(a) 1056.68 yen to the nearest yen

(b) 546.21 cm to the nearest 10 cm

(c) 23.35 mm to the nearest mm

(d) 621 317 to the nearest 100.

Look at the last digit before the decimal point, 6. The digit to its right is also 6. As 6 > 5, we round the digit before the decimal point to 7.

A. (a) 1056|.68 yen ≈ 1057 yen

The digit we are rounding is 4, which is followed by 6. As 6 > 5 we round 4 up to 5.

(b) 54|6.21 ≈ 550 cm

The digit we are rounding is 3, and the digit following it (the first digit after the decimal point) is also 3. As 3 < 5 we leave the digit we are rounding unchanged.

(c) 23|.35 mm ≈ 23 mm

The digit we are rounding is 3, and it is followed by 1. As 1 < 5 the digit we are rounding is unchanged.

(d) 621 3|17 ≈ 621 300

In part (d) of Worked example 1.4, you need to replace the last two digits '1' and '7' by zeros in order to keep the number the correct size. The 3 represents 300, so 317 to the nearest 100 is 300, and therefore '1' and '7' must be replaced by '00'.

You may find it easier to visualise the rounding process using a number line. For example for part (c) above:

23.35 is closer to 23 than to 24, so 23.35 mm = 23 mm to the nearest mm.

1A Place order structure of numbers

You might find it useful to remember the 'place order' (or 'place value') of numbers when considering degrees of accuracy. It is also useful when making sure the rounded value is the same order of magnitude (size) as the original number (millions must remain millions and thousands must remain thousands, etc.).

1	0	0	0	0	0	0	.	0	0	0
millions	hundreds of thousands	tens of thousands	thousands	hundreds	tens	units		tenths	hundredths	thousandths

Exercise 1.2

1. (a) Tom is 168.5 cm tall. Give his height to the nearest centimetre.

    (b) A film lasts for one hour and forty-seven minutes.
        Round this time to the nearest five minutes.

    (c) There were 3241 people at a hockey match.
        Give the number to the nearest hundred.

    (d) A camera costs 219 AUD. Round this price to the nearest
        10 dollars.

    (e) The area of a field is 627.5 m². Give this area to the nearest
        square metre.

    (f) A sheep weighs 75.45 kg. Give the mass to the nearest kilogram.

2. Round these numbers to the nearest 10.

    (a) 49   (b) 204   (c) 319

    (d) 2153   (e) 20 456

3. Round these numbers to the nearest 100.

    (a) 346   (b) 2011   (c) 85

    (d) 67 863   (e) 708 452

4. Calculate the following values using your GDC.
    Give your answer to the nearest integer.

    (a) $\sqrt{4.56}$ (b) 3.17^3 (c) $15\sin 60°$ (d) $\pi \times 6^2$

Some exam questions may ask you to give your answer to a specified number of decimal places, so you need to know how to do this. **However**, remember that if a specific degree of accuracy has **not** been requested, you **must** give the answer to three significant figures (see the section on 'Significant figures' below).

Decimal places

Standard calculators can give you answers to several **decimal places** (**d.p.**). A GDC can give you answers to as many as nine decimal places!

For most practical purposes, nine decimal places is far too many figures, so you need to be able to round to a given number of decimal places.

To round a decimal number, you can use the decimal point as your first reference, and then use the number line, the '< or ≥ 5' rule, or your GDC to round up or down appropriately.

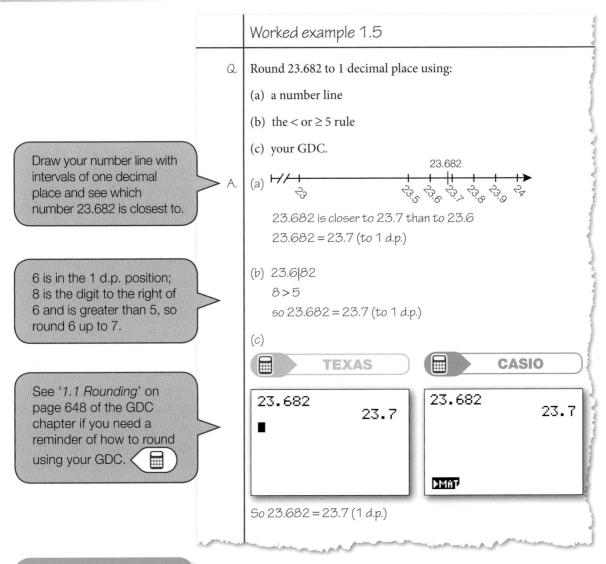

Worked example 1.5

Q. Round 23.682 to 1 decimal place using:

(a) a number line

(b) the < or ≥ 5 rule

(c) your GDC.

Draw your number line with intervals of one decimal place and see which number 23.682 is closest to.

A. (a)

23.682 is closer to 23.7 than to 23.6

23.682 = 23.7 (to 1 d.p.)

6 is in the 1 d.p. position; 8 is the digit to the right of 6 and is greater than 5, so round 6 up to 7.

(b) 23.6|82

8 > 5

so 23.682 = 23.7 (to 1 d.p.)

(c)

See '1.1 Rounding' on page 648 of the GDC chapter if you need a reminder of how to round using your GDC.

TEXAS

23.682
          23.7

CASIO

23.682
          23.7

▶MAT

So 23.682 = 23.7 (1 d.p.)

Can you use equals signs in these approximations? Or should you always use the 'approximately equal to' sign ≈ ?

When using your calculator, be practical: it is better use all the digits it provides in your calculations to get an accurate answer, but you do **not** need to write down every figure that your GDC gives you in each step of your working. Instead, store the long numbers in the memory of your GDC so they can be used in future calculations, but only **write down** a rounded value in your working (see '22.2D Using the GDC memory' on page 643 of the GDC chapter). Make sure you state the degree of accuracy that you have used when writing a rounded answer. It is fine to use abbreviations such as d.p. and s.f.

Exercise 1.3

1. Write the following numbers to
   (i) 1 decimal place; (ii) 2 decimal places.

   (a) 6.8152   (b) 153.8091   (c) 17.966   (d) 0.1592

2. Use your GDC to calculate the following.
   Give your answers to one decimal place.

   (a) $76.95 \times 2.1 \div 3.86$ (b) $(3.8 + 2.95)^2$ (c) $\sqrt{3^2 + 4^2 + 5^2}$

3. Use your GDC to calculate the following.
   Give your answers to two decimal places.

   (a) If $r = 6.8\,cm$, then $\pi r^2 =$

   (b) If $r = 3.2\,cm$ and $h = 2.9\,cm$, then $\pi r^2 h =$

   (c) If $r = 4.2\,cm$ and $h = 3.95\,cm$, then $\frac{1}{3}\pi r^2 h =$

Significant figures

On the instruction page of each examination paper for the IB Mathematical Studies SL course (the page on which you write your name), students are asked to give all final answers to an exact value, or to **three significant figures** if the question does not request a specific degree of accuracy.

Rounding to a certain number of **significant figures (s.f.)** is the most flexible system of rounding, as you can use it for numbers of any size as well as for numbers that have no decimal point. This means you can use it for very small numbers as well as for very large ones.

First we need to understand what is meant by 'significant figure':

- In a number that is greater than 1 (e.g. 143) the **first significant figure** is the **first (leftmost) digit** in the number, the **second significant figure** is the **second** digit from the left, and so on. So, in the number 143, '1' is the first significant figure, '4' is the second significant figure, and '3' is the third significant figure.

- In a number that is less than 1 (e.g. 0.0415), the first significant figure is the **first non-zero digit after the decimal point**, the second significant figure is the next digit to the right of the first significant figure, and so on. So, in the number 0.0415, '4' is the first significant figure, '1' is the second significant figure, and '5' is the third significant figure.

- In a number with figures on both sides of the decimal point (e.g. 78.2), the first significant figure is the first (leftmost) digit in the number, the second significant figure is the second digit from the left, and so on. So, in the number '78.2', '7' is the first significant figure, '8' is the second significant figure, and '2' is the third significant figure.

exam tip

You should practise rounding answers to three significant figures from the beginning of the course, so that you will be confident when you take the final examinations.

To round to **three significant figures**:

1. Find the third significant figure in the original number.

2. Look at the digit to the right and round the third significant figure according to the '< 5 or ≥ 5' rule.

3. Check the rounded number is the correct magnitude. If you need to, replace digits on the right of the third significant figure with zeros. Be careful to keep track of the number of digits that need to be replaced: the rounded number must be of the same magnitude as the original number (millions must remain millions, hundreds stay as hundreds, etc.)

For example, to round 6 214 789 to three significant figures:

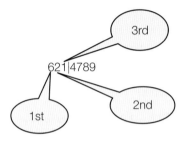

1 is the third significant figure and the next digit to the right is 4. As 4 < 5, you do not change the third significant figure.

Replace the '4', '7', '8' and '9' to the right of the third significant figure with zeros.

So 6 214 789 = 6 210 000 (3 s.f.).

hint

In Worked example 1.4 the answers were written using the symbol ≈ which means 'approximately equal to'. In this case no degree of accuracy was included with the answer so this symbol was used to indicate that the answer was rounded. So, 1056.68 yen ≈ 1057 yen indicates that 1057 is 'approximately equal to' and therefore states it is a rounded value. If the degree of accuracy was included, we would have used the = sign: 1056.68 = 1057 yen (to the nearest yen).

Notice that the answer is written as 6 214 789 = 6 210 000 (**3 s.f.**); it includes the comment '(3 s.f.)' at the end. This comment means 'to three significant figures' and indicates that the values are 'equal' *at that degree of accuracy*. The addition of the comment '(3 s.f.)' is required because 6 214 789 is not *exactly* equal to 6 210 000, so without it, the statement '6 214 789 = 6 210 000' would not actually be true. Some texts prefer to use the notation 6 214 789 → 6 210 000 (3 s.f.).

In some numbers, you will find that rounding the significant figure up means going from '9' to '10', which means you need to change both the significant figure and the number **before** it.

For example, to round 0.31972 to three significant figures:

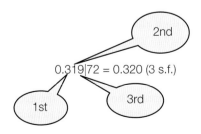

The third significant figure is 9. Because the next digit, 7, is greater than 5, 9 is rounded up to 10. In this case, you need to carry the '1' from '10'

over to the second significant figure (making it '2'), and you *must* keep a zero (the '0' from '10') in the position of the third significant figure, to maintain the degree of accuracy you were asked for. An answer of 0.32 would be incorrect, because it contains only **two** significant figures.

Worked example 1.6

Q. Round the following numbers to three significant figures.

(a) 0.00056384

(b) 4.607054

Find the third significant figure and look at the digit after it; as 8 > 5, round 3 up to 4.

A. (a)

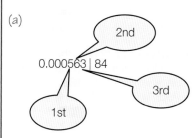

$0.00056384 = 0.000564$ (3 s.f.)

Remember to retain the zeros at the beginning of the number as they give the correct position for the later digits.

The third significant figure is '0'; as the next digit to the right is 7 and 7 > 5, round 0 up to 1.

(b)

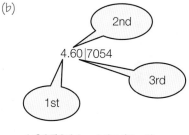

The '7', '0', '5' and '4' after the third significant figure are dropped.

$4.607054 = 4.61$ (3 s.f.)

Exercise 1.4

1. Write the following numbers to three significant figures.

   (a) 93.5159   (b) 108.011   (c) 0.0078388

   (d) 8.55581   (e) 0.062633

2. Use your GDC to calculate the following. Give your answers to 3 s.f.

   (a) $6.96 \times 2.15 \div 4.86$ (b) $(8.3 + 1.95)^3$

   (c) $\sqrt{6^2 + 5^2 + 4^2}$ (d) $\sqrt{6} + \sqrt{5} + \sqrt{4}$

3. Calculate the following, giving your answers to 3 s.f.

   (a) The area of a rectangle with a length of 6.9 cm and a width of 6.3 cm.

   (b) Use the formula $C = 2\pi r$ to calculate the radius of a circle with a circumference of 20 cm.

   (c) Use Pythagoras' theorem $a^2 + b^2 = c^2$ to calculate the length of the hypotenuse of a right-angled triangle whose shorter sides measure 7 cm and 5 cm.

4. Find the volume of this cone.
   Give your answer to three significant figures.

hint

You can look up the formula for the volume of a cone in the

Formula booklet. $a = \pi r^2$

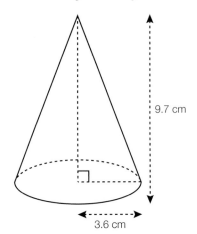

9.7 cm

3.6 cm

Important considerations for rounding

You can round numbers during a calculation, but be aware that if you round a number too early, you could significantly change the final answer.

The example below demonstrates this by calculating the volume of a cylinder using a rounded value for the area of its circular base, and comparing this to the volume obtained from using the exact area.

	Worked example 1.7
Q.	(a) Find the area of a circle with radius of 6.81 cm.
	(b) Write down your answer from (a) to three significant figures.
	(c) Use your answer from (b) to calculate the volume of a cylinder with base radius 6.81 cm and height 14.25 cm using the formula V = base area × height.

continued . . .

(d) Re-calculate the volume of the cylinder using the formula $V = \pi r^2 h$

(e) Find the difference between the answer to (c) and the answer to (d).

A. (a) Area of circle:

$$A = \pi r^2$$
$$= \pi \times 6.81^2 = 145.69\ldots cm^2$$

You can find the formula for the area of a circle in the Formula booklet. $a = \pi r^2$

(b) $146\,cm^2$ (3 s.f.)

In $145.69\ldots$, '5' is the third significant figure; as $6 > 5$, round 5 up to 6.

(c) $V = base \times height$
$$= 146 \times 14.25 = 2080.5\,cm^3$$

(d) $V = \pi r^2 h$
$$= \pi \times 6.81^2 \times 14.25$$
$$= 2076.15\ (2\ d.p.)$$

(e) $2080.5 - 2076.15 = 4.35\,cm^3$ (3 s.f.)

Worked example 1.7 helps to demonstrate the importance of rounding at an appropriate stage during a calculation. In part (d) no rounded values were used during the calculation; only the final value was rounded. But in part (c) a rounded value was used within the calculation. The answer from (c) is larger than that in (d); part (e) shows you the difference is $4.35\,cm^3$. Rounding during a calculation, rather than just at the end of the calculation, can lead to a less accurate estimate; in Worked example 1.7, rounding too early in the calculation led to an overestimate of the cylinder's volume.

If you had $2000\,cm^3$ of fluid, then either method (part (c) or (d)) would be sufficient for checking whether the bottle is big enough to hold the fluid: both answers are larger than the required $2000\,cm^3$.

You need to decide how accurate you need the answer to be in order to decide if it is acceptable to round during a calculation.

Estimation

Using a computer or a calculator gives you a very accurate answer to a problem. However, it is still important to be able to **estimate** the answer that you are expecting. This will help you to realise when you might have made a mistake, and to notice when other people make them too!

For example, Ed is shopping for his class barbecue. He buys 12 cartons of orange juice and 6 bottles of cola. The orange juice costs $1.42 a carton and the cola costs $1.21 a bottle.

In the drinks bottle example, the numbers for the volume are sufficiently close that the consequences of the value being wrong are not that important. Can you think of situations where rounding an answer too early could have serious consequences?

He estimates the bill as follows:

$$12 \times 1.42 \approx 12 \times 1.5$$
$$= (12 \times 1) + (12 \times 0.5)$$
$$= 12 + 6$$
$$= 18$$
$$6 \times 1.21 \approx 6 \times 1$$
$$= 6$$

Total = $24

At the cash register Ed is charged $177.66. This seems far too large a sum, and does not agree with Ed's estimate. What has gone wrong?

There is a record on the cash register of what was entered by the cashier:

$$12 \times 14.2 = 170.4$$
$$6 \times 1.21 = 7.26$$
$$\text{Total} = \$177.66$$

The cashier has put the decimal point for the price of the orange juice in the wrong place. The bill should be:

$$12 \times 1.42 = 17.04$$
$$6 \times 1.21 = 7.26$$
$$\text{Total} = \$24.30$$

If Ed had not made the estimate before he paid, he might not have questioned the amount he was charged and could have paid way too much!

To estimate quickly:

1. Round the numbers to simple values (choose values that will allow you to do the calculation using mental arithmetic).

2. Do the calculation with the simplified numbers.

3. Think about whether your estimate seems too big or too small.

Worked example 1.8

Q. Zita's mother has told her that she can redecorate her room. The room measures 5.68 m by 3.21 m. Zita wants to buy new carpet for the floor.

(a) Estimate the floor area of Zita's room to the nearest metre.

(b) Based on your answer from (a), what area of carpet do you suggest Zita should buy?

(c) Find the accurate floor area using your GDC and determine whether your suggestion in part (b) is sensible.

continued . . .

Use the '< or ≥ 5' rule to round each value in the calculation to the nearest metre.

A. (a) $5.68 \times 3.21 \approx 6 \times 3 = 18\,m^2$

One value was rounded up and the other was rounded down, so the result could be either too high or too low.

(b) To be sure that Zita buys enough carpet, it is best to assume that the estimate is too low. She probably needs to buy $19\,m^2$.

(c) Accurate calculation:

$5.68 \times 3.21 = 18.23\,m^2$ (2 d.p.)

so $18\,m^2$ would not have been enough; the suggestion to buy $19\,m^2$ was correct.

Exercise 1.5

1. Round each figure in these calculations to one significant figure, and use the rounded values to estimate an answer to the calculation. Check your estimate by using your GDC.

   (a) $5.8^2 \times 2.25$
   (b) $11.7 \times 2\pi$
   (c) $37.9 \div 5.16$

2. Nike measures the base of a parallelogram as 14.7 cm and its height as 9.4 cm.

   (a) Calculate the area of the parallelogram:

   (i) exactly
   (ii) to 1 d.p.
   (iii) to 3 s.f.

   (b) Nike estimates the answer as $15 \times 9 = 135\,cm^2$. Calculate the difference between the exact answer and her estimate.

hint

The formula for the area of a parallelogram is in the Formula booklet.

$a = \pi r^2$

3. (a) Write down the following figures to 1 s.f.:

   $m = 28.07$ $n = 13.23$ $p = 112.67$

   (b) If $q = \dfrac{25m}{n+p}$, use your answers from (a) to give an estimate of the value of q.

   (c) Use the accurate values in (a) to find an accurate value for q. Write down all the figures from your calculator display.

   (d) Calculate the difference between your estimate in (b) and the accurate answer in (c).

4. Winston estimated the area of a rectangular field as $12\,000\,\text{m}^2$. The exact measurements of the field were $383\,\text{m} \times 288\,\text{m}$.

(a) Calculate the area of the field using the exact measurements.

(b) What mistake do you think Winston made in his calculation?

Percentage errors

Estimating and rounding values involves error. It is important to establish a way of assessing the magnitude (size) of that error.

Sam estimates the number of people watching a football match. He thinks there are about 14 500. The gate receipts show that there were actually 14 861 people watching the match.

Deepa estimates that there were 380 people attending a school concert. The actual number was 349.

Who gave the better estimate?

$14861 - 14500 = 361$, so Sam's estimate was too low by 361 people.

$380 - 349 = 31$, so Deepa's estimate was too high by 31 people.

First impressions suggest that Deepa's estimate is better because the difference between the estimate and the actual value is smaller. But the sizes of the crowds were very different, so just looking at the differences does not give a fair comparison. To compare the results more fairly, we can use **percentage error**. The percentage error works out the difference between the estimate and the actual value **in relation to** the size of the actual value. The smaller the percentage error, the more accurate the estimate is.

 Percentage error $\varepsilon = \left| \dfrac{v_A - v_E}{v_E} \right| \times 100\%$, where v_A = approximate (estimated) value and v_E = exact value.

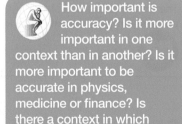

How important is accuracy? Is it more important in one context than in another? Is it more important to be accurate in physics, medicine or finance? Is there a context in which accuracy is not important?

The vertical bars around the fraction mean that we consider only positive values; for instance, if the difference between the exact and approximate values turns out negative, we just drop the minus sign.

Sam's percentage error is $\frac{14861 - 14500}{14861} \times 100 = 2.43\%$

Deepa's percentage error is $\frac{380 - 349}{349} \times 100 = 8.88\%$

So actually, Sam's estimate was the better one because the percentage error is smaller.

Error can also occur in the process of measuring. A physical measurement will always be a rounded value, because we do not have tools that are sensitive enough to measure continuous data to complete accuracy.

Q. At the beginning of a problem, Ben writes $\sqrt{13} = 3.6$.

He chooses to use the rounded answer of '3.6' rather than the exact value of $\sqrt{13}$ in the calculations that follow. So, instead of calculating $(2+\sqrt{13})^3$, he calculates $(2+3.6)^3$.

What is his percentage error?

> Substitute the exact value and the rounded value into the formula for percentage error.

A. $V_E = (2+\sqrt{13})^3$

$V_A = (2+3.6)^3$

> This percentage error is a result of Ben rounding the numbers during the calculations.

$$\text{Percentage error} = \frac{(2+\sqrt{13})^3 - (2+3.6)^3}{(2+\sqrt{13})^3}$$

$$= 0.297\%$$

Exercise 1.6

1. In each of these questions, calculate the percentage error. Give your answer to 3 s.f.

   (a) Anu estimates the length of a piece of rope to be 5.5 m. The accurate length is 5.65 m.

   (b) Miki types 3.96 into his calculator instead of 3.69.

   (c) Ali estimates the crowd at a basketball match as 4500. The true number is 4241.

   (d) Amy tells her mother that the call on her cell phone took only ten minutes. The call really took 14 minutes and 40 seconds.

2. Maria measures the diameter of a cylinder as 8.75 cm and its height as 5.9 cm.

   (a) Using the formula $V = \pi r^2 h$, calculate the volume of the cylinder to two decimal places.

   (b) More accurate measurements give the volume of the cylinder as 342.72 cm³. Calculate the percentage error between Maria's answer and the accurate value.

1.3 Expressing very large and very small numbers in standard form

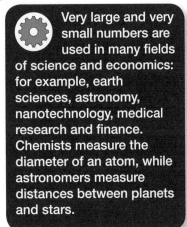

Very large and very small numbers are used in many fields of science and economics: for example, earth sciences, astronomy, nanotechnology, medical research and finance. Chemists measure the diameter of an atom, while astronomers measure distances between planets and stars.

Scientists, doctors, engineers, economists and many other people often use very large or very small numbers. For example:

- 'The galaxy of Andromeda is 2 000 000 light years from our galaxy.'

- 'A light year is approximately 9 460 000 000 000 km.'

- 'It is estimated that the volume of petrol reserves worldwide is 177 000 000 000 cubic metres.'

- 'The thickness of this strand of glass fibre is 0.000008 m.'

Modern computers and calculators help these people to work with such numbers, but the numbers can still be complicated to write out, to use and to compare. The numbers may also be too long for a calculator or spreadsheet to cope with and therefore need to be written in a shorter form.

Very small and very large numbers can be expressed in the form $a \times 10^k$ where $1 \leq a < 10$ and k is an integer. This is called **standard form** or **scientific notation**.

This notation is used to write numbers in a form that makes them:

- shorter

- easier to understand

- easier to compare

- able to fit onto a GDC or into a cell in a spreadsheet.

How to write a number in standard form

Large numbers

1. To write a very large number in standard form, first write down a value between 1 and 10 by inserting a decimal point after the first significant digit, e.g. for 13 000 write 1.3 (0.13 is less than 1, while 13.0, 130.00, etc. are all greater than 10).

2. Think about how many times you would need to **multiply** this new number by ten in order to get back to the original value, e.g. $1.3 \times 10 \times 10 \times 10 \times 10 = 13\,000$, so you need to multiply by 10 four times.

3. Then, rewrite the original number as the decimal value from step 1 multiplied by 10 raised to the power of the number of times you needed to multiply by 10, e.g. $13\,000 = 1.3 \times 10^4$.

For example, to write 5 120 000 in standard form:

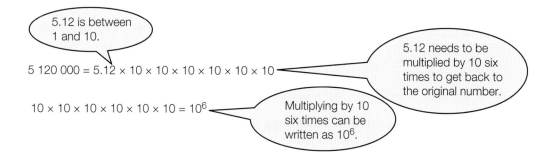

5.12 is between 1 and 10.

$5\ 120\ 000 = 5.12 \times 10 \times 10 \times 10 \times 10 \times 10 \times 10$

5.12 needs to be multiplied by 10 six times to get back to the original number.

$10 \times 10 \times 10 \times 10 \times 10 \times 10 = 10^6$

Multiplying by 10 six times can be written as 10^6.

So, 5 120 000 written in standard form is 5.12×10^6.

Another method is use the structure of the number in terms of place order:

10^6 (millions)	10^5 (hundreds of thousands)	10^4 (tens of thousands)	10^3 (thousands)	10^2 (hundreds)	10^1 (tens)	10^0 (units)
5	1	2	0	0	0	0

The first significant figure **5** has a place order in the millions and so indicates **5** million. It is in the 10^6 column, and this is the power of ten by which you need to multiply the value between 1 and 10.

Small numbers

1. To write a very small number in standard form, first write down a value between 1 and 10 by inserting a decimal point after the first significant digit (as you did for very large numbers), e.g. for 0.034 write 3.4.

2. Think about how many times you would need to **divide** the new number by 10 in order to get back to the original number, e.g. $3.4 \div 10 \div 10 = 0.034$, so you divide by 10 two times.

3. Then, rewrite the original number as the decimal value from step 1 multiplied by 10 raised to **negative** the number of times you need to divide by 10, e.g. $0.034 = 3.4 \times 10^{-2}$.

For example, to write 0.00684 in standard form:

$$0.00684 = 6.84 \div 10 \div 10 \div 10$$
$$= 6.84 \div 10^3$$
$$= 6.84 \times 10^{-3}$$

Alternatively, use the place order structure of the number:

10^0 (units)	. (decimal point)	10^{-1} (tenths)	10^{-2} (hundreths)	10^{-3} (thousanths)	10^{-4} (tenths of thousandths)	10^{-5} (hundredths of thousandths)
0	.	0	0	**6**	8	4

The first significant figure **6** represents **6** thousandths. It is in the 10^{-3} column, and this gives you the power of ten that you need.

Learning links

1B Negative indices and the standard form

In a number written in the form b^p, the superscript p is the **power** of b, also called the **index** or **exponent**. If p is a positive integer, it tells you the number of times to multiply by the number b. For example, $2^4 = 2 \times 2 \times 2 \times 2 = 16$.

Negative powers

If p is a **negative** integer, it tells you that you have a reciprocal, or $\frac{1}{b^p}$. Recall that a reciprocal is a fraction with 1 in the numerator. For example, $2^{-4} = \frac{1}{2^4} = \frac{1}{16}$ = 0.0625. Observe that

$$1 \div 2 \div 2 \div 2 = \frac{1}{2} \div 2 \div 2$$

$$= \frac{1}{2 \times 2} \div 2 \div 2 = \frac{1}{2 \times 2 \times 2} \div 2.$$

$$= \frac{1}{2 \times 2 \times 2 \times 2} = \frac{1}{2^4}$$

So 2^{-4} is the same as the fraction $\frac{1}{2^4}$.

This is an example of one of the laws of indices: $b^{-m} = \frac{1}{b^m}$.

How does this apply to the standard form?

The standard form is $a \times 10^k$ where $1 \le a < 10$ and k is an integer, which means that you have to **multiply** a by 10 raised to a power. Any small number that is less than 1 can always be written as $a \div 10^m$ or $a \times \frac{1}{10^m}$ where $1 \le a < 10$ and m is a **positive** integer. Using the law of indices above, this is the same as $a \times 10^{-m}$. In other words, we multiply by a **negative** power of 10 to indicate that we are really dividing by a power of 10.

Changing a number from standard form to ordinary form (decimal form)

To write a **large** number given in standard form $a \times 10^k$ as an ordinary number, **multiply** a by ten k times. For example:

$$7.904 \times 10^3 = 7.904 \times 10 \times 10 \times 10 = 7904$$

Here, $a = 7.904$ and $k = 3$. So multiply 7.904 by 10 three times (which is the same as multiplying by 1000).

To write a **small** number given in standard form $a \times 10^{-m}$ as an ordinary number, **divide** a by ten m times. For example:

$$3.816 \times 10^{-5} = 3.816 \div 10 \div 10 \div 10 \div 10 \div 10 = 0.00003816$$

Here, $a = 3.816$ and $m = 5$. So divide 3.816 by 10 five times (which is the same as dividing by 100 000).

It is possible to set your calculator to do all its calculations in standard form. Every time you use your GDC the screen will display the answer in the form that you have set. This can be useful if you often use very large or very small numbers, but not when you are doing calculations with more ordinary-sized numbers.

 See '*1.2 Answers in standard form*' on page 650 of the GDC chapter to find out how to do operations in the form $a \times 10^k$ with your GDC.

If a calculation is to be done in the standard form $a \times 10^k$, make sure that you know which key to use on your GDC to enter the exponent k. It will be marked **EE** or **EXP.**

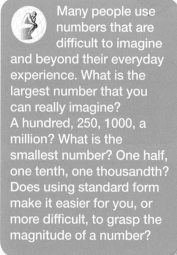

Many people use numbers that are difficult to imagine and beyond their everyday experience. What is the largest number that you can really imagine? A hundred, 250, 1000, a million? What is the smallest number? One half, one tenth, one thousandth? Does using standard form make it easier for you, or more difficult, to grasp the magnitude of a number?

exam tip

Be careful not to write 'calculator language' in your working or answer rather than true mathematical notation. For instance, do not put 8.12E6 in your solution; instead, write 8.12×10^6. In examinations you will be expected to give answers in correct mathematical notation.

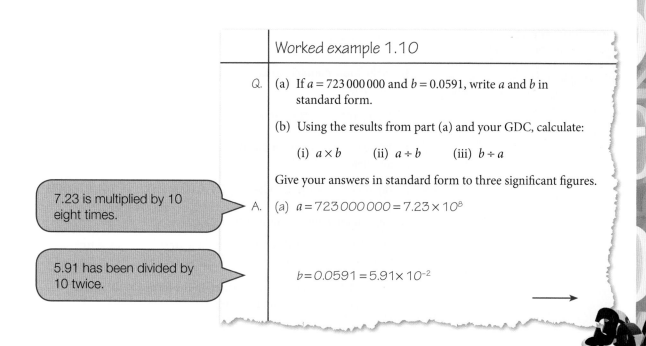

Worked example 1.10

Q. (a) If $a = 723\,000\,000$ and $b = 0.0591$, write a and b in standard form.

(b) Using the results from part (a) and your GDC, calculate:

(i) $a \times b$ (ii) $a \div b$ (iii) $b \div a$

Give your answers in standard form to three significant figures.

A. (a) $a = 723\,000\,000 = 7.23 \times 10^8$

7.23 is multiplied by 10 eight times.

$b = 0.0591 = 5.91 \times 10^{-2}$

5.91 has been divided by 10 twice.

continued . . .

(b)

 TEXAS

```
7.23E8*5.91E-2
            42729300
7.23E8/5.91E-2
    1.223350254E10
5.91E-2/7.23E8
    8.17427386E-11
■
```

 CASIO

```
7.23E8×5.91E-2
            42729300
7.23E8÷5.91E-2
    1.223350254E+10
5.91E-2÷7.23E8
    8.174273859E-11
▶MAT
```

(i) 4.27×10^7

(ii) 1.22×10^{10}

(iii) 8.17×10^{-11}

> If numbers are very big or very small, the GDC gives the answers in standard form automatically.

> Make sure you write the answers down using the correct notation! You would not get any marks if you write 8.17E–11.

Exercise 1.7

1. Fill in the missing values of n, e.g. if $34\,500 = 3.45 \times 10^n$, then $n = 4$.

   (a) $628 = n.28 \times 10^2$

   (b) $53\,000 = 5.3 \times 10^n$

   (c) $0.00282 = 2.82 \times 10^n$

   (d) $3\,640\,000 = 3.n4 \times 10^6$

   (e) $0.0208 = 2.n8 \times 10^{-2}$

hint

By 'decimal form' we mean an 'ordinary number'; so you need to write the number out in full as it would appear if not written in standard form. For example, 1.25×10^4 in 'decimal form' would be $12\,500$.

2. Write out the following numbers in decimal form.

   (a) 1.25×10^4 (b) 3.08×10^3 (c) 2.88×10^8

   (d) 4.21×10^{-2} (e) 9.72×10^{-3} (f) 8.38×10^{-6}

3. Write these numbers in the form $a \times 10^k$ where $1 \le a < 10$ and k is an integer.

   (a) $62\,100$ (b) 2100 (c) $98\,400\,000$ (d) 52

4. Write these numbers in the form $a \times 10^k$ where $1 \le a < 10$ and k is an integer.

   (a) 0.727 (b) 0.0319 (c) 0.00000257 (d) 0.000408

5. Look at the following numbers:

   398×10^1 0.17×10^3 2.4×10^{-3} 3.8×10^{-5}

   370×10^2 0.02×10^2 1.2×10^2

   (a) Which numbers are **not** written in the form $a \times 10^k$ where $1 \le a < 10$ and k is an integer?

   (b) Rewrite the numbers from part (a) in the form $a \times 10^k$ where $1 \le a < 10$ and k is an integer.

   (c) Put all the numbers in ascending (increasing) order.

6. Use your GDC to calculate the following. Give each answer in the form $a \times 10^k$ where $1 \le a < 10$ and k is an integer. Round 'a' to three significant figures.

For example, $(3.81 \times 10^{-2})^2 = 0.00145161 = 1.45 \times 10^{-3}$ (3 s.f.)

(a) $(8.5 \times 10^3) \times (3.73 \times 10^6)$ (b) $(5.997 \times 10^2) \div (6.063 \times 10^3)$

(c) $(7.71 \times 10^{-2}) \div (1.69 \times 10^7)$ (d) $(1.24 \times 10^{-3})^2$

(e) $\sqrt{(6.59 \times 10^9)}$ (f) $(7.01 \times 10^{-3})^3$

7. Given that $m = 3.9 \times 10^3$ and $n = 6.8 \times 10^{-4}$, calculate the following, giving your answer in the form $a \times 10^k$ where $1 \le a < 10$ and k is an integer.

(a) $m + n$ (b) $m - n$ (c) $m \times n$ (d) $m \div n$

8. If the speed of light is approximately $300\,000\,\text{km s}^{-1}$ and $\text{time} = \dfrac{\text{distance}}{\text{speed}}$, calculate the time that light takes to get from:

(a) Earth to Jupiter, when they are $5.88 \times 10^8\,\text{km}$ apart

(b) Mars to Venus, when they are $2.22 \times 10^8\,\text{km}$ apart

(c) Saturn to the sun, when they are $1.43 \times 10^9\,\text{km}$ apart.

Give your answers to the nearest minute. As all the figures have been rounded, these answers are only estimates.

9. The area of the Taman Negara park in Malaysia is $4.34 \times 10^3\,\text{km}^2$. The area of Central Park in New York is $3.41 \times 10^6\,\text{m}^2$. How many times can you fit Central Park into Taman Negara?

1.4 SI units

The international system of units (Système International d'Unités), or **SI units**, was adopted in 1960. The system is based on seven essential, or 'base', units for seven 'base' quantities that are independent of each other. The SI system forms a fundamental part of the language of science and commerce across the world.

Base quantity	Base unit	Symbol
Length	metre	m
Mass	kilogram	kg
Time	second	s
Electric current	ampere	A
Temperature	kelvin	K
Amount of substance	mole	mol
Intensity of light	candela	cd

Time

The SI unit for time is seconds, but it is often convenient to work in minutes, hours, days, weeks, months or years.

Learning links

1C Working with decimals and time

It is important to remember that hours and minutes work in parts of 60, not parts of 10 or 100. Therefore, when we say '25.6 minutes', the '.6' does not represent 6 seconds. To convert 0.6 minutes to a number of seconds, think of it as 0.6 of a minute, that is, 0.6 of 60 seconds. So, multiply 60 by 0.6 to get $0.6 \times 60 = 36$ seconds.

Worked example 1.11

Q. Fiona works for herself and needs to earn $20,000 per year.

(a) How much does she have to earn each month?

(b) How much does she have to earn each week?

(c) If she actually works 1000 hours per year, how many minutes is this? How many seconds?

There are 12 months in a year, so divide her yearly earnings by 12. For currencies it makes sense to round to 2 decimal places.

A. (a) $\$20\,000 \div 12 = \$1666.67$ (to 2 d.p.)

There are 52 weeks in a year, so divide her yearly earnings by 52.

(b) $\$20\,000 \div 52 = \$384.62$ (to 2 d.p.)

There are 60 minutes in an hour, so multiply the number of hours by 60 to get the number of minutes.

(c) $1000 \times 60 = 60\,000$ minutes

There are 60 seconds in a minute, so multiply the number of minutes by 60 to get the number of seconds.

$60\,000 \times 60 = 3\,600\,000$ seconds

Exercise 1.8

1. Convert these units of time:

   (a) 6 minutes 35 seconds to seconds

   (b) 562 seconds to minutes and seconds

   (c) 78 hours to days and hours

   (d) 6500 seconds to hours, minutes and seconds

   (e) 12 days 5 hours and 15 minutes to minutes

   (f) 6 hours, 7 minutes and 10 seconds to seconds

Temperature

The SI unit for temperature is the **kelvin** (K). This is the most important **scientific** measure of temperature, although in everyday life we use Celsius (°C) or Fahrenheit (°F). One kelvin has the same magnitude as one degree Celsius, but 0 K is at −273.15°C.

	Kelvin	Celsius	Fahrenheit
Freezing point of water	273.15	0°	32°
Boiling point of water	373.15	100°	212°

To convert a temperature in kelvins (K) to a temperature in Celsius (°C), use the formula:

$$T_C = T_K - 273.15$$

To convert a temperature in Celsius (°C) to a temperature in Fahrenheit (°F), use the formula:

$$T_F = \frac{9}{5}T_C + 32$$

To convert a temperature in Fahrenheit (°F) to a temperature in Celsius (°C), use the formula:

$$T_C = \frac{5}{9}(T_F - 32)$$

Worked example 1.12

Q. (a) The weather forecast in Houston, Texas, tells you that today's temperature will be 90°F. Give this temperature in degrees Celsius.

   (b) The temperature in Stockholm on 1 January was −5°C. Give this temperature in degrees Fahrenheit.

continued . . .

A. (a) $T_C = \dfrac{5}{9}(T_F - 32)$

$T_C = \dfrac{5}{9}(90 - 32) = 32.2\,^{\circ}C$

> Substitute $90 = T_F$ into the formula for converting Fahrenheit to Celsius.

(b) $T_F = \dfrac{9}{5}T_C + 32$

$T_F = \dfrac{9}{5} \times (-5) + 32 = 23\,^{\circ}F$

> Substitute $-5 = T_C$ into the formula for converting Celsius to Fahrenheit.

Exercise 1.9

1. The table gives temperatures from cities around the world. The temperatures were recorded in January. Some are in measured in degrees Celsius and others in degrees Fahrenheit. Convert the units and complete the table.

City	Miami	Riga	Milan	Bahrain	Lima	Perth	Moscow
Celsius (°C)		−2	7		25		−12
Fahrenheit (°F)	82			65		90	

Other units

You also need to be able to use units that are closely related to the SI base units; these units are not official SI units, but are very commonly used.

Length	Mass	Volume
millimetre (mm)	milligram (mg)	millilitre (ml), $1\,cm^3$
centimetre (cm)		
metre (m)	gram (g)	
kilometre (km)	kilogram (kg)	litre (l), $1000\,cm^3$
	tonne (t), $1000\,kg$	

> Is the fact that these prefixes are derived from Latin and Greek part of what makes mathematics a 'universal language'? Or does the use of the Système International in mathematics seem more relevant to this point?

You will find it easier to use these units if you remember the meaning of the prefixes milli- and kilo-:

- 'mille' means one thousand in Latin; a millimetre is $\frac{1}{1000}$ of a metre
- 'centum' means one hundred in Latin; a centimetre is $\frac{1}{100}$ of a metre
- 'khilloi' means one thousand in Greek; a kilogram is 1000 grams, a kilometre is 1000 metres.

Derived units

There is no unit for volume among the seven SI base units. Volume is an example of a derived quantity with a **derived unit**; a unit defined in terms of the SI base units by means of a formula. The most common derived units are the following:

Derived quantity	Derived unit	Symbol
Area	square metre	m^2
Volume	cubic metre	m^3
Speed/velocity	metre per second	$m\,s^{-1}$
Acceleration	metre per second per second	$m\,s^{-2}$
Density	kilogram per cubic metre	$kg\,m^{-3}$

Speed, acceleration, force and density are all examples of quantities we come across in everyday life that use derived units. For example, evaluation of the force created by acceleration is important in crash testing and vehicle safety.

You can often work out what formula was used to generate the derived units. For example, the unit of 'area' is square metre ($m^2 = m \times m$), and 'm' is the SI unit for 'length', so area = length × length was the formula used.

When you use derived units, you are actually using simple formulae. For example:

$$\text{speed } (m\,s^{-1}) = \frac{\text{distance (m)}}{\text{time (s)}}$$

$$\text{density } (kg\,m^{-3}) = \frac{\text{mass (kg)}}{\text{volume } (m^3)}$$

Worked example 1.13

Q. (a) Jared cycles 38 km in 3 hours and 20 minutes. What is his speed?

(b) If Jared continues at this speed, how long will it take him to cycle another 25 km? Give your answer to the nearest minute.

First convert the 20 minutes to hours to get the time in the same units: $\frac{20}{60} = \frac{1}{3}$. Then substitute values into the formula for speed.

A. (a) $speed = \dfrac{distance}{time}$

Jared's speed $= 38 \div 3\dfrac{1}{3} = 11.4\ km\,h^{-1}$

Rearrange the formula $speed = \dfrac{distance}{time}$ to calculate the time from distance and speed. Then substitute in the distance given in the question and your answer from part (a).

(b) $time = \dfrac{distance}{speed} = \dfrac{25}{11.4} = 2.193$

0.193 hours $= 0.193 \times 60 \approx 12$ minutes, so it will take 2 hours 12 minutes.

Exercise 1.10

1. Using the formula $\text{speed} = \dfrac{\text{distance}}{\text{time}}$, calculate:

   (a) the speed of a car that travels $95\,\text{km}$ in $2\frac{1}{2}$ hours

   (b) the number of hours it takes to travel $37.4\,\text{km}$ at $5.2\,\text{km}\,\text{h}^{-1}$

   (c) the distance travelled if you go at a speed of $11\,\text{km}\,\text{h}^{-1}$ for 2 hours 40 minutes.

2. (a) On the first day of their trek, Noah and his friends travel $21\,\text{km}$ in eight hours. What is their average speed?

   (b) On the second day they travel $18\frac{1}{2}\,\text{km}$ in seven hours. Are they travelling faster or slower on the second day?

   (c) What is their average speed over the whole two-day trek?

Conversion between different units

If you are asked to convert from one unit to another, look at the units very carefully.

Remember that you cannot convert units of length into units of volume, or units of mass into units of temperature. You can only convert between units of the same *type* of measure. So you can change a length measure in one unit to a length measure in another unit, e.g. mm to km, and so on.

Most conversions will rely on you knowing how to get from one unit to another. The conversion of some common units are useful to know.

$$\xleftarrow{\div 100}$$
$$1\,\text{m} = 100\,\text{cm}$$
$$\xrightarrow{\times 100}$$

$$\xleftarrow{\div 10}$$
$$1\,\text{cm} = 10\,\text{mm}$$
$$\xrightarrow{\times 10}$$

$$\xleftarrow{\div 1000}$$
$$1\,\text{m} = 1000\,\text{mm}$$
$$\xrightarrow{\times 1000}$$

$$\xleftarrow{\div 1000}$$
$$1\,\text{kg} = 1000\,\text{g}$$
$$\xrightarrow{\times 1000}$$

$$\xleftarrow{\div 60}$$
$$1\,\text{hour} = 60\,\text{minutes}$$
$$\xrightarrow{\times 60}$$

$$\xleftarrow{\div 60}$$
$$1\,\text{minute} = 60\,\text{seconds}$$
$$\xrightarrow{\times 60}$$

Sometimes, the units given can guide you to the method you should use to convert them.

Worked example 1.14

Q. (a) The mass of a child is $21\,\text{kg}$. Give the child's mass in standard form in grams.

(b) A computer program runs for $4000\,\text{s}$. Give the time in hours, minutes and seconds.

(c) The area of a circle is $5.25\,\text{m}^2$. Give the answer in cm^2.

$\longrightarrow$

continued . . .

A. (a) To get from kg to g, multiply by 1000.

$1\,kg = 1000\,g$
$21\,kg = 21 \times 1000\,g = 21\,000\,g$

Convert into standard form.

$21\,000 = 2.1 \times 10^4$
so the child's mass is $2.1 \times 10^4\,g$

(b) To convert seconds to minutes, divide by 60.

$4000 \div 60 = 66.667$ minutes

To convert 66 minutes to hours, divide by 60.

$66 \div 60 = 1.1$ hours

To convert a fraction of an hour (0.1) to minutes, multiply by 60.

$0.1 \times 60 = 6$ minutes

To convert a fraction of a minute (0.667) to seconds, multiply by 60.

$0.667 \times 60 = 40$ seconds

See Learning links 1C on page 28 for a reminder about decimals and time.

So $4000\,s = 1$ hour, 6 minutes, 40 seconds

(c) To convert from m to cm, multiply by 100.

$1\,m = 100\,cm$

Remember that to calculate an area, you need to multiply two lengths together. Each of these lengths must be converted to centimetres, so you need to multiply by 100 twice.

$1\,m^2 = (100\,cm)^2 = 100 \times 100\,cm^2$
$5.25\,m^2 = 5.25 \times 100 \times 100 = 52\,500\,cm^2$

In part (b) of Worked example 1.14, you could have used your GDC to convert 4000 s into hours, minutes and seconds:

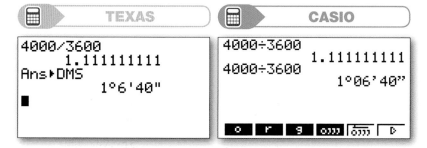

TEXAS

```
4000/3600
        1.111111111
Ans▶DMS
        1°6'40"
■
```

CASIO

```
4000÷3600
        1.111111111
4000÷3600
        1°06'40"
```

See '1.3 Time in hours, minutes and seconds' on page 651 of the GDC chapter for a reminder of how to do this, if you need to.

Worked example 1.15

Q. Esmé has a wooden box that measures
24 cm × 15 cm × 11 cm. Calculate the volume
of the box in:

(a) mm³   (b) cm³   (c) litres

A. (a) <u>Method 1:</u>

240 mm × 150 mm × 110 mm
= 3 960 000 mm³

<u>Method 2:</u>

24 cm × 15 cm × 11 cm
= 3960 cm³ = 3960 × (10 mm)³
= 3960 × 10 × 10 × 10 = 3 960 000 mm³

(b) $V = 24\,cm × 15\,cm × 11\,cm = 3960\,cm^3$

(c) $V = 3960 ÷ 1000 = 3.96$ litres

> Convert to mm before doing the calculation: 1 cm = 10 mm, so multiply each measurement by 10.

> Work out the answer in cm³ first, then convert to mm³. To change cm³ to mm³, you need to multiply by 10 three times (as you multiply three lengths when calculating volume).

> The lengths are already in cm, so there is no need to convert.

> 1000 cm³ = 1 litre, so divide the answer from (b) by 1000.

Exercise 1.11

In questions 1–5, convert the units as instructed.

For example, if the question says '5.75 litres to ml', give the answer as '5750 ml'.

1. (a) 3500 mm to m   (b) 276 cm to mm
   (c) 4800 m to km   (d) 352 m to cm

2. (a) 5.8 kg to g   (b) 30 g to kg
   (c) 1260 mg to g   (d) 1 kg to mg

3. (a) 4.5 m² to cm²   (b) 685 cm² to m²
   (c) 1.4 km² to m²   (d) 120 mm² to cm²

4. (a) 12 m³ to cm³   (b) 24 000 cm³ to m³
   (c) 1.3 cm³ to mm³   (d) 0.5 m³ to cm³

5. (a) 7900 ml to litres   (b) 3.95 litres to ml
   (c) 83.3 litres to cm³   (d) 687 ml to cm³

6. (a) A rectangle has a length of 2.5 m and a width of 2.8 m.
Give the area of the rectangle in (i) cm²; (ii) m².

(b) A cylinder has a height of 1.29 m and a radius of 45 cm. Using the formula $V = \pi r^2 h$, give the volume of the cylinder in (i) cm³; (ii) m³.

(c) A triangle has a base of length 12.5 cm and a height of 53 mm. What is the area of the triangle in cm²?

7. You have 7 m of ribbon that you want to cut into lengths of 18 cm.

(a) How many pieces of ribbon will you have?

(b) How much ribbon will you have left over?

8. You want to buy tiles to cover an area 3 m long and 1.5 m wide. You choose tiles that are 6 cm square. How many tiles will you need to buy?

9. A large bucket has a volume of $8\frac{1}{2}$ litres. You need to measure out cupfuls of 160 cm³.

(a) How many cupfuls will you measure?

(b) How much liquid will you have left over?

10. (a) Timmi is making a path round the edge of her garden. Calculate the area of the path (the non-shaded region).

(b) The concrete path is 8 cm deep. Calculate the volume of concrete that Timmi needs in cubic metres.

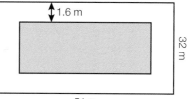

Summary

You should know:

- the definitions of the natural numbers $\mathbb{N}$, integers $\mathbb{Z}$, rational numbers $\mathbb{Q}$ and real numbers $\mathbb{R}$

- how to round numbers to a given number of decimal places or significant figures, and that this process is called approximation

- how to calculate percentage error using the formula
$$\varepsilon = \left| \frac{v_A - v_E}{v_E} \right| \times 100\%$$
where v_E is the exact value and v_A is the approximate value

- how to sensibly estimate the answer to a calculation, and how to use your estimate to check solutions obtained from a GDC or computer

- how to express numbers in the standard form $a \times 10^k$ where $1 \le a < 10$ and k is an integer, and how to perform calculations with numbers in this form

- what the SI (Système International) is and give examples of these units as well as other basic units of measurement, such as kilogram (kg), metre (m), second (s), litre (l), metres per second (m s⁻¹) and degrees Celsius (°C).

Mixed examination practice

Exam-style questions

1. Copy and complete the table. One box has been completed for you.

	11	$\frac{1}{11}$	$\sqrt{11}$	−11
$\mathbb{N}$				
$\mathbb{Z}$				
$\mathbb{Q}$				
$\mathbb{R}$			✓	

2. Put the following numbers into the correct set in the given Venn diagram:

π, 12, sin (30°), 0.02, 0, −2

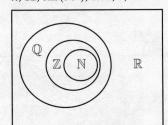

3. Calculate each the following and decide which type of number the answer is. For example,

$(14 + 5) \div 7 = 2\frac{5}{7}$ is a rational number.

(a) $(6 + 8) \div (9 − 2)$

(b) $6 + (8 \div 9) − 2$

(c) $2^3 \times 2^6 \div 2^8$

(d) $2 \times \pi \times 6.8$

(e) $(\sqrt{2})^2 + (\sqrt{3})^2 + (\sqrt{5})^2$

(f) 40% of −90

(g) $3(8 − \frac{1}{3}) − 5(12 − \frac{2}{3})$

(h) If $6(x + 3) = x − 2$ then $x = ?$

4. In this question, give your answers to one decimal place.

(a) Using the formula $A = \frac{1}{2}(a + b)h$, where a and b are the lengths of the parallel sides and h is the height, calculate the area of the trapezium.

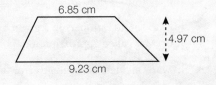

6.85 cm

4.97 cm

9.23 cm

(b) Using the formula $A = \frac{1}{2}(b \times h)$, where b is the base and h is the height, calculate the area of the triangle.

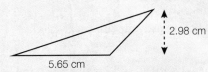

2.98 cm

5.65 cm

(c) Using the formula $C = 2\pi r$, where r is the radius, calculate the perimeter of the semi-circle.

2.5 m

5. Suppose that $A = \pi(R^2 - r^2)$, where $R = 19.29$ and $r = 11.01$.

   (a) Estimate the values of R, r and π to one significant figure.

   (b) Use your answers in (a) to estimate a value for A.

   (c) Calculate an accurate value for A, using the exact values for R and r. Give your answer to 3 s.f.

6. Calculate $\dfrac{1 + \sqrt{8.01}}{1.2^2}$, giving your answer to (i) one decimal place; (ii) three significant figures.

7. Given that the diameter of a molecule of C_{60} (buckminsterfullerene) is 1.1×10^{-9} m, how many molecules would fit along a line 1 cm long?

8. Use the formula density $= \dfrac{\text{mass}}{\text{volume}}$ to calculate the following. Include units in your answers.

   (a) 1 m^3 of plastic weighs 958 kg. What is its density?

   (b) Change 1 m^3 into cm^3.

   (c) What is the mass of 10 cm^3 of this plastic?

Buckminsterfullerene.

9. Osmium is the densest known solid. The density of osmium is $22\,610$ kg m^{-3}.

   (a) What is the mass of 0.5 m^3?   (b) What is the volume of a piece with a mass of 100 g?

Past paper questions

1. A problem has an **exact** answer of $x = 0.1265$.

   (a) Write down the **exact** value of x in the form $a \times 10^k$ where k is an integer and $1 \le a < 10$.

   (b) State the value of x given correct to **two** significant figures.

   (c) Calculate the percentage error if x is given correct to **two** significant figures.   *[Total 6 marks]*

2. (a) Calculate $\dfrac{77.2 \times 3^3}{3.60 \times 2^2}$.   *[1 mark]*

   (b) Express your answer to part (a) in the form $a \times 10^k$ where $1 \le a < 10$ and $k \in \mathbb{Z}$.   *[2 marks]*

   (c) Juan estimates the length of a carpet to be 12 metres and the width to be 8 metres. He then estimates the area of the carpet.

      (i) Write down his estimated area of the carpet.   *[1 mark]*

      When the carpet is accurately measured it is found to have an area of 90 square metres.

      (ii) Calculate the percentage error made by Juan.   *[2 marks]*

      [Total 6 marks]

Chapter 2 Solving equations

In this chapter you will learn:

- how to use a GDC to solve linear equations with one variable
- how to use a GDC to solve pairs of linear equations with two variables
- how to use a GDC to solve quadratic equations.

Algorithms are the building blocks of the modern world. Examples of algorithms include: the fundamental instructions for a computer; the procedure that a pharmaceutical firm follows in researching a new drug; and the strategy that a company uses to organise deliveries of letters and parcels all over the world.

The words 'algorithm' and 'algebra' both come from the work of the same mediaeval Arab mathematician, Al-Khwarizmi, who was a scholar at the House of Wisdom in Baghdad. Al-Khwarizmi wrote a textbook called *Hisab al-jabr w'al-muqabala*, which contained the first explanations of some of the techniques that are still used in modern algebra.

'Al-jabr' became the word **algebra**, a method of generalising problems in arithmetic.

Al-Khwarizmi's own name became the word **algorithm**, a term describing a powerful scientific way of solving problems.

In this chapter you will meet some of the oldest and most frequently used algorithms: those used to solve linear and quadratic equations.

Teachers are often asked, 'Why do we have to learn how to solve quadratic equations?' This is a question that is already thousands of years old!

About 3500 years ago, Egyptians and Babylonians (in present-day Iraq) wanted to know how to calculate the sides of a square or rectangle with any given area; these problems involved quadratic equations that had to be solved to find the lengths that they needed.

In modern algebra, if you want to find the dimensions of a rectangle which has one side 5 m longer than the other and whose area is 108 m², you could create an equation from the formula for the area of a rectangle:

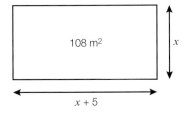

$$A = \text{length} \times \text{breadth}$$

$$x(x + 5) = 108$$

$$x^2 + 5x = 108$$

The Egyptians did not use algebraic methods like those above. They solved the problems using a set procedure — an algorithm. The solutions were collected in tables, so that the sages and engineers could look up solutions for different shapes and different areas.

Today, the problems are still very similar; but instead of using a prepared table to solve your equations, you can use algebra, a calculator or a computer.

2.1 Linear equations

You can recognise a **linear equation** from its **general form**:

$$y = mx + c \qquad \text{or} \qquad ax + by + c = 0$$

The highest power of x (also called the 'order') in a linear equation is 1. When plotted on a graph, a linear equation takes the form of a straight line: as you can see on the graph below, the linear equations $y = 5x - 3$ and $3x + 4y - 12 = 0$ each give a straight line.

Plotted on the same graph is the equation $y = 2^x - 1$, which does **not** give a straight line. This is not a linear equation because it cannot be written in either of the general forms above; neither general form contains x as an exponent (a power). Make sure you do not confuse $2x$, which is linear, with 2^x, which is not.

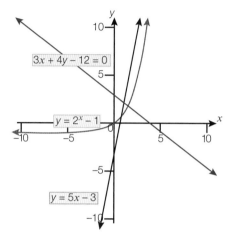

Exercise 2.1

1. Identify which of these equations are linear equations and which are not.

   (a) $y = 3x$ (b) $y = \dfrac{2}{x} + 4$ (c) $y = 7x^2 - 3$

   (d) $x = 9 - 5y$ (e) $x - y - \dfrac{3}{4} = 0$ (f) $y = -8$

2. Which of these are graphs of linear functions?

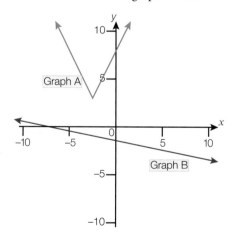

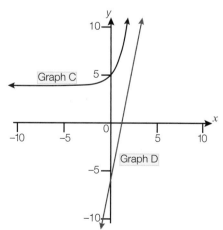

Rearranging linear equations

You need to be able to rearrange linear equations into different forms. Rearranging an equation can be used to find its solution, and is a skill required so that you can enter equations into your GDC in the correct format.

Worked example 2.1

Q. (a) Rearrange $y = 5x - 3$ into the form:

   (i) $y - mx = c$ (ii) $y - mx + c = 0$

(b) Rearrange $3x + 4y - 12 = 0$ into the form:

   (i) $mx + by = c$

   (ii) $by = mx + c$

   (iii) $y = \dfrac{mx + c}{d}$

> Subtract $5x$ from both sides of the equation.

> Add 3 to both sides of the equation from (i).

> Add 12 to both sides of the equation.

> Subtract $3x$ from both sides of the equation from (i).

> Divide both sides of the equation from (ii) by 4.

A. (a) (i) $y - 5x = -3$

   (ii) $y - 5x + 3 = 0$

(b) (i) $3x + 4y = 12$

   (ii) $4y = -3x + 12$

   (iii) $y = \dfrac{-3x + 12}{4}$

Learning links

2A Things to remember when rearranging equations

To rearrange equations, you need to remember some important points about algebra:

1. Letters are used to represent unknown values; these are called the **variables**.

2. Each equation is made up of different **terms** that are separated by either a '+' or '−' operator or the '=' sign. The '×' and '÷' operators do **not** separate terms; they form part of the term.

continued . . .

3. To make a variable the 'subject' of the equation, you have to get that variable on its own on one side of the '=' sign.

4. You might need to apply the **inverse** operation ('undo it') to make the variable the subject of the equation.

5. You need to apply the same operations to both sides of the equation to keep it balanced.

6. Remember the **BIDMAS** order of operations: deal with brackets first (by expanding them), then indices (powers or exponents can be reversed by taking the equivalent root), then multiplication and division (if both are present, do them from left to right), and finally addition and subtraction (if both are present, do them from left to right).

Exercise 2.2

1. The following are all linear equations.
   Rearrange them into the general form $y = mx + c$.

   (a) $x - y + 4 = 0$
   (b) $3x + y = 7$
   (c) $x - 9y = 15$

   (d) $5(3 - x) - 2y = 0$
   (e) $11(x - y) = 10$
   (f) $2(x - 3y - 4) = 5$

   (g) $\dfrac{1}{2}x + \dfrac{2}{3}y = 9$
   (h) $\dfrac{5x}{y-1} = \dfrac{4}{3}$
   (i) $\dfrac{y-7}{x} = \dfrac{2}{9}$

2. The following are all linear equations.
   Rearrange them into the form $ax + by + c = 0$.

   (a) $y = 5x + 4$
   (b) $y = \dfrac{1}{2}(x - 5)$
   (c) $3(2 - x) = 2y$

   (d) $3(x - 2) = 4(y + 1)$
   (e) $\dfrac{2y}{3} = 3x$
   (f) $\dfrac{1 - 5x}{2} = y$

Solving linear equations

Traditionally, people used graphs or algebra to solve linear equations. Today, you can solve linear equations using your GDC.

To gain confidence in using your GDC accurately, it is a good idea to try solving some simple equations using algebra first, and then check the answers using your GDC. See Learning links 2B on page 42 if you need a reminder of how to solve linear equations algebraically or graphically.

hint

When you are asked to **solve** an equation, you are being asked to find the numerical value that makes the equation true after you replace all instances of the letter with the value; such a value is called a **solution** to the equation.

2B Solving linear equations using algebra

To solve an equation using algebra, remember the following points:

- When solving an equation you need to make the variable the subject.

- Make sure you keep the equation balanced by doing the same to both sides of the '=' sign.

$$\frac{4(x+3)}{2} = 24$$

> In this example, 'x' is the variable, so we need to make this the subject, i.e. get it on its own.

$$4(x+3) = (4 \times x) + (4 \times 3)$$

$$= 4x + 12$$

> By the order of operations, we first need to expand (multiply out) the bracket on the lefthand side.

$$\frac{4x+12}{2} = 24$$

> Multiply each term on both sides of the '=' sign by 2 (to get rid of the fraction).

$$4x + 12 = 48$$

> Subtract 12 from both sides.

$$4x = 36$$

$$x = 9$$

> Then divide both sides by 4.

So the solution is $x = 9$.

- Check that the solution is correct by substituting the value for x in the original equation:

$$\frac{4(9+3)}{2} = \frac{4 \times 12}{2} = \frac{48}{2} = 24$$

> Substitute in $x = 9$.

Therefore the solution is correct.

2C Solving linear equations using a graph

You can solve a linear equation by plotting its graph, in the general form $y = mx + c$, on the a set of **axes** (**x-axis** and **y-axis**).

Suppose we wanted to find the solution of the equation $5x - 3 = 22$.

- Rewrite the equation in the general form $y = mx + c$

and plot the graph of this equation:

$$y = 5x - 3$$

continued . . .

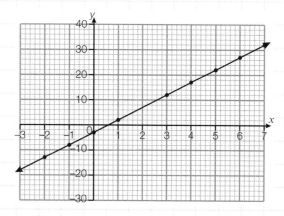

- Use the graph of $y = mx + c$ to find the value of x at which the original equation is true.

From the graph,
$y = 22$ when $x = 5$.
$5x - 3 = y = 22$

If $5x - 3 = 22$, and $y = 5x - 3$, then $y = 22$. Find 22 on the y-axis. At the point where $y = 22$ meets the graph of $y = 5x - 3$, read off the x-coordinate from the x-axis (you might find it helpful to draw the line $y = 22$). The x-coordinate is the solution.

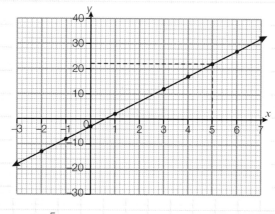

$x = 5$

- Check your answer by substituting the value of x back into the original equation.

$5x - 3 = 22$

If $x = 5$, then

$5x - 3 = 5 \times 5 - 3$

$\qquad = 25 - 3 = 22$

The solution is correct.

Worked example 2.2

Q. Solve the following equations using algebra, and check your solutions using your GDC.

(a) $5x - 8 = -14$

(b) $\frac{1}{2}y + 12 = 2y - 3$

(c) $3(x + 1) = 5(x - 2)$

(d) $\frac{3 - 2x}{4} = 5$

Add 8 to both sides then divide both sides by 5.

A. (a) $5x - 8 = -14$

$5x = -6$

$x = -1.2$

Check the answer using your GDC. (See '2.1(b) *Solving linear equations using an equation solver*' on page 653 of the GDC chapter if you need a reminder).

```
TEXAS
5X-8+14=0
■X=-1.199999999...
 bound={-1E99,1...
■left-rt=0
```

```
CASIO
Eq:5X-8=-14
   X=-1.2
Lft=-14
Rgt=-14

REPT
```

Add 3 to both sides, subtract $\frac{1}{2}y$ from both sides, then multiply by $\frac{2}{3}$.

(b) $\frac{1}{2}y + 12 = 2y - 3$

$15 = \frac{3}{2}y$

$10 = y$

Check the answer using your GDC.

```
TEXAS
0.5X+12-2X+3=0
■X=10
 bound={-1E99,1...
■left-rt=0
```

```
CASIO
Eq:0.5X+12=2X-3
   X=10
Lft=17
Rgt=17

REPT
```

Expand the brackets on each side. Combine the terms containing the variable on one side of the equation, and move the constants to the other side.

(c) $3(x + 1) = 5(x - 2)$

$3x + 3 = 5x - 10$

$13 = 2x$

$6.5 = x$

$\longrightarrow$

continued . . .

> Check the answer using your GDC.

TEXAS	CASIO

3(X+1)-5(X-2)=0
∎X=6.5
  bound={-1ᴇ99,1…
∎left-rt=0
	Eq:3(X+1)=5(X-2)
	  X=6.5
	Lft=22.5
	Rgt=22.5
	
	REPT

> Multiply both sides by 4 to get rid of the fraction first. Add $2x$ to both sides, then subtract 20 from both sides. Divide both sides by 2.

(d) $\dfrac{3-2x}{4}=5$

$3-2x=20$

$-17=2x$

$-8.5=x$

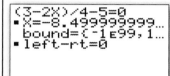

> Check the answer using your GDC.

TEXAS	CASIO

(3-2X)/4-5=0
∎X=-8.499999999…
  bound={-1ᴇ99,1…
∎left-rt=0
	Eq:(3-2X)÷4=5
	  X=-8.5
	Lft=5
	Rgt=5
	
	REPT

Exercise 2.3

Solve the following linear equations and check your answer using a GDC.

1. (a) $5m + 8 = 13$ (b) $0.2z - 12 = 2$

   (c) $6 - 2y = 8$ (d) $3 - 0.5x = -5$

2. (a) $6m - 2 = 3m + 8$ (b) $5 - 2f = 3 + 8f$ (c) $7x - 4 = 10 + 2x$

3. (a) $5(x + 1) = 3(2 - x)$

   (b) $0.4(z - 2) = 1.2(5 - z)$

   (c) $-2(y + 5) = 3(3 - y)$

4. (a) $\dfrac{x+2}{5} = 3$ (b) $\dfrac{y-3}{2} = \dfrac{y}{5}$

   (c) $\dfrac{m+1}{3} = \dfrac{4-m}{2}$ (d) $\dfrac{2x+5}{3} = \dfrac{3-4x}{2}$

2.2 Pairs of linear equations

In some situations you may have two **unknowns** that need to be found. If there are two conditions involving the unknowns, you can write an equation for each. For example:

> Dean buys 3 chocolate bars and 4 cokes for $12.
>
> Poppy buys 5 chocolate bars and 1 coke for $3.

Let x dollars be the price of each chocolate bar and y dollars the price of each coke drink. Then we know that:

$$3x + 4y = 12 \text{ and}$$

$$5x + y = 3$$

This forms a pair of linear equations.

A **pair of linear equations** means 'two linear equations containing two values that you do not know'.

Pairs of linear equations are also called **simultaneous equations** because both equations are true at the same time (i.e. simultaneously).

Solving pairs of linear equations

You can solve pairs of linear equations, but instead of having to find the value of one unknown, you need to find the values of two unknowns. Again, traditional methods include drawing a graph or using algebra but you can also use your GDC. For a reminder of the more traditional methods, see Learning links 2D and 2E on page 47.

For most GDCs you will need both equations to be in their general form in order to use them (for example $y = mx + c$). Make sure you are confident in rearranging equations because your GDC cannot do it for you. (See Learning links 2A on page 10 if you need a reminder of how to rearrange equations.)

Worked example 2.3

Q. (a) Use your GDC to plot the graph of each equation and hence solve the following pair of linear equations:

$$y + x = 2 \qquad \text{and} \qquad y + 3x = 0$$

A. (a)
$$y + x = 2 \qquad\qquad\qquad y + 3x = 0$$
$$y = 2 - x \qquad\qquad\qquad y = -3x$$
$$y_1 = -x + 2 \qquad\qquad\qquad y_2 = -3x$$

Rearrange the equations so that they are both in the general form $y = mx + c$.

continued . . .

 Use your GDC to solve. See '2.2 (a) Solving pairs of linear equations using a graph' on page 653 of the GDC chapter if you need a reminder.

See '2.2 (a) Solving pairs of linear equations using a graph' on page 653

TEXAS

CASIO

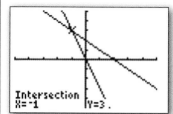

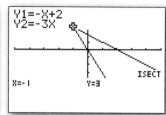

$x = -1$ and $y = 3$.

Write down the answer in the appropriate format.

Q. (b) Use your GDC to solve the following pairs of linear equations using an algebraic method:

$$5x + 2y = 13 \qquad \text{and} \qquad y = x - 4$$

Rewrite each equation in the form $ax + by = c$.

A. (b) $5x + 2y = 13$ $y = x - 4$
(The equation is already $-x + y = -4$
in the required format.)

Use your GDC to solve. See '2.2 (b) Solving pairs of linear equations using an equation solver' on page 655 of the GDC chapter if you need a reminder.

TEXAS

CASIO

Write down the answer in the appropriate format.

$x = 3$ and $y = -1$

Learning links

2D Solving pairs of linear equations using algebra

Using **elimination**, solve the equations $x + 2y = 12$ and $x - y = -3$.

1. Number each equation:

$$x + 2y = 12 \quad (1)$$
$$x - y = -3 \quad (2)$$

continued . . .

2. Subtract one equation from the other (or add them) to remove one of the unknowns.

$$x - x + 2y - (-y) = 12 - (-3)$$
$$3y = 15$$
$$y = 5$$

> In this example, (1) – (2) will eliminate x and leave us with just y.

3. Substitute this value of y into one of the original equations to find the value of x.

$$y = 5 \Rightarrow x - 5 = -3$$
$$x = 2$$

> Use equation (2).

4. So the solution is $x = 2$ and $y = 5$.

Using **substitution**, solve the equations $5x + 2y = 13$ and $y = x - 4$.

1. Number the equations as before:

$$5x + 2y = 13 \quad (1)$$
$$y = x - 4 \quad (2)$$

> In this example, it is more convenient to substitute (2) into (1). So, in equation (1) 'y' is replaced by '$x - 4$'.

2. Substitute one equation into the other to eliminate one of the unknowns.

$$5x + 2(x - 4) = 13$$
$$5x + 2x - 8 = 13$$
$$7x = 13 + 8$$
$$7x = 21$$
$$x = 3$$

3. Substitute the value of 'x' into one of the original equations.

$$x = 3 \Rightarrow y = x - 4 = 3 - 4 = -1$$

> Here we have used equation (2).

So the solution is $x = 3$ and $y = -1$.

2E Solving pairs of linear equations using graphs

You can solve pairs of linear equations by plotting their graphs, in the general form $y = mx + c$, on the same set of **axes** (**x-axis** and **y-axis**).

Suppose we wanted to solve the following pair of linear equations: $2x + y = 8$ and $x - y = 1$.

continued . . .

1. Plot them on the same set of axes.

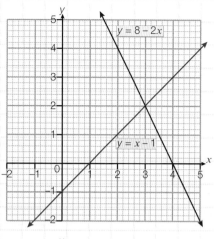

2. Find the **intersection** of the lines (the point where the two lines cross); this is where the x and y values are the same for both equations. The x and y coordinates are the solutions to the equations, so $x = 3$ and $y = 2$.

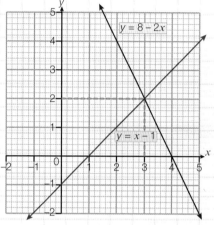

3. Check the answer by substituting these values into the original equations:

$$2x + y = 8$$
$$2 \times 3 + 2 = 8$$
and
$$x - y = 1$$
$$3 - 2 = 1$$

Exercise 2.4

Solve the following pairs of linear equations with your GDC.

1. (a) $y = x + 5$ and $y = 2x - 3$

   (b) $y = 3x - 5$ and $y = 10 - 2x$

   (c) $y = 5 - 2x$ and $4x + 3y = 14$

   (d) $2x + 3y = 42$ and $3x = 4y - 5$

   (e) $5x + 3y + 11 = 0$ and $2x - 4y = 10$

   (f) $2x + 7y - 9 = 0$ and $3x - 5y = 6$

   (g) $y + 2 = x$ and $y = 1.8x - 4.88$

   (h) $7x - 6y + 12 = 0$ and $4x + 3y - 9 = 0$

Do you think that it is easier to work out the solution to a problem if you can see it as a picture? Think about solving pairs of linear equations: which method is the clearest for you? Using algebra, graphs or technology (GDC)? After you have solved the problem, which method has given you the best understanding of the answer?

2. (a) $0.78s + 0.54t = 1.96$ and $3s - 2t = 23$

(b) $0.59s + \dfrac{1}{3}t = \dfrac{9}{7}$ and $1.7s = 3.1t + 8.4$

(c) $-8s + 4t + \dfrac{7}{6} = 0$ and $s - \dfrac{2}{3}t = \dfrac{8}{11}$

(d) $0.125s + 0.61t - 45 = 0$ and $\dfrac{1}{4}s - 1.15t = 11$

Solving practical problems involving pairs of linear equations

Pairs of linear equations can be used to solve practical problems that you might come across in everyday life.

Worked example 2.4

Q. One day, Kazuo orders three drinks and two pizzas from a pizza restaurant in town. The total cost comes to $7.95. The next day, Kazuo orders five drinks and three pizzas. This time he pays $12.42. He expects his friends to pay him back for these purchases. But what is the cost of one drink? And what is the cost of one pizza?

> Read the question, and decide on letters for the unknown quantities that you are trying to find.

A. Let x be the cost of a drink and y the cost of a pizza (in dollars).

> Translate the statements in the problem into algebraic equations: you know that on the first day Kazuo bought three drinks $(3x)$ and two pizzas $(2y)$ for $7.95, so you can write this as an equation: $3x + 2y = 7.95$.

Equation for the first day: $3x + 2y = 7.95$
Equation for the second day: $5x + 3y = 12.42$

> Solve the pair of equations using your preferred method; here we have used the equation solver on the GDC.

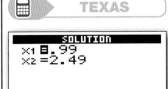 TEXAS

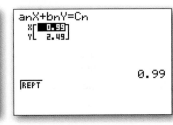 CASIO

continued . . .

Write down the answer.

$x = 0.99$ and $y = 2.49$

Kazuo can tell his friends that a drink cost $0.99 and a pizza cost $2.49.

Exercise 2.5

1. Two litres of milk and three loaves of bread cost 101 roubles. Three litres of milk and one loaf of bread cost 85 roubles.

   Using the information above, we can form the equation:

   $2m + 3b = 101$

   where m is the price of a litre of milk and b is the price of a loaf of bread in roubles.

   (a) Form another equation using the information from above.

   (b) Hence solve the pair of equations to find the values of m and b.

2. Zainab and Zahra bought some chocolates from the duty free shop in Dubai.

   Zainab bought 5 bars of Miniature Snickers and 3 bars of Twix Classics for a total of 126 AED.

   Zahra bought 6 bars of Miniature Snickers and 2 bars of Twix Classics for a total of 100 AED.

   Zainab's purchases can be represented by the equation:

   $5s + 3t = 126$

   where s is the price (in AED) of a Snickers bar and t is the price of a Twix bar.

   (a) Write an equation to represent Zahra's purchases.

   (b) Solve the pair of linear equations to find the price of each bar of chocolate.

3. The sum of two numbers is 97 and the difference between them is 23.

   By representing the larger number as x and the smaller one as y, write two separate equations for the sum and difference of the two numbers. Solve the equations to find both numbers.

4. Anton and Simone went to a music shop. They decided to buy the same CDs and DVDs. Anton bought five CDs and three DVDs for £104.92. Simone bought two CDs and seven DVDs for £128.91.

An equation for Anton's purchases can be written as:

$$5c + 3d = 104.92$$

where c and d are the unit costs in pounds of the CDs and DVDs, respectively.

(a) Write another equation to represent Simone's purchases.

(b) Hence solve the pair of equations to find the unit costs of the CDs and DVDs.

5. Three packs of batteries and a calculator cost £23.47. Five packs of batteries and seven calculators cost £116.45. Solve the appropriate simultaneous equations to find the costs of one pack of batteries and one calculator.

6. New Age Computers sells two models of laptop: easy-click and smooth-tab. Three easy-click and four smooth-tab laptops cost $2987. Two easy-clicks and five smooth-tabs cost $3123.

(a) Form a pair of linear equations to represent this information.

(b) Solve the equations to find the unit cost of each type of laptop.

7. Two adults and five children pay a total of $120 for a coach journey. Three adults and seven children pay a total of $172.50 for the same coach journey.

Find the total cost of tickets for eight adults and 11 children travelling on the same coach journey.

8. A mathematics test consists of shorter and longer questions. Each shorter question is worth 6 marks and each longer question is worth 11 marks.

Mrs Pavlov sets a test with 15 questions and a total of 120 marks. By forming the appropriate equations and solving them, find the number of questions of each type on this test.

9. In the diagram below, the straight line ST, with equation $3x - y + 7 = 0$, intersects the coordinate axes at the points S and T.

(a) Find the coordinates of the points S and T.

A different straight line, with equation $2x + y + 3 = 0$, intersects the line ST at the point R.

(b) Find the coordinates of the point R.

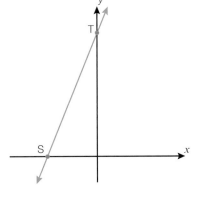

2.3 Quadratic equations

Quadratic equations can be recognised by the x^2 term, which they always contain.

The general form of a **quadratic equation** is $ax^2 + bx + c = 0$, where $a \neq 0$ (but b and c can be zero).

hint

Remember that $\neq$ means 'is not equal to' or 'does not equal'.

For example, the following equations are quadratic:

$2x^2 + 3x - 4 = 0$ The equation has $a = 2$, $b = 3$ and $c = -4$.

$x^2 - 4x = 0$ The equation has $a = 1$, $b = -4$ and $c = 0$.

$4x^2 - 49 = 0$ The equation has $a = 4$, $b = 0$ and $c = -49$.

When plotted on a graph, a quadratic equation $y = ax^2 + bx + c$ forms a curve that has one turning point and a central line of symmetry. This type of curve is called a **parabola**.

To plot the graph of a quadratic equation, it needs to be rearranged into the general form $y = ax^2 + bx + c$. If a is positive, the curve will have a minimum point; if a is negative, the curve will have a maximum point.

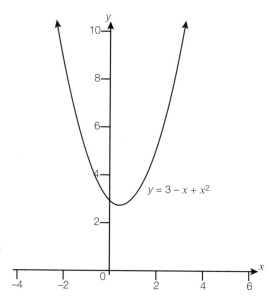

Minimum point because a is positive

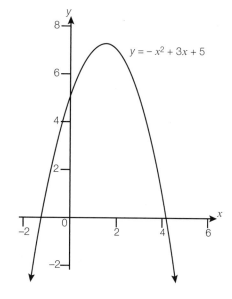

Maximum point because a is negative

A parabola is a very important shape.

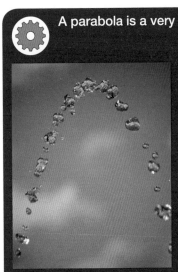

- If you throw a ball, the ball takes the path of a parabola; you can use this fact to predict the best angle at which to serve a tennis ball.
- Satellite dishes are parabolic, because this shape concentrates all the radio waves into one focal point.
- The jets of water from a fountain also follow a parabolic shape; this is helpful in predicting the paths of large quantities of water.
- The parabola is a useful shape in engineering. When you pass bridges, have a look at their shape and see how many of these are parabolic.

FF >> *You will learn more about parabolas in Chapter 18.*

Worked example 2.5

Q. Look carefully at the following equations. Identify the quadratic equations and rearrange them into the form $ax^2 + bx + c = 0$.

(a) $x^2 = 5 - 2x$ (b) $3 + x^3 = 5x$ (c) $3 - 2x = \dfrac{4}{x^2}$

(d) $4 + x(x + 2) = 0$ (e) $x^2 = 7$ (f) $11 = x^2 + 2x^{-1}$

> Add $2x$ to both sides, and subtract 5 from both sides.

A. (a) $x^2 = 5 - 2x$ is a quadratic equation.
   Rearranging gives $x^2 + 2x - 5 = 0$

(b) $3 + x^3 = 5x$ is not a quadratic equation because it contains an x^3 term.

> The x^2 term is dividing the number 4, so we actually have $\frac{1}{x^2}$ or x^{-2}, not x^2. (See Learning links '1B' on page 24 if you need a reminder of negative indices.)

(c) $3 - 2x = \dfrac{4}{x^2}$ is not a quadratic equation because it contains x^{-2} rather than x^2.

> Expanding the brackets gives you an x^2 term.

(d) $4 + x(x + 2) = 0$ is a quadratic equation.
   Rearranging gives:
   $4 + x^2 + 2x = 0$
   $x^2 + 2x + 4 = 0$

This equation contains the reciprocal of $x\left(\frac{1}{x}\right)$ so to write it in the general form of a quadratic equation, where we have bx, we would need to multiply through by x. Doing so creates the following equation: $11x = x^3 + 2$, which is not a quadratic because the highest power of x is 3, not 2.

continued . . .

(e) $x^2 = 7$ is a quadratic equation.

Rearranging gives $x^2 - 7 = 0$

(f) $11x = x^2 + 2x^{-1}$ is not a quadratic equation, it is cubic

$$11x = x^2 + 2\frac{1}{x}$$

Multiplying each side by x:

$$11x^2 = x^3 + 2$$
$$x^3 - 11x^2 + 2$$

Exercise 2.6

1. Determine which of the following are quadratic equations.

   (a) $5x^2 = 7$
   (b) $4 - x^2 = 0$
   (c) $x^2 + x^3 - 7x = 5$

   (d) $x^2 - 11x + 28 = 0$
   (e) $\dfrac{5}{x^2} + 3x - 2 = 0$
   (f) $10 - x - 9x^2 = 0$

   (g) $3x^2 + \dfrac{5}{x} - 6 = 0$
   (h) $0 = 1 + x + x^2$
   (i) $-x^2 - 4(x + 1) = 0$

2. Six graphs are shown below. Indicate which of them represent quadratic functions.

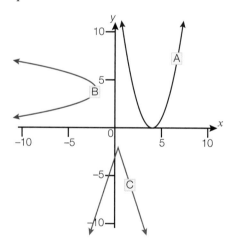
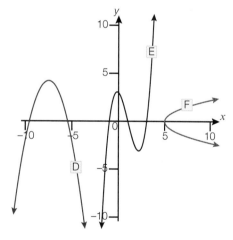

3. The equations of some quadratic functions are given below. Indicate whether the parabola will have a minimum or maximum point.

   (a) $y = 2x - x^2$
   (b) $y = x^2 - 10x + 2$
   (c) $y = 2x^2 + 3x - 5$
   (d) $y = 56 + x - 7x^2$

4. Rearrange the following quadratic equations into the general form $ax^2 + bx + c = 0$.

   (a) $x^2 = -x$
   (b) $x^2 - 2x = 3$
   (c) $4x^2 = 4 - x$

   (d) $6 - x^2 = -5x$
   (e) $x^2 + 5x - 8 = 7$
   (f) $8 - 6x = 15 - x^2$

Solving quadratic equations

Remember that the **solution**(s) of an equation are the numerical value(s) for the variables that make the equation true.

To solve a quadratic equation, you need to find the value(s) of the unknown variable that makes the equation $ax^2 + bx + c = 0$, true. In other words, the value(s) of x that make $ax^2 + bx + c$ equal zero.

You might have noticed that we talked about the 'value(s)' of the unknown variable. The '(s)' signifies that there can be more than one value for the variable. For quadratic equations, there are actually three possible outcomes of solving the equation:

- no solution
- one solution
- two solutions.

When the equation has two solutions, this means that there are **two** values of the variable that will make the equation true. But be careful, you do **not** substitute both values into the equation at the same time! You substitute one **or** the other solution, and either one will be correct.

For example, the solutions to the quadratic equation $x^2 - 9x + 20 = 0$ are $x = 4$ and $x = 5$. It is wrong to substitute both 4 and 5 into the equation at the same time: $4^2 - (9 \times 5) + 20 \neq 0$.

Instead, you should substitute $x = 4$ into the equation to check it works, and then substitute in $x = 5$:

when $x = 4$, $(4 \times 4) - (9 \times 4) + 20 = 16 - 36 + 20 = 0$

and

when $x = 5$, $(5 \times 5) - (9 \times 5) + 20 = 25 - 45 + 20 = 0$

Both $x = 4$ and $x = 5$ are solutions.

Different maths books may use different names to refer to the solutions of quadratic equations. They are sometimes called 'zeros' or 'the **roots** of an equation' rather than 'solutions'.

Like the other types of equation we have met in this chapter, a quadratic equation can be solved using algebra, by drawing a graph or using your GDC. The GDC makes it much quicker to solve the equation. However, it is a good idea to also know how to solve quadratic equations using the more traditional methods of algebra or by drawing a graph, so that you can use one method to find the answer and another to check the answer.

For more about how to use the more traditional methods to solve quadratic equations, see Learning links 2F and 2G on pages 58–59.

There are two different ways you can use your GDC to solve quadratic equations. You can plot a graph and see where the graph crosses the x-axis, or you can use an equation solver.

It is a good idea to learn both algebraic and graphical methods on your GDC and become comfortable with using them. In examinations, questions can be set that test your knowledge of either.

Worked example 2.6

Q. Solve the equation $x^2 - 4x - 5 = 0$, where the solutions are integers.

Use your GDC to draw the graph; make sure you can see the whole curve. See section '2.3(a) Solving quadratic equations using a graph' on page 656 of the GDC chapter if you need a reminder of how to do this.

A.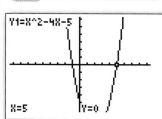

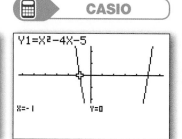

hint

Write down the answer appropriately.

$x = -1$ or $x = 5$

Remember that an integer is any whole number: positive, negative or zero.

Confirm your results using the equation solver on your GDC. See section '2.3(b) Solving quadratic equations using an equation solver' on page 657 of the GDC chapter if you need a reminder of how to do this.

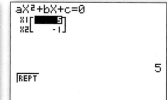

$x = -1$ or $x = 5$

Answer is confirmed.

Worked example 2.7

Q. Solve the equation $2x^2 - 5x + 1 = 0$, where the solutions are not integers.

Use your GDC to draw the graph as in Worked example 2.6.

A.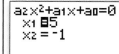

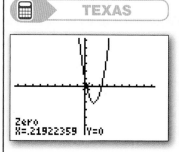

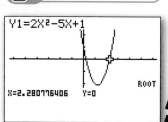

continued . . .

Write down the answers to three significant figures.

$x = 0.219$ (3 s.f.)

$x = 2.28$ (3 s.f.)

Confirm your results using the equation solver on your GDC as in Worked example 2.6.

TEXAS

$a_2x^2 + a_1x + a_0 = 0$
$x_1 \blacksquare 2.280776406$
$x_2 = .2192235936$

MAIN MODE COEF STO F◀▶D

CASIO

$aX^2 + bX + c = 0$
$x_1 [2.2807]$
$x_2 [0.2192]$

2.280776406

REPT

Answer is confirmed.

$x = 0.219$ (3 s.f.)

$x = 2.28$ (3 s.f.)

Learning links

2F Solving quadratic equations using algebra

When the equation is given in the form $(x - p)(x - q) = 0$

Suppose that you are asked to solve $(x - 5)(x + 1) = 0$.

One of the brackets, $(x - p)$ or $(x - q)$, must equal zero because only multiplying by zero will give zero! Write an equation making each bracket equal to zero to work out the possible values of x.

$5 - 5 = 0$

So, if $(x - 5) = 0$ then $x = 5$

$-1 + 1 = 0$

Or if $(x + 1) = 0$, then $x = -1$

Hence the solutions to this equation are $x = 5$ or $x = -1$.

When the equation is given in the form $ax^2 + bx + c = 0$ and $a = 1$

Suppose that you are asked to solve $x^2 - 2x - 3 = 0$.

This equation needs to be factorised before it can be solved. To **factorise** means to put into brackets so when $a = 1$, factorising means that $ax^2 + bx + c$ becomes $a(x + p)(x + q)$. In this example, you need to think about what value of p and what value of q would add together to give you -2 (the number 'b' in front of x) and multiply together to give you -3 (the **constant** 'c')

$\longrightarrow$

continued . . .

In this case, $p = -3$ and $q = 1$ would work, because

$$-3 + 1 = -2$$

$$-3 \times 1 = -3$$

So we can rewrite $x^2 - 2x - 3 = 0$ as

$$(x - 3)(x + 1) = 0$$

and then use the process shown in the previous example to find that

$$x = 3 \text{ or } x = -1$$

Be careful when factorising because the relationship is more complicated than demonstrated here when $a \neq 1$.

exam tip

Don't worry if you find it difficult to factorise. You can always use one of the other methods to solve the equation.

2G Solving quadratic equations using a graph

Suppose we wanted to solve the equation $-2x^2 - 3x = -5$.

1. First make sure that the terms are arranged in the general form $ax^2 + bx + c = 0$.

   $$2x^2 + 3x - 5 = 0$$

Add $2x^2 + 3x$ to both sides of the original equation.

2. Plot the graph of $y = ax^2 + bx + c$

   $$y = 2x^2 + 3x - 5$$

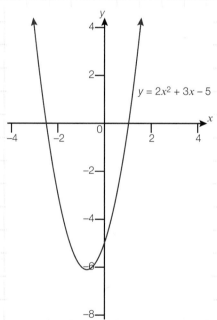

3. You know that the solution(s) to the equation $ax^2 + bx + c = 0$ is the value of x that makes it true; the equation is true when $y = 0$. On any graph, $y = 0$ where the graph crosses the x-axis; the x-values at these points are the solutions. This means that a quadratic equation could have the following number of solutions:

   - **zero**, if the graph does not meet the x-axis at all

   - **one**, if the graph meets the x-axis at only one place

   - **two**, if the graph crosses the x-axis at two points.

   In the example, the graph cuts the x-axis at the two points $(-2.5, 0)$ and $(1, 0)$.

   This means that the quadratic equation $2x^2 + 3x - 5 = 0$ has two solutions:

   $$x = -2.5 \text{ or } x = 1$$

Exercise 2.7

1. Solve the following quadratic equations using your GDC.

   (a) $3x^2 + x - 4 = 0$

   (b) $7x^2 - 18x + 8 = 0$

   (c) $-6x^2 - 11x + 10 = 0$

   (d) $-0.5x^2 + 4.8x + 6 = 0$

   (e) $\frac{1}{3}x^2 - 5x + 1 = 0$

   (f) $-\frac{5}{7}x^2 + \frac{2}{3}x + 1 = 0$

2. Rearrange these quadratic equations to the general form, and then solve them using your GDC.

   (a) $2x^2 + 3x = 2$

   (b) $3x^2 = 9 - 11x$

   (c) $13 = x^2 + 7x$

   (d) $3 - 6x^2 = 7x$

   (e) $x(4x - 5) = 8$

   (f) $4 - x(9x + 1) = 0$

3. Solve the following quadratic equations.

   (a) $1.5x^2 - 2.3x - 4.7 = 0$

   (b) $8x^2 + 13x = 11$

   (c) $x(2x - 7) = 5$

   (d) $4.1x^2 - 17x + 3.2 = 0$

   (e) $x + 2 = \frac{1}{x}$

   (f) $x = \frac{6}{3x + 1}$

Solving practical problems involving quadratic equations

At the beginning of this chapter, you saw an example of the type of problem considered by Egyptian engineers thousands of years ago. Quadratic equations are still very useful in solving practical problems you might encounter in everyday life. For example, you can use quadratic equations to find out the area of a rectangular or circular space for a given perimeter, or estimate the time it takes for a stone to fall to the bottom of a well.

> It is helpful to sketch a diagram. We know that there is 30 m of fencing for three sides because the fourth side is the wall. The pen is a rectangle, so we know that one side will be the same length as the wall and the other two sides will be the same length as each other. If we label the shorter sides x, then we know that the fencing needed for the two shorter edges is $2x$. The rest of the fence can be used for the edge opposite the wall. We can write an expression for this length:
>
> $30 - 2x$.

Worked example 2.8

Q. A farmer has 30 m of fencing to make a safe rectangular enclosure (a 'pen') for his lambs. He can use a wall to make one side, and the fencing to make the other three sides. He would like the area of the enclosure to be 108 m². Find the length and width of this pen.

A.
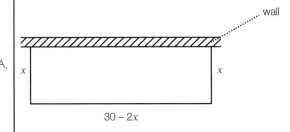

continued . . .

continued . . .

Substitute the variables for the sides of the rectangle into the formula for the area of a rectangle.

Area of rectangle = length × width

Area = $x(30 - 2x)$

We know the area must equal 108 m² so we can write an equation to solve.

$x(30 - 2x) = 108$

If you multiply out the brackets and rearrange, you will see that this is a quadratic equation.

$30x - 2x^2 = 108$
$-2x^2 + 30x - 108 = 0$

Use your GDC to solve.

TEXAS

CASIO

a₂x²+a₁x+a₀=0
x1 ◼9
x2 =6

MAIN MODE COEF STO F◄►D

aX²+bX+c=0
x1[◼ 9]
x2[6]

REPT

9

Two solutions are possible.

$x = 9$ or $x = 6$

Remember to find the length of the other side, $30 - 2x$, for each value of x.

If $x = 9$, then $30 - 2x = 30 - 2 \times 9 = 12$ m
If $x = 6$, then $30 - 2x = 30 - 2 \times 6 = 18$ m

If $x = 9$, the dimensions are 9 m by 12 m.
If $x = 6$, the dimensions are 6 m by 18 m.

Exercise 2.8

1. The product of two consecutive positive integers is 306. If the smaller number is n, write an equation in the form $an^2 + bn + c = 0$ to represent the product of the numbers. Hence solve the equation to find the two numbers.

2. The length of a rectangle is 7 cm more than its width. It has a diagonal of length 13 cm.

   (a) Write down a quadratic equation in x, using the information you have been given. (*Hint*: You may use Pythagoras' theorem.)

   (b) Solve this equation to find the dimensions of the rectangle.

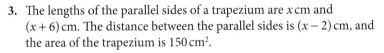

3. The lengths of the parallel sides of a trapezium are x cm and $(x + 6)$ cm. The distance between the parallel sides is $(x - 2)$ cm, and the area of the trapezium is 150 cm².

   (a) Form a quadratic equation in terms of x for the area of the trapezium.

   (b) Solve the equation to find x.

   (c) Hence find the dimensions of the trapezium.

4. A stone is thrown directly upwards. The height of the stone above ground level, h metres, after t seconds is given by the formula:

   $$h = 13 + 8t - 1.9t^2$$

   (a) Calculate the time it takes for the stone to reach a height of 20 m above the ground.

   (b) How long does it take before the stone hits the ground?

Summary

You should know:

- how to recognise the following types of equation:
  - linear equations have one unknown and the general form $y = mx + c$ or $ax + by + c = 0$
  - pairs of linear equations contain two unknowns, e.g. x and y
  - quadratic equations have one unknown and the general form $ax^2 + bx + c = 0$ where $a \neq 0$ (but b and c can be 0)
- that rearranging equations is required in order to solve them, even if using your GDC
- how to use your GDC to solve:
  - linear equations with one variable
  - pairs of linear equations with two variables
  - quadratic equations

  by

  - drawing a graph
  - using the equation solver

  and be confident using both methods.

Mixed examination practice

Exam-style questions

1. Solve the equation $2(x - 3) + 5x = 36$.

2. Solve the following pairs of simultaneous equations:

   (a) $x + 2y = 3$ and $4x + 3y = 2$

   (b) $3x + 7y - 20 = 0$ and $11x - 8y + 5 = 0$

   (c) $5x + 8y + 2 = 0$ and $6x - y + 19 = 0$

3. Solve the following quadratic equations:

   (a) $(7x - 2)(3x - 1) = 0$ (b) $x^2 - 3x - 9 = 0$

   (c) $x^2 + 2x = 34$ (d) $x^2 = 7x + 15$ (e) $7.5x^2 - 6x = 9.8$

4. Igor and Irishka are returning from a trip to India. They have bought presents for their friends and family.

   Igor bought 4 bracelets and 3 pendants for 5529 INR (rupees).

   Irishka bought 2 bracelets and 5 pendants for 6751 INR.

   (a) Form two simultaneous equations, using the information given.

   (b) Solve the pair of equations to find the price of each bracelet and each pendant.

5. The line with equation $y = mx + c$ passes through the points with coordinates $(1, -5)$ and $(4, 4)$.

   (a) Write down two equations to represent the fact that the line passes through the two points given above.

   (b) Solve the equations to find the values of m and c.

   (c) Does the point $(-4, 11)$ lie on this line?

6. Safe Power supplies electricity to the Ahmed household. The bill for a three-month period consists of two parts: a fixed (standing) charge and a usage charge. The total charge per quarter, C, in pounds can be represented as $C = a + bn$, where a is the fixed charge per quarter, b is the unit charge (per kWh used), and n is the number of units (kWh) used in that quarter.

   Last quarter the Ahmeds used 820 units of electricity and paid £106.24.

   In the previous quarter they used 650 units and paid £85.84.

   (a) Write down two equations in the variables a and b.

   (b) Find the values of a and b.

   (c) How much can the Ahmeds expect to pay next quarter if their estimated electricity usage is 745 units in the next three months?

7. A rectangular field has length 18 m longer than its width. If the area of the field is 760 m², calculate the dimensions of the field.

8. A ball is projected vertically into the air from ground level. After t seconds, the ball reaches a height of h metres. The equation for the flight of the ball can be expressed as:

$$h = 11t - 2.3t^2$$

   (a) How long does it take the ball to reach a height of 10 metres?

   (b) Calculate the time it takes for the ball to return to ground level.

Past paper questions

1. A store sells bread and milk. On Tuesday, 8 loaves of bread and 5 litres of milk were sold for $21.40. On Thursday, 6 loaves of bread and 9 litres of milk were sold for $23.40.

   If b = the price of a loaf of bread and m = the price of one litre of milk, Tuesday's sales can be written as $8b + 5m = 21.40$.

   (a) Using simplest terms, write an equation in b and m for Thursday's sales.

   (b) Find b and m.

   (c) Draw a sketch, in the space provided, to show how the prices can be found graphically.

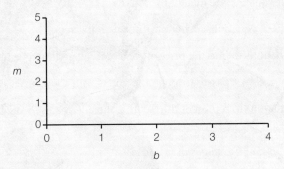

[May 2007, Paper 1, Question 12] (© IB Organization 2007) [6 marks]

2. *It is not necessary to use graph paper for this question.*

   (a) Sketch the curve of the function $f(x) = x^3 - 2x^2 + x - 3$ for values of x from −2 to 4, giving the intercepts with both axes.

   [3 marks]

   hint

   $f(x)$ is function notation and you will cover this in Chapter 17; for this question, just think of it as '$y =$'.

   (b) On the same diagram, sketch the line $y = 7 - 2x$ and find the coordinates of the point of intersection of the line with the curve.

   [3 marks]

[Nov 2007, Paper 2, Question 1(ii) (a),(b)] (© IB Organization 2007)

Chapter 3 Arithmetic and geometric sequences and series

A mosaic from within the Sultan Qaboos Grand Mosque, Mustat, Oman.

In this chapter you will learn:

- about arithmetic sequences and series, and their applications
- about geometric sequences and series, and their applications.

Patterns are everywhere. Some people recognise them most easily in art, others in music or poetry. There are also patterns in numbers that can help you to understand mathematical ideas better.

3.1 Arithmetic sequences

A **sequence** is an ordered list of numbers. In some sequences, the numbers have a regular pattern to them. Look at the sequences below. Each has been represented as a graph that plots the **position** of each **term** in the sequence against the term's **value**. If you look at either the list of numbers or the graph, you will see that there is a pattern in each sequence, and you can use this pattern to predict the next few numbers.

1. 4, 7, 10, 13, 16, …

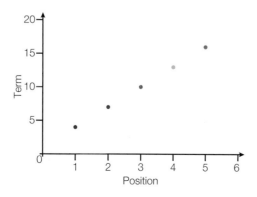

2. $1, \dfrac{1}{2}, \dfrac{1}{3}, \dfrac{1}{4}, \dfrac{1}{5}, \ldots$

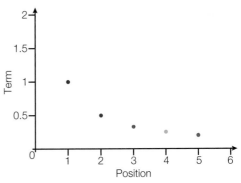

3. $\dfrac{1}{3}, 1, 3, 9, 27, \ldots$

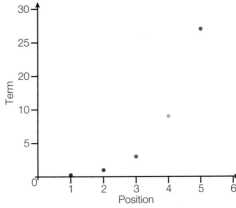

4. $50, 45, 40, 35, 30, \ldots$

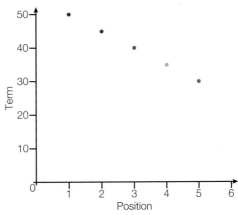

5. $512, 256, 128, 64, 32, \ldots$

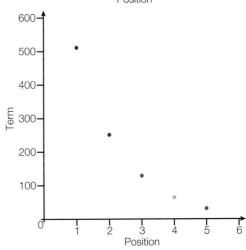

6. 1, 3, 6, 10, 15, …

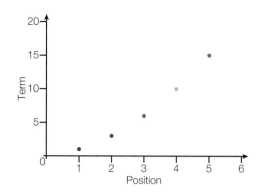

Look at either the number pattern or the graph. To get the next term, in which sequence would you:

- subtract 5?

- multiply by 3?

- divide by 2?

- add 3?

Two of the sequences are more complicated. Which are they? Can you find a pattern and describe how each of these sequences is built up?

Look again at the graphs of sequence 1 and sequence 4:

1.

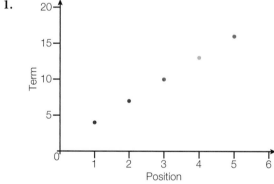

4.

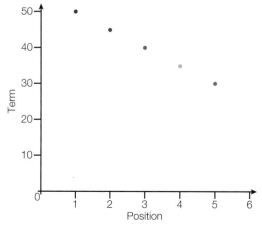

Notice that for each sequence, the plotted points lie along a straight line; the line is increasing in the case of sequence 1 and decreasing in the case of sequence 4. A sequence like 1 or 4 above is called an **arithmetic sequence** or **arithmetic progression**: the number pattern starts at a particular value and then increases, or decreases, by the same amount from each term to the next. This fixed **difference** between consecutive terms is called the **common difference** of the arithmetic sequence.

Look at sequence 1:

The sequence starts at 4, and increases by 3 for each subsequent term.

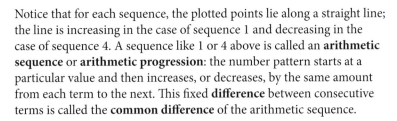

$7 - 4 = 10 - 7 = 13 - 10 = 16 - 13 = 3$, so **3** is the common difference of this sequence.

Now look at sequence 4:

The sequence starts at 50, and decreases by 5 for each subsequent term.

$45 - 50 = 40 - 45 = 35 - 40 = 30 - 35 = -5$, so **−5** is the common difference for this sequence.

Exercise 3.1

1. Which of the following are arithmetic sequences?

    (a) 1, 2, 4, 8, 16, …

    (b) 2, −2, 4, −4, 8, …

    (c) 2, 9, 16, 23, 30, …

    (d) 14, 8, 2, −4, −10, …

    (e) 2, 3, 5, 8, 13, …

    (f) 5, 12, 19, 26, 33, …

2. For each of the following arithmetic sequences, state the common difference and find the next three terms.

    (a) 5, 8, 11, __, __, __, …

    (b) 2, −1, −4, __, __, __, …

    (c) 350, 317, 284, __, __, __, …

    (d) 189, 210, 231, __, __, __, …

    (e) 28.7, 32.9, 37.1, __, __, __, …

    (f) $\frac{1}{2}, \frac{5}{4}, 2$, __, __, __, …

    (g) $\frac{4}{7}, \frac{26}{21}, 1\frac{19}{21}$

    (h) $2x + 7, x - 2, -11$, __, __, __, …

The nth term of an arithmetic sequence

We may want to know the value of a particular term in an arithmetic sequence, for example, the tenth term. We can use algebra to represent the terms of a sequence using the letter u and the position of each term in the sequence by a subscript number:

Position	1	2	3	4	...	$n-1$	n
Term	u_1	u_2	u_3	u_4	...	u_{n-1}	u_n

u_1 = first term, u_2 = second term, u_3 = third term and so on. A general term in a sequence is called the nth term. A term that is at position n in the sequence would be represented by u_n, and the term before u_n would be represented by u_{n-1}.

There is a general formula to calculate the nth term of an arithmetic sequence:

 $u_n = u_1 + (n-1)d$, where d is the common difference.

The general formula allows you to calculate the value of any term in an arithmetic sequence, so long as you know the value of the starting term (u_1) and the common difference (d).

Worked example 3.1

Q. (a) If $u_1 = 5$ and $d = 4$, find u_8 and u_{14}.

(b) For the sequence 8, 7.5, 7, 6.5, ... calculate u_9 and u_{50}.

Substitute the given values of u_1, d and n into the formula for the general term u_n. First, let $n = 8$.

A. (a) $u_n = u_1 + (n-1)d$

$u_8 = 5 + (8-1) \times 4 = 5 + 7 \times 4 = 33$

Substitute $n = 14$ into the formula.

$u_{14} = 5 + (14-1) \times 4 = 5 + 13 \times 4 = 57$

Identify the values of u_1 and d for this sequence.

(b) In this sequence, $u_1 = 8$ and $d = -0.5$.

Substitute $n = 9$ into the formula for the general term u_n.

$u_9 = 8 + (9-1) \times (-0.5) = 8 - 4 = 4$

Substitute $n = 50$ into the formula.

$u_{50} = 8 + (49-1) \times (-0.5) = 8 - 24 = -16$

Learning links

3A Deriving the formula for the nth term of an arithmetic sequence

The pattern in an arithmetic sequence can be used to analyse its structure and to find the general rule that allows you to calculate the value of any term in the sequence.

Look the sequence 5, 9, 13, 17, 21, ...

The first term is 5, and the common difference is +4.

Write out the terms in a way that helps you to spot a pattern:

		Or	What is done to u_1
The first term	$u_1 = 5$	$u_1 = 5$	
The second term	$u_2 = 5 + 4 = 9$	$u_2 = 5 + 4$	Adding one 4
The third term	$u_3 = 9 + 4 = 13$	$u_3 = 5 + 4 + 4$	Adding two 4s
The fourth term	$u_4 = 13 + 4 = 17$	$u_4 = 5 + 4 + 4 + 4$	Adding three 4s

Notice that to get u_3, you have to add 4 to the first term and then add 4 again, i.e. you need to add 2 lots of 4 to the first term.

To get u_4 you have to add 3 lots of 4 to the first term.

The pattern shows that the number of times you need to add 4 is one fewer than the term number:

$$u_4 = u_1 + (4 - 1) \times 4$$

Now replace the numbers with letters: n for the position of the term in the sequence and d for the common difference. Then according to the pattern, to find any term (at the nth position) in the sequence, you:

take the first term, u_1, and then add the common difference, d, one time fewer than the term number that you need.

This is easier to write as a formula:

$$u_n = u_1 + (n - 1) \times d$$

Let us check using a different sequence.

Consider the sequence 100, 95, 90, 85, 80, ...

The common difference is −5. Substitute the values of n and d into the formula and see if you get the correct values for the terms of the sequence:

$u_1 = 100$
$u_2 = 100 + (2 - 1) \times (-5) = 100 - 5 = 95$
$u_3 = 100 + (3 - 1) \times (-5) = 100 - 10 = 90$
$u_4 = 100 + (4 - 1) \times (-5) = 100 - 15 = 85$

It works!

This is true for all arithmetic sequences.

Exercise 3.2

1. In each of the following sequences, you are given the first term u_1 and the common difference d. Find the requested terms of the sequence using the formula for the nth term.

   (a) $u_1 = 7$, $d = 6$; find the 19th and 27th terms.

   (b) $u_1 = 36$, $d = 21$; find the 20th and 40th terms.

   (c) $u_1 = 84$, $d = -13$; find the 3rd and 17th terms.

   (d) $u_1 = -23$, $d = 11$; find the 16th and 34th terms.

   (e) $u_1 = -156$, $d = 29$; find the 10th and 18th terms.

   (f) $u_1 = 1080$, $d = -15.6$; find the 8th and 21st terms.

   (g) $u_1 = 268$, $d = -16$; find the 41st and 69th terms.

   (h) $u_1 = 59.4$, $d = 12.3$; find the 31st and 55th terms.

   (i) $u_1 = \dfrac{3}{7}$, $d = \dfrac{1}{5}$; find the 18th and 27th terms.

2. For each of the following arithmetic sequences, calculate the terms indicated.

   (a) 2, 5, 8, … ; 7th and 11th terms

   (b) 16, 23, 30, … ; 20th and 31st terms

   (c) 35, 39, 43, … ; 9th and 40th terms

   (d) 0, −4, −8, …. ; 23rd and 30th terms

   (e) 2, −7, −16, … ; 11th and 29th terms

   (f) 120, 77, 34, … ; 10th and 27th terms

   (g) 0.62, 0.79, 0.96, … ; 18th and 35th terms

   (h) $\dfrac{5}{9}, \dfrac{29}{36}, \dfrac{19}{18}, \dots$; 7th and 21st terms

   (i) $5x + 2$, $6x + 7$, $7x + 12$, … ; 13th and 20th terms

Using the formula to find values other than u_n

The general formula can be used in a number of different ways depending on what you know about the sequence and what you want to find out.

If you know the value of the first term and the value of any other term in the sequence, you can work out the common difference, even if you do not have all the terms of the sequence.

If you know at least three consecutive terms (terms next to each other) in a sequence then you can work out the common difference easily. If you also know the last term of the sequence, you can work out how many terms there are in the sequence.

Worked example 3.2

> There are two ways of answering this question.

Q. The fourth term of an arithmetic sequence is 17. The first term is 5.

Find the common difference.

> Look at the way the sequence is set up.

A. Method 1:

5   _?_   _?_   17, _?_, _?_...

> To get the 4th term, we add 3 lots of the common difference to the first term. So you know that between 5 and 17, d was added three times. Write this as an equation.

$$3d = 17 - 5$$

> Solve for d.

$$3d = 12$$
$$d = 4$$

> Use the general formula for u_n and substitute in the values you know.

Method 2:
$$u_n = u_1 + (n-1)d$$
$$u_1 = 5 \text{ and } u_4 = 17, \text{ so } 17 = 5 + (4-1) \times d$$
$$17 = 5 + 3d$$

> Solve for d.

$$17 - 5 = 3d$$
$$12 = 3d$$
$$d = 4$$

Worked example 3.3

Q. Find the common difference and the number of terms in the sequence 49, 43, 37, ... , 1.

> The common difference is easy to work out first.

A. $d = 43 - 49 = -6$

> There are several different ways to calculate the number of terms in the sequence.

Method 1:

> Use the formula for the general term u_n.
>
> Substitute the information that you know into the formula.

$u_n = u_1 + (n-1)d$
$1 = 49 + (n-1) \times (-6)$

> This is a linear equation in the variable n.
>
> Solve for n.
>
> So 1 is the 9th term of the sequence.

$1 = 49 - 6(n-1)$
$6(n-1) = 49 - 1$
$6(n-1) = 48$
$n - 1 = 8$
$n = 9$

 Solving linear equations was covered in Chapter 2.

There are 9 terms in the sequence.

> Use the recursion mode of your GDC to enter the common difference repeatedly.
>
> See section '3.1 (a) Finding the number of terms in an arithmetic sequence using the recursion mode to enter the common difference repeatedly' on page 658 of the GDC chapter for a reminder, if you need to.

Method 2:

TEXAS	CASIO

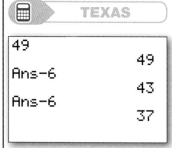

1 is the 9th term.
So there are 9 terms in the sequence.

Use the formula for a general term and an appropriate equation solver on your GDC.

Substitute known values into the formula.

Rearrange the formula so that the equation equals zero.

Use your GDC to solve. See section '*2.1 (b) Solving linear equations using an equation solver*' on page 653 of the GDC chapter if you need to.

Write the answer down appropriately.

continued . . .

Method 3:

$$u_n = u_1 + (n-1)d$$
$$1 = 49 + (n-1) \times (-6)$$

$$6(n-1) - 48 = 0$$

TEXAS	CASIO

6(X-1)-48=0
▪ X=9
  bound={-1ᴇ99,1…
▪ left-rt=0
	Eq:6(X-1)=48
	   X=9
	Lft=48
	Rgt=48
	
	REPT

There are 9 terms in the sequence.

Sometimes you might know two terms in a sequence that are neither the first term nor consecutive terms. In these circumstances, it is a little more complicated to calculate the common difference, but it is still possible. You can use the formula for the general term u_n, and the terms that you *do* know, to write a pair of linear equations to solve.

Worked example 3.4

Q. If the third term of an arithmetic sequence is 12 and the eighth term is 27, find the first term and the common difference.

Substitute known values into the formula for the general term u_n; this gives a pair of linear equations with the unknowns u_1 and d.

A.
$$u_n = u_1 + (n-1)d$$
$$u_3 = u_1 + (3-1)d, \text{ so } 12 = u_1 + 2d$$
$$u_8 = u_1 + (8-1)d, \text{ so } 27 = u_1 + 7d$$

Now you have a pair of simultaneous equations with two unknown quantities to find.

$$u_1 + 2d = 12$$
$$u_1 + 7d = 27$$

continued . . .

Solve using **your** preferred method.

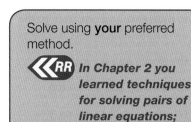

«RR *In Chapter 2 you learned techniques for solving pairs of linear equations; you will need to use one of those techniques here.*

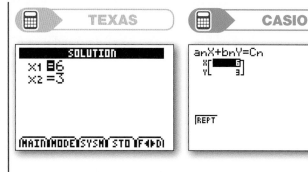

Write down the answer appropriately.

$u_1 = 6$ and $d = 3$

Exercise 3.3

1. In the following arithmetic sequences you are given the first term and one other term of the sequence. Find the common difference in each case.

   (a) $u_1 = 7$ and $u_{18} = 58$ (b) $u_1 = 45$ and $u_{10} = 117$

   (c) $u_1 = -17$ and $u_{22} = 214$ (d) $u_1 = 25.9$ and $u_{30} = -40.8$

   (e) $u_1 = 87$ and $u_{25} = -240.6$ (f) $u_1 = -40$ and $u_{17} = 88$

   (g) $u_1 = -135$ and $u_{18} = 307$ (h) $u_1 = 19.7$ and $u_{31} = -43.3$

   (i) $u_1 = 66.1$ and $u_{50} = -27$ (j) $u_1 = 19.84$ and $u_{102} = 76.703$

2. Find the number of terms in each of the following arithmetic sequences. You are given the first three terms and the last term in each case.

   (a) $5, 7, 9, \ldots, 75$ (b) $15, 18, 21, \ldots, 93$

   (c) $64, 77, 90, \ldots, 649$ (d) $-6, 7, 20, \ldots, 488$

   (e) $49, 60, 71, \ldots, 643$ (f) $80.8, 75.9, 71, \ldots, -404.3$

   (g) $37.95, 34.3, 30.65, \ldots, -126.3$

   (h) $126.4, 117.95, 109.5, \ldots, -498.9$

   (i) $167, 133, 99, \ldots, -1363$

   (j) $1083, 1064, 1045, \ldots, 0$

3. Find the first term in each of the following arithmetic sequences. In each case you are given the common difference and one term in the sequence.

(a) $d = 5$ and $u_{12} = 67$ (b) $d = 17$ and $u_{14} = 240$

(c) $d = -8$ and $u_{51} = 0$ (d) $d = -23$ and $u_{27} = -400$

(e) $d = 9.75$ and $u_{24} = 280.25$ (f) $d = -6.9$ and $u_{14} = 98.3$

(g) $d = 54$ and $u_{40} = 4096$ (h) $d = 13.6$ and $u_{33} = 523.2$

(i) $d = -10.1$ and $u_{78} = -572.7$

(j) $d = \frac{2}{3}$ and $u_{24} = 75\frac{1}{2}$

4. The fifth term of an arithmetic sequence is 9 and the eleventh term is 45.

(a) Denoting the first term by u_1 and the common difference by d, write down two equations in u_1 and d that fit the given information.

(b) Solve the equations to find the values of u_1 and d.

(c) Hence find the fiftieth term of the sequence.

5. The fourth term of an arithmetic sequence is 118 and the seventh term is 172.

(a) Find the first term and the common difference.

(b) Calculate the twentieth term of the sequence.

6. The ninth term of an arithmetic sequence is 36 and the twenty-first term is −168.

(a) Find the first term and the common difference.

(b) Calculate the thirty-seventh term.

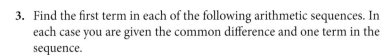

hint

The position of a term in a sequence has to be an integer.

7. In an arithmetic sequence the tenth term is −88.93 and the seventeenth term is −130.93.

(a) Determine the common difference and the first term.

(b) Find the fortieth term of the sequence.

(c) Is −178.52 a term in the sequence?

Solving practical problems involving arithmetic sequences

Patterns are seen in art, music and poetry. But patterns can also be found in many other contexts that may not be so obvious. For example, seating plans in theatres and sports arenas, or the growth of a child all display patterns.

You can apply what you have learned about arithmetic sequences to practical situations like these as well as many others.

As the distance Maya runs increases by a fixed amount each week, her training pattern is an example of an arithmetic sequence with $u_1 = 5$ and $d = 3$. There are two ways you could answer the questions.

Use the recursion mode on your GDC until there are three terms on the screen.

The third term is 11.

Substitute known values into the formula for the general term: $u_1 = 5$, $d = 3$, and $n = 3$.

Substitute $u_1 = 5$ and $d = 3$ into the formula for the general term. We are looking for the value of n for which $u_n > 25$. We need to solve the inequality $5 + 3(n - 1) > 25$. There are several ways you can do this.

Use an equation solver on your GDC. The inequality sign ($>$) needs to be replaced by an $=$ sign, so that we can treat it as a linear equation.

Worked example 3.5

Q. Maya is training for a marathon. She builds up her fitness by running an extra 3 km each week. She runs 5 km the first week.

(a) How far will she run in the third week?

(b) In which week will she run more than 25 km?

A. (a) <u>Method 1:</u>

 TEXAS   CASIO

Maya runs 11 km in the third week.

<u>Method 2:</u>
$$u_n = u_1 + (n - 1)d$$
$$u_3 = 5 + (3 - 1) \times 3 = 11 \text{ km}$$

(b) $u_n = 5 + 3(n - 1)$
$$5 + 3(n - 1) > 25$$

 Return to Chapter 2 for a reminder of how to solve linear equations using your GDC if you need to.

<u>Method 1:</u>

 TEXAS   CASIO

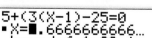
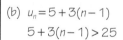

continued . . .

The answer given by the GDC is 7.67, but the question asks for 'which week', so take $n = 8$. (You can check that $n = 7$ gives 23 m, which is less than 25.)

Maya runs more than 25 km in the 8th week.

Method 2:

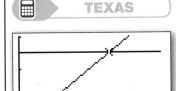 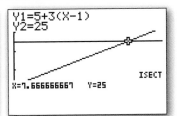

Use your GDC to draw the graph of the sequence $y_1 = 5 + 3(x - 1)$ and the line $y_2 = 25$. The point of intersection tells us the value of x for which the sequence equals 25.

The GDC gives the x-coordinate of the intersection as 7.67. Round this up to 8 to get the value of n.

Maya runs more than 25 km in the 8th week.

Exercise 3.4

hint

Note in Worked example 3.5 that n is a number of weeks and must be a natural number, so the answer should be rounded up to the next natural number.

1. Jamie is collecting Pokemon cards. In the first month he collected 12 cards, and he plans to collect an additional 7 cards every month. The total number of cards in his collection each month forms an arithmetic sequence.

    (a) How many cards will Jamie have in the sixth month?

    (b) How long will it take Jamie to collect 96 cards?

2. Rosetta has bought a new Russian language phrase-book. She has decided to learn some new Russian words every week. In the first week she learned 10 new words. She learned 19 new words in the second week and 28 new words in the third week. The number of new Russian words Rosetta learns each week forms an arithmetic sequence.

    (a) How many new words will Rosetta learn in the eleventh week?

    (b) During which week will Rosetta learn 181 new words?

3. Sally has 30 weeks of training before her next sporting event. In the first week she trains for 45 minutes. The lengths of time she trains every week form an arithmetic sequence. Each week she trains four minutes longer than in the previous week.

(a) How long will Sally train in the fourteenth week?

(b) After which week will Sally be training longer than two hours?

(c) How long will she train in the final week before the sporting event?

4. Mr Mensah owns several cocoa plantations. Each year he plans to harvest 18 tonnes more cocoa beans than in the previous year. In the first year he harvested 42 tonnes, the following year 60 tonnes, the year after that 78 tonnes, and so on.

(a) How many tonnes of cocoa beans does Mr Mensah expect to harvest in the sixth year?

(b) In which year will Mr Mensah's harvest exceed 300 tonnes of cocoa beans?

5. Veejay works as a car salesman. His monthly commission forms an arithmetic sequence. In the tenth month he earned 2150 rupees. In the twenty-first month he earned 3800 rupees.

(a) How much commission did Veejay earn in the first month?

(b) In which month is his commission expected to exceed 6000 rupees?

3.2 Arithmetic series: the sum of an arithmetic sequence

If you add up the terms of an arithmetic sequence, the result is called an **arithmetic series**:

$$S = u_1 + u_2 + u_3 + u_4 + u_5 + \ldots + u_{n-1} + u_n$$

You can use arithmetic **series** to solve different problems.

Let us return to Maya training for a marathon (Worked example 3.5). She builds up her fitness by running an extra 3 km each week. She runs 5 km in the first week.

Maya now wishes to know the total distance that she has run in her first eight weeks of training. How can she find this out?

She could write down the distance run in each of the eight weeks and add these numbers up:

$$S = 5 + 8 + 11 + 14 + 17 + 20 + 23 + 26 = 124 \text{ km}$$

To do this, she first needs to work out each term in the sequence. This is easy when there are only eight terms, but if Maya wanted to know the total distance run in a year (52 weeks), it would be a long task to work out every term of the sequence and then add them all up!

There are much quicker ways of calculating the sum of an arithmetic series, using either algebra or your GDC.

Using algebra to calculate the sum of an arithmetic series

The sum of an arithmetic series with n terms is given by the formula

$$S_n = \frac{n}{2}(u_1 + u_n)$$

hint

This is the formula to use if you know the first term, the last term, and the total number of terms. It is most helpful when there are lots of terms in the sequence, because you don't need to work out every term in order to get the sum!

Maya could work out the total distance run in the first eight weeks of training as $S_8 = \frac{8}{2}(5+26) = 124$ km

Exercise 3.5

1. For each of the following arithmetic series, you are given the first term u_1 and the last term u_n. Find the sum of the first n terms in each series using the formula $S_n = \frac{n}{2}(u_1 + u_n)$.

   (a) $u_1 = 7$ and $u_{20} = 64$ (b) $u_1 = 35$ and $u_{32} = 376$

   (c) $u_1 = -80$ and $u_{29} = 32$ (d) $u_1 = 79$ and $u_{40} = -194$

   (e) $u_1 = 46.1$ and $u_{24} = 225.5$ (f) $u_1 = -20$ and $u_{18} = -362$

A reminder of how to rearrange equations was provided in Learning links 2A on page 40 of Chapter 2.

2. For each of the following arithmetic series, you are given the last term and the sum of the first n terms. Use the formula $S_n = \frac{n}{2}(u_1 + u_n)$ to work out the first term of each series. (*Note:* you may have to rearrange the formula.)

	Last term (u_n)	Number of terms (n)	Sum of series
(a)	5	10	185
(b)	119	20	1430
(c)	158	14	1302
(d)	−160	24	−1632
(e)	−7	30	1095
(f)	0	32	4960

What if you do not know the last term in the series whose sum you want to find? You cannot use the formula. There is another formula for the sum of an arithmetic series. This formula uses the common difference d instead of the last term:

$$S_n = \frac{n}{2}\left[2u_1 + (n-1)d\right]$$

In the case of Maya's training (Worked example 3.5), the total distance she runs in the first eight weeks can be calculated using this formula as follows:

$$S_8 = \frac{8}{2}\left[2 \times 5 + (8-1) \times 3\right]$$
$$= 4 \times [10 + 21]$$
$$= 124 \text{ km}$$

Exercise 3.6

1. Use the formula $S_n = \dfrac{n}{2}\left[2u_1 + (n-1)d\right]$ to find the sum of each of the following arithmetic series.

   (a) $u_1 = 14$, $d = 8$ and $n = 10$ (b) $u_1 = 33$, $d = 16$ and $n = 18$

   (c) $u_1 = -5$, $d = 27$ and $n = 21$ (d) $u_1 = 30$, $d = -19$ and $n = 20$

   (e) $u_1 = -28$, $d = 1.5$ and $n = 40$ (f) $u_1 = 14$, $d = 8$ and $n = 10$

   (g) $u_1 = 53$, $d = -7$ and $n = 29$ (h) $u_1 = 80.52$, $d = -13.75$ and $n = 30$

2. Use the formula $S_n = \dfrac{n}{2}\left[2u_1 + (n-1)d\right]$ to find the sum of each of the following series. For each series you are given the first three terms and the number of terms in the sum.

   (a) $8 + 15 + 23 + \ldots$; 12 terms   (b) $9 + 20 + 31 + \ldots$; 20 terms

   (c) $56 + 70 + 84 + \ldots$; 26 terms   (d) $145 + 95 + 45 + \ldots$; 28 terms

   (e) $35 + 18 + 1 + \ldots$; 15 terms   (f) $12.5 + 20 + 27.5 + \ldots$; 18 terms

   (g) $6.75 + 5.5 + 4.25 + \ldots$; 30 terms

   (h) $3.172 + 4.252 + 5.332 + \ldots$; 36 terms

Learning links

3B Deriving the formula $S_n = \dfrac{n}{2}(u_1 + u_n)$ for the sum of an arithmetic series

Using Maya's training example (Worked example 3.5), let us try to spot a pattern in the numbers by writing the sequence forwards and then backwards:

sequence written forwards

$$
\begin{array}{ccccccccccccccc}
S & = & 5 & + & 8 & + & 11 & + & 14 & + & 17 & + & 20 & + & 23 & + & 26 \\
S & = & 26 & + & 23 & + & 20 & + & 17 & + & 14 & + & 11 & + & 8 & + & 5
\end{array}
$$

sequence written backwards

We can see pairs of numbers. Notice that each pair adds up to the same value (31).

Adding each pair of numbers together, we get

$$(5 + 26) + (8 + 23) + (11 + 20) + \ldots + (26 + 5)$$
$$= 31 + 31 + 31 + \ldots + 31$$

until we have 8 lots of 31. So the sum is

$$8 \times 31 = 248$$

continued . . .

Notice we have used the same sequence of numbers twice (forwards and backwards), so we need to divide by 2:

$S = 248 \div 2 = 124$

With the same reasoning as above but using letters instead of numbers, we have

sequence written forwards →

$$
\begin{array}{ccccccccccccc}
S_n & = & u_1 & + & u_2 & + & u_3 & + & \cdots & + & u_{n-2} & + & u_{n-1} & + & u_n \\
S_n & = & u_n & + & u_{n-1} & + & u_{n-2} & + & \cdots & + & u_3 & + & u_2 & + & u_1
\end{array}
$$

← sequence written backwards

We have created n pairs of numbers and each pair has the same total, which is equal to $(u_1 + u_n)$. So, adding the sum of the two series together we get n lots of $(u_1 + u_n)$:

$2S_n = n(u_1 + u_n)$

Therefore $S_n = \dfrac{n}{2}(u_1 + u_n)$.

3C Deriving the formula $S_n = \dfrac{n}{2}\left[2u_1 + (n-1)d\right]$ for the sum of an arithmetic series

Let's use Maya's sequence again. In the bottom row, we have replaced the numbers with letters: n for the position of the term in the sequence, and d for the common difference.

$S = 5 \quad + 8 \quad\quad + 11 \quad\quad\quad + \ldots + 23 \quad\quad\quad\quad\quad\quad\quad + 26$

$S = 5 \quad + (5 + 3) \quad + (5 + 3 + 3) \quad + \ldots + (5 + 3 + 3 + 3 + 3 + 3 + 3) \quad + (5 + 3 + 3 + 3 + 3 + 3 + 3 + 3)$

$S = u_1 \quad + (u_1 + d) \quad + (u_1 + 2d) \quad\quad + \ldots + (u_1 + (n-2)d) \quad\quad\quad\quad + (u_1 + (n-1)d)$

Writing the sequence forwards and backwards we get:

sequence written forwards →

$$
\begin{array}{ccccccccc}
S_n = & u_1 & + & (u_1 + d) & + & (u_1 + 2d) + \ldots & + & (u_1 + (n-2)d) & + & (u_1 + (n-1)d) \\
S_n = & (u_1 + (n-1)d) & + & (u_1 + (n-2)d) & + & (u_1 + (n-3)d) + \ldots & + & (u_1 + d) & + & u_1
\end{array}
$$

← sequence written backwards

If we add each pair together then there are n pairs of numbers, and each pair adds up to the same total: $2u_1 + (n-1)d$. So we have n lots of $2u_1 + (n-1)d$ altogether, and we get

$2S_n = n[2u_1 + (n-1)d]$

Dividing by 2 then gives $S_n = \dfrac{n}{2}\left[2u_1 + (n-1)d\right]$.

Using your GDC to calculate the sum of an arithmetic series

You can use your GDC to calculate the sum of a given number of terms in an arithmetic sequence. There are two main methods:

- using the GDC recursion mode

- using the 'sum' and 'seq' functions on your GDC.

Using the recursion mode on your GDC

To calculate the total distance that Maya runs in eight weeks of training:

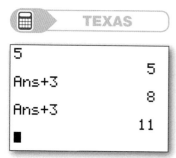

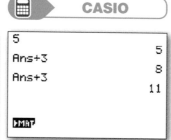

Use your GDC in recursion mode to output each term in the sequence as far as the number of terms requested.

$5 + 8 + 11 + 14 + 17 + 20 + 23 + 26 = 124$ km

Write down the numbers displayed on the right-hand side of the screen and add them together.

Using the 'sum' and 'seq' functions on your GDC

A function for summing the terms of a sequence is available on your GDC. See '*3.2 Finding the sum of an arithmetic sequence using the 'sum' and 'seq' functions*' on page 659 of the GDC chapter for a reminder if you need to.

To calculate the total distance that Maya runs in eight weeks of training:

If $u_1 = 5$ and $d = 3$, $u_n = 5 + 3(n - 1)$

First, put the known values into the formula for the nth term of an arithmetic sequence,
$u_n = u_1 + (n - 1)d$.

Enter the right-hand side of the formula into your GDC and enter the required parameters.

= 124 km

Worked example 3.6

Q. Consider the sequence consisting of all the odd numbers from 1 to 99:

$$1, 3, 5, 7, 9, \ldots , 97, 99$$

It is an arithmetic sequence with $u_1 = 1$ and $d = 2$.

(a) How many terms are there?

(b) What is the total if you add all the terms up?

> Using algebra: first put the known values into the formula for an arithmetic sequence.

A. (a) $u_n = u_1 + (n-1)d$

$99 = 1 + 2(n-1)$

> Rearrange and solve for n.

$98 = 2(n-1)$

$49 = n-1$

$n = 50$

There are 50 terms in the sequence.

> Check the answer using your GDC. See '2.1 (b) Solving linear equations using an equation solver' on page 653 if you need to.

 TEXAS

 CASIO

```
1+2(X-1)-99=0
▪X=50
 bound=▪-1ᴇ99,1…
▪left-rt=0
```

```
Eq:99=1+2(X-1)
     X=50
Lft=99
Rgt=99

REPT
```

> The answers match.

There are 50 terms in the sequence.

> Using algebra: since we know the last term, we can substitute the known values into the formula $S_n = \dfrac{n}{2}(u_1 + u_n)$ for the sum of an arithmetic series.

(b) $S_{50} = \dfrac{50}{2}(1+99)$

$= 25 \times 100$

$= 2500$

 TEXAS

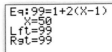 CASIO

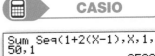

> Check your answer using the 'sum' and 'seq' functions on your GDC. See '3.2 Finding the sum… using the 'sum' and 'seq' functions' on page 659 if you need to.

The sum of the sequence is 2500.

Exercise 3.7

Use algebra to answer the questions below, and check your answers with your GDC.

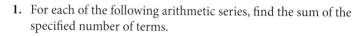

exam tip

Using a GDC can be quite complicated for this type of problem so you should also know how to calculate (or check) your answer using algebra.

1. For each of the following arithmetic series, find the sum of the specified number of terms.

   (a) $7 + 15 + 23 + \dots$ (24 terms)

   (b) $38 + 51 + 64 + \dots$ (16 terms)

   (c) $150 + 127 + 104 + \dots$ (40 terms)

   (d) $4.97 + 8.19 + 11.41 + \dots$ (36 terms)

   (e) $\frac{3}{4} + \frac{19}{20} + 1\frac{3}{20} \dots$ (15 terms)

2. For the following arithmetic series you are given the first three terms and the last term. In each case find the number of terms and the sum of the series.

   (a) $14 + 27 + 40 + \dots + 261$ (b) $86 + 115 + 144 + \dots + 985$

   (c) $7 + 8.35 + 9.7 + \dots + 31.3$ (d) $93 + 76 + 59 + 42 + \dots + (-400)$

   (e) $12\frac{1}{2} + 15\frac{1}{4} + 18 + \dots + 95$

3. Find the sum of each of the following series:

   (a) The first 80 positive integers.

   (b) All the even numbers between 23 and 243.

   (c) All multiples of 3 between 2 and 298.

   (d) The non-multiples of 7 between 1 and 99 inclusive.

   (e) All common multiples of 5 and 6 between 1 and 1000.

4. The eighth term of an arithmetic sequence is 216 and the seventeenth term is 369. Find the:

   (a) first term   (b) common difference

   (c) sum of the first 40 terms.

5. The first term of an arithmetic series is 28. The common difference is 6.

   (a) Find the sum of the first 20 terms of the series

   (b) The sum of the first n terms of the series is 5800. Show that n satisfies the equation

   $$3n^2 + 25n - 5800 = 0$$

   (c) Hence solve the equation to find n.

Solving practical problems by summing arithmetic series

Arithmetic series appear in the real world. An example that you might have come across is simple interest. Simple interest is a type of financial investment used in which an initial monetary value is invested and earns interest. The amount of money increases in a straight line as the rate of increase stays the same. For example, if Luca put $500 into a saving account that earned 1% interest a year, she would earn $5 a year ($1\% \times 500 = 5$). So, at the end of the first year she would have $500 + \$5 = \$505$. At the end of the second year she would have $\$505 + \$5 = \$510$. At the end of 5 years she would have $\$500 + \$5 + \$5 + \$5 + \$5 + \$5 = \$525$ in her savings account. It can also be useful to know long it will be before a particular total is reached. You can apply the formulae learned in this chapter to find out this kind of information.

Make sure that you start the solution to each problem by writing down the values that you know and can identify what it is that you need to find.

Worked example 3.7

Start by writing down what you know and then what you need to find out: we have the first term ($u_1 = 2$) and the common difference (+2). We need to find the sum of the amount saved in the first 13 weeks (this is denoted by S_{13}).

Q. Oscar decides that he will save an extra €2 each week. He saves €6 the first week and €8 the next.

(a) How much will he have saved over the first 13 weeks?

(b) How long will it take him to save €300?

A. (a) $u_1 = 6, d = 2$

Using algebra: because we don't know the last term (the amount Oscar saved in week 13), we use the formula $S_n = \dfrac{n}{2}[2u_1 + (n-1)d]$ for the sum of an arithmetic sequence and substitute in the values we have.

$$S_{13} = \frac{13}{2}[2 \times 6 + (13-1) \times 2]$$
$$= \frac{13}{2}[12 + 24]$$
$$= 13 \times 18$$
$$= 234$$

Oscar will save €234 over the first 13 weeks.

Check the answer using your GDC.

Substitute the values of u_1 (6) and d (2) into the formula for the nth term of an arithmetic sequence: $u_n = u_1 + (n-1)d$.

$u_1 = 6, d = 2$
$u_n = 6 + 2(n-1)$

continued . . .

Use the 'sum' and 'seq' functions on your GDC. See page 659 of the GDC chapter if you need a reminder.

 TEXAS

sum(seq(6+2(X−1▸
234
■

 CASIO

Sum Seq(6+2(X−1),X,1,
13,1
234

List L→M Dim Fill Seq ▸

The answer matches.

Oscar will save €234 over the first 13 weeks.

We know the first term and the common difference. This time we want to find the number of terms in the sequence (n) when the sum of the sequence (S_n) is 300.

(b) $u_1 = 6, d = 2$

Using algebra: we can substitute the values we know into the appropriate formula for the sum of an arithmetic series:

$S_n = \dfrac{n}{2}\big[2u_1 + (n-1)d\big]$.

$$S_n = \frac{n}{2}\big[2 \times 6 + (n-1) \times 2\big]$$

$$300 = \frac{n}{2}\big[2 \times 6 + (n-1) \times 2\big]$$

Rearrange the equation to solve for n.

$$300 = \frac{n}{2}\big[2 \times 6 + (n-1) \times 2\big]$$

$$= \frac{n}{2}\big[12 + 2n - 2\big]$$

$$= \frac{n}{2}\big[10 + 2n\big]$$

$$= 5n + n^2$$

$$n^2 + 5n - 300 = 0$$

This is a quadratic equation. Solve using your preferred method.

 See Chapter 2 for methods of solving quadratic equations.

 TEXAS

 CASIO

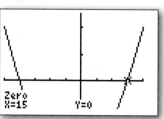

Zero
X=15   Y=0

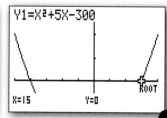

Y1=X²+5X−300

X=15   Y=0   ROOT

$n = 15$ or $n = -20$

continued . . .

Remember that n is a number of weeks, so it must be a positive integer. Therefore the solution of -20 is not possible.

It will take Oscar 15 weeks to save €300.

Check using algebra.

By factorising:
$$n^2 + 5n - 300 = 0$$
$$(n - 15)(n + 20) = 0$$
$$n = 15$$

You could also have used your GDC by plotting the graph of $S_n = \dfrac{n}{2}\left[2u_1 + (n - 1)d\right]$ and the line $y = 300$ on the same axis to find the point of intersection. (See '2.3 (a) Solving quadratic equations using a graph' on page 656 of the GDC chapter if you need to.)

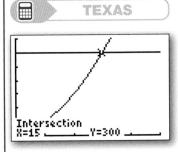

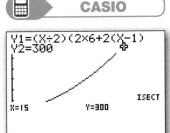

The graphs intersect at $n = 15$. The answers match.

It will take Oscar 15 weeks to save €300.

The German mathematician Carl Friedrich Gauss (1777–1855) was a child prodigy, able to correct his father's arithmetic at the age of three. His teacher at the village school in Braunschweig, Lower Saxony, found it very hard to find sums to occupy him. One day, he asked Gauss to add up all the numbers from 1 to 100. Gauss was only seven years old, but within minutes he had the answer: the first one hundred natural numbers add up to 5050. He had used the same pattern explained in Learning links 3B to add up an arithmetic series:

| S | $=$ | 1 | $+$ | 2 | $+$ | 3 | $+$ | 4 | $+$ | ... | $+$ | 98 | $+$ | 99 | $+$ | 100 |
| S | $=$ | 100 | $+$ | 99 | $+$ | 98 | $+$ | 97 | $+$ | ... | $+$ | 3 | $+$ | 2 | $+$ | 1 |

This gives 100 pairs of numbers that add up to 101. But the series has been used twice, so $S_{100} = \frac{1}{2} \times 100 \times 101 = 5050$. Gauss became one of the most influential and innovative mathematicians of his time, and his ideas still inspire mathematicians today.

Is this a proof of Gauss's method of summing an arithmetic series? Or does a mathematical proof have to use algebra? It is said that mathematical proof and scientific proof are quite different. Try to think of ways in which they are alike, and ways in which they differ.

Exercise 3.8

1. Mrs Gomez has decided to save towards her daughter Alejandra's university education. She will pay €400 into a savings account on Alejandra's sixth birthday, then €550 on her seventh birthday, and so on, increasing the deposit by €150 each year. When Alejandra is sixteen, the last deposit will be made, and all the interest that has accumulated will be added.

   (a) How much will Mrs Gomez pay into the account on Alejandra's tenth birthday?

   (b) What will be the total amount of money in the account immediately after Alejandra's twelfth birthday?

   (c) What is the total amount of money Alejandra can expect to have in her savings account before interest is added?

2. Ali and Husain are recruiting students into a new Mathematics Club at their school. Each week they plan to recruit two more new members than in the previous week. In the first week they gained three new members; the next week they recruited five new members, the week after that seven new members, and so on.

   (a) Show that they can expect to recruit 21 new members in the 10th week.

   (b) What is the expected **total** membership of the Club in the 20th week (excluding Ali and Husain)?

   (c) In which week is the total membership (excluding Ali and Husain) expected to exceed 80?

3. Carmen has decided to save money over a period of two years. She saves $1 in the first week, $3 in the second week, $5 in third week, and so on, with her weekly savings forming an arithmetic series.

   (a) Find the amount that she saves in the last week of the first year.

   (b) Calculate her total savings over the complete two-year period.

4. Adebayo started receiving pocket money when he was twelve years old. His first monthly pocket money was 2000 nairas. This increased each month by 250 nairas.

   (a) Calculate the total pocket money he received in the first year.

   Adebayo has been saving all his pocket money so far. After three years of saving he decides to buy himself a treat for 60,000 nairas.

   (b) How much of his savings over the three years will remain after he spends the 60,000 nairas?

3.3 Geometric sequences

A geometric sequence is a list of numbers with a pattern, but this pattern is different from that of an arithmetic sequence.

Recall these example sequences from the beginning of section 3.1.

3. $\dfrac{1}{3}$, 1, 3, 9, 27, ...

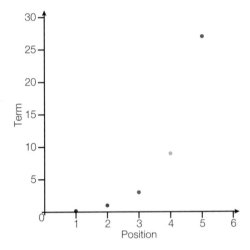

5. 512, 256, 128, 64, 32, ...

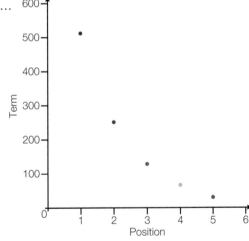

The graphs of these sequences are curves rather than straight lines. The curve is increasing in the case of sequence 3 and decreasing in the case of sequence 5.

Such sequences are called **geometric sequences**: the number pattern starts at a particular value and is then **multiplied**, or **divided**, by the same amount each time. This fixed multiplier from each term to the next is called the **common ratio** of the geometric sequence.

Look closer at sequence 3:

The sequence starts at $\frac{1}{3}$, and is multiplied by 3 for each subsequent term.

$$\underset{\frac{1}{3}}{} \overset{\times 3}{\frown} \underset{1}{} \overset{\times 3}{\frown} \underset{3}{} \overset{\times 3}{\frown} \underset{9}{} \overset{\times 3}{\frown} \underset{27}{}$$

Dividing each term by the value of the term before it, we get $\frac{1}{\frac{1}{3}} = \frac{3}{1} = \frac{9}{3} = \frac{27}{9} = 3$, so **3** is the common ratio of this sequence.

Now look at sequence 5:

The sequence starts at 512, and is multiplied by $\frac{1}{2}$ for each subsequent term.

$\frac{256}{512} = \frac{128}{256} = \frac{64}{128} = \frac{32}{64} = \frac{1}{2}$, so $\frac{1}{2}$ is the common ratio of this sequence.

Exercise 3.9

1. Which of the following sequences are geometric sequences?

    (a) 2, 22, 222, 2222, …

    (b) 1, 10, 100, 1000, …

    (c) 1, 4, 16, 25, 36, …

    (d) $84, 56, 37\frac{1}{3}, 24\frac{8}{9},…$

    (e) $5, 5^2, 5^3, 5^4, …$

    (f) $3 + y, 6 + y, 12 + y, 24 + y, …$

    (g) $2, -4a, 8a^2, -16a^3, …$

    (h) $x^3, x^6, x^9, x^{12}, …$

2. Find the next three terms in each of the following geometric sequences.

    (a) 4, 8, 16, __, __, __, …

    (b) 200, 120, 72, __, __, __, …

    (c) 729, 243, 81, __, __, __, …

    (d) 30.5, 36.6, 43.92, __, __, __, …

3. Find the missing terms in the following geometric sequences.

    (a) 480, 360, __, 202.5, __, …

    (b) __, __, 12.5, 25, 50, …

    (c) −6, __, __, −162, −486, …

    (d) $1, \frac{1}{5}, $ __, __, __, …

The *n*th term of a geometric sequence

The pattern in a geometric sequence can lead to a formula for calculating the value of any term. The formula for the general term of a geometric sequence, known as the *n*th term, is given by:

$$u_n = u_1 \times r^{n-1}, \text{ where } r \text{ is the common ratio.}$$

For example, the sequence 512, 256, 128, 64, 32, … has:

- $u_1 = 512$
- $u_2 = 512 \times (\frac{1}{2})^1 = 256$
- $u_3 = 512 \times (\frac{1}{2})^2 = 128$
- $u_4 = 512 \times (\frac{1}{2})^3 = 64$
- and $u_7 = 512 \times (\frac{1}{2})^{7-1} = 512 \times (\frac{1}{2})^6 = 8$

If you know the first term and the common ratio, you can use the formula for the general term to calculate the value of any term in the sequence.

Worked example 3.8

Q. Consider the sequence 2, 3, 4.5, …

(a) Confirm that this is a geometric sequence.

(b) Write down the values of u_1 and r.

(c) Calculate u_7.

> Check the ratio between consecutive terms; is it constant?

A. (a) $\dfrac{3}{2} = 1.5, \dfrac{4.5}{3} = 1.5$

The ratio is the same, so this is a geometric sequence.

> u_1 is the first term and r is the common ratio between terms.

(b) $u_1 = 2$ and $r = 1.5$

> Substitute known values into the formula: multiply the first term by the common ratio (7 − 1 =) 6 times.

(c) $u_7 = 2 \times (1.5)^6 = 22.8$ (3 s.f.)

You can use the formula to find other values too, depending on what information you start with. For instance, if you know the value of two terms of a geometric sequence, you can use the formula to find the common ratio and the first term.

Worked example 3.9

There are two ways you can approach this problem.

Q. In a geometric sequence, the second term is 2 and the fifth term is -16. Find:

(a) the common ratio

(b) the first term.

Draw the sequence.

A. <u>Method 1:</u>

(a)

?   2   ?   ? -16

$u_2 = 2$ and u_5 is -16.

To get from u_2 to u_5 you need to multiply by the common ratio 3 times. We can write this as an equation and solve for r.

$$2 \times r^3 = -16$$
$$r^3 = -8$$
$$r = -2$$

To go from the 1st term to the 2nd term, you multiply by r; so to go from the 2nd term to the 1st term, divide by r.

(b) $u_2 = 2, r = -2$

$2 \div -2 = -1$

$u_1 = -1$

Use the general formula $u_n = u_1 \times r^{n-1}$. For $u_2 = 2$ substitute $n = 2$ into the formula. For $u_5 = -16$ substitute $n = 5$ into the formula to give two equations.

<u>Method 2:</u>

(a) $u_n = u_1 \times r^{n-1}$

$u_2 = u_1 \times r = 2 \ (1)$

$u_5 = u_1 \times r^4 = -16 \ (2)$

 RR *Return to Chapter 2 for methods of solving pairs of linear equations if you need to.*

We have a pair of linear equations. Here, we solve by elimination. Divide equation (2) by equation (1) to find r.

$u_1 r = 2$

$u_1 r^4 = -16$

$$\dfrac{u_1 r^4}{u_1 r} = \dfrac{-16}{2}$$

$r^3 = -8$

$r = -2$

Substitute the value of r into either one of the equations above.

(b) $u_1 \times (-2) = 2$

$u_1 = 2 \div (-2) = -1$

$u_1 = -1$

3D Deriving the formula for the nth term of a geometric sequence

Take the sequence $\frac{1}{3}$, 1, 3, 9, 27, 81, …

The first term is $\frac{1}{3}$, and the common ratio is 3.

Write out the terms in a way that helps you to spot a pattern:

		Or	What is done to u_1
The first term	$u_1 = \dfrac{1}{3}$	$u_1 = \dfrac{1}{3}$	
The second term	$u_2 = \dfrac{1}{3} \times 3 = 1$	$u_2 = \dfrac{1}{3} \times 3$	Multiplying by one 3
The third term	$u_3 = 3 \times 1 = 3$	$u_3 = \dfrac{1}{3} \times 3 \times 3$	Multiplying by two 3s
The fourth term	$u_4 = 3 \times 3 = 9$	$u_4 = \dfrac{1}{3} \times 3 \times 3 \times 3$	Multiplying by three 3s

The pattern shows that if you want to find the value of the nth term in the sequence, u_n, take the value of the first term, u_1, and multiply by the common ratio, r, $(n-1)$ times, that is, one time fewer than the term's position.

Exercise 3.10

1. Consider the sequence 10, 15, 22.5, …

    (a) Confirm that this is a geometric sequence.

    (b) Write down the values of u_1 and r.

    (c) Calculate u_{10} to 1 decimal place.

2. (a) In a geometric sequence, $u_3 = 3$ and $u_7 = 48$. Find r, u_1 and u_{10}.

    (b) In a geometric sequence, $u_3 = 3$ and $u_6 = 81$. Find r, u_1 and u_{10}.

3. The second term of a geometric sequence is 5 and the fourth term is 20.

    (a) Find the first term and the common ratio.

    (b) Use these values to calculate the 12th term.

4. For each of the following geometric sequences, find the common ratio and the specified term.

   (a) 3, 12, 48, … ; 10th term

   (b) 64, 96, 144, … ; 20th term

   (c) 90, 288, 921.6, … ; 18th term

   (d) 1, 1.5, 2.25, … ; 16th term

   (e) 180, −198, 217.8, … ; 12th term

   (f) −45, −99, −217.8, … ; 21st term

5. The following sequences are all geometric. For each, calculate the common ratio and three more terms.

   (a) 2, 3, …   (b) −1, 2, …

   (c) 100, 50, …   (d) 1, 1.1, …

Finding the position of a term in a geometric sequence

You can determine the position of a term by any of the following methods:

- drawing a diagram

- trial and improvement

- using your GDC to plot graphs

- using your GDC's equation solver.

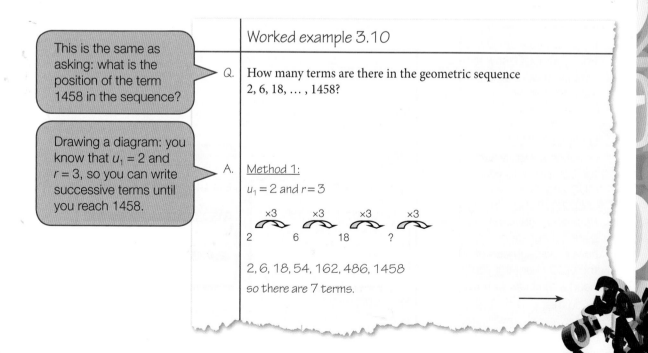

This is the same as asking: what is the position of the term 1458 in the sequence?

Drawing a diagram: you know that $u_1 = 2$ and $r = 3$, so you can write successive terms until you reach 1458.

Worked example 3.10

Q. How many terms are there in the geometric sequence 2, 6, 18, … , 1458?

A. Method 1:

$u_1 = 2$ and $r = 3$

$$\overset{\times 3}{\frown}\ \overset{\times 3}{\frown}\ \overset{\times 3}{\frown}\ \overset{\times 3}{\frown}$$
2   6   18   ?

2, 6, 18, 54, 162, 486, 1458

so there are 7 terms.

continued . . .

Use **trial and improvement** by substituting different values of n into the formula.

exam tip

Make sure you write down all your working.

Method 2:

$u_1 = 2$ and $r = 3$

$u_n = u_1 \times r^{n-1}$

$u_n = 2 \times 3^{n-1} = 1458$

Try

$n = 5$: $2 \times 3^4 = 162$, too low

$n = 8$: $2 \times 3^7 = 4374$, too high

$n = 7$: $2 \times 3^6 = 1458$, correct answer

So 1458 is the 7th term.

Method 3:

Use your GDC to plot graphs: you want to find the value of n when $2 \times 3^{n-1} = 1458$. Plot the graphs of $y = 2 \times 3^{n-1}$ and $y = 1458$ and find the point that the two graphs intersect. See '19.2 (a) Solving unfamiliar equations using a graph' on page 684 of the GDC chapter for a reminder of how to do this if you need to.

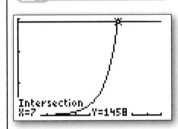

From GDC: $n = 7$

If you got your answer from your GDC, say so when you write down your answer.

Method 4:

$2 \times 3^{n-1} = 1458$

Use your GDC's equation solver: enter the equation into your GDC and solve. See section '19.2 (b) Solving unfamiliar equations using an equation solver' on page 685 of the GDC chapter if you need a reminder of how to do this.

From GDC: $n = 7$

Exercise 3.11

1. Use the equation solver on your GDC to find the number of terms in each geometric sequence.

   (a) $2, 4, 8, \ldots , 512$

   (b) $1.2, 1.44, \ldots , 2.0736$

   (c) $1600, 160, 16, \ldots , 0.016$

   (d) $81, 27, 9, \ldots , \dfrac{1}{27}$

   (e) $1, 0.1, 0.01, \ldots , 0.00001$

   (f) $1, \dfrac{3}{4}, \dfrac{9}{16}, \ldots , \dfrac{729}{4096}$

2. Use the graphing function on your GDC to find the number of terms in each of the following geometric sequences.

	First term	Common ratio	Last term
(a)	100	0.8	40.96
(b)	24	1.5	273.375
(c)	8	2	8192
(d)	40	$\dfrac{1}{2}$	$\dfrac{5}{128}$
(e)	160	$\dfrac{1}{4}$	$\dfrac{5}{524288}$
(f)	243	$\dfrac{1}{3}$	$\dfrac{1}{243}$

3. The first term of a geometric sequence is $80\,400$ and the common ratio is 1.05. Given that $u_n = 97\,726.7025$, use the method of trial and improvement to find the value of n.

4. For each of the following geometric sequences you are given the first term, the common ratio and u_n. Use an appropriate method to determine the value of n.

   (a) $u_1 = 8, r = 2, u_n = 16\,384$

   (b) $u_1 = 3, r = 6, u_n = 839\,908$

   (c) $u_1 = 4, r = \dfrac{1}{2}, u_n = 0.0625$

   (d) $u_1 = 256, r = \dfrac{1}{4}, u_n = \dfrac{1}{64}$

   (e) $u_1 = \dfrac{8}{81}, r = \dfrac{3}{2}, u_n = \dfrac{27}{16}$

   (f) $u_1 = -48, r = 2, u_n = -1536$

3.4 Geometric series: the sum of a geometric sequence

If you add up the terms of a geometric sequence you get a **geometric series**.

Geometric series are important in financial calculations as well as in many other practical situations.

You can calculate the sum of a geometric series by adding all the values together but as you are multiplying by a common ratio each time, the sum can get very large very quickly and it is much more convenient to use a formula.

There are two formulae for the sum of a geometric series

$$S_n = \frac{u_1(r^n - 1)}{r - 1} = \frac{u_1(1 - r^n)}{1 - r}, \; r \neq 1$$

exam tip

The two formulae give exactly the same answer, but it is easier to use $S_n = \frac{u_1(r^n - 1)}{r - 1}$ if $r > 1$ and $S_n = \frac{u_1(1 - r^n)}{1 - r}$ if $r < 1$.

hint

The $\neq$ symbol in the formula above means 'not equal to'. Here r cannot equal 1 because this would make the denominator zero, and you cannot divide by zero.

There is a legend about a Chinese emperor who wished to reward the wise man who had invented the game of chess. The emperor promised the wise man whatever he desired. The wise man asked for 'one grain of rice on the first square of the chess board, two grains on the second and four grains on the third, until the chessboard is filled'. How much rice is that in total? Was it a sensible promise for the emperor to have made?

Learning links

3E Deriving the formula for the sum of a geometric sequence

Suppose that a university student, who did not have very much money, asked his grandmother to help him out with a very small amount of money each day. He thought she wouldn't miss a few cents each day but that if he saved it, it would help him a lot.

$\longrightarrow$

continued . . .

He asked her to give him:

1 cent on 1 April

2 cents on 2 April

4 cents on 3 April ...

and to continue this pattern until the end of the month (30 days).

The amounts of money given each day form a geometric sequence with $u_1 = 1$ and $r = 2$. Looking at the first few terms it looks like his idea is a very good one, it won't cost his grandmother that much money at all.

How much would his grandmother have given him by the end of April?

The sum after 30 days can be calculated by adding up the amounts he got each day.

$$S = 1 + 2 + 4 + 8 + 16 + \ldots$$

$$S = 2^0 + 2^1 + 2^2 + 2^3 + 2^4 + \ldots + 2^{29}$$

To add up a geometric series, we can use the pattern in the numbers. If the value of each term in the series is doubled and then written below the original series, you can see that most of the terms are the same.

$$S = 1 + 2 + 4 + 8 + 16 + \ldots + 2^{28} + 2^{29} \qquad (1)$$
$$ \times 2 \quad \times 2 \quad \times 2 \quad \times 2 \quad \times 2$$
$$2S = 2 + 4 + 8 + 16 + 32 + \ldots + 2^{29} + 2^{30} \qquad (2)$$

So, subtracting one sequence from the other makes most terms cancel out and gives you a simple way of calculating the answer. (2) − (1) gives:

$$2S - S = (2 + 4 + 8 + 16 + \ldots + 2^{29} + 2^{30}) - (1 + 2 + 4 + 8 + 16 + \ldots + 2^{29})$$

That is, $S = 2^{30} - 1$ (where 2^{30} is r^n and 1 is u_1).

So $S = 1073741823$ cents, which is 10,737,418.23 dollars!.

Luckily for her, the student's grandmother was a mathematician and she recognised the geometrical pattern and disagreed with his idea!

We can use a similar trick to calculate the sum of a general geometric series: multiply the series by its common ratio and write the result below the original series; then subtract the two series, which makes most terms cancel and leads to the following two formulae for the sum: $S_n = \dfrac{u_1(r^n - 1)}{r - 1} = \dfrac{u_1(1 - r^n)}{1 - r}$, $r \neq 1$

Worked example 3.11

Q. Consider the geometric sequence $-1, 2, -4, 8, -16, \ldots$

(a) Write down the values of u_1 and r.

(b) Find the tenth term.

(c) Find the sum of the first ten terms.

> Use the formula
> $u_n = u_1 \times r^{n-1}$.
> Substitute in the values
> from (a), and substitute
> in $n = 10$.

A. (a) $u_1 = -1, r = -2$

(b) $u_n = u_1 \times r^{n-1}$

$u_n = (-1) \times (-2)^{n-1}$

$u_{10} = (-1) \times (-2)^9 = (-1) \times (-512) = 512$

(c)

> Use the formula
> $S_n = \dfrac{u_1(r^n - 1)}{r - 1}$.
> Substitute in the values of
> u_1, r, and $n = 10$.

$S_n = \dfrac{(-1)\left((-2)^n - 1\right)}{(-2) - 1}$

$S_{10} = \dfrac{(-1)\left((-2)^{10} - 1\right)}{(-2) - 1} = 341$

> You can use either of
> the formulae $\dfrac{u_1(r^n - 1)}{r - 1}$ or
> $\dfrac{u_1(1 - r^n)}{1 - r}$, but if you use
> the second version, be
> especially careful when
> entering the negative signs
> into your calculator.

$S_n = \dfrac{(-1)\left(1 - (-2)^n\right)}{1 - (-2)}$

$S_{10} = \dfrac{(-1)\left(1 - (-2)^{10}\right)}{1 - (-2)}$

$= \dfrac{(-2)^{10} - 1}{3} = 341$

 TEXAS   CASIO

> Check using your GDC.
> See section '3.3 Finding
> the sum of the geometric
> series using the list
> function' on page 661 of
> the GDC chapter.

L1	L2	L3	1
-1	------	------	
2			
-4			
8			
-16			
32			
-64			

L1(1) = -1

	List 1	List 2	List 3	List 4
SUB				
9	-256			
10	512			
11	341			
12				

| Sum | Prod | Cuml | % | Δ | ▷ |

From GDC: Sum = 341

Worked example 3.12

Q. Consider the geometric sequence 3, 2.4, 1.92, 1.536, ...

(a) Write down the value of u_1.

(b) Show that $r = 0.8$.

(c) Calculate S_8.

Calculate the ratio using the second and first terms (you could have calculated the ratio between any two consecutive terms).

A. (a) $u_1 = 3$

(b) $r = 2.4 \div 3 = 0.8$

$r < 1$, so use the formula
$$S_n = \frac{u_1(1-r^n)}{1-r}$$
(Alternatively, you could use the list function on your GDC, as per the check in Worked example 3.11.)

(c) $S_n = \dfrac{u_1(1-r^n)}{1-r} = \dfrac{3(1-0.8^n)}{1-0.8}$

$S_8 = \dfrac{3(1-0.8^8)}{1-0.8} = 12.5$ (3 s.f.)

Exercise 3.12

1. Use the formula $S_n = \dfrac{u_1(r^n - 1)}{r - 1}$ to calculate the sum of each of the following geometric series.

   (a) $u_1 = 2$, $r = 2$; first 10 terms

   (b) $u_1 = 0.3$, $r = 5$; first 8 terms

   (c) $u_1 = 1.465$, $r = 7$; first 11 terms

   (d) $u_1 = \dfrac{5}{8}$, $r = 4$; first 9 terms

   (e) $u_1 = 1$, $r = 1.2$; first 12 terms

   (f) $u_1 = 3.6$, $r = 2.06$; first 21 terms

2. Use the formula $S_n = \dfrac{u_1(1-r^n)}{1-r}$ to calculate the sum of the first 20 terms of each of these geometric series.

   (a) $u_1 = 500$, $r = 0.2$

   (b) $u_1 = 1200$, $r = \dfrac{1}{4}$

   (c) $u_1 = 4$, $r = -\dfrac{3}{4}$

   (d) $u_1 = 84$, $r = -\dfrac{1}{2}$

   (e) $u_1 = 20.6$, $r = 0.565$

   (f) $u_1 = 800$, $r = 0.01$

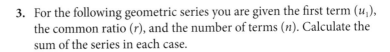

3. For the following geometric series you are given the first term (u_1), the common ratio (r), and the number of terms (n). Calculate the sum of the series in each case.

(a) $u_1 = 4, r = 2, n = 10$

(b) $u_1 = 16, r = 1.5, n = 18$

(c) $u_1 = -81, r = 0.9, n = 20$

(d) $u_1 = 1.25, r = 3, n = 22$

(e) $u_1 = 358, r = 0.95, n = 30$

4. For each of the following geometric series, find the common ratio and hence calculate the sum of the specified number of terms.

(a) $10 + 20 + 40 + \ldots$; first 20 terms

(b) $3 + 9 + 27 + \ldots$; first 24 terms

(c) $128 + 64 + 32 + \ldots$; first 18 terms

(d) $4 + 4.8 + 5.76 + \ldots$; first 16 terms

(e) $6.25 + 1.25 + 0.25 + \ldots$; first 10 terms

(f) $2^3 + 2^4 + 2^5 + \ldots$; first 20 terms

(g) $7^3 + 7^6 + 7^9 + \ldots$; first 24 terms

5. The third term of a geometric sequence is 144 and the sixth term is 9.216. Given that all the terms in the sequence are positive, calculate:

(a) the common ratio

(b) the sum of the first 16 terms of the sequence.

6. Take the geometric series $1000 + 500 + 250 + \ldots$

(a) Write down u_1 and r.

(b) Calculate the sum of the first 10 terms.

7. The first three terms of a geometric series are $32 + 16 + 8 + \ldots.$ Calculate the sum of the first 14 terms. Give your answer three decimal places.

8. A geometric series has $u_2 = 15$ and $u_4 = 135$.

(a) Write down the values of u_1 and r.

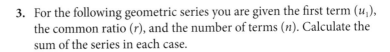
hint

(b) Calculate the sum of the first 16 terms. Write down all the figures on your GDC screen.

$\in$ is set notation and means 'belongs to', so $k \in \mathbb{Z}$ means that k is within the set of integers denoted by $\mathbb{Z}$.

(c) Give the answer to three significant figures.

(d) Write the answer to part (c) in the form $a \times 10^k$, where $1 \le a < 10$ and $k \in \mathbb{Z}$.

Solving practical problems involving geometric sequences and series

Many practical problems can be solved using geometric sequences and series, especially in situations where there is growth or decay that does not follow a straight line ('nonlinear').

 You will see more examples in Chapter 4 and Chapter 19.

Worked example 3.13

Q. The heating is switched off in a school laboratory. An experiment is set up to look at the growth in a population of fruit flies. As the temperature in the laboratory is low, it is found that the population is only growing by 30% per day.

On Monday there are 20 fruit flies.

(a) How many fruit flies will there be on Friday?

(b) How long will it be before the population exceeds 500 fruit flies?

> The population growing by 30% per day means that each day the population is $(100 + 30)\%$ times the previous day's population.

A. $r = 130\% = 1.3$

> If Monday is the first day, then Friday is the fifth day and so $n = 5$.

(a) $u_n = u_1 \times r^{n-1} = 20 \times 1.3^{n-1}$

> Substitute known values into the general formula. Round the answer to the nearest integer (the number of fruit flies is discrete data and so must be a whole number).

$u_5 = 20 \times 1.3^4 = 57.122 \approx 57$

> We are looking for the smallest n for which $u_n > 500$.
>
> As in Worked example 3.10, there are four main ways in which you could do this: we show three of them.

(b) $20 \times 1.3^{n-1} > 500$

$\longrightarrow$

continued . . .

Trial and improvement.

<u>Method 1:</u>

Try

$n = 10: 20 \times 1.3^9 = 212$ (3 s.f.)

$n = 15: 20 \times 1.3^{15} = 787$ (3 s.f.)

$n = 14: 20 \times 1.3^{13} = 606$ (3 s.f.)

$n = 13: 20 \times 1.3^{12} = 466$ (3 s.f.)

So $n = 14$ is the first day on which the population will exceed 500.

<u>Method 2:</u>

Use your GDC as in Worked example 3.10 to plot $y = 20 \times 1.3^{x-1}$ and $y = 500$. Find the x-value of their intersection and round up to the next integer.

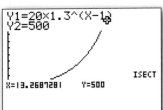

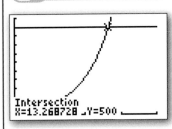

From GDC: intersection at $x = 13.3$

So $n = 14$

<u>Method 3:</u>

Use the equation solver on your GDC as you did in Worked example 3.10 using the equation $20 \times 1.3^{n-1} = 500$.

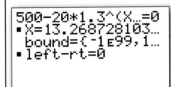

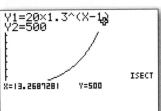

From GDC: solution is $x = 13.3$

So $n = 14$

Exercise 3.13

1. The first time that Sim counts a population of beetles there are 20. A month later there are 35 beetles. The population grows as a geometric sequence. How many beetles are there after 12 months? Give your answer to three significant figures.

2. A business makes a profit of 50,000 AUD in 2005. In 2006, the profit is 60,000 AUD. If the profit continues to grow as a geometric sequence, what is the profit in 2010? Give your answer to three significant figures.

3. The Kumars lived in a rented four-bedroom property from January 2000 until December 2009.

(a) Given that their yearly rent formed a geometric sequence, complete the table below.

Year	Annual rent (£)
2000	8990
2001	9170
2002	
2003	
2004	
2005	
2006	
2007	
2008	
2009	

(b) What was the total amount of rent paid over the 10-year period?

4. Miles joined the Apollo Golf and Gym Club in January 2005. The annual fee was £672 then. Since 2005 the fees have increased steadily by 4% every year.

(a) How much was the membership fee in 2010?

(b) How much in total did Miles pay in membership fees from 2005 to 2010?

Summary

You should know

- what an arithmetic sequence and series is

- what a geometric sequence and series is

- how to use the formulae for the nth term and the sum of the first n terms, of an arithmetic and a geometric sequence

- some common applications of arithmetic and geometric sequences and series in the real world.

Mixed examination practice

Exam-style questions

1. The first three terms of an arithmetic sequence are 24, 41, 58, …

   (a) State the common difference.

   (b) Work out the 20th term of the sequence.

   (c) Find the sum of the first 20 terms of the sequence.

2. The 5th term of an arithmetic sequence is 42 and the 9th term is 64.

   (a) Write two equations involving the first term u_1 and the common difference d.

   (b) Solve the equations to find the first term and the common difference.

3. Jasmine has been collecting stamps for a while. She collected 7 stamps in the first month, 11 stamps in the following month, 15 stamps in the month after that, and so on, in an arithmetic sequence.

   (a) How many stamps did she collect in the 12th month?

   (b) What was her **total** collection after 24 months?

   (c) How many more stamps did she collect altogether in her third year than in her second year?

   (d) After how many months will her total collection exceed 500 stamps?

4. The first term of a geometric sequence is 400 and the fourth term is 204.8.
   All the terms are positive numbers.

   (a) Find the common ratio.

   (b) Find the sum of the first 18 terms.

5. A ball is dropped onto a hard surface. It bounces up 2 m the first time. Each bounce after that reaches a height that is 85% of the one before. What height will the ball reach on the seventh bounce?

6. Marthe starts a savings account for her son. On his first birthday she puts €120 in the account, on his second birthday she deposits €126, and on his third birthday €132.30.

   (a) Explain why the common ratio for this geometric series is 1.05.

   (b) How much money will Marthe put in her son's account on his fifth birthday? On his tenth birthday?

   (c) How much money will he have in his account at the end of ten years?

   Note: The answers to (b) and (c) are financial, so remember to round them to two decimal places.

7. Tomasz is training for a 50 km bicycle race. He cycles 5 hours in the first week, and plans to increase the training time by 10% each week.

   (a) Show that he will cycle for 5.5 hours the second week.

   (b) How long will he cycle in the fifth week?

   (c) He trains for 12 weeks. What is his total training time?

   Give all your answers to three significant figures.

8. Mei is starting a new job. Her starting salary is $30,000, and she is told that it will increase each year. She can choose one of the following:

   Option 1: an annual increase of $500

   Option 2: an increase of 2% each year

   Mei plans to stay in the job for five years. Which option should she choose?

9. (i) Francine is repaying a loan she took out to buy a car. Her monthly repayments form an arithmetic series. She repaid $450 in the first month, $445 in the second month, $440 in the third month, and so on.

   (a) How much will Francine repay in the 30th month?

   (b) What is the total amount she will have repaid after three years?

   (ii) Bradley bought an identical car at the same time as Francine. However, his loan repayments were different. He repaid $600 in the first month, $592 in the second month, $584 in the third month, and so on.

   (a) What is the total amount Bradley will have repaid after three years?

   (b) In which month will the repayment amount be the same for Francine and Bradley?

10. Super Bricks is a new building company. The company produced 140 000 bricks in the first month. The volume of production is expected to rise at a monthly rate of 8%.

   (a) What is the expected monthly volume of production at the end of the first year of production?

   (b) What is the estimated total volume of production over the first twelve months?

   A rival company Brick Works produced 250 000 bricks in the first month. Responding to a rise in demand, the company plans to increase production at a monthly rate of 4%.

   (c) Show that over the next six months, Brick Works will produce more than 1.6 million bricks.

Past paper questions

1. The first three terms of an arithmetic sequence are

   $2k + 3, 5k - 2$ and $10k - 15$.

   (a) Show that $k = 4$. [3 marks]

   (b) Find the values of the first three terms of the sequence. [1 mark]

   (c) Write down the value of the common difference. [1 mark]

   (d) Calculate the 20th term of the sequence. [2 marks]

   (e) Find the sum of the first 15 terms of the sequence. [2 marks]

   [Total 9 marks]

[Nov 2006, Paper 2, Question 4(i)] (© IB Organization 2006)

2. A geometric progression G_1 has 1 as its first term and 3 as its common ratio.

   (a) The sum of the first n terms of G_1 is 29 524. Find n. [3 marks]

   A second geometric progression G_2 has the form $1, \dfrac{1}{3}, \dfrac{1}{9}, \dfrac{1}{27}, \ldots$

   (b) State the common ratio for G_2. [1 mark]

   (c) Calculate the sum of the first 10 terms of G_2. [2 marks]

   (d) Explain why the sum of the first 1000 terms of G_2 will give the same answer as the sum of the first 10 terms, when corrected to three significant figures. [1 mark]

   (e) Using your results from parts (a) to (c), or otherwise, calculate the sum of the first 10 terms of the sequence $2, 3\dfrac{1}{3}, 9\dfrac{1}{9}, 27\dfrac{1}{27}, \ldots$

   Give your answer **correct to one decimal place**. [3 marks]

   [Total 10 marks]

[May 2007, Paper 2, Question 4(ii)] (© IB Organization 2007)

3. The first term of an arithmetic sequence is 0 and the common difference is 12.

   (a) Find the value of the 96th term of the sequence. [2 marks]

   The first term of a geometric sequence is 6. The 6th term of the geometric sequence is equal to the 17th term of the arithmetic sequence given above.

   (b) Write down an equation using this information. [2 marks]

   (c) Calculate the common ratio of the geometric sequence. [2 marks]

   [Total 6 marks]

[May 2008, Paper 1, Question 8] (© IB Organization 2008)

4. A National Lottery is offering prizes in a new competition. The winner may choose one of the following.

Option one: $1000 each week for 10 weeks.

Option two: $250 in the first week, $450 in the second week, $650 in the third week, increasing by $200 each week for a total of 10 weeks.

Option three: $10 in the first week, $20 in the second week, $40 in the third week, continuing to double for a total of 10 weeks.

(a) Calculate the amount you receive in the tenth week, if you select:

    (i) option two;

    (ii) option three. *[6 marks]*

(b) What is the total amount you receive if you select **option two**? *[2 marks]*

(c) Which option has the greatest total value? Justify your answer by showing all appropriate calculations. *[4 marks]*

[Total 12 marks]

[May 2002, Paper 2, Question 2] (© *IB Organization 2002*)

Chapter 4 Financial mathematics

In this chapter you will learn:

- about currency conversions
- about simple and compound interest
- how to use geometric sequences and series in a financial context
- about annual inflation and depreciation.

The stock market.

The investment of money, the trading of money, and the best way of looking after your money — these are important concerns all over the world, and understanding them helps people to make sensible decisions about their lives.

This chapter demonstrates how your knowledge about numbers and sequences can help you gain a better understanding of money matters.

4.1 Currency conversions

A currency is the system of money in use in a particular country. Over time, different countries have developed different currencies with distinctive names and values that depend on the history and geography of that country.

When you travel from one country to another, you will need to change (or convert) one currency into another.

The value of a country's currency relative to other currencies can also affect the trade and prosperity of that country.

- In some countries, the basic unit of currency is divided into smaller units. For example, £1 = 100 pence, $1 = 100 cents. So answers to financial questions involving such currencies should be given to **two decimal places**, for example as $5.34.

- In other countries, the basic unit of currency is not split into smaller parts; examples include the Japanese yen. So answers to financial questions involving such currencies should be given to the **nearest whole number**.

Some common currencies are listed in the table below, along with their symbols.

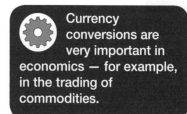

Currency conversions are very important in economics — for example, in the trading of commodities.

Currency	Three-letter abbreviation	Symbol
Australian dollar	AUD	$
Canadian dollar	CAD	$
European euro	EUR	€
Hong Kong dollar	HKD	$
Indian rupee	INR	₹
Japanese yen	JPY	¥
US dollar	USD	$
UK pound	GBP	£

Currency exchange rates

To change one currency to another you need to know the **exchange rate**. The exchange rate is also called the 'foreign-exchange rate', 'forex rate' or 'FX rate'. It is the ratio between the values of two currency units, a number that you can use to exchange one currency for another.

Exchange rates vary constantly; they can be affected by trade, the politics and stability of a country, and natural catastrophes.

Newspapers and websites provide up-to-date tables of rates. An example of an exchange-rate table, taken from http://www.x-rates.com/, is shown on page 112.

Notice that, in the table on page 112, the exchange rates are given to six significant figures. You can use these numbers to calculate the amount that you will pay or receive in a transaction, but for most currencies you would express the final amount to two decimal places.

This particular table has the 'from' currencies arranged in columns and the 'to' currencies arranged in rows. This means that the number in the first column and second row of the table, 0.775915, is the exchange rate from CAD to EUR, that is, the number of Canadian dollars for each Euro. Be aware that other tables may be arranged differently, with the 'from' currencies in rows and the 'to' currencies in columns.

In financial questions set in examinations, you will be expected to give answers to two decimal places, unless you are given different instructions. If you forget to do this, you will be given a one-mark penalty for that examination paper.

What effects might fluctuations in a country's currency value have on international trade? For example, if a currency becomes relatively expensive, it could make that country's exports more difficult to sell.

To work out the amount of currency that you will get when you exchange currency 1 for currency 2, you multiply by the exchange rate:

amount of currency 2 = amount of currency 1 × exchange rate

	CAD	EUR
CAD	1	1.2888
EUR	0.775915	1

Wednesday, January 12, 2011

Modified from http://www.x-rates.com

> In the table above, the exchange rate from EUR to CAD (4th column, 3rd row) is 1 EUR = 1.2888 CAD

> First, calculate how much money she has left.

> The exchange rate from CAD to EUR (3rd column, 4th row) is 1 CAD = 0.775915 EUR

Worked example 4.1

Q. (a) Zara is planning to travel from France to Canada. She has €1800 to change into Canadian dollars. How many dollars can she buy if she exchanges the currencies according to the table alongside?

(b) During her holiday, Zara spends $1600 of her Canadian dollars. If she changes her remaining dollars back into euros when she gets home, according to the table above, how many euros will she have?

A. (a) 1800 EUR = 1800 × 1.2888 CAD
         = 2319.84 CAD (2 d.p.)

(b) $2319.84 − $1600 = $719.84

719.84 CAD = 719.84 × 0.775915 EUR
           = 558.53465 EUR

So she will get €558.53 (2 d.p.)

Exercise 4.1

1. Use the given exchange-rate table to answer the following questions. Round your answers to two decimal places.

	USD	GBP	CAD	EUR	AUD
USD	1	1.57137	1.01378	1.30656	0.993413
GBP	0.636387	1	0.645161	0.831483	0.632195
CAD	0.9864	1.55	1	1.2888	0.979903
EUR	0.765363	1.20266	0.775915	1	0.760322
AUD	1.00662	1.58178	1.0205	1.31523	1

Wednesday, January 12, 2011

Source: **http://www.x-rates.com**

(a) How many CAD can be exchanged for 1200 AUD?

(b) How many GBP can be exchanged for 1500 CAD?

(c) How many AUD can be exchanged for 800 USD?

(d) How many EUR can be exchanged for 750 GBP?

(e) How many USD can be exchanged for 2450 EUR?

2. Yuki is travelling from Japan to Canada on business. In Tokyo the bank is quoting an exchange rate of 1 JPY = 0.01205 CAD.

   (a) If she changes ¥120,000 into Canadian dollars, how many dollars will she receive?

   (b) She spends $885 in Canada. How many dollars does she have left?

   (c) She changes her Canadian money back into Japanese yen when she returns. Assuming that the exchange rate has remained the same, how many yen does she have now? (Give your answer to the nearest yen.)

3. Jean is going on holiday. He is travelling from Geneva to Sicily. He takes 950 CHF (Swiss francs) with him, and changes it into euros at his hotel.

   The hotel exchange rate is 1 CHF = 0.76715 EUR.

   (a) How many euros does he receive?

   (b) At the end of the two-week holiday he has €125 left. How many Swiss francs will he get back? Two weeks later the hotel exchange rate is 1 CHF = 0.821567 EUR.

Buying and selling currency

Currency can be bought and sold like any other commodity. If you visit a bureau de change, you will see the current rates of exchange displayed on a board like this.

Country	Currency	We buy	We sell
Australia	AUD	1.697	1.460
Euro zone	EUR	1.299	1.132
Hong Kong	HKD	12.89	11.34
Japan	JPY	139.7	121.0
Switzerland	CHF	1.638	1.411
USA	USD	1.683	1.472

The rates in this table were taken from a British newspaper published in 2011, so they are relative to GBP (Great Britain Pounds). In other words, they give the number of units of each currency for each pound sterling. The 'We **buy**' column gives the rates used when you change other currencies **to** GBP; the 'We **sell**' column gives the rates that apply when you change money **from** GBP to other currencies.

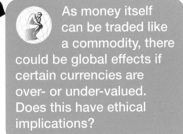

As money itself can be traded like a commodity, there could be global effects if certain currencies are over- or under-valued. Does this have ethical implications?

You can also buy and sell currency through banks and brokers. These are businesses being run for profit, and there are two ways in which they can make a profit from currency exchange:

1. The broker charges **commission**, which is a percentage of the value of the transaction. You pay the commission to the broker for the money that you exchange.

2. The bank buys currency from customers at one rate, and sells it at a lower rate. The difference in price will be the bank's profit.

For example, Marc and Annie are travelling from Cardiff in Wales to Hong Kong. They decide to take £1250 each, but go to different banks to change the currency.

Marc's bank quotes an exchange rate of 1 GBP = 12.39 HKD, and charges 2% commission in the original currency.

This means that the amount of commission he pays is $0.02 \times £1250 = £25$.

The exchange rate is applied to the remaining £1250 − £25 = £1225, giving $1225 \times 12.39 = 15{,}177.75$ HKD.

Annie decides to buy from a bank that charges no commission.

The bank is selling at a rate of 1 GBP = 11.46 HKD, so her £1250 becomes $1250 \times 11.46 = 14{,}325$ HKD.

After the trip they return to Wales with 3700 HKD each, and sell their currency back to their respective banks.

Marc's bank again charges 2% commission and uses the same exchange rate as before: 1 GBP = 12.39 HKD.

So the amount of commission he pays is $0.02 \times \$3700 = \$74$, and the amount of money remaining to be exchanged is $\$3700 − \$74 = \$3626$.

Applying the exchange rate then gives $3626 \div 12.39 = 292.66$ GBP.

Annie's bank is buying at a rate of 1 GBP = 13.29 HKD, so her $3700 becomes $3700 \div 13.29 = 278.40$ GBP.

In this example, even though Marc was charged commission, he had the better deal in both directions of conversion. This will not always be the case, so it is usually worth checking to see where you can get the best deal for a particular transaction.

Exercise 4.2

1. Jung lives in Singapore and is travelling to Thailand. She wants to change 1600 Singapore dollars (SGD) into Thai baht (THB).

   The bank in Singapore charges 2% commission in dollars and quotes an exchange rate of 1 SGD = 23.910 THB.

   (a) Calculate the number of Thai baht that Jung will receive.

   (b) In Bangkok she buys a hat for 85 THB. What did it cost in SGD, according to the exchange rate given above?

2. Cara lives in Scotland and travels to the Netherlands. Her bank quotes her an exchange rate of £1 = €1.17 and charges her £3 in commission. Cara changes £150 into euros.

   (a) How many GBP does Cara have left to exchange after she has paid the commission?

   (b) How many euros does Cara receive from the bank?

   (c) In the Netherlands, Cara buys 750 g of cheese for her grandfather. If the cheese costs €12.80 per kilogram, calculate the cost of this gift in GBP.

For questions 3–5, use the exchange rates in the following table.

Question 3		Question 4		Question 5	
USA/EUR exchange		EUR/GBP exchange		GBP/HKD exchange	
We buy	We sell	We buy	We sell	We buy	We sell
0.75863	0.72596	0.87504	0.83736	12.3768	11.8438

3. Mike travels from the USA to Spain. He changes $900 into euros at his bank.

   (a) Use the table above to calculate the number of euros that he receives, assuming that no commission is charged.

   Mike's flight is cancelled, and he changes the euros back into dollars.

   (b) Using the same table, how many dollars does the bank give him back?

   (c) How much money has Mike lost by changing his money twice?

4. Anya travels from Greece to England. She needs to change €1200 into GBP. She has a choice to make.

   (a) Bank A charges 1.6% commission in euros and offers an exchange rate of 1€ = £0.851483. Calculate the number of GBP she would receive from bank A.

   (b) Bank B buys and sells GBP at the rates shown in the table above, with no commission charged. Calculate the number of GBP that Anya would receive from bank B.

   (c) Which bank should Anya choose?

5. Nic is flying from England to Hong Kong.

   (a) He changes £240 into Hong Kong dollars. If the bank is selling at the rate shown in the table above, how many HKD does he receive?

   (b) On his return to England, he has 780 HKD left to change back into pounds. If the bank is buying at the rate shown in the table above, how many GBP does he receive?

"That piggy bank is for my college fund."

Investment, and the earning of interest from investments, happens all over the world. However, it is important to realise that not all societies have the same attitude to financial investments and treat them in the same way. For example, Islamic law does not allow the charging of interest or fees for loans of money. Therefore Islamic banking operates in a different way.

4.2 Compound interest

If you have saved or earned some money, you will want to keep it in a safe place. It would be even better if, while that money is being looked after, it generates more money and your original sum increases.

The sum of money that you deposit (pay into the bank) is called the **capital**. You can earn **interest** on that capital while it is in the bank.

There are two types of interest:

- **simple interest**, where the interest is calculated on only the original sum deposited

- **compound interest**, where the interest is calculated on the original sum plus all the interest previously accumulated.

In this course we will focus on compound interest.

Imagine that your friend Shane has saved 800 AUD, and needs to decide on the best way to protect it and use it to finance his future travel plans.

Shane has identified three different options, and asks you for your advice.

- *Option* 1: He puts the money in a safe place at home, and adds any more money that he saves to his original sum.

- *Option* 2: He puts the money in a bank for a year. The bank is offering him an annual **interest rate** of 4% on his deposit. At the end of the year, he can withdraw the interest to spend or leave the deposit in the bank to earn more interest; however, Shane will only ever get interest on the initial deposit. This is an example of simple interest.

- *Option* 3: He puts the money in the bank for several years. The bank offers him a lower interest rate of 3.5% annually, but after one year it calculates the interest, adds the amount to Shane's deposit, and then the following year pays interest on both the original deposit and the interest that it has already earned. This is an example of compound interest.

Let's look at what will happen to Shane's $800 deposit over a few years, assuming that he makes no withdrawals or further deposits (numbers are rounded to the nearest dollar):

Shane's savings	Option 1	Option 2	Option 3
End of year 1	800 AUD	$800 \times 4\% = 32$ $800 + 32 = 832$ AUD	$800 \times 3.5\% = 28$ $800 + 28 = 828$ AUD
End of year 2	800 AUD	$800 + 32 + 32 = 864$ AUD	$828 + (828 \times 3.5\%) = 828 + 29 = 857$ AUD
End of year 3	800 AUD	$800 + 32 + 32 + 32 = 896$ AUD	$857 + (857 \times 3.5\%) = 857 + 30 = 887$ AUD

Putting these numbers on a graph makes it easier to see what will happen in the future.

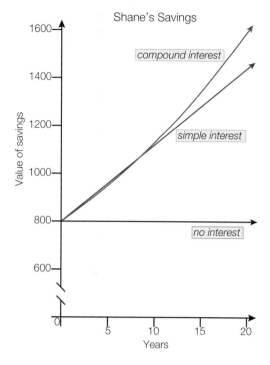

Shane's Savings

Value of savings

compound interest

simple interest

no interest

Years

Shane's dilemma illustrates three different ways of looking after money:

- Option 1 earns no interest on the capital of 800 AUD. The value of the savings does not increase.

- Option 2, **simple interest**, earns interest on the capital, but that interest is not 'reinvested'. The value of the savings increases in a straight line; the rate of increase stays the same.

- Option 3, **compound interest**, earns interest on the capital, and that interest is reinvested by being added to the capital to form a new base for future interest calculations. The value of the savings increases **exponentially**.

 You will meet exponential growth in Chapter 19.

What is your advice to Shane?

Now we look at the mathematical structure of Options 2 and 3 in more detail.

With **simple interest**, as long as you keep the original deposit in the bank, it will continue to earn the same amount of interest year after year.

In Shane's case, his 800 AUD deposit will earn $800 \times 4\% = 32$ AUD of interest every year. So at the end of 5 years he will have earned $5 \times 32 = 160$ AUD interest, and his total balance will be $800 + 32 + 32 + 32 + 32 + 32 = 800 + (5 \times 32) = 960$ AUD.

Note that his total balance from one year to the next can be viewed as an **arithmetic sequence** with first term 800 and common difference 32.

 You met sequences in Chapter 3.

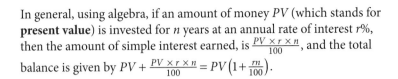

In general, using algebra, if an amount of money PV (which stands for **present value**) is invested for n years at an annual rate of interest $r\%$, then the amount of simple interest earned, is $\frac{PV \times r \times n}{100}$, and the total balance is given by $PV + \frac{PV \times r \times n}{100} = PV\left(1 + \frac{rn}{100}\right)$.

Applying these formulae to Shane's case, we take $PV = 800$, $r = 4$ and $n = 5$. So:

$$\text{interest earned} = \frac{800 \times 4 \times 5}{100} = 160 \text{ AUD}$$

$$\text{total balance} = 800 \times \left(1 + \frac{4 \times 5}{100}\right) = 960 \text{ AUD}$$

With **compound interest**, as long as you make no withdrawals, the amount of interest earned will increase from year to year.

This is easier to understand if we do the interest calculations year by year. In Shane's case:

	Total balance
Beginning of year 1	800 AUD
End of year 1	$800 + 800 \times \dfrac{3.5}{100} = 828 \text{ AUD}$
End of year 2	$\left(800 + 800 \times \dfrac{3.5}{100}\right) + \left(800 + 800 \times \dfrac{3.5}{100}\right) \times \dfrac{3.5}{100} = 856.98 \text{ AUD}$

In general, using algebra, we can work out a formula for the account balance after n years.

If an amount of money PV is invested for n years at an annual rate of interest $r\%$, then:

	Total balance	Formula
Beginning of year 1	PV	PV
End of year 1	$PV + PV \times \dfrac{r}{100} = PV\left(1 + \dfrac{r}{100}\right)$	$PV\left(1 + \dfrac{r}{100}\right)$
End of year 2	$PV\left(1 + \dfrac{r}{100}\right) + PV\left(1 + \dfrac{r}{100}\right) \times \dfrac{r}{100}$ $= PV\left(1 + \dfrac{r}{100}\right)\left(1 + \dfrac{r}{100}\right)$ (by taking out a factor of $PV\left(1 + \dfrac{r}{100}\right)$ from the first line)	$PV\left(1 + \dfrac{r}{100}\right)^2$
End of year n		$PV\left(1 + \dfrac{r}{100}\right)^n$

Note that the total balance from one year to the next can be viewed as an **geometric sequence** with first term PV and common ratio $\left(1+\frac{r}{100}\right)$.

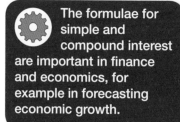

The total balance after n years is referred to as the **future value** of the investment, denoted by FV.

The general formula for compound interest is:

$$FV = PV\left(1+\frac{r}{100k}\right)^{kn}$$ where $FV =$ future value, $PV =$ present value, $n =$ number of years, $r\% =$ annual rate of interest, and $k =$ number of compounding periods per year.

So far we have considered only the situation where interest is calculated at the end of each year, that is, $k = 1$. But often interest is calculated at more frequent intervals, such as quarterly ($k = 4$) or monthly ($k = 12$).

Applying the formula to Shane's example, we take $PV = 800$, $r = 3.5$, $k = 1$, and $n = 5$. Then we get:

$$FV = 800\times\left(1+\frac{3.5}{100}\right)^{5} = 950.15 \text{ AUD}$$

The interest that Shane will have earned over five years is $950.15 - 800 = 150.15$ AUD.

Here are some important points to remember when calculating compound interest:

- Think about when you are investing the money; this is usually taken to be the beginning of year 1.

- Think about when you are being asked for the total balance or interest earned; this is usually at the end of a certain year, which is the 'n' in the formula.

- Look at the time intervals at which interest is calculated; interest may be calculated yearly, half-yearly, quarterly, monthly or daily.

Note that if Shane invests his $800 at the same compound interest rate but calculated quarterly or monthly rather than yearly, he will end up with different amounts at the end of five years.

Think carefully about compound interest. Would it be good for your savings or pension, but bad for your credit card? Do you always read the small print?

Investing 800 AUD at 3.5% compounded quarterly yields:

$$FV = 800\times\left(1+\frac{3.5}{100\times4}\right)^{4\times5} = 800\times\left(1+\frac{3.5}{400}\right)^{20} = 952.27 \text{ AUD}$$

Investing 800 AUD at 3.5% compounded monthly yields:

$$FV = 800\times\left(1+\frac{3.5}{100\times12}\right)^{12\times5} = 800\times\left(1+\frac{3.5}{1200}\right)^{60} = 952.75 \text{ AUD}$$

By compounding more frequently, a little more interest has been earned.

The compound interest formula $FV = PV\left(1+\frac{r}{100k}\right)^{kn}$ can be used to solve many of the financial questions that you are likely to meet.

Worked example 4.2

Q. Twins Paco and Peta are given 12,000 pesos each by an aunt.

(a) Paco decides to invest his money in a bank that is offering 4.8% interest compounded yearly. How much money will he have in the bank after five years?

(b) Peta decides to invest her money in another bank that is offering 4.6% interest compounded every three months (quarterly). How much money will she have in the bank after five years?

(c) Which twin has made the better investment?

> Use the compound interest formula with $PV = 12000$, $r = 4.8$, $k = 1$ and $n = 5$.

A.
(a) Paco: $FV = 12000 \times \left(1+\dfrac{4.8}{100}\right)^5 = 15170\,pesos$

> Use the compound interest formula with $PV = 12000$, $r = 4.6$, $k = 4$ and $n = 5$.

(b) Peta: $FV = 12000 \times \left(1+\dfrac{4.6}{100 \times 4}\right)^{4 \times 5}$

$= 12000 \times \left(1+\dfrac{4.6}{400}\right)^{20} = 15083\,pesos$

(c) Paco has made the better investment.

Worked example 4.3

Q. Jan invests 950 euros in a bank that pays 3.8% interest compounded yearly. How many years will it take for his investment to double?

> Write down the formula for compound interest and substitute in the given values. Here, $k = 1$.

A. $FV = PV\left(1+\dfrac{r}{100k}\right)^{kn}$

$FV = 950\left(1+\dfrac{3.8}{100}\right)^n$

> We want to find the value of n for which $FV = 2 \times PV$.

$2 \times 950 = 950\left(1+\dfrac{3.8}{100}\right)^n$

$\longrightarrow$

> After dividing both sides of the equation by 950, we have an equation to solve for n.

continued . . .

$$2 = (1 + 0.038)^n$$

> Use your GDC to plot the graphs of $y = (1 + 0.038)^x$ and $y = 2$ and look for their intersection. See section '19.2(a) Solving unfamiliar equations using a graph' on page 684 of the GDC chapter if you need reminding how.

exam tip

Logarithms are not in the syllabus, but if you are confident in using them, you can use them to solve equations like this one.

> There are several ways to find n. Here are two.

> Trial and improvement.

Method 1:

Try

$n = 20: (1 + 0.038)^{20} = 2.108$, too high

$n = 18: (1 + 0.038)^{18} = 1.957$, too low

$n = 19: (1 + 0.038)^{19} = 2.031$, close to 2

It will take 19 years for Jan's investment to double.

Method 2:

 TEXAS

 CASIO

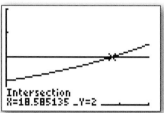

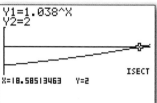

Intersection is at $x = 18.6$

So it will take 19 years.

Exercise 4.3

1. Astrid has inherited 40,000 euros from her great aunt. She has decided to invest the money in a savings account at an interest rate of 6% **per annum**.

   Find how much the investment will be worth after five years if interest is compounded:

   (a) yearly

   (b) quarterly (every three months)

   (c) monthly.

2. Kyle has just retired from his job. He was given a **lump sum** pension of 500,000 AUD and decided to save his money in a deposit account which pays 4% interest rate per annum.

   Find how much his savings will be worth after one year if the interest is compounded:

   (a) quarterly   (b) monthly   (c) weekly.

3. Richard invests $3800 in a bank account at $r\%$ interest compounded annually. He hopes to save $5000 in five years. What is the minimum value of r needed for him to meet his target?

4. Mr Woodward saw the following advertisement in a timber investment brochure.

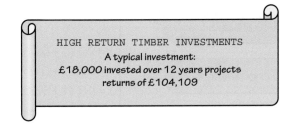

HIGH RETURN TIMBER INVESTMENTS
A typical investment:
£18,000 invested over 12 years projects
returns of £104,109

He decided to follow up on the opportunity, but wants to know what the annual interest rate is. Calculate the interest rate for him, assuming that interest is compounded yearly.

5. Mrs Simpson invests a lump sum of $100,000 in an offshore business. She is promised an interest rate of 4.2% compounded annually.

   (a) How long will it take for the investment to double?

   (b) If it takes n years for the investment to treble, find the value of n.

6. Dr Chapman saw the following advertisement in a newspaper.

Fix your savings for the next 10 years:
   • Earn a competitive fixed rate of 3.6% per annum
   • Invest from £1000 to £2 million
   • Withdrawals and closures are not allowed
   • Strictly limited offer

He decided to invest £64,000 for the advertised term of 10 years.

   (a) Assuming that interest is compounded annually, what will his investment be worth after 5 years?

   (b) Will he be able to double his investment over the 10-year period? Justify your answer.

4.3 The GDC and financial mathematics

Most GDCs have a built-in program that can help you to solve the financial problems that you might come across in exercises, examinations and real life. See '4.1 The financial App, TVM' on page 661 of the GDC chapter for how to use this App.

Once you have loaded the program, you will see a screen containing a list of variables. You need to read the question carefully and input the values for the different variables.

exam tip

This is one of the programs that you are allowed to use in IB examinations. If it is not on your GDC already, you should be able to download it from the website for your brand of GDC.

The letters and symbols used in the program should be familiar to you if you have already solved financial problems using the compound interest formula:

N or n = number of time periods (usually years)	
I% = interest rate	
PV = present value	
PMT = extra payments into the account each year	
FV = future value	
P/Y = number of interest payments made into the account each year	
C/Y = number of compounding periods each year	

TEXAS

```
N=0
I%=0
PV=0
PMT=0
FV=0
P/Y=1
C/Y=1
PMT:END BEGIN
```

CASIO

```
Compound Interest:End
n  =0
I% =0
PV =0
PMT=0
FV =0
P/Y=12          ↓
 n  I%  PV PMT FV AMT
```

Keep the following points in mind when you use the TVM program:

- Write down the answers to the calculations clearly.

- You must not use 'calculator language' in projects and examinations, so quote the compound interest formula in your solutions.

- You may find it helpful to list the values required by the program as you read the question.

- For investments, PV must be entered as a **negative** quantity: you have invested the money, so it is no longer in your account — the bank has it!

- To get the answer using a TEXAS GDC, highlight the quantity that you want to find, then press ALPHA, SOLVE.

- To get the answer using a CASIO GDC, press the Function key for the quantity that you want.

hint

You might find it interesting to look up 'compound interest' on the internet. A search will turn up many websites, some explaining the mathematics, and some giving simple examples similar to the ones in this book.

Worked example 4.4

Q. | Marie has \$680 to invest. Suppose that she puts it in a bank account that pays 3.7% interest compounded annually.

(a) How much money will she have at the end of 10 years?

(b) How long will it take to double her investment?

(c) Marie would like her investment to double in 15 years. At what rate does her account need to earn interest if she is to achieve this?

continued . . .

A. (a) $FV = PV\left(1 + \dfrac{r}{100k}\right)^{kn}$

Substitute the given values into the compound interest formula. Here $k = 1$.

$$FV = 680\left(1 + \dfrac{3.7}{100}\right)^n = 680 \times 1.037^n$$

Substitute in $n = 10$.

$$FV = 680 \times (1 + 0.037)^{10} = 977.90$$

 TEXAS   CASIO

```
N=10
I%=3.7
PV=-680
PMT=0
■FV=977.904572
P/Y=1
C/Y=1
PMT:END BEGIN
```

```
Compound Interest
FV =977.904572



REPT        AMT     GRPH
```

We want to find the value of n for which $FV = 2 \times PV$, so use the compound interest formula to write down the equation that we need to solve.

(b) $2 \times 680 = 680 \times (1 + 0.037)^n$

Divide both sides by 680.

$$2 = (1 + 0.037)^n$$

Solve the equation by trial and improvement or by plotting graphs and finding their intersection.

From GDC: $n = 19.08$

 TEXAS   CASIO

```
■N=19.0781826
I%=3.7
PV=-680
PMT=0
FV=1360
P/Y=1
C/Y=1
PMT:■ BEGIN
```

```
Compound Interest
n  =19.0781826



REPT        AMT     GRPH
```

Check the answer using the TVM program on your GDC.

Now r is the unknown value that we want to find.

(c) $FV = 680\left(1 + \dfrac{r}{100}\right)^n$

We want FV to be $2 \times PV$ when $n = 15$, so write down the equation to solve for r.

$$2 \times 680 = 680\left(1 + \dfrac{r}{100}\right)^{15}$$

Divide both sides by 680.

$$2 = \left(1 + \dfrac{r}{100}\right)^{15}$$

continued . . .

> From GDC: $r = 4.73$
>
> So the account needs to earn interest at 4.73%.

Solve the equation by trial and improvement or plotting graphs and finding their intersection.

Check your answer using the TVM program.

 TEXAS

```
N=15
·I%=4.729412282
PV=-680
PMT=0
FV=1360
P/Y=1
C/Y=1
PMT:     BEGIN
```

 **CASIO**

```
Compound Interest
I% =4.729412282


REPT        AMT      GRPH
```

As you can see, the TVM program is particularly useful when solving questions like (b) and (c) in Worked example 4.4.

Worked example 4.5

Q. In part (a) of Worked example 4.4, Marie invested her money at 3.7% compound annually. She could also invest her money at a rate of 3.6% compounded monthly.

What would be the difference in her investment amounts under the two schemes after 10 years?

Substitute the given values into the compound interest formula.

A. $FV = PV\left(1 + \dfrac{r}{100k}\right)^{kn}$

$FV = 680\left(1 + \dfrac{3.6}{100 \times 12}\right)^{12n} = 680 \times 1.003^{12n}$

Substitute in $n = 10$.

$FV = 680 \times (1 + 0.003)^{120} = 974.14$

Calculate the difference between this answer and the answer to Worked example 4.4(a).

£977.90 − £974.14 = £3.76

 TEXAS

```
N=10
I%=3.6
PV=-680
PMT=0
·FV=974.1388751
P/Y=1
C/Y=12
PMT:     BEGIN
```

CASIO

```
Compound Interest
FV =974.1388751


REPT        AMT      GRPH
```

977.90 − 974.14 = 3.76 GBP

The GDC's TVM program is also very useful for solving loan-related problems, such as working out the monthly repayment for a mortgage or a car-purchase loan. In this case, the program's variables have the following meaning:

 hint

There are also many websites that contain 'compound interest calculators', which can help you to predict how investments will change over time depending on different interest rates or different compounding periods. They can also work out the regular payment amounts needed to repay a loan.

- N or n = number of time periods (instalments)

- I% = interest rate

- PV = total loan amount, which should be entered as a **positive** number

- PMT = payment amount per period; this is the quantity you want to find

- FV = **0**, because at the end of the lifetime of the loan, you want to owe nothing

- P/Y = number of payments per year

- C/Y = number of interest compounding periods per year, usually the same as P/Y

For example, suppose Lukas needs to take out a loan for €9000, and the local bank offers him a loan at 4.5% interest per annum, to be paid back over 5 years in monthly instalments.

Entering n = 5 × 12, I% = 4.5, PV = 9000, FV = 0, P/Y = 12 and C/Y = 12 into his GDC, Lukas finds that PMT = 167.79. This means that his monthly repayment amounts will be €167.79.

The total amount he will have repaid at the end of the five years (60 instalments) is €167.79 × 60 = €10,067.23. So the total interest that the bank will earn from him is €1067.23.

Note that if Lukas had waited until the end of the five years to pay everything back, interest would have accrued on all of the €9000 for five years. Assuming the interest is compounded annually, he would have owed $9000\left(1+\frac{4.5}{100}\right)^5 = 9000 \times 1.045^5 = $ €11,215.64 at the end of five years, to be paid off in one go (of which €2215.64 is interest). By repaying in monthly instalments, each month Lukas reduces the outstanding debt on which interest accrues, so overall he ends up paying less; this process of gradually decreasing a debt by paying it back in regular instalments is called **amortisation**.

Exercise 4.4

Try using your GDC to answer the investment-related questions in Exercise 4.3.

The following questions are all concerned with loan repayment problems.

The table on page 127 shows monthly repayment amounts for a loan of £5000 (APR = annual percentage rate). Use the information from the table to answer questions 1–3.

	8.4% APR	9.9% APR	12.9% APR
36 months	£156	£160	£166
48 months	£122	£125	£132
60 months	£101	£104	£111
90 months	£74	£77	£85
120 months	£60	£64	£72
180 months	£48	£52	£60
240 months	£42	£46	£55
300 months	£38	£43	£53

1. (a) Find the monthly repayment on a loan of £5000 at 9.9% per annum taken over 120 months.

   (b) Calculate the total amount to be repaid on a loan of £35,000 taken over 60 months at a rate of 12.9% per annum.
   (*Hint*: £35,000 is seven times £5000.)

2. Two friends, Arthur and Ken, both took out loans of £40,000. Arthur was offered his loan at 9.9% per annum, to be repaid over 60 months.

   (a) Work out Arthur's monthly repayment.

   (b) Calculate Arthur's total repayment on his loan over the 60 months.

   Ken's loan was at 8.4% per annum over 90 months.

   (c) Work out Ken's monthly repayment.

   (d) Which of the two friends had the better deal? Explain your answer.

3. Margaret is buying a car for £25,000. She pays a 10% deposit and takes out a loan at 8.4% per annum over 48 months.

   (a) How much deposit did she pay?

   (b) How much did she borrow?

   (c) Work out her monthly repayment.

   (d) Calculate the total interest paid on the loan.

4. Mr and Mrs Alonso are planning to go on a cruise to celebrate their silver wedding anniversary. They need an extra €4380 to complete their payment, and decide to ask their bank for a loan. They agree to repay over 5 years at 6.8% per annum.

   (a) Calculate the value of the monthly repayment.

   (b) Find the total amount repaid over the five years.

   (c) Find the total amount of interest charged.

   (d) Would they have got a better deal if, for the same loan amount of €4380, they had opted for repayment over 3 years at 7.2% per annum? Justify your answer.

5. Jeremy is looking for a new car and wants to buy either a Nissan Pathfinder or a Nissan X-Trail. He printed the following advertisements from a website. However, some of the data was not legible.

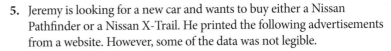

	MONTHLY PAYMENTS	CUSTOMER DEPOSIT	CASH PRICE	TOTAL AMOUNT OF CREDIT	TOTAL AMOUNT PAYABLE	DURATION
	?	?	£29,580	£13,958	£31,066	36 months

	MONTHLY PAYMENTS	CUSTOMER DEPOSIT	CASH PRICE	TOTAL AMOUNT OF CREDIT	TOTAL AMOUNT PAYABLE	DURATION
	£539	£17,024	£34,560	?	?	36 months

(a) For the Nissan X-Trail, calculate the monthly payments and the customer deposit.

(b) For the Nissan Pathfinder, calculate the total amount Jeremy needs to borrow and the total amount payable on the loan.

The following table shows monthly repayments for a $1000 loan taken over different periods and at different rates. Use the information from the table to answer questions 6 and 7.

Loan term (years)	Monthly repayments per $1000							
	Annual interest rate							
	6.00%	6.25%	6.50%	6.75%	7.00%	7.25%	7.50%	8.00%
3	30.42	30.54	30.65	30.76	30.88	30.99	31.11	31.34
5	19.33	19.45	19.57	19.68	19.80	19.92	20.04	20.28
10	11.10	11.23	11.35	11.48	11.61	11.74	11.87	12.13
12	9.76	9.89	10.02	10.15	10.28	10.42	10.55	10.82
15	8.44	8.57	8.71	8.85	8.99	9.13	9.27	9.56
20	7.16	7.31	7.46	7.60	7.75	7.90	8.06	8.36
25	6.44	6.60	6.75	6.91	7.07	7.23	7.39	7.72
30	6.00	6.16	6.32	6.49	6.65	6.82	6.99	7.34

6. The Johnsons take out a loan for $8000 over 5 years at a rate of 7.5% per annum. Calculate:

(a) the value of the monthly repayment

(b) the total amount paid over the five years

(c) the amount of interest charged.

7. Mr and Mrs Freeman are planning to refurbish their house at a cost of $39,500. They decide to take out two separate loans.

Mr Freeman is offered a loan for $20,500 at 6.5% per annum over 12 years.

Mrs Freeman is offered a loan for the remaining amount at 7.25% over 10 years.

(a) How much in total will the couple pay for the loan?

(b) What will be the total interest charged on the loan?

(c) Would Mr and Mrs Freeman get a better deal if they went for a third offer of a joint loan for the whole amount of $39,500 at 8% per annum over 10 years? Justify your answer.

8. Yuko takes out a loan for ¥43,000 over three years at a rate of 2.17% per annum. Find:

(a) the value of the monthly repayment

(b) the total amount paid over the three years

(c) the amount of interest charged.

(4.4) Inflation

In England, a litre of milk cost about 19 pence in 1968; it cost approximately 79 pence in 2009.

In America, a bottle of ketchup cost 22 cents in 1966; fifteen years later it cost 99 cents.

The steady rise in prices, and consequent fall in the quantity of goods that the same amount of money can buy, is called **inflation**. Over the past 120 years, inflation in most industrialised countries has been at around 3% a year.

Cumulative Inflation by
Decade Since 1913
© InflationData.com

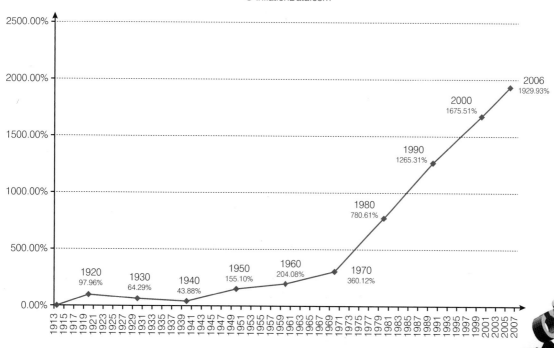

There have been periods of time in certain countries when changes in prices were very drastic. For example, Germany at the time of the Weimar Republic in the 1920s experienced hyperinflation, where prices rose so rapidly that money lost most of its value before it could be spent. In America, following the Wall Street crash of 1929, negative inflation (**deflation**) meant that stock prices dropped suddenly, causing massive unemployment and severe economic depression.

Governments calculate inflation using a statistic called the Consumer Price Index (CPI). This number is estimated by looking at a 'basket' of goods that people use most commonly. The rate at which the cost of those goods in the basket changes over time gives a measure of inflation.

Inflation calculations can be done using the compound interest formula with $k = 1$, $FV = PV\left(1 + \frac{r}{100}\right)^n$, or a GDC's TVM program.

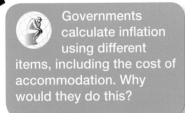

Governments calculate inflation using different items, including the cost of accommodation. Why would they do this?

Inflation rates vary with the price fluctuations of different commodities. Some commodities, such as oil, have a more variable rate than others.

Use the compound interest formula. In this case r = annual rate of inflation, and remember that because it is inflation $k = 1$.

Worked example 4.6

Q. In 1990, the average price of a barrel of oil was $23.19. If price inflation occurred at an average rate of 3% after 1990, what would a barrel of oil have cost in 2010?

A. $FV = PV\left(1 + \dfrac{3}{100}\right)^n$

$FV = 23.19(1 + 0.03)^{20} = \$41.88$

In 2010, the average price of a barrel of oil was actually $53.48, even more than expected from a 3% inflation rate.

Worked example 4.7

Q. If the inflation rate in Canada this year is 2.35%, calculate the likely cost of a 450 CAD laptop computer:

(a) one year ago   (b) in four years' time.

Substitute the given values into the compound interest formula and set $k = 1$.

A. (a) $FV = PV\left(1 + \dfrac{r}{100}\right)^n$

$= PV\left(1 + \dfrac{2.35}{100}\right)^n = PV \times 1.0235^n$

$\longrightarrow$

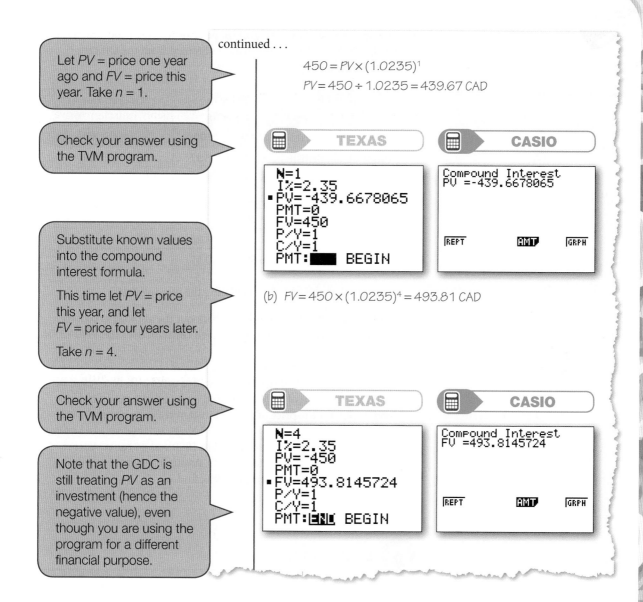

continued . . .

$$450 = PV \times (1.0235)^1$$
$$PV = 450 \div 1.0235 = 439.67 \ CAD$$

Let PV = price one year ago and FV = price this year. Take $n = 1$.

Check your answer using the TVM program.

Substitute known values into the compound interest formula.

This time let PV = price this year, and let FV = price four years later.

Take $n = 4$.

Check your answer using the TVM program.

Note that the GDC is still treating PV as an investment (hence the negative value), even though you are using the program for a different financial purpose.

(b) $FV = 450 \times (1.0235)^4 = 493.81 \ CAD$

Exercise 4.5

1. A house cost £198,000 twenty years ago. If the rate of inflation has remained at 4% per year over the past twenty years, find the present cost of the house.

2. Florence bought her car six years ago for €45,850. If inflation has caused the price of cars to increase by 2.8% each year, what would it cost her to buy the car now?

3. Phoenix Communications bought a new IT system for $3.4 million twelve years ago. If the rate of inflation has been a steady 1.98% per year over the past twelve years, calculate how much the system would have cost them now.

4. The table below shows the average price of selected products in the UK in 1990 and 2004 (information obtained from the Office for National Statistics).

Commodity	Price in £ per kg		Overall rate of inflation, %
	1990	2004	1990–2004
Rump steak, British	8.13	8.97	10.3
Cod fillets	5.74	8.64	?
Sugar, granulated	0.62	0.74	?
Cheese, Cheddar	3.30	5.67	71.8
Apples, eating	1.03	1.25	?
Carrots	0.59	0.57	?

(a) Complete the table by calculating the missing data.

(b) For each of the commodities, work out the annual percentage rate of inflation, assuming it stayed constant over the 1990–2004 period.

5. In 1980 the price of 100 g of instant coffee was $1.01. As a result of inflation, the price of coffee increased by 3.16% per year. Find how long it took for the price of 100 g of instant coffee to rise to $1.88.

6. The average price of a litre of petrol in 1990 was 44 cents. After n years, the price increased to 81 cents. Assuming that the steady year-on-year inflation rate was 6.29%, find n.

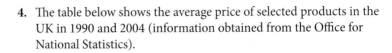 **4.5** Depreciation

If you buy a new bicycle, does it gain value with time? Or does it lose value? Most manufactured goods lose value as they get older. So a bicycle that cost 20,000 INR (Indian rupees) could be worth only 16,500 INR three years later. This reduction in value is called **depreciation**.

Depreciation is important to individuals because they would generally have to sell an item for much less than they paid for it originally. It is important to businesses, because any new equipment that they buy will be worth less from year to year.

As with inflation, you can calculate depreciation using the compound interest formula with $k = 1$, which is $FV = PV\left(1 + \frac{r}{100}\right)^n$. But note that as the value is decreasing each year, the interest rate r will be **negative**.

Worked example 4.8

Q. Reena buys a new bicycle for 25,000 INR. She knows that the value of the bicycle will depreciate by 6% each year. What will her bicycle be worth in eight years' time?

> Substitute the given values into the formula, remembering that r is negative and $k = 1$.

A. $FV = PV\left(1+\dfrac{r}{100}\right)^n$

$= PV\left(1+\dfrac{-6}{100}\right)^n = PV \times 0.94^n$

> Substitute in $PV = 25000$ and $n = 8$.

$25000 \times 0.94^n = 15239$ INR

> Check your answer using the TVM program.

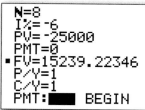

Worked example 4.9

Q. José runs a printing business in Chile. He decides to buy a new printing press at a cost of 4500 pesos. The value of the press depreciates at a rate of 10% each year. How long will it take before the press is worth half the amount that José paid for it?

> Substitute the given values into the formula.
>
> Again, r is negative, as the value of the printing press is decreasing and $k = 1$.

A. $FV = PV\left(1+\dfrac{r}{100}\right)^n$

$= 4500\left(1+\dfrac{-10}{100}\right)^n = 4500 \times 0.9^n$

> We want to find the value of n for which $FV = 0.5 \times PV$.

$0.5 \times 4500 = 4500 \times 0.9^n$

$\longrightarrow$

continued . . .

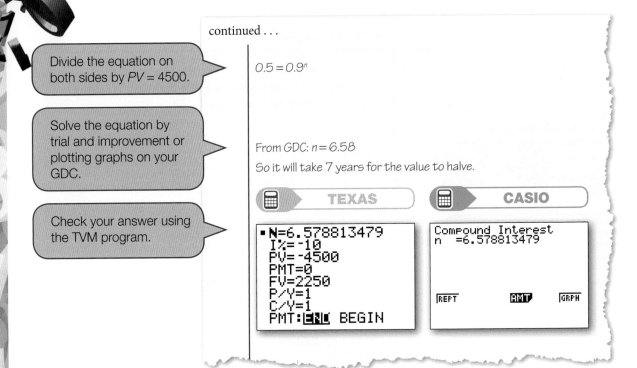

Divide the equation on both sides by $PV = 4500$.

$0.5 = 0.9^n$

Solve the equation by trial and improvement or plotting graphs on your GDC.

From GDC: $n = 6.58$
So it will take 7 years for the value to halve.

Check your answer using the TVM program.

TEXAS
```
▪N=6.578813479
 I%=-10
 PV=-4500
 PMT=0
 FV=2250
 P/Y=1
 C/Y=1
 PMT:END BEGIN
```

CASIO
```
Compound Interest
n  =6.578813479



[REPT]      [AMT]    [GRPH]
```

Exercise 4.6

1. A laser printer was bought new for £454.80. The printer depreciates in value at 18% per year.

   (a) Find the printer's value after three years.

   (b) How much of its value will be lost after five years?

2. Christopher bought his car in May 2005 for $49,995. The rate of depreciation is estimated to be a steady 21% per year.

   (a) How much was Christopher's car worth in May 2010?

   (b) How much of the car's original value did he lose?

   (c) Is it worth selling his car in May 2012 for $10,000? Justify your answer.

3. I buy a car for €43,000 and keep it for n years. The value of the car after n years is €22,016. If the car's value has been depreciating at a constant rate of 21% per annum, find the value of n.

4. A drinks company bought new laboratory equipment for $168,000. It is estimated that at the end of its useful life, the value of the equipment will be $22,750. If the yearly rate of depreciation is 17.5%, find the length of the useful life of the equipment.

5. A company buys a new communication system for $350,000. It is estimated that for the first three years, the rate of depreciation will be 20% per annum. After three years the rate of depreciation changes to a constant r% per annum, until the system is scrapped for $12,000 at the end of ten years' service.

(a) Work out the estimated value of the system after three years.

(b) Find the value of r.

(c) How long did it take for the system to lose half of its value?

Summary

You should know:

- how to carry out currency conversions

- what compound interest is and that it can be calculated yearly, half-yearly, quarterly or monthly

- that compound interest is an application of geometric sequences and series in a financial context

- how to use the GDC's financial package (TVM) to answer finance-related questions

- the concepts of annual inflation and depreciation.

Mixed examination practice

Exam-style questions

1. Frederique is travelling from Canada to Moscow. She changes 800 Canadian dollars (CAD) into Russian rubles (RUB). The exchange rate is 1 CAD = 29.7044 RUB.

   (a) How many rubles does she receive?

   On her return Frederique has 7000 rubles left. She decides to change them back into Canadian dollars.

   (b) Assuming that the exchange has remained the same, how many CAD will she receive for her remaining rubles?

2. Andriano invested $9100 in a five-year investment scheme at the beginning of 2001. Interest was compounded monthly at an annual rate of 7%.

   (a) What was the investment worth after two years?

   (b) How much overall interest did Andriano receive at the end of the five-year period?

3. A school minibus cost £23,500 when bought new in August 2008. Its value depreciated at an annual rate of 18% over the next three years.

   (a) Work out the value of the minibus in August 2011.

   (b) Calculate the percentage loss in value of the minibus over the three-year period.

4. Zubair invests a lump sum of 180,000 ZAR (South African rands) in a Guaranteed Savings Scheme. The annual interest rate is estimated at 4.8%.

   (a) What is the value of the investment after three years?

   (b) How long will it take for the investment to double?

   (c) If it takes n years for the investment to treble, find the value of n.

5. Stephanie is paying back a loan she took out to buy a car. She has renegotiated special payment terms on the outstanding amount, $5950. She has arranged to pay $300 in the first month, $294 the next month, and so on, reducing her payment by 2% each month.

   (a) How many months will it take Stephanie to pay off the outstanding amount?

   (b) What is the value of her last monthly payment?

6. The following is an extract from a national newspaper (in April 2010) about the rise in school fees:

   'Private school fees have risen by 42% over the last five years due to inflation.'

   It is assumed that the annual rate of inflation is r% and has stayed constant over the past five years.

   (a) Find the value of r to two decimal places

   (b) Given that the fees at Donna's school were $40,000 in April 2010, work out what Donna's school fees were in:

   (i) April 2008   (ii) April 2006.

7. Mr Abban plans to buy a new car for £25,995. He applies to the bank for a loan repayable over a period of three years at 5.9% per annum. The loan schedule is shown below, with some of the information missing. Calculate each of the three missing items on the loan schedule.

Cash Price £25,995
£2,995 Deposit
followed by 1 Payment of £651.76
and 35 monthly payments of
£....(a)......
Total Interest charged for the loan £.......(b).....
Total Amount Payable £.....(c).......
Borrowing Rate 5.9% per annum

8. Jennifer bought her new BMW 3-Series car for £27,245. Her brother James bought his new Mercedes C-Class for £29,015.

The salesman claimed that:

- The BMW 3-Series is worth around 70% of its new price after three years.

- The Mercedes C-Class is worth 86% of its initial purchase price after one year.

(a) What will Jennifer's car be worth after three years, based on the salesman's claim?

(b) What is the **annual** depreciation rate of the BMW?

(c) How much of its value did James's car lose after a year, according the salesman's claim?

(d) If James sold his car three years later for £20,000, what was the equivalent **annual** rate of depreciation?

(e) Based on the salesman's claim, was James better off selling his car or not? Explain your answer.

Past paper questions

1. On Vera's 18th birthday she was given an allowance from her parents. She was given the following choices.

- Choice A: $100 every month of the year

- Choice B: a fixed amount of $1100 at the beginning of the year, to be invested at an interest rate of 12% per annum, compounded monthly

- Choice C: $75 the first month and an increase of $5 every month thereafter

- Choice D: $80 the first month and an increase of 5% every month thereafter

(a) Assuming that Vera does not spend any of her allowance during the year, calculate, for each of the choices, how much money she would have at the end of the year. *[8 marks]*

(b) Which of the choices do you think that Vera should choose? Give a reason for your answer. *[2 marks]*

(c) On her 19th birthday, Vera invests $1200 in a bank that pays interest at $r\%$ per annum compounded annually. Vera would like to buy a scooter costing $1452 on her 21st birthday. What rate will the bank have to offer her to enable her to buy the scooter? *[4 marks]*

[Total 14 marks]

[Nov 2002, Paper 2, Question 3] (© *IB Organization 2002*)

2. Annie is starting her first job. She will earn a salary of $26,000 in the first year and her salary will increase by 3% every year.

   (a) Calculate how much Annie will earn in her 5th year of work. *[3 marks]*

   Annie spends $24,800 of her earnings in her first year of work. For the next few years, inflation will cause Annie's living expenses to rise by 5% per year.

   (b) (i) Calculate the number of years it will be before Annie is spending more than she earns.

   (ii) By how much will Annie's spending be greater than her earnings in that year? *[6 marks]*

   [Total 9 marks]

[May 2006, Paper 2, Question 4(ii)] (© *IB Organization 2006*)

3. *Give all answers in this question correct to the **nearest** dollar.*

   Clara wants to buy some land. She can choose between two different payment options.

   Both options require her to pay for the land in **20** monthly instalments.

   - Option 1: The first instalment is $2500. Each instalment is $200 more than the one before.

   - Option 2: The first instalment is $2000. Each instalment is 8% more than the one before.

   (a) If Clara chooses option 1,

       (i) write down the values of the second and third instalments;

       (ii) calculate the value of the final instalment;

       (iii) show that the **total amount** that Clara would pay for the land is $88,000. *[7 marks]*

   (b) If Clara chooses option 2,

       (i) find the value of the second instalment;

       (ii) show that the value of the fifth instalment is $2721. *[4 marks]*

   (c) The price of the land is $80,000. In option 1 her total repayments are $88,000 over the 20 months. Find the annual rate of simple interest which gives this total. *[4 marks]*

   (d) Clara knows that the **total amount** she would pay for the land is not the same for both options. She wants to spend the least amount of money. Find how much she will save by choosing the cheaper option. *[4 marks]*

   [Total 19 marks]

[May 2008, Paper 2, Question 10] (© *IB Organization 2008*)

4. Sven is travelling to Europe. He withdraws $800 from his savings and converts it to euros. The local bank is buying euros at $1 : €0.785 and selling euros at $1 : €0.766.

(a) Use the appropriate rate above to calculate the amount of euros Sven will receive.

(b) Suppose the trip is cancelled. How much will he receive if the euros in part (a) are changed back to dollars?

(c) How much has Sven lost after the two transactions? Express your answer as a percentage of Sven's original $800.

[**May 2006, Paper 1, Question 10**] (© *IB Organization 2006*)

5. Emma places €8000 in a bank account that pays a nominal interest rate of 5% per annum, compounded quarterly.

(a) Calculate the amount of money that Emma would have in her account after 15 years. Give your answer correct to the nearest euro. *[3 marks]*

(b) After a period of time she decides to withdraw the money from this bank. There is €9058.17 in her account. Find the number of months that Emma had left her money in the account. *[3 marks]*

[**May 2008, Paper 1, Question 8**] (© *IB Organization 2008*)

2 Descriptive statistics

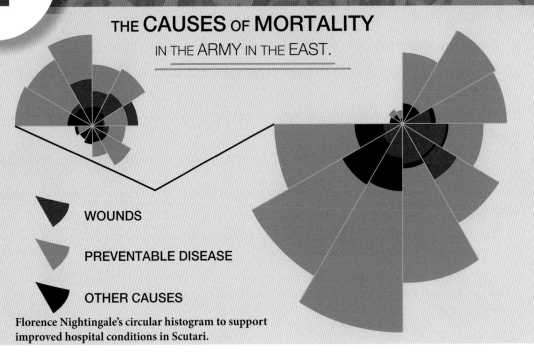

THE CAUSES OF MORTALITY
IN THE ARMY IN THE EAST.

- WOUNDS
- PREVENTABLE DISEASE
- OTHER CAUSES

Florence Nightingale's circular histogram to support improved hospital conditions in Scutari.

In 1854, Russia was at war with Turkey. England and France went to Turkey's aid and sent soldiers to fight in the Crimea. Conditions were dreadful, and soldiers of all the armies were dying of hunger and disease as well as from wounds sustained in battle.

Florence Nightingale went to Scutari, one of the worst hospitals, and was appalled by the conditions that she found there. However, before she could make improvements, she faced the difficult task of convincing the authorities in London that improvements were necessary.

While she was growing up, Florence loved mathematics and had special tutors to help her study. She was only eight when she drew her first statistics diagram. While at Scutari, she kept careful records of all the patients, documenting the reasons for their death or recovery. She realised that pages of figures and tables are difficult to interpret and to explain. So she drew one of the first circular histograms, or 'rose diagrams', to illustrate the causes of soldiers' death during the war.

The diagram has twelve sectors, one for each month of the year. The largest area, the outer layer coloured blue, shows the deaths from infectious but preventable diseases. The red areas show the deaths from wounds, and the black areas are for 'all other causes'.

The impact was immediate: pages of figures were condensed into a single, clear graphic image. It is fair to imagine that Florence Nightingale's diagram was an important part of her campaign to improve the conditions in military hospitals, and helped her to achieve the transformation for which she is remembered.

Prior learning topics

It will be easier to study this topic if you:

- know how to collect data
- are able to use tally marks to create a frequency table for data
- can recognise and interpret bar charts, pie charts and pictograms
- can draw your own bar charts, pie charts and pictograms.

Chapter 5 Classification and display of data

The world is flooded with data. There is more information available now than there has ever been before, and much of it is available to anyone who wishes to access it. This abundance of easily accessible information is fantastic but can also create problems. A mass of data can be difficult to make sense of until it has been organised into a form that has meaning.

Statistics is the branch of mathematics that organises data and presents it in a format that is understandable and useful. It is concerned with the ways in which to analyse data, and how to show the significance of that data after it has been analysed.

When presented with a large quantity of data, one of the first decisions you need to make is how to classify the data. If you do a seaside survey for your Biology coursework, you will have pages filled with information: lengths and masses, colours and numbers, areas and names of species. How many of these pieces of information can you put together? Can you compare the area of seaweed with its mass, or the colour of a shell with its diameter?

In this chapter, you will study some of the diagrams that you can use to make data easier to understand.

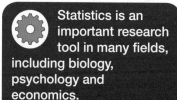

Statistics is an important research tool in many fields, including biology, psychology and economics.

5.1 Classifying data

The first thing you need to do when faced with a collection of data is to classify it. The type of data that you are working with will determine the kind of diagram you will use to present it and the calculations that you can do with it.

Qualitative data is data that cannot be counted — for example, the colour of a leaf.

Quantitative data is data that comes from counting or measuring. The mass of a shell, the length of a stream, and the number of birds in a flock are all examples of quantitative data.

Quantitative data can be classified as either discrete or continuous.

Discrete data can take only certain distinct values, such as whole numbers, or fall into distinct categories. For example, the number of birds in a flock is discrete data: you can count 7 or 8 birds, but not 7½ birds. The units of measurement for discrete data cannot be split into smaller parts. Be careful — for example, shoe size in the UK is measured in whole and half sizes so it is possible to have a shoe size of 6 or 6½. Discrete data might not always be a whole number. UK shoe size is restricted to a whole number or the half sizes between those whole numbers and no other division is possible, so it is discrete data.

Continuous data can take any values within a certain range of real numbers. This type of data usually comes from measuring. For example, the length of a bird's wing could be 10 cm, 10.1 cm, 10.12 cm, 10.12467 cm or any other value from 10 cm to 50 cm depending on the species of bird and the degree of accuracy to which the measurement was taken. You can choose how accurately you measure the data. For example, the length of a bird's wing can be measured in centimetres or millimetres; the mass of a pebble can be measured in grams or kilograms.

Populations, samples and bias when collecting data

It is important that any data is collected with a clear purpose. A large quantity of information is very difficult to analyse unless you have decided what question(s) you are seeking to answer, and why you are asking it. You also need to decide on the population that you are studying, and how you are going to take samples from that population.

The **population** is the particular group of objects or people that are being studied. For instance, if you are studying the distribution of a particular kind of shellfish, the population would consist of all the shellfish of that type in the region you are looking at. You could also study different **variables** relating to that species, such as their mass or the depth of water in which they are found.

Populations can be very large, such as all the people in your town, all the plants in a park, or all the cars sold by a local dealer, so it might not be practical to collect data for the whole population. Once you have decided on the population and the question(s) that you want to answer, you will need to think about how you are going to choose samples from this population that are of a practical size to collect and to analyse.

A **sample** is part of the population being studied. It should be chosen with care because if you choose badly the data that you obtain could be of little or no use.

A **representative sample** is a small proportion of the population that is supposed to be representative of the whole population being studied.

A **random sample** is a sample chosen in such a way that all members of the population have an equal chance of being selected.

exam tip

You will not be set any questions on sampling in your examinations, but learning about sampling can be useful for projects.

A **biased sample** is a sample chosen by a method where some members of the population are more likely to be selected than others; this will result in distorted or unfair data.

Suppose that you are doing a survey at your school that asks 'should we replace the swimming pool with a basketball court?'. Then:

- the **population** consists of all the students in your school

- to collect a **representative sample**, you would need to select students in order to make sure that you get a cross-section of opinions; so make sure you have students from each year, an equal mixture of sporty and non-sporty students, a variety of ability levels, both sexes, mixture of interests, etc.

- to collect a **random sample**, use a method of selection where every student has an equal chance of being chosen (name out of a hat, date of birth, etc.)

- you would be collecting a **biased sample** if you survey only your friends or if you survey only the basketball team.

So, for any statistical collection of data that you plan, you need to ask the following questions:

- Have I decided on a clear research question?

- Have I defined the population?

- Have I chosen a method of taking samples that will not be biased?

> Data needs to be looked at critically. Any data should be scrutinised for the reason that it was collected and for **bias**. Try asking yourself 'Who paid for the data to be collected and analysed?'.

Worked example 5.1

Q. | Javed wants to study the statistics of the Athletics World Championships, with a particular interest in the high jump competition. Copy and complete the table to give an example of possible parameters of his survey.

Type of data	Example
Qualitative data	
Quantitative data	
Discrete data	
Continuous data	
Population	
Variables	
Representative sample	
Random sample	
Biased sample	

→

continued . . .

> There are other possibilities, these are just some options.

A.

Type of data	Example
Qualitative data	The names of the countries taking part.
Quantitative data	The number of attempts each athlete makes.
Discrete data	The number of athletes in each team.
Continuous data	The height of the 'personal best' jump for each athlete.
Population	All the athletes competing in the high jump competition.
Variables	Each athlete's age, number of years on the team.
Representative sample	Javed goes through the team lists, and chooses athletes that represent a cross-section of each team.
Random sample	Each athlete is assigned a number, and Javed selects his sample by using a random number generator.
Biased sample	Javed picks his favourite athletes.

Exercise 5.1

1. State whether each of the following examples of quantitative data is discrete or continuous:

   (a) the time it takes to run 100 metres

   (b) the number of runs scored in a cricket match

   (c) the distance jumped by Philip in the Olympic triple jump

   (d) the number of words in the first sentence on each page of a book

   (e) the number of items found in the pencil cases of students in a class

   (f) the length of the footprints of children in a school

   (g) the mass of each potato in a sack

   (h) the number of electrons in the outer shell of different atoms

   (i) the number of leaves on each branch of a tree

   (j) the arm spans of basketball players in a team.

5.2 Simple discrete data

Simple discrete data consists of a list of individual values. The data can be organised by putting it into a **frequency table**. Frequency tables list each variable (measurement) and its corresponding frequency, and make it easier to see the shape, or distribution, of the data.

> Frequency tables can sometimes include a tally chart but it is not essential.

Worked example 5.2

Q. Dee asks all the children at her younger brother's school how many siblings they have. Put her results into a frequency table and include a tally chart. What does her data say about the number of siblings?

A.

Number of siblings	Tally	Frequency
0	IIII IIII II	12
1	IIII IIII IIII IIII I	21
2	IIII IIII IIII	14
3	IIII IIII	9
4	IIII	4
Total number of children questioned		60

The table shows that 21 children have only one brother or sister, while 4 children have 4 brothers or sisters each. The most common number of siblings from this sample is 1.

The best diagrams for displaying discrete data are pie charts and bar charts.

Bar charts for discrete data have **gaps** between adjacent bars. They are usually drawn with vertical bars where the discrete data (or categories) are plotted along the horizontal axis and frequency is plotted on the vertical axis. You can also have horizontal bars (where the discrete variable is plotted on the vertical axis and the frequency on the horizontal axis) but this is less common and more likely to be seen in newspapers or magazines than in mathematics books.

Pie charts display the data as parts of a whole, where the circle represents the total frequency of your data and the sectors represent different measurements. You plot data on a pie chart by calculating the frequency of a given measurement as a fraction of the whole and converting it into degrees (so that it is a fraction of 360°).

Let's see how Dee could display her data.

Dee displays her data in a bar chart:

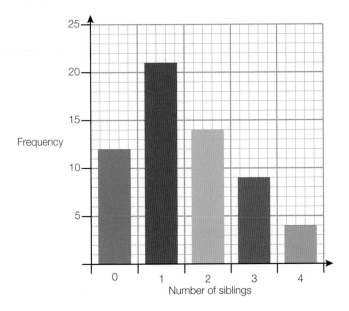

Dee also used a pie chart to display her data like this:

Number of siblings

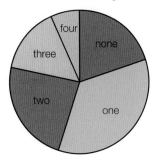

Exercise 5.2

In each question you are given a set of discrete data. Draw up a frequency table, bar chart and pie chart to summarise the data. Make a statement about your data.

1. The homework marks (out of 10) of 25 students:

   9, 8, 7, 7, 6, 7, 6, 7, 10, 5, 10, 8, 6, 9, 7, 5, 9, 8, 8, 5, 6, 10, 9, 5, 7

2. The number of rejects in each of 36 batches of laptop batteries:

   1, 0, 0, 2, 5, 1, 3, 0, 0, 2, 0, 0, 0, 0, 2, 1, 4, 2,

   3, 3, 3, 4, 1, 3, 5, 0, 0, 2, 4, 4, 3, 2, 3, 1, 1, 2

3. The number of home runs in 17 baseball matches:

   28, 23, 24, 24, 25, 26, 26, 27, 27, 27, 27, 28, 28, 28, 31, 31, 34

5.3 Grouped discrete data

When you have a large sample of discrete data with a big difference between the smallest data value and the largest data value, you might find that the total frequency is spread thinly across the many values between the smallest and largest values. When this happens, a frequency table like the one created for Dee in Worked example 5.2 might not be very informative. It would lead to a very long frequency table that will not show clearly any shape or pattern in the data, making it difficult to analyse.

Grouping the data into 'groups' makes it easier to summarise discrete data when the data set is large and/or there is a big difference between the smallest and the largest values. Preferably, the data set should be divided into five to fifteen groups, but the number of groups to take will depend on the size of the sample and the spread of the data. It is easier to make a fair analysis of the distribution of the frequency if the size of each group (the range of data values it includes) is equal. For example, each group might cover four data values. Remember however, that although **grouped data** allows us to see general patterns more clearly, some detail will be lost.

exam tip

You can group the data using unequal sized groups where one group might cover ten values and another includes five, but the data needs to be handled slightly differently in order to make a fair analysis.

Worked example 5.3

Q. Ahmed records the project marks of 50 IB students on the Mathematical Studies course:

7	14	16	10	20	10	19	13	8	14
15	8	13	17	11	17	11	15	20	12
14	18	6	11	12	13	6	11	12	17
20	9	13	7	15	12	11	14	11	20
11	17	15	18	8	14	13	19	17	9

Enter the data into a grouped frequency table and comment on the results.

There are 50 data values ranging from 7 to 20, so it is sensible to group the data. We have chosen to use seven equal-sized groups (even though two of them will have no entries in them); other groups are possible. Each group includes three values; for example, the group 6–8 includes the marks of 6, 7 and 8.

A.

Marks	Tally	Frequency
0–2		0
3–5		0
6–8	‖‖‖ ‖	7
9–11	‖‖‖ ‖‖‖ ‖	11
12–14	‖‖‖ ‖‖‖ ‖‖‖‖	14
15–17	‖‖‖ ‖‖‖	10
18–20	‖‖‖ ‖‖‖	8
Total frequency		50

continued . . .

> From the frequency table, it is not possible to see how many students scored 6 marks, or 7 marks, or 8 marks; we can only see that there are seven people altogether whose marks are in the 6–8 group, so some detail has been lost because the data has been grouped. However, we can see a general pattern that suggests students tend to score between 9 and 17 marks.

A bar chart can be used to display grouped discrete data. Here, the groups are plotted along the horizontal axis; again, there should be spaces between the bars to indicate that the data is discrete. The frequency table in Worked example 5.3 can be converted to the following bar chart:

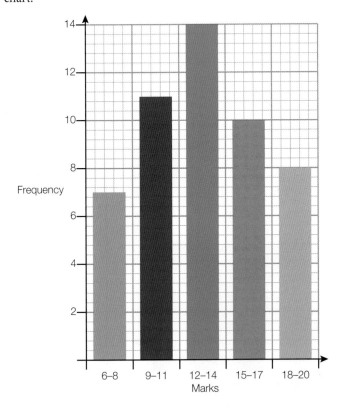

Exercise 5.3

1. The following data shows the number of students enrolled on the Mathematical Studies course in 28 accredited IB schools:

    15, 24, 20, 11, 15, 12, 8, 20, 11, 21, 18, 5, 10, 5, 13, 11, 4, 10, 4, 9,

    12, 12, 14, 14, 5, 15, 17, 4, 18, 13, 13, 21, 9, 11, 12, 14, 15, 21, 4, 24

    Complete a frequency table with groups 0–4, 5–9, 10–14, etc.

2. The number of a certain band's CDs that were sold per month over 2.5 years are as follows:

52, 51, 71, 49, 50, 68, 52, 65, 48, 51, 67, 56, 58, 65, 68,

66, 66, 52, 67, 62, 67, 59, 74, 65, 70, 57, 64, 71, 67, 54

Complete a frequency table with groups, 45–49, 50–54, 55–59, etc.

In questions 3–6, draw a bar chart to represent the given set of data.

3. Examination marks of a group of students:

Exam mark	1–20	21–40	41–60	61–80	81–100
Number of students	3	5	6	12	8

4. Age of teachers, in completed years, at a high school:

Age of teachers	21–30	31–40	41–50	51–60
Frequency	12	23	17	8

5. Length of service, in full years, of head-teachers in a sample of county schools:

Length of service(years)	0–6	7–13	14–20	21–27	28–34
Frequency	9	18	25	12	6

6. The number of books borrowed from a school library by a group of students in an academic year:

Number of books	0–3	4–7	8–11	12–15	16–19
Number of students	3	6	15	11	7

5.4 Grouped continuous data

Continuous data can take infinitely many possible values depending on the degree of accuracy used in the measurement. Therefore, the total frequency will be spread very thinly across many data values and it is important to group the data before we can summarise it in a frequency table.

Grouping continuous data is not as straightforward as grouping discrete data; it can be quite difficult to define the smallest and largest value of each group because they can take an infinite number of values! Groups of continuous data are usually called **classes** instead, and the smallest and largest values of each class are called the class **boundaries**. The boundaries are defined by a given set of parameters and values are assigned to each class based on these parameters. There should be no gaps between the boundaries, so that no data values will be missed.

There are two main conventions for defining the class boundaries. Whichever one you use, the important point to remember is that all data should be able to fit into a class, and that no data value should be able to fit into more than one class.

Convention 1:

lower boundary ≤ data value < upper boundary

In the first convention, the boundaries of a class are chosen so that all the measurements in that class are smaller than the upper boundary but greater than or equal to the lower boundary.

For example, the following frequency table gives the heights of 40 plants. The height of each plant was measured to the nearest centimetre, and then recorded. The data has been grouped in such a way that:

$0 \leq h < 5$ is the class containing all plant heights greater than or equal to 0 cm but less than 5 cm (it is often written simply as 0–5),

$5 \leq h < 10$ is the class containing all plant heights greater than or equal to 5 cm but less than 10 cm (it is often written simply as 5–10), and so on.

Height h (cm)	Frequency
$0 \leq h < 5$	5
$5 \leq h < 10$	7
$10 \leq h < 15$	13
$15 \leq h < 20$	8
$20 \leq h < 25$	5
$25 \leq h < 30$	2

Note that with this convention, the upper limit of each class is the same as the lower limit of the next class. This makes sure that all data values will fit into a class.

Convention 2:

lower boundary $- x \leq$ data value $<$ upper boundary $+ x$

In the second convention, there is a gap between the limits of consecutive classes as if you were grouping discrete data. But, each class actually begins or ends in the middle of the gap; any value that falls into a gap between two classes is rounded up or rounded down using the '< 5 or ≥ 5 rule', to the closest class limit. x in the example above indicates the appropriate degree of accuracy to which the class boundaries are defined.

For example, the masses of players in a football competition were measured before the tournament began. The mass of each player was measured in kilograms to an accuracy of one decimal place, and the masses were grouped to the nearest kilogram; so using the '< 5 or ≥ 5 rule', $x = 0.5$.

The following frequency table was compiled using the second convention of defining class boundaries:

61–65 is the class containing all masses greater than or equal to 60.5 kg (which will be rounded up to 61 kg) and less than 65.5 kg (which will be rounded down to 65 kg),

66–70 is the class containing all masses greater than or equal to 65.5 kg and less than 70.5 kg,
    and so on.
So the actual class boundaries are 60.5 (61 − 0.5), 65.5 (65 + 0.5), 70.5 (70 + 0.5) and so on, that is, values that lie in the middle of the gap between the upper limit of one class and the lower limit of the next.

Mass (kg)	Frequency
61–65	8
66–70	15
71–75	21
76–80	14
81–85	6
86–90	2

Be careful — sometimes data will be grouped according to a method that is neither of the two conventions described above. The boundaries of a class may be chosen so that all measurements in that class are less than or equal to the upper boundary and strictly greater than the lower boundary. For example:

Time (minutes)	Frequency
$40 < t \leq 50$	7
$50 < t \leq 60$	13
$60 < t \leq 70$	10
$70 < t \leq 80$	6
$80 < t \leq 90$	3

Always look carefully at how the classes are defined in a grouped frequency table.

As with discrete data, grouping continuous data will result in the loss of some original information. After the data is grouped, you can only tell how many items there are in each class, but not their original values.

Grouping the data does give a clearer overall picture, however, and prepares the data for any subsequent calculations.

Exercise 5.4

Each question gives the results of 30 students participating in a particular event on College Sports Day. Draw up a frequency table for each set of data, using appropriate classes.

1. 100 m race times in seconds:

17.72	16.95	17.07	18.17	22.59	19.54	17.83	25.19	21.68	19.27
23.4	13.85	19.07	21.26	21.3	20.71	18.6	13.84	14.7	16.55
16.65	22.92	20.48	30.58	24.81	17.64	21.04	18.04	13.89	12.02

2. Shot put distances in metres:

10.55	7.6	8.91	9.3	8.6	6.31	11.25	11.62	11.41	9.56
6.73	9.3	7.96	7.58	13.67	5.47	7.2	8.2	6.62	5.81
12.35	6	10	6.17	11.17	7.97	14.04	6.82	9.16	9.19

3. Long jump distances in metres:

1.95	5.36	2.76	3.91	4.13	4.81	4.2	4.66	4.87	4.17
2.49	2.79	3.91	5.65	5.94	4.96	3.9	4.44	4.9	4.37
5.3	6.05	3.65	6.1	4.52	4.45	6.49	3.93	3.76	6.34

4. 400 m race times in seconds:

78.03	68.21	79.06	61.16	66.51	72.22	73.13	64.03	72.12	64.49
75.13	68.96	68.54	73.44	68.14	72.49	67.52	73.1	74.77	67.13
81.38	74.1	69.23	75.67	70.45	81.38	72.44	67.12	76.77	72.18

5. Javelin distance in metres:

26.29	32.67	41.36	39.93	39.55	38.08	32.5	37.24	29.28	27.45
32.55	37.38	33.92	35.72	44.97	33.98	42.08	29.42	35.92	41.02
40.23	36.82	33.09	32.25	48.79	32.46	47.24	26.61	37.82	30.48

5.5 Mid-interval values and upper and lower boundaries

You have already seen that grouped data is useful to identify general patterns but that the detail of the data is lost. What if you wanted to calculate some statistics about the data but you are only given the grouped frequency table? How can you do this without the detailed data? The mid-interval value allows you to **estimate** statistical values of the data.

In grouped data, the **mid-interval value** is the value that is half-way between the upper and lower boundaries of the group or class. It is the 'average' value of that particular group. When using the mid-interval value to make conclusions about our data, we assign the frequency for that group to this value as it is easier to deal with a 'representative' value for that group than it would be to deal with all the values of that group. This is why it only allows you to *estimate* statistical data, because not all points in that group will really be at the mid-interval value.

 You will learn about measures of central tendencies (averages) in Chapter 6.

To calculate the mid-interval value for discrete data:

- The lower boundary of a group is the lowest value in that group.

- The upper boundary of a group is the highest value in that group.

- To find the mid-interval value of a group, add the upper and lower boundaries and divide the sum by two.

For example, for the group 12–14 in a set of discrete data:

- The lowest value is 12, so the lower boundary is 12.
- The highest value is 14, so the upper boundary is 14.
- $(12 + 14) \div 2 = 13$, so the mid-interval value is 13.

To calculate the mid-interval value for continuous data, the definition of the mid-interval value depends on how the data has been rounded and which convention has been used to define the classes.

Look again at the example of plant heights from the previous section. The classes are:

$0 \le h < 5$, $5 \le h < 10$, $10 \le h < 15$, $15 \le h < 20$, etc. and were defined using convention 1.

- The lower class boundaries are 0, 5, 10, …
- The upper class boundaries are 5, 10, 15, …
- Use the same sum as for discrete data to find the mid-interval value [(lowest class boundary + highest class boundary) ÷ 2]:
  $(0 + 5) \div 2 = 2.5$ is the mid-interval value for the first class;
  $(5 + 10) \div 2 = 7.5$ is the mid-interval value for the second class, and so on.

> The upper and lower boundaries are harder to define for continuous data than they are for discrete data, and often different statisticians will come up with different answers! Think about why this situation has arisen.

In summary, the full calculations for the plant height data are:

Height (cm)	Class boundaries	Frequency	Class width	Mid-interval value
$0 \le h < 5$	0–5	5	$5 - 0 = 5$	$(0 + 5) \div 2 = 2.5$
$5 \le h < 10$	5–10	7	5	7.5
$10 \le h < 15$	10–15	13	5	12.5
$15 \le h < 20$	15–20	8	5	17.5
$20 \le h < 25$	20–25	5	5	22.5
$25 \le h < 30$	25–30	2	5	27.5

Look again at the masses of the footballers from the previous section. The classes are:

61–65, 66–70, 71–75, etc. were defined using convention 2.

So in this case the lowest boundary is not, for example, 61 but is instead 60.5 because any value between 60.5 and 61 would have been rounded up to 61. Similarly, the highest boundary is not, for example, 65 but is instead 65.5 because any value between 65 and 65.5 would have been rounded down to 65.

- The lower class boundaries are 60.5, 65.5, 70.5, …
- The upper class boundaries are 65.5, 70.5, 75.5, …
- Use the same sum as before: $(60.5 + 65.5) \div 2 = 63$ is the mid-interval value for the first class; $(65.5 + 70.5) \div 2 = 68$ is the mid-interval value for the second class, and so on.

The full calculations for the footballers' mass data are:

Mass (kg)	Class boundaries	Frequency	Class width	Mid-interval value
61–65	$60.5 \leq w < 65.5$	8	$65.5 - 60.5 = 5$	$(60.5 + 65.5) \div 2 = 63$
66–70	$65.5 \leq w < 70.5$	15	5	68
71–75	$70.5 \leq w < 75.5$	21	5	73
76–80	$75.5 \leq w < 80.5$	14	5	78
81–85	$80.5 \leq w < 85.5$	6	5	83
86–90	$85.5 \leq w < 90.5$	2	5	88

Remember the following points:

- If you have collected your own data and then organised it into classes, make sure that you have described the upper and lower boundaries of each class accurately.

- If you are using someone else's data, look at it carefully and make sure that you understand how they have defined the upper and lower class boundaries.

Exercise 5.5

1. The following table shows the times (in seconds) taken to run the 110-hurdles race in a decathlon competition.

   Copy and complete the table by filling in the class boundaries, class width and mid-interval values

Time (s)	Class boundaries	Frequency	Class width	Mid-interval value
$18 \leq t < 20$	18–20	3	2	$(18 + 20) \div 2 = 9$
$20 \leq t < 22$		4		
$22 \leq t < 24$		6		
$24 \leq t < 26$		10		
$26 \leq t < 28$		3		
$28 \leq t < 30$		2		

2. Copy and complete tables like the one below for the sets of discrete data given in questions 3–6 of Exercise 5.3.

	Class boundaries	Frequency	Class width	Mid-interval value

3. Use your answers in Exercise 5.4 to complete tables like the one above for the sets of continuous data given in each question of the exercise.

5.6 Frequency histograms

To understand grouped continuous data and get a good idea of its shape, the most useful diagram is often a frequency **histogram**.

A frequency histogram is not the same as a bar chart, although they may look similar. In a histogram, the frequency of a data class is represented by the **area** of the bar, whereas in a bar chart it is represented by the height of the bar.

In a histogram, the width of a bar is defined by the lower and upper boundaries of that class of data. Since we are looking at continuous data, the upper boundary of each class will be the same as the lower boundary of the next class, so there will be **no gaps** between adjacent bars.

In this course we will consider only histograms which have bars of **equal width**, meaning that all the data classes have equal size. Note that if every bar has the same width, then the area of each bar is directly proportional to the height of that bar, and so the frequency of that data class will be represented by the height of the bar, just as it is in bar charts for discrete data. Bear in mind, though, that in histograms with bars of unequal width, the frequency of a data class is **not** directly represented by the bar height.

Also be aware that some histograms may look as if they have gaps between the bars – but that would be because some of the data classes are empty.

You can draw histograms by hand or by using your GDC or a computer graphing package. See section '*5.2 Drawing a histogram*' on page 664 of the GDC chapter for a reminder of how to use your GDC if you need to.

When drawing a histogram by hand, you would plot the class intervals along the horizontal axis and the frequency for each data class along the vertical axis to get the bars. A GDC constructs a histogram using the **mid-interval** value and frequency of each class to draw the bars.

Let us plot histograms for the plant heights and footballers' mass data given in section 5.4.

exam tip

Any histograms that you encounter in examinations will have class intervals of equal width.

Plant heights:

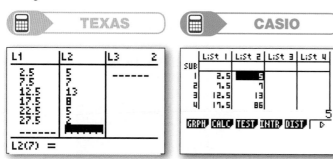

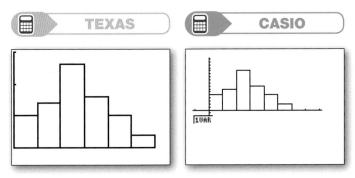

Footballers' masses:

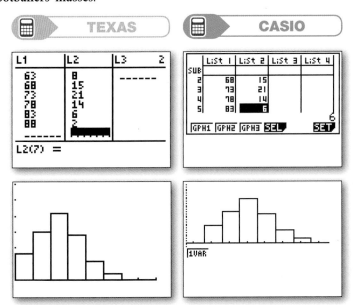

If you draw the histogram by hand or with a computer statistics package, you will be able to add more detail to your graph, such as labelling the axes and giving it a title:

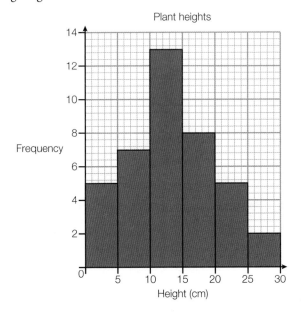

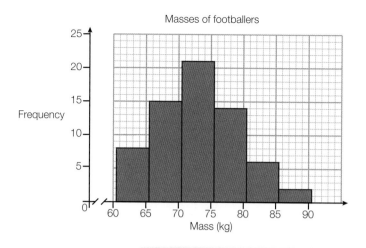

Masses of footballers

Frequency / *Mass (kg)*

Worked example 5.4

Q. Every day at noon, Fingal records the rainfall at his home near Sligo. The rainfall is measured in millimetres. These are his results for July 2012:

87	48	108	69	78	89	18	23	5	13	25	41	32
76	132	136	49	95	105	48	10	15	21	38	49	62
61	42	35	18	14								

Use the data to:

(a) complete a frequency table   (b) draw a histogram.

> Here, we have grouped the data using classes of width 20. This gives seven classes, which is a reasonable number.

A.

Rainfall	Tally	Frequency
$0 \leq r < 20$	IIII	5
$20 \leq r < 40$	IIII III	8
$40 \leq r < 60$	IIII I	6
$60 \leq r < 80$	IIII	5
$80 \leq r < 100$	III	3
$100 \leq r < 120$	II	2
$120 \leq r < 140$	II	2
Total		31

> Use a tally chart to find the frequency for each class.

> Plot the histogram by hand.

July rainfall

Frequency / *Rainfall (mm)*

Exercise 5.6

Each question presents a set of data. Copy and complete the given frequency table and hence draw the corresponding frequency histogram.

1. The number of days spent on revision for a final examination by a group of students:

   10, 34, 37, 33, 12, 15, 34, 34, 34, 13, 28, 23, 34, 11, 13,

   36, 23, 38, 31, 16, 16, 36, 26, 28, 12, 19, 19, 33, 19, 12

Number of days	Tally	Frequency
10–14		
15–19		
20–24		
25–29		
30–34		
35–39		

2. The thickness, in mm, of books on a library shelf:

   11, 19, 49, 36, 63, 38, 56, 23, 26, 10, 38, 51, 86, 43, 83, 80, 63, 71, 28, 18,

   80, 22, 70, 12, 68, 57, 21, 59, 68, 55, 47, 50, 62, 68, 46, 80, 21, 19, 14, 29

Thickness (mm)	Tally	Frequency
0–14		
15–29		
30–44		
45–59		
60–74		
75–89		

3. The time, to the nearest minute, taken to complete a given homework assignment:

   43, 79, 85, 70, 71, 60, 78, 79, 77, 82, 80, 91, 57, 67, 75,

   54, 64, 86, 69, 84, 72, 89, 79, 85, 63, 60, 74, 89, 62, 88,

   80, 69, 63, 92, 93, 70, 80, 59, 81, 89, 42, 93, 56, 65, 82

Time (minutes)	Tally	Frequency
$40 < t \leq 50$		
$50 < t \leq 60$		
$60 < t \leq 70$		
$70 < t \leq 80$		
$80 < t \leq 90$		
$90 < t \leq 100$		

   Note: the classes here are defined differently from either of the two conventions described in section 5.4.

4. The masses to the nearest gram of a random selection of apples before they are bagged on a farm:

Mass (g)	Frequency
151–190	2
191–230	12
231–270	17
271–310	6
311–350	3

Mass (g)	Class boundaries	Class width	Mid-interval value	Frequency
151–190	150.5–190.5	$190.5 - 150.5 = 40$	$(150.5 + 190.5) \div 2 = 170.5$	2
191–230				
231–270				
271–310				
311–350				

5. The volume of fuel (to the nearest litre) bought by 50 different drivers at a filling station in a two-hour period:

Volume (litres)	Frequency
20–39	5
40–59	12
60–79	20
80–99	9
100–119	4

Volume (litres)	Class boundaries	Class width	Mid-interval value	Frequency
20–39				5
40–59				12
60–79				20
80–99				9
100–119				4

6. A country's monthly iron ore production in millions of tonnes (for this question select your own classes):

8.3, 7.5, 8.6, 8.7, 8.9, 8.0, 7.5, 7.2, 7.6, 7.7, 8.1, 8.2, 8.2, 8.5,

7.9, 8.3, 8.1, 8.2, 8.3, 8.2, 8.3, 7.7, 8.3, 8.7, 8.5, 7.9, 8.1

Iron ore production (millions of tonnes)	Tally	Frequency

7. The masses of 30 tennis balls were recorded at the beginning of a tournament. The masses of the balls, in grams, are listed as follows:

56.1, 56.7, 55.3, 57.2, 56.2, 58.4, 58.1, 55.8, 59.3, 55.4,
58.0, 57.7, 58.3, 57.3, 57.0, 57.9, 56.9, 59.4, 58.1, 57.7,
57.1, 55.9, 56.7, 58.5, 56.6, 57.1, 57.8, 56.4, 57.8, 58.5

Mass, w (grams)	Class boundaries	Class width	Mid-interval value	Frequency
$55.0 < w \leq 55.5$				
$55.5 < w \leq 56.0$				
$56.0 < w \leq 56.5$				
$56.5 < w \leq 57.0$				
$57.0 < w \leq 57.5$				
$57.5 < w \leq 58.0$				
$58.0 < w \leq 58.5$				
$58.5 < w \leq 59.0$				
$59.0 < w \leq 59.5$				

Note: the classes here are defined differently from either of the two conventions described in section 5.4.

5.7 Cumulative frequency

Cumulative frequency is the total frequency up to a certain data value. For grouped data, you can calculate the cumulative frequency at the upper boundary of each data class by adding the frequency of that class to the cumulative frequency up to the class before. In other words, you keep track of the 'running total' of the frequency at each class boundary, showing how the frequency accumulates. The cumulative frequency allows you to make general statements about your data, for example '60% of children in my school have at least one pet'.

Cumulative frequency tables

To make a cumulative frequency table, you add an extra column to a frequency table. This column is used to keep track of the running total.

Worked example 5.5

Q. Add cumulative frequencies to the table of IB project marks that Ahmed compiled in Worked example 5.3 and make some observations about the data.

A.

> In the 'cumulative frequency' column you add the frequency of the class to the cumulative frequency of the class before it.

Marks	Frequency	Cumulative frequency
0–2	0	0
3–5	0	0
6–8	7	7
9–11	11	18
12–14	14	32
15–17	10	42
18–20	8	50
Total frequency	50	

> (0 + 0)
>
> (0 + 7)
>
> (7 + 11)
>
> (18 + 14)
>
> (32 + 10)
>
> (42 + 8)

> The value at the end of the cumulative frequency column is the same as the total frequency.

From the cumulative frequency you can see that:

18 students gained 11 marks or fewer.

32 students gained 14 marks or fewer.

42 students gained 17 marks or fewer.

Exercise 5.7

1. The following table shows the hammer throw distances recorded in a competition. Complete the cumulative frequency table

Distance d (metres)	Frequency	Cumulative frequency
$55 < d \le 60$	5	
$60 < d \le 65$	7	
$65 < d \le 70$	5	
$70 < d \le 75$	8	
$75 < d \le 80$	8	
$80 < d \le 85$	9	
$85 < d \le 90$	3	

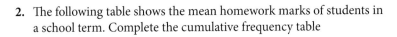

2. The following table shows the mean homework marks of students in a school term. Complete the cumulative frequency table

Mark (%)	Frequency	Cumulative frequency
20–29	1	
30–39	2	
40–49	5	
50–59	10	
60–69	12	
70–79	4	
80–89	3	

3. Complete the following cumulative frequency table.

Test mark (%)	Frequency	Cumulative frequency
31–40	2	
41–50	6	
51–60	9	
61–70	15	
71–80	10	
81–90	7	
91–100	3	

Cumulative frequency curves (ogives)

Once you have created a cumulative frequency table, you can use it to draw a cumulative frequency curve or graph. This graph has a distinctive 'S-shape', and is sometimes called an **ogive**. You can use the curve to answer questions about the data up to a certain data value and you can use it make estimates about the data such as what frequency a certain data value might occur at, or what the frequency is likely be of a particular data value. This can useful if you want to use existing data to make predictions about data in the future.

You can also use the cumulative curve to estimate the 'average' data value. This is the data value at which 50% of the total frequency lies and the one you expect to occur most often. This is called the **median**. You can also use the cumulative curve tell you at what data point 25% of the frequency lies (the **lower quartile**), and where 75% of it lies (**upper quartile**). These three values can help you to spot patterns in your data.

 You will learn more about the median and other measures of central tendency (averages) in Chapter 6, and more about quartiles in Chapter 7.

When you draw a cumulative frequency curve:

1. Mark the values of the **upper** class boundaries along the horizontal axis.

2. Plot the cumulative frequency values along the vertical axis.

3. Label the axes clearly.

4. Give the graph a title.

When using the graph to estimate the median or the values of the quartiles:

1. Draw a dashed line straight across from the vertical axis until you meet the cumulative curve.

   (a) For the median, the value on the vertical axis will be at '50% × total frequency'.

   (b) For the lower quartile, the value will be '25% × total frequency'.

   (c) For the upper quartile, the value will be '75% × total frequency'.

2. From the point where you meet the curve, draw a straight vertical line (dashed) down to the horizontal axis and read off the value.

It is important that you include these dashed lines in your working to demonstrate how you obtained each value.

	Worked example 5.6
Q.	The total lung capacity (TLC) of 120 female members of a sports club was recorded. The data was grouped into classes of width 0.25 litres and the cumulative frequency was calculated. Draw a cumulative frequency curve of the data and make observations about the data.

Capacity (litres)	Frequency	Cumulative frequency
3.00–3.25	0	0
3.25–3.50	4	4
3.50–3.75	11	15
3.75–4.00	23	38
4.00–4.25	32	70
4.25–4.50	21	91
4.50–4.75	13	104
4.75–5.00	8	112
5.00–5.25	5	117
5.25–5.50	3	120

continued . . .

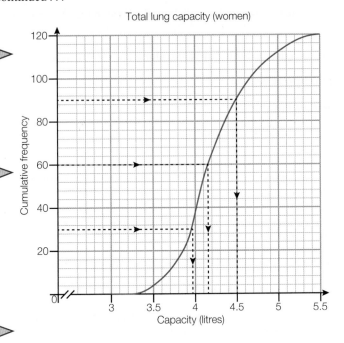

Total lung capacity (women)

The lung capacity, in litres, is plotted on the horizontal axis and the cumulative frequency on the vertical axis.

The first point plotted is (3.25, 0), the second is (3.50, 4), the third is (3.75, 15), and so on, up to the final point (5.50, 120). Note that the x-coordinates of the plotted points are the upper class boundaries.

Draw a horizontal line from 60 on the vertical axis to the curve, and then vertically down to the horizontal axis. The dashed line reaches the horizontal axis somewhere between 4.1 and 4.2, so an estimate for the median would be 4.15 litres.

To obtain these estimates, you would draw a vertical line from the relevant value on the horizontal axis (3.6 litres or 4.8 litres) **up** to the curve and then horizontally to the left until you reach the vertical axis.

A. From the graph it is possible to read off estimates for a number of statistical data:

- The TLC achieved by 50% of the women (60 women) is about 4.15 litres. This is an estimate of the **median**.
- The TLC achieved by 75% of the women (90 women) is about 4.5 litres. This is the **upper quartile**.
- The TLC achieved by 25% of the women (30 women) is about 3.95 litres. This is called the **lower quartile**.

From the cumulative frequency curve it is also possible to estimate that, for example:

- About 8 women have a TLC of less than 3.6 litres.
- About 105 women have a TLC of less than 4.8 litres.
- 15 (= 120 − 105) women have a TLC greater than 4.8 litres.

exam tip

If you draw your cumulative frequency graph by hand, the values that you estimate from it may differ from those given by a software package or GDC. If you estimated values for the median and quartiles by drawing lines correctly on your graph, the examiner will accept those values because you have shown how you obtained them.

Worked example 5.7

Q. A company has 180 employees, and the company record summarises their salaries as follows:

Salary s ($,000)	Frequency	Cumulative frequency
$10 \le s < 15$	8	8
$15 \le s < 20$	13	21
$20 \le s < 25$	19	
$25 \le s < 30$	26	
$30 \le s < 35$	32	
$35 \le s < 40$	35	
$40 \le s < 45$	20	
$45 \le s < 50$	13	
$50 \le s < 55$	10	
$55 \le s < 60$	4	

(a) Complete the cumulative frequency column.

(b) Draw a cumulative frequency curve to represent the information.

(c) Use the graph to find an estimate for the median salary.

(d) Use the graph to calculate the percentage of the employees with:

    (i) a salary below $22,000

    (ii) a salary above $58,000.

(e) Use your graph to estimate the upper quartile and the lower quartile.

> Calculate the cumulative frequency in each row by adding the frequency in that row to the cumulative frequency of the previous row.

A. (a)

Salary s ($,000)	Frequency	Cumulative frequency
$10 \le s < 15$	8	8
$15 \le s < 20$	13	$8 + 13 = 21$
$20 \le s < 25$	19	$21 + 19 = 40$
$25 \le s < 30$	26	$40 + 26 = 66$
$30 \le s < 35$	32	$66 + 32 = 98$
$35 \le s < 40$	35	$98 + 35 = 133$
$40 \le s < 45$	20	$133 + 20 = 153$
$45 \le s < 50$	13	$153 + 13 = 166$
$50 \le s < 55$	10	$166 + 10 = 176$
$55 \le s < 60$	4	$176 + 4 = 180$

$\longrightarrow$

continued . . .

(b)

Employee salaries

Cumulative frequency vs *Salary ($,000)*

Use the upper class boundaries and corresponding cumulative frequencies to plot the curve.

(c)

Employee salaries

Cumulative frequency vs *Salary ($,000)*

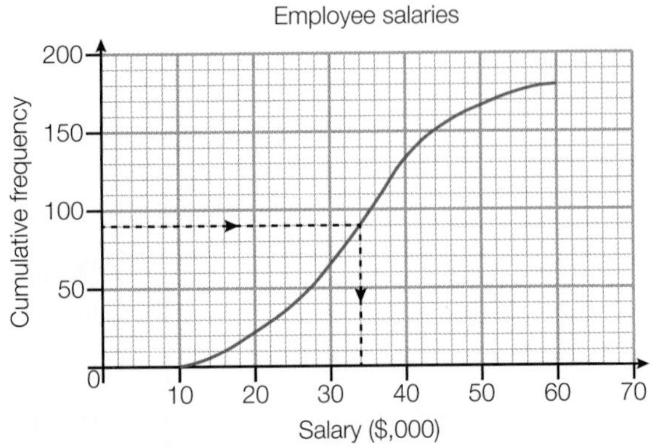

The median salary is approximately $34,000.

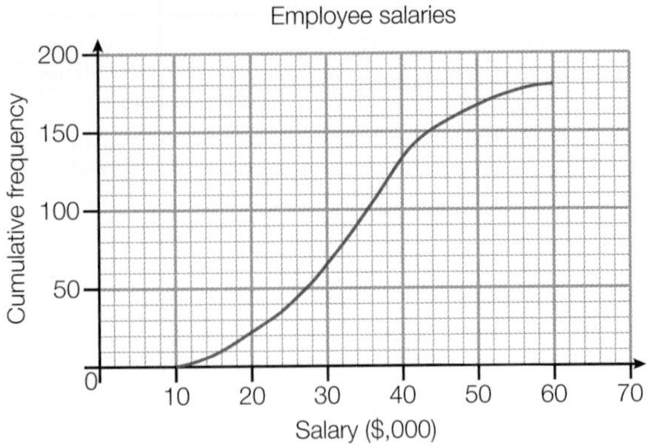

50% × 180 = 90. On the cumulative frequency graph, draw a line horizontally across from 90 on the vertical axis to the curve, and then vertically down until it meets the horizontal axis.

(d)

Employee salaries

Cumulative frequency vs *Salary ($,000)*

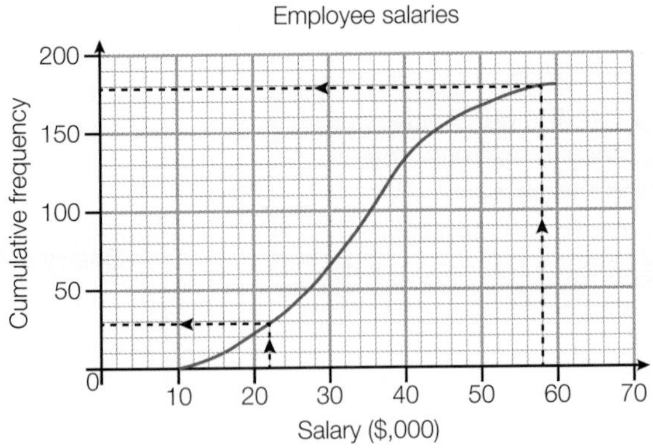

(i) Approximately 28 employees earn less than $22,000:

$$\frac{28}{180} \times 100\% = 15.6\%$$

So, about 16% (to the nearest per cent) of employees earn less than $22,000.

Draw a line vertically up from $22,000 on the horizontal axis to the curve, and then horizontally to the left to the vertical axis. This tells you that up to 28 employees earn less than $22,000. The question asks what 'percentage' of employees, so you need to work out what percentage of 180 employees 28 is.

continued . . .

Draw a line vertically up from 58 on the horizontal axis to the curve, and then horizontally to the left until it hits the vertical axis.

(ii) Approximately 179 employees earn less than $58,000, so around $180 - 179 = 1$ employee earns more than $58,000:

$$\frac{1}{180} \times 100\% = 0.556\%$$

1% of employees (to the nearest percent) earn more than $58,000.

(e)

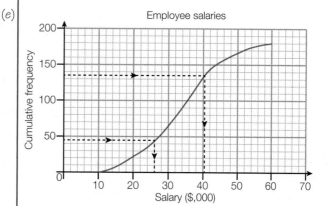

Employee salaries

$75\% \times 180 = 135$;
$25\% \times 180 = 45$.

Draw lines horizontally across from 135 and 45 on the vertical axis to the curve, and then vertically down until they meet the horizontal axis.

The upper quartile of salaries is about $40,500. The lower quartile of salaries is about $26,000.

This means 75% of employees earn up to $40,500 and about 25% of employees earn $26,000 or less.

Exercise 5.8

1. The following table shows the times achieved by Olympic gold medallists in the men's 100-metres final from 1896 to 2008.

Time (seconds)	Frequency	Cumulative frequency
$9.60 \le t < 10.00$	20	
$10.00 \le t < 10.40$	30	
$10.40 \le t < 10.80$	12	
$10.80 \le t < 11.20$	14	
$11.20 \le t < 11.60$	2	
$11.60 \le t < 12.00$	0	
$12.00 \le t < 12.40$	1	
$12.40 \le t < 12.80$	2	

(a) Complete the cumulative frequency table.

(b) Draw a cumulative frequency curve to represent the information.

(c) Find an estimate of the median time.

2. The following table shows the distances achieved by medallists in the women's long jump in the Olympic Games from 1948 to 2008.

Distance, d (metres)	Frequency	Cumulative frequency
$5.50 \leq d < 5.75$	3	
$5.75 \leq d < 6.00$	1	
$6.00 \leq d < 6.25$	5	
$6.25 \leq d < 6.50$	4	
$6.50 \leq d < 6.75$	7	
$6.75 \leq d < 7.00$	11	
$7.00 \leq d < 7.25$	15	
$7.25 \leq d < 7.50$	1	

(a) Complete the cumulative frequency table.

(b) Draw a cumulative frequency curve to represent the information.

(c) Find an estimate for the median distance achieved.

(d) Find estimates for the lower quartile and the upper quartile.

3. The hand spans of 60 female students are represented on the cumulative frequency diagram below.

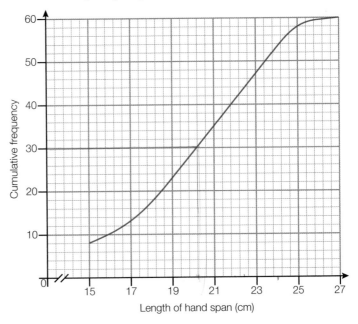

(a) Find an estimate of the median length of hand span.

(b) Estimate the number of students with a hand span less than 22.5 cm.

(c) Calculate the percentage of students with a hand span greater than 24 cm.

5.8 Box and whisker diagrams

The picture below shows how cumulative frequency curves are related to another sort of statistical diagram called a **box and whisker diagram** or box plot.

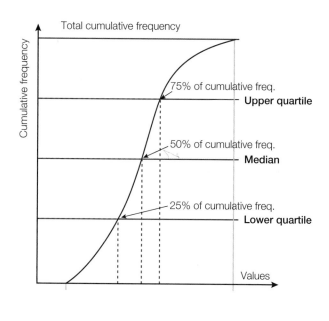

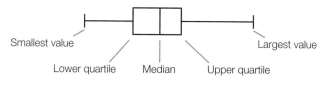

A box and whisker diagram summarises five important values from a set of data, and gives you a simple picture of the data. It is also useful when you have two or more sets of data and wish to make comparisons between them.

The information displayed by a box and whisker diagram is sometimes called a **five-figure summary**. The five figures are:

- the smallest value (minimum) of the data
- the lower quartile (Q_1)
- the median (Q_2)
- the upper quartile (Q_3)
- the largest value (maximum) of the data.

Revisiting the example on total lung capacity in the previous section (Worked example 5.6), the five figures are:

- minimum 3.25 litres
- lower quartile 3.95 litres

- median 4.15 litres

- upper quartile 4.5 litres

- maximum 5.5 litres

You can use your GDC to draw box and whisker diagrams. See section '5.3 *Drawing a box and whisker diagram*' on page 665 of the GDC chapter if you need a reminder of how to do this.

The box and whisker diagram for the lung capacity data looks like this:

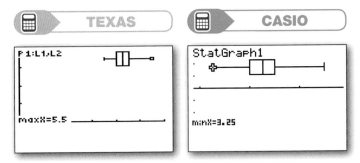

If you are drawing the box and whisker diagram on paper (from scratch or by copying it from your calculator), remember to put in a heading and, more importantly, a scale.

Note that:

- half, or 50%, of the data lies between Q_1 and Q_3

- a quarter, or 25%, of the data lies between the smallest value and Q_1

- three quarters (75%) of the data lies between the smallest value and Q_3 (note that this also means that a quarter of the data lies between Q_3 and the largest value).

Exercise 5.9

1. For each of the following sets of data, draw a box and whisker diagram by hand.

    (a) Minimum mark (%):   35
            Lower quartile: 48
            Median: 56.5
            Upper quartile: 67
            Maximum mark: 82

    (b) Minimum distance (m):   10
            Lower quartile: 22
            Median: 48
            Upper quartile: 65
            Maximum distance: 86

(c) Minimum time (s): 12.0
   Lower quartile: 17.0
   Median: 18.8
   Upper quartile: 21.3
   Maximum time: 25.2

(d) Minimum height (m): 61.2
   Lower quartile: 68.2
   Median: 71.8
   Upper quartile: 73.5
   Maximum height: 81.4

2. Use your GDC to draw box and whisker diagrams for the following sets of data. State the five-figure summary in each case.

   (a) 59, 35, 64, 43, 83, 46, 51, 71, 54, 61, 89, 77, 47, 71, 74, 84, 76, 54, 51, 86, 61, 65, 63

   (b) 49.4, 48.8, 42.6, 49.1, 45.6, 45.3, 50.6, 35.5, 45.6, 48.5, 52.1, 32.9, 56.8

   (c) 33.72, 39.87, 48.51, 23.05, 41.93, 36.76, 43.9, 40.74, 28.07, 49.1, 54.73, 53.16

   (d) 141.13, 84.6, 188.44, 172.45, 175.82, 152.03, 155.83, 166.07, 159.94, 163.01, 150.08, 117.09, 133.81, 152.64, 171.24, 111.98, 142.78, 119.22

Using box and whisker diagrams

The box and whisker diagrams below are being used to compare the marks of two study groups. The upper diagram gives the five-figure summary for the group studying IB Chemistry HL. The lower diagram presents the five-figure summary for a group of students studying IB Physics HL.

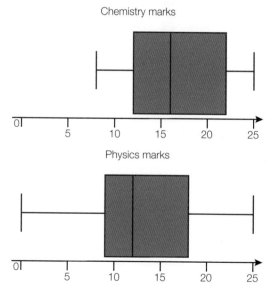

Chemistry marks

Physics marks

These diagrams show that:

- The median mark for Chemistry is higher than that for Physics.

- The distance between Q_1 and Q_3 is smaller for Physics than for Chemistry.

- The lowest mark in Physics is lower than the lowest mark in Chemistry. (In fact, the lowest Physics mark is so low that it has skewed the diagram; an unusually low or high value in the data is called an **outlier**, a piece of data that is so different from the rest that it can cause a distortion in calculations done with the data.)

- The top marks are the same for each study group.

Worked example 5.8

Q. As part of her project, Cécile counts the number of words in the sentences of a newspaper. The box and whisker diagram for her data is shown below. Use it to write down:

(a) the maximum and minimum number of words in a sentence

(b) the median number of words in the newspaper sentences

(c) the upper quartile (Q_3) and the lower quartile (Q_1).

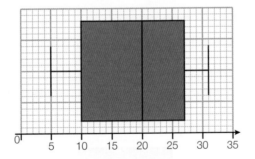

A. (a) The maximum number of words in a sentence is 31; the minimum number is 5.

> Look at the right and left ends of the whiskers.

(b) The median number of words is 20.

> Look at the vertical line inside the box.

(c) The upper quartile is 27 and the lower quartile is 10.

> Look at the right and left ends of the box.

Worked example 5.9

Q. Every day at noon, Fingal records the temperature at his home near Sligo. The temperatures are expressed in degrees Celsius (°C) to the nearest degree. These are his results for July 2012.

21	13	17	16	20	12	15	22	14	20	22	14	16
12	13	12	18	21	15	15	13	12	21	22	16	15
22	21	21	18	14								

Use the data to:

(a) make a frequency table

(b) draw a box and whisker diagram on your GDC

(c) find the values of the lower quartile, median and upper quartile using your GDC.

Make a tally chart. To avoid losing any detail, we do not group the data.

A. (a)

Temperature (°C)	Tally	Frequency
12	||||	4
13	|||	3
14	|||	3
15	||||	4
16	|||	3
17	|	1
18	||	2
19		0
20	||	2
21	|||||	5
22	||||	4
Total		31

Draw a box and whisker diagram using your GDC. See section '*5.3 Drawing a box and whisker diagram*' on page 665 of the GDC chapter if you need a reminder of how to do this.

(b)

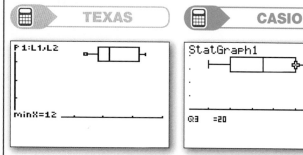

TEXAS	CASIO
P1:L1,L2 ... minX=12	StatGraph1 ... Q3 =20

Read off the median and quartiles and write down the answers appropriately.

(c) From GDC: $Q_1 = 14$, Med $= 17$, $Q_3 = 20$

Exercise 5.10

1. The examination results of students in a class are summarised in the following box and whisker diagram.

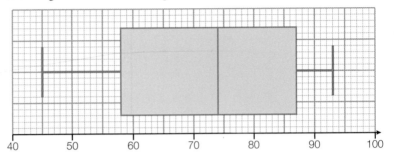

Using the information from the diagram, find:

(a) the minimum and maximum scores

(b) the median

(c) the lower quartile

(d) the upper quartile.

2. The box and whisker diagram below shows the heights of members of a sports club.

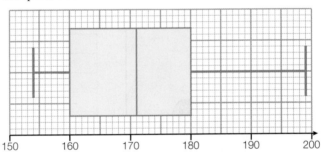

From the diagram, write down:

(a) the median

(b) the highest and lowest values

(c) the lower quartile and the upper quartile.

3. The following list shows the total number of tries scored by each team in a rugby league.

16	17	21	16	15	14	23	15	23	15	14	21	17
15	22	20	21	17	18	18	15	20	22	22	14	19
14	14	18	22	23	19	18	20	19	21	21	17	23
19	20	18	14	21	18	16	19	18	16	16		

(a) Copy and complete the given frequency table.

Number of tries	Tally	Frequency
14		
15		
16		
17		
18		
19		
20		
21		
22		
23		
Total		

(b) Draw a box and whisker diagram.

(c) Give the values of the lower quartile, median and upper quartile found with your GDC.

Summary

You should know:

- the classification of data as qualitative or quantitative, and the classification of quantitative data as discrete or continuous

- how to draw up frequency tables and present simple discrete data

- how to deal with grouped discrete or continuous data and draw up frequency tables

- how to define upper and lower class boundaries and mid-interval values

- how to use a GDC to draw frequency histograms

- how to produce cumulative frequency tables and curves for grouped discrete or continuous data

- how to find medians and (upper and lower) quartiles from cumulative frequency curves

- how to draw box and whisker diagrams using your GDC and find five-figure summaries.

Mixed examination practice

Exam-style questions

1. The following table shows the number of items in customers' shopping baskets at a check-out.

Number of items	1–3	4–6	7–9	10–12	13–15	16 or more
Number of shoppers	2	10	12	10	8	5

Draw a bar chart to represent the data.

2. The heights of 36 students, to the nearest centimetre, are given in the list below:

172, 162, 175, 172, 173, 175, 175, 162, 168, 166, 163, 179,

182, 171, 175, 186, 169, 165, 168, 172, 171, 164, 165, 170,

169, 168, 172, 170, 177, 175, 169, 166, 187, 162, 175, 161

(a) Complete the following frequency table.

Height h (cm)	Tally	Frequency
$160 < h \leq 165$		
$165 < h \leq 170$		
$170 < h \leq 175$		
$175 < h \leq 180$		
$180 < h \leq 185$		
$185 < h \leq 190$		

(b) Draw a frequency histogram to represent the data.

3. The following data represents the distances, in metres, recorded in a triple jump competition:

8.7	8.57	7.53	7.1	7.99	10.89	6.15	9.23	8.97	11.05
7.56	7.09	10.35	9.38	6.79	11.23	9.93	11.69	9.19	9.08
10.71	7.75	10.46	11.45	10.46	6.38	10.25	8.92	6.25	12.34

(a) Complete the frequency table.

Distance d (metres)	Frequency
$5.00 \leq d < 6.50$	
$6.50 \leq d < 8.00$	
$8.00 \leq d < 9.50$	
$9.50 \leq d < 11.00$	
$11.00 \leq d < 12.50$	

(b) Create a cumulative frequency table and hence use your table to draw a cumulative frequency curve.

(c) Use the appropriate summary data from your answer in part (b) to draw a box and whisker diagram.

4. The cumulative frequency graph shown below represents the time taken to travel to school by a group of 94 students.

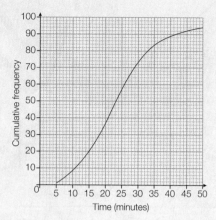

From the graph, answer the following questions.

(a) Write down the median time.

(b) Write down the lower quartile and the upper quartile for the times taken to travel to school.

(c) Estimate the number of students who take longer than 38 minutes to travel to school.

(d) Given that the minimum and maximum times are 5 minutes and 50 minutes, respectively, draw and label a box and whisker diagram for the data.

5. The scores of all the students who sat a mock examination are summarised in the cumulative frequency curve below.

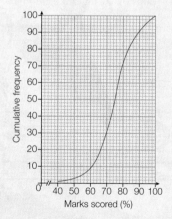

(a) From the graph, find:

   (i)   the number of students sitting the examination

   (ii) the median examination mark

   (iii) the upper and lower quartile marks.

(b) How many students scored between 61% and 75% inclusive?

(c) Given that the minimum score was 40% and the maximum was 100%, draw and label a box and whisker diagram for the data.

(d) Any student scoring more than 84% was awarded a Level 7. Estimate the number of students who were awarded a Level 7.

6. The test results of 25 students in Group A1 are displayed in the box and whisker diagram below.

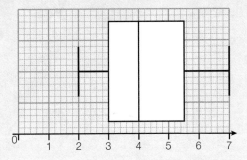

(a) Find the range of the results (that is, the difference between the maximum and minimum marks).

(b) Find the lower quartile and the upper quartile mark.

(c) What is the median mark?

The test results of students in Group A2 are as follows:

1, 3, 3, 4, 4, 4, 4, 4, 5, 5, 5, 5, 5, 5, 5, 5, 5, 6, 6, 6, 6, 7, 7, 7

(d) Represent these results in a box and whisker diagram.

(e) Compare the results of the two groups by citing two differences in their performance.

7. The performance of two Year 12 groups in the same test is illustrated on the two box and whisker diagrams below.

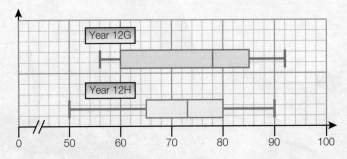

(a) Complete the following table of summary statistics.

	Year 12G	Year 12H
Median		
Lower quartile		
Upper quartile		

(b) Use the results from part (a) to compare the performance of the two groups in the test.

Past paper questions

1. A random sample of 200 females measured the length of their hair in cm. The results are displayed in the cumulative frequency curve below.

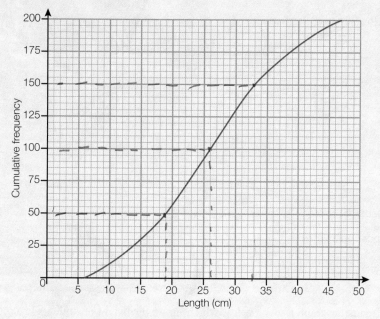

    (a) Write down the median length of hair in the sample. [1 mark]

    (b) Find the interquartile range for the length of hair in the sample. [2 marks]

    FF ⟫ **The interquartile range is the difference between Q_1 and Q_3. You will learn more about this in Chapter 7.**

    (c) Given that the shortest length was 6 cm and the longest 47 cm, draw and label a box and whisker plot for the data on the grid provided below.

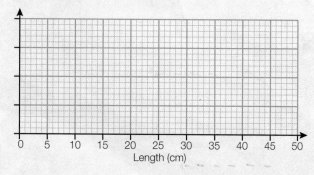

    [3 marks]

    [May 2008, Paper 1, Question 13] (© *IB Organization 2008*)

2. (a) State which of the following sets of data are discrete.

    (i) Speeds of cars travelling along a road.

    (ii) Numbers of members in families.

(iii) Maximum daily temperatures.

(iv) Heights of people in a class measured to the nearest cm.

(v) Daily intake of protein by members of a sporting team.

The boxplot below shows the statistics for a set of data.

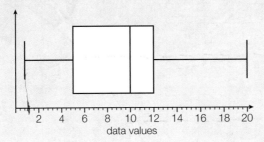

(b) For this data set write down the value of

(i) the median

(ii) the upper quartile

(iii) the minimum value present

[6 marks]

[May 2007, Paper 1, Question 2(a)(b)] (© *IB Organization 2007*)

3. A cumulative frequency graph is given below which shows the height of students in a school.

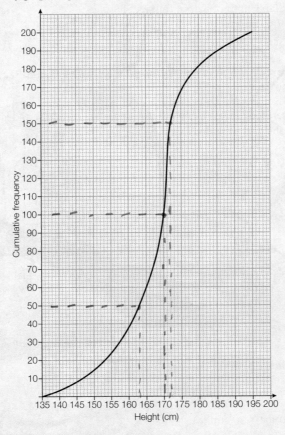

(a) Write down the median height of the students.   [1 mark]

(b) Write down the 25th percentile.   [1 mark]

(c) Write down the 75th percentile.   [1 mark]

The height of the tallest student is 195 cm and the height of the shortest student is 136 cm.

(d) Draw a box and whisker plot on the grid below to represent the heights of the students in the school.

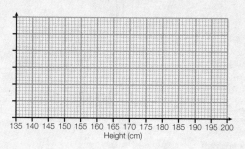

135 140 145 150 155 160 165 170 175 180 185 190 195 200
Height (cm)

[3 marks]

[**May 2009, Paper 1, Question 5**] (© *IB Organization 2009*)

exam tip

The 25th and 75th percentiles are the same as the lower and upper quartile.

Chapter 6

Measures of central tendency

In this chapter you will learn:

- several ways of measuring central tendency (mean, median and mode)
- how to find the median for simple discrete data
- how to find the mean and mode for simple discrete data, for grouped discrete data and for continuous data
- how to calculate an estimate for the mean from grouped data
- how to recognise the modal class.

"Add the numbers, divide by how many numbers you've added and there you have it-the average amount of minutes you sleep in class each day."

Can you describe yourself as 'average'? Do you know anyone whom you think is average? Is this concept helpful to organisations such as insurance companies, public health bodies or governments?

The word 'average' is often used to summarise a whole set of data, or even an entire population, with one single number.

In statistics, the everyday word 'average' is one example of a **measure of central tendency**.

The three most common ways of describing the average of a population or sample of data are described below:

- The **median** is the central (middle) value of a data set whose values have been arranged in order of size.

- The **mean** is the sum of all the data values divided by the total number of data values in the set.

- The **mode** is the data value that occurs most frequently.

To see the difference between these three measures, let's look at how they are calculated for a given set of data.

Suppose that Rita records the length of time that she spends on every assignment that her Maths teacher sets over the course of one term. She would like to know the 'average' length of time that she takes to complete her homework. She measures her times to the nearest minute.

In one term the times are 43, 51, 53, 52, 75, 95, 36, 43, 37, 67, 87, 58 and 56 minutes.

First, she puts the times in order from least to greatest time; then she picks out the middle value. This gives her the **median**. This is 53 minutes.

36, 37, 43, 43, 51, 52, **53**, 56, 58, 67, 75, 87, 95

> There are 13 data values. The central value is '53' because there are the same number of values above it as there are below it (six above and six below).

Next, she adds up all the times and divides by the total number of assignments she was set (13). This gives the **mean**:

$$(43 + 51 + 53 + 52 + 75 + 95 + 36 + 43 + 37 + 67 + 87 + 58 + 56) \div 13$$
$$= 753 \div 13$$
$$= 57.9 \text{ minutes.}$$

She also looks for the value that occurs most frequently, this is the **mode**. This is 43 minutes, as this time is listed twice and all other times are only recorded once.

43, 51, 53, 52, 75, 95, 36, 43, 37, 67, 87, 58, 56

Rita's results are:

Mean	57.9 minutes
Median	53 minutes
Mode	43 minutes

You can see that each measure of central tendency gives a slightly different answer. Which one should Rita use?

Rita's mean is the highest measure of the three at 57.9 minutes. If you look at the list of data, you can see that it is influenced by two values, 87 and 95, that are considerably larger than any of the other values.

Adolph Quetelet, (1796–1874) was born in Ghent (in present-day Belgium). He was a gifted student and was interested in poetry, art and languages as well as mathematics and astronomy. In 1823 he went to Paris to study astronomy and the theory of probability, returning to Belgium to give his first lectures on probability in 1824. From this time on, he worked hard to find a mathematical way of describing 'the average man', but could not find one measure that was suitable for all sets of data and situations. His work was fundamental to the later development of statistics, and to understanding the way in which statistical results can be used.

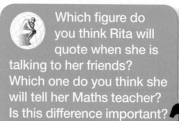

Which figure do you think Rita will quote when she is talking to her friends? Which one do you think she will tell her Maths teacher? Is this difference important?

In finding the median, the two larger values are balanced by two lower values when ordering the data.

Rita's mode is quite a lot lower than either the median or the mean and, looking at all the data points, does not seem like a very good representation of the average time.

Rita can use any of the three values, which are all correct, but as they are all different you can see why she can't simply just say the 'average'. She needs to decide which measure to use in a given situation, and be able to explain why she has chosen that particular measure.

There are different methods of working with the mean, median and mode that depend on the type of data being analysed.

6.1 Finding the median for simple data

The median is the middle value when the data is presented in an ordered list. So, if the data is presented as a simple list of numbers, then to find the median:

1. Put the numbers in order of size, usually from smallest to largest.

2. Identify what position the middle value is in as follows:

   (a) If the total frequency is an **odd number**, use the formula $\frac{1}{2}(n+1)$, where n is the (odd) number of data values. For example:

   1, 5, 8, 9, 9, **9**, 9, 10, 11, 14, 15

There are 11 data values so $n = 11$; substitute this into the formula: $11 + 1 = 12$, and $12 \div 2 = 6$, so the sixth value is the middle value and the value at this position is the median.

$n = 11$, so $\frac{1}{2}(11+1) = 6$

Value at position 6 is 9.
The median is 9.

   (b) If there is an **even number** of data values, then there will be **two** middle values and the median is calculated by working out the mean of these two values. The two middle values are those that are on either side of the value obtained by using the formula $\frac{1}{2}(n+1)$. For example:

   2, 3, 4, 6, **7, 8**, 9, 10, 10, 12

There are 10 data values so $n = 10$; substitute this into the formula: $10 + 1 = 11$, and $11 \div 2 = 5.5$. The positions either size of 5.5 are the 5th position and the 6th position; the two middle values are 7 and 8.

Find the mean of the two middle values:
$(7 + 8) \div 2 = 7.5$.
The median is 7.5.

You can also use your GDC to find the median of a list of numbers. See section '6.1 (a) Finding the mean, median, quartiles and standard deviation for a simple list of data (single variable, no frequency)', on page 666 of the GDC chapter if you need a reminder of how. In the list of statistics provided by your GDC, the median is labelled 'Med' or 'Q_2'.

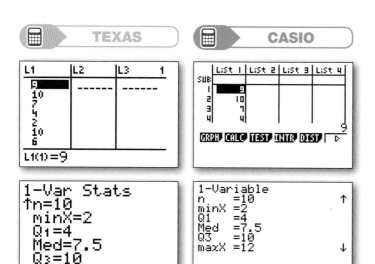

Exercise 6.1

1. The following data shows the number of misprints in different chapters of a draft copy of a new textbook:

    2, 3, 0, 1, 5, 7, 1, 3, 0, 4, 5, 5, 0, 8, 1, 2, 6, 6

    Find the median number of misprints per chapter of the book.

2. The list below shows the number of revision lessons attended by each student of a Mathematics class before a mock examination:

    2, 5, 5, 4, 8, 9, 2, 3, 6, 7, 8, 3, 7, 9, 4, 6, 7, 3, 7, 8, 9, 5, 6

    Find the median number of revision lessons attended by a student.

3. The prices of 'super value tyres' stocked by a garage are shown below:

    £33, £29, £35, £40, £45, £46, £47, £47, £53, £54, £64, £66, £50

    Find the median price of the tyres stocked in the garage.

6.2 Finding the mean for discrete and continuous data

When you calculate the median, you are not interested in the actual values of *all* the data given; you are only interested in the central value(s).

A measure that *does* consider all the values in the data set is the **mean**.

The formula for finding the mean is as follows:

The mean $\bar{x}$ of a set of data $x_1, x_2, ..., x_n$ is $\bar{x} = \dfrac{\sum\limits_{i=1}^{k} f_i x_i}{n}$, where $n = \sum\limits_{i=1}^{k} f_i$

x_i is the value at the general position i.

f_i is the frequency of the value at position i.

$\sum\limits_{i=1}^{k} f_i x_i$ tells you that you need to multiply each data value (x_i) by its frequency (f_i), and then add all the products together.

$\sum\limits_{i=1}^{k} f_i$ represents the sum of all the frequencies, which is the same as the total number of data values.

Simple data

Simple data is considered to be a list of just one variable where each variable only has a frequency of 1. So, for example, 4, 5, 9, 10 is a simple list of data. To find the mean of a simple list of values, add up all the values and divide by the total frequency.

For example, take the numbers 9, 10, 7, 4, 2, 10, 6, 12, 3, 8.

There are 10 of them. So the mean is:

$$(9 + 10 + 7 + 4 + 2 + 10 + 6 + 12 + 3 + 8) \div 10 = \frac{71}{10} = 7.1$$

Even if the data is discrete, it is not unusual for the mean to have a value that is not a whole number, or not the same as any of the values in the original list. For example, the number of children in every family is discrete data, but according to United Nations figures, the mean number of children in a family in 2011 was 2.5. In this context, this value represents that most families in the United Nations have between 2 and 3 children, not that some people can have half a child!

You can use your GDC to calculate the mean of a simple list of data. See section '*6.1 (a) Finding the mean, median, quartiles and standard deviation for a simple list of data (single variable, no frequency)*' on page 666 of the GDC chapter if you need a reminder of how. In the list of statistical data on your GDC, the mean is labelled as $\bar{x}$.

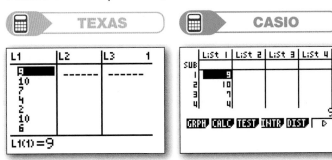

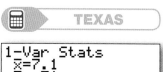
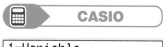
```
1-Var Stats
x̄=7.1
Σx=71
Σx²=603
Sx=3.314949304
σx=3.144837039
↓n=10
■
```

```
1-Variable
x̄      =7.1
Σx     =71
Σx²    =603
σx     =3.14483703
sx     =3.3149493
n      =10              ↓
```

Discrete data organised in a frequency table

Suppose that the sizes of shoes sold in a ladies' shoe shop in San Gimignano are collected in a frequency table. To find the mean size of shoes sold, you could write out all the values (repeating each one according to its frequency) and then add them up as we did with the list of simple data in the previous section. But it is easier and quicker to use the formula:

$$\bar{x} = \frac{\displaystyle\sum_{i=1}^{k} f_i x_i}{n}.$$

Worked example 6.1

Q. A new shoe design is coming to the shop in San Gimignano for the new season. The manager wants to make sure he can meet demand but cannot afford to over-order stock. He has been keeping a record of how many women buy shoes of each size and he wants to know which size is the most popular. Calculate the mean shoe size of the women who shop in his store.

A.

Shoe size, x_i	Frequency, f_i	Size × frequency $x_i \times f_i$
34	7	$34 \times 7 = 238$
35	11	$35 \times 11 = 385$
36	15	$36 \times 15 = 540$
37	19	$37 \times 19 = 703$
38	23	$38 \times 23 = 874$
39	25	$39 \times 25 = 975$
40	18	$40 \times 18 = 720$

The calculation $\displaystyle\sum_{i=1}^{k} f_i x_i$ is demonstrated in the third column of the table.

Each shoe size is multiplied by its frequency.

$\longrightarrow$

continued . . .

Shoe size, x_i	Frequency, f_i	Size × frequency $x_i \times f_i$
41	13	$41 \times 13 = 533$
42	8	$42 \times 8 = 336$
43	3	$43 \times 3 = 129$
Total	**142**	5433

The product of $x_i \times f_i$ for each shoe size is added together to give the value of $\sum_{i=1}^{k} f_i x_i$

$n = \sum_{i=1}^{k} f_i$ is shown at the bottom of the second column

$$\bar{x} = \frac{\sum_{i=1}^{k} f_i x_i}{n} = \frac{5433}{142} = 38.3$$

Substitute the values of $\sum_{i=1}^{k} f_i x_i$ and n into the formula for calculating the mean.

The mean shoe size sold is 38.3.

Using your GDC, you would just need to enter the shoe size as one list of data and the frequency as a second list of data. Your GDC can then calculate the mean (and other statistics) for you. See section '6.1 (b) *Finding the mean, median, quartiles and standard deviation for grouped data (single variable with frequency)*' on page 667 of the GDC chapter for a reminder of how to do this.

TEXAS

L1	L2	L3	2
34	7	------	
35	11		
36	15		
37	19		
38	23		
39	25		
40	18		

L2(1)=7

```
1-Var Stats
x̄=38.26056338
Σx=5433
Σx²=208567
Sx=2.223917626
σx=2.216073095
↓n=142
```

CASIO

	List 1	List 2	List 3	List 4
SUB				
1	34	7		
2	35	11		
3	36	15		
4	37	19		

GRPH CALC TEST INTR DIST ▷

```
1-Variable
x̄    =38.2605633
Σx   =5433
Σx²  =208567
σx   =2.21607309
sx   =2.22391762
n    =142          ↓
```

Grouped discrete data

To calculate the mean of grouped data, you use the same formula as before:

$$\overline{x} = \frac{\displaystyle\sum_{i=1}^{k} f_i x_i}{n}$$

But, the mean calculated from a table of grouped data will always be an **estimate** of the true mean.

If the data has been grouped, you need a single value that can represent all the data within a given group. A sensible value to choose as the group representative would be the one half-way between the class boundaries: the **mid-interval value**.

Look again at Ahmed's table data from Worked example 5.3. Suppose we want to find an estimate of the mean mark. The first thing we need to do is identify the mid-interval value for each group. This value will be substituted into the formula for the mean as the 'x_i' value.

Recall from Chapter 5 that once data is grouped it loses some detail.

Return to section 5.5 if you need a reminder of how to calculate the mid-interval value of a group when using discrete data.

Marks	Frequency, f_i	Mid-interval value, x_i	$x_i \times f_i$
0–2	0	1	$0 \times 1 = 0$
3–5	0	4	$0 \times 4 = 0$
6–8	7	7	$7 \times 7 = 49$
9–11	11	10	$11 \times 10 = 110$
12–14	14	13	$14 \times 13 = 182$
15–17	10	16	$10 \times 16 = 160$
18–20	8	19	$8 \times 19 = 152$
Total	**50**		**653**

Using the formula and substituting in known values:

$$\overline{x} = \frac{\displaystyle\sum_{i=1}^{k} f_i x_i}{n} = 653 \div 50 = 13.1$$

Therefore an estimate of the mean mark is 13.1.

You can use your GDC to calculate the mean of grouped data in much the same way as you would for a simple list of data with frequency: simply enter the mid-interval in one list and the frequency in another list. See '*6.1 (b) Finding the mean, median, quartiles and standard deviation for grouped data (single variable with frequency)*' on page 667 of the GDC chapter if you need a reminder.

exam tip

In examinations, if a question is dealing with grouped data, it will always say 'Find an estimate of the mean'. Do not worry about this wording — the examiner is just acknowledging that the data has been grouped, so that not every one of the original values will be used.

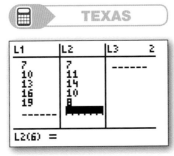
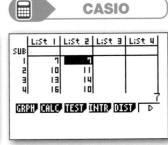

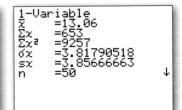

Grouped continuous data

Refer back to section 5.5 if you need a reminder of how to calculate the mid-interval value of a class when using grouped continuous data.

As with grouped discrete data, the mean of grouped continuous data will also be an estimate. The calculation is very similar to the method for grouped discrete data, but you need to take care to use the correct class boundaries when calculating the mid-interval value.

For example, let's revisit the data on the mass of footballers from section 5.4. To find the mean mass, you first need to identify the class boundaries, then the mid-interval values, and then do the appropriate calculations for the formula:

$$\overline{x} = \frac{\sum_{i=1}^{k} f_i x_i}{n}$$

Mass (kg)	Class boundaries	Mid-interval value, x_i	Frequency, f_i	$x_i \times f_i$
61–65	60.5–65.5	$(60.5 + 65.5) \div 2 = 63$	8	$63 \times 8 = 504$
66–70	65.5–70.5	68	15	$68 \times 15 = 1020$
71–75	70.5–75.5	73	21	$73 \times 21 = 1533$
76–80	75.5–80.5	78	14	$78 \times 14 = 1092$
81–85	80.5–85.5	83	6	$83 \times 6 = 498$
86–90	85.5–90.5	88	2	$88 \times 2 = 176$
Total			**66**	**4823**

So $\overline{x} = \dfrac{\sum_{i=1}^{k} f_i x_i}{n} = 4823 \div 66 = 73.1$. The mean mass is 73.1 kg.

You can use your GDC in the same way as you did for discrete grouped data.

TEXAS

L1	L2	L3	1
63	8	------	
68	15		
73	21		
78	14		
83	6		
88	2		

L1(7)=

CASIO

	List 1	List 2	List 3	List 4
SUB				
1	63	8		
2	68	15		
3	73	21		
4	78	14		

8

GRPH CALC TEST INTR DIST ▷

```
1-Var Stats
x̄=73.07575758
Σx=4823
Σx²=355019
Sx=6.293612405
σx=6.24575154
↓n=66
■
```

```
1-Variable
x̄    =73.0757575
Σx   =4823
Σx²  =355019
σx   =6.24575154
sx   =6.2936124
n    =66          ↓
```

Worked example 6.2

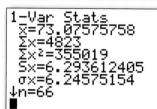

RR We learned about histograms in Chapter 5. See section '*5.2 Drawing a histogram*' on page 664 of the GDC chapter for a reminder of how to use your GDC if you need to.

Q. Fifty people were asked to say when they think a time period of one minute had elapsed. The times they estimated were recorded to the nearest second. The results are listed below.

Time (s)	50–52	53–55	56–58	59–61	62–64	65–67	68–70
Frequency	6	8	11	9	8	6	2

(a) Use the table to draw a histogram on your GDC.

(b) Estimate the mean value of the results.

(c) Use the histogram and mean value to comment on your results.

A. (a)

Enter the mid-interval values in one list and the frequencies in another.

Time (s)	50–52	53–55	56–58	59–61	62–64	65–67	68–70
Frequency	6	8	11	9	8	6	2
Mid-interval x_i	51	54	57	60	63	66	69

TEXAS

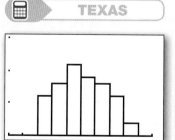

CASIO

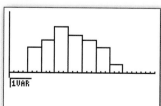

1VAR

continued . . .

(b)

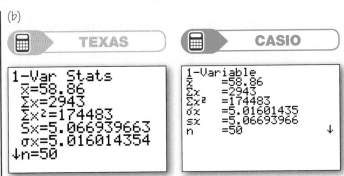

TEXAS

```
1-Var Stats
x̄=58.86
Σx=2943
Σx²=174483
Sx=5.066939663
σx=5.016014354
↓n=50
```

CASIO

```
1-Variable
x̄      =58.86
Σx     =2943
Σx²    =174483
σx     =5.01601435
sx     =5.06693966
n      =50        ↓
```

Use your GDC to get an estimate of $\bar{x}$.
Write down the answer appropriately.

The mean is estimated to be 58.9 seconds.

(c) The histogram is skewed towards the left, and the mean is less than 60 seconds. This indicates that most of the people taking part in the experiment underestimated the length of a minute.

exam tip

Data is sometimes described as **skewed** to the left or to the right. This is not a term that will appear in the examinations, but you may meet it when reading other books.

Exercise 6.2

1. The price of a 4th generation iPod Touch 8GB in ten different shops is shown below.

   £164, £166.21, £167.00, £169.99, £167,

   £170.00, £172.00, £174.00, £174.99, £179.99

   Calculate the mean price for this model of iPod.

2. In 2010, the countries with GDP per capita in the top ten of the world had the following GDP figures:

$82,600	$69,900	$62,100	$57,000	$54,600
$51,600	$49,600	$48,900	$141,100	$179,000

   Calculate the mean per capita GDP of these countries.

3. The sizes in KB of emails in a person's inbox are listed below.

   10, 10, 15, 2, 27, 3, 323, 38, 4, 4, 4, 4, 439, 6, 6, 6, 7, 8, 926

   Calculate the mean size of these emails.

4. (a) The following table shows the distribution of ages of 22 horses from the same race-course.

Age (years)	2	3	4	5	6	7
Frequency	3	4	8	3	2	2

   Calculate the mean age of the horses.

(b) The following table shows the carrying mass of the same horses.

Carrying mass (lbs)	110	112	113	114	115	116
Frequency	1	2	2	1	1	2
Carrying mass (lbs)	118	120	121	122	123	126
Frequency	3	5	1	1	2	1

Calculate the mean carrying mass of these horses.

5. The table below shows the number of goals scored by top goal-scorers in the English Premier League for the 2010 football season.

Number of goals	10	11	12	13	15	17	18	20
Frequency	8	1	4	6	1	1	1	2

(a) Find the total number of goals scored by these players.

(b) Calculate the mean number of goals scored.

The list of top 40 goal-scorers in the same season contains the following additional information:

Number of goals	7	8	9
Frequency	4	5	7

(c) Calculate the overall mean number of goals scored by the players from the list of top 40 goal-scorers.

6. The table below shows the price list of cars stocked by a car dealer.

	4-Door Sedan	2-Door Coupe	Hatchback
1	$9,990	$11,990	$9,985
2	$11,965	$12,490	$10,990
3	$11,965	$14,990	$12,115
4	$11,965	$15,605	$12,115
5	$11,965	$15,605	$12,605
6	$12,295	$16,995	$13,155
7	$12,295	$17,200	$13,300
8	$12,445	$18,275	$13,895
9	$13,200	$18,575	
10	$13,200	$18,999	
11	$13,359		
12	$13,365		

(a) Using the prices from the table, calculate the mean and median prices for the three types of car.

Average	Type of car		
	4-Door Sedan	2-Door Coupe	Hatchback
Mean price($)			
Median price ($)			

(b) Which of the two measures do you think is better for comparing the prices of the types of cars? State your reason.

(c) Explain why your answers from part (a) may not be a fair way of comparing the average prices of the cars. Suggest a fairer method.

7. The bar chart below shows the marks scored by students in a French spelling test.

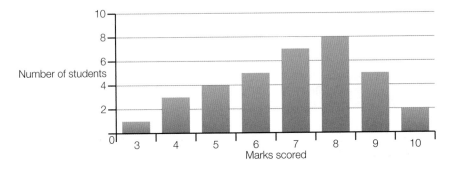

(a) How many students took the test?

(b) What was the mean mark scored by the students?

(c) Which mark represents the median score?

8. The consumption of softwood throughout the UK for the period 2000–2009 is shown in the table below. The figures are given in thousands of green tonnes.

(*Source*: http://www.forestry.gov.uk/forestry/HCOU-4UBEJZ)

Mass, m (thousands of green tonnes)	Frequency
$500 < w \leq 750$	16
$750 < w \leq 1000$	4
$1000 < w \leq 1250$	0
$1250 < w \leq 1500$	5
$1500 < w \leq 1750$	5
$1750 < w \leq 2000$	1
$2000 < w \leq 2250$	3
$2250 < w \leq 2500$	4
$2500 < w \leq 2750$	2

(a) What is the estimated total consumption of softwood by the UK in the given period?

(b) Calculate an estimate of the mean mass of softwood consumed in the given period.

9. The table below shows the average price per litre of fuel in 194 countries in 2010. Fuel prices refer to the pump prices of the most widely sold grade of gasoline. Prices have been converted from the local currency to US dollars.

(*Source*: http://data.worldbank.org)

Fuel price per litre, p (USD)	Frequency
$0.00 < p \leq 0.40$	12
$0.40 < p \leq 0.80$	16
$0.80 < p \leq 1.20$	70
$1.20 < p \leq 1.60$	52
$1.60 < p \leq 2.00$	39
$2.00 < p \leq 2.40$	3
$2.40 < p \leq 2.80$	2

Work out an estimate of the mean price per litre of fuel in 2010 across these countries.

10. The table from Exercise 5.8, question 1, showing the times of Olympic gold medallists in the men's 100-metres final from 1896 to 2008 has been reproduced below.

Time (seconds)	Frequency
$9.60 \leq t < 10.00$	20
$10.00 \leq t < 10.40$	30
$10.40 \leq t < 10.80$	12
$10.80 \leq t < 11.20$	14
$11.20 \leq t < 11.60$	2
$11.60 \leq t < 12.00$	0
$12.00 \leq t < 12.40$	1
$12.40 \leq t < 12.80$	2

Calculate an estimate of the mean winning time.

6.3 Identifying the mode or modal class

The mode is the value that occurs most frequently in a set of data. If the data is grouped, then the class with the largest frequency is called the **modal** class.

If you have made a frequency table for the data, the mode or modal class will correspond to the highest frequency in that table. For example, look at the data on the number of siblings from Worked example 5.2:

Number of siblings	Frequency
0	12
1	21
2	14
3	9
4	4
Total number of children questioned	60

> The largest frequency is 21, so the mode is 1 sibling.

The mode is 1.

If you have drawn a bar chart or histogram to display the data, the mode or modal class is the data value or data class with the highest bar.

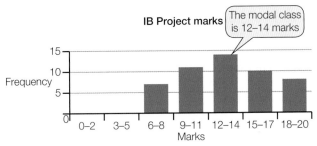

IB Project marks

> The modal class is 12–14 marks

6.4 Comparing the median, mean and mode

At the beginning of this chapter, Rita calculated the mean, median and mode for the time spent on her Maths assignments, and obtained three different answers.

This outcome occurs quite often, especially for sets of values that are very spread out, or where the data is sparse. It is important to be aware of how and why these 'averages' can be so different, and be able to choose the most appropriate value to summarise a particular data set.

Suppose that Rita asks her classmates to count the number of music downloads they make in one month. She collects the following data:

19, 23, 15, 16, 17, 13, 21, 12, 18, 20, 12, 14, 10, 22, 12

She finds that:

Mean	16.3
Median	16
Mode	12

Governments, aid agencies, corporations, in fact most organisations, gather data about their clients or customers to use in assessing what has been achieved and in planning for the future. It is important that statistics should always be used with an understanding of where and how the data has been collected, and how the statistical measures have been calculated. It is too easy to think that figures look reasonable, when in fact they have been calculated to mislead.

She and her classmates discuss the results. Ari says that they should not use the mode; it is low in comparison with the other figures and does not give a good representation of the other data. Niamh is worried about the median; it seems high in relation to the mode, and she thinks it does not give any indication that there are a lot of low figures in the data set. The class as a whole decides that the best measure for this data set is the mean, because it has used all the figures and taken into account both high and low numbers. This is the result of their discussion for this particular data set; a different group of people could come to a different conclusion and decide to choose the median as the best measure. The important point is that you think about and are able to explain any differences in the values of the three measures.

Rita's data on music downloads was discrete. We now look at an example where the data is continuous. Similar problems can arise if the three measures of central tendency give different values.

Suppose that a forestry company wanted to know the average growth of a group of trees. They measured the heights of those trees in successive years. The frequency table below gives the heights of the trees in 2012.

Height (m)	Frequency
5–9	12
10–14	18
15–19	18
20–24	8
25–29	3
Total	59

To help calculate the mean, we add extra columns for the mid-interval values x_i and the products $f_i x_i$.

Height (m)	Frequency (f_i)	Mid-interval value (x_i)	$f_i \times x_i$
5–9	12	7	84
10–14	18	12	216
15–19	18	17	306
20–24	8	22	176
25–29	3	27	81
Total	59		863

The mean is $863 \div 59 = 14.6\,\text{m}$.

The mode can be found by looking at the first table: there are actually two modal classes, 10–14 m and 15–19 m, which have the same frequency. Data sets with two modes are described as **bimodal**.

In this case, neither the mean nor the mode is a good measure of central tendency:

- The mean is influenced too much by the heights of the three tall trees.
- Since there are two modes, this measure is not very useful.

When presenting statistics, a responsible organisation will make it clear how the data was collected, which statistical measure is being used to summarise it, and why. They will also use the correct terms. For example, a development agency might collect many small donations from individuals as well as some large ones from corporations. Using the median to represent the 'average' donation will allow them to balance these small contributions against the large ones; if they use the mean, it may make the large donations seem too important.

Sometimes it is possible to calculate unknown values within your data set if you know the mean, median or mode.

> There are six numbers, so the median is the mean of the 3rd and 4th ones, which are 16 and p. Solve the equation for p.

> Now we only have one unknown left, q. We can use the information about the mean to find it.

Worked example 6.3

Q. The following set of ordered numbers has mean and median both equal to 16.5.

$$12, 15, 16, p, 18, q$$

Find the values of p and q.

A. $\dfrac{16+p}{2} = 16.5$

$16 + p = 33$

$p = 17$

Mean $= (12 + 15 + 16 + 17 + 18 + q) \div 6 = 16.5$

$(12 + 15 + 16 + 17 + 18 + q) = 16.5 \times 6$

$78 + q = 99$

$q = 21$

Worked example 6.4

Q. A clinic recorded the blood pressure of its patients as follows:

Blood pressure (mmHg)	70–79	80–89	90–99	100–109	110–119	120–129
Frequency	8	11	15	19	22	18

Blood pressure (mmHg)	130–139	140–149	150–159	160–169	170–179
Frequency	17	15	12	9	6

(a) Write down the total number of patients.

(b) Calculate an estimate of the mean blood pressure.

(c) Write down the modal class.

(d) An 'ideal' blood pressure is considered to lie between 90 and 120 mmHg. What percentage of patients had an 'ideal' blood pressure?

> Add all the frequencies to get the total number.

> To estimate the mean, we first need to identify the class boundaries and the mid-interval values.

A. (a) $8 + 11 + 15 + 19 + 22 + 18 + 17 + 15 + 12 + 9 + 6 = 152$

(b) The boundaries of the first class are 69.5 and 79.5, so the mid-interval value is $(69.5 + 79.5) \div 2 = 74.5$. The second class has boundaries 79.5 and 89.5, with mid-interval value 84.5, and so on. $\longrightarrow$

continued . . .

Use your GDC to calculate the mean. See section '*6.1 (b) Finding the mean, median, quartiles and standard deviation for grouped data ...*' on page 667 of the GDC chapter if you need a reminder of how.

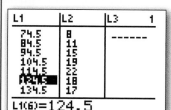 TEXAS

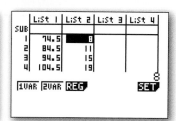 CASIO

Write down the answer appropriately.

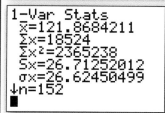

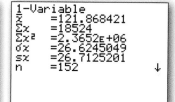

The modal class is the class with the highest frequency.

The mean is 122 mmHg (3 s.f.)

(c) The modal class is 110–119 mmHg.

The number of people with blood pressure between 90 and 120 mmHg is the number of people in the classes 90–99, 100–109 and 110–119.

(d) $15 + 19 + 22 = 56$

$$\text{Percentage} = \frac{56}{152} \times 100 = 36.8\%$$

Exercise 6.3

1. For each of the following sets of data, find:

   (i) the mean   (ii) the median   (iii) the mode

   and then compare the three averages.

   (a) 5, 7, 3, 2, 1, 2, 8

   (b) 70, 57, 57, 61, 64, 70, 69

   (c) 29, 28, 27, 38, 29, 35, 29

   (d) 110, 140, 160, 110, 105, 109, 120, 107, 111, 107

   (e) 33, 44, 37, 48, 50, 42, 47, 42, 44, 40, 36

2. The mean of the following twelve numbers is 30.

   30, 27, 28, 33, 27, x, 27, 32, 33, 31, 29, 31

   (a) Determine the value of x.

(b) Find the median.

(c) What is the modal value?

(d) Which of the two measures, the median or the mode, summarises the data better?

3. The mean of the following twelve numbers is 18.

    11, 20, 19, x, 18, 10, 19, 20, 13, 21, 11, 19

    (a) Determine the value of x.

    (b) Find the median.

    (c) Find the mode.

    (d) Which of the two measures, the median or mode, summarises the data better?

4. For each of the following sets of data you are given the mean value. Determine the value of:

    (i) x (ii) the median   (iii) the mode.

    (a) $2x$, 13, 18, 19, $2x$, x, 17, 12; mean $= 13$

    (b) 12, 16, $2x$, 18, 23, 18, 26, 24, x, $2x$; mean $= 19$

    (c) 7, 11, 7, x, 9, 14, 16, 11, $2x$, $4x$; mean $= 11$

5. For a certain class, the number of student absences from school during the summer term is shown on the table below.

Absences (days)	0	1	2	3	4	5	6	7
Frequency	8	6	3	3	2	1	1	1

    (a) State the total number of students in the class.

    (b) Calculate the total number of absences.

    (c) Find the mean number of absences.

    (d) State the modal number of absences.

    (e) Determine the median number of absences.

    (f) Discuss which of the averages is more likely to be used when:

        (i) comparing attendance among different groups

        (ii) dealing with targeted individual attendance.

6. The scores of the top 26 golfers for rounds 1 and 2 in a major tournament are given below.

    Round 1:

Score	66	68	69	70	71	72	73	74	75
Number of golfers	1	3	2	4	5	2	5	2	2

Round 2:

Score	68	69	70	71	72	73	74	75	78
Number of golfers	1	8	1	5	4	4	1	1	1

(a) Copy and complete the following table of summary statistics for the first two rounds of the competition.

	Round 1	Round 2	Rounds 1 and 2 combined
Mean			
Mode			
Median			

(b) Compare the performance of the golfers in the two rounds.

(c) Which of the three measures better describes the overall performance of the golfers?

7. For each of the following sets of grouped data:

(i) Work out an estimate of the mean.

(ii) State the modal group.

(a) The time taken by a group of 15-year-old students to complete a homework task:

Time (minutes)	Number of students
27–33	3
34–40	6
41–47	13
48–54	10
55–61	8
62–68	7
69–75	3

(b) The circulation of a group of daily newspapers:

Circulation, c, (thousands)	Frequency
$0 \leq c < 150$	50
$150 \leq c < 300$	35
$300 \leq c < 450$	7
$450 \leq c < 600$	4
$600 \leq c < 750$	1
$750 \leq c < 900$	0
$900 \leq c < 1050$	1

Summary

You should know:

- that the three measures of central tendency are the mean, median and mode

- how to calculate the mean, median and mode for simple discrete data

- how to calculate an estimate of the mean, and to identify the modal class, for grouped discrete or continuous data

- that the mean, median and mode for the same set of data might be different but are all 'correct'; you need to choose which measure to use and explain why.

Mixed examination practice

Exam-style questions

1. The scorecard of the first innings of a county cricket club is shown below.

Batsman	Number of runs
1	36
2	33
3	22
4	51
5	
6	30
7	30
8	27
9	17
10	7
11	1

Mean number of runs 28

(a) What was the total number of runs scored by the team?

(b) Work out the number of runs scored by the fifth batsman.

(c) Determine the median number of runs.

2. The bar chart shows the performance of two groups in their Mathematical Studies mock examination.

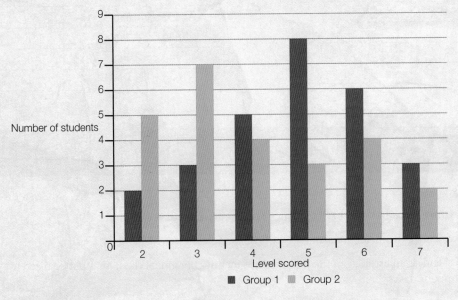

(a) How many students took the examination in each group?

(b) What was the mean grade for each of the groups?

(c) Compare the performance of the two groups of students.

(d) Find the combined mean for the two groups.

3. The following table shows the distances achieved by medal winners in the women's long jump in the Olympic Games from 1948 to 2008. (It is a copy of the data from Exercise 5.8 question 2.)

Distance, d (metres)	Frequency
$5.50 \leq d < 5.75$	3
$5.75 \leq d < 6.00$	1
$6.00 \leq d < 6.25$	5
$6.25 \leq d < 6.50$	4
$6.50 \leq d < 6.75$	7
$6.75 \leq d < 7.00$	11
$7.00 \leq d < 7.25$	15
$7.25 \leq d < 7.50$	1

Work out an estimate of the mean distance jumped by these athletes.

4. The table below summarises the populations of 48 African countries in 2005.

Population, p (in millions)	Number of countries
$0 < p \leq 10$	27
$10 < p \leq 20$	11
$20 < p \leq 30$	3
$30 < p \leq 40$	3
$40 < p \leq 50$	1
$50 < p \leq 60$	1
$60 < p \leq 70$	1
$70 < p \leq 80$	1

(a) What is the estimated total population of the 48 countries?

(b) Calculate an estimate of the mean population of these countries.

One of the countries omitted from the list has a population of 138 million people.

(c) Use your result from part (a) to calculate the overall mean for the 49 countries.

5. Each of the following sets of data has been listed in numerical order. The mean and the median have been given. Determine the values of x and y in each case.

(a) 37, 38, 39, x, 39, 43, 45, y (mean is 41, median is 39)

(b) 11, x, 14, 14, y, 19, 19, 20 (mean is 16, median is 16)

(c) 42, 42, 43, x, y, 48, 50, 53, 55, 56 (mean is 48, median is 47)

6. The number of merit awards received by a group of students in one month is shown below.

Number of merits	0	1	2	3	4	5	6
Frequency	2	15	17	10	9	5	3

(a) Find the total number of students in the group.

(b) Calculate the total number of merits.

(c) Find the mean number of merits.

(d) State the modal number of merits.

(e) Determine the median number of merits.

(f) Compare the three averages, indicating which of them is a better summary measure of the number of merits.

7. The table below shows the number of sixes scored by 30 cricketers in their professional careers.

Number of sixes	0	1	2	3	4	5	6	7	8	14
Frequency	3	4	4	5	2	4	2	4	1	1

(a) Find the mean number of sixes.

(b) State the modal number of sixes.

(c) Determine the median number of sixes.

Past paper questions

1. The histogram below shows the amount of money spent on food each week by 45 families.
The amounts have been rounded to the nearest 10 dollars.

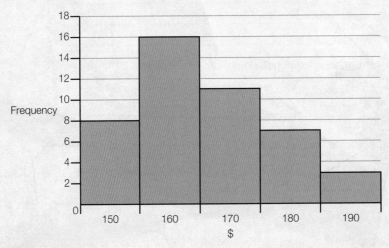

(a) Calculate the mean amount spent on food by the 45 families.

(b) Find the **largest possible amount** spent on food by a single family in the **modal** group.

(c) State which of the following amounts could **not** be the total spent by all families in the modal group:

    (i) $2430   (ii) $2495   (iii) $2500   (iv) $2520   (v) $2600

[6 marks]

[May 2006, Paper 1, Question 5] (© *IB Organization 2006*)

2. The temperatures in °C, at midday in Geneva, were measured for eight days and the results are recorded below.

7, 4, 5, 4, 8, T, 14, 4

The mean temperature was found to be 7°C.

  (a) Find the value of T.   *[3 marks]*

  (b) Write down the mode.   *[1 mark]*

  (c) Find the median.   *[2 marks]*

[Nov 2009, Paper 1, Question 1] (© *IB Organization 2009*)

3. The figure below shows the lengths in centimetres of fish found in the net of a small trawler.

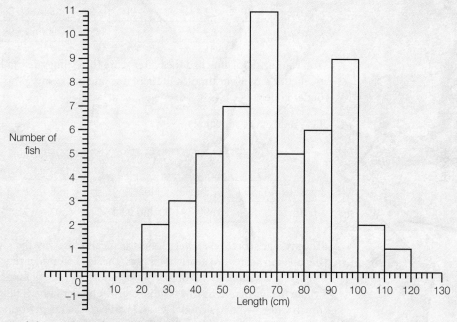

  (a) Find the total number of fish in the net.   *[2 marks]*

  (b) Find (i)   the modal length interval

           (ii) the interval containing the median length

           (iii) an estimate of the mean length.   *[5 marks]*

[May 2007, Paper 2, Question 1(a),(b)] (© *IB Organization 2007*)

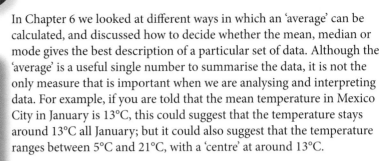

Chapter 7 Measures of dispersion

In this chapter you will learn:

- the different ways of measuring the dispersion of a set of data
- how to calculate the range, interquartile range and standard deviation.

In Chapter 6 we looked at different ways in which an 'average' can be calculated, and discussed how to decide whether the mean, median or mode gives the best description of a particular set of data. Although the 'average' is a useful single number to summarise the data, it is not the only measure that is important when we are analysing and interpreting data. For example, if you are told that the mean temperature in Mexico City in January is 13°C, this could suggest that the temperature stays around 13°C all January; but it could also suggest that the temperature ranges between 5°C and 21°C, with a 'centre' at around 13°C.

This chapter looks at various methods of calculating the **dispersion** of a set of data; this is an estimate of how 'spread out' (i.e. dispersed) the data is. This will give you an indication of how well the mean, median or mode represents the data overall.

Jaime and her father enjoy playing golf together. They also enjoy arguing about who is the better golf player.

Here are their scores over the past eight games:

| Jaime | 90 | 92 | 92 | 90 | 87 | 91 | 86 | 85 |
| Father | 90 | 83 | 95 | 93 | 86 | 88 | 96 | 82 |

You can see that Jaime had the better score three times, her father had the better score four times, and there was one tied game. Who is the better golfer?

Let's look at the statistics:

	Mean	Median	Mode	Range (highest score − lowest score)
Father	89	89	None	96 − 82 = 14
Jaime	89	90	90 and 92	92 − 85 = 7

The average scores reveal very little: the mean scores are the same, and the median scores are nearly the same. The last column of the table, 'Range', gives more useful information: Jaime has a small range of scores, which means that her game is quite consistent; her father's range is much wider — he has good days and bad days, so his performance is more variable. Does this extra information help you to decide who is the better golfer?

A measure of central tendency (median, mean or mode) gives you one piece of information about the data set, but it is also important to know how spread out the data is. If the spread of data is small, the mean or median gives a more accurate measure than if the data is widely dispersed.

7.1 Range and interquartile range

The simplest way of measuring the spread of a set of data is to subtract the lowest value from the highest value. This is called the **range**. The range can be calculated for any set of data, though it may not always provide useful information: when one or two data values are unusually high or low (outliers), the range will give an unrealistically large value for the spread.

Another number measures the spread about (above and below) the **median** and is obtained by subtracting the lower quartile from the upper quartile. It is called the **interquartile range** (IQR); it measures the spread of the central 50% of data values. The interquartile range is often used in preference to the range because it is not affected by outliers, but it still doesn't take into account all of the data. The formula for interquartile range is given in your Formula booklet as:

$$IQR = Q_3 - Q_1$$

You know from Chapter 5 that:

- half (50%) of the data lies between Q_1 and Q_3; we now know this is called the interquartile range

- a quarter (25%) of the data lies between the smallest value and Q_1

- three quarters (75%) of the data lies between the smallest value and Q_3 (note that this also means that a quarter of the data lies between Q_3 and the largest value).

For both the range and the interquartile range:

- A smaller measure of spread tells you that the data values lie close to the 'average value'.

- A larger measure of spread tells you that the data is more widely dispersed from the 'average value'.

We now look at how to find the interquartile range for different types of data sets.

Simple data

For **simple data** with an **even number** of values:

- Put the numbers in order.

- Divide the set into two halves.

- Find the median for each **half**; these will be the quartiles Q_1 and Q_3.

- Subtract the lower quartile from the upper quartile to get the interquartile range: $IQR = Q_3 - Q_1$.

In Chapter 5 you learned how to use a cumulative frequency curve to find the values of the upper and lower quartiles.

You learned how to find the median in Chapter 6.

For example, take the numbers 12, 8, 9, 14, 15, 10, 16, 18, 19, 13, 9, 11.

Put them in order and divide into two halves, then find the median of each half: 8, 9, 9, 10, 11, 12 | 13, 14, 15, 16, 18, 19

Lower half: 8, 9, **9**, **10**, 11, 12

$Q_1 = (9 + 10) \div 2 = 9.5$

> Find the lower quartile by taking the median of the lower half; as there is an even number of values, this is obtained by finding the mean of the third and fourth values.

Upper half: 13, 14, **15**, **16**, 18, 19

$Q_3 = (15 + 16) \div 2 = 15.5$

The interquartile range is $Q_3 - Q_1 = 15.5 - 9.5 = 6$.

> Find the upper quartile by taking the median of the upper half in the same way as you did with the lower half.

For **simple data** with an **odd number** of values:

- Put the numbers in order.

- Find the median of the **whole** data set; the median separates the data set into two halves.

- Look at each half, **not including the median of the whole set**, and find the median for the **lower** half and then for the **upper** half; the medians for the two halves will be the quartiles Q_1 and Q_3.

- Subtract the lower quartile from the upper quartile to get the interquartile range: $IQR = Q_3 - Q_1$.

For example, take the numbers 9, 10, 7, 4, 2, 10, 6, 12, 3, 8, 5.

Put them in order and find the median, then divide the list into two halves and find the median of each half:

2, 3, 4, 5, 6, **7**, 8, 9, 10, 10, 12

> Median is the central value of the ordered data, which is 7.

Lower half (7 not included): 2, 3, **4**, 5, 6.

$Q_1 = 4$

> Find the lower quartile by taking the median of the lower half; as there is an odd number of values, the median is the central value.

Upper half (7 not included): 8, 9, **10**, 10, 12.

$Q_3 = 10$

> Find the upper quartile by taking the median of the upper half; the median is the central value.

The interquartile range is $Q_3 - Q_1 = 10 - 4 = 6$.

Grouped data

For grouped data organised in a grouped frequency table, it is best to use a **cumulative frequency graph** to find the quartiles and the interquartile range. You learned how to do this in Chapter 5.

Here is a quick reminder: let us revisit the data on the mass of footballers from section 5.4. We use the frequency table to draw a cumulative frequency curve.

hint

Remember to plot the **upper boundary** of each class against the cumulative frequency.

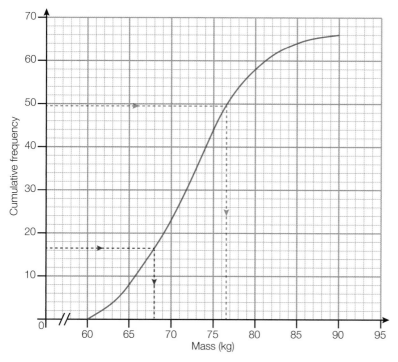

Mass (kg)	Frequency	Cumulative frequency
61–65	8	8
66–70	15	23
71–75	21	44
76–80	14	58
81–85	6	64
86–90	2	66

There are 66 footballers in total, so:

- Lower quartile represents a quarter of the total frequency, so this is a frequency of $\frac{1}{4} \times 66 = 16.5$ (or you could do 25% × 66).

- Upper quartile represents three quarters of the total frequency, so this is a frequency of $\frac{3}{4} \times 66 = 49.5$ (or you could do 75% × 66).

Draw horizontal lines from 16.5 and 49.5 on the vertical axis until they meet the curve; then from each intersection draw a vertical line down to the horizontal axis and read off the value. This gives:

- $Q_3 = 76.5$

- $Q_1 = 68$

You can then use the values of Q_1 and Q_3 to calculate the interquartile range:

$$IQR = Q_3 - Q_1 = 76.5 - 68 = 8.5$$

If the points used to plot a cumulative frequency graph are joined with straight lines rather than with curves, will your answers change? Would it matter? Some statisticians prefer using straight lines to join plotted points, to show that they are making no assumptions about the spread of data between successive points.

Note that with grouped data, your GDC does **not** provide a reliable way to calculate the upper and lower quartiles. It is much better to use a cumulative frequency graph.

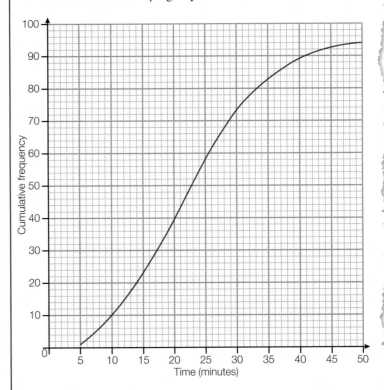

Worked example 7.1

Q. The cumulative frequency graph shown below represents the times taken to travel to school by a group of 94 students.

From the graph:

(a) Write down the median time.

(b) Calculate the interquartile range for the times taken to travel to school.

(c) Estimate the number of students who take longer than 38 minutes to travel to school.

(d) Given that the minimum and maximum times are 5 minutes and 50 minutes respectively, draw a box and whisker diagram for the data.

 You learned about box and whisker diagrams in Chapter 5.

continued . . .

A.

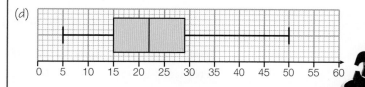

We draw lines on the cumulative frequency graph to find the answers.

Draw a line horizontally across from 47 on the vertical axis to the curve, and then vertically down until it meets the horizontal axis.

(a) $50\% \times 94 = 47$

Median = 22 minutes.

Draw lines horizontally across from 23.5 and 70.5 on the vertical axis to the curve, and then vertically down until they meet the horizontal axis.

(b) $25\% \times 94 = 23.5$, $75\% \times 94 = 70.5$

From the graph, $Q_1 = 15$, $Q_3 = 29$

so IQR = $29 - 15 = 14$ minutes.

Draw a line vertically up from 38 on the horizontal axis to the curve, and then horizontally to the left until it hits the vertical axis.

(c) 87 students take less than 38 minutes to travel to school, so $94 - 87 = 7$ take longer than 38 minutes.

Use the median, upper and lower quartiles, and maximum and minimum values to construct the box and whisker diagram.

(d)

Exercise 7.1

1. For each of the following sets of data, determine:

   (i) the median (ii) the range (iii) the interquartile range.

   (a) 6.77, 6.67, 6.72, 6.66, 6.60, 7.06, 7.04, 7.01, 6.96, 6.81, 6.80

   (b) 226, 222, 224, 222, 220, 235, 235, 234, 232, 227, 227, 247, 241

   (c) 65, 86, 64, 50, 77, 96, 72, 66, 72, 65, 77, 69, 75, 73

   (d) 14.3, 22.3, 14.1, 19.2, 11.7, 30.9, 21.7, 13.6, 17.2, 20.1, 18.6, 25.1

   (e) 580, 550, 300, 350, 300, 344, 500, 263, 330, 230, 330, 196, 200, 608

   (f) 97.9, 96.9, 99.4, 98.1, 97.7, 97.1, 95.9, 96.7, 98.5, 96.6, 97.1

2. For each of the following sets of data, calculate:

   (i) the median (ii) the range (iii) the interquartile range.

   (a) The number of goals scored over a football season per match:

Number of goals	0	1	2	3	4	5
Number of matches	10	11	9	5	3	2

   (b) The height of students in a class of 14- and 15-year-olds:

Height (cm)	154	157	165	171	175	176	181
Frequency	5	9	12	6	7	8	3

   (c) The number of marks scored by a class in a maths test:

Marks	60	61	62	63	64	65	66
Frequency	3	5	6	13	7	2	1

   (d) The number of emails a class of students receive in a day:

Number of emails	0	1	2	3	4	5	6
Number of students	1	9	11	13	8	4	2

   (e) The mass of passengers' luggage on a flight from Paris to New York:

Mass of luggage (kg)	25	26	27	28	29	30	31	32
Frequency	3	7	9	11	10	28	2	1

   (f) The price of 1997 three-door Alfa Romeos in Rome:

Price ($)	1349	1499	1599	1849	2399	2899	3349	3399	5799
Frequency	15	18	20	22	25	12	8	7	3

3. For each of the following cumulative frequency curves, estimate:

(i) the median (ii) the lower and upper quartiles (iii) the interquartile range.

(a)

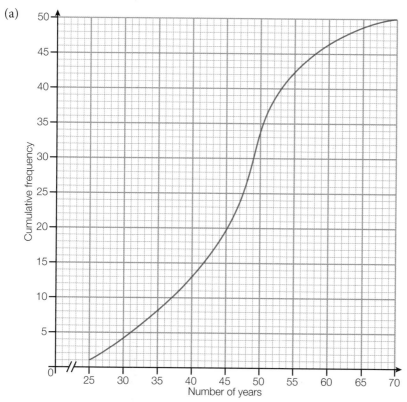

(b)

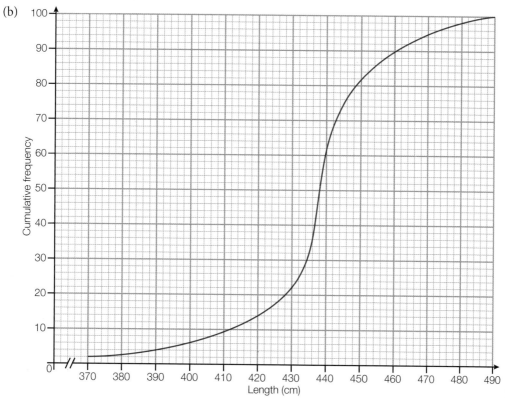

(c)

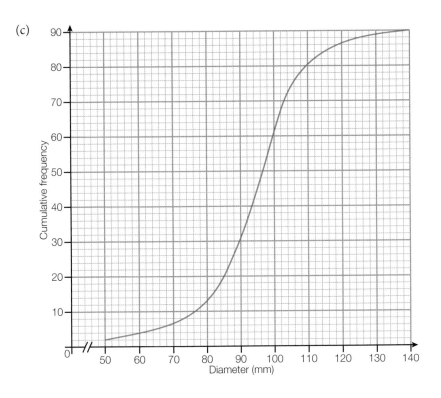

7.2 Standard deviation

The **standard deviation** is another measure of spread about the 'average'. It tells you the spread of the data about the **mean** value. The standard deviation measures the 'average' distance of all the data points from the mean. It takes into account **all** of the data in the set. The smaller the standard deviation, the closer the data values are to the mean and the more representative the mean is of the data set.

We will look at how to calculate the standard deviation for various types of data. There is a formula that can be used to calculate the standard deviation, but it is quicker to use a statistics program on your GDC.

Simple data

The Formula booklet does not contain a formula for the standard deviation, and in the examinations you are expected to use your GDC. However, to understand what the standard deviation means, you might find it helpful to calculate a few without using a statistical program on your calculator. See Learning links 7A if you would like to see how to calculate the standard deviation using more traditional methods.

7A Calculating the standard deviation step by step

The standard deviation is based on finding the distance between each data value and the mean, and then averaging those distances.

To do this:

1. Calculate the mean value of the data.

2. Find the distance of each data value from the mean.

3. Square these distances.

4. Calculate the mean of all the squared distances; that is, add them up and divide by the total number of values. The result is called the **variance**.

5. Take the square root of your result in the previous step. This is the standard deviation.

The steps are easier to follow if you put the calculations in a table. For example, taking the six values 1, 2, 4, 11, 12 and 15, we first find their mean:

$$\bar{x} = (1 + 2 + 4 + 11 + 12 + 15) \div 6 = 7.5$$

Then we calculate the distances of each value from the mean, and their squares, in a table:

x	$(x - \bar{x})$	$(x - \bar{x})^2$
1	$1 - 7.5 = -6.5$	42.25
2	$2 - 7.5 = -5.5$	30.25
4	$4 - 7.5 = -3.5$	12.25
11	$11 - 7.5 = 3.5$	12.25
12	$12 - 7.5 = 4.5$	20.25
15	$15 - 7.5 = 7.5$	56.25
Total		173.5

The variance is $173.5 \div 6 = 28.916\ldots$

So the standard deviation is $\sqrt{28.916\ldots} = 5.38$ (3 s.f.)

If you have a large data set, this would be a long calculation. You can save time by using a spreadsheet or other software package.

Worked example 7.2

Q. The following diagrams show two sets of data.

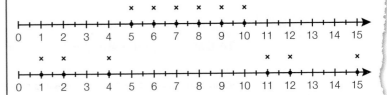

For both data sets the mean is 7.5. Calculate the standard deviation for both data sets and determine which mean is a more accurate representation of the data set.

Use your GDC to calculate the standard deviation. For a reminder of how to do this, see '6.1 (a) Finding the mean, median, quartiles and standard deviation for a simple list of data...' on page 666 of the GDC chapter.

A.

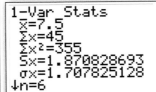 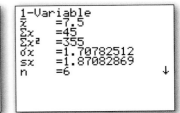

The standard deviation for the first set of data is $\sigma_x = 1.71$ (3 s.f.)

Write down the answer appropriately.

Use your GDC to calculate the standard deviation of the second set of data.

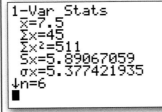

The standard deviation of the second set of data is
$\sigma_x = 5.38$ (3 s.f.)

Write down the answer appropriately.

The standard deviation of the first set of data is much lower than the standard deviation of the second set of data. This suggests that the data values in the first set are more closely distributed around the mean; this can also be seen in the diagrams. The mean of 7.5 is a more accurate representation of the average value in the first set of data than it is in the second. Since 5.38 is more than three times as big as 1.71, the spread of data about the mean is more than three times greater in the second set than in the first set.

GDC

Your GDC actually gives two standard deviation values: s_x and σ_x. In this course we will only be using the value σ_x, so be careful that you read off the correct result from your GDC.

Discrete data organised in a frequency table

For ungrouped data in a table, you can calculate the standard deviation with your GDC by entering the data values in List 1 and the frequencies in List 2. See '*6.1 (b) Finding the mean, median, quartiles and standard deviation for grouped data…*' on page 667 of the GDC chapter if you need a reminder of how.

For example, recall Dee's table of the number of siblings of her brother's schoolmates from Worked example 5.2.

Number of siblings	Frequency
0	12
1	21
2	14
3	9
4	4
Total number of children questioned	60

The standard deviation is used in many statistical applications. It plays a key role in understanding the normal distribution (see Chapter 11), a distribution that is widely used in fields as diverse as finance, psychology, quality control and population studies.

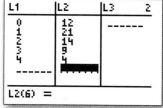

From GDC, $\sigma_x = 1.16$.

Grouped discrete or continuous data

For grouped data in a frequency table, enter the **mid-interval values** of the data classes in List 1 and the frequencies in List 2. Again, see section *6.1 (b)* on page 667 of the GDC chapter if you need to.

For example, let's revisit the table showing heights of trees from section 6.4.

Height (m)	Mid-interval value	Frequency
5–9	7	12
10–14	12	18
15–19	17	18
20–24	22	8
25–29	27	3
Total		59

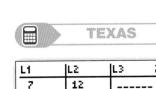

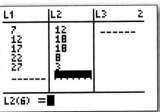

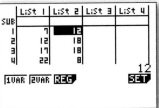

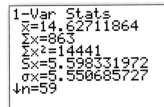

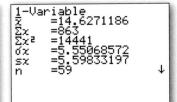

> **exam tip**
>
> To estimate the mean or standard deviation for a grouped data set, remember to always use the mid-interval value.

From GDC, $\sigma_x = 5.55$ (3 s.f.).

Exercise 7.2

1. The table below shows data from Meteogroup UK for 19 July 2011 across 11 towns and cities.

Town/city	Sunshine (hours)	Rainfall (inches)	Temperature (°C)	
			Minimum	Maximum
Edinburgh	1.0	0.12	11	19
Glasgow	3.6	0.01	13	19
Hull	2.8	0.51	13	20
Ipswich	6.9	0.03	11	21
Leeds	6.0	0.00	12	21
Lincoln	1.9	0.24	11	20
London	1.6	0.55	11	19
Manchester	0.4	0.24	12	16
Southampton	3.3	0.28	11	23
St Andrews	3.5	0.63	11	20
Stornoway	0.0	0.02	11	13

Source: Meteogroup UK.

Calculate the mean and standard deviation across all 11 locations for:

(a) hours of sunshine

(b) amount of rainfall in inches

(c) minimum temperature

(d) maximum temperature.

2. A five-day temperature forecast across nine cities is shown in the table below.

Temperature (°C)	14	15	16	17	18	19	20	21	22
Frequency	2	1	5	7	13	10	4	2	1

Using the information from the table above, calculate:

(a) the mean temperature for the five-day period

(b) the corresponding standard deviation for the data.

3. The price and number of bookings for various cruises in a three-month period are represented in the table below.

Price (£)	Number of bookings
1700	12
1850	18
2150	24
2530	26
2880	35
3100	15
3500	12
4300	6
5600	2

(a) Calculate the mean cost of a cruise.

(b) Calculate the standard deviation of the cost of these cruises.

4. The maximum spectator numbers for two different football leagues are shown below. Calculate the mean and standard deviation of attendances across the stadia for each league.

(a)

Attendance n (thousands)	Number of stadia
$10 \leq n < 26$	8
$26 \leq n < 42$	12
$42 \leq n < 58$	15
$58 \leq n < 74$	9
$74 \leq n < 90$	5

(b)

Attendance n (thousands)	Number of stadia
$10 \leq n < 26$	11
$26 \leq n < 42$	17
$42 \leq n < 58$	5
$58 \leq n < 74$	2
$74 \leq n < 90$	4
$90 \leq n < 106$	1

5. The performance of a group of students in a History project is illustrated in the table below. Calculate the mean and standard deviation of the students' scores.

Score (out of 70)	Number of students
21–25	3
26–30	7
31–35	15
36–40	20
41–45	7
46–50	4
51–55	4
56–60	1
61–65	4

7.3 Using the interquartile range and standard deviation to make comparisons

Once you have collected data and calculated the mean, median, interquartile range and/or the standard deviation, what do you do with this information? Statistical values such as these are useful for making general statements about your data, which in turn could be used to draw conclusions or predict future data.

Two IB students, Abi and Ben, are analysing the statistical information that they have gathered on a Biology field trip. They are studying shellfish and want to find out if limpets are larger when they are closer to the sea. They measure the diameter of groups of limpets at different points on a beach. Before they compare the different groups, they want some reassurance that the samples they've collected for each area are representative of the limpets in that area. For one group of 80 limpets, they collected the following results.

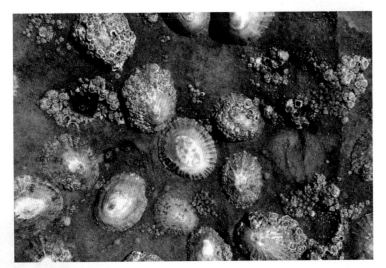
A group of limpets.

Diameter d (cm)	Frequency
$0 < d \leq 1$	7
$1 < d \leq 2$	12
$2 < d \leq 3$	15
$3 < d \leq 4$	19
$4 < d \leq 5$	17
$5 < d \leq 6$	10
Total	80

Abi drew a cumulative frequency curve and calculated the median and interquartile range of the data:

- Median = 3.3 cm

- Interquartile range = 2.3 cm

Ben calculated the mean and standard deviation:

- Mean = 3.21 cm

- Standard deviation = 1.48 cm

Ben and Abi looked at the frequency table to find the modal class:

- Modal class is $3 < d \leq 4$

From this information we can see that the mean and median are close together, and both of these values lie within the modal class. This suggests that the limpets within the sample are all similar sized (suggesting they fairly represent the size of limpets in that area); but be careful – these values on their own are not proof that their sample is good. They need further support.

By drawing a histogram, Abi and Ben could see that the data is not symmetrical but is very slightly leaning towards higher values. But we can also see that it is not distorted completely to one direction either (as it would be if most of the data were concentrated at one end of the range of values), nor is it distorted by the data being very spread out.

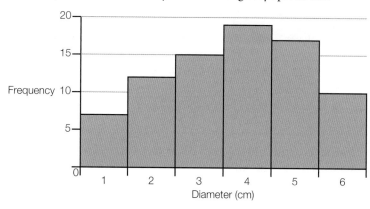

The box and whisker diagram also seems to suggest that the data leans slightly towards the higher values:

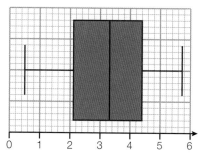

In their research, scientists often compare populations from around the world to understand more about the topic they are studying. Linking up with another IB college to share data would enable students to take advantage of working this way too.

exam tip

When you use your GDC to draw a histogram or box and whisker plot, the scale will not be shown on the axes, so you will need to define this in what you write down.

The interquartile range tells us that the central 50% of data (the 'box' in the box and whisker diagram) spans about 2.3 cm.

The standard deviation is small, which means that the data is quite closely clustered around the mean.

From the above combined analyses of this data set, you could say that it is highly likely that Abi and Ben have collected a good sample on their field trip. The sizes are not biased in one direction and the data is close to the measure of central tendency, which suggests the mean or median shell size taken from this sample is a good representation of the shell size of all limpets in this area.

Worked example 7.3

Q. An ornithologist weighed 12 adult male sparrows (*Passer domesticus*) in spring and again in autumn. The masses were recorded in grams.

Spring mass (g)	36.6	33.7	25.2	31.4	28.0	27.8	38.0	26.4	26.3	34.1	30.6	26.0
Autumn mass (g)	35.3	38.7	34.5	29.8	31.9	33.6	32.6	29.6	32.2	30.7	33.5	38.9

(a) Calculate the mean and standard deviation of the masses in spring and the masses in autumn.

(b) Comment on your results.

> Calculate the mean and standard deviation of the spring masses using your GDC. See '6.1 (a) Finding the mean, median, quartiles and standard deviation for a simple list of data…' on page 666 of the GDC chapter if you need a reminder.

A. (a)

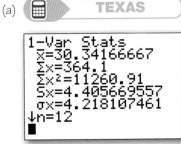

```
1-Var Stats
x̄=30.34166667
Σx=364.1
Σx²=11260.91
Sx=4.405669557
σx=4.218107461
↓n=12
```

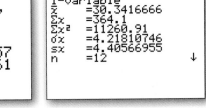

```
1-Variable
x̄      =30.3416666
Σx     =364.1
Σx²    =11260.91
σx     =4.21810746
sx     =4.40566955
n      =12          ↓
```

$\bar{x} = 30.3\,g$, $\sigma_x = 4.22\,g$

continued . . .

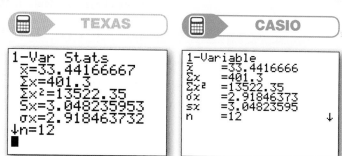

Calculate the mean and standard deviation of the autumn masses using your GDC.

$\bar{x} = 33.4\,g$, $\sigma_x = 2.92\,g$

Compare the means.

Compare the standard deviations.

(b) In autumn the mean mass of the birds is greater than it is in spring. In spring the standard deviation is larger, suggesting that the data is more spread out. So the autumn masses are both heavier and more consistent.

This data supports the hypothesis that in autumn birds are heavier because they have gained mass over the summer when food is abundant. In spring, birds have just gone through a period of limited food sources during the winter and so are less able to gain mass. However, some birds may have retained more mass through the winter because of access to bird feeders or habitats with plenty of grain and seeds, which could account for the greater spread of masses in the spring.

Exercise 7.3

1. The following data shows the number of goals scored by each of the ten teams in the ANZ Netball Championship during the 2010 and 2011 seasons.

| 2010 season | 621 | 646 | 599 | 533 | 662 | 664 | 684 | 677 | 647 | 758 |
| 2011 season | 571 | 594 | 679 | 651 | 696 | 717 | 644 | 682 | 681 | 704 |

(a) Calculate:

(i) the mean number of goals scored per team in each season

(ii) the standard deviation of the number of goals scored per team in each season.

(b) Use your answers from part (a) to compare the goal-scoring performance of the teams in the two seasons.

2. Mrs Chan has two IB Mathematical Studies groups. The marks scored by her students in the last class test are shown below

Group MS-A	25	68	93	30	42	22	33	35	35	67	77	50	97	98	95
Group MS-B	53	70	52	27	57	52	77	48	87	50	40	62	58	78	50

(a) Calculate:

  (i) the median mark for each group

  (ii) the quartiles and hence the interquartile range of the test marks for each group.

(b) Use your answers from above to compare the performance of the two groups in the test.

3. The following are the waiting times in minutes for blood tests at two separate laboratories.

Lab A	52	43	44	42	51	51	57	47	52	50	41	44	42	47	52	54	45	49
	50	42	43	40	46	49	54	44	51	51	43	47	46	59	58	58	50	51
Lab B	52	39	40	40	59	55	56	44	49	50	37	38	40	55	58	57	45	49
	51	39	38	39	52	55	57	44	53	53	42	40	43	51	55	62	47	51

(a) Create a grouped frequency table for each set of data.
  (*Hint*: you can use the groups 37–39, 40–42, 43–45, etc.)

(b) Construct separate cumulative frequency tables for the two sets of data.

(c) Draw cumulative frequency curves for the two sets of data.

(d) From your curves, estimate the median and the interquartile range of the waiting times at each laboratory.

(e) Use your results from part (d) to compare the waiting times for blood tests in the two laboratories.

4. The following table shows ten countries ranked by population in 2011.

Rank	Country	Population (millions)
1	China	1337
2	India	1189
3	United States	311
4	Indonesia	246
5	Brazil	203
6	Pakistan	
7	Nigeria	166
8	Bangladesh	159
9	Russia	139
10	Japan	127
Mean		406

(a) Given that the mean population of the ten countries was 406 million, find an estimate of the population of Pakistan in 2011.

(b) Determine the median population of the ten countries.

(c) Calculate the standard deviation of the populations.

5. The world mid-year population for 2011 of people under 90 years old by age and sex is summarised in the table below.

Age	Male (millions)	Female (millions)
0–14	949	885
15–29	901	859
30–44	745	725
45–59	539	549
60–74	275	303
75–89	83	119

(a) Work out estimates for the mean and standard deviation of the male population and of the female population.

(b) Calculate the combined mean and standard deviation.

(c) Use your answers from parts (a) and (b) to fill in the following table:

	Males	Females	Combined
Mean			
Standard deviation			

(d) Comment on the differences and similarities between the male and female population distributions.

Summary

You should know:

- that the dispersion of a data set estimates how spread out the data set is, and therefore indicates how good a representation of the data the measure of central tendency is

- that there are three ways of measuring dispersion: range, interquartile range and standard deviation

- how to calculate the range, interquartile range and standard deviation

- how to make sensible comments about your data based on these values and the additional support of histograms, cumulative frequency curves and/or box and whisker diagrams.

Mixed examination practice

Exam-style questions

1. The mean of the 12 numbers listed below is 7.

   5, x, 10, 6, 9, 10, y, 3, 8, 9, 1, 8

   (a) Write a simplified equation connecting x and y.

   (b) Given that the mode of the numbers is 8 and $x < y$, find the values of x and y.

   (c) Hence find the median of the numbers.

   (d) Determine the lower and upper quartiles.

   (e) Find the interquartile range.

2. The table below shows the tuition fees for 65 schools in the USA.

Fees F (US dollars)	Number of schools
$5{,}000 \le F < 10{,}000$	2
$10{,}000 \le F < 15{,}000$	4
$15{,}000 \le F < 20{,}000$	8
$20{,}000 \le F < 25{,}000$	8
$25{,}000 \le F < 30{,}000$	25
$30{,}000 \le F < 35{,}000$	18

   (a) In which interval does the median lie?

   (b) What is the modal group?

   (c) Work out an estimate of the mean value of the tuition fees.

   (d) Construct a cumulative frequency graph for the data.

   (e) Use your graph to estimate the following values:

   (i) the median   (ii) the interquartile range.

   (f) Given that the minimum and maximum tuition fees are \$5000 and \$35,000 respectively, draw a box and whisker diagram to represent the given data.

3. The following table shows the time spent in the staff room by teachers during one lunch break.

Time (minutes)	Frequency	Cumulative frequency
0–4	1	1
5–9	4	5
10–14	7	12
15–19	6	18
20–24	4	x

Time (minutes)	Frequency	Cumulative frequency
25–29	10	32
30–34	y	34
35–39	9	43
40–44	5	48

Determine the values of x and y.

4. The following table shows the number of text messages received by a group of students in a 24-hour period.

Number of text messages	Frequency	Cumulative frequency
3	1	1
4	3	4
5	c 4	8
6	6	14
7	9	23
8	10	33
9	8 d	41
10	6	47
11	3 f	50

(a) How many students were there in the group?

(b) Work out the values of c, d, e and f.

5. Data on the US field production of crude oil (in millions of barrels) between 1920 and 2010 is displayed in the diagram below.

(*Source*: U.S. Energy Information (2012); http://www.eia.gov/)

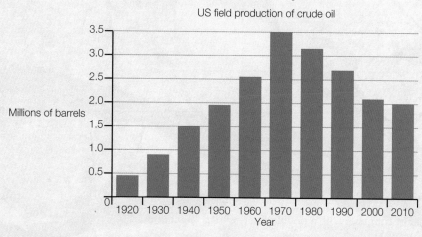

US field production of crude oil

(a) Find an estimate of the total volume of crude oil produced in the given years.

(b) Work out the mean volume of crude oil produced per year.

6. An Under-16s Youth Football League has 12 teams in Division One and 13 teams in Division Two. At the end of the 2010 season, the mean number of points earned by the teams was 32.5 for Division One and 36 for Division Two.

   After a disciplinary hearing, six of the Division One matches were cancelled at the end of the season. As a result, all 18 points earned by the teams in these matches (3 for each match) were withdrawn.

   (a) Work out the reduced mean number of points for teams in Division One after the disciplinary hearing.

   (b) What is the combined mean number of points for both divisions after the disciplinary hearing?

7. The graph below is the cumulative frequency graph of the populations of 50 countries with between 8 million and 56 million people.

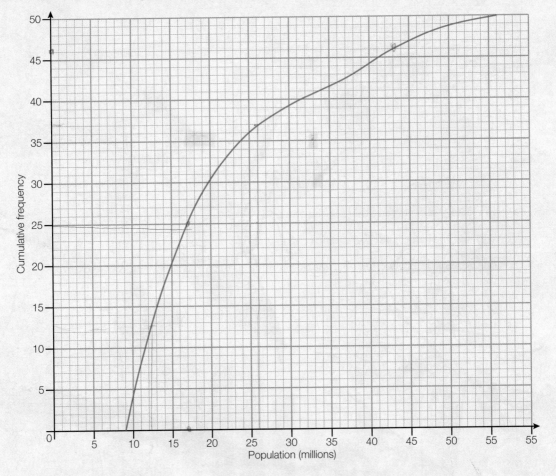

   (a) Use the graph to estimate:

       (i)   the median population

       (ii) the number of countries with a population less than 43 million

       (iii) the percentage of countries with a population greater than 36 million.

   (b) Draw a box and whisker diagram to represent the population distribution of these countries.

8. 90 students were asked how long it took them to get ready for school in the morning. Their responses are summarised in the table below.

Time t (minutes)	$10 \leq t < 15$	$15 \leq t < 20$	$20 \leq t < 25$	$25 \leq t < 30$	$30 \leq t < 35$	$35 \leq t < 40$
Frequency	6	14	16	34	18	2

(a) In which interval does the median lie?

(b) What is the modal group?

(c) Calculate estimates for the mean and standard deviation of the times.

(d) Draw a frequency histogram to represent the data.

(e) Use your answers from above to comment on the data.

9. The table below summarises the weights of 22 male and 22 female foxes.

Weight w (lbs)	Frequency	
	Male	Female
$0 \leq w < 15$	6	7
$15 \leq w < 30$	7	6
$30 \leq w < 45$	1	1
$45 \leq w < 60$	1	4
$60 \leq w < 75$	5	3
$75 \leq w < 90$	2	1

(a) Draw two separate frequency histograms to represent the information.

(b) Write down the modal groups for the weights of the foxes.

(c) Calculate estimates of the mean and standard deviation of the weights.

The box and whisker diagrams for the data are shown below.

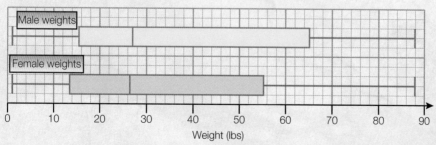

(d) Use the information from the diagrams to comment on the differences/similarities between the weights of the male and female foxes.

10. The following histogram shows the distances travelled by salesmen of an advertising company during a randomly chosen week.

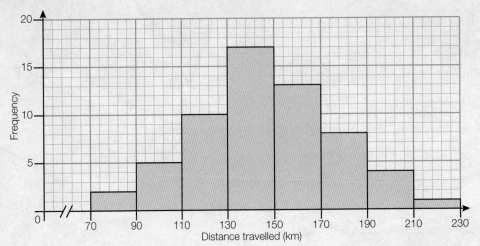

(a) Determine the total number of journeys made by the salesmen during the week.

(b) Write down the interval containing:

   (i)   the modal distance

   (ii) the median distance

(c) Work out estimates of:

   (i)   the mean distance travelled

   (ii) the standard deviation of the distances

(d) Use your answers from above to comment on the journeys made by the salesmen.

11. The cumulative frequency diagram below shows the lengths of the arm spans of members of a sports club.

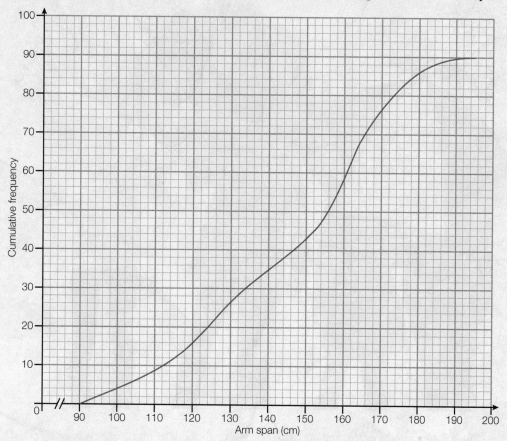

(a) From the graph, find:

(i) the median length   (ii) the interquartile range of the lengths.

(b) Draw a box and whisker diagram to represent the data.

The graph was drawn from the following table:

Length L (cm)	Frequency
$90 \leq L < 105$	6
$105 \leq L < 120$	u
$120 \leq L < 135$	13
$135 \leq L < 150$	v
$150 \leq L < 165$	24
$165 \leq L < 180$	w
$180 \leq L < 195$	4

(c) Using information from the graph, find the values of u, v and w.

(d) Calculate an estimate of the mean length of the arm spans.

3 Logic, sets and probability

1899: the United States patents office predicts that, 'Everything that can be invented, has been invented.' (A misquote attributed to Charles Holland Duell, Commissioner of the US Patent Office, 1899.)

1943: the Chairman of IBM predicts that there will, 'only be a world market for maybe five computers.' (Commonly attributed to Thomas J. Watson, Chairman of International Business Machines (IBM), 1943.)

1992: spare capacity on cell phones is used to send messages in text. It is predicted to be useful as a portable paging system for people who use their cars as an office, but for no-one else.

These examples suggest that we are not very good at predicting the future, and yet forecasting and prediction is now a central part of everyone's lives.

Who uses probability?

- Every time that you use something new, take a prescribed tablet, or decide what you are going to do tomorrow, your decision may have been made based on probabilities.

- Will your hockey match take place tomorrow? It depends on the weather forecast.

- What style of T-shirts will be fashionable next year? It depends on the trend forecasters and marketing teams of big corporations.

'Perfect accuracy (in forecasting) is not obtainable', say Richard Brealey and Stewart Myers in the journal *Finance*. 'But the need for planning in business is vital.' (*Source*: Richard Brealey and Stewart Myers, *Principles of Corporate Finance* (McGraw Hill, 1988).) Businesses must utilise accurate forecasting methods.

Chapter 8 Set theory and Venn diagrams

Organising **sets** or groups of objects that share characteristics is a way of remembering them and of understanding them. To do this, mathematicians use set theory to describe different groups and **Venn diagrams** to illustrate the sets. Venn diagrams are useful for practical problems and for numerical ones.

Set theory was developed by Georg Cantor (1845–1918) and revolutionised almost every mathematical field that was being studied at that time. Although his ideas were initially regarded as controversial and contentious, they have since been universally recognised for their importance and their impact on the study of mathematics.

Georg Cantor.

Venn diagrams were developed by the English mathematician John Venn (1834–1923). He taught logic and probability theory at Cambridge University and developed a method of using intersecting circles to illustrate and explain his ideas to students. In his later career he wrote a book called 'The Logic of Chance' that was influential in the study of statistical theory. He was also very skilled at building machines, including one that bowled cricket balls.

> **In this chapter you will learn:**
>
> - how to use the notation of set theory including elements, intersection, union, complement and subsets
> - how to construct and interpret Venn diagrams with simple applications
> - how to solve problems using Venn diagrams.

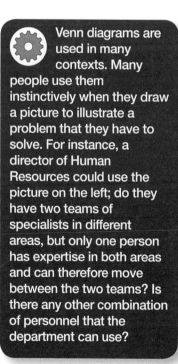

Venn diagrams are used in many contexts. Many people use them instinctively when they draw a picture to illustrate a problem that they have to solve. For instance, a director of Human Resources could use the picture on the left; do they have two teams of specialists in different areas, but only one person has expertise in both areas and can therefore move between the two teams? Is there any other combination of personnel that the department can use?

How do you organise your study books – by subject, by size, by colour or by weight? Do you have any books that can be used in more than one subject? Where do you put those books?

Johan organises his books by subject; he has three on History, three on Economics and one that is relevant to both Economics and History.

A Venn diagram can be used to illustrate the overlap:

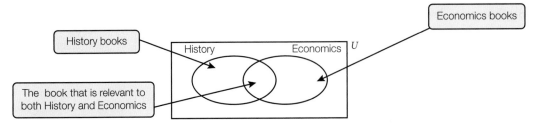

Venn diagrams are always enclosed in a rectangle. This rectangle is called the **universal set** and defines the numbers or objects that you are considering. The letter U next to the rectangle indicates that this is a universal set.

When written out, sets are always contained within curly brackets. Two or more sets are identical if they contain the same items or elements in any order. For example, $\{H_2, H_1, H_3\} = \{H_3, H_1, H_2\} = \{H_1, H_2, H_3\}$.

In the set of Johan's books:

the number of books relevant to History, $n(H) = 4$,

the number of books relevant to Economics, $n(E) = 4$,

the number of books relevant to History and Economics, $n(H \text{ and } E) = 1$,

and the number of books relevant to History or Economics or both, $n(H \text{ or } E) = 7$.

The Venn diagram will now look like this:

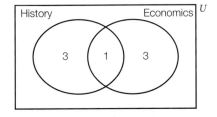

The last two statements can be written as:

$n(H \text{ and } E) = n(H \cap E) = 1$	The symbol for 'and' is $\cap$ and is called the **intersection**.
$n(H \text{ or } E) = (H \cup E) = 3 + 3 + 1 = 7$	The symbol for 'or' is $\cup$ and is called the **union**.

Johan also has two Mathematics books but there is no overlap between these and his History books so the Venn diagram for Johan's books relevant to History and to Mathematics looks like this:

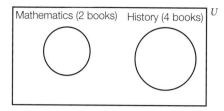

From the diagram you can see that the sets are separate; there is no overlap. So:

the number of History books, $n(H) = 4$

and the number of Mathematics books, $n(M) = 2$,

then the number of History or Mathematics books, $n(M \cup H) = 2 + 4 = 6$.

As there are no books that can be used for both Mathematics and History, $n(H \cap M) = \varnothing$.

A set with no members in it is called an **empty set** and the symbol for an empty set is $\varnothing$.

An empty set is not the same as {0}; this is a set containing the number zero so it is not empty.

Johan's friends Magda, Iris, Erik and Piotr all play hockey. Erik and Piotr play in the same team as Johan. The universal set in this example is 'all Johan's friends'.

The Venn diagram looks like this:

$U = \{$all Johan's friends$\}$

$A = \{$Johan's friends who play hockey$\} = \{$M, I, E, P$\}$

$B = \{$friends in the same team as Johan$\} = \{$E, P$\}$

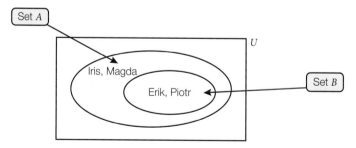

Notice that set B is completely enclosed by set A. Set B is called a **subset** of set A; all the members of B are also in A.

You can use some extra notation:

M $\in$ A means that Magda is a member, or element, of set A.

I $\notin$ B means that Iris is not a member of set B, as she is not in the same hockey team as Johan.

$B \subset A$ means that B is a subset of A. Every element of B is enclosed within set A.

An empty set is also a subset of all other sets.

Summary of notation

{}	curly brackets	lists the members of a set
U	universal set	defines the field being considered
$n(A)$		number of elements in a set A
$\in$	element	a member of a set
$\notin$	not an element	not a member of a set
$\varnothing$	empty set	a set with no elements or members
$\cap$	intersection	$A \cap B$ is the overlap of set A and set B (A and B)
$\cup$	union	$A \cup B$ contains all the elements of A and of B (but without any repeats) (A or B)
$\subset$	subset	a set that is equal to or enclosed by another set

exam tip

In examinations, questions are unlikely to contain more than two or three subsets in any universal set.

Exercise 8.1

1. Write the following statements, using set notation:

   (a) x is a member of set A

   (b) x is not a member of set A

   (c) B is a subset of C

   (d) C union D

   (e) A intersection B.

2. Write the following statements, using set notation:

   (a) the elements of set A are x, y and z

   (b) the number of elements in both sets A and B is 3

   (c) set B consists of the vowels, a, e, i, o, u

   (d) the number of elements in set A is 5.

8.2 Venn diagrams with numbers

Venn diagrams are a good way of organising sets of numbers so that you can see the links between them.

Let $U = \{1, 2, 3, \ldots, 9, 10\}$ All the integers from 1 to 10.

$A = \{2, 4, 6, 8, 10\}$ All the even natural numbers between 1 and 10 inclusive, i.e. including 10.

$B = \{2, 3, 5, 7\}$ All the prime numbers between 1 and 10.

Before you fill in the Venn diagram, think about the following:

2 is in both set A and set B, so goes in the overlap of A and B.

1 and 9 are in neither set A nor set B, so they go outside the circles.

3, 5 and 7 are prime but not even, so they go inside set B but outside set A.

6, 4, 8 and 10 are even but not prime numbers, so they go inside set A but outside set B.

Now the numbers are organised, the diagram shows that:

$n(U) = 10$

$n(A) = 5$

$n(B) = 4$

$5 \notin$ set A (Remember $\notin$ means 'is not a member'.)

$9 \notin$ set A or set B

$2 \in$ set A and set B (Remember $\in$ means 'is a member'.)

$A' = \{1, 3, 5, 7, 9\}$ A' means the **complement** of A, which consists of all the numbers that are not in set A.

You can see that set theory can be expressed in **notation**, in **set language** or by using **diagrams**.

The table below shows the notation and explains it using diagrams, based on the example above.

Set notation	Set language	Meaning	Venn diagram	Answer
$A \cup B$	A union B.	Everything that is in either or both sets.		{2, 3, 4, 5, 6, 7, 8, 10}
$A \cap B$	A intersection B.	Everything that is in the overlap of both sets.		{2}
A'	The complement of A.	Everything that is not in set A.		{1, 3, 5, 7, 9}
$(A \cup B)'$	The complement of $(A \cup B)$.	Everything that is not in set A or set B.		{1, 9}
$A \cap B'$	The intersection of A and the complement of B.	The overlap between A and everything that is not in B.		{4, 6, 8, 10}
$A' \cup B$	The union of B with the complement of A.	Everything that is in B or not in A.		{1, 2, 3, 5, 7, 9}
$(A \cap B)'$	The complement of A intersection B.	Everything that is not in the overlap of A and B.		{1, 3, 4, 5, 6, 7, 8, 9, 10}

RR *In Chapter 1, the definitions of numbers are given using set language. Natural numbers were defined as $\mathbb{N} = \{0, 1, 2, 3, 4, 5, ...\}$.*

Using this notation you can see that, for this course, natural numbers include zero and all the positive counting numbers from one to infinity.

If integers are defined as $\mathbb{Z} = \{..., -3, -2, -1, 0, 1, 2, 3, 4, ...\}$, then you can see the difference between the definitions very quickly.

Worked example 8.1

Q. Let $U = \{-5, -4, -3, -2, -1, 0, 1, 2, 3, 4, 5\}$ (all the integers from -5 to $+5$),

$A = \{-5, -4, -3, -2, -1\}$ (negative integers from -5 to $+5$),

$B = \{-4, -2, 0, 2, 4\}$ (even integers from -5 to $+5$).

(a) Draw the Venn diagram.

(b) Use the diagram to answer the following questions.

   (i) Is $A \cap B$ an empty set?

   (ii) List the elements of $A \cup B$.

   (iii) List the elements of $A \cap B'$.

   (iv) Find $n(A)$, $n(A \cap B)$ and $n((A \cup B)')$.

   (v) Describe the set $A \cap B$ in words.

A. (a)

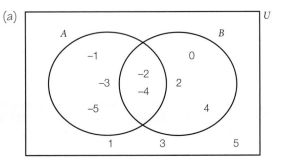

'A intersection B' is not an empty set, because it contains the numbers -2 and -4.

(b) (i) $A \cap B \neq \varnothing$

'A union B' consists of all the numbers that are in A and/or B.

(ii) $A \cup B = \{-5, -4, -3, -2, -1, 0, 2, 4\}$

All the numbers that are in A and not in B.

(iii) $A \cap B' = \{-1, -3, -5\}$

(iv) $n(A) = 5$

$n(A \cap B) = 2$

All those numbers that are not in A or B.

$n((A \cup B)') = 3$

(v) $A \cap B$ contains numbers that are both negative and even.

Exercise 8.2

1. (a) If $P = \{1, 4, 8, 12, 20, 32, 52, 84\}$, state $n(P)$.

    (b) If $Q = \{$square numbers less than 40$\}$, state $n(Q)$.

    (c) If $R = ($prime numbers between zero and 30$\}$, state $n(R)$.

2. Two sets of real numbers A and B are defined as follows:

    $A = \{9, 10, 11, 12, 13, 14, 15\}$

    $B = \{5, 6, 7, 8, 9, 10, 11\}$

    List the elements of sets $A \cup B$ and $A \cap B$.

3. Copy this Venn diagram three times.

    (a) On one copy, shade the area that represents $P \cap Q$.

    (b) On another copy, shade the area that represents $(P \cap Q)'$.

    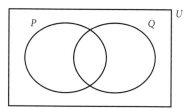

    (c) On the third copy, shade the area that represents the complement of $(P \cup Q)$.

4. The universal set U is the set of integers from 1 to 64 inclusive. A and B are subsets of U such that:

    A is the set of square numbers,

    B is the set of cubed numbers.

    List the elements of the following sets:

    (a) A (b) B (c) $A \cup B$ (d) $A \cap B'$.

8.3 Applications of set theory and Venn diagrams

Venn diagrams can be useful when solving practical problems.

Worked example 8.2

Q. There are 40 students at an IB school who are studying either Chemistry, Biology or both. 25 students are studying Chemistry and 19 students are studying Biology. 4 students are studying both subjects. How many students study just Chemistry or just Biology?

$\longrightarrow$

If people work in international teams and have to communicate quickly, diagrams can be a quick way of ensuring that everyone understands an idea, even if they are not working in their first language. Some people remember ideas better if they see them as a picture too.

continued . . .

A. Let U = {students studying Chemistry and/or Biology}
   = 40

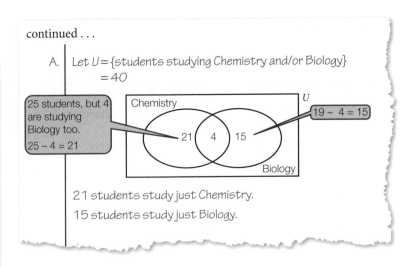

25 students, but 4 are studying Biology too.
25 − 4 = 21

19 − 4 = 15

21 students study just Chemistry.
15 students study just Biology.

Worked example 8.3

Q. Of the same group of 40 students, 12 take History, 18 take Economics and 5 take both subjects. How many students do not take History or Economics?

A. Let U = {students studying History and/or Economics}

7 + 5 + 13 = 25
40 − 25 = 15
There are 15 students who do not take History or Economics.

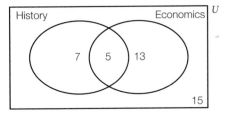

There are 15 students who do not take History or Economics.

Worked example 8.4

Q. There are 32 students at a party. 12 students say that they only like chocolate-pecan ice cream and 10 students say that they only like strawberry-and-cookies ice cream. 8 students do not like either. How many students like both?

A.

There are 32 students, so
$$12 + x + 10 + 8 = 32$$
$$x + 30 = 32$$
$$x = 2$$

Two students like both chocolate-pecan and strawberry-and-cookies ice cream.

Exercise 8.3

1. The universal set U is defined as:

   $U = \{x \in \mathbb{Z}: 41 \leq x \leq 50\} \equiv \{$all the integers from 41 to 50 inclusive$\}$

   Subsets X and Y of U are defined as:

   $X = \{$multiples of 6$\}$

   $Y = \{$multiples of 7$\}$.

   (a) List the elements of:

        (i) $X \cap Y$ (ii) $X \cap Y'$.

   (b) Find $n((X \cap Y)')$.

   (c) Illustrate the information from (a) on copies of this Venn diagram.

hint

Here is a reminder of what these symbols mean:
≥ greater than or equal to;
≤ less than or equal to;
≡ equivalent to.

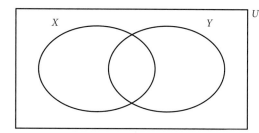

2. Let U be the set of all positive integers from 5 to 55 inclusive.

   A, B and C are subsets of U such that:

   A is the set of prime numbers contained in U,

   B is the set of multiples of 11 contained in U,

   C contains all the positive integers that are factors of 55.

   (a) List all the members of set A.

   (b) Write down all the members of:

        (i) $B \cup C$ (ii) $A \cap B \cap C$.

3. The universal set U is defined as all positive integers between 11 and 43 inclusive.

   A, B and C are subsets of U such that:

   $A = \{$factors of 36$\}$, $B = \{$multiples of 4$\}$ and $C = \{$multiples of 6$\}$.

   (a) Find $n(B)$.

   (b) List the elements in $A \cap B \cap C$.

   (c) List the elements in $A \cap B'$.

4. During a school's Sports Day activities, students participated in Track and Field events.

$U = \{$Track and Field events$\}$

$T = \{$Track events, mainly running$\}$

$F = \{$Field events, mainly jumping, throwing, etc.$\}$

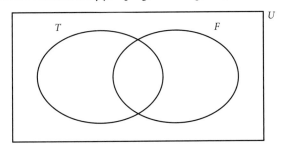

On three separate copies of the Venn diagram from above, shade the following regions. Write in words what each region represents.

(a) $T \cap F'$ (b) $(T \cap F)'$

5. In the Venn diagram, sets A and B are subsets of the universal set U.

U is defined as the positive integers between 1 and 12 inclusive.

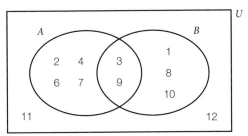

(a) Find:

   (i) $n(A)$ (ii) $n(A \cap B)$.

(b) List the elements in:

   (i) $(A \cup B)'$ (ii) $A' \cap B$.

8.4 Venn diagrams with three sets

Venn diagrams can be used to solve problems with three sets. The notation and definitions for three sets are the same as those with two sets, but the diagrams are more complicated.

Most problems with three sets give you a diagram like this:

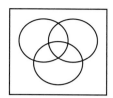

But you need to read the questions carefully, because you may get one like this:

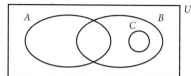

Or like this:

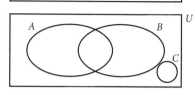

In some problems the Venn diagram has already been completed, and can be used to answer questions.

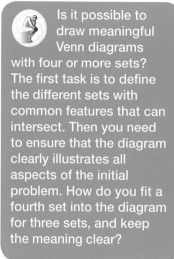

Is it possible to draw meaningful Venn diagrams with four or more sets? The first task is to define the different sets with common features that can intersect. Then you need to ensure that the diagram clearly illustrates all aspects of the initial problem. How do you fit a fourth set into the diagram for three sets, and keep the meaning clear?

Worked example 8.5

Q. In this diagram the universal set $U = \{1, 2, 3, 4, 5, 6, 7, 8, 9, 10\}$

$A = \{3, 4, 6, 8, 10\}$

$B = \{7, 8, 10\}$

$C = \{2, 5, 6, 7, 8, 9\}$

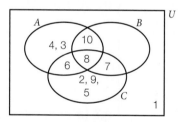

Use the diagram to list the elements in the following sets and shade their position on the Venn diagram:

A. (a) $A \cap B = \{8, 10\}$

(a)
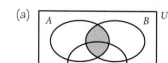

continued . . .

(b) $A \cap B \cap C = \{8\}$

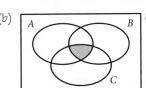

(c) $A \cup C = \{2, 3, 4, 5, 6, 7, 8, 9, 10\}$

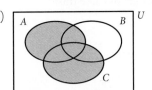

(d) $A' = \{1, 2, 5, 7, 9\}$

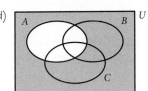

(e) $(A \cup B)' = \{1, 2, 5, 9\}$

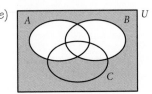

(f) $A' \cap B = \{7\}$

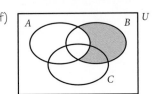

(g) $(A' \cap B) \cap C = \{7\}$

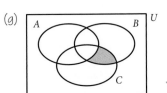

Worked example 8.6

Q. There are 50 people in a band. The conductor wants to know who can play the saxophone, who can play the trumpet and who can play the drums.

He discovers that:

2 people can play all three instruments,

5 people can play the saxophone and the trumpet,

1 person can play the saxophone and the drums,

3 people can play the trumpet and the drums,

22 people can play the trumpet,

15 people can play the drums,

18 people can play the saxophone.

How many people cannot play any of these instruments?

> To complete the Venn diagram you should start in the middle and work outwards. In this example the information has been given in the correct working order, but many questions may not do this. So look for the information that goes in the centre first!

> Start with two people in the centre, $n(S \cap T \cap D) = 2$

> Then look at the other intersections: 5 people play saxophone and trumpet, so put a 5 in the overlap of just S and T.

> 1 person plays saxophone and drums, so put a 1 in the overlap of just S and D; similarly for the 3 people who play trumpet and drums.

A.
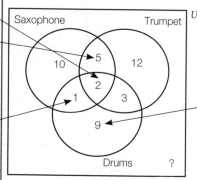

> 15 people play the drums but $1 + 2 + 3 = 6$ have already been included in the intersections with saxophone and trumpet, leaving 9. Do the same to get 10 in S only and 12 in T only.

There are 42 people in the band who play saxophone, trumpet or drums.

There are $50 - 42 = 8$ people who do not play any of these instruments.

Exercise 8.4

1. Use set notation to represent the shaded region in the following Venn diagrams:

(a)
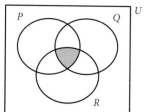

(b)
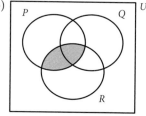

(c)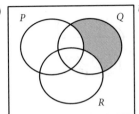

(d)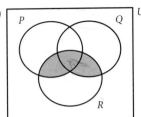

2. The universal set U is defined as $U = \{a, c, e, f, g, h, j, k\}$.

   B, T and S are subsets of U such that:

   $B = \{a, c, f, g\}$

   $T = \{c, e, g, h\}$

   $S = \{f, g, h, j\}$.

   The information from above is illustrated on the Venn diagram:

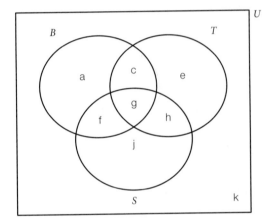

   From the Venn diagram, list the elements of each of the following regions:

   (a) $B \cap T \cap S$

   (b) $(B \cap T)'$

   (c) $(B \cap T)' \cap S$

   (d) $B \cap (T \cup S)$.

3. 60 teachers were asked which sports programmes they watched on TV during one evening after school.

   18 watched Athletics (A),

   27 watched Cricket (C),

   20 watched Soccer (S),

   3 watched all three sports programmes,

   1 watched Cricket and Soccer only,

   4 watched Athletics and Soccer only,

   5 watched Athletics and Cricket only.

(a) Draw a Venn diagram to illustrate the relationship between the sports programmes.

(b) On your diagram indicate the number of teachers belonging to each region.

(c) Determine the number of teachers who did not watch any of the three sports programmes mentioned above.

4. 72 students were asked which subject they revised over the weekend.

21 revised Mathematics (M) only,

8 revised French (F) only,

11 revised Physics (P) only,

2 revised all three subjects,

3 revised Mathematics and French,

5 revised French and Physics,

7 revised Mathematics and Physics.

(a) Represent the above information on a Venn diagram, indicating the number of students belonging to each region.

(b) How many students revised neither Mathematics nor French nor Physics?

You should know:

- the foundations of set theory including what is meant by elements, intersection, union, complement and subsets

- the different ways of expressing set theory: set notation, set language and Venn diagrams

Set notation	Set language	Meaning	Venn diagram
$A \cup B$	A union B.	Everything that is in either or both sets.	
$A \cap B$	A intersection B.	Everything that is in the overlap of both sets.	
A'	The complement of A.	Everything that is not in set A.	
$(A \cup B)'$	The complement of $(A \cup B)$.	Everything that is not in set A or set B.	
$A \cap B'$	The intersection of A and the complement of B.	The overlap between A and everything that is not in B.	
$A' \cup B$	The union of B with the complement of A.	Everything that is in B or not in A.	
$(A \cap B)'$	The complement of A intersection B.	Everything that is not in the overlap of A and B.	

- about Venn diagrams with simple applications and problems that can be solved by using them.

Mixed examination practice

Exam-style questions

1. The following data represents the results from a survey of students in the same tutor group:

   U = {students in tutor group}, $n(U) = 50$

   H = {History students}, G = {Geography students}

   $n(H) = 16$, $n(G) = 24$, $n(H \cap G) = 2$.

   (a) Explain in words what the region $(H \cup G)'$ represents.

   (b) State the value of $n(H \cap G)'$.

   (c) Draw a Venn diagram to represent the data from above, indicating the number of students in each region of the diagram.

2. A survey was carried out on 40 students about when they did their homework over the weekend. The results are shown below:

   F = {homework done on Friday night}

   S = {homework done on Saturday/Sunday}

   $n(F) = 20$, $n(S) = 29$.

   (a) State the value of $n(F \cap S)$.

   (b) What does $(F \cup S)'$ mean? Explain why $n(F \cup S)' = 0$.

   (c) Draw a Venn diagram to represent the data from above, indicating the number of students in each region of the diagram.

3. 100 Mathematics teachers who attended a conference were asked which programme of study they had taught in the last 18 months. Their responses are illustrated on the Venn diagram below:

   U = {Mathematics teachers at conference}

   A = {teachers who have taught on the Advanced Level programme}

   B = {teachers who have taught on the IB Diploma programme}

   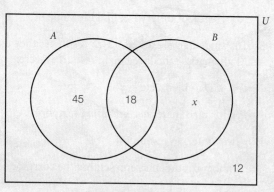

   (a) Describe the region denoted by x using:

       (i) words   (ii) set notation.

   (b) State the value of x.

   (c) Find: (i) $n((A \cap B)')$ (ii) $n((A \cup B)')$.

4. A survey which asked 120 people about what types of books and materials they read most recently in their local library provided the following results:

71 read fiction books (F),

54 read non-fiction books (N), including textbooks,

44 read reference books (R), including journals and newspapers,

20 read both fiction and reference,

8 read reference and non-fiction but not fiction,

15 read fiction and non-fiction but not reference,

x people read all three types of materials,

10 read none of the types of materials mentioned above.

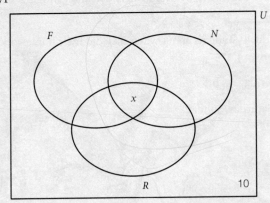

(a) Show that $n(F \cap R \cap N') = 20 - x$.

(b) Find, in terms of x, $n(N \cap R' \cap F')$.

(c) Complete the Venn diagram, indicating the number of people corresponding to each region.

(d) Hence, or otherwise, find the value of x.

5. 100 students were asked which resources they used during their revision for their final examination in Mathematics. The three main resources were:

$C = \{$CDs, videos, etc.$\}$

$P = \{$printed materials, including textbooks, etc.$\}$

$W = \{$web/internet resources$\}$

The number of students representing the corresponding regions are:

$n(P) = 51$ $n(C \cap W) = 13$

$n(W) = 32$ $n(C \cap P \cap W) = 6$

$n(C) = 63$ $n[(C \cup P)' \cap W] = 6$

$n(P \cap C) = 24$ $n(C \cup P \cup W)' = 4$

Complete the Venn diagram below using the information given above.

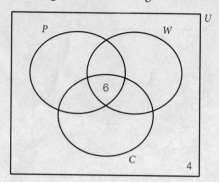

6. The principals of 180 colleges were asked where they advertised for teachers to fill vacant positions. Their responses are illustrated on the Venn diagram below, where:

L = {local newspapers}

N = {national newspapers}

W = {web/internet}

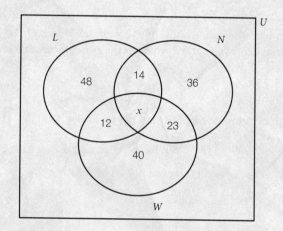

(a) Given that $n(L \cup N \cup W)' = 0$, determine the value of x.

(b) From the information in the Venn diagram, write down the number of principals who advertised:

(i) in both local newspapers and on the internet

(ii) in local newspapers and/or on the internet

(iii) in both national newspapers and on the internet but not in local newspapers

(iv) in local and/or national newspapers but not on the internet.

7. The following Venn diagram shows the number of students who study Biology (B), Chemistry (C) and Physics (P) in a college.

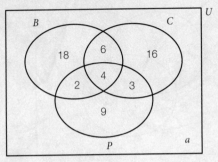

(a) Find:

    (i) $n(B \cap C \cap P)$ (ii) $n(C \cup P)$.

Given that $n(U) = 100$, find:

(b) the value of a

(c) $n(B')$.

8. The Mathematics Enrichment Club in a school runs sessions on Mondays (M), Wednesdays (W) and Fridays (F). A number of students were asked which of the enrichment sessions they had attended during the previous week.

8 students attended on Monday only,

6 students attended on Monday and Wednesday but not on Friday,

7 students attended on Monday and Friday but not on Wednesday,

3 students attended on Wednesday and Friday but not on Monday,

20 students did not attend any of the sessions.

(a) Illustrate the above information on a Venn diagram.

Given that:

25 students attended on Monday,

24 students attended on Wednesday,

35 students attended on Friday,

(b) find the number of students who attended all three sessions during the week

(c) find the total number of students in the group

(d) hence complete the Venn diagram from part (a).

9. 300 tourists were asked which attractions they had seen while in London.

Most of them had seen Buckingham Palace (*B*), Trafalgar Square (*T*) and Westminster Abbey (*W*).

25 people had seen all three attractions,

52 people had seen both Trafalgar Square and Westminster Abbey,

28 people had seen Buckingham Palace and Westminster Abbey but not Trafalgar Square,

88 people had seen exactly two of the three attractions,

211 people had seen Buckingham Palace or Trafalgar Square,

199 people had seen Trafalgar Square or Westminster Abbey,

49 people had seen other attractions, but none of the three places listed above.

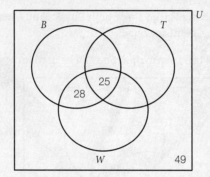

Use the information from above to complete the Venn diagram, indicating the number of people representing each of the regions.

10. 120 customers in a music shop were asked about the genre of music they had just bought from the shop. The three main genres were Classical (*C*), Folk (*F*) and Pop (*P*).

4 customers bought all three genres of music,

60 customers bought Pop or Folk music but not Classical,

59 customers bought Pop music,

30 customers bought at least two of the three genres of music,

7 customers bought Pop and Classical but not Folk music,

10 customers bought both Classical and Folk music,

25 customers bought none of these three genres of music.

Illustrate the information from above on a Venn diagram, indicating the number of customers for each region.

Past paper questions

1. At a certain school there are 90 students studying for their IB diploma. They are required to study at **least one** of the subjects: Physics, Biology or Chemistry.

   50 students are studying Physics,

   60 students are studying Biology,

   55 students are studying Chemistry,

   30 students are studying both Physics and Biology,

   10 students are studying both Biology and Chemistry but not Physics,

   20 students are studying all three subjects.

   Let x represent the number of students who study both Physics and Chemistry but not Biology. Then $25 - x$ is the number who study Chemistry only.

   The figure below shows some of this information and can be used for working.

   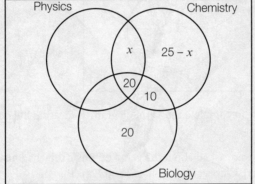

   (a) Express the number of students who study Physics only, in terms of x.

   (b) Find x.

   (c) Determine the number of students studying **at least two** of the subjects.

   [Total 6 marks]

   [May 2006, Paper 1, Question 13] (*© IB Organization 2006*)

2. A school offers three activities, basketball (B), choir (C) and drama (D). Every student must participate in at least one activity.

   16 students play basketball only,

   18 students play basketball and sing in the choir but do not do drama,

   34 students play basketball and do drama but do not sing in the choir,

   27 students are in the choir and do drama but do not play basketball,

(a) Enter the above information on the Venn diagram below.   *[2 marks]*

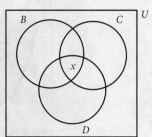

99 of the students play basketball, 88 sing in the choir and 110 do drama.

(b) Calculate the number of students x participating in all three activities.   *[1mark]*

(c) Calculate the total number of students in the school.   *[3 marks]*

[Total 6 marks]

[Nov 2007, Paper 1, Question 8] *(© IB Organization 2007)*

Chapter 9 Logic

In this chapter you will learn:

- about the principles of symbolic logic
- how propositions are defined and their notation
- about compound statements, their truth tables and Venn diagrams
- how to use truth tables to test arguments, and the concepts of logical equivalence, contradiction and tautology
- how converse, inverse and contrapositive statements are constructed.

William Jevons' logic piano.

The logic piano was built for William Jevons (1835–1882) and is now in the Museum of the History of Science in Oxford, England. It was designed to create **truth tables** for up to four **propositions** at a time. William Jevons' friend, John Venn, could see no practical use for it as he could think of no set of propositions that would need a mechanical device to interpret them. Nevertheless, Jevons used the logic piano in both his teaching and his personal studies.

But what is logic? What are truth tables? Logic is described as the science of thinking, of reasoning, and of proof. It should not be confused with the everyday meaning of 'logical thinking' that is commonly used by people to describe a sensible route of thinking, or 'common sense'; here it is a specific mathematical process. It is the careful study of the patterns of arguments, particularly those that start with a true **statement** and go on to a valid conclusion. Truth tables are diagrams that help to interpret and draw conclusions from the logical process.

The study of logic began centuries ago. In India, Medhatithi Gautama (*c.* 6th century BCE) developed logic for religious and philosophical arguments. In Greece, the philosopher Aristotle introduced the concept of syllogisms. In China, the Mohist school encouraged an interest in logic and the solving of logical puzzles.

This chapter is an introduction to Mathematical Logic, a topic in mathematics that is concerned with the study of formal reasoning and mathematical proof.

You will encounter logic in other fields. For example, it is part of the study of law, computing, language and politics.

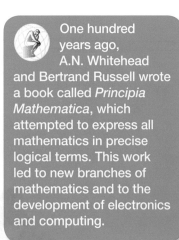

One hundred years ago, A.N. Whitehead and Bertrand Russell wrote a book called *Principia Mathematica*, which attempted to express all mathematics in precise logical terms. This work led to new branches of mathematics and to the development of electronics and computing.

9.1 Propositions

Mathematical logic is based on statements, which are also known as propositions.

A **proposition** is a statement that is either true (T) or false (F); it cannot be both true and false **at the same time**. For any proposition, it is the clarity of the statement that is important.

For instance, 'All men are mortal' and 'The flower is blue' are both clear statements, and therefore propositions.

A proposition cannot be a question, an instruction or an opinion.

For example:

'The sun is shining.'   is a statement and therefore a proposition.
'Is the sun shining?'   is a question and therefore not a proposition.
'How beautiful the sun is!'   is an opinion, not a proposition.
'Tell the sun to shine.'   is an instruction, not a proposition.

hint

In determining if a statement is a proposition, it does not matter if it is a 'true' or 'false' statement; for example:

'All men are mortal' is a proposition that is always true.

'This flower is blue' is a proposition that may be true or may be false.

'The Earth is flat' is a proposition, even though it is factually incorrect.

Worked example 9.1

Q. | Look at these statements and decide which ones are propositions.

Notice that mathematical statements can also be propositions.

(a) Do all cats have tails?

(a) No — This is a question.

(b) $7 > 4$

(b) Yes — This is a statement so it is a proposition.

(c) Logic is important.

(c) No — This is an opinion.

(d) Kuala Lumpur is the capital of Malaysia.

(d) Yes — This is a statement so it is a proposition.

(e) Can cows see in colour?

(e) No — This is a question.

(f) $4.8 \notin \mathbb{R}$

(f) Yes — This is a statement, so it is a proposition, even though it is false (4.8 is a real number).

$\longrightarrow$

continued . . .

(g) Mammals live on land.

(h) Our sun is a star.

(i) Write a letter.

(j) That was a good song.

(g) Yes
> This is a statement, so it is proposition, even though some mammals live in the sea.

(h) Yes
> This is a statement so it is a proposition.

(i) No
> This is an instruction.

(j) No
> This is an opinion.

Exercise 9.1

1. Consider the following statements and decide which ones are propositions. In the case of a proposition, indicate whether it is true or false.

   (a) A dollar is a unit of currency.

   (b) Come back home!

   (c) All square numbers are odd numbers.

   (d) There are 12 months in a year.

   (e) China is an Asian country.

   (f) Where is Anna?

   (g) iPods can store music.

   (h) Three little birds.

   (i) 2 is a prime number.

   (j) Is this what you are looking for?

Symbolic notation

Writing out propositions in full takes time and is often not very useful. It is easier to assign each proposition a letter, and give a single definition of that letter. The usual letters used are p, q, r, s.

For example, the proposition 'all cats have tails' can be defined by writing:

p: All cats have tails.

Similarly,

q: 4.8 is a real number.

r: Our sun is a star.

There are many other symbols in symbolic notation that are used to show the relationship between multiple propositions; you will be introduced to these as you progress through the chapter.

Negation

Negation is the opposite of the original proposition, and means 'not'. The symbol for 'not' is ¬. (Note that there are other symbols for 'not': ~ *p*, *p*′ or $\bar{p}$; you might recognise ′ from set notation.)

So, for the proposition *p*: It is raining,

the negation is ¬*p*: It is not raining.

¬(¬*p*): It is not not raining. This means the same as 'it is raining'.

You can also think of negation in terms of diagrams. The Venn diagram below shows you that everything that is false is not true. The truth table gives you another visual picture. Truth tables list each statement in symbolic notation at the top of a column in the table, and indicate if they are true (T) or false (F) in each cell of the table.

 You learned about Venn diagrams in Chapter 8.

 Truth tables are covered in more depth in section 9.4, page 268

not *p*

p	¬*p*	¬(¬*p*)
T	F	T
F	T	F

From the truth table you can see that:

if *p* is true, ¬*p* is not true (so it is false) and therefore 'not not *p*' is true;

if *p* is false, ¬*p* is true (because it is the opposite) and therefore 'not not *p*' is false.

9.2 Compound statements

Propositions can be connected to form **compound statements**.

Take the following propositions:

- It is raining.
- I have my umbrella.
- It is sunny.

You could say:

- It is raining **and** I have my umbrella.
- It is raining **or** it is sunny.
- It is **not** raining **and** it is sunny.
- It is raining **or** it is sunny, **but not both**.

Each of these is a compound statement that uses different words to connect the two propositions and produces a statement with a different meaning from the original propositions.

Notice that the key words that connect each proposition are: 'and', 'or', 'not', 'or … but not both'.

If the original proposition is a compound statement, the resulting **negation** ($\neg$) is not considered a compound statement. However, the negation is still an important part of many compound statements.

Conjunction, disjunction and exclusive disjunction

Conjunction, disjunction and exclusive disjunction are the technical terms for the words that connect two propositions to make a compound statement. They look complicated but the ideas they express are simple and you are already familiar with them from set theory. Each term has a symbol called a **connective** that allows you to write the whole statement.

For the following explanations of each connective, we have used a truth table and a Venn diagram to demonstrate their meaning. The truth tables illustrate the different combinations that are possible in each situation.

This use of Venn diagrams in a different context shows how powerful they are and how clearly they can illustrate ideas.

Conjunction

When two propositions are connected by the word 'and', the compound statement is called a **conjunction**. The logic symbol for 'and' is '$\wedge$'.

For the propositions p: It is raining

q: I have my umbrella

the compound statement 'It is raining and I have my umbrella' becomes $p \wedge q$.

p can be either true (T) or false (F).

q can be either true or false.

This means there are four possible combinations that could occur with the propositions p and q (note that only one can occur at any one time):

- both propositions are true: p is true, and q is true   (1)
- both propositions are false: p is false, and q is false   (2)
- one proposition is true and
  the other false: p is true, and q is false   (3)
                                   p is false, and q is true.   (4)

The four different situations can be illustrated much more easily using a truth table or a Venn diagram, which allow you to see under what circumstances $p \wedge q$ is true. If you start with T, T, F, F in the column 'p', then you can complete the rest of the columns accordingly.

p	q	$p \wedge q$
T	T	T
T	F	F
F	T	F
F	F	F

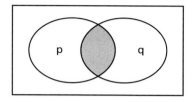

You can see from the truth table and the Venn diagram that for $p \wedge q$ to be true, **both** p and q must be true. If either p or q, or both, are false, then the whole combined proposition is false.

It might help you to recognise that a conjunction in logic is similar to an intersection in set theory. If you compare the Venn diagram for a **conjunction** with the Venn diagram for the **intersection** of two sets you will see that they look the same.

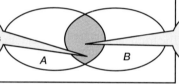

In logic, if A is the statement 'it is raining' and B is the statement 'I have my umbrella' then the shaded region represents the conjunction statement 'It is raining and I have my umbrella': $A \cap B$

In set theory, if A is the set 'it is raining' and B is the set 'I have my umbrella' then the shaded region is the intersection of A and B, 'It is raining and I have my umbrella': $A \cap B$

 You learned about intersection in set theory in Chapter 8.

In set theory, $A \cap B$ means 'the intersection of A and B' or 'A and B'.

In logic, $p \wedge q$ means 'p and q'.

Disjunction

When two propositions are connected by the word 'or', the compound statement is called a **disjunction**. The logic symbol for 'or' is '$\vee$'. A compound statement with a disjunction is true when either one, or both, of the propositions are true.

For the propositions p: It is raining

                           q: It is sunny

the compound statement 'It is raining or it is sunny' becomes $p \vee r$.

Both the truth table and the Venn diagram below show that for $p \vee q$ to be true, either p or q must be true. $p \vee q$ is only false if **both** p and q are false.

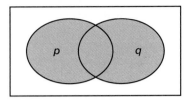

p	r	$p \vee r$
T	T	T
T	F	T
F	T	T
F	F	F

Again, it might help you to recognise that a disjunction in logic is similar to a union in set theory. In set theory, $A \cup B$ means 'the union of A and B' or 'A or B'. In logic, $p \vee q$ means 'p or q'.

Exclusive disjunction

When two propositions are connected by the phrase 'or, but not both', the compound statement is called an **exclusive disjunction**. The logic symbol for 'or, but not both' is '$\veebar$'.

For the propositions p: It is raining

                    r: It is sunny

the compound statement 'It is raining or it is sunny, but not both' becomes $p \veebar r$.

The truth table and Venn diagram below show that for $p \veebar r$ to be true, **either** p is true **or** r is true, but p and r should **not both** be true.

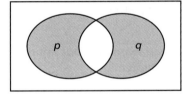

p	r	$p \veebar r$
T	T	F
T	F	T
F	T	T
F	F	F

Summary

Compound statement	Symbol	What it means	When it is true
Negation	$\neg p$	not p	True when p is false.
Conjunction	$p \wedge q$	p and q	True when both p and q are true.
Disjunction	$p \vee q$	p or q	True when either p or q, or both p and q, are true.
Exclusive disjunction	$p \veebar q$	p or q, but not both	True when either p or q is true, but not both.

So far we have explained compound statements where each of the propositions consists of words. However, compound statements can be created from propositions that use numbers as well as from those that use words. You should be able to work with both kinds. You also need to be able to interpret a proposition from symbolic notation into words, and from words into symbolic notation.

Q. p: x is a square number

q: $x > 4$

(a) Express these compound statements in symbols:

   (i) x is not a square number

   (ii) x is a square number and x is greater than 4

   (iii) x is a square number or x is greater than 4, but not both

(b) Express these compound statements in words:

   (i) $p \vee q$ (ii) $\neg p \wedge \neg q$ (iii) $\neg p \veebar q$

'x is not a square number' is the opposite of the proposition p, so it is the negation of p.

A. (a) (i) $\neg p$

The connective in the compound statement is 'and', which means this is a conjunction.

   (ii) $p \wedge q$

The connective in the compound statements is 'or, but not both', which means this is an exclusive disjunction.

   (iii) $p \veebar q$

$\vee$ is the symbolic notation for disjunction, which means 'or'.

(b) (i) x is a square number or x is greater than 4.

$\neg p$ indicates that it is the negation of p, the opposite, which is that x is not a square number; $\wedge$ indicates a conjunction 'and'; and $\neg q$ indicates that it is the negation of q, which is x is not greater than 4. Put it all together.

Be careful – the opposite of $x > 4$ is **not** simply $x < 4$; if x is not greater than 4 it could be equal to 4, or less than 4. The true opposite of $x > 4$ is 'x is not greater than 4'.

   (ii) x is not a square number and x is not greater than 4.

$\neg p$ indicates that x is not a square number; $\veebar$ is the symbolic notation for exclusive disjunction, which means 'or, but not both'; q is $x > 4$. Put it all together; the 'but not both' comes at the end of the statement whilst the connective 'or' goes between the two propositions.

   (iii) x is not a square number or x is greater than 4, but not both.

Exercise 9.2

1. The propositions p, q, and r are defined as follows:

   p: Ken plays tennis.

   q: The sun is shining.

   r: It is hot.

   Write these sentences in symbolic notation:

   (a) Ken does not play tennis.

   (b) It is hot, or Ken plays tennis, but not both.

   (c) The sun is shining and it is hot.

   (d) It is not hot and the sun is shining.

2. The propositions p, q and r are defined as follows:

   p: x is a prime number.

   q: $x < 100$.

   r: x is a 2-digit number.

   Write in words the following statements:

   (a) $\neg p$ (b) $p \wedge q$ (c) $\neg p \vee r$

   (d) $\neg p \vee \neg r$ (e) $\neg(p \wedge q)$

3. Three logic propositions are given below.

   p: Jenny hates football.

   q: Jenny watches Sky Sports.

   r: Jenny watches the Comedy Channel.

   Write the following symbolic statements in words:

   (a) $p \wedge \neg q$ (b) $\neg p \wedge q$ (c) $q \veebar r$

4. Propositions p, q and r are defined as follows:

   p: Simon is good at Mathematics.

   q: Simon does homework regularly.

   r: Simon has passed his Mathematics test.

   Write symbolic statements for the following sentences:

   (a) Simon does his homework regularly and he is good at Mathematics.

(b) Simon does not do homework regularly and has failed his Mathematics test.

(c) Either Simon is not good at Mathematics or he does not do homework regularly.

(d) Simon is not good at Mathematics and he has failed his Mathematics test.

9.3 Implication and equivalence

Implication and equivalence create compound statements where one proposition leads into another.

Implication

When two propositions are connected by the words 'If…, then…' the compound statement is called an **implication**. The logic symbol for 'if…, then…' is '$\Rightarrow$'.

For example, consider the propositions:

p: You play my favourite music.

q: I buy you a soda.

The compound statement, '**If** you play my favourite music **then** I buy you a soda', becomes: $p \Rightarrow q$

p is called the antecedent and q is called the consequent.

exam tip

It is important to use the words 'If…, then…' and not 'therefore'. 'It is raining therefore I have my umbrella' is not the same as 'If it is raining, then I have my umbrella'. 'Therefore' suggests a different relationship between the rain and the umbrella.

The truth table shows that $p \Rightarrow q$ is always true unless p is true and q is false.

In general, an implication is only false if the first proposition is true and the second proposition is false.

If the first implication is false, then the truth of the second is not relevant; it can be true or false, and the overall implication statement is true.

p	q	$p \Rightarrow q$
T	T	T
T	F	F
F	T	T
F	F	T

Another way to understand the argument is to think it through as shown below; an argument that involves a promise will help you to remember.

p	q	What does this mean in words?	What is the truth of the implication $p \Rightarrow q$?
T	T	If you play my favourite music, then I buy you a soda.	True. You play my favourite music and I buy you a soda.
T	F	If you play my favourite music, then I do not buy you a soda.	False. You play my favourite music but I do not buy you a soda. According to the implication statement, q cannot be false if p is true, so the overall statement is false.
F	T	If you do not play my favourite music, then I buy you a soda.	True. You do not play my favourite music but I can still buy you a soda. The second statement is not relevant because the first is false; q could still be true even if p is false so the original implication statement is still true.
F	T	If you do not play my favourite music, then I do not buy you a soda.	True. You do not play my favourite music so I do not buy you a soda. Again the truth of the second statement is not relevant because the first statement is false; q could be true or false if p is false, so the implication statement '$p \Rightarrow q$' is still true.

Equivalence

When two propositions are connected by the words 'If and only if...' the compound statement is called an **equivalence**. The logic symbol for 'if and only if' is the double headed arrow '$\Leftrightarrow$'.

When two propositions p and q are such that $p \Rightarrow q$ (if p then q) and $q \Rightarrow p$ (if q then p), the propositions are said to be equivalent.

For example, consider the propositions:

  p: Ella passes her exams.

  q: Her mother cooks her favourite meal.

$p \Rightarrow q$ says that if Ella passes her exams then her mother cooks her favourite meal.

$q \Rightarrow p$ says that if her mother cooks her favourite meal then Ella passes her exams.

The two statements can be put together, and the compound statement becomes:

$p \Leftrightarrow q$: 'If and only if Ella passes her exams her mother cooks her favourite meal.'

$q \Leftrightarrow p$: 'If and only if her mother cooks her favourite meal, Ella passes her exams'.

p	q	$p \Leftrightarrow q$
T	T	T
T	F	F
F	T	F
F	F	T

Equivalence is only true if the first proposition implies the second and the second implies the first. In other words, an equivalence is only true if both p and q are true or both p and q are false.

Worked example 9.3

Q. Consider the following logic statements:

p: x is a square number.

q: $x > 0$.

Write the following logic statements in words:

(a) $p \Rightarrow \neg q$ (b) $\neg p \Rightarrow \neg q$ (c) $\neg p \Leftrightarrow q$.

A. (a) If x is a square number, then x is not greater than zero.

(b) If x is a not a square number, then x is not greater than zero.

(c) If and only if x is a not a square number, x is greater than zero.

Summary

Compound statement	Symbolic notation	What it means	When it is true
Implication	$p \Rightarrow q$	'If…, then…'	True unless p is true and q is false.
Equivalence	$p \Leftrightarrow q$	'If and only if…'	True when both p and q are true or both p and q are false.

Exercise 9.3

1. Three logic propositions are defined as follows:

p: Veejay revises for his test.

q: Veejay attends football training.

r: Veejay passes his test.

Write in words the following symbolic statements:

(a) $q \veebar r$ (b) $p \wedge \neg q$ (c) $\neg p \wedge q$

(d) $p \Rightarrow \neg q$ (e) $p \Rightarrow r$ (f) $\neg p \Rightarrow \neg r$.

2. Consider the following logic statements:

p: The weather is cloudy.

q: I will ride my bike into town.

r: I will take my umbrella.

Write the following in symbolic notation:

(a) If the weather is cloudy, then I will take my umbrella.

(b) If I ride my bike into town, then I will not take my umbrella.

(c) If I do not ride my bike into town, then it is cloudy.

3. Suppose *p* represents 'a triangle is isosceles' and *q* represents 'a triangle has two equal sides.' Write the following statements using symbolic notation:

(a) If a triangle is isosceles then it has two equal sides.

(b) If a triangle does not have two equal sides, then it is not isosceles.

(c) A triangle is isosceles if and only if it has two equal sides.

4. Let *p* represent: *x* is a quadrilateral.

Let *q* represent: *x* is 2-D shape which has a pair of parallel sides.

Let *r* represent: *x* is a parallelogram.

Write in words the following symbolic statements and indicate whether they are true or false:

(a) $(p \wedge q) \Rightarrow r$ (b) $r \Rightarrow p$

(c) $r \Rightarrow q$ (d) $(p \wedge q) \Leftrightarrow r$

9.4 Using truth tables

As you have seen, a truth table helps you to consider every possible outcome for any logical statement. The short truth tables that we have used as diagrams to explain and illustrate the connectives between two propositions can be expanded to illustrate a logical argument and to test its truth.

p	*q*	¬*p*	*p* ∧ *q*	*p* ∨ *q*	*p* ⊻ *q*	*p* ⇒ *q*	*p* ⇔ *q*
T	T	F	T	T	F	T	T
T	F	F	F	T	T	F	F
F	T	T	F	T	T	T	F
F	F	T	F	F	F	T	T

The tables look complicated, but if you work carefully and use the basic rules column by column, you should be able to build them with confidence.

Tables for two propositions

If there are two propositions then there are only four possible combinations of the two propositions, and the first two columns of the truth table are always the same:

- both propositions are true: p is true, and q is true (1)
- both propositions are false: p is false, and q is false (2)
- one proposition is true and the other false: p is true, and q is false (3)
  p is false, and q is true. (4)

p	q
T	T
T	F
F	T
F	F

If you write this in the columns as shown above, it makes the rest of a larger table easier to construct. Extra columns can be added for each part of the argument, with the last column used for the final summary.

The following examples show you how to build up the truth tables that you have already met for two propositions, and how to use them to test logical statements. For example, is the statement 'if I revise for my test, then I will go and play football' the same as the statement 'if I go and play football, then I will revise for my test'? In logic terms, is $p \Rightarrow q$ the same statement as $q \Rightarrow p$?

 You will learn more about logical equivalence in section 9.5.

Here is a reminder of the connectives you have met so far:

Compound statement	Symbolic notation	What it means	When it is true
Negation	$\neg p$	not p	True when p is false.
Conjunction	$p \wedge q$	p and q	True when both p and q are true.
Disjunction	$p \vee q$	p or q	True when either p or q or both p and q are true.
Exclusive disjunction	$p \veebar q$	p or q, but not both	True when either p or q is true, but not both.
Implication	$p \Rightarrow q$	'If…, then…'	True unless p is true and q is false.
Equivalence	$p \Leftrightarrow q$	'If and only if…'	True when both p and q are true or both p and q are false.

*Testing if **p** ⇒ **q** is logically equivalent to **q** ⇒ **p***

You may think that $p \Rightarrow q$ is exactly the same as, or logically equivalent to, $q \Rightarrow p$. You can check using truth tables. Create a truth table for $p \Rightarrow q$; this will have the columns p, q, and $p \Rightarrow q$. Create a truth table for $q \Rightarrow p$; this will have the columns q, p, and $q \Rightarrow p$.

Start both tables with the four possible combinations of p and q shown on page 269, and then work out the truth of the statement in the third column. We have already worked through the table for $p \Rightarrow q$ in the section on implication statements. Let's work through the truth table for $q \Rightarrow p$:

> Fill in the first two columns as per the general table for two propositions on page 269.

p	q	$q \Rightarrow p$
T	T	T
T	F	T
F	T	F
F	F	T

> If q is true and p is true, then $q \Rightarrow p$ is true.

> If q is false, then the truth of p is not relevant and $q \Rightarrow p$ is true. This also applies to the last row.

> If q is true then p cannot be false; so $q \Rightarrow p$ is false.

hint

For $q \Rightarrow p$ consider the first term to be the second term, i.e. in this case q acts like a p and q acts like a p.

p	q	$p \Rightarrow q$
T	T	T
T	F	F
F	T	T
F	F	T

p	q	$q \Rightarrow p$
T	T	T
T	F	T
F	T	F
F	F	T

Look at the final columns in the two tables. They are not the same, so $p \Rightarrow q$ and $q \Rightarrow p$ are not logically equivalent.

Testing if $\neg(p \wedge q)$ is logically equivalent to $\neg p \wedge \neg q$

Logical statements can look as though they should follow the usual rules of algebra, especially if they contain brackets. But this is not necessarily the case.

Take the following statements:

is $\neg(p \wedge q)$ logically equivalent to $\neg p \wedge \neg q$?

If we followed the usual rules of algebra we would expect these statements to be equivalent as they both 'read' as 'not p and not q'. Let's use truth tables to check if they are **logically** equivalent.

Set up two truth tables, one for $\neg(p \wedge q)$ and one for $\neg p \wedge \neg q$. Start with the set columns for p and then q in both tables. For the $\neg(p \wedge q)$ table add the column '$p \wedge q$'. For the $\neg p \wedge \neg q$ table, $\neg p$ and $\neg q$ each have their own column. End each table with the overall statement.

> $p \wedge q$ is only true when both p and q are true; $\neg(p \wedge q)$ is only true when $p \wedge q$ is false.

p	q	$p \wedge q$	$\neg(p \wedge q)$
T	T	T	F
T	F	F	T
F	T	F	T
F	F	F	T

p	q	$\neg p$	$\neg q$	$\neg p \wedge \neg q$
T	T	F	F	F
T	F	F	T	F
F	T	T	F	F
F	F	T	T	T

> $\neg p \wedge \neg q$ is only true when p and q are false.

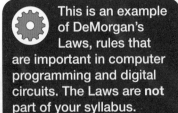

This is an example of DeMorgan's Laws, rules that are important in computer programming and digital circuits. The Laws are **not** part of your syllabus.

Look at the final columns. They are not the same, so the two statements are not logically equivalent.

Testing if $\neg(p \wedge q)$ is logically equivalent to $\neg p \vee \neg q$

We can use truth tables to show that $\neg(p \wedge q)$ is exactly the same as, or logically equivalent to, $\neg p \vee \neg q$.

p	q	$p \wedge q$	$\neg(p \wedge q)$
T	T	T	F
T	F	F	T
F	T	F	T
F	F	F	T

p	q	$\neg p$	$\neg q$	$\neg p \vee \neg q$
T	T	F	F	F
T	F	F	T	T
F	T	T	F	T
F	F	T	T	T

Look at the final columns. They are the same, so the two statements are logically equivalent:

$$\neg(p \wedge q) \equiv \neg p \vee \neg q$$

Exercise 9.4

1. Two propositions p and q are defined as follows:

   p: Donald passed his driving test.

   q: Debbie passed her driving test.

   (a) Write in symbolic form:

   (i) Both Donald and Debbie passed their driving tests.

   (ii) Both Donald and Debbie did not pass their driving tests.

   (b) Write the following statement in words: $\neg p \vee q$.

   (c) Copy and complete the following truth table for the logic statement $\neg p \vee q$.

p	q	$\neg p$	$\neg p \vee q$
T	T		
T	F		
F	T		
F	F		

2. Consider the statements:

   p: Arsenal defends well.

   q: Arsenal will win the match.

   (a) Write the following propositions using symbolic notation:

   (i) If Arsenal does not defend well they will not win the match.

   (ii) Arsenal will win the match if and only if they defend well.

(b) Copy and complete the truth table, using the information from the statement made in part (a) (i).

p	q	$\neg p$	$\neg q$	$\neg p \Rightarrow \neg q$
T	T			
T	F			
F	T			
F	F			

Tables for three propositions

The basic table is:

p	q	r
T	T	T
T	T	F
T	F	T
T	F	F
F	T	T
F	T	F
F	F	T
F	F	F

If you are using three propositions, then the possible combinations of the propositions increases from four to eight. The truth table needs to be set up so that all eight possible combinations are included. Recall that the usual letters to denote propositions are p, q, r, s; here we have used r to denote the third proposition.

If you always start with the same three columns and build the argument stage by stage, the tables are straightforward. Look at the pattern of T and F in the columns.

This table can now be used to construct the truth table for a compound statement involving three propositions, and to test whether the argument is true in every situation.

Is $p \wedge \neg q \Rightarrow r$ always true?

Add an extra column for $\neg q$, then one for $p \wedge \neg q$, and a final column for the whole statement. Work down each column row by row.

p	q	r	$\neg q$	$p \wedge \neg q$	$p \wedge \neg q \Rightarrow r$
T	T	T	F	F	T
T	T	F	F	F	T
T	F	T	T	T	T
T	F	F	T	T	F
F	T	T	F	F	T
F	T	F	F	F	T
F	F	T	T	F	T
F	F	F	T	F	T

> Remember that if the truth of the first statement is false then the truth of the second statement is irrelevant and the implication statement is true.

> '$p \wedge \neg q \Rightarrow r$' cannot be true if '$r$' is false, so the final statement is false.

The final column consists mainly of 'true' but there is also a 'false', so this argument is not true in **all** situations.

You can also use the truth tables to construct arguments when you are given the propositions in full.

Worked example 9.4

Q. p: It is cold.

q: The ice is thick.

r: I will go skating.

Use a truth table to test the statement, 'if and only if it is cold and the ice is thick, then I will go skating'.

'It is cold and the ice is thick' is written $(p \wedge q)$.

'If and only if it is cold and the ice is thick, then I will go skating' is written $(p \wedge q) \Leftrightarrow r$.

A.

p	q	r	$p \wedge q$	$p \wedge q \Leftrightarrow r$
T	T	T	T	T
T	T	F	T	F
T	F	T	F	F
T	F	F	F	T
F	T	T	F	F
F	T	F	F	T
F	F	T	F	F
F	F	F	F	T

Set up the first three columns as per the basic truth table for three propositions on page 272.

$(p \wedge q) \Leftrightarrow r$ is not a valid argument. The final column of the truth table contains both true and false conclusions. If an argument is valid the entries in the final column must all be true.

Exercise 9.5

1. For an IB Revision Course students have three choices:

   e: Economics

   m: Mathematics

   s: a Science subject.

   Students choose two subjects which **must** include Mathematics and either Economics or a Science subject, but not both.

   (a) Write the sentence above, using symbolic notation.

   (b) Write in words $\neg s \Rightarrow e$.

   (c) Complete the truth table.

e	s	$\neg e$	$\neg e \Rightarrow s$
T	T		
T	F		
F	T		
F	F		

exam tip

Questions using three propositions may be set with some of the columns partly filled in. You can use the short truth tables in your Formula booklet to help you complete them.

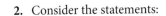

2. Consider the statements:

   p: It is the weekend.

   q: I will go to the cinema.

   (a) Write down, in words, the meaning of $q \Rightarrow \neg p$.

   (b) Complete the truth table.

p	*q*	$\neg p$	$q \Rightarrow \neg p$
T	T		
T	F		
F	T		
F	F		

3. Three propositions are defined as:

   p: The exam paper was easy.

   q: The grade boundaries were low.

   r: Joe performed well in the exam.

   Samantha says, 'If Joe performed well in the exam then either the exam paper was easy or the grade boundaries were low.'

   Complete the truth table for Samantha's statement and comment on the logical validity of the statement.

p	*q*	*r*	$p \veebar q$	$r \Rightarrow (p \veebar q)$
T	T	T		
T	T	F		
T	F	T		
T	F	F		
F	T	T		
F	T	F		
F	F	T		
F	F	F		

4. Let *p* represent: Boris is a rugby player, let *q* represent: Boris has the rugby ball and let *r* represent: Boris has a football.

   (a) Write the following using symbolic notation:

   (i) If Boris is a rugby player then he has the rugby ball.

   (ii) Boris has the rugby ball and he has not got a football.

   (iii) If Boris is not a rugby player then he has a football.

   (b) Write the following argument in words:

   $$\neg r \Rightarrow (p \vee q)$$

(c) Construct a truth table for the argument in part (b) using the values below for p, q, r and $\neg r$.

p	q	r	$\neg r$	$p \vee q$	$\neg r \Rightarrow (p \vee q)$
T	T	T	F		
T	T	F	T		
T	F	T	F		
T	F	F	T		
F	T	T	F		
F	T	F	T		
F	F	T	F		
F	F	F	T		

9.5 Logical equivalence, tautology and contradiction

Logical equivalence, **tautology** and **contradiction** are all tested using truth tables. In each case it is the final column of the table that is the most important as it will give you the result.

If you are testing two compound statements for **logical equivalence**, you are looking to see whether they are interchangeable. The statements may be in words or symbols but if one is true, so is the other. If one is false, then the other statement is false too.

A logical **tautology** is always true and is never shown to be false, even if the initial propositions are false.

A logical **contradiction** is never true and cannot be shown to be true.

Logical equivalence

You have already seen some examples of testing the logical equivalence of two statements by using two truth tables, one for each statement. It is best to concentrate on completing each table separately; if they are logically equivalent then the final column of both truth tables will be exactly the same. Some of the results may surprise you but if you think about a likely result and check your tables carefully, you will see that it is correct.

Not all the logic questions set in assignments or examinations use words; they may also be set as propositions that are not defined. Problems like this can be easier to work through than questions using words, as you do not have to think about whether the statements you are testing are true in a practical way and whether or not you agree with them.

hint

Do not get confused between the terms 'equivalence' and 'logically equivalent/logical equivalence'.

'Equivalence' is **one compound statement** connected by the symbol $\Leftrightarrow$ or by the words 'if and only if…'.

Logically equivalent is when **two compound statements** are exactly the same.

Worked example 9.5

Q. Is $(p \Rightarrow q)$ logically equivalent to $(\neg p \vee q)$?

A.

p	q	$p \Rightarrow q$
T	T	T
T	F	F
F	T	T
F	F	T

p	q	$\neg p$	$(\neg p \vee q)$
T	T	F	T
T	F	F	F
F	T	T	T
F	F	T	T

> Create two truth tables. One for $p \Rightarrow q$ and one for $(\neg p \vee q)$. Compare the final columns of the two tables.

The final columns are exactly the same, so the statements are logically equivalent:

$$(p \Rightarrow q) \equiv (\neg p \vee q)$$

Logical tautology

If a compound statement is always true, it is called a **tautology**. In this case all the values in the final column will be true. Some of the results may seem to be obvious but are worth looking at to help your understanding; others do not seem so obvious.

The first example is set using words, but the second is an illustration using the connections established in earlier sections of this chapter.

Worked example 9.6

Q. If q: swans are white

and

$\neg q$: swans are not white

show that $(q \vee \neg q)$ is a tautology.

A.

q	$\neg q$	$q \vee \neg q$
T	F	T
F	T	T

If q: swans are white

$\neg q$: swans are not white

then $(q \vee \neg q)$ tells you that all swans are white or not white – it is a tautology.

This truth table looks very complex. But if you use the techniques you learned for constructing tables with two propositions and then complete it column by column, you will see that it is straightforward. Make sure that you have a separate column for each part of the statement.

Q. Show that $\{(p \wedge q) \Rightarrow r\} \Leftrightarrow \{p \Rightarrow (q \Rightarrow r)\}$ is a tautology.

A.

p	q	r	$p \wedge q$	$(p \wedge q) \Rightarrow r$	$q \Rightarrow r$	$p \Rightarrow (q \Rightarrow r)$	$\{(p \wedge q) \Rightarrow r\} \Leftrightarrow \{p \Rightarrow (q \Rightarrow r)\}$
T	T	T	T	T	T	T	T
T	T	F	T	F	F	F	T
T	F	T	F	T	T	T	T
T	F	F	F	T	T	T	T
F	T	T	F	T	T	T	T
F	T	F	F	T	F	T	T
F	F	T	F	T	T	T	T
F	F	F	F	T	T	T	T

Use '$p \wedge q$' and '$(p \wedge q) \Rightarrow r$' for the first part of the argument; use '$q \Rightarrow r$' and '$p \Rightarrow (q \Rightarrow r)$' for the second part and '$\{(p \wedge q) \Rightarrow r\} \Leftrightarrow \{p \Rightarrow (q \Rightarrow r)\}$' for the complete statement.

Logical contradiction

This is the reverse of tautology. If a compound statement is always false, it is called a **contradiction**. When you complete the truth table all the results in the final column are false. As before, some of the results might appear to be obvious while others might be surprising.

Worked example 9.8

Q. If q: swans are white

$\neg q$: swans are not white

(a) show that $(q \wedge \neg q)$ is a contradiction.

A. (a)

q	$\neg q$	$q \wedge \neg q$
T	F	F
F	T	F

If q: swans are white

$\neg q$: swans are not white

then $(q \wedge \neg q)$ tells you that all swans are white and not white – it is a contradiction.

(b) Use a truth table to show that $(p \vee q) \wedge (\neg p \wedge \neg q)$ is a contradiction.

A. (b)

p	q	$\neg p$	$\neg q$	$p \vee q$	$\neg p \wedge \neg q$	$(p \vee q) \wedge (\neg p \wedge \neg q)$
T	T	F	F	T	F	F
T	F	F	T	T	F	F
F	T	T	F	T	F	F
F	F	T	T	F	T	F

The final column of the truth table contains only false conclusions, therefore the statement $(p \vee q) \wedge (\neg p \wedge \neg q)$ is a contradiction.

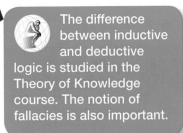

The difference between inductive and deductive logic is studied in the Theory of Knowledge course. The notion of fallacies is also important.

The study of logic helps when you are preparing presentations and essays. Theory of Knowledge essays are 1600 words long, so a logical structure will help you to organise the ideas you need together.

1. Consider the statements:

   p: Oliver likes horse riding.

   q: Ulrika likes skiing.

   For each of the symbolic statements, (a) to (e):

   (i) construct the corresponding truth table

   (ii) indicate whether the statement is a tautology, a contradiction, or neither.

   (a) $\neg(p \wedge \neg q)$

   (b) $p \vee \neg(p \wedge q)$

   (c) $(p \Rightarrow q) \wedge (\neg p \wedge q)$

   (d) $\neg(p \Rightarrow q) \Leftrightarrow (\neg p \vee q)$

   (e) $p \wedge (\neg q \wedge p)$

2. Three propositions are defined as follows:

   p: The bad weather continues.

   q: This week's cricket match will be cancelled.

   r: I will watch football.

   (a) Write in words the symbolic statements:

   (i) $\neg p \vee q$

   (ii) $\neg p \wedge \neg q$

   (iii) $\neg q \Leftrightarrow \neg p$

   (iv) $(p \wedge q) \veebar (q \wedge \neg p)$.

   (b) Construct truth tables for each pair of statements and indicate whether or not they are logically equivalent.

   (i) $p \Rightarrow q$ and $\neg p \vee q$

   (ii) $(p \wedge q) \wedge r$ and $p \wedge (q \wedge r)$

   (iii) $p \Leftrightarrow q$ and $(p \wedge q) \vee (\neg p \wedge \neg q)$

   (iv) $(p \Rightarrow q) \Rightarrow r$ and $p \Rightarrow (q \Rightarrow r)$

3. The two propositions p and q are defined as follows:

p: The internet is not working.

q: I check my emails.

(a) Write in words the following statements:

  (i) $p \Rightarrow \neg q$

  (ii) $\neg p \Rightarrow q$.

(b) Construct a truth table for the compound proposition given below.
   $(p \Rightarrow \neg q) \vee (\neg p \Rightarrow q)$

(c) Using your table from part (b) state whether the statement is a contradiction, a tautology, or neither.

9.6 Converse, inverse and contrapositive

The implication $p \Rightarrow q$ has three closely related statements: the **converse**, the **inverse** and the **contrapositive**.

If $p \Rightarrow q$, then $q \Rightarrow p$ is the converse

  $\neg p \Rightarrow \neg q$ is the inverse

  $\neg q \Rightarrow \neg p$ is the contrapositive.

Converse

To form the **converse** of the statement $p \Rightarrow q$, you **convert** p to q and q to p.

Take the propositions:

  p: Poppa eats spinach.

  q: Poppa is strong.

$p \Rightarrow q$ gives the statement, 'If Poppa eats spinach then Poppa is strong'.

$q \Rightarrow p$ gives the statement, 'If Poppa is strong then Poppa eats spinach'.

If $p \Rightarrow q$ is true, then $q \Rightarrow p$ is only true when both p and q are true, both p and q are false, or p is true and q is false. It is not true in every case.

p	q	$p \Rightarrow q$	$q \Rightarrow p$
T	T	T	T
T	F	F	T
F	T	T	F
F	F	T	T

hint

You might find it helpful to remind yourself of the truth table for implication in section 9.3.

Inverse

To form the **inverse** of the statement $p \Rightarrow q$, you **invert** p to its negative $\neg p$ and invert q to its negative $\neg q$.

Using the propositions:

    p: Poppa eats spinach.

    q: Poppa is strong.

$p \Rightarrow q$ gives the statement, 'If Poppa eats spinach then Poppa is strong'.

$\neg p \Rightarrow \neg q$ gives the statement, 'If Poppa does not eat spinach then Poppa is not strong'.

If $p \Rightarrow q$ is true, then $\neg p \Rightarrow \neg q$ is only true when both *p* and *q* are true, both *p* and *q* are false, or *p* is true and *q* is false. It is not true in every case.

p	*q*	$\neg p$	$\neg q$	$p \Rightarrow q$	$\neg p \Rightarrow \neg q$
T	T	F	F	T	T
T	F	F	T	F	T
F	T	T	F	T	F
F	F	T	T	T	T

Contrapositive

To form the **contrapositive** of the original statement, you combine both the converse and the inverse. The propositions are turned round, and then negated.

$p \Rightarrow q$ becomes $q \Rightarrow p$, then $\neg q \Rightarrow \neg p$

For example, consider the propositions:

    p: Poppa eats spinach.

    q: Poppa is strong.

$p \Rightarrow q$ gives the statement, 'If Poppa eats spinach then Poppa is strong'.

$\neg q \Rightarrow \neg p$ gives the statement, 'If Poppa is not strong then Poppa does not eat spinach'.

The result of combining the inverse and converse is that the contrapositive is now logically equivalent to the original statement.

'If Poppa eats spinach then Poppa is strong', is logically equivalent to, 'If Poppa is not strong then Poppa does not eat spinach', even if this seems unlikely given the propositions.

p	*q*	$\neg p$	$\neg q$	$p \Rightarrow q$	$\neg q \Rightarrow \neg p$
T	T	F	F	T	T
T	F	F	T	F	F
F	T	T	F	T	T
F	F	T	T	T	T

The logical equivalence between the converse, inverse and contrapositive can be seen clearly in their truth tables.

Truth tables for the converse and inverse

p	q	$\neg p$	$\neg q$	$p \Rightarrow q$	$q \Rightarrow p$	$\neg p \Rightarrow \neg q$
T	T	F	F	T	T	T
T	F	F	T	F	T	T
F	T	T	F	T	F	F
F	F	T	T	T	T	T

Truth tables for the contrapositive and the original implication

p	q	$\neg p$	$\neg q$	$p \Rightarrow q$	$\neg q \Rightarrow \neg p$
T	T	F	F	T	T
T	F	F	T	F	F
F	T	T	F	T	T
F	F	T	T	T	T

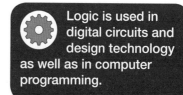

Logic is used in digital circuits and design technology as well as in computer programming.

Worked example 9.9

Q. Consider the propositions p: x is an even number.

                              q: x can be divided by 2.

Give the converse, inverse and contrapositive statements. What do you notice?

A. Original: $p \Rightarrow q$

> If x is an even number, then x can be divided by 2.

Converse: $q \Rightarrow p$

> If x can be divided by 2, then x is an even number.

Inverse: $\neg p \Rightarrow \neg q$

> If x is not an even number, then x cannot be divided by 2.

Contrapositive: $\neg q \Rightarrow \neg p$

> If x cannot be divided by 2, then x is not an even number.

For these specific propositions, the original statement, the converse, the inverse and the contrapositive are all true according to the rules of mathematical logic **and** the rules of arithmetic, for answers that are integers.

Worked example 9.10

Q. Let p and q represent the propositions

p: Henry practises his flute.

q: Henry plays in the band.

Write the following statements in symbols. Which statement is the converse? Which statement is the inverse?

(a) If Henry plays in the band, then Henry practises his flute.

(b) If Henry does not practise his flute, then Henry does not play in the band.

(c) Write the contrapositive of these propositions in words.

A. (a) $q \Rightarrow p$ This is the converse, as p and q have been reversed.
(b) $\neg p \Rightarrow \neg q$ This is the inverse, as both p and q have been negated.
(c) If Henry does not play in the band, then Henry does not practise his flute.

Exercise 9.7

1. Let p, q and r represent the propositions:

   p: The music is good.

   q: I feel like dancing.

   r: I dance to the music.

   Write the following in symbols and then in words:

   (a) the inverse of $p \Rightarrow r$

   (b) the converse of $p \Rightarrow r$

   (c) the contrapositive of $q \Rightarrow r$.

2. For each of the statements (a) to (e) write in words the corresponding:

   (i) inverse   (ii) converse   (iii) contrapositive.

   (a) If you listen attentively in class, then you perform well in tests.

   (b) If you like current affairs, then you listen to news regularly.

   (c) If you are taught by Mrs Brown, then you are brilliant at Logic.

   (d) If Sandra is unwell, then she cannot play in the netball match.

   (e) If Andrew is good at languages, then he can be a tourist guide.

3. Suppose p represents 'Grandma goes to the dentist' and q represents 'Grandma visits Aunt Sally'.

   (a) Write in words the converse of $p \Rightarrow q$.

   (b) Write the following proposition in symbolic form.

   'If Grandma does not visit Aunt Sally, then she goes to the dentist'.

   (c) Is the proposition in part (b) the inverse, converse or the contrapositive of the proposition in part (a)?

4. Jasmine makes the statement 'If a shape is a rectangle, then it is a parallelogram.'

   (a) For this statement, write in words its:

      (i)   converse

      (ii) inverse

      (iii) contrapositive.

   (b) Which of the statements in part (a) is true?

Summary

You should know:

- the basics of symbolic logic
- the definition of propositions and the symbolic notation used to describe them
- what compound statements are and the different types of connectives between them
- how to illustrate compound statements using truth tables and Venn diagrams
- how to use truth tables to test arguments
- how to use truth tables to demonstrate the concepts of logical equivalence, contradiction and tautology
- how to construct converse, inverse and contrapositive statements.

Mixed examination practice

Exam-style questions

1. Consider the following logic statements:

   p: My laptop is broken.

   q: My laptop is fixed.

   r: I will finish writing up my Portfolio task.

   (a) Write in words the following symbolic statements;

       (i) $\neg q \wedge \neg r$

       (ii) $q => r$

       (iii) $r \Leftrightarrow q$.

   (b) Write the following statements, using symbolic notation:

       (i)   My laptop is broken and it is not fixed.

       (ii) My laptop is broken and I will not finish writing up my Portfolio task.

2. Consider the following statements:

   p: New Year is approaching.

   q: I will shop for presents.

   (a) Write down, in words, the meaning of $p \Rightarrow q$.

   (b) Copy and complete the truth table.

p	q	$\neg p$	$\neg q$	$\neg p \Rightarrow \neg q$
T	T			
T	F			
F	T			
F	F			

3. Consider the following logic statements:

   p: I do not save enough money.

   q: I buy a new car.

   (a) Write the expression $\neg p \Rightarrow q$ as a logic statement.

   (b) Write the following statement in logic symbols:

       'I save enough money and I do not buy a new car.'

(c) Copy and complete the truth table.

p	q	$\neg p$	$\neg q$	$\neg p \Rightarrow q$	$\neg p \wedge \neg q$
T	T	F	F	F	F
T	F	F	T		
F	T	T	F		
F	F	T	T		

4. For each of the statements, write in words the corresponding:

   (i) inverse   (ii) converse   (iii) contrapositive.

   (a) If Elliot passes his driving test then his dad will buy him a new car.

   (b) If it snows heavily tonight then the roads will not be busy tomorrow morning.

   (c) If the recession continues then unemployment will remain high.

5. Consider the two propositions

   p: Ali goes to the Homework Club.

   q: Ali goes home early.

   Nadia says: 'If Ali goes to the Homework Club, then Ali does not go home early'.

   (a) Write Nadia's statement in symbolic form.

   (b) Write, in symbolic form, the contrapositive of Nadia's statement.

6. Three logic propositions are given below:

   p: x is a polygon.

   q: x has equal sides and equal angles.

   r: x is a regular polygon.

   Write in words the following symbolic statements and indicate whether they are true or false:

   (a) $q \Rightarrow r$ (b) $r \Leftrightarrow (p \wedge q)$ (c) $p \Leftrightarrow q$.

7. Let p and q be the statements

   p: Marco is a member of the debating society.

   q: Marco enjoys debating.

   (a) Consider the following logic statement:

   'If Marco is a member of the debating society then he enjoys debating.'

   (i) Write down in words the inverse of the statement.

   (ii) Write down in words the converse of the statement.

(b) Construct truth tables for the following statements:

   (i) $p \Rightarrow q$ (ii) $\neg p \Rightarrow \neg q$

   (iii) $p \vee \neg q$ (iv) $\neg p \wedge q$.

(c) Which of the statements in part (b) are logically equivalent?

Past paper questions

1. Complete the truth table for the compound proposition $(p \wedge \neg q) \Rightarrow (p \vee q)$.

p	q	$\neg q$	$(p \wedge \neg q)$	$(p \vee q)$	$(p \wedge \neg q) \Rightarrow (p \vee q)$
T	T	F	F		
T	F	T	T		
F	T	F		T	
F	F		F	F	

[Total 8 marks]

[Nov 2005, Paper 1, Question 11] (© IB Organization 2005)

2. (a) **Copy** and **complete** the table below by filling in the three empty columns.

p	q	$p \wedge q$	$p \vee q$	$\neg p$	$(p \vee q) \wedge \neg p$	$(p \vee q) \wedge \neg p \Rightarrow q$
T	T	T	T			
T	F	F	T			
F	T	F	T			
F	F	F	F			

[3 marks]

(b) What word is used to describe the argument $(p \vee q) \wedge \neg p \Rightarrow q$? [1 mark]

[Total 4 marks]

[May 2005, Paper 2, Question 3(ii)] (© IB Organization 2005)

3. The truth table below shows the truth-values for the proposition

$p \veebar q \Rightarrow \neg p \veebar \neg q.$

p	q	$\neg p$	$\neg q$	$p \veebar q$	$\neg p \veebar \neg q$	$p \veebar q \Rightarrow \neg p \veebar \neg q$
T	T	F	F		F	
T	F	F		T	T	T
F	T	T	F	T	T	T
F	F	T	T	F		T

(a) Explain the distinction between the compound propositions, $p \veebar q$ and $\neg p \veebar \neg q$.

(b) Fill in the four missing truth-values on the table.

(c) State whether the proposition $p \veebar q \Rightarrow \neg p \veebar \neg q$ is a tautology, a contradiction or neither.

[Total 6 marks]

[May 2007, Paper 1, Question 4] (© IB Organization 2007)

4. (a) (i) Complete the truth table below.

p	q	$p \wedge q$	$\neg(p \wedge q)$	$\neg p$	$\neg q$	$\neg p \vee \neg q$
T	T			F	F	
T	F			F	T	
F	T			T	F	
F	F			T	T	

(ii) State whether the compound propositions $\neg(p \wedge q)$ and $\neg p \vee \neg q$ are equivalent.　　*[4 marks]*

Consider the following propositions.

p: *Amy eats sweets*

q: *Amy goes swimming.*

(b) Write, in symbolic form, the following proposition.

Amy either eats sweets or goes swimming, but not both.　　*[2 marks]*

[Total 6 marks]

[May 2008, Paper 1, TZ2, Question 1] (© IB Organization 2008)

Chapter 10 Probability

In this chapter you will learn:

- what the sample space is and how to construct sample space diagrams
- how to calculate expected values
- how to calculate probabilities of events and their complements
- how to find the probabilities of combined, mutually exclusive and independent events
- how to use tree diagrams, Venn diagrams, sample space diagrams and tables of outcomes to calculate probabilities
- that probability 'with replacement' is not the same as probability 'without replacement'
- how to calculate conditional probability from sample space diagrams.

Liber de Ludo Aleae was written by the Italian physician and mathematician Girolamo Cardano (1501–1576), but it was not published until after his death. Do you think it is significant that probability can be determined by mathematics? Are there still occasions when people believe that they can determine their future by chance?

Two thousand years ago, Roman soldiers would settle disputes by tossing a coin. They believed that if the coin landed to show a 'head', the result was ordained by the state — or by the gods. Similarly, in India, people would roll dice and respect the decision made by the dice because they believed that was the outcome that the gods desired.

It was not until 1663 that a book was published on the mathematics of chance; it was called *Liber de Ludo Aleae*. The book demonstrated that the outcome of tossing a coin or rolling a dice could be predicted with some accuracy, and probability started to lose its mystery.

10.1 Introduction to probability

Probability is a measure of 'chance'. It gives a numerical representation of the likelihood that a result will be obtained. Probability can be measured as a percentage, a decimal or a fraction. For example, if there is a 1 in 4 chance of something happening, you could represent this in three ways.

25%

$\frac{1}{4}$

0.25

All probabilities lie between zero and one:

- If a result is certain then it has a probability of 1.

- If a result is impossible, it has a probability of 0.

The 'results' of a probability experiment are known as **outcomes**. An individual outcome being investigated is known as an **event**.

Probabilities are normally represented by the letter P with the event enclosed within parentheses. For example, P(red sock) = $\frac{1}{4}$.

Complementary events

If your local weather forecast tells you that there is a 65% chance of a storm tomorrow, what is the chance that there is no storm?

All the probabilities in any situation must add to a total of 1:

P(storm) = 0.65, so P(no storm) = 1 − 0.65 = 0.35

The probability that there is no storm is 35%.

The event 'there is no storm' is the **complement** of the event 'there is a storm'.

 In general, P(A') = 1 − P(A)

hint

A' is the notation to represent 'not A'

This can be illustrated using a Venn diagram:

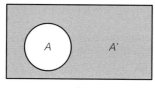

The complement of an event consists of all the possibilities that are not in the event.

When you are solving probability problems, it is often useful to look for complementary events, as it can make the calculations easier.

In a normal deck of playing cards, there are four suits: Hearts (red), Diamonds (red), Spades (black) and Clubs (black). Each suit is made up of 13 cards: 2 to 10, Jack, Queen, King and Ace.	*Worked example 10.1*
	Q. Sacha has a deck of cards. The probability of picking an ace is $\frac{4}{52}$. He picks a card at random. What is the probability that he does **not** pick an ace?
Sacha has subtracted the probability of picking an ace from one.	A. P(Ace) = $\frac{4}{52}$, so P(A') = 1 − $\frac{4}{52}$ = $\frac{48}{52}$

Exercise 10.1

See '24.2E Entering fractions' on page 644 of the GDC chapter for a reminder of how to use your calculator for calculations involving fractions if you need to.

1. The probability of Henry catching his school bus in the mornings is 0.99. What is the probability of Henry missing his bus?

2. Jess has a bag of sweets. The bag contains red, green and brown sweets; the probability of picking a green sweet is $\frac{6}{20}$ and the probability of picking a red sweet is $\frac{9}{20}$. Jess picks a sweet out of the bag randomly (without looking).

    (a) What is the probability of picking a brown sweet?

    (b) Find the probability of **not** picking a brown sweet.

3. There are 24 students in a class. Each student studies only one subject out of History, Geography or Politics. $\frac{5}{12}$ students study History and $\frac{4}{12}$ students study Geography. One student is selected at random to represent the class in the Student Forum.

    (a) What is the probability that the student chosen studies Politics?

    (b) Find the probability that the student chosen does **not** study Politics.

10.2 Sample space diagrams

If one of the Roman soldiers had thrown one coin, what is the probability that it showed a 'head'? As a coin has two sides and the 'head' is only on one side, the probability of throwing a head is 'one out of two' or $\frac{1}{2}$. This is written as P(Head) = $\frac{1}{2}$, where P(Head) means 'the probability of obtaining a head on one throw'. 'Obtaining a head on one throw' is known as an event. 'Obtaining a tail on one throw' is another event. Each of these events is a possible outcome (result) of throwing a coin.

If the Roman soldier had thrown two coins, what is the probability that he would have thrown two heads? 'The probability of obtaining two heads in two throws' is also called an event. It is a possible outcome of throwing two coins. There are other possible outcomes of throwing two coins, for example throwing a head on one coin and a tail on the other coin.

The complete set of possible outcomes from an experiment, such as throwing a die or a coin, is called the **sample space.**

In order to calculate the probability of a given event it is useful to draw a diagram that lists all the possible outcomes. This diagram is called a **sample space diagram**.

Die or dice? Die is the singular (one), dice is the plural and should be used when you have two or more. This convention is not always kept and 'dice' may be used for one die as well as for several.

Let's return to the Roman soldier who threw two coins; there are only four possible outcomes:

First coin = H; second coin = H

First coin = H; second coin = T

First coin = T; second coin = H

First coin = T; second coin = T

The sample space could be represented more neatly using a simple table:

1st throw	H	H	T	T
2nd throw	H	T	H	T

Or written as a set: {(H, H), (H, T), (T, H), (T, T)}

Both sample space diagrams tell us that there are only four possible outcomes, and if you are just as likely to get a H as a T, then the probabilities are as follows:

- P(throwing two heads with one coin) = P(H, H) = $\frac{1}{4}$ (one out of four)

- P(throwing one head and one tail) = P((H, T) or (T, H)) = $\frac{2}{4}$ = $\frac{1}{2}$ (two out of four)

- P(throwing two tails with two coins) = P(T, T) = $\frac{1}{4}$ (one out of four).

Note that in any sample space, all the probabilities will add to a total of one, e.g. $\frac{1}{4} + \frac{1}{2} + \frac{1}{4} = 1$.

Writing the sample space as a simple list or table is straightforward when the number of possible outcomes is quite small. But when there are lots of possible outcomes, other sample space diagrams might be more appropriate.

Examples of sample space diagrams

As you know, a sample space diagram is a way of listing all the possible outcomes. It can be as simple as a list of the possibilities or it can be much more complicated. The following examples show some of the ways that you can create your own diagram but it is not a comprehensive list. For some questions more than one type of diagram may be used. You can use any of the diagrams but it is important that you can understand any sample space diagram and that you include every possible outcome.

A grid sample space diagram

The grid consists of a vertical and a horizontal axis, like a graph. It is useful for showing the sample space for a **combined event**; a combined event is when two or more single events occur one after the other (for example throwing two coins, two dice, or throwing a coin and a dice).

The possible outcomes of each event are listed on the axes and the 'plotted' points show the various combinations of outcomes when two events occur together. It displays all the possible combinations so that you can see them clearly. A diagram like this is useful for problems that involve two dice. You can see in this example that if two dice are thrown, the possible value on each die is plotted along each axis. You can then circle the points you are interested in.

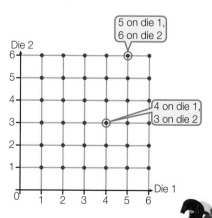

For example, suppose we wanted to know what the probability is of the event 'the sum of the two dice adds up to 6'. We would draw the space sample diagram as shown here and circle all relevant points; in this case there are 5 of them. The total number of points; is 36 (6 along the horizontal axis × 6 along the vertical axis). So the probability of a sum of 6 is 5 out of 36.

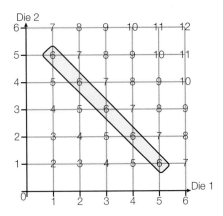

A tree diagram

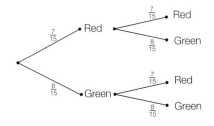

A **tree diagram** shows all the possible successive events in a problem; this is useful for **combined events**, where one event occurs after another. The probability of taking a certain 'branch' of the tree is written along that branch. The probabilities along each branch are multiplied together to get the final probability of a given combined event occurring.

Tables of outcomes

A simple table:

In a simple table, the possible outcomes of a **single event** (throwing only one die or one coin, etc.) are listed along with the probability of obtaining that outcome.

For example, when a fair six-sided die is thrown the possible outcomes are 1, 2, 3, 4, 5 or 6; these are listed as x. As the die is not biased, there is an equal probability of each outcome.

The die has six sides, so $P(1) = P(2) = \ldots = \frac{1}{6}$.

x	1	2	3	4	5	6
Probability	$\frac{1}{6}$	$\frac{1}{6}$	$\frac{1}{6}$	$\frac{1}{6}$	$\frac{1}{6}$	$\frac{1}{6}$

A two-way table:

Two-way tables display the frequency for two or more sets of data, and allow you to see all the different combinations of that data. They are often called **contingency** tables because within each cell they show the frequency for a given combination of events. These are useful for **combined events**. In this example, we have the number of boys and girls in a particular sports club who enjoy either tennis or athletics. This sample space allows you to calculate the probabilities for various different events.

For example, we can see from the table that 17 out of all 42 (40%) children liked to play tennis but only 5 out of 22 (23%) girls liked to play tennis.

	Tennis	Athletics	Total
Boys	12	8	20
Girls	5	17	22
Total	17	25	42

A pie chart

You know from Chapter 5 that pie charts display frequencies as parts of a whole, where the circle represents the total frequency of your data and the sectors represent different measurements. This is useful for **single events**. This chart shows the number of students who play in each section of their college orchestra.

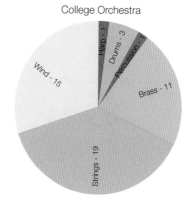

College Orchestra

A Venn diagram

A Venn diagram is a good way of displaying information. You know from Chapter 8 that a Venn diagram can be used to illustrate overlap between different sets of data (and you have been told in this chapter that the sample space can be written as a set).

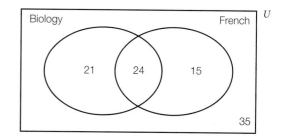

Exercise 10.2

1. Alexandra rolls two four-sided dice, both regular tetrahedra. She adds together the numbers on their bases.

    Copy and complete this sample space diagram.

	1	2	3	4
1	2			5
2				
3			6	
4		6		

exam tip

In an examination you can be asked to complete a sample space diagram, or to draw your own. If you draw your own, the examiner will mark any clear diagram and check to ensure that your answer to the problem matches it.

2. For the two vacancies of Head Girl and Deputy Head Girl there are three candidates on the voting list: Bryony, Paige and Rosalind. Complete a sample space diagram to illustrate the possible combinations of the candidates for the two positions.

3. The spinner below has four sectors, marked 1, 2, 3 and 4. Olaf spins the spinner twice and records the number facing the arrow each time. He then adds the two numbers together.

    Draw a sample space diagram to illustrate all the possible sums Olaf is likely to get.

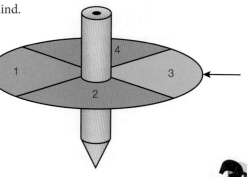

4. A triangular spinner has sectors labeled A, B and C. It is spun twice.

(a) What is the total number of possible outcomes?

(b) Complete a full sample space diagram for the possible outcomes.

The spinner is spun three times.

(c) What is the total number of possible outcomes?

10.3 Calculating probability and the expected value

You know that when you draw up a sample space diagram you are listing all the possible outcomes.

When tossing two coins, the event A (tossing two heads) can be written as:

$$A = \{(H, H)\}$$

There are four different ways that the coins can fall, so all the outcomes can be written as:

$$U = \{(H, H), (H, T), (T, H), (T, T)\}$$

From section 10.2, you know that:

$$P(H, H) = \tfrac{1}{4} \text{ (one out of four)}$$

$$P(H \text{ and } T) = \tfrac{2}{4} \text{ (two out of four)}$$

$$P(T, T) = \tfrac{1}{4} \text{ (one out of four)}$$

This leads us to a general formula for calculating probability:

$$P(A) = \frac{\text{number of outcomes in } A}{\text{total number of outcomes}} \quad \text{or} \quad P(A) = \frac{n(A)}{n(U)}$$

	Worked example 10.2
Q.	The numbers 1 to 10 are written on separate pieces of card and put into a bag. Sophie puts her hand in the bag and takes out a single card.
	(a) What is the probability that she picks a prime number?
	(b) What is the probability that she picks a multiple of 5?
	(c) What is the probability that she picks a zero?

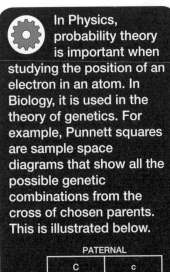

In Physics, probability theory is important when studying the position of an electron in an atom. In Biology, it is used in the theory of genetics. For example, Punnett squares are sample space diagrams that show all the possible genetic combinations from the cross of chosen parents. This is illustrated below.

PATERNAL

		C	c
		C	c
MATERNAL	C	CC	Cc
	c	cC	cc

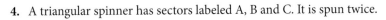

«« RR *U is the universal set; you learned about this in Chapter 8.*

continued . . .

(d) What is the probability that she picks a number from 1 to 10?

(e) What is the probability that she does not pick a prime number?

A. The sample space diagram in this case is easier to write out using sets:

$U = \{1, 2, 3, 4, 5, 6, 7, 8, 9, 10\}$

Prime numbers $= \{2, 3, 5, 7\}$

Multiples of 5 $= \{5, 10\}$.

> There is a total of ten numbers, 4 are prime numbers.

(a) $P(\text{prime number}) = \dfrac{4}{10}$

> There are two multiples of five.

(b) $P(\text{multiple of five}) = \dfrac{2}{10}$

> The universal set does not contain a zero.

(c) $P(\text{zero}) = 0$

> A number from 1 to 10 is certain.

(d) $P(1....10) = 1$

> If four numbers are prime, six are not (10 − 4); or you can use the fact that 'prime' and 'not prime' are complementary events and calculate $1 - \frac{4}{10}$.

(e) $P(\text{no prime number}) = \dfrac{6}{10}$

Worked example 10.3

Q. A die with eight faces (an octahedron) has one of a, b, c, d, e, f, g, h written on each face. The die is rolled and the letter on the top face is noted.

(a) Draw a sample space diagram.

(b) Calculate the probability that the die lands with 'f' on the top face.

(c) Calculate the probability that the die lands with a vowel on the top face.

(d) Calculate the probability that the die does not land with a vowel on the top face.

continued . . .

> The list of letters in the universal set is used as the space diagram.

A. (a) $U = \{a, b, c, d, e, f, g, h\}$

> There is only one 'f'.

(b) $P(f) = \dfrac{1}{8}$

> There are two vowels out of 8 letters.

(c) $P(vowel) = \dfrac{2}{8} = \dfrac{1}{4}$

> If there are two vowels, there must be $8 - 2 = 6$ consonants. (Note that you could also have subtracted the probability of getting a vowel from 1 to get the probability of 'not a vowel': $1 - \frac{1}{4} = \frac{3}{4}$.)

(d) $P(consonant) = \dfrac{6}{8} = \dfrac{3}{4}$

Worked example 10.4

Q. Two dice are thrown and the scores are added together. Calculate the following probabilities:

(a) P(total of six)

(b) P(total of at least eight)

(c) P(the two scores are the same)

(d) P(total of 1).

A.

> First you need to draw a sample space diagram. The best diagram for this problem is a sample space diagram where you can see all the possible combinations and outline the ones that you need in order to help you answer the questions.

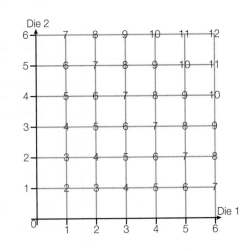

continued . . .

Circle all occurrences of '6'. There are five.

(a)

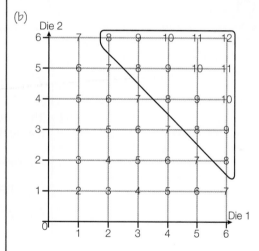

$$P(\text{total of six}) = \frac{5}{36}$$

'At least eight' means 'eight or more', so circle all occurrences of 8, 9, 10, 11 and 12. There are 15.

(b)

$$P(\text{total of at least eight}) = \frac{15}{36} = \frac{5}{12}$$

continued . . .

(c)

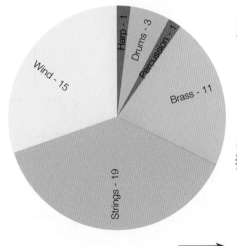

Die 2 / Die 1 grid showing sums:
Row 6: 7, 8, 9, 10, 11, 12
Row 5: 6, 7, 8, 9, 10, 11
Row 4: 5, 6, 7, 8, 9, 10
Row 3: 4, 5, 6, 7, 8, 9
Row 2: 3, 4, 5, 6, 7, 8
Row 1: 2, 3, 4, 5, 6, 7

$$P(\text{the two scores are the same}) = \frac{6}{36} = \frac{1}{6}$$

(d) $P(\text{total of } 1) = \dfrac{0}{36} = 0$

> 'The two scores are the same' means that the same number is on both dice. So this includes the outcomes (1, 1) (2, 2), (3, 3), etc., i.e. the sums 2, 4, 6, etc.

> The lowest possible total of the two dice is 2, so getting a score of 1 is impossible.

Worked example 10.5

Q. There are 50 people in the college orchestra. Use the pie chart to calculate the probability that:

(a) a person plays a string instrument

(b) a person plays a brass instrument

(c) a person does not play a wind instrument.

College Orchestra

Pie chart segments: Harp - 1, Drums - 3, Percussion - 1, Brass - 11, Wind - 15, Strings - 19

continued . . .

There are 50 people in the orchestra, but only 20 play a string instrument. (Note: the harp is a stringed instrument.)

A. (a) $P(string) = \dfrac{20}{50}$

There are 50 people in the orchestra, but only 11 play a brass instrument.

(b) $P(brass) = \dfrac{11}{50}$

If $\frac{15}{50}$ of the orchestra play a wind instrument, then $1 - \frac{15}{50}$ don't play a wind instrument. (Or you could do $50 - 15 = 35$, out of 50.)

(c) $P(not\ wind) = 1 - \dfrac{15}{50} = \dfrac{35}{50}$

Exercise 10.3A

1. There are 20 marbles in a bag. 8 of them are red, 7 are green and the remaining 5 are white. Sabel picks one of the marbles out of the bag without looking. Find the probability that the chosen marble is:

   (a) red

   (b) white or green

   (c) not green.

hint

If the marbles are red, white or green, then the event 'white or green' is the same as the event 'not red'.

2. Alfred tosses a coin and rolls a six-sided die. Copy and complete the following table of possible outcomes:

	1	2	3	4	5	6
Head	H1	H2				
Tail					T5	T6

   Calculate the probability that Alfred gets:

   (a) an even number   (b) a factor of 6

   (c) a head and a square number   (d) a tail or a prime number.

3. The letters of the word MATHEMATICS are written on different cards, shuffled and placed face down. One of the cards is picked at random. Calculate the probability that chosen card shows:

   (a) an A   (b) an M   (c) not a vowel.

4. Two dice are thrown and the scores are added up. Calculate the following probabilities.

    (a) P(total is 11)   (b) P(total is at most 10)

    (c) P(total is a square number)   (d) P(total is a prime number)

5. A school hockey team plays two matches. Each match could end in a win (W), a loss (L) or a draw (D).

    (a) List all the possible outcomes of the two matches. You may find it helpful to copy and complete the table below.

Match 1	W	W	W	L	L	L	D	D	D
Match 2									

    (b) What is the probability of drawing one match only?

    (c) Calculate the probability of not losing any of the matches.

6. The examination grades of a group of 30 IGCSE students are illustrated on the pie chart.

    A student is chosen at random from the group. Calculate the probability that the student scored:

    (a) a grade C

    (b) a grade B or better

    (c) a grade worse than grade C.

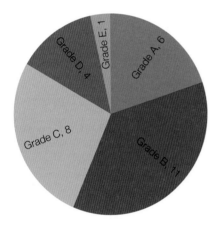

7. Ditmar rolls two six-sided dice. He then multiplies the two numbers showing. Complete the following sample space diagram for the outcomes.

	1	2	3	4	5	6
1						
2		4			10	
3						
4						
5		10			25	
6						36

    Using Ditmar's results from the sample space diagram, calculate the probability of the product being:

    (a) a square number   (b) a prime number

    (c) a cubed number   (d) a multiple of 3

    (e) a common multiple of 3 and 5.

8. A survey was carried out on a group of Physics and Chemistry students. The results are shown on the Venn diagram below.

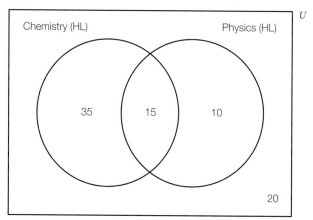

(a) How many students took part in the survey?

(b) If one of the students is chosen at random, calculate the probability that the student:

   (i)   studies Chemistry (HL)

   (ii)   studies both Chemistry (HL) and Physics (HL)

   (iii) does not study Physics (HL).

9. Three IB students, Andrew, Fareeda and Caitlin, all study History.

(a) Complete the table below to show all the possible combinations of levels of entry, at either Higher (HL) or Standard (SL) level.

Andrew	Fareeda	Caitlin
HL	HL	HL
HL	HL	SL
HL		

(b) What is the total number of possible combinations of choices for the three students?

(c) Find the probability that all three students study History at the same level.

(d) Calculate the probability that exactly two of the students study History at Standard Level.

(e) What is the probability that at least one of the students studies History at Higher Level?

Theoretical and experimental probability

Noah wants to know the probability that he will shoot a hoop successfully in basketball.

Safia wants to know the probability that she will throw two sixes when she throws two dice.

These are two different types of problem and will require different approaches.

The probability of success for Noah depends on how good a player he is and how successful he has been in the past. He calculates the probability **experimentally**, with figures he has collected himself. This is an example of **experimental** probability.

Safia can calculate the probabilities of a particular score on a non-biased die using the theory that all six faces are equally likely to occur $\left(\frac{1}{6}\right)$, so she can calculate her result **theoretically**.

	1	2	3	4	5	6
1	1,1	1,2	1,3	1,4	1,5	1,6
2	2,1	2,2	2,3	2,4	2,5	2,6
3	3,1	3,2	3,3	3,4	3,5	3,6
4	4,1	4,2	4,3	4,3	4,5	4,6
5	5,1	5,2	5,3	5,4	5,5	5,6
6	6,1	6,2	6,3	6,4	6,5	**6,6**

Using a sample space diagram, Safia knows that there are 36 different combinations that she should get based on theory if she throws two dice. Only one of these will give her (6,6):

$$P(6,6) = \frac{1}{30}$$

In general, for **theoretical probability**,

$$P(\text{event}) = \frac{\text{number of possible successful events}}{\text{total number of events}}$$

Worked examples 10.1–10.5 are all examples of **theoretical** probability.

But Noah cannot use theory to calculate his chances of success because his chances are **biased**; they depend on his experience and level of skill. He has to rely on his knowledge of past events. Noah has kept a record of his last 80 attempts at getting the ball through a hoop; each of the 80 attempts is called a 'trial'. He was successful 48 times.

In general, for **experimental probability**,

$$P(\text{success}) = \frac{\text{number of successful trials}}{\text{total number of trials}}$$

So for Noah, $P(\text{success}) = \frac{48}{80} = \frac{3}{5}$

Expected value

The expected value is what you would *expect* to get 'on average' within a given distribution based on a given probability. An expected value is a mean calculated from the probability and the number of events/trials.

In general:

Expected value = probability of success $\times$ number of trials

So, if Noah was to try to score a hoop 10 times, how many times would he *expect* to be successful?

Expected number of scores: $\dfrac{3}{5} \times 10 = 6$

Noah would expect to score 6 hoops in 10 attempts.

Similarly, if Safia was to throw two dice 12 times, how many times should she expect to throw two sixes?

Expected value $= \dfrac{1}{36} \times 12 = 0.333333\ldots$

So, we could say (rounding to the nearest whole number) that Sofia would not expect to roll two sixes at all in 12 throws of the dice.

Probability calculations can tell you what to expect but there will always be a variation between the calculated value and the actual value. If you only do a small number of trials, it is unlikely that the expected value will be a good reflection of the actual values because the expected value will be more affected by extremes. The more trials you do, the closer the actual result should be to the expected value.

 These are expected values. How true do you think they are? If you throw a fair coin 200 times, do you expect to get exactly 100 heads and 100 tails? Would more throws be more likely to give you exact values?

Worked example 10.6

Q. (a) If Safia throws two dice 180 times, how many times can she expect to throw (6,6)?

(b) If Noah makes 36 attempts to put the ball through the hoop, how many times will he be successful?

In general, expected value = probability × number of trials.

We know from earlier in this section that the theoretical probability of getting (6,6) is $\frac{1}{36}$. We need to calculate how many times out of 180 throws she is likely to get (6,6). So, we multiply the number of throws by the probability for one throw.

We know from earlier in the section that the probability of him scoring a hoop is $\frac{3}{5}$, so multiply this by the number of trials.

A. (a) $P(6,6) = \dfrac{1}{36}$

$= \dfrac{1}{36} \times 180$

$= 5$

Safia should get (6,6) five times.

(b) Since $P(\text{success}) = \dfrac{48}{80} = \dfrac{3}{5}$

$\dfrac{3}{5} \times 36 = 21.6$

He can expect to be successful 21.6 (22) times.

1. Frances tosses two coins. List all the possible outcomes.

   Use your list to work out the probability of getting:

   (a) two heads   (b) at least one tail.

   Frances tosses two coins simultaneously 120 times. How many times does she expect to get:

   (c) exactly one tail   (d) two heads   (e) at least one tail?

2. Emma tosses three coins. List all the possible outcomes.

   Use your list to calculate the probability of getting:

   (a) all heads   (b) exactly one tail

   (c) at least one head   (d) at most two tails.

   Emma repeats her experiment 96 times. How many times does she expect to get:

   (e) all heads   (f) at most two tails?

3. A survey was carried out on a sample of 300 patients in a hospital. The blood groups of the patients are shown in the table below.

Blood group	O	A	B	AB
Frequency	135	120	33	12

   (a) If a patient is chosen at random, what is the probability that the patient:

        (i) belongs to blood group A?

        (ii) does not belong to blood group O?

   (b) Out of 1300 patients in the hospital, how many of them would you expect to belong to:

        (i) blood group AB?   (ii) blood group B?

4. A survey of the regular means of transport to school was carried out on a sample of 100 students in a secondary school.

   (a) If a student is chosen at random, what is the probability that the student:

        (i) travelled to school by car   (ii) did not walk to school?

   (b) There are 1100 students in the school. How many do you expect to travel to school:

        (i) by bicycle?   (ii) not on foot?

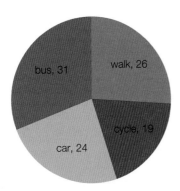

10.4 Mutually exclusive events

Two events are **mutually exclusive** if they cannot happen at the same time.

You cannot toss one coin and get a 'head' **and** a 'tail' at the same time.

You cannot run in the 400 m race with five other people and come both first **and** second in the same race.

These are mutually exclusive events. One **or** the other can happen but **not both** at the same time.

So, coming first in the 400 m race is mutually exclusive to coming second in the same race. This can be written as $P(A \cap B) = \varnothing$ using set notation; there are no elements in the set 'A and B' because A and B cannot happen at the same time. But you could come first *or* second; what is the probability of coming first *or* second? If the probability that you win the 400 m is 0.24 and the probability that you come second is 0.35, then you can calculate the probability that you come either first *or* second by adding the two probabilities together:

$P(\text{first}) + P(\text{second}) = 0.24 + 0.35 = 0.59$

This can be written as $P(A \cup B) = P(A) + P(B)$.

We can say that in any general probability situation, if you can add together the probabilities of two events **and** their intersection is an empty set with no elements in it, then the events you are working with are mutually exclusive.

For two mutually exclusive events, you **add** the probabilities because one **or** the other can occur but not both.

  In general, if $P(A) + P(B) = P(A \cup B)$, and $P(A \cap B) = \varnothing$, then the events are mutually exclusive.

‹‹RR You learned about set notation in Chapter 8.

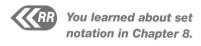

Some of the probability formulae are in the Formula booklet, so make sure you know where to look for them. It is important that you rely on your understanding of the probability rather than just on the formulae; this might help you spot an incorrect answer.

‹‹RR Remember from Chapter 8 that in set notation ∪ is 'union' ('or'), ∩ is 'intersection' ('and'), and ∅ is the empty set.

The Venn diagram illustrates two mutually exclusive events; there is no overlap between the sets.

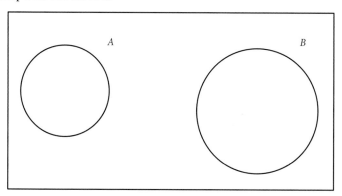

Exercise 10.4

1. A jar contains 9 red, 12 green and 11 yellow marbles. A marble is chosen at random. What is the probability of choosing:

   (a) a green marble?   (b) a yellow or red marble?

2. There are 7 apples, 3 plums and 6 pears in a fruit bowl. Gemma picks a fruit randomly from the bowl. Determine the probability of Gemma picking:

   (a) a pear

   (b) a plum

   (c) a pear or a plum.

3. There are 24 cars at a car park. 6 of them are estate cars and 4 of them coupés. One of the owners has just reported to the car park attendant that her car's wing mirror has been damaged.

   Calculate the probability that the damaged car:

   (a) is an estate car   (b) is a coupé car

   (c) is an estate or coupé   (d) not an estate car.

4. A school Lacrosse team is playing in a friendly match. The probability of winning is 0.6 and the probability of drawing is 0.25.

   (a) Find the probability of losing the match.

   (b) Work out the probability of winning or drawing.

   (c) Calculate the probability of not drawing the match.

5. There are 28 IB students working in a school library. 5 of them study Mathematics (HL) and 14 of them study Mathematics (SL).

   One of the students is using the photocopier. What is the probability that the student does:

   (a) Mathematics (HL)?

   (b) Mathematics (HL) or Mathematics (SL)?

   (c) neither Mathematics (HL) nor Mathematics (SL)?

6. The grade distribution of GCSE results for a secondary school in the UK for 2011 is shown below.

Grade	A*	A	B	C	D	E	F	G	U
% of entries	7.8	15.4	21.7	24.9	15.1	7.8	4.1	2.0	

   (a) Given that a U grade is a fail, find the percentage of entries which were failures.

(b) If one of the examination entries is selected at random, find the probability that it earned:

(i) a C grade or higher

(ii) an E grade or lower

(iii) an A or A*.

(c) The school registered 2000 entries in total. Calculate the expected number of:

(i) A or A* grades   (ii) A* to C grades.

10.5 Probability of combined events

Combined events are those that are not mutually exclusive; they are events that can happen at the same time or have some overlap. In these situations you can find the probability of getting 'A or B' or 'A and B'. The general formula for combined events is:

$$P(A \cup B) = P(A) + P(B) - P(A \cap B)$$

 Remember from Chapter 8 that in set notation $\cup$ is 'union' ('or') and $\cap$ is 'intersection' ('and').

A marketing company is doing a household survey. They survey 42 houses and find: 23 households with gas cookers, 17 households with electric cookers and five who use dual fuel cookers (cookers that use both gas and electricity). Seven other houses cook on oil-fired cookers. What is the probability that a household cooks with gas or electricity or both?

Using the formula, $P(A \cup B) = P(A) + P(B) - P(A \cap B)$:

If G represents gas and E represents electricity, then

$$P(G \cup E) = P(G) + P(E) - P(G \cap E)$$

From the original information, you can calculate that

$$P(G \cup E) = \frac{23}{42} + \frac{17}{42} - \frac{5}{42} = \frac{35}{42}$$

You might find this easier to visualise using a Venn diagram. The five dual fuel cookers go into the intersection (gas **and** electricity).

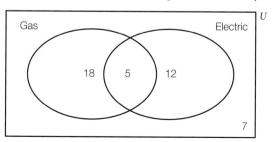

This is the formula for combined events, but remember that a good diagram can help you to understand a situation and complete the calculations without using the formula.

This formula is in the Formula booklet, but in examinations questions using formulae on their own will not be set. All questions will be set in context.

Households that cook with gas or electricity or both are in the **union** of 'gas', 'electricity' and 'gas and electricity'. Since $18 + 5 + 12 = 35$, there are 35 households cooking with gas or electricity or both, so $P(G \cup E) = \frac{35}{42}$.

Independent events

Two events are **independent** if the first one has no influence on the second.

The probability of getting a head when you throw a coin is $\frac{1}{2}$. What is the probability of getting a tail if you throw it again? It is still $\frac{1}{2}$, as the two events do not affect each other. They are independent. The probability of throwing a head **and** then another head can be calculated as follows:

$$P(\text{two heads}) = \frac{1}{2} \times \frac{1}{2} = \frac{1}{4}$$

For independent events, you **multiply** the probabilities of each event because you could have one **and** the other.

 In general, for independent events, $P(A \cap B) = P(A) \times P(B)$.

The formula can be used to test whether or not events are independent.

Let $U = \{$natural numbers from one to twenty$\}$

$A = \{$multiples of 5$\}$

$B = [$multiples of 4$\}$

Are A and B independent?

You can check by testing the probabilities.

$A = \{5, 10, 15, 20\}$

$B = \{4, 8, 12, 16, 20\}$

Only the number 20 occurs in both lists:

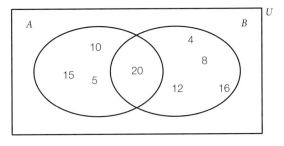

$P(A) = \frac{4}{20}$, $P(B) = \frac{5}{20}$ and $P(A \cap B) = \frac{1}{20}$

$P(A) \times P(B) = \frac{4}{20} \times \frac{5}{20} = \frac{1}{20} = P(A \cap B)$

A and B are proved to be independent.

Worked example 10.7

Q. In a local art competition, the probability that Barbara wins a prize for her design is 0.4 and the probability that Alan wins a prize for his photograph is 0.58. The probability that they both win a prize is 0.25.

(a) Find $P(A \cup B)$, the probability that either Alan or Barbara wins a prize.

(b) Are the events A and B independent? Explain your answer.

> A 'or' B means 'add' the probabilities. The events are combined, so use the formula $P(A \cup B) = P(A) + P(B) - P(A \cap B)$.

A. (a) $P(A \cup B) = 0.4 + 0.58 - 0.25 = 0.73$

> $P(A \cap B) = 0.25$ is given to you in the question as the probability that they both win a prize. The calculation $P(A) \times P(B)$ gives a different answer, so A and B are not independent.

(b) For events to be independent,
$P(A) \times P(B) = P(A \cap B)$.
$P(A) \times P(B) = 0.4 \times 0.58 = 0.232$
$P(A \cap B) = 0.25$ and $P(A) \times P(B) = 0.232$
so the events are not independent.

Can events be mutually exclusive and independent?

When you read a problem, you need to be quite clear that you understand the difference between mutually exclusive and independent events.

Mutually exclusive events cannot be independent. Look at the Venn diagrams and the formulae below.

Independent events

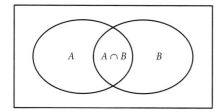

$P(A \cap B) = P(A) \times P(B)$

Mutually exclusive events

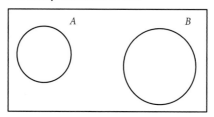

$P(A) + P(B) = P(A \cup B)$, and $P(A \cap B) = 0$

If A and B are mutually exclusive, then $P(A \cap B) = 0$. If they are independent and both occur with positive probability, then $P(A \cap B) = P(A) \times P(B) \neq 0$. Since $P(A \cap B)$ cannot be zero and non-zero at the same time, two events cannot be mutually exclusive and independent at the same time.

Worked example 10.8

Q. The numbers 2, 3, 4, 5, 6, 7, 8 and 10 are written out on eight separate pieces of paper. One number is chosen.

(a) Are the events 'choosing a 2' and 'choosing an odd number' mutually exclusive?

(b) Are the events 'choosing a 2' and 'choosing a prime number' mutually exclusive?

(c) Are the events 'choosing an even number' and 'choosing a prime number' independent?

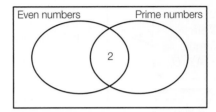

A. (a) 2 is an even number; if only one number is picked then an odd and an even number cannot be chosen at the same time, so these events are mutually exclusive.

(b) 2 is an even number and also a prime number, so choosing a 2 and choosing a prime number are not mutually exclusive events.

(c) If $E = \{2, 4, 6, 8, 10\}$ and $P = \{2, 3, 5, 7\}$:

$$P(E) = \frac{5}{8}, P(P) = \frac{4}{8} \text{ and } P(E \cap P) = \frac{1}{8}$$

$$P(E) \times P(P) = \frac{5}{8} \times \frac{4}{8} = \frac{5}{16} \neq \frac{1}{8}$$

The events are not independent

Exercise 10.5

1. For the two events A and B, $P(A \cup B) = 0.61$, $P(A) = 0.33$, $P(B) = 0.82$.

   (a) Find $P(A \cap B)$.

   (b) Explain with reasons whether the events A and B are independent.

2. The events A and B are mutually exclusive.
   $P(A) = 0.57$ and $P(B) = 0.26$. Find $P(A \cup B)$.

3. Gemma is ready for her driving test. The probability of her passing first time is 0.65. If she fails her first test, the probability of her passing on the second attempt is 0.85.

   (a) Calculate the probability of Gemma passing in exactly two attempts.

   (b) Find the probability of Gemma passing within two attempts.

4. Out of the 260 registered members of a golf club, 200 of them are male. 31 of the members are aged 65 or older. 55 of the female members are aged under 65.

   (a) If one of the golfers is selected at random, what is the probability that he or she is:

       (i) a male golfer under 65 years of age?

       (ii) a female golfer who is 65 or older?

   (b) Two of the golfers won awards in the last season. Calculate the probability that:

       (i) at least one of them is a female golfer and younger than 65

       (ii) neither of them is a male golfer older than 65.

5. Tim and Gary have carried out a survey of students resident in their neighbourhood. The number of students enrolled in different levels of education is summarised in the table below.

	Elementary School	High School	College
Frequency	370	170	190

   Three students from the neighbourhood have been nominated to be given awards for academic excellence and service in the local community.

   Calculate the probability that:

   (a) all three students are in High School

   (b) exactly two of the students are College students

   (c) at least one of the students is in Elementary School.

6. Jonah tosses a coin and rolls a six-sided die. Find the probability of Jonah getting:

   (a) a head on the coin and an even number on the die

   (b) a tail on the coin and a factor of 12 on the die.

7. Diego manages a football team. His team is playing a match. The team consists of a goalkeeper, four defenders, four midfield players and two strikers. At half time Diego decides to make two substitutions. If all the players have the same chances of being substituted, calculate the probability that:

   (a) the players to be substituted are not strikers

   (b) at least one striker is being substituted

   (c) at most one midfielder is being substituted

   (d) the goalkeeper is not being substituted.

10.6 Tree diagrams and Venn diagrams

Many probability questions can be solved by using tree diagrams or Venn diagrams. Both give a good picture of the information in a question and help you to move from there to a solution. In some problems it will be clear which diagram to choose; in others you may find that you can use either and it will depend on your personal preference. It is important to make sure that you are confident in using both and not afraid to move from one type of diagram to the other if it allows you to work through the original problem more easily.

Using tree diagrams

Tree diagrams allow you to see all the possible outcomes of successive events, and to calculate the probability of those events.

FF ⟫ *They are very useful in section 10.7.*

Priya has a bag containing 5 red balls and 3 blue ones. She picks out a ball, notes the colour and replaces the ball. She then takes out a second ball, notes the colour and puts the ball back in the bag.

Priya is doing two successive actions. The first action can be represented by the first two branches of the tree, and her second action can be represented by the branches that follow on from the first ones.

Using theoretical probability, Priya knows that $P(\text{red}) = \frac{5}{8}$ and $P(\text{blue}) = \frac{3}{8}$.

She can build her tree diagram like this:

The diagram shows all the possible combinations and allows Priya to calculate the probabilities.

$$P(\text{red, red}) = \frac{5}{8} \times \frac{5}{8} = \frac{25}{64}$$

> Red is followed by another red ('and'), so Priya has to *multiply*.

$$P(\text{red, blue}) = \frac{5}{8} \times \frac{3}{8} = \frac{15}{64}$$

$$P(\text{blue, red}) = \frac{3}{8} \times \frac{5}{8} = \frac{15}{64}$$

$$P(\text{blue, blue}) = \frac{3}{8} \times \frac{3}{8} = \frac{9}{64}$$

exam tip

Remember to **multiply** across the branches, and **add** down the branches.

$$P(\text{two different colours}) = \frac{5}{8} \times \frac{3}{8} + \frac{3}{8} \times \frac{5}{8} = \frac{25}{64}$$

Priya can check that she has covered every combination:

$$\frac{25}{64} + \frac{15}{64} + \frac{15}{64} + \cdots + \frac{9}{64} = 1$$

Two colours could be red first then blue (R **and** B) **or** blue first then red (B **and** R). '**And**' means that 'R and B' need to be multiplied, and 'B and R' need to be multiplied. '**Or**' indicates that you can't have both (R, B) and (B, R) at the same time, so they are mutually exclusive and their product probabilities must be *added*.

 Remember from section 10.1 that all probabilities of an experiment add up to 1.

The branches of a tree diagram do not have to show the same values.

Worked example 10.9

Q. | If the weather is fine, Mr Liu walks to work. The probability that he is late is 0.1.

If it rains, Mr Liu catches the bus and the probability that he is late is 0.3.

The probability of rain is 0.45.

(a) What is the probability that Mr Liu is late for work?

(b) From the tree diagram, calculate the probability that:

   (i)   Mr Liu catches the bus and is not late.

   (ii) Mr Liu walks to work and is late.

   (iii) Mr Liu is not late for work.

(c) Mr Liu works 255 days a year. On how many days does he expect **not** to be late?

In this situation, Mr Liu makes a decision dependent on the weather. So the first event is 'rain' or 'no rain' and the second event is 'late' or 'not late' depending on the outcome of the first event.

continued . . .

There are two ways that he can be late, if he travels by bus **or** if he walks.

Using the tree diagram: follow the branches that show it rains and he is late.

A. (a) $P(R, L) = 0.45 \times 0.3 = 0.135$

Using the tree diagram follow the branches that show it does not rain and he is late.

$P(R', L) = 0.55 \times 0.1 = 0.055$

It cannot rain **and** not rain, but it can rain **or** not rain, so the events are mutually exclusive and the probabilities are added.

$P(L) = 0.135 + 0.055 = 0.19$

This is the probability that it rains (he catches the bus) and he is not late. Follow the appropriate branches and multiply the probabilities.

(b) (i) $P(R, L') = 0.45 \times 0.7 = 0.315$

This is the probability that it does not rain (he walks to work) and he is late. Multiply the probabilities along the branch.

(ii) $P(R', L) = 0.55 \times 0.1 = 0.055$

'Late' and 'Not late' are complementary events so you can use your answer to part (a) here.

(iii) $P(L') = 1 - 0.19 = 0.81$

Use the probability from part (b)(iii).

(c) $P(L') = 0.81$

Expected value = frequency × probability.

$255 \times 0.81 \approx 207$

Mr Liu expects not to be late about 207 days of the year.

Exercise 10.6A

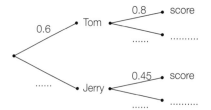

1. Tom and Jerry play for the same hockey team. The manager always selects either Tom or Jerry for the team. The probability of Tom being selected is 0.6. If he is selected, the probability of Tom scoring is 0.8. The probability of Jerry scoring is 0.45.

   (a) Copy and complete the tree diagram.

   (b) For the next match, calculate the probability of:

       (i)   Tom playing and scoring

       (ii) either Tom or Jerry scoring

       (iii) neither Tom nor Jerry scoring.

   (c) If Jerry plays in the next two successive matches, calculate the probability of:

       (i) scoring in just one of the matches

       (ii) scoring in at most one of the matches.

2. Kofi and Kojo are playing a game of tennis. The probability of Kofi serving an ace is 0.6. The probability of Kojo serving an ace is 0.55.

   Calculate the probability that:

   (a) both Kofi and Kojo serve aces

   (b) neither Kofi nor Kojo serves an ace

   (c) at least one of them serves an ace.

3. Leslie plays football. He plays either in midfield or as a striker. The probability of his playing in midfield is 0.3. When he plays in midfield the probability of scoring is 0.6. When he plays as a striker the probability of scoring is 0.9.

   (a) Copy and complete the tree diagram below.

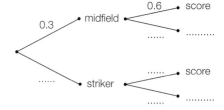

   If Leslie plays one match, calculate the probability of him:

   (b) scoring as a midfielder

   (c) scoring

   (d) playing as a striker and not scoring

   (e) not scoring.

4. Julius takes two penalty kicks in a game of rugby. For each kick the probability of scoring is equal to 0.85.

Draw a tree diagram, and hence calculate the probability of Julius:

(a) missing both kicks

(b) scoring once

(c) missing no more than once.

5. Kye has invited two friends, Carmen and Jermaine, to his birthday party in Milton Keynes. Carmen is travelling by car and Jermaine by train. The probability of Carmen arriving late is 0.34, while the probability of Jermaine being late is 0.28.

(a) Copy and complete the tree diagram.

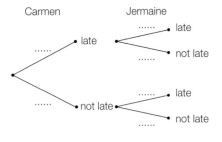

(b) Calculate the probability that:

(i) neither of the friends is late

(ii) both friends are late

(iii) only Carmen is late

(iv) only one of the friends is late.

Using Venn diagrams

In some situations it is easier to display the information you are given in a Venn diagram.

Worked example 10.10

Q. A school has 95 students who are taking their IB diploma this year. There are 45 students who study Biology and 39 who study French. There are 24 students who study both Biology and French. Draw a Venn diagram and calculate the probability that:

(a) a student studies Biology or French

(b) a student does not study Biology

(c) a student does not study Biology or French.

A.

The Venn diagram allows you to use the fact that 24 students are studying both subjects.

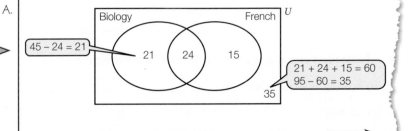

continued . . .

From the diagram:

'B or F' means the union of B and F, so

21 + 24 + 15 = 60

(a) $P(B \text{ or } F) = \dfrac{60}{95}$

'Not B' means everywhere in the diagram except B:
15 + 35 = 50

(b) $P(B') = \dfrac{50}{95}$

'Not F or B' means everywhere that is not F or not B. In this case it is outside both circles.

(c) $P(F' \text{ or } B') = \dfrac{35}{95} = \dfrac{7}{19}$

You can keep your answer as $\frac{35}{95}$ or write the fraction in its simplest form.

Exercise 10.6B

1. The sets A and B are subsets of U. They are defined as follows:

   $U = \{\text{prime numbers less than } 20\}$

   $A = \{\text{prime factors of } 30\}$

   $B = \{\text{prime factors of } 66\}$

   hint

   The prime factors of 12 are {2, 3}

   (a) Draw a Venn diagram to represent the relationship between sets U, A and B. List the elements of the sets in the corresponding regions of the Venn diagram.

   (b) Find the probability that a number chosen randomly from the universal set U is:

   (i) a factor of 55

   (ii) a factor of 39.

2. In a class of 24 students, 9 study History and 14 study Economics. Four of the students study neither History nor Economics.

   (a) Draw a Venn diagram to represent the information given above.

   (b) If a student is chosen at random, calculate the probability that the student:

   (i)   studies History or Economics

   (ii) does not study Economics

   (iii) studies Economics or History, but not both.

3. The Venn diagram below shows how many members of a Leisure Club are interested in bowling and line dancing.

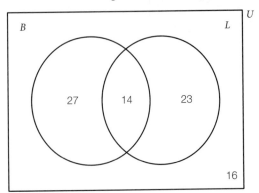

U = {all members of the club}

B = {members who enjoy bowling}

L = {members who enjoy line dancing}

(a) How many members does the club have?

(b) If one of the members decides to leave the club, what is the probability that she/he:

(i) enjoys line dancing

(ii) enjoys line dancing but not bowling

(iii) does not enjoy bowling

(iv) enjoys line dancing or bowling, but not both

(v) enjoys both line dancing and bowling, or neither?

10.7 Probability 'with replacement' and 'without replacement'

If a problem is in two stages, look carefully at the explanation.

Maryam has a bag of sweets. There are 7 red sweets and 8 green sweets. Without looking in the bag, Maryam picks out two sweets, one at a time. She has two choices once she has picked out her first sweet:

1. She can put the first sweet back in the bag before taking the second one; this is a problem 'with replacement' and the probabilities of selecting a sweet are the same for the first sweet and the second sweet.

2. She can eat the first sweet, and then take the second sweet. This has altered the probabilities for the second stage and is a problem 'without replacement'. The probability of selecting a sweet for the second time is different from the probability of selecting the first sweet.

Without replacement

Maryam has a bag of sweets. There are 7 red sweets and 8 green sweets. Without looking in the bag, Maryam takes out a sweet and eats it. She then takes another sweet and eats that.

(a) What is the probability that she eats two green sweets?

(b) What is the probability that she eats two different coloured sweets?

This problem is similar to the example in section 10.6 where Priya is picking coloured balls, so the best diagram to use is a tree diagram. However, Maryam has *eaten* the first sweet instead of *replacing* it. The number of sweets in the bag is now different; therefore the probabilities will be different when she takes a second sweet.

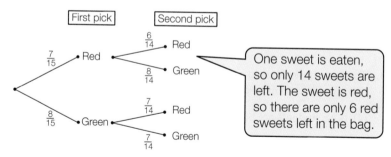

Using the tree diagram:

(a) $P(G, G) = \dfrac{8}{15} \times \dfrac{7}{14} = \dfrac{4}{15}$

> There are 15 sweets and 8 are green so the probability of picking a green sweet is $\frac{8}{15}$. After one green sweet is eaten, there are only 14 sweets left in total and only 7 green sweets, so the probability of picking a green sweet has changed to $\frac{7}{14}$.

(b) $P(R, G \text{ or } G, R) = \dfrac{7}{15} \times \dfrac{8}{14} + \dfrac{8}{15} \times \dfrac{7}{14} = \dfrac{8}{15}$

> There are two ways to pick two different colours: red then green, **or** green then red.

With replacement

If Maryam does not eat the first sweet but puts it back in the bag, the problem is different. This is now a probability question 'with replacement' so the probabilities on the tree diagram do not change.

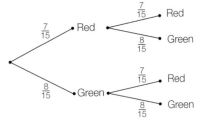

Using the tree diagram the probabilities are now:

(a) $P(G, G) = \dfrac{8}{15} \times \dfrac{8}{15} = \dfrac{64}{225}$

(b) $P(R, G \text{ or } G, R) = \dfrac{7}{15} \times \dfrac{8}{15} + \dfrac{8}{15} \times \dfrac{7}{15} = \dfrac{112}{225}$

Exercise 10.7

1. A bag contains 9 yellow marbles and 4 blue marbles. A marble is taken from the bag and its colour noted but it is **not** replaced. Another marble is then taken. Calculate the probability that:

    (a) at least one of the marbles is yellow

    (b) the marbles are of different colours

    (c) neither marble is blue.

2. A bag contains 12 red marbles and 8 green marbles. A marble is taken from the bag and its colour noted. It is then replaced. Another marble is then taken and its colour noted. Calculate the probability that:

    (a) both marbles are green

    (b) the marbles are of different colours

3. There are 18 students in a class, 8 boys and 10 girls. A teacher asks for two volunteers to hand out some books. Calculate the probability that:

    (a) both students are boys

    (b) neither of the students is a boy

    (c) at least one of the students is a girl.

4. A jar contains 7 red marbles, 5 green marbles and 3 blue marbles. Alice takes a marble, notes its colour and puts it back in the jar. She then takes another marble. Calculate the probability that:

    (a) the marbles are of the same colour

    (b) the marbles are of different colours

    (c) there is at least one blue marble.

5. A bag contains 12 soft-centred sweets and 8 hard-centred ones. Without looking, Robert takes a sweet from the bag, eats it and then takes another one. Calculate the probability that:

   (a) neither of the sweets is soft-centred

   (b) not more than one of the sweets is hard-centred

   (c) there is at least one of each type of sweet.

6. The table below shows the breakdown of the examination results in Mathematical Studies for an IB College.

Level	3	4	5	6	7
Frequency	2	8	12	7	3

   If one student is chosen at random, calculate the probability that the student achieved:

   (a) a Level 6 or 7   (b) a Level 4 or higher.

   Two students are selected randomly. With the aid of a tree diagram, calculate the probability that:

   (c) both of them achieved Level 7s

   (d) just one of them achieved a Level 7

   (e) at least one of them achieved a Level 7.

7. Terry likes playing snooker. The values of the seven coloured balls are as follows:

Colour	red	yellow	green	brown	blue	pink	black
Points value	1	2	3	4	5	6	7

   Terry picks two of the snooker balls randomly and calculates the total points score. Neither ball is replaced.

   (a) Draw a sample space diagram to show the list of possible sums.

   (b) Calculate the probability of picking two balls with a total points score:

      (i)   equal to 8

      (ii) not greater than 10

      (iii) not less than 12.

8. The table below shows the orders placed by a group of 140 passengers in an airport café.

	Bagel	Croissant	Toast	Total
Tea	26	18	33	
Coffee	34	12	17	
Total				

(a) A catering officer asks one of the customers what they have just ordered. What is the probability that the customer:

   (i)   did not order a croissant

   (ii) ordered tea

   (iii) ordered coffee but not toast?

(b) Mr and Mrs Knight have just finished their meal at the café. What is the probability that:

   (i)   they both had coffee and a bagel

   (ii) neither of them had toast

   (iii) at least one of them had a croissant?

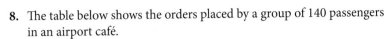

10.8 Conditional probability

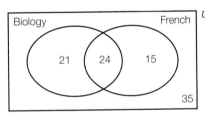

Look at this Venn diagram again:

The diagram shows that 39 out of 95 students are taking French, so:

$$P(\text{French}) = \frac{39}{95}$$

But suppose that you ask a slightly different question.

'Given that a student is studying French, what is the probability that they are also studying Biology?' The extra information 'given that' alters the problem; it is an example of **conditional probability**, where you are given some additional information that you need to use in your calculation.

The word 'given' in the question tells you that you are solving a conditional probability question.

Look at the Venn diagram again. The probability is no longer calculated from all the students at the college; you calculate the probability using the number of students who are studying French as the total. 39 are studying French, and 24 students are studying French and Biology. So, the probability that a student studies Biology given that they study French:

$$P(B \mid F) = \frac{24}{39}$$ 'B | F' means 'B given F'

In general terms we can say that the probability of A given B is equal to the probability of 'A and B' divided by the probability of B. The general formula for conditional probability is shown below.

$$\text{In general, } P(A \mid B) = \frac{P(A \cap B)}{P(B)}$$

You are asked about another friend. What is the probability that he is studying French given that he is **not** studying Biology?

You can approach this in two ways:

1. Look at the Venn diagram. 15 students study only French, and 50 students $(15 + 35)$ do not study Biology, so $P(F \mid B') = \frac{15}{50}$.

2. Or you can use the formula:

$$P(F \mid B') = \frac{P(\text{French and no Biology})}{P(\text{no Biology})} = \frac{\dfrac{15}{95}}{\dfrac{50}{95}} = \frac{15}{50}$$

In both cases: $P(F \mid B') = \dfrac{15}{50}$

exam tip

Make sure you remember that in conditional probability the denominator will change depending on the conditions. Focus on the words instead of the formula.

Worked example 10.11

Q. Zoe has a drawer containing 5 pink socks and 7 blue socks. Without looking, she picks out a sock, puts it on her bed and takes out another sock.

The tree diagram looks like this:

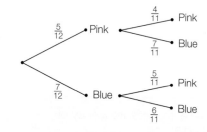

(a) What is the probability that Zoe picks out two socks of the same colour?

(b) Given that she picks out two socks that are the same colour, what is the probability that they are both blue?

She could pick out (pink, pink) $(\frac{5}{12} \times \frac{4}{11})$ **or** (blue, blue) $(\frac{7}{12} \times \frac{6}{11})$. Remember that once the first sock has been picked, there are only 11 socks left and one less of the selected colour.

A. (a) $P(\text{same colour}) = \dfrac{5}{12} \times \dfrac{4}{11} + \dfrac{7}{12} \times \dfrac{6}{11} = \dfrac{31}{66}$

continued . . .

continued . . .

The word 'given' in the question indicates that the probability is conditional. Use the general formula $P(A \mid B) = \dfrac{P(A \cap B)}{P(B)}$ and substitute in the appropriate values obtained from part (a).

(b) $P(\text{both blue} \mid \text{same colour}) = \dfrac{P(\text{both blue})}{P(\text{same colour})}$

$P(\text{both blue}) = \dfrac{7}{12} \times \dfrac{6}{11} = \dfrac{7}{22}$

$P(\text{same colour}) = \dfrac{31}{66}$ (from part (a))

$P(\text{both blue} \mid \text{same colour}) = \dfrac{7}{22} \div \dfrac{31}{66} = \dfrac{21}{31}$

exam tip

Answering a conditional probability question involves reading the question carefully, and then creating a good sample space diagram. If you do this successfully, you may not need to use the formula.

Worked example 10.12

Q. This table shows the hair colour of 64 children at a nursery.

	Brown	Blonde	Black
Boy	10	15	7
Girl	8	19	5

Use the sample space diagram to answer the following questions; you do not need to use the formula.

(a) What is the probability that a child has blonde hair?

(b) Given that a child has blonde hair, what is the probability that it is a girl?

Using the table, the total frequency of blonde is 34 (15 + 19).

A. (a) $P(\text{Blonde}) = \dfrac{15 + 19}{64} = \dfrac{34}{64} = \dfrac{17}{32}$

There are 19 blonde girls and a total of 34 blonde children.

(b) $P(\text{Girl} \mid \text{Blonde}) = \dfrac{19}{34}$

Worked example 10.13

Q. 100 members of a film club are asked which type of film they like watching: animation, thrillers or romances.

The results are given on this Venn diagram. Only six members like all three genres.

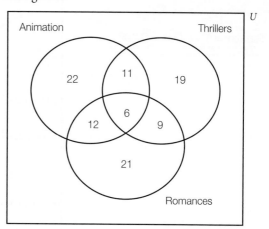

(a) What is the probability that someone likes watching animated films?

(b) Given that they like watching animated films, what is the probability that they also enjoy romances? Do not use the formula.

> Using the Venn diagram:
> 22 + 11 + 12 + 6 = 51 people out of 100 like animated films.

A. (a) $P(\text{animation}) = \dfrac{51}{100}$

> Using the Venn diagram:
> of the 51 people who like animations, 12 + 6 = 18 people also like romances.

(b) $P(R \mid A) = \dfrac{18}{51}$

Worked example 10.14

Q. The results of a conditional probability calculation can be unexpected.

Suppose that there is a disease that affects one person in every thousand. It is curable but the treatment is unpleasant. A test has been developed that gives a positive result for the presence of the disease in 97% of the people who have the disease and 4% of those who do not. Is it a reliable test?

> If you were given these figures by a doctor, would you take the test? After looking at the mathematics on the next page, would you change your mind?

continued . . .

This is the tree diagram:

A.

P(disease) = $\frac{1}{1000}$ = 0.001

P(no disease) = 1 − 0.001 = 0.999

$$P(\text{positive test}) = 0.001 \times 0.97 + 0.999 \times 0.04 = 0.04093$$

$$P(\text{disease} \mid \text{positive test}) = \frac{0.001 \times 0.97}{0.04093} = 0.0237 \text{ or } 2.37\%$$

There is a 2.37% chance that someone with a positive test result has the disease. The test needs to be much more reliable than this if it is to be useful.

Exercise 10.8

1. The following table shows the number of IB students studying Physics and Economics in a College. It is also known that none of the Physics students studies Economics.

	Physics	Economics
Standard Level	28	46
Higher Level	12	14

(a) One of the students is chosen at random, calculate the probability that the student studies:

   (i) Physics or Economics at Higher Level

   (ii) at Higher Level, given that the student studies Physics.

(b) It is known that Anna studies Economics. What is the probability that she studies Economics at Standard Level?

2. Out of 100 students at a Language School, 43 study Russian and 59 study Chinese. 17 of the students study neither Russian nor Chinese.

(a) Represent the given information on a fully labelled Venn diagram.

(b) How many of the students study both Russian and Chinese?

(c) A student is chosen at random from the school. Calculate the probability that the student studies:

    (i)   both Chinese and Russian

    (ii)   Chinese, given that he or she does not study Russian

    (iii) Russian, given that he or she studies Chinese.

3. The following table shows the results of a survey carried out among all the Year 12 students in a school. The table shows the number of students who had eaten breakfast at home or had lunch at school on the last day of term.

		Breakfast	
		Yes	No
School lunch	Yes	42	65
	No	25	18

Find the probability that a Year 12 student, chosen at random on that day:

(a) had breakfast and school lunch

(b) had school lunch, given that they had breakfast

(c) did not have breakfast, given that they did not have school lunch.

Summary

You should know:

- the basic principles of probability

    – a certain result has a probability of 1

    – an impossible result has a probability of 0

    – all probabilities lie between 0 and 1

    – the results of a probability experiment are called outcomes and an individual outcome being investigated is an event

    – the probabilities of all possible outcomes of a probability experiment add up to 1

    – if an event A' is complementary to A, their probabilities add up to 1 ($P(A') = 1 - P(A)$).

continued ...

- what a sample space is and how to construct sample space diagrams

- how to calculate theoretical and experimental probabilities, and that the general formula for calculating probability is $P(A) = \dfrac{\text{number of outcomes in } A}{\text{total number of outcomes}}$.

- what the expected value is and how to calculate it

- how to recognise and calculate the probability of combined, mutually exclusive and independent events

- how to use tree diagrams, Venn diagrams, sample space diagrams and tables of outcomes to calculate probabilities

- that probability 'with replacement' is not the same as probability 'without replacement'

- how to calculate conditional probability using sample space diagrams (and the formula as well).

Mixed examination practice

Exam-style questions

1. The sample space diagram for rolling a **biased** six-sided die is shown below.

x	1	2	3	4	5	6
$P(x)$	a	0.3	0.2	0.1	$2a$	a

   (a) Work out the value of a.

   (b) Calculate the probability of rolling a 5.

   (c) Find the probability of not rolling a 5.

2. One letter is chosen at random from the word CALCULUS. What is the probability of choosing the letters L or C?

3. The letters of the word BOTANICAL are written on nine separate cards and placed on a table. Nikolai picks one of the cards at random.

   Calculate the probability he picks a card with the letter:

   (a) A   (b) T   (c) A or T.

4. 60 IB students were asked to name their favourite subjects. The pie chart illustrates the responses given by the students.

   If one of the students is picked at random, find the probability that the student chose:

   (a) Economics

   (b) French or History

   (c) neither Geography nor Philosophy.

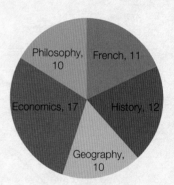

5. Out of 80 university students, 48 of them were over 18 years old and 32 of them had cars. 20 of the over-18-year-olds had cars.

   (a) Complete the following table based on the information from above.

	Over 18's	18 or under	Total
Have cars			
Do not have cars			
Total			80

   One of the 80 students is chosen at random. What is the probability that the student:

   (b) is not over 18 years old and owns a car

   (c) does not own a car?

6. Twin sisters, Wing and Nam, are entered for the Senior Mathematics Challenge. They could each win a Gold Certificate, a Silver Certificate, a Bronze Certificate or nothing. Given that each of them wins a certificate, complete a full sample space diagram for the possible outcomes.

Wing	Gold	Gold							
Nam	Gold								

   (a) What is the total number of possible outcomes?

   (b) What is the probability of:

      (i)   both sisters winning bronze certificates?

      (ii) neither of them winning a gold certificate?

      (iii) the sisters winning different certificates?

7. A survey of 140 football fans was carried out at the Stadio Olimpico in Rome. They were asked whether they lived in Rome and, if they did, which football team they supported.

   $U = \{\text{football fans}\}$
   $R = \{\text{residents of Rome}\}$
   $L = \{\text{Lazio fans}\}$
   $n(R \cup L) = 134$
   $n(R) = 110$
   $n(R \cap L) = 42$

   (a) Draw a Venn diagram to represent the information from above.

   (b) If one of the football fans is selected at random, calculate the probability that the fan:

      (i)   supports Lazio

      (ii) lives in Rome, given that the fan does not support Lazio

      (iii) supports Lazio, given that the fan does not live in Rome.

8. A group of students were asked whether they owned iPhones or iPads. Their responses are illustrated on the Venn diagram.

   $U = \{\text{students surveyed}\}$
   $D = \{\text{students who owned iPads}\}$
   $E = \{\text{students who owned iPhones}\}$

   (a) How many students were surveyed?

   (b) If two student are chosen at random, find the probability that:

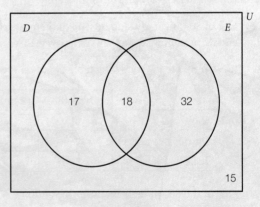

      (i)   both students own an iPad

      (ii) both students own iPhones, given that they own iPads

      (iii) both students own iPhones, given that they do not own iPads.

9. The table below shows the number of teachers who have played any of the following types of sports in the previous week. Each teacher has played only one of the types of sports indicated.

	Male	Female	Total
Baseball		10	39
Basketball	20		
Hockey	14	19	
Total	63		110

(a) Copy and complete the table from above.

(b) If two teachers are chosen at random, calculate the probability that:

   (i) only one of them has played hockey

   (ii) both of them have played baseball, given that they are both female teachers

   (iii) they are male teachers, given that they play hockey or basketball.

10. Seventy Economics students and teachers were asked which Economics magazine they had read in the past month. Their responses are shown in the table below. Each of the respondents had read only one of the three magazines indicated.

	The Economist	*MoneyWeek*	*New Economy*
Student	32	8	17
Teacher	6	3	4

(a) If a student is chosen at random, what is the probability that this student has read either *The Economist* or *MoneyWeek*?

(b) If two teachers are chosen at random, find the probability that at least one of them has read *New Economy*.

(c) If two of the students and teachers are chosen randomly, calculate the probability that:

   (i) they are both teachers, given that they have not read *The Economist*

   (ii) they are both students, given that they have either read *MoneyWeek* or *New Economy*.

11. In a group of 30 students, 20 study French, 7 study German and 6 study neither French nor German.

(a) If one student is chosen at random, calculate the probability that the student:

   (i) studies both French and German

   (ii) studies German, given that he/she does not study French.

(b) Two of the students have decided to enrol on a Russian language course. Find the probability that:

   (i) both students study French, given that they study either French or German but not both

   (ii) both of them study German, given that they do not study French.

12. The Venn diagram below shows how 48 teachers at a Sixth Form College travelled to school in one month.

U = {48 teachers in the college}
W = {teachers who walked to school}
C = {teachers who travelled to school by car}
B = {teachers who rode to school by bike}

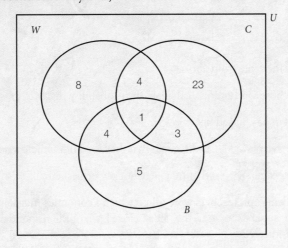

(a) One of the 48 teachers is asked how he/she travelled to school. Write in words what the following probabilities mean:

(i) $P(W \mid B)$

(ii) $P(C \mid B')$

(iii) $P(B' \mid W \cap C)$.

(b) Calculate all the probabilities in part (a).

4 Statistical applications

In 1747 the government of Sweden conducted its first population census to find out how many citizens were living in the country. Today, governments all over the world use regular censuses to collect data about their citizens so that they have sufficient information to plan the services needed now and in the future.

Once information has been collected, it needs to be displayed in a meaningful way and then analysed if it is to be used constructively. Initially called 'State mathematics', the branch of mathematics that deals with the collection, organisation, presentation and analysis of data is now known as 'Statistics'. This chapter introduces three statistical techniques that have become increasingly influential.

For example, when the data on smoking habits of lung cancer patients was analysed, people came to realise that the connection or 'correlation' was too strong to have occurred by chance. Now the health ministries of most countries discourage their citizens from smoking because the risks are considered to be unacceptably high.

However, some authorities have argued that our reliance on statistical inference is now too great and is stopping us from taking events seriously that the statistics tell us are unlikely. In his book *Black Swan*, Nassim Nicholas Taleb suggests that the reliance of banks and trading firms on analysis based on the normal distribution means that they do not allow for very unlikely events (which he calls 'black swan events'), and this can lead them to ignore positive developments and to make very large mistakes when they encounter negative events.

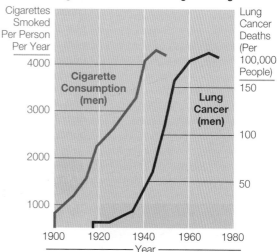

Source: National Institutes of Health.

Prior learning topics

It will be easier to study this topic if you have already completed:

- Topic 2 (Chapters 5–7)
- Chapter 10

Chapter 11 The normal distribution

In this chapter you will learn:

- about the normal distribution and the concept of a random variable
- about the parameters σ and μ
- about properties of the normal distribution, such as the bell shape and the symmetry about $x = \mu$
- how to draw the normal distribution curve and areas under it on a diagram
- how to do normal probability calculations by using diagrams and your GDC
- how to do inverse normal calculations.

Every year Nando weighs his lambs before taking them to market. He can only take lambs above a certain mass, and any that are too light are left behind. He finds that most of his lambs are approximately the same mass, but some are heavier and some are lighter.

If Nando drew a histogram of the masses of his lambs, it would look like this:

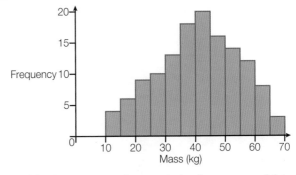

The shape of this histogram is characteristic of many sets of data that involve continuous variables such as height, length, time, blood pressure, or other quantities that are measured rather than counted.

 Recall from Chapter 5 that discrete data can be counted, while continuous data comes from measuring.

The masses of the lambs cluster around a central value; there are few lambs that are very heavy or very light, so the frequencies for masses near the middle of the range are higher than those for masses near the ends of the range. This creates a 'bell shaped' histogram, and you can see immediately that high or low values occur less frequently than those that are close to the central value.

This 'bell-shaped' distribution of frequencies is called the **normal distribution**, and it has been known and used for nearly three hundred years.

11.1 The normal distribution curve

The graph of the normal distribution looks like this:

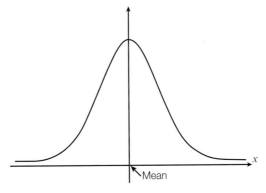

The vertical 'axis' in the middle marks the position of the **mean**. x is the value of the continuous variable X being measured and is plotted along the horizontal axis.

You will have noticed straight away several properties of the normal distribution:

- It is symmetrical about the mean.

- The maximum height of the curve occurs at the mean.

- If you think of the height as representing 'frequency', then you can see that the mean, median and mode are all the same.

 The mean, median and mode were defined in Chapter 6.

The normal distribution has other special properties that make it useful in many different areas of statistics; it is particularly useful in the study of probabilities.

Two of these special properties are:

- The total area under the curve equals 1.

- The horizontal axis is an **asymptote** of the curve; the curve approaches the horizontal axis but never touches it.

To work with the normal distribution, you need to know the mean and standard deviation of the population from which data is being collected.

 You met the standard deviation in Chapter 7. It is a measure of spread around the mean of a set of data.

As the area under the normal distribution curve is equal to 1, you can use any partial area to calculate the probability of obtaining a particular range of data values.

 All probabilities have values between 0 and 1; see Chapter 10.

There is special notation for normal distributions. Suppose you are measuring a variable X (e.g. height, length or time). X is called a **random variable** because its value can be different each time it is observed; it is a **continuous random variable** if it can take any value within a certain interval of real numbers (which is the case when X is a measurement of some quantity). If the continuous random variable X follows a normal distribution, we write:

$$X \sim \mathrm{N}(\mu, \sigma^2)$$

where:

- N denotes the normal distribution

- μ (the Greek letter 'mu') stands for the mean

- σ is the standard deviation.

You say this as 'the variable X is normally distributed with a mean of μ and a standard deviation of σ'.

Pierre Simon Laplace (1749–1827) discovered his mathematical talents when he entered Caen University, in France, at the age of 16. He studied the mathematical and scientific techniques current at that time, moving to Paris when he was 19. As the scientific instruments in the eighteenth century were not very accurate, scientists worked by taking a series of measurements and then calculating their mean. Laplace proved that the mean of many observations is described by a 'bell-shaped' curve and that even when the original distribution is not normal, the mean of the repeated samples will be. He also proved that the larger the number of samples, the better the fit to the normal distribution.

A normal distribution with a mean of 23 and a standard deviation of 3.7 is written as:

$$X \sim N(23, 3.7^2)$$

Relationship between the shape of the curve and the mean and standard deviation

The normal distribution curve is always bell-shaped, but the exact shape of the 'bell' is controlled by the values of the mean and the standard deviation.

In the graph below, notice that a small standard deviation gives a curve that is tall and thin, while a large standard deviation gives a curve that is low and wide. In all cases, the total area under the curve equals 1.

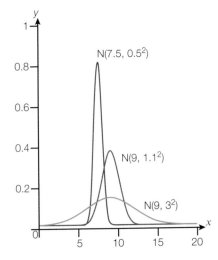

The following graph shows three normal distribution curves with the same standard deviation but different mean values. The curves all have the same maximum height. Changing the value of the mean does not change the shape of the curve but moves it to a different place along the horizontal axis.

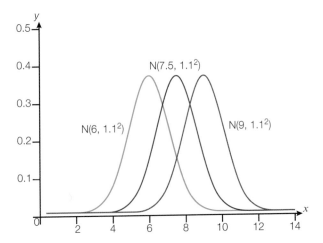

If you keep the mean at the same value but change the standard deviation, you will see that the curve remains centred at the same location on the horizontal axis, but its shape becomes more peaked or flatter depending on the value of the standard deviation: a small standard deviation gives a tall and narrow curve, while a large standard deviation gives a low, flat and wide curve.

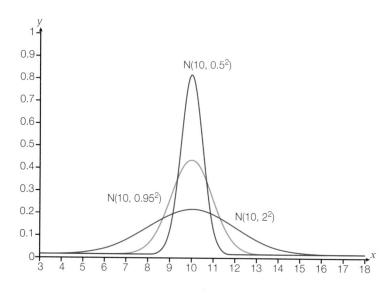

Symmetry of the normal distribution curve

Understanding the symmetry of the normal distribution curve will be very important in learning how to use the curve for calculating probabilities.

When drawing the curve, there are two common ways of marking the x-axis.

1. Mark the mean on the x-axis and put a sensible scale of x values around it. Write the distribution beside the curve.

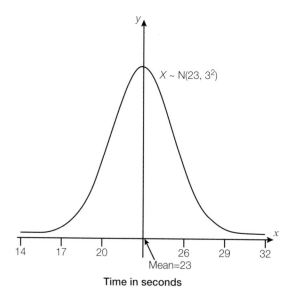

2. In some situations it is more relevant to mark the mean on the *x*-axis together with a certain number of standard deviations to the right and left of the mean. For instance, normal curves generated by spreadsheets or GDCs will usually show four standard deviations in each direction.

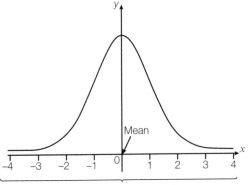

By the symmetry of the curve, 50% of the population lies to the right of the mean and 50% lies to the left; in other words, 50% of data values are expected to lie above the mean and 50% below the mean.

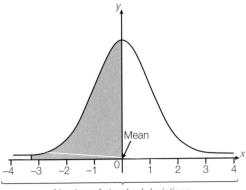

For applications, it is useful to remember what percentage of the population lies within a certain number of standard deviations of the mean:

Approximately **68%** of the distribution lies between **−1** and **+1** standard deviations from the mean.

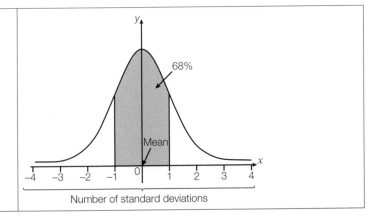

Approximately **95%** of the distribution lies between **−2** and **+2** standard deviations from the mean.	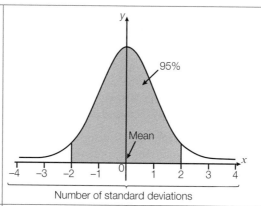
Approximately **99%** of the distribution lies between **−3** and **+3** standard deviations from the mean.	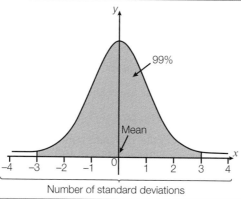

11.2 Probability calculations using the normal distribution

The symmetry and general properties of the normal distribution make it suitable for use in many different fields. Modern statistics packages have made it easy to do calculations with the normal distribution, even if you do not understand the detailed mathematics behind it.

For example, the distribution of masses of Nando's lambs has a mean of 41.1 kg and a standard deviation of 13.5 kg. Nando can only send lambs to market if they have a mass of at least 33 kg. He can estimate the **proportion** of his lambs that can go to market by making a sketch like the following:

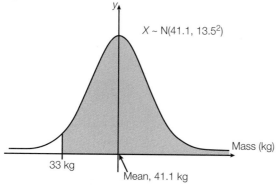

The proportion of lambs with a mass of 33 kg or more is represented by the area under the curve to the right of $x = 33$.

> **Sets of data that come from measurements can often be approximated very well by the normal distribution. These include measurements of physical, psychological, biological and economic phenomena, and so the normal distribution is used in disciplines ranging from physics and biology to finance and business.**

When doing calculations with the normal distribution, it is always a good idea to draw clear diagrams showing the area that you are using to solve a problem.

As the total area under the curve is 1, you can use any partial area that you have shaded under the curve to estimate the **proportion** of your data that lies within that range of x values or, equivalently, the **probability** of your data taking on those values.

Your graphical calculator has a program that will perform the area calculations, but in order to enter all the data correctly you should sketch a diagram first. Before you do anything with your GDC, read the question carefully, and identify the area under the normal curve corresponding to the probability that you have been asked to calculate. Express the distribution in the form $X \sim N(\mu, \sigma^2)$, and check $\geq$ and $\leq$ symbols in the question with particular care. Then draw a bell-shaped curve, and on your diagram:

- mark the mean
- mark the lower and upper boundaries relevant to the question
- shade in the area that you need to find.

For example, if Nando wants to estimate the number of lambs whose mass is between 33 kg and 48 kg, he would shade in the following area under his normal curve: the lower boundary would be $x = 33$, and the upper boundary would be $x = 48$.

GDC

Be careful not to confuse normal **cdf** with normal **pdf**.

The cdf (cumulative distribution function) gives an area under the curve, i.e. the probability that you are calculating.

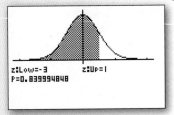

The pdf (probability density function) gives the y-coordinate of a point on the normal curve corresponding to a given value of x.

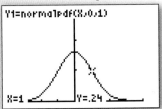

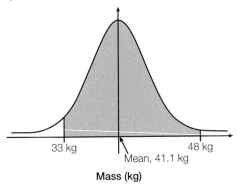

Mass (kg)

A hand-drawn diagram on which you have shaded the required area will help to ensure that you have understood the question. Now use a GDC.

Areas under the normal distribution curve are calculated by your GDC by drawing a graph (see section *11.1 (a)* on page 669 of the GDC chapter) or with the **normal cumulative distribution** (ncd) **function** (see section *11.1 (b)* on page 670 of the GDC chapter).

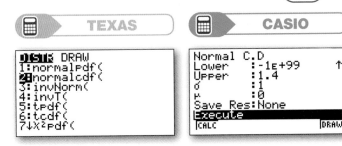

Standard normal distribution N(0, 1²)

A normal distribution with a mean of 0 and a standard deviation of 1 is called the **standard normal distribution**.

By default, the program on your GDC calculates areas for the standard normal distribution. This means that if the question you want to answer involves the standard normal distribution, you will only need to enter the upper and lower boundaries.

Worked example 11.1

Q. (a) If $X \sim N(0, 1^2)$, find the probability that X is 1.15 or less; this is written as $P(X \leq 1.15)$.

A.

> Sketch a diagram first, either by hand or on a GDC or computer. Shade the area under the curve to the **left** of 1.15 because we are looking for $X \leq 1.15$.

> Calculate the probability using your GDC; you can use either method *11.1 (a)* on page 669 or method *11.1(b)* on page 670 of the GDC chapter. There is no lower boundary defined in the question, so enter a very large **negative** number such as −1E99 on your GDC. Enter 1.15 as the upper boundary.

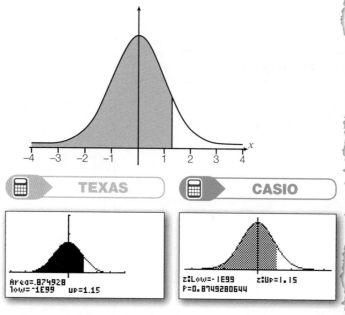

From GDC: $P(X \leq 1.15) = 0.875$

Q. (b) If $X \sim N(0, 1^2)$, find $P(X \geq -1.9)$.

A.

> Sketch a diagram and shade the area under the curve to the **right** of −1.9.

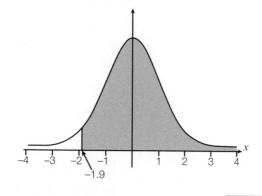

continued . . .

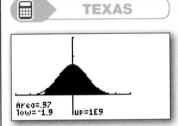

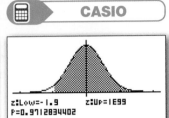

From GDC: $P(X \le 1.15) = 0.971$

Q. (c) If $X \sim N(0, 1^2)$, find the probability that X lies between -1.5 and 0.7.

A.

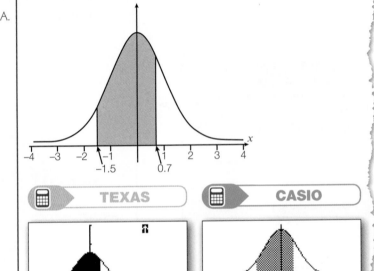

$P(-1.5 \le X \le 0.7) = 0.691$

Use your GDC to calculate the probability by drawing a graph or using the ncd function. Enter −1.9 as the lower boundary. This time there is no upper boundary defined in the question, so use a very **large** positive number such as 1E9 or 1E99.

Sketch a diagram. Shade the area under the curve between $x = -1.5$ and $x = 0.7$.

Use your GDC to calculate the probability; enter the given lower and upper boundaries into your GDC.

Exercise 11.1

1. Assume that $X \sim N(0, 1^2)$. For each of the given probabilities, sketch the normal distribution curve and indicate, by shading and labelling, the required area.

   (a) $P(X \ge 1.7)$ (b) $P(X \le 0.9)$

   (c) $P(0 \le X \le 0.9)$ (d) $P(0.8 \le X \le 1.9)$

   (e) $P(X \ge -0.8)$ (f) $P(X \le -1.9)$

   (g) $P(-2.5 \le X \le -0.5)$ (h) $P(-0.5 \le X \le 2.5)$

   (i) $P(0.5 \le X \le 2.5)$ (j) $P(-1.0 \le X \le 0)$

2. Calculate each of the probabilities in question 1.

3. (a) Sketch, shade and label the following areas, given that $X \sim N(0, 1^2)$.

   (i) $P(X \geq 1.5)$ (ii) $P(X \leq -1.5)$

(b) Comment on the relationship between the two areas.

(c) Calculate both probabilities.

4. Given that $X \sim N(0, 1^2)$, what is the connection between the three probabilities $P(X \leq -2)$, $P(-2 \leq X \leq 2)$ and $P(X \geq 2)$?

General normal distribution $N(\mu, \sigma^2)$

In most problems the normal distribution will not be the standard one with mean 0 and standard deviation 1.

You can still calculate probabilities using your GDC, but now you will need to enter the mean and standard deviation as well as the lower and upper boundary values. On most GDCs, you enter the values of μ and σ **after** the lower and upper limits. It is still essential to draw a diagram to visualise the area you are calculating.

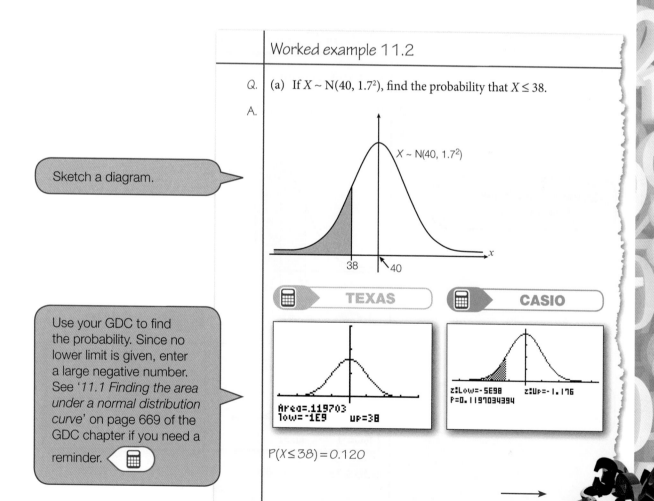

Worked example 11.2

Q. **(a)** If $X \sim N(40, 1.7^2)$, find the probability that $X \leq 38$.

A.

Sketch a diagram.

$X \sim N(40, 1.7^2)$

38 40

TEXAS   **CASIO**

Use your GDC to find the probability. Since no lower limit is given, enter a large negative number. See '11.1 Finding the area under a normal distribution curve' on page 669 of the GDC chapter if you need a reminder.

Area=.119703
low=-1E9   up=38

z:Low=-5E98   z:Up=-1.176
P=0.1197034394

$P(X \leq 38) = 0.120$

continued . . .

Q. (b) If $X \sim N(150, 12^2)$, find the probability that $X \le 158$.

A.

$X \sim N(150, 12^2)$

150 158

From the diagram, you can predict that the answer should be greater than 0.5.

Use your GDC to calculate the probability.

TEXAS

Area=.747508
low=-1E9   lup=158

CASIO

z:Low=-8.3E7   z:Up=0.6666
P=0.7475074625

$P(X \le 158) = 0.748$

Q. (c) If $X \sim N(45, 9^2)$, find $P(36 \le X \le 54)$.

A.

$X \sim N(45, 9^2)$

36   54
45

Shade the area between $x = 36$ and $x = 54$.

Use your GDC to calculate the probability.

TEXAS

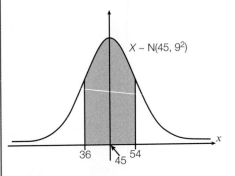

Area=.682689
low=-1   lup=1

CASIO

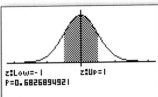

z:Low=-1   z:Up=1
P=0.6826894921

$P(36 \le X \le 54) = 0.683$

Exercise 11.2

1. For each of the following probabilities, sketch the normal distribution curve and indicate, by shading and labelling, the required areas.

   (a) $X \sim N(7, 2^2)$

       (i) $P(X \geq 9)$ (ii) $P(X \leq 11.5)$

       (iii) $P(X \leq 4.8)$ (iv) $P(5.4 \leq X \leq 8.2)$

   (b) $X \sim N(48, 9^2)$

       (i) $P(36 \leq X \leq 52)$ (ii) $P(55 \leq X \leq 75)$

       (iii) $P(25 \leq X \leq 48)$ (iv) $P(22 \leq X \leq 32)$

2. Calculate each of the probabilities in question 1.

3. Given that $X \sim N(2.4, 3^2)$, calculate the following probabilities. Remember to shade the required area before using your GDC.

   (a) $P(X \leq -2)$ (b) $P(-2 \leq X \leq 0)$ (c) $P(-2 \leq X \leq 2.4)$

   (d) $P(-1 \leq X \leq 6.6)$ (e) $P(X \geq 5.7)$

4. Let X be a normally distributed variable with a mean of 3 and a standard deviation of 2. What is $P(X \geq 6)$?

11.3 Solving practical problems with the normal distribution

The calculation of probabilities often comes up in the context of solving practical problems. The bell-shaped distribution is a good model for a wide range of 'real world' situations, as Adolphe Quetelet found out in his quest for the 'average man'.

Suppose that one year Nando finds that his lambs have a mean mass of 35.8 kg, with a standard deviation of 2.05 kg. As usual, Nando can only send his lambs to market if they have a mass of at least 33 kg. What is the probability that a lamb has a mass of less than 33 kg? If Nando has 150 lambs, how many lambs do you expect he will have to keep back?

We assume that X, the random variable representing the mass of a lamb, follows a normal distribution. So:

$X \sim N(35.8, 2.05^2)$

The probability that a lamb has a mass of less than 33 kg is given by the area under the curve to the left of $x = 33$:

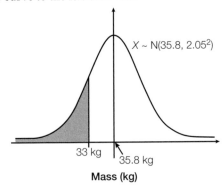

On your GDC, enter a large negative number (such as −1E9) for the lower boundary, 33 for the upper boundary, 35.8 for μ, and 2.05 for σ.

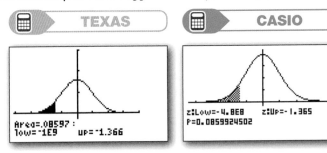

Hence $P(X < 33) = 0.0860$.

As Nando has 150 lambs in total, the expected number that are below 33 kg is $150 \times 0.0860 = 13$. So Nando expects to keep 13 lambs because they are not heavy enough to go to market.

Worked example 11.3

Q. A manufacturer calculates that the lifetime of his laptop batteries is normally distributed with a mean life of 28 months and a standard deviation of 7.5 months.

The manufacturer gives a 12-month guarantee on each battery.

(a) What is the probability that a battery will last at least 28 months?

(b) What is the probability that a battery will last more than 38 months?

(c) What is the probability that a battery will last less than 12 months?

(d) The manufacturer makes 5000 batteries each month. How many batteries can he expect will be returned under the terms of his guarantee?

continued . . .

(e) The company accountant thinks that the figure in (d) is too high. Should the manufacturer aim to make the standard deviation larger or smaller?

> Write down the distribution.

A. Let X be the lifetime of a battery; then
$X \sim N(28, 7.5^2)$

> To answer this question, you do not really need to use a calculator because you know the distribution is symmetrical about the mean.

(a) The mean of the distribution is 28, so by the symmetry of the normal distribution, $P(X \geq 28) = 0.5$

TEXAS

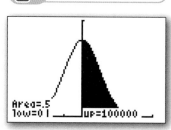

CASIO

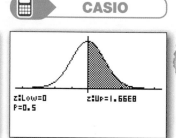

> Check your answer on your GDC. See section 11.1 on pages 669-670 of the GDC chapter if you need a reminder.

(b)

> We want the area to the right of 38. Sketch the curve and this area.

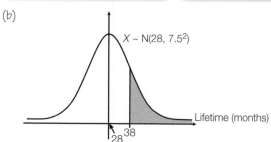

TEXAS

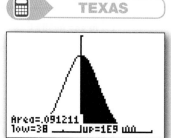

CASIO

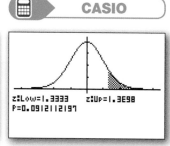

$P(X \geq 38) = 0.0912$

(c)

> We want the area to the left of 12.

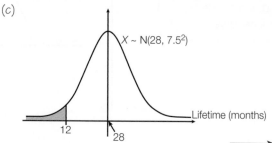

continued . . .

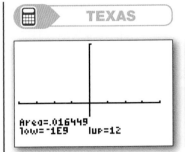

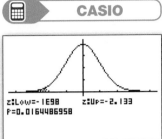

$P(X < 12) = 0.0164$

Notice that here the GDC has calculated the probability but not displayed the shaded curve. Be aware that sometimes your GDC might not give the expected output; but as long as you entered the calculation correctly, it should still produce the correct answer.

(d) Among 5000 batteries, the expected number that will be returned is $5000 \times 0.0164 = 82$.

Remember from Chapter 10 that expected value = probability × frequency. The probability of a battery being returned is $P(X < 12)$, which we found in (c).

(e) The manufacturer should aim to make the standard deviation smaller. For instance, if he reduces it to 6 months, only 19 batteries will be returned under the guarantee:

If $X \sim N(28, 6^2)$, then $P(X < 12) = 0.00383$

$5000 \times 0.00383 = 19.15$

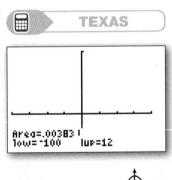

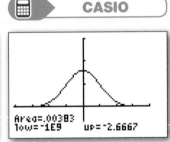

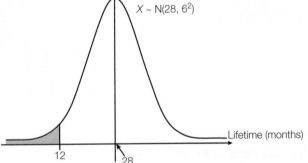

The standard deviation measures the spread around the mean; if σ is smaller, values will be more tightly clustered around the mean and so the probability of getting much shorter lifetimes will be lower.

Exercise 11.3

1. A survey of a sample of Australian cattle dogs determined the mean longevity to be 13.4 years with a standard deviation of 2.4 years.

   Miki is an Australian cattle dog. Estimate the probability of Miki living:

   (a) beyond 10 years

   (b) between 12 and 17 years

   (c) no more than 18 years.

2. The masses of adult African elephants belonging to a certain herd is known to be normally distributed with a mean of 5.5 tons and a standard deviation of 0.4 tons.

   (a) Bingo is an African elephant belonging to the above-mentioned herd. Estimate the probability of his mass being:

   (i) less than 6 tons   (ii) greater than 4.5 tons

   (iii) between 5.2 and 6.2 tons.

   (b) Out of a population of 100 adult elephants, estimate how many would be expected to have a mass of:

   (i) between 4.8 and 6.8 tons   (ii) less than 7 tons.

   (c) Do you expect any of the elephants to have a mass of more than 8 tons?

3. The reaction times of a sample of students were found to be normally distributed with a mean of 222 milliseconds and a standard deviation of 41 milliseconds.

   (a) What proportion of the students had a reaction time greater than 240 milliseconds?

   (b) What is the percentage of students with reaction times between 200 and 300 milliseconds?

   (c) If a student is chosen at random, what is the probability of his or her reaction time being less than 180 milliseconds?

   (d) Out of a student population of 600, how many of them do you expect to have a reaction time of less than 180 milliseconds?

4. Milk prices in a farming community were found to be normally distributed with a mean price of 24.99 cents per litre and a standard deviation of 2.51 cents per litre.

   Estimate the percentage of farms for which the price of a litre of milk is:

   (a) less than 30 cents

   (b) more than 20 cents

   (c) between 28 and 32 cents.

> Is the normal distribution relied upon too much? Is it always a good model for continuous data collected in a wide range of contexts? It can be argued that the normal distribution does not give enough importance to events that occur on the 'edges' of a population. It is used extensively in international finance, but can it predict unusual events and warn us when the system is heading towards crisis?

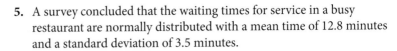

5. A survey concluded that the waiting times for service in a busy restaurant are normally distributed with a mean time of 12.8 minutes and a standard deviation of 3.5 minutes.

   On one particular evening, the restaurant served 240 customers. Estimate the number of customers who were served after waiting:

   (a) longer than 18 minutes

   (b) less than 5 minutes

   (c) between 10 and 15 minutes.

   The manager decided to give free desserts to all customers who waited for more than 20 minutes.

   (d) Estimate the number of customers out of the total of 240 who received the free desserts.

6. The IQ test scores of students in a school were found to be normally distributed with a mean of 110 and a standard deviation of 12.

   (a) Estimate the **proportion** of students in the school with IQ test scores:

   (i) above 90   (ii) below 80

   (iii) below 125   (iv) above 130.

   (b) Given that the student population is 1600, estimate the **number** of students with IQ test scores between:

   (i) 85 and 125   (ii) 130 and 140.

11.4 Inverse normal calculations

If you are given a probability value (a number between 0 and 1), your GDC can calculate the value a such that $P(X \le a)$ equals the known probability; this is called a **left tail** calculation. It can also find the value b such that $P(X \ge b)$ equals the known probability, which is called a **right tail** calculation. In either case, the GDC is performing an **inverse** calculation: it is working backwards, reversing the sort of calculations you have been doing in sections 11.2 and 11.3. See '11.2 Inverse normal calculations' on page 671 of the GDC chapter for a reminder of how to use your GDC to calculate inverse normal calculations.

For inverse normal calculations, it is even more helpful to draw a diagram, as this enables you to predict whether the answer should be greater than or less than the mean.

First, you need to establish whether you are looking at the left or right tail of the normal distribution. Then, shade the area that represents the probability you have been given.

Remember that by the symmetry of the normal curve, exactly half the area lies on each side of the mean. So if the given probability is greater than 0.5, the area must extend across the line of symmetry. Conversely, if the given probability is less than 0.5, the area must lie entirely on one side of the mean:

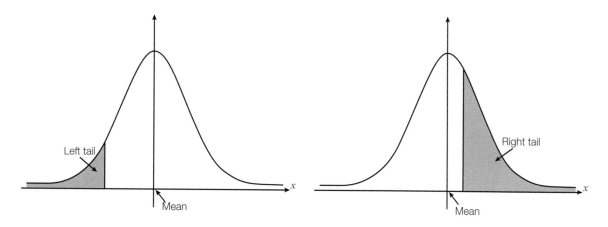

If the given probability is **less than 0.5** and you are looking for a **left tail** value, the answer should be to the **left** of the mean (the value is less than the mean). If the given probability is **less than 0.5** and you are looking for a **right tail** value, the answer should be to the **right** of the mean (the value is greater than the mean).

If the given probability is **greater than 0.5** and you are looking for a **left tail** value, the answer should be to the **right** of the mean (the value is greater than the mean). If the given probability is **greater than 0.5** and you are looking for a **right tail** value, the answer should be to the **left** of the mean (the value is less than the mean).

Inverse standard normal distribution

Recall that the standard normal distribution has mean 0 and standard deviation 1, denoted by $N(0, 1^2)$.

In this case, if the given probability is **less than 0.5** and you are looking for a **left tail** value, the answer should be **negative**; if the given probability is **less than 0.5** and you are looking for a **right tail** value, the answer should be **positive**.

If the given probability is **greater than 0.5** and you are looking for a **left tail** value, the answer should be **positive**; if the given probability is **greater than 0.5** and you are looking for a **right tail** value, the answer should be **negative**.

By default, your GDC does inverse calculations with the standard normal distribution, so if the question you want to answer is about the standard normal distribution, the only number you need to enter is the given probability.

On most TEXAS GDCs, the default setting is to calculate a left tail value. On most CASIO GDCs, you have the option of choosing a right tail or a left tail.

Worked example 11.4

Q. If $X \sim N(0, 1^2)$, find the value of a for which $P(X \le a) = 0.88$.

A.

Sketch the graph. $P(X \le a)$ tells you that you should be looking at a left tail. Since $0.88 > 0.5$, a must lie to the right of the mean so that the area extends across the central line of symmetry.

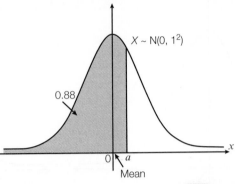

$X \sim N(0, 1^2)$

0.88

0 a

Mean

Enter the number 0.88 into the inverse normal function on your GDC. See section *11.2 Inverse normal calculations* on page 671 of the GDC chapter if you need to.

TEXAS

```
invNorm(0.88
        1.174986791
```

CASIO

```
Inverse Normal
Data     :Variable
Tail     :Left
Area     :0.88
σ        :1
μ        :0
Save Res:None
None LIST
```

```
Inverse Normal
 xInv=1.17498679
```

The GDC gives $a = 1.17$.

Worked example 11.5

Q. If $X \sim N(0, 1^2)$, find the value of b for which $P(X \ge b) = 0.65$.

A.

Sketch the graph. $P(X \ge b)$ tells you that you should be looking at a right tail. Since $0.65 > 0.5$, b must lie to the left of the mean so that the area extends across the central line of symmetry.

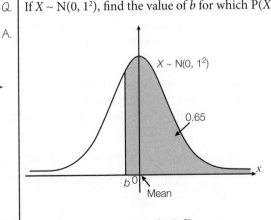

$X \sim N(0, 1^2)$

0.65

b 0

Mean

continued . . .

continued . . .

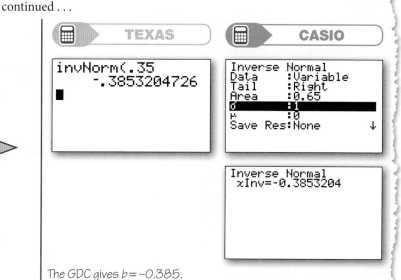

Use the inverse normal calculation on your GDC. On a CASIO GDC, choose 'right tail' and enter 0.65.

On a TEXAS GDC, because it only deals with left tails, you need to calculate the area of the left tail first. Remember that the total area under the curve is 1, and the right tail area is given as 0.65, so the left tail area = 1 − 0.65 = 0.35 and this is the number that you enter into the GDC.

The GDC gives $b = -0.385$.

(Note: the negative sign shows you that the value of b is below the value of the mean.)

Inverse general normal distribution

For distributions $N(\mu, \sigma^2)$ where μ is not 0 or σ is not 1, you can use your GDC for inverse calculations just as you did for the standard normal distribution, but now you also need to enter the values of the mean and standard deviation **after** the value of the probability.

Worked example 11.6

Q. If $X \sim N(5, 0.6^2)$, find the value of c for which $P(X \geq c) = 0.37$.

A.

Sketch a normal curve with mean 5 and standard deviation 0.6. $P(X \geq c)$ tells you that you are looking at a right tail. Since $0.37 < 0.5$, c must lie to the right of the mean. Shade in the relevant area.

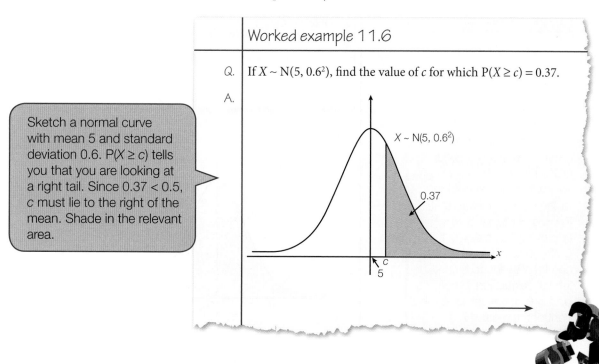

$X \sim N(5, 0.6^2)$

0.37

continued . . .

Again, since this is a right tail, for a TEXAS GDC you need to calculate the area of the left tail first:

left tail area = 1 − 0.37 = 0.63

so this is the number that you enter, followed by the values of μ and σ. See section '*11.2 Inverse normal calculations*' on page 671 of the GDC chapter if you need to.

TEXAS

```
invNorm(0.63,5,⊪
        5.199112011
■
```

CASIO

```
Inverse Normal
Data      :Variable
Tail      :Right
Area      :0.37
σ         :0.6
μ         :5
Save Res:None      ↓
None LIST
```

```
Inverse Normal
  xInv=5.19911201
```

From GDC: *c* = 5.12

Worked example 11.7

Q. If $X \sim N(17, 2.2^2)$, find the values of *d* and *e* for which $P(X \le d) = 0.1$ and $P(d \le X \le e) = 0.72$.

Finding *d* is a left tail calculation. Use the inverse nomal calculation on your GDC.

A.

TEXAS

```
invNorm(0.1,17,⊪
        14.18058655
■
```

CASIO

```
Inverse Normal
  xInv=14.1805866
```

From GDC: *d* = 14.2

Sketch the graph on your GDC. From P(*d* ≤ X ≤ *e*), we know that *e* should lie to the right of *d*. Note that P(X ≤ *d*) + P(*d* ≤ X ≤ *e*) = P (X ≤ *e*), so P(X ≤ *e*) = 0.1 + 0.72 = 0.82. The value of *e* can then be found by a left tail calculation. Since 0.82 > 0.5, *e* must lie to the right of the mean 17.

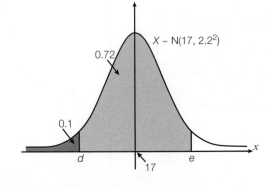

continued . . .

 TEXAS

 CASIO

Enter 0.82, $\mu = 17$ and $\sigma = 2.2$ in a left tail calculation to find e using the inverse normal calculation on your GDC.

```
invNorm(0.82,17▶
        19.01380318
```

```
Inverse Normal
  xInv=19.0138032
```

From GDC: $e = 19.0$

Worked example 11.8

Q. In a certain year, Nando estimates that 5% of his lambs have not reached the required mass for market. The mean mass of the lambs this year is 38 kg and the standard deviation is 2.85 kg. What is the minimum mass requirement for lambs to be sent to market this year?

A.

Sketch the graph. Let a be the minimum mass required. If 5% of the lambs cannot be sent to market, the proportion of underweight lambs is 0.05, which means that $P(X \le a) = 0.05$.

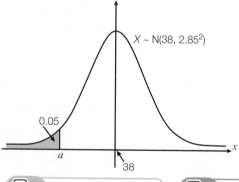

$X \sim N(38, 2.85^2)$

0.05

a

38

TEXAS

CASIO

Use the inverse normal calculation on your GDC. Enter 0.05, $\mu = 38$ and $\sigma = 2.85$ on your GDC for a left tail calculation to find a.

```
invNorm(0.05,38▶
        33.31216717
```

```
Inverse Normal
Data    :Variable
Tail    :Left
Area    :0.05
σ       :2.85
μ       :38
Save Res:None          ↓
LEFT RIGHT CNTR
```

```
Inverse Normal
  xInv=33.3121672
```

The minimum mass required is 33.3 kg.

Exercise 11.4

1. It is known that a random variable X is normally distributed with mean 45 and standard deviation 9. Find $P(28 \leq X \leq 66)$.

2. The BMI (body mass index) of a group of women is believed to be normally distributed with a mean of 23 and a standard deviation of 3. If a woman is chosen at random from the group, what is the probability that her BMI is no greater than 26?

3. The masses of teachers in a certain school are normally distributed with mean 65 kg and standard deviation 9.3 kg.

    (a) Mr Lee teaches at the school. What is the probability that he has a mass of more than 75 kg?

    (b) 80% of teachers in the school have a mass of less than m kg. Determine the value of m.

4. The masses of a sample of pet rabbits are normally distributed with mean 2.6 kg and standard deviation 0.4 kg. If one of the rabbits is chosen at random, what is the probability that it has a mass of between 2 kg and 3 kg?

5. Michelle has bought a sack of potatoes from the market. The masses of the potatoes are known to be normally distributed with mean of 350 g and a standard deviation of 20 g.

    (a) Michelle takes a potato randomly out of the sack. Find the probability that it has a mass of:

    (i) more than 380 g   (ii) less than 390 g

    (iii) between 320 g and 405 g.

    (b) 10% of the potatoes have a mass of less than w grams.

    (i) Sketch, shade and label a normal distribution curve to represent this information.

    (ii) Hence determine the value of w.

6. Mr Gonzalez is a tomato farmer. The masses of the tomatoes from his farm are normally distributed with a mean of 160 grams and a standard deviation of 15 grams. Mr Gonzalez wants to categorise his tomatoes according to mass. The lightest 10% are to be classed as 'small', the heaviest 10% as 'large' and the rest as 'medium'. Given that the medium tomatoes weigh between x grams and y grams, find the values of x and y.

7. Zara bought a large box of table tennis balls for a regional tournament. The diameter of the balls was assumed to be normally distributed with mean 44 mm and standard deviation 1.8 mm. Zara rejected 3% of the balls for being undersized and 2% for being oversized. She decided to use the remaining balls for the tournament. What was the range of diameters of the balls which Zara declared fit for the tournament?

11A Transforming a normal variable to a standardised normal variable

As you have seen, it is particularly easy to do calculations with the standard normal distribution $N(0, 1^2)$ on the GDC, as you do not need to enter the values of μ and σ. In the days before calculators and computers, people would look up normal distribution probabilities (areas under the curve) and inverse normal values from tables compiled especially for the standard normal distribution.

Any normal distribution can be **standardised**, that is, transformed to the standard normal distribution. In fact, this is what your GDC does when you give it the mean and standard deviation of a general normal distribution.

How does it do that?

Suppose that $X \sim N(2, 0.5^2)$. If we plot this normal curve on the x- and y-axes, it looks like:

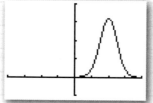

The curve is centred at the mean 2, which lies to the right of 0.

If we subtract the mean from each x value, then the curve will be shifted left by 2 units so that it is centred at 0:

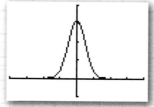

This curve is narrower and taller than the standard normal distribution curve, because its standard deviation is less than 1. We can make the curve have exactly the same shape as the standard normal curve if we divide all x values by the standard deviation 0.5 (i.e. multiply them by 2):

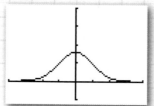

continued . . .

So, by subtracting the mean from each value of the random variable X and then dividing by the standard deviation, we have obtained a variable $z = \frac{x-\mu}{\sigma}$ which follows the **standard** normal distribution. In fact, for any particular value x taken by the random variable X, the value $z = \frac{x-\mu}{\sigma}$ represents the **number of standard deviations** that x is away from the mean; $z = \frac{x-\mu}{\sigma}$ is often called the 'z-score' of x.

So, if $X \sim N(2, 0.5^2)$:

- For $x = 3.5$, $z = \frac{3.5-2}{0.5} = 3$, so the value 3.5 is 3 standard deviations above the mean.

- For $x = 1.75$, $z = \frac{1.75-3}{0.5} = -2.5$, so the value 1.75 is 2.5 standard deviations below the mean.

- Similarly, calculating $P(X \leq 3.2)$ is the same as calculating $P(Z \leq \frac{3.2-2}{0.5}) = P(Z \leq 2.4)$ where $Z \sim N(0, 1^2)$.

Worked example

Q. The time taken to go through the security check at an airport is found to be normally distributed with a mean of 25 minutes and a standard deviation of 5.25 minutes.

(a) What is the probability that a passenger will wait for less than 20 minutes?

(b) Ben is late and only has 34 minutes to get through security and out to the departure lounge. What is the probability that he will not be able to board his plane?

(c) The airport wants to advertise that 90% of its passengers are through the security checks within x minutes. What is the value of x?

A. (a)

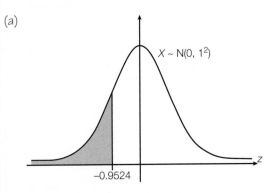

If a passenger waits for 20 minutes, the z-score is $\frac{20-25}{5.25} = -0.9524$.
We want to find $P(Z < -0.9524)$.

continued . . .

continued . . .

> Enter the value −0.9524 into your GDC. There's no need to enter μ and σ. Use your GDC; see section '11.1' on pages 669-670 of the GDC chapter if you need to.

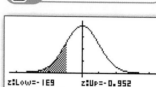

The probability that a passenger waits for less than 20 minutes is 0.170.

(b)

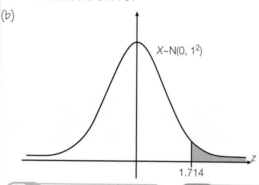

$X \sim N(0, 1^2)$

> Sketch the normal curve. 34 minutes gives a z-score of $\frac{34-25}{5.25} = 1.714$. We want to find $P(Z > 1.714)$.

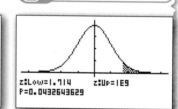

> Use your GDC to calculate the probability.

The probability that Ben cannot board his plane is 0.0432.

(c)

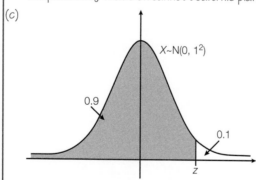

$X \sim N(0, 1^2)$

0.9

0.1

> Sketch the normal curve. We are given that $P(X \le x) = 0.9$. This is an inverse normal calculation. In terms of $Z \sim N(0, 1^2)$, we first find $P(Z \le z) = 0.9$.

> Use the inverse normal calculation on your GDC (see section '11.2' on page 670 if you need to). Again, enter just the probability 0.9, without μ and σ.

The GDC gives $z = 1.282$.

continued . . .

> **Convert the value of z to a value of x.**

$$z = \frac{x - \mu}{\sigma}$$

$$1.282 = \frac{x - 25}{5.25}$$

$$x = 1.282 \times 5.25 + 25 = 31.7$$

So 90% of passengers are through the security checks within 32 minutes.

Summary

You should know:

- the concept of a random variable
- about the normal distribution, its parameters μ and σ, the bell shape, and its symmetry about $x = \mu$
- the diagrammatic representation of the normal distribution curve and areas under the curve
- how to carry out normal probability calculations using area diagrams and your GDC
- how to carry out inverse normal calculations and when they should be used.

Mixed examination practice

Exam-style questions

1. It is known that a random variable is normally distributed with a mean of 50 and standard deviation of 5.

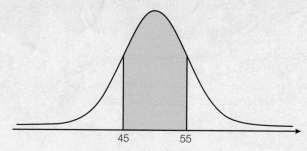

   (a) State the following probabilities:

       (i) $P(45 \leq X \leq 55)$ (ii) $P(40 \leq X \leq 60)$.

   (b) Find the following probabilities:

       (i) $P(X \leq 68)$ (ii) $P(X \geq 43)$.

2. It is known that a random variable X is normally distributed with mean 45 and standard deviation 9. Find $P(28 \leq X \leq 66)$.

3. A random variable X is normally distributed with mean 410 and standard deviation 29. Find:

   (a) $P(X \leq 380)$ (b) $P(X \geq 430)$ (c) $P(350 \leq X \leq 450)$.

4. The Ryder family usually book taxis from the company Quick Cabs. The waiting times for a taxi are known to be normally distributed with a mean waiting time of 19 minutes and a standard deviation of 4 minutes. Tom Ryder has just booked a taxi from Quick Cabs. Find the probability that the taxi will arrive:

   (a) in less than 25 minutes   (b) in more than 10 minutes   (c) in 5 to 20 minutes.

5. The distances thrown in a javelin competition can be assumed to be normally distributed with a mean distance of 64.28 metres and standard deviation of 5.31 metres.

   (a) Work out the probability of a randomly chosen competitor throwing the javelin beyond 70 metres.

   After the first round, only 15% of the competitors progressed to the next round of the competition.

   (b) Determine the minimum throwing distance needed to qualify for the next round.

   Twenty-four people took part in the javelin competition. Yurek's throw was 60.7 metres.

   (c) Estimate the number of competitors who performed better than Yurek.

6. The masses of drivers at a bus depot are normally distributed with mean 78 kg and standard deviation 4.7 kg.

   (a) If one of the drivers is picked at random, find the probability that the driver weighs:

       (i)   more than 65 kg   (ii)   less than 85 kg.

   (b) 60% of the drivers at the depot weigh more than m kg. Determine the value of m.

7. The volume of hot chocolate dispensed from a drinks machine is known to follow a normal distribution with mean 250 ml and standard deviation 8 ml. You are 'underserved' if the volume of dispensed drink is less than 230 ml.

   (a) If Melanie uses the machine once, calculate the probability that she will not be underserved.

   (b) Tia and Maria have just used the drinks dispenser. Calculate the probability that:

      (i) neither of them has been 'underserved'

      (ii) at least one of them has been 'underserved'.

   (c) If the dispensing unit is adjusted and the standard deviation changes to 6 ml, do you expect more or fewer customers to be underserved? Explain your answer.

Past paper questions

1. A manufacturer makes wooden sticks with a mean length of 5 m. The lengths are normally distributed with a standard deviation of 10 cm.

   (a) Calculate the values of **a**, **b** and **c** shown on the graph below.

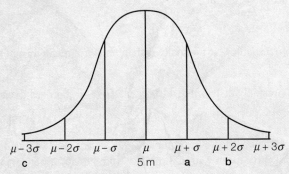

$$\mu-3\sigma \quad \mu-2\sigma \quad \mu-\sigma \quad \mu \quad \mu+\sigma \quad \mu+2\sigma \quad \mu+3\sigma$$
$$\textbf{c} \qquad\qquad\qquad\qquad 5\,\text{m} \quad \textbf{a} \qquad \textbf{b}$$

[3 marks]

exam tip

In the examination, you will **not** be asked to calculate the mean or standard deviation using the inverse normal calculation, so part (c) is no longer within the scope of the syllabus. But we thought that you might find it interesting to try solving this problem using the methods in Learning links 11A.

   (b) What is the probability that a stick chosen at random will measure more than 4.85 m? *[3 marks]*

   (c) The manufacturer sets the machine to make different sticks with a mean length of 3.5 m. It is known that 90% of the sticks will be less than 3.8 m in length. What is the standard deviation of these lengths? *[4 marks]*

[Nov 2004, Paper 2, Question 7(ii)] (© IB Organization 2004)

2. The weights of cats form a normal distribution about a mean weight of 3.42 kg with a standard deviation of 0.82 kg.

   The local veterinarian has collected data for 150 cats that have attended the surgery.

   (a) (i) Write down the percentage of cats that will weigh within 1 standard deviation of the mean. *[1 mark]*

      (ii) How many of the cats that visit the surgery will weigh within 1 standard deviation of the mean? *[2 marks]*

(b) (i) On a suitable bell-shaped diagram, shade in the area corresponding to all cats weighing less than 2 kg.

[1 mark]

(ii) Calculate the standardised normal value z corresponding to 2 kg.

[2 marks]

(iii) What percentage of cats will weigh less than 2 kg?

[2 marks]

(c) Calculate the percentage of cats that will weigh between 2 kg and 4.8 kg.

[3 marks]

(d) The probability of a cat weighing more than w kg is 2.5%. Find w.

[3 marks]

[**May 2004, Paper 2, Question 7(i)**] (© *IB Organization 2004*)

exam
tip

Part (b)(ii) is no longer on the syllabus so you will not have to answer questions like this in an examination. However, you might enjoy trying it with the help of Learning links 11A.

Chapter 12 Correlation

In Darrell Huff's book *How to Lie with Statistics*, he refers to a study that claimed that non-smoking college students gained better grades than students who smoked. The study concluded that 'smoking leads to poor college grades'. Huff questioned the findings of the study, arguing that there are other interpretations besides this obvious one. For instance, instead of smoking being the cause of poor grades, perhaps 'low grades depressed the students and caused them to smoke', or maybe 'students with lower grades were more sociable and therefore more likely to smoke'. Measuring the relationship between two sets of data is a useful tool to establish how one variable changes with another, but it is limited; it does not tell you *why* this relationship exists. The data in the study clearly showed a relationship between smoking and poor grades, but it does not explain why this relationship exists.

12.1 The concept of correlation

There are many situations in which a statistician might like to know if two variables are related and how they are related.

Data that consists of measurements of two variables taken from each individual in a sample is called **bivariate data**; the relationship between the two variables is referred to as the **correlation**. An example of bivariate data is the mass and height of boys on a basketball team; or the size and rate of photosynthesis of a leaf.

For bivariate data we try to classify one of the two variables as 'independent' and the other as 'dependent'. The **independent variable** is the one that can be controlled by the person conducting the experiment or study; it is hypothesised to 'cause' some kind of effect to the dependent variable. The **dependent variable** is the variable that is just observed without being controlled, and is supposed to show the 'effect'.

For example:

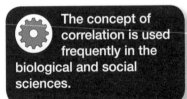
The concept of correlation is used frequently in the biological and social sciences.

- Is the stretch of someone's hand dependent on his or her height? The independent variable is the person's height, and the dependent variable is the length of their hand span.

- If a company spends more on advertising, will it sell more of its product? The independent variable could be the money spent on advertising each month, and the dependent variable would be the total monthly sales.

- Is your IB Mathematical Studies grade related to the hours of music that you listen to? The dependent variable is the IB grade and the independent variable is the average number of hours per week spent listening to music.

Exercise 12.1

1. In each of the following situations, identify which is the independent variable and which is the dependent variable and comment on whether you expect any correlation between them.

   (a) The amount of alcohol Terry consumes and his reaction time.

   (b) The number of people in a household and the monthly expenditure on food.

   (c) Saba's body mass and the number of hours she spends exercising each week.

   (d) The amount of time Dave spends exercising in the gym and his blood sugar level.

   (e) The value of a second-hand car and the mileage on the car's odometer.

   (f) The length of a person's middle finger and their sprint time/speed.

   (g) The screen size of an LED TV set and its price.

12.2 Scatter diagrams

The table below lists the Mathematical Studies grades (x) of students in an IB class and the number of hours of music that each student listens to each week (y).

x	2	3	3	5	5	7	2	3	4	6	5	5	4	6	5
y	11	14	15	16	16	19	13	10	13	18	19	12	18	17	11

Can you tell from the numbers if there is any relationship between how much music they listen to and the grade they achieve?

A diagram plotting these pairs of (x, y) values makes it easier to see a possible relationship:

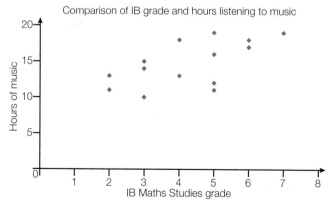

From the diagram you can see that there is a possible connection between a student's grade and the hours of music that they listen to.

This diagram is called a **scatter diagram** (also called a scatter graph or scatter plot). Scatter diagrams help to illustrate the connection between the two variables of a bivariate data set. For each pair of data values, one value is plotted along the *x*-axis and the other along the *y*-axis.

In general, you plot the independent variable along the *x*-axis and the dependent variable along the *y*-axis; in other words, the *x*-coordinate of each plotted point is a data value of the independent variable, and the *y*-coordinate is the corresponding data value of the dependent variable.

A scatter diagram shows the type of connection between the two variables. There are three principal types of correlation: positive, negative or zero (no) correlation.

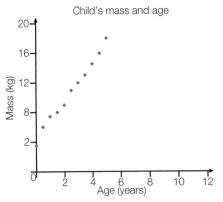

Positive correlation:
The dependent variable increases as the independent variable increases (*y* increases with *x*).

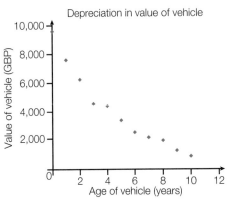

Negative correlation:
The dependent variable decreases as the independent variable increases (*y* decreases with *x*).

No correlation:
The points seem to be scattered randomly and no pattern can be seen.

Correlation and causation

Although the diagram for IB Maths Studies grade and hours spent listening to music tells you there is a possible connection between the two variables, can you really say that listening to music improves your grade? Or could it be that students with higher grades generally have more time to listen to music?

It is very important not to confuse correlation with causation. This is an extremely common mistake. Does listening to music *cause* your higher maths grade? If two things tend to happen together, it does not necessarily mean that one caused the other, even if you would like that to be the case!

You should always question any correlation that you find, and ask yourself if the relationship is truly causative. Could there be a third factor that is influencing both of the variables?

For instance, suppose a doctor is claiming that his studies show that heart disease is linked to decaying teeth. His figures show that the worse someone's teeth are, the more likely that person is to have heart disease.

But does having bad teeth actually cause heart disease? Or could it be that people who do not look after their teeth also tend to take little or no exercise and have a bad diet?

Exercise 12.2

1. For each of the following scatter diagrams, identify:

   (i) the type of correlation

   (ii) the independent variable

   (iii) the dependent variable.

   (a) The relationship between the height and arm span of a group of students:

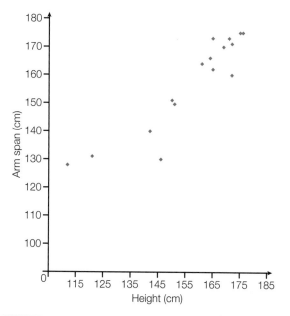

 How do you distinguish between correlation and causation? Firstly, to isolate the relationship you are interested in, it is important to identify all the variables that might be involved, and fix all variables other than the two being examined at the same level. In the bad teeth and heart disease example, the gender, age, diet and exercise habits of subjects would need to be kept constant across the sample. But how easy is this to achieve in practice?

(b) The relationship between the age and price of second-hand cars.

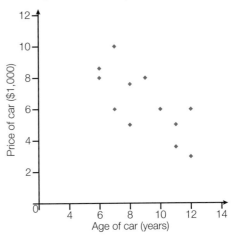

(c) The relationship between the mock and final examination scores of a group of students:

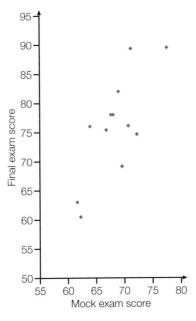

(d) The relationship between the hours of sunshine per day and the maximum temperature across eleven different cities:

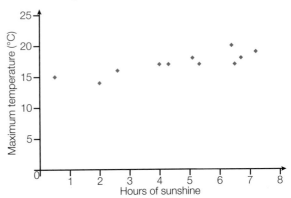

(e) The relationship between the number of goals conceded and the number of points scored by teams in a football league:

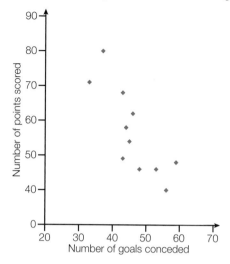

The **line of best fit** on a scatter diagram is drawn to give the best representation of the correlation between the two variables. The line of best fit is the one that has an approximately even spread of the data points either side of it.

Lines of best fit can be drawn by hand, on your GDC, or using a spreadsheet program on a computer.

If you have already plotted a scatter diagram on graph paper, you can draw a line of best fit by taking a long transparent ruler and adjusting its position so that the scattered points look as balanced as possible on either side of the line.

The line should be drawn so that it goes directly through the **mean point**. This is the point whose x-coordinate is the mean of the data values plotted along the x-axis and whose y-coordinate is the mean of the data values plotted along on the y-axis.

Looking again at the data on IB Mathematical Studies grade (x) and the number of hours per week (y) that a student spends listening to music:

x	2	3	3	5	5	7	2	3	4	6	5	5	4	6	5
y	11	14	15	16	16	19	13	10	13	18	19	12	18	17	11

Mean of x-values: $\bar{x} = \dfrac{65}{15} = 4.33$

Mean of y-values: $\bar{y} = \dfrac{222}{15} = 14.8$

 RR *The mean is the sum of all the data values divided by the total frequency of data values. See Chapter 6.*

So the mean point of this set of bivariate data is (4.33, 14.8).

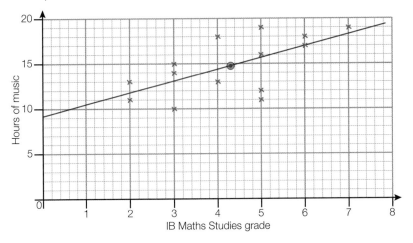
Draw a line on the scatter diagram. It must pass through the mean point (4.33, 14.8), and the other plotted points should look approximately evenly distributed above and below it.

If you use your GDC or a computer program to draw a line of best fit, it will use similar principles to those used to draw it by hand. Using your GDC can be a quicker way to establish if there is a correlation between two variables than plotting a scatter diagram by hand, but if you are specifically asked to draw a scatter diagram, you should do it by hand. (See section '12.1 Drawing a scatter diagram of bivariate data' on page 672 of the GDC chapter if you need a reminder of how to use your GDC to draw a scatter diagram).

Exercise 12.3

1. For each of the following sets of data, plot a scatter diagram by hand, and draw the line of best fit. Remember to include the mean point.

(a)

Minimum temperature (°C)	10	10	11	8	7	7	11	10	10	11
Hours of sunshine	5.3	4.1	3.5	5.4	6.7	6.5	4	4.3	2.6	2

(b)

Number of goals scored	78	69	60	72	55	59	51	49	48	45	56
Number of points scored	80	71	71	68	62	58	54	49	48	47	47

(c)

Height (cm)	148	162	161	152	167	172	176	179	172	157
Circumference of neck (cm)	11	26	30	30	32	30	33	41	33	35

(d)

Population (millions)	9.4	10.8	4.9	5.6	7.2	5.8	3.4	9.8	4.1	6.3
Income per capita (US$,000)	23	20	36	31	22	27	44	14	33	21

(e)

Exam paper 1 mark (%)	86	74	74	83	64	88	88	86	70	84	85
Exam paper 2 mark (%)	94	80	73	95	42	95	85	82	71	73	89

12.4 Pearson's product moment correlation coefficient, *r*

When you are analysing bivariate data, a hand-drawn scatter diagram can only give an approximate idea of the strength of the correlation. Moreover, fitting a line by hand is often not going to be very accurate, and different people are likely to draw different lines and come to slightly different conclusions. It is clear that a more dependable method is needed.

Pearson's product moment correlation coefficient (PMCC) is a complicated name for a simple idea. It is a number, usually denoted by *r*, which can take any value between −1 and +1. Its sign indicates the type of correlation, and its magnitude (size) indicates the strength of correlation.

- $r = +1$ means that there is perfect positive correlation

- $r = 0$ means that there is no correlation

- $r = -1$ means that there is perfect negative correlation.

Values of *r* calculated from data usually lie between +1 and −1 and can be roughly interpreted as follows:

$r = -1$	Perfect negative correlation
$-1 < r \leq -0.75$	Strong negative correlation
$-0.75 < r \leq -0.5$	Moderate negative correlation
$-0.5 < r \leq -0.25$	Weak negative correlation
$-0.25 < r < 0$	Very weak negative correlation
$r = 0$	No correlation
$0 < r < 0.25$	Very weak positive correlation
$0.25 \leq r < 0.5$	Weak positive correlation
$0.5 \leq r < 0.75$	Moderate positive correlation
$0.75 \leq r < 1$	Strong positive correlation
$r = 1$	Perfect positive correlation

exam tip

If $-0.5 < r < 0.5$, it is difficult to draw a line of best fit that has any meaning, because the data is just too scattered. It is important to keep this in mind if you are going to use scatter diagrams in your project.

Calculating the PMCC using your GDC

It is much quicker and easier to use your GDC to calculate the value of *r* than it is to do it by hand. (See Learning links 12A if you want to know how it is done by hand.)

For example, let us use the data below:

Distance, *x* (km)	4	8	5	10	6
Time, *y* (minutes)	15	35	12	40	24

Plot the data on a scatter diagram and draw the line of best fit:

(See '*12.2 Finding the product moment correlation coefficient and the equation of the regression line y on x*' on page 674 of the GDC chapter for a reminder of how to do this.)

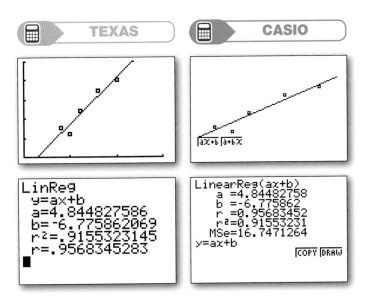

TEXAS

CASIO

From GDC: $r = 0.957$ (3 s.f.)

As well as the value of r, the linear regression function gives you more information:

- It tells you the equation of the line of best fit, $y = ax + b$. For this example, $a = 4.84$ and $b = -6.78$, so the equation of the line is $y = 4.84x - 6.78$.

- It also displays r^2, called the 'coefficient of determination', which measures the strength of correlation but doesn't indicate what type it is.

 You will learn more about linear regression in section 12.5.

Calculating the PMCC using a spreadsheet

It is convenient to use a spreadsheet program on a computer to investigate the correlation between two variables. The steps are generally as follows:

1. Enter the x values in column A and the y values in Column B.

2. Select the cells containing the data and choose the scatter graph option; the scatter plot will then be drawn by the software.

3. Choose the option to add the line of best fit; this is usually called a **trend line**. If you select the options to 'display equation on chart' and to 'display R-squared value on chart', then the program will draw the line of best fit and label it.

Karl Pearson (1857–1936) was interested in biometry, the use of mathematical methods to study biology. His work was founded on the concept that the scientific method is more 'descriptive' than 'explanatory', and he developed statistical methods to provide accurate mathematical descriptions of biological data. Between 1893 and 1912 he wrote 18 papers entitled *Mathematical Contributions to the Theory of Evolution*. Pearson emphasised the idea that correlation can be measured. In 1911 he established the world's first university statistics department at University College, London.

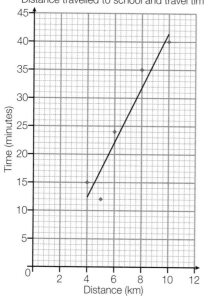

Distance travelled to school and travel time

$y = 4.8448x - 6.7759$
$R^2 = 0.9155$

If you take the square root of the R^2 value displayed on the spreadsheet chart, you will get the PMCC, $r = 0.957$.

Learning links

12A Calculating the PMCC by hand

In most cases you will calculate r using a GDC, a statistics package on a computer, or a spreadsheet. However, it is often easier to gain understanding of an idea if you do a few calculations 'by hand' rather than relying on a calculator or computer.

The formula for the PMCC is:

$$r = \frac{s_{xy}}{s_x \times s_y}$$

where

- s_{xy} is the **covariance** of x and y

- s_x is the standard deviation of the x values

- s_y is the standard deviation of the y values.

> **RR** s_x and s_y are an alternative to the notation σ_x and σ_y for standard deviations, which you may see in other statistics textbooks; recall that we also used σ to denote standard deviations in Chapters 7 and 11.

continued . . .

The formulae for s_x and s_y are as follows:

$$s_x = \sqrt{\frac{\sum x^2}{n} - \bar{x}^2} \qquad s_y = \sqrt{\frac{\sum y^2}{n} - \bar{y}^2}$$

 Recall from Chapter 6 that the $\sum$ symbol means 'add up all the values of'. So $\sum x^2$ means 'add up all the values of x squared'.

Covariance is another measure, related to the standard deviation, of the connection between two variables. The formula for the covariance is

$$s_{xy} = \frac{\sum xy}{n} - \bar{x} \times \bar{y}$$

Let's take a simple example to see how the PMCC can be calculated 'by hand'.

Five IB students decided to see if there was any correlation between the distance that they travelled to school and the duration of the journey. All five students travelled by bus.

Distance, x (km)	4	8	5	10	6
Time, y (minutes)	15	35	12	40	24

The scatter diagram of their data shows that there is positive correlation between the two variables.

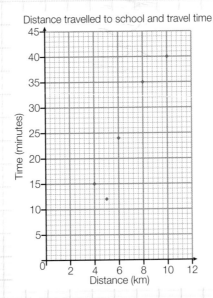

Distance travelled to school and travel time

The most organised way of doing the calculation is to draw up a table listing all the values you need in order to apply the formulae.

continued . . .

x	y	xy	x^2	y^2
4	15	60	16	225
8	35	280	64	1225
5	12	60	25	144
10	40	400	100	1600
6	24	144	36	576
Totals 33	126	944	241	3770

$$\bar{x} = \frac{33}{5} = 6.6 \qquad \bar{y} = \frac{126}{5} = 25.2$$

Then substitute values into the formulae:

$$s_{xy} = \frac{\sum xy}{n} - \bar{x} \times \bar{y} = \frac{944}{5} - 6.6 \times 25.2 = 22.48$$

$$s_x = \sqrt{\frac{\sum x^2}{n} - \bar{x}^2} = \sqrt{\frac{241}{5} - 6.6^2} = 2.154$$

$$s_y = \sqrt{\frac{\sum y^2}{n} - \bar{y}^2} = \sqrt{\frac{3770}{5} - 25.2^2} = 10.907$$

Hence

$$r = \frac{22.48}{2.154 \times 10.907} = 0.957$$

The value of r is close to $+1$, showing that there is strong positive correlation between the distance travelled to school and the time taken.

Exercise 12.4

1. Determine the value of Pearson's product moment correlation coefficient r in each of the following cases.

(a)

x	1	4	6	1	10	5	2	10
y	20	18	13	23	10	18	18	13

(b)

x	600	515	618	551	493	595	515
y	21	29	64	69	13	9	77

(c)

x	344	269	194	171	339	221	349	330	272
y	165	185	262	300	170	180	99	95	173

(d)

x	70	50	35	48	78	68	69	39	73	44	35	46
y	54	38	41	37	70	54	63	41	58	33	29	48

(e)

x	9.8	1.7	10.7	7.4	6.2	3.4	9.3	7.1	10.1	9.3
y	20.5	5.2	22.1	14.3	15.3	11.9	22.6	18.8	18.6	17

12.5 Regression line of y on x

The **regression line** is another type of line of best fit for a set of bivariate data. It is obtained by minimising the sum of the squared distances between the data points and the line. It takes into account the distance of each point from the line of fit and then takes the square of this distance and minimises the total of all the squared distances so that the line represents the data as closely as possible.

The phrase 'y on x' just means that the scatter diagram is drawn with x as the independent variable and y as the dependent variable, and that the squared distances being minimised are distances from the line in the y direction.

The regression line has an equation in the form $y = mx + c$.

Calculating the regression line using a GDC

You will be expected to use a GDC to find the regression line in all exercises and examinations. When you calculate r (the PMCC) using your GDC you will get the equation of the regression line at the same time, so the instructions are identical. (See '*12.2 Finding the product moment correlation coefficient and the equation of the regression line y on x*' on page 674 of the GDC chapter if you need to.)

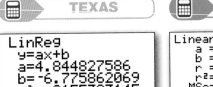

When you read the equation of the regression line from the screen, remember that 'a' is the slope of the line (the gradient, m) and 'b' is the y-intercept (c).

So the equation (to three significant figures) is $y = 4.84x - 6.78$.

If data collected from a scientific experiment suggests that there is a connection between two variables, plotting a graph to make a visual check is a good starting point. However, to determine the type and strength of the correlation, and be able to make predictions based on the findings, we need to use formulae and precise calculations to obtain quantitative results such as the PMCC and the regression line. This is an approach that has been used widely across all the sciences.

12B Calculating the regression line by hand

You will be expected to use a GDC to find the regression line in all exercises and examinations; but, as usual, you might find the idea easier to understand if you practise a few calculations by hand.

The formula for the regression line is:

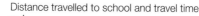

$$y - \bar{y} = \frac{s_{xy}}{(s_x)^2}(x - \bar{x})$$

where, as defined in Learning links 12A, s_{xy} is the covariance of x and y, s_x is the standard deviation of the x values, $\bar{x}$ is the mean of the x values, and $\bar{y}$ is the mean of the y values.

This formula is outside the IB Mathematical Studies syllabus, but if you want to know more about where it came from, you can find the explanation in any statistics textbook.

Let's revisit the example from Learning links 12A about the relationship between journey distance and travelling time:

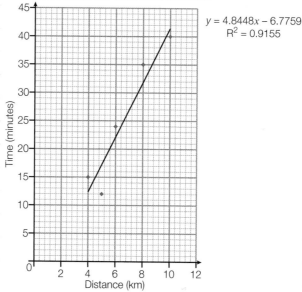

Distance travelled to school and travel time

$y = 4.8448x - 6.7759$
$R^2 = 0.9155$

We already calculated the following quantities in Learning links 12A:

$$\bar{x} = 6.6, \ \bar{y} = 25.2, \ s_x = 2.154, \ s_{xy} = 22.48$$

So the equation of the regression line is:

$$y - 25.2 = \frac{22.48}{(2.154)^2}(x - 6.6)$$

$$y - 25.2 = 4.845(x - 6.6)$$

$$y - 25.2 = 4.845x - 31.98$$

$$y = 4.85x - 6.78 \ (3 \text{ s.f.})$$

Worked example 12.1

Q. At a local garage, Pim collected data on cars with 1.4L engines. For cars in his sample that are of the same make and model, he looked at the relationship between the age of the car and its value. He expects a negative correlation, as older cars generally cost less than newer ones.

Age of car (years)	3	5.5	4	2	6	1.5
Value of car (€)	8850	6500	7995	9150	5495	9950

Help Pim find:

(a) the product moment correlation coefficient for his data

(b) the equation of the regression line.

> Let the independent variable x be the age of a car, because we expect that it has an effect on the dependent variable, y, which would be the value of the car.

A.

TEXAS   CASIO

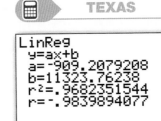

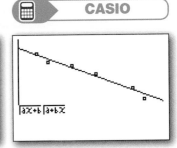

> Use your GDC to find r and the slope and y-intercept of the regression line. See section '12.2 Finding the product moment correlation…' on page 674 of the GDC chapter if you need to.

(a) From GDC: $r = -0.984$, so there is a strong negative correlation between the age of the car and its re-sale value.

(b) $y = -909x + 11300$ (to 3 s.f.)

Exercise 12.5

You are expected to use your GDC to answer all the questions in this exercise.

1. Tasia has collected the following data on the ages of 12 married couples. He is investigating whether there is a correlation between the age of the husband and the age of the wife.

Age of husband (x years)	65	70	49	55	60	56	79	73	43	72	79	53
Age of wife (y years)	59	66	35	48	61	39	77	46	35	71	74	53

(a) Find the equation of the regression line of y on x.

(b) Calculate the correlation coefficient r of the data.

(c) Comment on the value of r.

2. Katarina is investigating the relation between a person's arm span and the length of their forearm. The sample data collected from 11 students is shown in the table below.

Arm span (x cm)	160	150	179	184	169	160	157	163	157	173	174
Length of forearm (y cm)	26	23	25	31	25	24	27	27	24	25	26

(a) Find the equation of the regression line of y on x.

(b) Calculate the correlation coefficient r of the data.

(c) Comment on the value of r.

3. The following table shows the population and income per capita of ten countries from the same economic zone.

Country	1	2	3	4	5	6	7	8	9	10
Population, x (millions)	4.49	14.86	7.5	3.76	2.59	9.15	6.70	10.18	4.67	7.95
Income per capita, y (USD)	682	189	353	668	950	266	355	230	491	287

(a) Write down Pearson's product moment correlation coefficient, r, of the data.

(b) Comment on your value of r.

(c) Find the equation of the regression line of y on x.

(d) Use your equation to estimate the income per capita of a country from the same zone with a population of 5.5 million.

4. Jamil is investigating the relationship between the arm span and the length of the right foot of his friends. His sample data is illustrated in the table below.

Arm span, x (cm)	167	171	167	152	173	126	170	160	173	182
Length of right foot, y (cm)	24	25	24	23	26	19	23	25	26	26

(a) Write down the equation of the regression line of length of right foot (y) on arm span (x).

(b) Use your equation from part (a) to predict the length of the right foot corresponding to an arm span of 165 cm.

(c) Write down the correlation coefficient, r.

(d) Describe the nature of the correlation between arm span and length of right foot, based on Jamil's data.

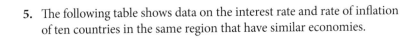

5. The following table shows data on the interest rate and rate of inflation of ten countries in the same region that have similar economies.

Country	1	2	3	4	5	6	7	8	9	10
Interest rate, x (%)	5.50	8.25	9.25	4.00	3.25	20.00	3.50	12.50	9.50	6.00
Inflation rate, y (%)	5.30	8.49	9.40	5.24	1.80	14.13	3.10	8.39	7.80	5.40

(a) Write down the correlation coefficient, r, of the data.

(b) The equation of the line of regression of y on x is of the form $y = mx + c$. Determine the values of m and c.

(c) A similar country has an interest rate of 16.00%. Estimate the inflation rate for this country.

> Can you reliably use the equation of the regression line to make predictions? Even if you are working beyond the range of the original data?

12.6 Using the equation of the regression line

The equation of the regression line can be used to estimate values that are not in the original data. This can be very useful if the data you have collected contains insufficient detail or if you wish to make a prediction about some values that you have not collected.

However, you must be very careful: it is easy to get unreasonable values out of the equation of the regression line, leading to nonsense predictions.

In general, do **not** use the regression line to predict new values if:

- the correlation is weak: $-0.5 < r < +0.5$

- the predicted values are outside the range of the data values already collected (this is called **extrapolation**).

> **exam tip**
>
> This is a mistake made by many students doing a statistical project. If your bivariate data show weak correlation, make sure that you comment on this.

Here is an example where a seemingly good set of data can lead to a false prediction.

The table shows a subset of data collected by a weather balloon. The data consists of the different temperatures recorded as the balloon rises.

Temperature, x (°C)	16.6	21.0	21.0	23.4	20	17.8	15.0	10.3	4.7	−0.8
Height, y (m)	1700	1850	1920	1960	2440	2740	3140	3660	4270	4880

The scatter graph shows a strong correlation, and the value of r confirms this.

Scatter graph: PMCC:

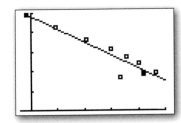

```
LinReg
 y=ax+b
 a=-132.7292686
 b=4833.666103
 r²=.8869791724
 r=-.9417957169
```

From the GDC, the correlation coefficient is $r = -0.942$ and the equation of the regression line is $y = -133x + 4830$ (3 s.f.).

For a height of 5000 m ($y = 5000$), the equation of the regression line gives $x = \dfrac{5000 - 4830}{-133} = -1.28$, i.e. a temperature of $-1.28°C$.

For a height of 10 000 m ($y = 10000$), the equation gives

$x = \dfrac{10000 - 4830}{-133} = -38.9$, i.e. a temperature of $-38.9°C$.

However, when the entire data set is plotted (see graph below), you can see that the linear equation we found fits only those data points with height less than 12 000 m. At higher altitudes, this equation would give temperature values that are far from the real measurements.

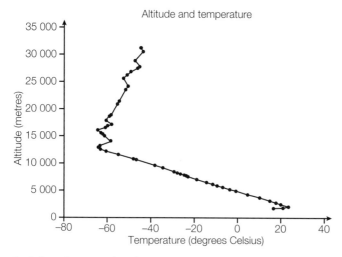
Altitude and temperature

Real data; figure used with permission from Houghton Mifflin Harcourt.

Exercise 12.6

You are expected to use your GDC to answer all the questions in this exercise.

1. The performance of eleven students on two examination papers in History is shown in the table below.

Paper A ($x\%$)	90	71	91	71	65	98	70	86	95	80	75
Paper B ($y\%$)	82	82	86	63	81	95	76	91	98	92	71

   (a) Calculate the product moment correlation coefficient, r, of the data.

   (b) What does the value of r suggest about the relationship between scores on the two examination papers?

   (c) Hayley, a student from another class, has taken only Paper A. She scored 83%. Estimate Hayley's anticipated score on Paper B.

   (d) Joe's score on Paper B was 68%. Calculate an estimate of Joe's score on Paper A.

2. The table shows data on the GDP per capita and the unemployment rate (as a percentage of the labour force) of 10 countries.

Country	1	2	3	4	5	6	7	8	9	10
GDP per capita, x ($,000)	50.5	48.1	31.4	50.1	44.4	44.6	27.9	48.5	37.0	22.1
Unemployment rate, y (%)	4.10	7.89	7.40	7.82	9.52	6.00	16.40	14.30	8.20	6.30

(a) Determine the equation of the regression line of y on x.

(b) Use your equation to estimate the GDP per capita of a country with an unemployment rate of 6.8%.

(c) Estimate the unemployment rate of a country with a per capita GDP of $34,500.

(d) Find the correlation coefficient r.

(e) Comment on the value of r.

3. The total number of points gained by the top ten teams in the English Premier League for the 2009/2010 and 2010/2011 seasons is shown in the following table.

Team	Points	
	2009/2010 (x)	2010/2011 (y)
Manchester United	85	80
Chelsea	86	71
Manchester City	67	71
Arsenal	75	68
Tottenham	70	62
Liverpool	63	58
Everton	61	54
Fulham	46	49
Aston Villa	64	48
Sunderland	44	47

Jessica wants to determine whether there is a correlation between the points gained by these ten teams in the two successive seasons. She thinks there is bound to be a strong positive correlation between the points gained by each team in the two seasons.

(a) By calculating the coefficient of correlation, comment on the accuracy of Jessica's assertion.

(b) The equation of the regression line of y on x is $y = mx + c$. Determine the values of m and c.

Hull City gained 30 points in the 2009/2010 season but they were relegated at the end of the season and so did not play in the same division during the next season.

Jessica decided to use the equation from part (b) to estimate the number of points Hull City would have gained if they had stayed in the same division for the 2010/2011 season.

(c) What is Jessica's estimate?

(d) Comment on the reliability of the answer in part (c).

Summary

You should know:

- what bivariate data is and how to plot it on a scatter diagram
- the concept of correlation and the line of best fit
- how to draw a line of best fit by hand, passing though the mean point on the scatter diagram
- how to calculate Pearson's product moment correlation coefficient, r, using your GDC
- how to interpret values of r in terms of strong or weak, positive, zero or negative correlation
- how to find the regression line of y on x
- how and when to use the regression line for prediction purposes.

Mixed examination practice

Exam-style questions

1. Bethan is investigating the mileage of second-hand cars and their prices. The results of her investigation on a sample of ten cars are shown in the table.

Mileage	65 000	118 000	66 000	41 000	73 000	105 000	79 000	91 000	87 000	59 000
Price (US dollars)	9,295	6,495	10,295	14,495	12,995	5,995	9,995	8,995	7,995	14,495

The diagram shows the scatter graph of her data.

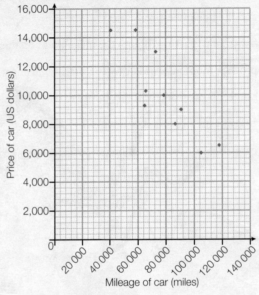

(a) State the independent and dependent variables.

(b) Comment on the correlation between the variables.

(c) State the mean mileage and the mean price of the cars.

(d) The point on the scatter diagram representing the mean mileage and the mean price of the cars can be represented as $(\bar{m}, \bar{p})$. Copy the scatter diagram onto graph paper and draw the line of best fit, indicating the point $(\bar{m}, \bar{p})$.

2. The table shows the attendance during a school term and the end-of-term test scores of 12 students.

Attendance (%)	76	83	76	91	54	97	48	97	89	90	84	91
Test score (%)	54	50	57	72	39	75	36	59	59	65	59	72

(a) Draw a scatter diagram by hand to illustrate the data. Include the line of best fit on your diagram.

(b) State the type of correlation.

(c) Determine the linear correlation coefficient, r, of the data and hence comment on the strength of the correlation.

3. The following table shows the distances (in metres) thrown by ten athletes who participated in both a javelin and a discus competition.

Javelin, x (m)	54.5	33.7	50.6	61.9	49.3	45.9	38	46.1	52.8	62
Discus, y (m)	44.8	37.12	51.76	62.64	34.08	26.08	38.64	31.68	48.64	62.8

(a) Find the equation of the regression line of y on x.

(b) Find the linear correlation coefficient, r, of the data.

(c) Comment on the value of r.

4. Jensen is investigating the relationship between the cross-sectional area (in mm^2) and the current rating (in amperes) of some copper conductors. His results are illustrated in the table below.

Cross-sectional area, x	1	1.5	2.5	4	6	10	16
Current rating, y	15	19.5	27	36	46	63	85

(a) Write down the correlation coefficient, r.

(b) Describe the nature of the correlation between cross-sectional area and current rating of these copper conductors.

(c) Write down the equation of the regression line of current rating (y) on cross-sectional area (x) of the copper conductors.

(d) Use your equation from part c) to predict the current rating of a copper conductor with a cross-sectional area of 3.5 mm^2.

(e) Comment on the suitability of using the regression line equation obtained in part (c) to predict the current rating of a copper conductor with cross-sectional area 18.5 mm^2.

5. The weather section of a newspaper lists the minimum and maximum daytime temperatures (in degrees Celsius) of 11 cities:

Minimum, x	1	6	3	7	6	0	0	4	3	2	8
Maximum, y	12	7	10	9	11	15	15	11	9	15	10

(a) Write down the correlation coefficient, r, of the data.

(b) The equation of the regression line of y on x is of the form $y = mx + c$. Determine the values of m and c.

(c) Comment on the suitability of using the regression line equation from part (b) to predict the maximum daytime temperature of a city from the same region with a minimum temperature of 15°C.

(d) Another city in the same region had a minimum temperature of 5°C on the same day. Estimate the maximum temperature.

6. The following table shows 52-week highest and lowest prices (in sterling pence) of the shares of nine companies listed in the FTSE 100 on 13 March 2012.

Highest, x	1228	1754	2347	1207	3344	1491	645	420	3194
Lowest, y	940	787	1412	740	2138	900	464	301	2543

Mr Lawrence believes that there is a strong positive correlation between the highest and lowest share prices.

(a) By calculating Pearson's product moment correlation coefficient for the data, comment on the validity of Mr Lawrence's assertion.

(b) Determine the equation of the regression line of y on x.

(c) One of the listed companies in the FTSE 100 had a highest share price of 1564 pence. Estimate its lowest share price over the 52-week period.

(d) Work out an estimate of the maximum share price of another company with a lowest share price of 2300 pence over the 52-week period.

7. The following table shows the finishing times (in seconds) of some athletes who competed in both the 100 m and the 200 m races in a track and field event.

100 m time, x	13.3	14.1	14.7	16.4	14.2	15.8	16.3	15.3	15.4	15.7
200 m time, y	25.9	25.4	25.6	29.8	24.9	27.1	31.0	29.2	30.1	29.4

(a) Find the correlation coefficient r.

(b) Comment on the value of r.

(c) Determine the equation of the regression line of y on x.

Serginio and Tunde participated in the same event.

Serginio ran the 100 m race in 15.12 seconds, but he did not compete in the 200 m race due to an injury.

Tunde was disqualified from the 100 m race due to a false start but finished the 200 m race in 26.1 seconds.

(d) Use your equation from part (c) to estimate:

(i) Serginio's finishing time if he had run the 200 m race

(ii) Tunde's finishing time if he had run the 100 m race.

Past paper questions

1. In an experiment a vertical spring was fixed at its upper end. It was stretched by hanging different weights on its lower end. The length of the spring was then measured. The following readings were obtained.

Load x (kg)	0	1	2	3	4	5	6	7	8
Length y (cm)	23.5	25	26.5	27	28.5	31.5	34.5	36	37.5

(a) Plot these pairs of values on a scatter diagram taking 1 cm to represent 1 kg on the horizontal axis and 1 cm to represent 2 cm on the vertical axis. *[4 marks]*

(b) (i) Write down the mean value of the load ($\bar{x}$). *[1 mark]*

   (ii) Write down the standard deviation of the load. *[1 mark]*

   (iii) Write down the mean value of the length ($\bar{y}$). *[1 mark]*

   (iv) Write down the standard deviation of the length. *[1 mark]*

(c) Plot the mean point ($\bar{x}, \bar{y}$) on the scatter diagram. Name it L. *[1 mark]*

It is given that the covariance S_{xy} is 12.17.

(d) (i) Write down the correlation coefficient, r, for these readings. *[1 mark]*

   (ii) Comment on this result. *[2 marks]*

(e) Find the equation of the regression line of y on x. *[2 marks]*

(f) Draw the line of regression on the scatter diagram. *[2 marks]*

(g) (i) Using your diagram or otherwise, estimate the length of the spring when a load of 5.4 kg is applied. *[1 mark]*

   (ii) Malcolm uses the equation to claim that a weight of 30 kg would result in a length of 62.8 cm. Comment on his claim. *[1 mark]*

[Total 18 marks]

[Nov 2006, Paper 2, TZ0, Question 3] (© IB Organization 2006)

2. Tania wishes to see whether there is any correlation between a person's age and the number of objects on a tray which could be remembered after looking at them for a certain time.

She obtains the following table of results.

Age (x years)	15	21	36	40	44	55
Number of objects remembered (y)	17	20	15	16	17	12

(a) Use your graphic display calculator to find the equation of the regression line of y on x. *[2 marks]*

(b) Use your equation to estimate the number of objects remembered by a person aged 28 years. *[1 mark]*

(c) Use your graphic display calculator to find the correlation coefficient r. *[1 mark]*

(d) Comment on your value for r. *[2 marks]*

[Total 6 marks]

[Nov 2007, Paper 1, TZ0, Question 14] (© IB Organization 2007)

Chi-squared hypothesis testing

As you learned in Chapter 12, Pearson's product moment correlation coefficient can be used to test the strength of connection between two variables in a set of bivariate data.

There are many other situations in which you might want to test if two or more variables are dependent on each other. For example, in a trial of a new fertiliser the manufacturer wants to find out whether the fertiliser actually has an effect on the growth of crops; in other words, is the yield of a plot where the new chemical has been applied significantly higher than the yield of the control plot?

Karl Pearson developed a statistical method called the chi-squared (χ^2) test for independence, which can be used to determine if a result is significant. This test could be used to determine if the yield in the treated plot is significantly greater than that in the control plot and thus indicate if the new chemical works.

To take another example, suppose you want to know whether the choice of a second language for the IB diploma is independent of gender. Assuming this were the case, you would expect the proportions of boys and girls choosing each language to be the same. You could test your assumptions using the chi-squared (χ^2) test. You would collect the real data on how many boys and girls choose each language option and compare these numbers with the 'expected' numbers. Then you would determine if the real data deviates enough from the expected to say that students' language choices might depend on gender.

13.1 The χ^2 statistic

The χ^2 statistic is a goodness-of-fit test. In general, the χ^2 **statistic** is defined as:

$$\chi^2 = \sum \frac{(f_O - f_E)^2}{f_E}$$

where f_O is an observed frequency, f_E is the corresponding expected frequency, and the Σ symbol indicates 'add up all the separate calculations'.

At its most basic level, the χ^2 test is used to check if the frequencies of collected data values (observed frequencies) differ significantly from what you would 'expect' to find (expected frequencies). In other words, it can be used to assess how good the 'fit' is between the observed frequency distribution and a 'theoretical' distribution. The theoretical or expected distribution could be based on known probabilities, the normal distribution, complete randomness, or some other distribution that you suspect is appropriate.

The χ^2 statistic is not difficult to calculate and the calculations can be done quickly on your GDC. (See '*13.1 The χ^2 test for independence*' on page 675 of the GDC chapter for a reminder if you need to.)

Learning links

13A Calculating the χ^2 statistic

To gain an understanding of the method and what the results mean, it is best to work through the following examples by hand.

Jon needs some random numbers for his project, but has left his calculator at school. He writes down 100 single figures chosen from the numbers 0 to 9. Are the figures he has written down really random? How good is the fit between the numbers he has chosen 'at random' and numbers that are truly randomly generated?

Suppose these are Jon's results:

Number	0	1	2	3	4	5	6	7	8	9
Frequency	12	7	9	14	6	7	14	13	8	10

How close is this distribution of frequencies to the 'theoretical' one?

We will use the formula $\chi^2 = \sum \dfrac{(f_O - f_E)^2}{f_E}$ where f_O is an observed frequency and f_E is the corresponding expected frequency.

First, we need to work out the 'expected frequencies' assuming that the numbers are truly randomly selected. Using probability theory, under the assumption of complete randomness each of the ten numbers from 0 to 9 is equally likely to be chosen, so each number should come up $\dfrac{1}{10} \times 100 = 10$ times.

We then calculate the discrepancy between observed and expected frequencies as follows:

Number	0	1	2	3	4	5	6	7	8	9
Observed frequency f_O	12	7	9	14	6	7	14	13	8	10
Expected frequency f_E	10	10	10	10	10	10	10	10	10	10
Difference $f_O - f_E$	+2	−3	−1	+4	−4	−3	+4	+3	−2	0

You might think that adding up the differences will give a good representation of the discrepancy between observed and expected frequencies; however, in this case the differences add up to zero because the positive and negative values cancel each other out. To get around this cancellation problem, we square the differences, making them all non-negative, before adding them up:

continued . . .

Number	0	1	2	3	4	5	6	7	8	9
Observed frequency f_O	12	7	9	14	6	7	14	13	8	10
Expected frequency f_E	10	10	10	10	10	10	10	10	10	10
Difference $f_O - f_E$	+2	−3	−1	+4	−4	−3	+4	+3	−2	0
Squared difference $(f_O - f_E)^2$	4	9	1	16	16	9	16	9	4	0

We find that the sum of the squared differences, $\sum (f_O - f_E)^2$, is 84. To obtain a measure of discrepancy that is of roughly the same magnitude as the individual frequencies, we divide this sum by the expected frequencies, 10, to get 8.4.

So, in Jon's random number case, $\chi^2 = 8.4$.

The critical χ^2 value

But what does the value of the χ^2 statistic mean?

Let's use the example from Learning links 13A: Jon needs some random numbers for his project; he writes down 100 single figures chosen from the numbers 0–9.

These are Jon's results:

Number	0	1	2	3	4	5	6	7	8	9
Frequency	12	7	9	14	6	7	14	13	8	10

If all 100 figures were truly chosen at random, you would expect each number from 0–9 to have a probability of 0.1 (there are 10 numbers, so the probability of selecting any one number is 1 out of 10). In Learning links 13A we compared the frequency of Jon's numbers with the expected frequencies and calculated that $\chi^2 = 8.4$. What does this value of 8.4 mean? 8.4 is a measure of the discrepancy between the real frequencies and the expected frequencies. Is this measure of discrepancy 'significant' enough for us to say that Jon's numbers are not really random and that he was actually biased in favour of certain numbers and against others?

To decide if the χ^2 statistic is large enough to conclude that the discrepancy between the observed frequencies and the expected/theoretical frequencies is significant, we compare it with a **critical χ^2** value. This critical value depends on the number of **degrees of freedom** and the **significance level** at which you choose to work.

You can interpret the results as follows:

- if calculated χ^2 statistic > critical value, the result is significant and the expected/theoretical distribution **is not a good fit** of the observed data

- if calculated χ^2 statistic < critical value, the result is not significant and the expected/theoretical distribution **is a good fit** of the observed data.

The significance level is usually denoted by the Greek letter α (alpha). It is the greatest acceptable **probability of incorrectly** deciding that the result is significant when actually it is insignificant, i.e. thinking the theoretical distribution is not a good fit for the observed data when it actually is. So, if you choose a significance level of 5%, then there will be at most a 5% chance that you will state your data is significant when actually it is not. The lower α is, the more stringent the criterion will be for a 'significant' discrepancy, and the more confident you can be that your decision is correct.

Tables are available that give χ^2 critical values for various degrees of freedom and significance levels, and you read off your critical χ^2 from this table. There is a small table at the end of this chapter, on page 404.

 We will see how to calculate the number of degrees of freedom later in the chapter.

In Jon's random number example, the number of degrees of freedom is 9. He can look up the χ^2 critical values for 9 degrees of freedom in a set of tables. The critical values for significance levels 10%, 5% and 1% (α = 0.1, 0.05 and 0.01) are as follows:

$$\chi^2_{10\%} = 14.68 \quad \chi^2_{5\%} = 16.92 \quad \chi^2_{1\%} = 21.67$$

At the 5% significance level, Jon's $\chi^2_{calc} = 8.4$ and $\chi^2_{5\%} = 16.92$.

Since 8.4 < 16.92, the result is not significant, which means that there is **not** enough evidence to claim that Jon's numbers are not random. Therefore, the χ^2 test has informed us that Jon's chosen numbers are likely to be random.

p-value

As well as comparing the calculated χ^2 statistic with a critical value, you can also find the '*p*-value' associated with the χ^2 statistic and the number of degrees of freedom. The ***p*-value** is the **probability** of getting a discrepancy as large as the calculated χ^2 statistic **if** the theoretical distribution were correct. Therefore, the smaller the *p*-value, the less likely it is that the observed frequencies and the theoretical distribution are a good fit and the more likely it is that the discrepancy between the observed and theoretical frequencies is significant.

You can interpret the results as follows:

- when the *p*-value < significance level, the result is significant and the theoretical distribution is **not a good fit** of the observed distribution

- when the *p*-value > significance level, the result is not significant and the theoretical distribution **is a good fit** of the observed distribution.

In an examination you will always be given the critical value of χ^2 that you need.

For Jon's χ^2_{calc} value of 8.4 and 9 degrees of freedom, $p = 0.494$. (You can find this value using a GDC or a spreadsheet program on a computer; see '13.1 The χ^2 test for independence' on page 675 of the GDC chapter for a reminder if you need to.) Since $0.494 > 0.05$, at the 5% significance level there is **not** enough evidence to claim that Jon's numbers are not random. (This agrees with our earlier conclusion obtained by comparing with the critical value.)

In summary

For a goodness-of-fit test:

- If $\chi^2_{calc} > \chi^2_{critical}$, then you can say that the result is significant and the theoretical distribution is not a good fit for the data; if $\chi^2_{calc} < \chi^2_{critical}$, then you can say that there is not enough evidence to suggest the result is significant, and the theoretical distribution is a good fit for the data.

- If p-value < significance level, then you can say that the result is significant and the theoretical distribution is not a good fit for the data; if p-value > significance level, then you can say that there is not enough evidence to suggest the result is significant, and the theoretical distribution is a good fit for the data.

Worked example 13.1

Q. Finn and Edda are playing a game with an eight-sided die. Edda wins if she rolls an odd number; Finn wins if he rolls an even number. Edda keeps losing the game, and is sure that the dice is biased towards even numbers. From the results below, is there enough evidence to support Edda's claim?

Number	1	2	3	4	5	6	7	8
Frequency	4	5	6	9	6	9	0	3

> This is a goodness-of-fit test where the 'theoretical distribution' is based on assuming that the die is balanced. First, calculate the expected frequencies.

A. If the die is balanced, each number should appear with equal probability $\frac{1}{8}$.

The total frequency is $4 + 5 + 6 + 9 + 6 + 9 + 0 + 3 = 42$,

so each number is expected to occur $42 \times \frac{1}{8} = 5.25$ times.

> Calculate the squared differences between the observed and expected frequencies.

Number	1	2	3	4	5	6	7	8
f_O	4	5	6	9	6	9	0	3
f_E	5.25	5.25	5.25	5.25	5.25	5.25	5.25	5.25
$f_O - f_E$	−1.25	−0.25	0.75	3.75	0.75	3.75	−5.25	−2.25
$(f_O - f_E)^2$	1.5625	0.0625	0.5625	14.0625	0.5625	14.0625	27.5625	5.0625

continued . . .

Use the formula to find the χ^2 statistic.

$$\sum (f_0 - f_E)^2 = 63.5$$

$$\chi^2_{calc} = \sum \frac{(f_0 - f_E)^2}{f_E} = \frac{63.5}{5.25} = 12.1$$

Look up the critical value from a table. The number of degrees of freedom is $8 - 1 = 7$.

For 7 degrees of freedom, $\chi^2_{5\%} = 14.1$.

Since $12.1 < 14.1$, at the 5% significance level there is not enough evidence to say that the die is unbalanced; maybe Edda is just having an unlucky day.

Let's try a different significance level.

For 7 degrees of freedom, $\chi^2_{10\%} = 12.017$.

Since $12.1 > 12.017$, at the 10% significance level we can conclude that the die is unbalanced.

Check the p-value as well.

For $\chi^2_{calc} = 12.1$ and 7 degrees of freedom, $p = 0.0975$.

As $0.0975 > 0.05$, the evidence for bias is not strong enough at the 5% significance level.

But, as $0.0975 < 0.1$, the evidence is strong enough at the 10% significance level.

Degrees of freedom

In the example where Jon was writing down random numbers chosen from 0–9, the table had 10 'cells' containing the observed frequencies. Since he wrote down a total of 100 numbers, the sum of the frequencies is 100. For the first 9 cells to be filled, any frequency values could have gone into them; but once they have been filled, the value of the final cell is completely determined as it must contain a frequency that would give a total frequency of 100 numbers. Therefore, the final cell has 'no freedom' so the number of degrees of freedom in this situation is 9 (10 cells – 1 cell).

In general, for a goodness-of-fit test where you are comparing a list of observed frequencies against a theoretical distribution:

degrees of freedom = number of frequencies to be compared – 1

Now let's consider more complicated situations.

A car dealer has collected data about the age of his customers and the colour of car they choose. Is colour choice independent of age, or is there any relationship between the two variables? His data, collected from 63 customers, can be presented in a **two-way contingency table** as follows:

		Age group				
		20–30	31–40	41–50	50+	Total
Colour	Green	2	3	6		14
	Red	7	4	4		18
	Grey	2	4	8		16
	Blue					15
Total		13	15	20	12	63

 You learned about two-way tables in Chapter 10, section 10.2.

The cells containing the observed frequencies are arranged in four columns and four rows; each column represents a different age group, and each row represents a different choice of car colour. Note that if the totals of every row and column are known, then once the cells in the first three rows and first three columns have been filled, the values in the remaining (blank) cells are completely determined, because they need to give the correct total for each row and column. Thus there is no freedom in choosing the values to go into the cells of the fourth row and fourth column. The number of degrees of freedom in this case is the number of cells in the first three rows and first three columns: $3 \times 3 = 9$.

The general formula for calculating the degrees of freedom for a two-way contingency table, provided that the total frequency of each row and each column is known, is similar to the formula for a single list of observed frequencies:

degrees of freedom = (number of rows − 1) × (number of columns − 1)

hint

Don't confuse contingency tables with the tables of critical values for the χ^2 test.

In the next section you will see how to use the χ^2 test for independence on a two-way table.

Exercise 13.1

1. For each of the following (two-way) contingency tables, calculate the number of degrees of freedom.

(a)

	B_1	B_2
A_1	64	134
A_2	91	174

(b)

	B_1	B_2	B_3
A_1	48	24	14
A_2	34	16	10

(c)

	B_1	B_2	B_3	B_4
A_1	45	95	63	28
A_2	20	109	57	18
A_3	45	50	104	29

(d)

	B_1	B_2
A_1	24	35
A_2	37	52
A_3	57	41
A_4	79	58

13.2 The χ^2 test for independence

In Nariko's town, people say that it is better if you get Ms B as your examiner for the driving test; she is believed to pass more people than Miss C or Mr A.

Nariko decides to collect some actual results from the test centre, and analyse them to determine whether there is any truth to the common belief.

To check if pass/fail rates in the driving test are dependent on the examiner, Nariko uses a χ^2 test. First, she puts the data she collected in a two-way table:

Observed frequencies	Mr A	Ms B	Miss C	Total
Pass	28	38	35	101
Fail	20	10	18	48
Total	48	48	53	149

At first glance, Mr A and Ms B conducted the same number of tests (48), but Ms B passed 28 more people than she failed whereas Mr A passed only 8 more people than he failed. This seems to suggest that the rumours in town are true. However, Nariko is a statistician and knows that it is important to avoid being swayed by opinion; so she starts by assuming that there is no dependence or bias.

All χ^2 tests start from the assumption that the two factors being tested are **independent**. This independence is stated as the **null hypothesis**, usually denoted by H_0.

Nariko's null hypothesis is:

H_0: the pass rate is independent of the examiner who conducts the test.

In contrast, the **alternative hypothesis** (H_1) is:

H_1: the pass rate is dependent on the examiner who conducts the test.

To apply the χ^2 test, Nariko then needs to calculate the **expected frequencies**, which are the frequencies that should occur if the factors were truly independent. These expected frequencies are calculated using probability theory (see Chapter 10).

From the rightmost column of Nariko's table above, you can see that the pass rate (proportion of passes) is $\frac{101}{149}$ and the failure rate is $\frac{48}{149}$.

exam tip

In examinations, all your calculations for the χ^2 test may be done on the GDC. If you use the χ^2 test in your project, you can use either the formula or your GDC.

Therefore, if these rates are **independent** of which examiner conducts the driving test, then all three examiners would be expected to pass (and fail) the same proportion of candidates.

Since Mr A examined 48 candidates, $48 \times \frac{101}{149} = 32.5$ of them would be expected to pass, and $48 \times \frac{48}{149} = 15.5$ would be expected to fail.

Ms B examined the same number of people as Mr A, so her expected frequencies of pass and fail are the same as for Mr A.

Miss C examined 53 candidates, so $53 \times \frac{101}{149} = 35.9$ would be expected to pass, and $53 \times \frac{48}{149} = 17.1$ would be expected to fail.

The table of expected frequencies is shown on the left.

In general, the expected frequency to go in each cell of the table can be found from the following formula:

$$\text{expected frequency} = \frac{\text{row total} \times \text{column total}}{\text{total}}$$

Expected frequencies	Mr A	Ms B	Miss C
Pass	32.5	32.5	35.9
Fail	15.5	15.5	17.1

For instance, the cell for 'Mr A, Pass' has row total 101 and column total 48, so the expected frequency is $\frac{101 \times 48}{149} = 32.5$ (3 s.f.). The cell for 'Miss C, Fail' has row total 48 and column total 53, hence the expected frequency is $\frac{48 \times 53}{149} = 17.1$.

Now Nariko has two tables, one showing the observed frequencies from the data she collected, and the other showing the expected values that she calculated using probability theory.

Observed frequencies	Mr A	Ms B	Miss C
Pass	28	38	35
Fail	20	10	18

Expected frequencies	Mr A	Ms B	Miss C
Pass	32.5	32.5	35.9
Fail	15.5	15.5	17.1

Each table contains two rows and three columns of numbers, so the number of degrees of freedom $= (2 - 1) \times (3 - 1) = 1 \times 2 = 2$.

Using her GDC, Nariko finds that $\chi^2_{\text{calc}} = 4.89$.

For 2 degrees of freedom, the tables give the critical value at the 0.05 significance level as $\chi^2_{5\%} = 5.991$. Since $\chi^2_{\text{calc}} < \chi^2_{5\%}$, Nariko concludes that she does **not** have enough evidence to reject H_0. In other words, the data does not support the claim that the pass rate is dependent on the examiner.

To confirm the result obtained by comparing χ^2_{calc} and χ^2_{critical}, Nariko also finds the p-value using her GDC: it is $p = 0.087$. Because $0.087 > 0.05$, this confirms that she should accept the null hypothesis of pass rates and examiners being independent.

hint

If χ^2_{calc} had been large enough that Nariko could reject the null hypothesis, then she would be accepting the alternative hypothesis, i.e. that there is a relationship between the examiner and the pass rate on the driving test.

Remember that even when the chi-squared test indicates that there is dependence between two factors, it does not tell you what kind of relationship it is. So even if Nariko's data did show enough evidence of dependence, the χ^2 test would not tell Nariko that Ms B was more likely to pass people than the other examiners — just that there was some relationship between the examiner and the likelihood of passing.

Significance level

You have already seen in Worked example 13.1 that the significance level chosen can make a difference to your conclusion.

For Nariko's driving test data, the p-value of 0.087 was greater than 0.05, so at the 5% significance level Nariko accepts the null hypothesis. However, since $0.087 < 0.1$, at the 10% significance level Nariko would **reject** the null hypothesis and conclude that there is dependence between pass rate and examiner. If you look up the critical χ^2 value for $\alpha = 0.1$ and 2 degrees of freedom, you will find that $\chi^2_{10\%} = 4.605$. As $\chi^2_{calc} = 4.89 > 4.065$, this also tells us that we can reject the null hypothesis.

The most commonly chosen significance level is 5%, but 1%, 2.5% and 10% are also used.

Knowing how it can drastically affect the conclusions of the test, make sure that you always state the significance level (or check that you are using the right level given in the question) when you are analysing data with the chi-squared test.

5% is the significance level most commonly used in IB examination questions.

In applying the χ^2 test, you use probability theory to do calculations. Can this be considered a rigorous application of mathematics to science? In statistics, is it ever possible to give a definite answer, or is it enough that you always remain aware of the restrictions, biases or flaws that may exist? When you read the results of a statistical survey, do you keep this in mind and take it into account while you interpret the conclusions?

Exercise 13.2

1. Calculate the expected frequencies for each of the following contingency tables.

(a)

	B_1	B_2
A_1	64	134
A_2	91	174

(b)

	B_1	B_2	B_3
A_1	48	24	14
A_2	34	16	10

(c)

	B_1	B_2	B_3	B_4
A_1	45	95	63	28
A_2	20	109	57	18
A_3	45	50	104	29

(d)

	B_1	B_2
A_1	24	35
A_2	37	52
A_3	57	41

13.3 Using your GDC to calculate the χ^2 statistic

The questions in Exercises 13.1 and 13.2 can be worked through without using any statistical functions on your GDC. In this section, we show you how to find the χ^2 statistic and the p-value with your GDC. See '13.1 The χ^2 test for independence' on page 675 of the GDC chapter for details. As you will see, it is very convenient to use your GDC when you need to perform a χ^2 test for a project or assignment or to answer an examination question.

Suppose you want to find out whether there is a link between hair colour and eye colour. Do most people with black hair have brown eyes?

The following data is collected from a sample of 63 people.

	Black hair	Brown hair	Blonde hair
Blue eyes	5	7	12
Brown eyes	15	10	2
Green eyes	3	4	5

1. State the hypotheses. Remember that the null hypothesis, H_0, always assumes **independence** of the factors.

   H_0: the colour of a person's eyes is independent of the colour of their hair.
   H_1: the colour of a person's eyes is dependent on the colour of their hair.

2. Decide on the significance level that you are going to use.

   The data will be tested at the 5% significance level.

3. Enter the table of observed values into matrix A on your GDC. The table of data has 3 rows and 3 columns, so you need a matrix with the same dimensions.

exam tip

Matrices (plural of 'matrix') are not in the IB Mathematical Studies syllabus. You only need them for entering data values from two-way tables into your GDC.

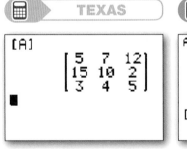

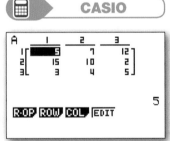

GDC

See section '13.2 viewing the contents of a matrix' on page 677 of the GDC chapter if you need to.

Take a look at matrix B, which contains the expected frequencies. Note that the GDC sets this up automatically; you don't need to do any calculations.

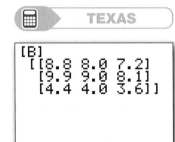

4. Ask your GDC to calculate the χ^2 statistic.

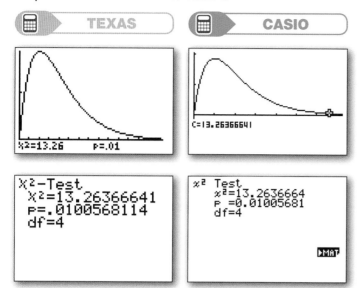

Your GDC will give you χ^2_{calc}, the p-value and the degrees of freedom 'df'.

5. Compare χ^2_{calc} and $\chi^2_{5\%}$. Since df = 4, you can look up the critical value $\chi^2_{5\%}$ from a table (or, if this is an examination question, $\chi^2_{5\%}$ will be given to you). In this case:

$$\chi^2_{5\%} = 9.49$$

$$\chi^2_{calc} = 13.3$$

$$\chi^2_{calc} > \chi^2_{5\%}$$

So reject H_0 and accept H_1: the colour of someone's eyes is dependent on the colour of their hair.

6. As an alternative to step 5, or to confirm the conclusion drawn there, compare the p-value with the significance level.

Here $p = 0.01 < 0.05$, so reject H_0 and conclude that eye colour is dependent on hair colour.

Remember that the χ^2 statistic is a measure of the **deviation** between the observed and expected frequencies. Therefore:

- If the observed and expected values are all exactly the same, then $\chi^2_{calc} = 0$.

- If the observed and expected values are close together, the value of χ^2_{calc} will be small. If χ^2_{calc} is **smaller** than the value of $\chi^2_{critical}$ for the associated degrees of freedom and significance level, then **accept** H_0.

- If the observed and expected values are very different, the value of χ^2_{calc} will be large. If χ^2_{calc} is **larger** than the value of $\chi^2_{critical}$, then **reject** H_0.

The p-value is a measure of how **likely** you are to get your value of χ^2_{calc} if H_0 were true. Therefore:

- If the p-value is **more** than the significance level, you don't have enough evidence to doubt the validity of H_0, so **accept** H_0.

- If the p-value is **less** than the significance level, then **reject** H_0.

The χ^2 test is a widely used technique in the social sciences as well as in biology, psychology, geography and many other fields. It can be used to answer questions such as: Do men and women tend to vote for different political parties? How effective is a new vaccine? Is there a connection between the colour of cars and the number of accidents in which they are involved?

exam tip

In an examination, you will expected to do the calculations for a χ^2 test on your GDC, so the questions will test your **understanding** of the results that your calculator produces.

Worked example 13.2

Q. Katya has collected data about the types of movie that students in her year group particularly enjoy. She predicts that the preferences will be the same for boys and girls.

Here are her results:

	Adventure	Romance	Comedy	Animation
Male	11	3	9	8
Female	6	9	7	7

(a) State Katya's null hypothesis and her alternative hypothesis.

(b) Find the expected frequency for the number of females who prefer adventure movies.

(c) Using your GDC, find the chi-squared statistic for Katya's data.

(d) Using your GDC, find the p-value for this data.

(e) Show that the number of degrees of freedom for this data is 3.

(f) If $\chi^2_{5\%} = 7.815$, give Katya's conclusion.

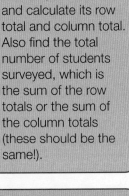

Remember that the null hypothesis always assumes independence.

Look at the cell for 'Female, Adventure' and calculate its row total and column total. Also find the total number of students surveyed, which is the sum of the row totals or the sum of the column totals (these should be the same!).

Use a matrix with 2 rows and 4 columns to enter the data into your GDC. Then calculate the χ^2 statistic. See section '13.1 The χ^2 test for independence' on page 675 if you need a reminder.

A. (a) H_0: the choice of favourite movie type is independent of gender.

H_1: the choice of favourite movie type depends on gender.

(b) Row total $= 6 + 9 + 7 + 7 = 29$

Column total $= 11 + 6 = 17$

Total frequency $= 60$

so expected frequency $= \dfrac{29 \times 17}{60} = 8.22$

(c)

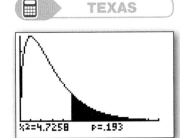

TEXAS

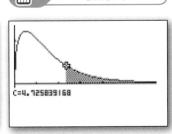

CASIO

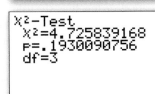

$\chi^2_{calc} = 4.73$

continued . . .

Read off the *p*-value from the screen.

(d) From GDC: $p = 0.193$

Use the formula for a two-way table.

(e) $df = (4-1) \times (2-1) = 3 \times 1 = 3$

Compare χ^2_{calc} with the given critical value $\chi^2_{5\%}$. Or compare the *p*-value with the significance level 5%.

(f) $4.73 < 7.815$, i.e. $\chi^2_{\text{calc}} < \chi^2_{5\%}$

so Katya accepts the null hypothesis.

$p = 0.193 > 0.05$ leads to the same conclusion.

Therefore Katya concludes that the choice of favourite movie type is independent of gender.

Exercise 13.3

1. For each of the following contingency tables, calculate:

(i) the degrees of freedom   (ii) the χ^2 statistic   (iii) the *p*-value.

(a)

	B_1	B_2
A_1	64	134
A_2	91	174

(b)

	B_1	B_2	B_3
A_1	48	24	14
A_2	34	16	10

(c)

	B_1	B_2	B_3	B_4
A_1	45	95	63	28
A_2	20	109	57	18
A_3	45	50	104	29

(d)

	B_1	B_2
A_1	24	35
A_2	37	52
A_3	57	41
A_4	79	58

2. Calculate the chi-squared statistic for each of the following sets of data.

(a)

	B_1	B_2	B_3
A_1	259	280	388
A_2	130	219	210

(b)

	P	Q	R
A	86	153	52
B	79	73	35
C	33	21	28

(c)

	P	Q	R
A	23	25	30
B	33	51	46
C	61	73	30
D	86	104	46

(d)

	M	N
P	50	25
Q	80	38
R	45	37
S	61	40

3. Jocelyn wants to investigate whether high performance (at grade A* or A) in GCSE is dependent on gender. She has collected the following data to help her with her investigation.

	A*	A
Boys	77	161
Girls	109	209

She decides to set up a chi-squared test.

(a) State the null hypothesis.

(b) Find the number of degrees of freedom.

(c) Determine the chi-squared statistic for this data.

The χ^2 critical value at 5% level of significance is 3.84.

(d) State whether or not Jocelyn should reject the null hypothesis, justifying your answer clearly.

4. The table below shows data on a sample of drivers involved in motor vehicle accidents, categorised according to gender and age. Karim wants to test whether there is an association between the age and gender of drivers involved in accidents.

	Younger drivers	Older drivers
Male	217	508
Female	115	360

A chi-squared test at the 10% level of significance is performed.

(a) State the null hypothesis.

(b) State the number of degrees of freedom.

(c) Determine the chi-squared statistic for this data.

The χ^2 critical value at 10% level of significance is 4.61.

(d) What conclusion can Karim draw from this test? Give a reason for your answer.

5. A librarian carried out a survey on the genre of books borrowed from the library by readers of different ages. The results are summarised below.

	Fiction	Non-fiction	Other
Under 21	32	18	50
22–40	61	19	36
Over 40	23	37	44

Set up a suitable null hypothesis and test it at the 5% level of significance. You may take the χ^2 critical value for this test to be 9.49.

13.4 Restrictions on using the χ^2 test

When you are analysing data you have collected yourself or data that is given to you, there are some issues to bear in mind before applying the χ^2 test for independence.

- The categories for each variable must be mutually exclusive, i.e. they cannot occur at the same time.

 You learned about mutually exclusive events in Chapter 10.

- The **expected** frequencies should not be too small:

  – In a 2×2 contingency table, no cell should contain an expected frequency of 5 or less.

  – In a larger contingency table (one with more than two rows or two columns), no cell should contain an expected frequency of 1 or less, and no more than 20% of the expected frequencies should be less than 5.

  – If there are expected frequencies in a table that do not satisfy the above conditions, combine cells so that the required limits are reached.

exam tip

- If the number of degrees of freedom is 1, the usual formula for the χ^2 statistic is believed to overestimate the amount of deviation between observed and expected values. This overestimation is reduced by applying the **Yates continuity correction**.

Summary

You should know:

- what the χ^2 test for independence is and how to calculate it

- what the critical χ^2 value and p-value are and how to use them

- how to use contingency tables to analyse dependency between two variables

- how to formulate a null and an alternative hypothesis

- how to calculate expected frequencies and degrees of freedom

- the meaning of the significance level

- how to determine if you should reject or accept the null hypothesis

Below is an example of a table of chi-squared values. In the examination you will always be given the values you need to use, and will not have to read them off a table like this.

Table of chi-squared critical values

		Significance level				
		0.10	**0.05**	**0.025**	**0.01**	**0.001**
	1	2.706	3.841	5.024	6.635	10.828
	2	4.605	5.991	7.378	9.210	13.816
	3	6.251	7.815	9.348	11.345	16.266
	4	7.779	9.488	11.143	13.277	18.467
Degrees of freedom	**5**	9.236	11.070	12.833	15.086	20.515
	6	10.645	12.592	14.449	16.812	22.458
	7	12.017	14.067	16.013	18.475	24.322
	8	13.362	15.507	17.535	20.090	26.125
	9	14.684	16.919	19.023	21.666	27.877
	10	15.987	18.307	20.483	23.209	29.588

Mixed examination practice

Exam-style questions

1. The table below shows cell phone ownership for different age groups.

	18–34	35–54	55+
Own cell phone	440	590	707
Do not own cell phone	28	86	362

Use a χ^2 test at the 5% significance level to test whether cell phone ownership is independent of age. Show all stages of your test, including the null and alternative hypotheses, number of degrees of freedom and the expected frequencies.

2. The table below shows the voting behaviour of a sample of workers. Omar wants to test whether voting behaviour is associated with the type of work that voters do.

	Party		
	PPP	**CPP**	**SLP**
Manual workers	37	24	44
Non-manual workers	57	30	19

A chi-squared test at the 10% level of significance is performed.

(a) State the null hypothesis.

(b) State the number of degrees of freedom.

(c) Determine the chi-squared statistic for this data.

The χ^2 critical value at the 10% level of significance is 4.61.

(d) What conclusion can Omar draw from this test? Give a reason for your answer.

3. Mrs Elwood, the Director of Studies in a secondary school, is analysing the school's GCSE results to investigate whether low performance in Mathematics (at grade F or lower) is independent of gender. The table shows the number of low grades and failures in the most recent examination session.

	F	G	U
Boys	43	22	13
Girls	31	14	9

Mrs Elwood uses the chi-squared test at the 5% level of significance.

(a) State a suitable null hypothesis, H_0.

(b) State the number of degrees of freedom.

(c) Determine the chi-squared statistic for this data.

The χ^2 critical value at the 5% significance level is 5.99.

(d) State whether or not Mrs Elwood will reject the null hypothesis, justifying your answer clearly.

4. A salesman has collected the following data on the sales of smart phones and other cell phones.

		Smart phones	Other cell phones
Age group	18–34	252	188
	35–54	235	355
	55+	165	542

He wishes to test whether ownership of smart phones depends on age.

To do so he performs a chi-squared test at the 5% level of significance.

(a) State the null hypothesis.

(b) State the number of degrees of freedom.

(c) Determine the chi-squared statistic for this data.

The χ^2 critical value at the 5% level of significance is 5.99.

(d) What conclusion can be drawn from this test? Give a reason for your answer.

5. A study was conducted by a polling agency to determine whether there is a relationship between voting behaviour and age of voters. The data gathered is shown below.

		Age of voters			
		18–24	25–34	35–54	55+
Political party	Action Party	204	343	354	429
	Progress Party	412	380	462	406
	National Party	227	124	280	154

Set up a suitable null hypothesis and test it at the 5% level of significance. You may take the χ^2 critical value for the data to be 12.59.

6. The performance of 200 students in their IB Mathematics examinations is shown in the table. A chi-squared test is applied to the data to test whether high performance is related to the level at which the subject was studied.

	Level 7	Level 6	Level 5
Mathematical Studies	50	23	11
Mathematics SL	29	26	9
Mathematics HL	20	19	13

(a) State the null hypothesis, H_0, for this data.

(b) Calculate the expected numbers of Level 5, Level 6 and Level 7 grades for Mathematics HL.

Using a 5% level of significance the p-value was found to be 0.0806 correct to 3 significant figures.

(c) State whether the null hypothesis, H_0, should be accepted. Justify your answer.

7. The Road Safety Committee of a Local Authority has collected the following data:

	Age in years				
	≤ 19	**20–24**	**25–44**	**45–64**	**≥ 65**
Drivers in accidents	21	40	46	14	10
Drivers not in accidents	42	60	68	69	31

Set up a suitable null hypothesis and test it at the 5% level of significance. Perform your test using the p-value and confirm your result using the chi-squared test statistic. You may take the χ^2 critical value for the data to be 7.78. Show all the relevant stages of your test.

Past paper questions

1. Manuel conducts a survey on a random sample of 751 people to see which television programme type they watch most from the following: Drama, Comedy, Film, News. The results are as follows.

	Drama	**Comedy**	**Film**	**News**
Males under 25	22	65	90	35
Males 25 and over	36	54	67	17
Females under 25	22	59	82	15
Females 25 and over	64	39	38	46

Manuel decides to ignore the ages and to test at the 5% level of significance whether the most watched programme type is independent of **gender**.

(a) Draw a table with 2 rows and 4 columns of data so that Manuel can perform a chi-squared test.

[3 marks]

(b) State Manuel's null hypothesis and alternative hypothesis. *[1 mark]*

(c) Find the expected frequency for the number of females who had "Comedy" as their most-watched programme type. Give your answer to the nearest whole number. *[2 marks]*

(d) Using your graphic display calculator, or otherwise, find the chi-squared statistic for Manuel's data.

[3 marks]

(e) (i) State the number of degrees of freedom available for this calculation.

(ii) State the critical value for Manuel's test.

(iii) State his conclusion. *[3 marks]*
[Total 12 marks]

[Nov 2007, Paper 2, TZ0, Question 4(ii)] (© *IB Organization 2007*)

2. The local park is used for walking dogs. The sizes of the dogs are observed at different times of the day. The table below shows the numbers of dogs present, classified by size, at three different times last Sunday.

$$
\begin{array}{c} \\ \text{Morning} \\ \text{Afternoon} \\ \text{Evening} \end{array}
\begin{array}{ccc} \text{Small} & \text{Medium} & \text{Large} \\ \left(\begin{array}{ccc} 9 & 18 & 2 \\ 11 & 6 & 13 \\ 7 & 8 & 9 \end{array} \right) \end{array}
$$

(a) Write a suitable null hypothesis for a χ^2 test on this data.

(b) Write down the value of χ^2 for this data.

(c) The number of degrees of freedom is 4. Show how this value is calculated.

The critical value, at the 5% level of significance, is 9.488.

(d) What conclusion can be drawn from this test? Give a reason for your answer.   *[Total 6 marks]*

[May 2007, Paper 1, TZ0, Question 8] (© *IB Organization 2007*)

3. 200 people of different ages were asked to choose their favourite type of music from the choices Popular, Country and Western and Heavy Metal. The results are shown in the table below.

Age/Music choice	Popular	Country and Western	Heavy Metal	Totals
11–25	35	5	50	90
26–40	30	10	20	60
41–60	20	25	5	50
Totals	85	40	75	200

It was decided to perform a chi-squared test for independence at the 5% level on the data.

(a) Write down the null hypothesis.   *[1 mark]*

(b) Write down the number of degrees of freedom.   *[1 mark]*

(c) Write down the chi-squared value.   *[2 marks]*

(d) State whether or not you will reject the null hypothesis, giving a clear reason for your answer.   *[2 marks]*
     [Total 6 marks]

[May 2008, Paper 1, TZ1, Question 5] (© *IB Organization 2008*)

5 Geometry and trigonometry

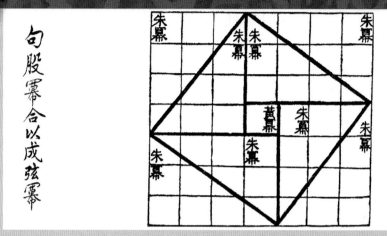

An ancient Chinese diagram illustrating Pythagoras' theorem.

The study of geometry, and in particular the mathematics of right-angled triangles, goes back to the earliest civilisations.

Every time that you use Pythagoras' theorem, or solve a triangle using trigonometry, imagine yourself back with a student sitting on a mat in Babylon, or puzzling out the answer in ancient China, India or Egypt.

Pythagoras' theorem is named after Pythagoras of Samos (~ 569–475 BCE), a Greek who worked in the eastern Mediterranean and southern Italy. However, his particular proof is just one amongst many.

A Chinese textbook (*Zhou Bi Suan Jing*) contains a description of the same theorem and examples of how to apply it to practical problems. This dates from an era of about 300 BCE.

There are early sets of **Pythagorean triples** on a clay tablet from Babylon that dates from ~1800 BCE, and the theorem is well documented in early Indian sources. Builders in Egypt, in the time of the Pharaohs, used a rope stretcher based on the 3,4,5 triangle to create a right angle.

Trigonometry was probably developed to support the study of astronomy. The prediction of eclipses was always important, as religious ceremonies had to be timed to coincide with them. The earliest documented evidence of the use of the sine is about 500 CE, in India in the time of Aryabhata I.

Did all these scholars have the same ideas in isolation? Or did they communicate with each other and pass theories and techniques along trade routes and seaways? Was the mathematics they used waiting for them to discover it? Or did they all invent it and then tell each other about it? Historians and archaeologists know that there was much more communication in those early times than previously thought. Does this explain the exchange of ideas more than 2000 years ago?

Prior learning topics

It will be easier to study this topic if you:

- know the basic geometric concepts: point, line, plane and angle
- recognise simple two-dimensional shapes such as circles, triangles, quadrilaterals and combinations of these
- know how to calculate the areas and perimeters of simple and compound shapes
- know Pythagoras' theorem and how to use it
- know how to plot coordinates in two dimensions
- know how to find the midpoints of lines on a graph and the distance between two points on a graph.

Chapter 14 Equation of a line in two dimensions

In this chapter you will learn:

- about the gradient (m) of a line and how to calculate it
- how to identify parallel lines ($m_1 = m_2$) and perpendicular lines ($m_1 \times m_2 = -1$)
- about the y-intercept (c) of a line
- more about the equation of a line in two dimensions given in either form: $y = mx + c$ or $ax + by + d = 0$

Euclid (~ 300 BCE) was a Greek mathematician who worked in Alexandria in Egypt. Whilst leading the mathematical school in Athens, he wrote a textbook in 13 parts called *The Elements* in which he collected together all the mathematics known at that time. Euclid's reputation is founded on the way he collated, and improved, theorems and ideas that were current then, which was mainly geometry. *The Elements* was the standard textbook for mathematicians until about 150 years ago. Euclid can be described as the most important mathematics teacher of all time.

The Elements begins with definitions and five postulates, or axioms. The first postulate states that it is possible to draw a straight line between any two points. This may seem obvious to you as you have drawn lines on pieces of paper since you were young. But consider that any straight line is constructed from an infinite number of points on that line and to draw a straight line on a flat piece of paper, you only need two pieces of information. With those two pieces of information you can draw a line that is unique.

You need:

- either a point on the line and its direction or gradient,
- or two points on the line.

This was groundbreaking at the time but is something that we take for granted today, and students often question why we need to learn it. There is a story about someone who had begun to learn geometry with Euclid who wondered a similar thing. After he had learned the first theorem, the student asked Euclid, 'What shall I get by learning these things?' Euclid responded by asking his slave to, 'Give him three pence since he must make gain out of what he learns.'

EUCLIDES

14.1 The gradient of a line

The **gradient** of a line describes the 'steepness' or slope of that line. A very steep line has a large gradient, while a shallow slope has a small gradient.

The gradient is defined as: $m = \dfrac{\text{change in vertical distance}}{\text{change in horizontal distance}}$

m is the letter that represents the gradient of a line in the general linear equation $y = mx + c$.

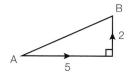

The vertical change from A to B is +2.

The horizontal change from A to B is +5.

$m = \dfrac{2}{5}$

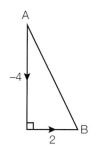

The vertical change from A to B is −4.

The horizontal change from A to B is +2.

$m = \dfrac{-4}{2} = -2$

A line that 'slopes downwards' has a negative gradient.

Calculating the gradient from the coordinates of the points on the line

If a line is plotted on a graph, the gradient can be calculated using the **coordinates** of points on that line. Be careful though and look at the scale of the graph, both horizontally and vertically. In the graph below, two units on the horizontal axis is the same as two units on the vertical axis, but this might not always be the case.

hint

A Cartesian plane (below) is a system of two axes on a flat expanse. It is named after René Descartes, who originated it.

AC is 2 units long,

BC is 4 units long.

$m_{AB} = \dfrac{4}{2} = 2$

DF is 1 unit long,

EF is 4 units long.

$m_{ED} = \dfrac{-1}{4} = -\dfrac{1}{4}$

Note that the line DE slopes downwards so it has a negative gradient. F is −1 along the y-axis from D.

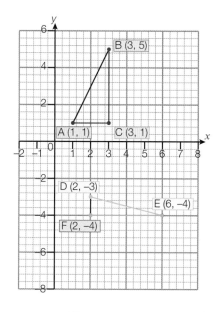

Using the general coordinates (x_1, y_1) and (x_2, y_2), the vertical distance from A to B in the graph below is $y_2 - y_1$ and the horizontal distance from A to B is $x_2 - x_1$.

The suffixes to x and y must be in the same order. This will ensure that the gradient has the correct sign.

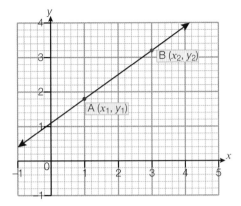

The gradient can be calculated as:

$$m = \frac{\text{change in vertical distance}}{\text{change in horizontal distance}} = \frac{y_2 - y_1}{x_2 - x_1}$$

Therefore, if you are given the coordinates of two points on a line, you can calculate its gradient in one of two ways:

The calculations of gradients can be important in civil engineering. The trans-Canada highway is engineered so that gradients in the road (any inclines or declines) are kept at about 6%. This helps to regulate traffic speed and flow.

1. Draw a graph, plot the points and calculate the vertical and horizontal changes.

2. Use the formula $m = \dfrac{y_2 - y_1}{x_2 - x_1}$.

Worked example 14.1

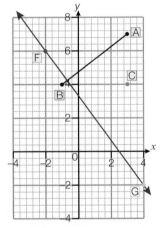

Q. (a) Find the gradient of the line joining the points A(3, 7) and B(−1, 4).

continued . . .

(b) A line passes through the points F(−2, 6) and G(4, −2). Calculate the gradient of the **line segment** FG.

(c) C is the point (3, 4). Calculate the gradients of the lines AC and BC.

A.

Substitute the coordinates into the formula for the gradient:
$$m = \frac{y_2 - y_1}{x_2 - x_1}.$$

(a) $m_{AB} = \dfrac{7-4}{(3-(-1))} = \dfrac{3}{4}$

$$m = \frac{3}{4}$$

Notice that FG 'slopes backwards' so this gradient is negative.

(b) $m_{FG} = \dfrac{6-(-2)}{(-2)-4} = \dfrac{8}{-6} = -\dfrac{4}{3}$

$$m = -\frac{4}{3}$$

When trying to divide by zero, your calculator may return the answer, 'Syntax ERROR' or 'Ma ERROR'.

(c) $m_{AC} = \dfrac{7-4}{3-3} = \dfrac{3}{0}$.

This is incalculable. The gradient of a vertical line is undefined. The symbol ∞ is used to denote this.

AC is a vertical line and so has an undefined gradient.

The gradient of any horizontal line is zero.

$$m_{BC} = \frac{4-4}{3-(-1)} = \frac{0}{4} = 0$$

BC is a horizontal line.

The next worked example shows how to calculate gradients of parallel lines and of lines that are **perpendicular** to each other.

Worked example 14.2

Q. (a) Plot the points A(1, 1), B(3, 5), C(2, 4), D(8, 1), E(−4, −5) and F(−1, 1) on a graph and join the points A to B, C to D and E to F.

(b) Calculate the gradients of the line segments AB, CD and EF.

(c) Which two lines are parallel? Look at their gradients and comment.

(d) Which two lines are perpendicular?

continued . . .

A. (a)

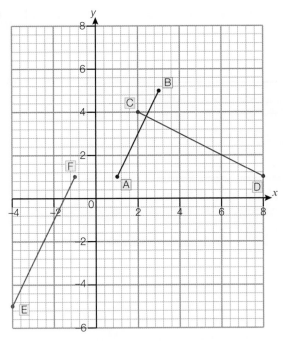

(b) $m_{AB} = \dfrac{4}{2} = 2$

$m_{CD} = \dfrac{3}{-6} = -\dfrac{1}{2}$

$m_{EF} = \dfrac{6}{3} = 2$

(c) AB and EF are parallel; they have the same gradient.

> Remember that lines are parallel if they go in the same direction but never touch; the shortest distance between them is constant. You can see that AB and EF are parallel.

(d) AB and CD are perpendicular.

$m_{AB} \times m_{CD} = 2 \times -\dfrac{1}{2} = -1$

EF and CD are also perpendicular.

> Two lines are perpendicular if they form a right angle where they intersect. If $m_1 \times m_2 = -1$ then the lines are perpendicular.

Gradient summary

- Horizontal lines have a gradient of 0.

- Vertical lines have a gradient that is undefined.

- Parallel lines have the same gradient, $m_1 = m_2$.

- The gradients of two lines that are perpendicular multiply to give −1: $m_1 \times m_2 = -1$.

Exercise 14.1

1. Plot the following sets of points and hence calculate the gradient of each of the lines joining the points.

(a) (2, 0) and (0, 2)

(b) (1, 7) and (3, 15)

(c) (−2, 3) and (6, −8)

(d) (−4, −5) and (0, 7)

(e) (8, −9) and (12, 10)

2. Plot the following points on a graph: A(−1, 2), B(1, 3), C(5, 0) and D(1, −2). Join the points to form a quadrilateral ABCD.

(a) Calculate the gradients of the line segments AB, BC, CD and AD.

(b) Which two of the line segments are parallel? Look at their gradients. Comment on the connection between their gradients.

(c) Name a pair of perpendicular line segments. Look at their gradients. Comment on the connection between their gradients.

3. (a) Draw the line segments AE, CD, CE, DE, DF and GF on a copy of this grid. Hence calculate the gradient of each of them.

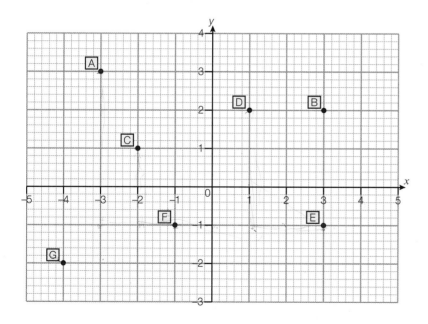

(b) Which of the line segments from above are parallel? Comment on the relationship between their gradients.

(c) Which of the line segments from above are perpendicular? Comment on the relationship between their gradients.

4. (a) Calculate the gradients of each of the following line segments.

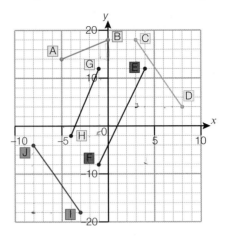

(b) Indicate, with reasons, which two of the line segments are:

(i) parallel

(ii) perpendicular.

$y = mx + b$

14.2 The *y*-intercept

The point where a line crosses the *y*-axis is called the **y-intercept**. This is often denoted by the letter *c*.

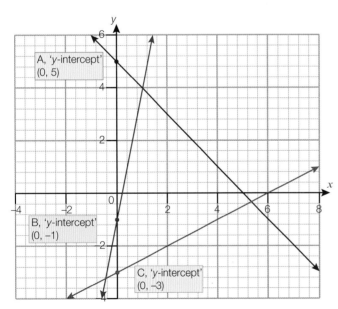

A is the point (0, 5)

B is the point (0, −1)

C is the point (0, −3)

If you are asked to give the coordinates of the *y*-intercept, the *x*-coordinate will always be 0.

Finding the equation of a straight line

The equation of a straight line describes the condition (or rule) that links the x- and y-coordinates to create that line. For some lines it is simple to look at the diagram or the coordinates and note the link.

If the points (5, 4), (4, 3) and (2, 1) are plotted on a graph, they form a line. What is the rule that connects the x- and y-coordinates?

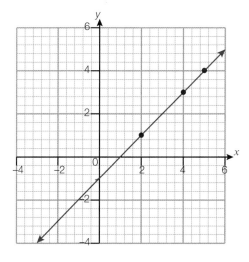

(x, y)	x	y in terms of x
(2, 1)	2	$2 - 1 = 1$
(4, 3)	4	$4 - 1 = 3$
(5, 4)	5	$5 - 1 = 4$

The y-coordinate is always one less than the x-coordinate.

The equation of the line is $y = x - 1$.

Look at the gradient and y-intercept on the graph.

The gradient $= 1$.

The y-intercept is $(0, -1)$.

The points (2, 0), (2, 5) and (2, −3) are plotted on a graph. Find the rule that connects them.

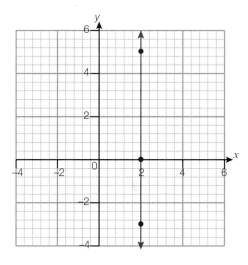

x	y
2	−3
2	0
2	5

The x-coordinate is always 2; only the y-coordinate changes.

The equation of the line is $x = 2$.

The graph shows that the line is vertical.

The gradient of the line is ∞.

The graph does not cross the y-axis, so there is no y-intercept.

Worked example 14.3

Q. Plot the points (4, 3), (2, 2) and (0, 1) on a graph and look for the rule that connects the x- and y-coordinates.

(a) Calculate the gradient of the line and the y-intercept.

(b) What connection do the gradient and the y-intercept have with the rule/equation?

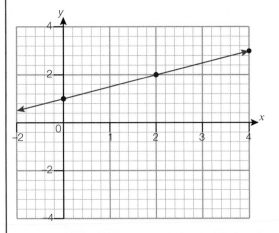

A.

x	y	(x, y)	y in terms of x
0	1	(0, 1)	$\frac{1}{2} \times 0 + 1 = 1$
2	2	(2, 2)	$\frac{1}{2} \times 2 + 1 = 1 + 1 = 2$
4	3	(4, 3)	$\frac{1}{2} \times 4 + 1 = 2 + 1 = 3$

The rule that connects the x- and y-coordinates is $y = \frac{1}{2}x + 1$.

Check this rule for $x = 3$:
$$y = \frac{1}{2} \times 3 + 1 = \frac{5}{2}$$
You can confirm this value by looking at the graph.

Get the information from the graph.

(a) The gradient of the line is $\frac{1}{2}$.

The y-intercept of the line is (0, 1).

(b) The gradient has the same value as the number (**coefficient**) multiplying the x.

The intercept has the same value as the **constant**.

Exercise 14.2

1. Plot the following sets of points on a graph. Determine the rule connecting the x- and y-coordinates of the points and hence find the equation of the line passing through the points.

   (a) $(-1, -2), (0, 0), (2, 4)$

   (b) $(-1, -1), (0, 1), (1, 3)$

   (c) $(1, 2), (2, 5), (3, 8)$

   (d) $(2, 3), (3, 7), (4, 11)$

   (e) $(1, -3), (2, -6), (3, -9)$

   (f) $(1, -2), (2, -5), (3, -8)$

   (g) $(-2, 6), (0, 4), (4, 0)$

2. By selecting two or three suitable points on the line, determine the equation of each of the following straight lines in the graphs (a) to (e). The lines are coloured red.

(a)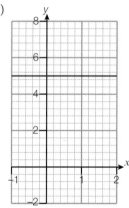

(b)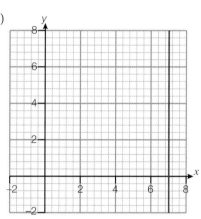

(c)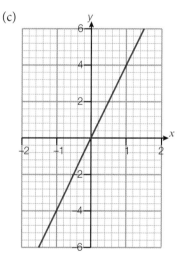

(d)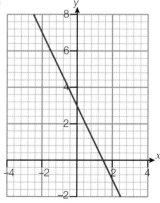

(e)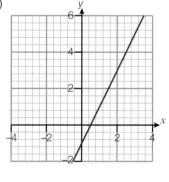

3. Find the equations of line A, line B and line C.

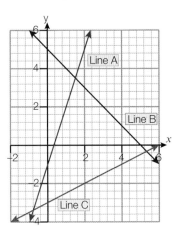

14.4 The equation of a straight line

The general equation of a straight line can be given in different forms. In this course you should be able to recognise:

$$y = mx + c \qquad \text{the 'gradient-intercept' form}$$
$$ax + by + d = 0 \qquad \text{the 'general' form.}$$

The 'gradient-intercept' form: $y = mx + c$

hint

If the equation is $y = mx - c$ then '$-c$' represents the y-intercept.

If the equation is in this form 'm' represents the gradient and '$+ c$' represents the y-intercept.

Depending on the information that you are given, you can find the equation of a particular line, as shown in the examples below.

Worked example 14.4

Q. The gradient of a line is $\dfrac{4}{3}$ and the line crosses the y-axis at $(0, -2)$. Find the equation of the line.

A. If the gradient is $\dfrac{4}{3}$ then $m = \dfrac{4}{3}$.

If the line crosses the y-axis at $(0, -2)$ then the y-intercept is -2.

So, the equation of the line is $y = \dfrac{4}{3}x - 2$.

Worked example 14.5

In this case, the intercept has not been given and must be calculated by substituting known values into $y = mx + c$ and solving the equation for c.

Q. The gradient of a line is −3, and the line passes through the point (2, 5). Find the equation of the line.

Replace y by the value of the y-coordinate of the point, x by the value of the x-coordinate and m by the value of the gradient.

A. $y = mx + c$

$5 = -3 \times 2 + c$

$5 = -6 + c$

$11 = c$

The equation of the line is $y = -3x + 11$.

Worked example 14.6

Q. A line passes through the points A(−3, 4) and B(1, −6). Find the equation of the line AB.

The line is passing through two points but the gradient and the y-intercept have not been given, so we need to calculate them.

A. $m = \dfrac{y_2 - y_1}{x_2 - x_1}$

$m = \dfrac{(-6-4)}{(1-(-3))}$

$= \dfrac{-10}{4} = \dfrac{-5}{2}$

Once the gradient has been calculated, you can substitute known values into $y = mx + c$ to solve for c. Choose either A or B as the point. The result will be the same whichever point you use.

Using point A:

$4 = \dfrac{-5}{2} \times -3 + c$

$4 = \dfrac{15}{2} + c$

$4 - \dfrac{15}{2} = c$

$\dfrac{-7}{2} = c$

The equation of the line is $y = -\dfrac{5}{2}x - \dfrac{7}{2}$.

The 'general' form: $ax + by + d = 0$

The general form of a linear equation is $ax + by + d = 0$, where a, b and d are integers.

The general form can be useful because you can use it to write an equation without rational numbers (fractions). If you are given the gradient-intercept form of an equation and it contains fractions, you can rearrange it into the general form to remove the fractions and make it easier to work with. You can also rearrange the general form into the gradient-intercept form.

RR *You were reminded how to rearrange equations in Learning links 2A in Chapter 2.*

Worked example 14.7

Q. Rearrange the following equations into the form $ax + by + d = 0$.

(a) $y = -2x - 1$ (b) $\dfrac{1}{2}y = 4x - 3$ (c) $\dfrac{y}{3} = -\dfrac{x}{2} + 2$

A. (a) $y = -2x - 1$

Add $2x$ to both sides of the equation.

$y + 2x = -1$

Add 1 to both sides of the equation.

$y + 2x + 1 = 0$

(b) $\dfrac{1}{2}y = 4x - 3$

Multiply each term by 2.

$y = 8x - 6$

Subtract $8x$ and add 6 to both sides of the equation.

$y - 8x + 6 = 0$

(c) $\dfrac{y}{3} = -\dfrac{x}{2} + 2$

Multiply each term by 6, the common denominator of $\dfrac{1}{2}$ and $\dfrac{1}{3}$.

$2y = -3x + 12$

Add $3x$ and subtract 12 from both sides of the equation.

$3x + 2y - 12 = 0$

Worked example 14.8

Q. A straight line passes through the points A(3, 4) and B(5, 10).

(a) Find the gradient of the line segment AB.

(b) Find the equation of the line AB. Give your answer in the form $y = mx + c$.

$\longrightarrow$

continued . . .

(c) Find the equation of the line parallel to AB that passes through the point C(−2, 1).

(d) Find the equation of the line perpendicular to AB that passes through the point D(0, −1). Give your answer in the form $ax + by + d = 0$.

> Calculate the gradient using the formula $m = \dfrac{y_2 - y_1}{x_2 - x_1}$.

A. (a) $m_{AB} = \dfrac{4-10}{3-5} = \dfrac{-6}{-2} = 3$

> Use one of the points to substitute values into the gradient-intercept equation; solve the equation for c.

(b) Using A(3, 4)

$$y = mx + c$$
$$4 = 3 \times 3 + c$$
$$4 - 9 = c$$
$$-5 = c$$

Equation of AB is
$$y = 3x - 5$$

> If the lines are parallel, you know that $m = 3$ and you can substitute this value and the coordinates of point C into $y = mx + c$ to solve for c.

(c) If lines are parallel, then $m = 3$ for both lines

Using C(−2, 1)
$$1 = 3 \times -2 + c$$
$$1 = -6 + c$$
$$7 = c$$

Equation of line through C is
$$y = 3x + 7$$

> $m_1 \times m_2 = -1$
> $3 \times -\dfrac{1}{3} = -1$

(d) If $m = 3$, the gradient of the perpendicular line $= -\dfrac{1}{3}$

> Substitute the coordinates of point D into $y = mx + c$ to solve for c.

Using D (0, −1)
$$-1 = -\dfrac{1}{3} \times 0 + c$$
$$-1 = c$$

Equation of line through D is
$$y = -\dfrac{1}{3}x - 1$$

> Rearrange $y = mx + c$ into the general form $ax + by + d = 0$. Multiply each term by 3 to remove the fraction.

$$3y = -x - 3$$
$$x + 3y + 3 = 0$$

Descartes demonstrated that geometric problems could be described in terms of algebra, and algebra problems in terms of geometry. Does this tell you that some problems can be seen from two entirely different viewpoints?

Exercise 14.3

1. Find the equation of the straight line through the given point with the given gradient.

(a) (3, 7); 6

(b) (0, 8); 4

(c) (−2, 4); −5

(d) $(1, 0); -3$

(e) $\left(\dfrac{3}{4}, -3\right); 2$

(f) $\left(-5, \dfrac{3}{4}\right); \dfrac{5}{7}$

2. Find the equation of the straight line passing through the following pairs of points.

(a) $(0, 4)$ and $(-2, 8)$

(b) $(-3, 5)$ and $(7, 3)$

(c) $(2, -1)$ and $(9, 0)$

(d) $\left(7, \dfrac{1}{3}\right)$ and $\left(11, \dfrac{5}{6}\right)$

(e) $(-6, -3)$ and $(-1, 4)$

(f) $\left(\dfrac{1}{2}, \dfrac{3}{4}\right)$ and $(0, -1)$

3. The points A and B have coordinates $(2, 5)$ and $(4, 9)$ respectively. A straight line l_1 passes through A and B.

(a) Find the equation of line l_1 in the form $ax + by + d = 0$.

The line l_2 passes through the point $(3, -5)$ and has gradient $\dfrac{2}{7}$.

(b) Find the equation of l_2

4. Find the equation of the line that is:

(a) parallel to the line $y = 7x - 1$ and passes through the point $(2, -9)$

(b) passes through the point $(-4, 7)$ and is parallel to the line $5x + 2y = 3$

(c) passes through $\left(3, \dfrac{1}{5}\right)$ and is parallel to the line $11 - 3x - 2y = 0$

(d) parallel to the line $5x = 9 - 8y$ and passes through the origin.

5. Find the equation of the line passing through the point:

(a) $(6, -1)$ and perpendicular to the line $y = 3x$

(b) $(11, 15)$ and perpendicular to the line $7x = 2y$

(c) $(0, 9)$ and perpendicular to the line $4x - 3y = 13$

(d) $\left(-\dfrac{1}{5}, 0\right)$ and perpendicular to the line $3x + 2y - 12 = 0$.

6. (a) Find the gradient of the line joining the points $A(-1, 2)$ and $B(3, 4)$.

(b) Hence find the equation of the line AB in the form $y = mx + c$.

(c) Find the equation of the line CD, perpendicular to AB and passing through point $C(5, 9)$.

7. Find the equation of each of the following lines in the form
$y = mx + c$.

(a)
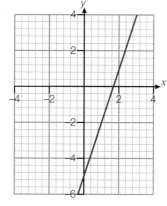

(b)
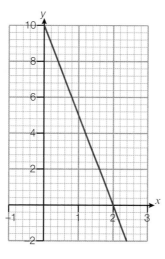

(c)
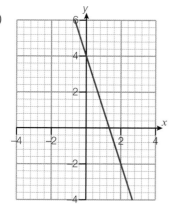

(d)
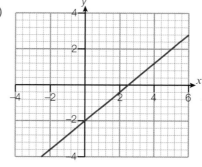

8. (a) Find the gradient of the line joining the points A(1, −2) and B(3, −4).

(b) Hence find the equation of the line joining the points A and B in the form $y = mx + c$.

(c) Rearrange the equation of the line to the form $ax + by + d = 0$, where a, b and d are integers.

14.5 Drawing a straight line graph from an equation

The equation of a line gives the unique rule that allows you to draw that line, and that line only.

Using $y = mx + c$

There are three methods for drawing a straight line graph using $y = mx + c$. You can:

1. Use the values of m and c.

2. Calculate a table of values using the equation and plot them.

3. Use your GDC.

To draw the line with equation $y = -\frac{1}{2}x + 3$

Method 1:

$m = -\frac{1}{2}$, $c = 3$, so the line passes through the point $(0, 3)$ with a gradient of $-\frac{1}{2}$.

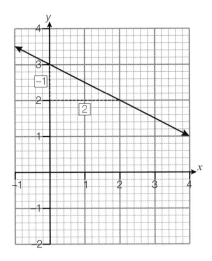

Method 2:

Draw up a table of values and then plot the points. It is helpful to calculate at least three points, as this will confirm that you have a straight line.

x	-2	0	4
$-\dfrac{1}{2}x + 3 = y$	$-\dfrac{1}{2}(-2) + 3 = 4$	$-\dfrac{1}{2} \times 0 + 3 = 3$	$-\dfrac{1}{2} \times 4 + 3 = 1$

Plot the points $(-2, 4)$, $(0, 3)$ and $(4, 1)$.

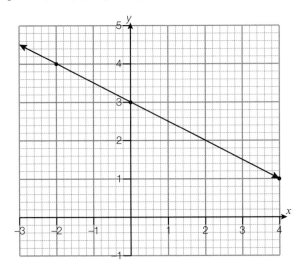

Method 3:

Using your GDC (see '*22.2.G Graphs*' on page 645 and '*14.1 Accessing the table of coordinates from a plotted graph*' on page 678 of the GDC chapter for a reminder if you need to):

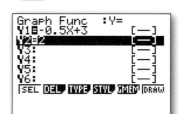

i. Enter the equation.

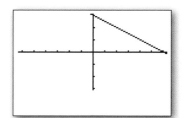

ii. Draw the line.

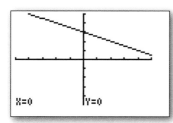

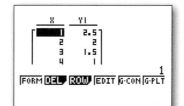

iii. Use the table to check the coordinates of your points.

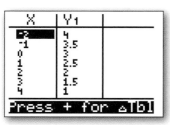

Using $ax + by + d = 0$

There are three methods for drawing a straight line graph using $ax + by + d = 0$. You can:

1. Use the equation to find the intercepts on the x- and y-axes.

2. Rearrange the general equation into the gradient-intercept form and use the values of m and c.

3. Rearrange the general equation into the gradient-intercept form and use your GDC.

To draw the line with equation $3x - 4y - 12 = 0$

Method 1:

Find the intercepts on the x- and y-axes by calculating the points where $x = 0$ and $y = 0$ and drawing a line through those points.

$$\text{When } x = 0, 3x = 0 \qquad -4y - 12 = 0$$
$$\text{so } 3x - 4y - 12 = 0 \Rightarrow \qquad -4y = 12$$
$$y = -3 \qquad \text{Plot } (0, -3)$$

$$\text{When } y = 0, 4y = 0 \qquad 3x - 12 = 0$$
$$\text{so } 3x - 4y - 12 = 0 \Rightarrow \qquad 3x = 12$$
$$x = 4 \qquad \text{Plot } (4, 0)$$

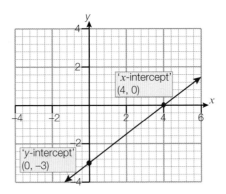

Method 2:

Rearrange into the gradient-intercept form with y as the subject of the equation, then use the values of m and c to draw the line.

$$3x - 4y - 12 = 0$$

Add $4y$ to both sides of the equation.

$$3x - 12 = 4y$$

Divide each term by 4.

$$\tfrac{3}{4}x - 3 = y$$

If $y = \tfrac{3}{4}x - 3$, draw the line with an intercept of $(0, -3)$ and gradient of $\tfrac{3}{4}$.

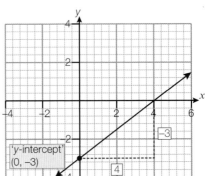

Method 3:

When using your GDC, you must use the equation in the form
$y = mx + c$ so, from method 2 above, draw $y = \frac{3}{4}x - 3$ on your GDC and
transfer the line onto your graph paper, using the table function.

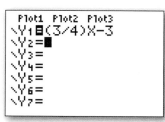

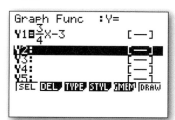

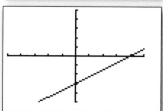

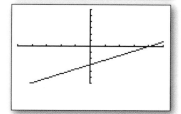

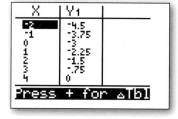

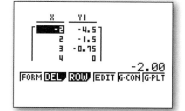

Worked example 14.9

Q. | Draw a Cartesian plane with axes $-6 \le x \le 6$ and $-8 \le y \le 6$.

(a) On the Cartesian plane, draw the line given by the equation $y - 2x + 7 = 0$.

(b) Rearrange the equation of the line into the gradient-intercept form.

(c) Write down the gradient of the line.

(d) Find the equation of a line parallel to the original, which passes through the point $(-2, 1)$. Draw this line.

(e) Find the equation of a line perpendicular to the original that passes through the point $(-1, 4)$. Draw this line.

To draw the line with equation $y - 2x + 7 = 0$, find when the line crosses each axis.

When $x = 0$, $y = -7$.

When $y = 0$, $x = 3.5$.

The line is drawn through $(0, -7)$ and $(3.5, 0)$.

The gradient-intercept form is $y = mx + c$. Add $2x$ to both sides and subtract 7 from both sides.

In the form $y = mx + c$, m is the gradient.

If the new line is parallel then its gradient is also $+2$. Substitute $x = -2$ and $y = 1$ into $y = mx + c$ and solve for c.

If the new line is perpendicular, then the gradients multiplied together should equal -1. Create an equation to solve.

Substituting $x = -1$ and $y = 4$ into $y = mx + c$ and solve for c.

continued . . .

A. (a) See (a) in dark blue in the graph below for line $y - 2x + 7 = 0$.

(b) $y - 2x + 7 = 0$

$\Rightarrow y = 2x - 7$

(c) The gradient of line is $+2$.

(d) $1 = 2 \times (-2) + c$

$1 = -4 + c$

$c = 5$

The new equation is $y = 2x + 5$

See line (d) in pink on the graph below.

(e) $m_2 \times 2 = -1$

$m_2 = -\dfrac{1}{2}$

$4 = -\dfrac{1}{2} \times -1 + c$

$4 = \dfrac{1}{2} + c$

$c = 3.5$

The new equation is $y = -\dfrac{1}{2}x + 3.5$

See line (e) in green on the graph below.

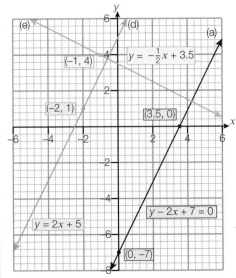

Exercise 14.4

1. Draw the lines of the equations given below.

    (a) $y = 2x - 3$ (b) $y = 1.5x + 4$

    (c) $y = 6 - x$ (d) $y = 10 - 7x$

    (e) $2y = 8 + 5x$ (f) $5y = 3x - 9$

2. Draw the following lines:

    (a) $4y = 3x - 12$ (b) $x + y = 7$

    (c) $2x + 3y = 6$ (d) $6y - 7 = 5x$

    (e) $3x + 4y - 2 = 0$ (f) $4x - y - 3 = 0$

    (g) $7x + 3y - 4 = 0$

3. (a) Draw the line with the equation $y = 3x + 4$.

    (b) Find the equation of the line parallel to $y = 3x + 4$ that passes through the point (2, 7).

4. (a) Draw the line with the equation $y = 4 - 5x$.

    (b) Find the equation of the line parallel to $y = 4 - 5x$ and passing through the point (−1, 2).

    (c) Find the equation of the line passing through the point (3, 8) which is perpendicular to the line $y = 4 - 5x$.

5. Solve the following simultaneous equations. In each case use your GDC to draw the pair of straight lines and write down the point of **intersection**.

    (a) $y = 7x - 4$ and $y = 4$ (b) $y = 4x - 1$ and $y = -2x + 2$

    (c) $y = 6 - 5x$ and $y = 4x - 12$ (d) $3y + x = 1$ and $5y = x + 7$

    (e) $x - 2y = 2$ and $3x - 4y = 8$ (f) $2x + 3y - 7 = 0$ and
                                                    $15x - 7y - 9 = 0$

Chapter 2 gives methods for solving pairs of linear equations. One of the methods described uses a graph, and the solution is found where the two lines intersect.

Summary

You should know:

- how to calculate the gradient and y-intercept of a line
- that the equation of a line in two dimensions can be given in two forms:
  - the gradient-intercept form, $y = mx + c$
  - the general form, $ax + by + d = 0$
- that parallel lines have the same gradient ($m_1 = m_2$) and two lines are perpendicular if the product of their gradients is -1 ($m_1 \times m_2 = -1$)
- how to use information from a graph to create an equation of the line
- how to draw a graph using the equation of the line.

Mixed examination practice

Exam-style questions

1. Find the equation of the straight lines through the point $(-3, 7)$ with the following gradients:

    (a) 2

    (b) -5

    (c) $-\dfrac{3}{4}$ (Leave your answer to part (c) in the form $ax + by + c = 0$.)

2. The graph below shows four lines; A, B, C and D. Write down the equation of each of the lines in the form $y = mx + c$.

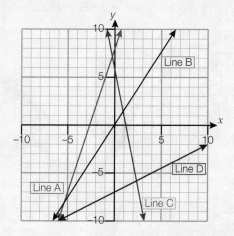

3. The points C and D have coordinates $(-1, -8)$ and $(1, 2)$ respectively.

    (a) Find the gradient of the line joining the points C and D.

    (b) Hence find the equation of the line joining the points C and D in the form $y = mx + c$.

4. The line L_1 has the equation $2y + 3x = 6$.

    (a) Draw the graph of line L_1.

    (b) Find the equation of the line L_2 which passes through the point $(-3, 0)$ and is perpendicular to the line L_1.

    (c) Determine the equation of line L_3, passing through the point $(4, -7)$ and parallel to L_1.

5. The line L_1 has the equation $4x + 5y - 20 = 0$.

   (a) Draw the graph of line L_1.

   (b) Write down the equation of any line which is:

      (i) parallel to L_1

      (ii) perpendicular to L_1.

   A second line, L_2, has equation $20y - 15x - 18 = 0$.

   (c) Draw the graph of line L_2.

   (d) Find the point of intersection of the two lines.

   (e) Hence state the solutions of the following pair of simultaneous equations:

      $4x + 5y - 20 = 0$ and $20y - 15x - 18 = 0$.

Past paper questions

1. (a) Write down the gradient of the line $y = 3x + 4$.   *[1 mark]*

   (b) Find the gradient of the line which is perpendicular to the line $y = 3x + 4$.   *[1 mark]*

   (c) Find the equation of the line which is perpendicular to $y = 3x + 4$ and which passes
       through the point (6, 7).   *[2 marks]*

   (d) Find the coordinates of the point of intersection of these two lines.   *[2 marks]*

                                                                        [Total 6 marks]

[May 2008, Paper 1, TZ2, Question 6] (© *IB Organization 2008*)

2. Three points are given A(0, 4), B(6, 0) and C(8, 3).

   (a) Calculate the gradient (slope) of line AB.   *[2 marks]*

   (b) Find the coordinates of the **midpoint**, M, of the line AC.   *[2 marks]*

   (c) Calculate the length of line AC.   *[2 marks]*

   (d) Find the equation of the line BM giving your answer in the form $ax + by + d = 0$
       where a, b and $d \in \mathbb{Z}$.   *[5 marks]*

   (e) State whether the line AB is perpendicular to the line BC showing clearly your
       working and reasoning.   *[3 marks]*

                                                                       [Total 14 marks]

[Nov 2006, Paper 2, TZ0, Question 2] (© *IB Organization 2006*)

hint

In question 2, part (b), the midpoint M
is halfway along the line AC.

Chapter 15 Trigonometry

Trigonometry is a practical application of mathematics that is used in fields as diverse as navigation, engineering, map-making and building.

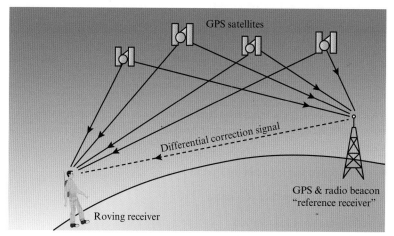

GPS satellites

Differential correction signal

GPS & radio beacon "reference receiver"

Roving receiver

In the most basic terms, a receiver of a global positioning system (GPS) dermines where it is on Earth by calculating the distance between at least three satellites in space and the receiver on the ground (artwork adapted from http://www.thegeeksclub.com/how-gps-works/).

Trigonometry uses the fact that, as long as the shape of a triangle does not change, the ratios of its sides remain the same.

In this diagram, triangles ADE and ABC are similar; the angle $x°$ is the same for both. So,
$$\frac{a}{b} = \frac{d}{c} = \frac{e}{f}.$$

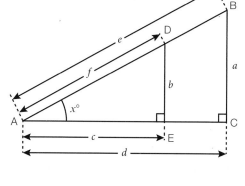

In any **right-angled triangle**, the sides are given the same names:

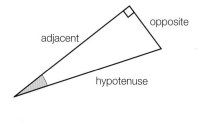

adjacent
opposite
hypotenuse

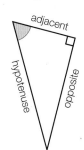

adjacent
hypotenuse
opposite

The **hypotenuse** is always opposite the right angle (no matter how the triangle is oriented). It is the longest side.

The opposite side is opposite the given angle.

The adjacent side is beside the given angle.

15.1 Trigonometric ratios

There are three standard ratios that have values programmed into your GDC. Their full names are **sine**, **cosine** and **tangent**, but these are frequently shortened to sin, cos and tan, respectively. The short versions are printed on your calculator keys.

The ratios are defined as:

$$\sin(e)\ \theta = \frac{\text{opposite}}{\text{hypotenuse}} \qquad \cos(ine)\ \theta = \frac{\text{adjacent}}{\text{hypotenuse}} \qquad \tan(gent)\ \theta = \frac{\text{opposite}}{\text{adjacent}}$$

When you are using a **trigonometric ratio**, the most important step is choosing the correct one! Once you have identified the correct ratio to use:

- write down the formula for that ratio

- insert the values that you know

- complete your calculation.

If you are solving a problem that involves right-angled triangles, you can use trigonometry to find:

- the length of **a side**, given that you know the length of one other side and the size of an angle

- the size of **an angle,** given that you know the lengths of two sides.

For example, to find side x in the triangle ABC below first check the information:

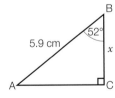

o(pposite) no ✗

a(djacent) yes (x) ✓

h(ypotenuse) yes (5.9cm) ✓

Use CAH = cosine.

$$\cos\theta = \frac{\text{adjacent}}{\text{hypotenuse}}$$

$$\cos 52° = \frac{x}{5.9}$$

$$x = 5.9 \times \cos 52°$$

$$x = 3.63\ \text{cm}$$

If you know the lengths of two sides and need to know the length of the third side, use **Pythagoras' theorem**.

If you need a reminder of how to use the trigonometric keys on your GDC, see section '*22.2B The second and third functions of a calculator key*' on page 642 of the GDC chapter.

Worked example 15.1

Q. For the given triangle, calculate:

(a) the size of angle x

(b) the length of the adjacent side.

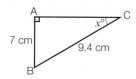

> o – yes; a – no; h – yes; so use sin ratio. Substitute in known values and solve for x.

A. (a) $\sin x = \dfrac{opposite}{hypotenuse}$

$\sin x = \dfrac{7}{9.4} = 0.7447$

$x = 48.1°$

> To get the angle in degrees, you need to use inverse sin; this is the $\sin^{-1}$ key on your GDC.

 TEXAS CASIO

```
7/9.4
        .7446808511
sin⁻¹(Ans
        48.13169377
```

```
7÷9.4
        0.7446808511
sin⁻¹ Ans
        48.13169377

►MAT
```

> Pythagoras' theorem states that 'the square on the hypotenuse is equal to the sum of the squares on the other two sides.'
>
> $c^2 = a^2 + b^2$
>
>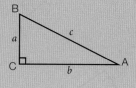

(b) $AC^2 = 9.4^2 - 7^2$

$AC^2 = 39.36$

$AC = \sqrt{39.36}$

$AC = 6.27\,cm$

> You know the lengths of two sides.
>
> Use Pythagoras' theorem to find the length of the third side.

Worked example 15.2

Q. In the triangle XYZ, $Y\hat{X}Z = 32°$ and $YZ = 3.9\,cm$.

(a) Find the length of XZ, the hypotenuse.

(b) Calculate the length of XY.

> First, sketch a diagram and label it with the information from the question. Then identify the ratio needed and solve the equation.

A.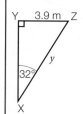

continued . . .

To find XZ, you are using the opposite side and the hypotenuse. Choose SOH.

(a) $\sin\theta = \dfrac{opposite}{hypotenuse}$

$\sin 32° = \dfrac{3.9}{y}$

$y = \dfrac{3.9}{\sin 32°}$

$y = 7.36\ m$

Using Pythagoras' theorem.

(b) $XY^2 = XZ^2 - YZ^2$

$ = 7.36^2 - 3.9^2$

$XY = 6.24\ m$

GDC

Remember to use the square root ($\sqrt{}$) key.

Exercise 15.1

1. For each of the following triangles work out the length of the side labelled x.

(a)
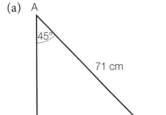

(b)
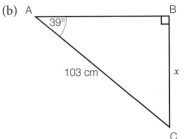

(c)
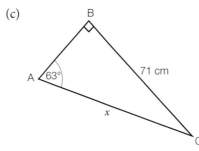

(d)
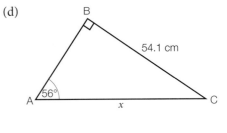

(e)
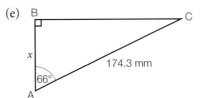

(f)
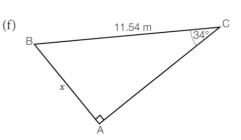

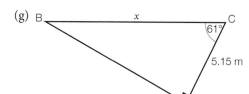

(g)

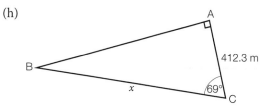

(h)

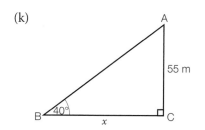

(i)

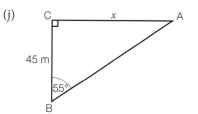

(j)

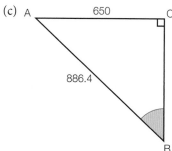

(k)

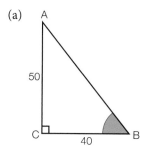

(l)

2. Calculate the size of the shaded angle in each of the triangles below.

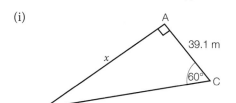

(a)

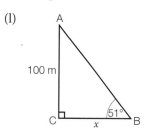

(b)

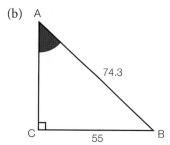

(c)

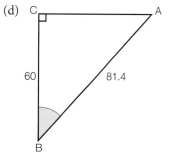

(d)

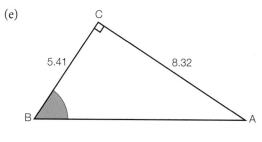

(e)

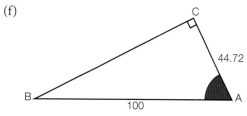

(f)

15 Trigonometry   439

Always sketch a clear diagram for problem-solving questions involving trigonometry.

3. Triangle PQR is isosceles with PQ = PR = 35 cm. Angle QP̂R = 84°. Find the length of the perpendicular from P to QR.

4. A ladder 6 metres long leans against a vertical wall. The ladder makes an angle of 54° with the wall. How far up the wall does the ladder reach?

5. A ladder 8 metres long is placed against a vertical wall. If the ladder reaches 6.3 metres up the wall, calculate the angle the ladder makes with the wall.

6. Germaine is flying a kite. She pins the end of the kite string to the ground so that the string is pulled straight as the wind pushes on the kite. If the length of the kite string is 7.8 metres and the kite has a vertical height of 5.9 metres above the ground, what angle does the string of the kite make with the horizontal ground?

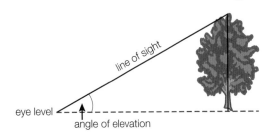

If you draw a diagram for problems that use these terms, it will help you to identify the correct angle.

15.2 Angles of elevation and depression

If you lie on the ground so that the base of a tree is at eye level and look up, the angle that you look through is called the **angle of elevation**.

If you lie on the ground at a cliff top and look down at a boat on the water, the angle that you look through is called the **angle of depression**.

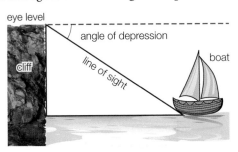

Worked example 15.3

Q. Una is lying down on flat ground, 360 m from the base of a television mast. If the angle of elevation from Una to the top of the mast is 13.0°, how high is the mast?

A.

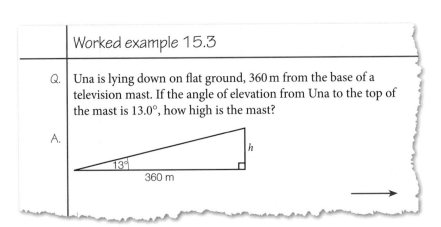

continued . . .

$$\tan x = \frac{opposite}{adjacent}$$

$$\tan 13° = \frac{h}{360}$$

$$h = \tan 13° \times 360$$

$$h = 83.1\,m$$

o – yes

a – yes

h – no

Use TOA.

 TEXAS

```
tan(13)*360
        83.11254881
```

 CASIO

```
tan (13)×360
        83.11254881
```
▶MAT

Worked example 15.4

Q. Alexis is lying down on top of a hill, looking at a garage in the village below. If the hill is 563 m high, and the village is 2.25 km away, calculate the angle of depression.

A.

The angle of depression between two points = the angle of elevation between those points; from the diagram you can see that the angles are alternate angles, which means they are the same size.

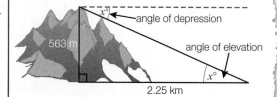
563 m

angle of depression
angle of elevation
$x°$
2.25 km

o – yes; a – yes; h – no.
Use TOA.

$$\tan x = \frac{opposite}{adjacent}$$

Make sure the units of distance are the same.

$$\tan x = \frac{563}{2250}$$

$$x = 14.0°$$

$$x = \text{angle of depression} = 14.0°$$

Summary

This flow chart can help you to choose the correct trigonometric ratio for any given problem.

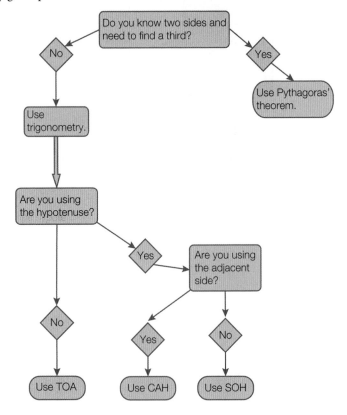

Exercise 15.2

1. From a point on a boat, the angle of elevation to the top of a vertical cliff is 32°. If the horizontal distance of the boat from the bottom of the cliff is 1650 metres, calculate the vertical height of the cliff.

2. A coastguard is standing on a cliff. From the top of the cliff he measures the angle of depression of an approaching fishing trawler to be 26°. The distance between the coastguard and the fishing trawler is 1750 metres.

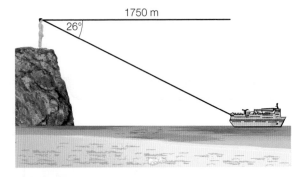

Given that the coastguard is 1.89 metres tall, find the vertical height of the cliff above the trawler.

3. From a point A, the angle of elevation of the top, B, of a tall building is 24°. From another point C on the opposite side of the building, the angle of elevation of the top of the building is 15°. It is known that the distance between A and B is 175 m.

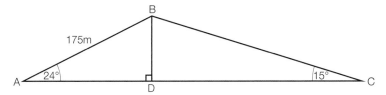

(a) Calculate the height of the building.

(b) Find the distance between the points A and C.

15.3 Harder trigonometry problems

In a practical problem, right-angled triangles can be difficult to identify. It may be necessary to draw in an extra line so that you can use right-angled trigonometry.

Worked example 15.5

Q. Find the height of this trapezium:

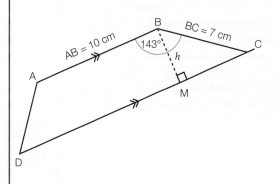

Sketch in the line BM; this is the perpendicular height of the trapezium. You can see this creates the right-angled triangle BMC.

You can use the angle relationships formed between parallel lines to find angle $M\hat{B}C$. $A\hat{B}M$ and $B\hat{M}C$ are alternate angles, so are equal. This leaves you with a right-angled triangle, with angle 53° adjacent to the side whose length you want to find. Use cos.

A. $A\hat{B}M = B\hat{M}C = 90°$

$M\hat{B}C = 143 - 90 = 53°$

$\cos 53° = \dfrac{h}{7}$

$h = 4.21 \text{ cm}$

Worked example 15.6

Q. Three friends are hiking. They start at Amville and walk 6.3 km due north to Brent. They plan to turn east and walk another 8.2 km to Cosford. At Brent, one of the friends twists his ankle so the group decides to take the shortest route to the road that runs directly from Amville to Cosford. How far will they have to walk to reach the road?

Sketch a diagram.

A.

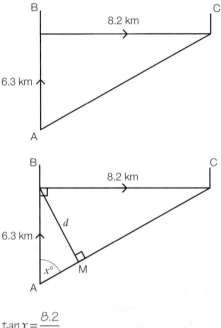

Draw the route from B to the road AC and mark the angle that you need to calculate. Label the point where the extra line meets the line AC as M. This creates the right-angled triangle ABM.

Use the triangle ABC to calculate x.

$$\tan x = \frac{8.2}{6.3}$$

$$x = 52.5°$$

Use the triangle ABM and the angle x to calculate d.

$$\sin 52.5° = \frac{d}{6.3}$$

 TEXAS   **CASIO**

GDC

```
tan⁻¹(8.2/6.3)
        52.46519086
sin(Ans)*6.3
        4.995795108
■
```

```
tan⁻¹ (8.2÷6.3)
        52.46519086
sin Ans×6.3
        4.995795108
□

JUMP DEL ▶MAT MATH
```

Do not round the answer to the angle calculation too soon. Leave all the figures in your GDC and use them all. (See '22.2C The Ans/ANS key' and '22.2D Using the GDC memory' on page 643 in the GDC chapter if you need a reminder of how.)

Give the final answer to 3 s.f.

$d = 5.00\,\text{km}$ (3 s.f.)

Exercise 15.3

For these questions, if you are not given a diagram, make sure that you draw a clear picture for yourself.

1. In the triangle below, PQ = 56.6 cm, SR = 110 cm and QP̂S = 45°.

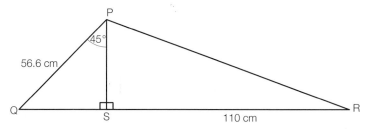

   Calculate:

   (a) the length of PS   (b) the length of QS

   (c) the size of angle QP̂R.

2. Arif, Ben and Chanika are standing in the playground. Arif is standing at point A. Ben is standing 86 m directly north of Arif at point B. Chanika is standing 119 m due east of Arif.

   Chanika looks at Arif and then turns through an angle of *x* degrees to walk towards Ben.

   (a) Calculate the distance between Arif and Chanika.

   (b) Determine the value of *x*.

3. ABCD is the plan of a trapezoidal garden. Angles BÂD and AD̂C are 56° and 45° respectively. Given that the length of CD is 85 m, calculate the length of AB.

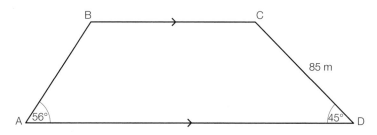

4. Luca and Sasha are playing on a rectangular playing field ABCD. The lengths of AB and BC are 150 m and 80 m respectively. They part, with Luca walking directly along AB and Sasha walking along the diagonal AC. Find the angle between their two routes.

5. David is standing at a point D on the bank of a river. Emma is standing directly opposite David on the other bank at point E. Francis is standing at point F on the same bank as Emma but 70 m downstream along a straight stretch of the river. The angle between DE and DF is 28°. What is the width of the river between David and Emma?

15.4 The sine rule

If you work with triangles that have no right angle, you need new rules and formulae.

To make the formulae easy to use, the triangles are always labelled according to the following convention.

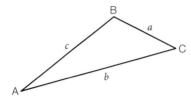

Side 'a' is opposite angle A.

Side 'b' is opposite angle B.

Side 'c' is opposite angle C.

You can use this convention with other letters too, for example:

side 'x' is opposite angle X.

In the standard ABC triangle, the sine rule states that:

$a=\pi r^2$ $\dfrac{a}{\sin A} = \dfrac{b}{\sin B} = \dfrac{c}{\sin C}$ (use to find the length of a side) or $\dfrac{\sin A}{a} = \dfrac{\sin B}{b} = \dfrac{\sin C}{c}$ (use to find the size of an angle)

The sine rule has three ratios but you only need two for each calculation. To make sure that you have the correct pairs, look for one ratio that has two known values and one ratio containing the side or angle that you are looking for.

In the example below, there is one known and one unknown quantity in each ratio, so you **cannot** use the sine rule.

$$\frac{129}{\sin A} = \frac{150}{\sin B} = \frac{c}{\sin 28°}$$

If you fill in the known values and cannot find a complete ratio that you can use for the calculation, use the cosine rule (see section 15.5).

Worked example 15.7

Q. Find the length of side AB.

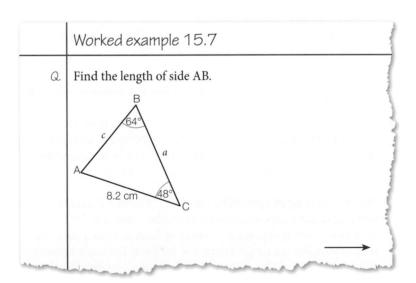

---

continued . . .

A. $\dfrac{a}{\sin A} = \dfrac{b}{\sin B} = \dfrac{c}{\sin C}$

$\dfrac{a}{\sin A} = \dfrac{8.2}{\sin 64°} = \dfrac{c}{\sin 48°}$

$\dfrac{8.2}{\sin 64°} = \dfrac{c}{\sin 48°}$

$c = \dfrac{8.2 \times \sin 48°}{\sin 64°}$

$c = 6.78\,\text{cm}$

> Substitute known values into all the ratios before you decide which pair you need. You need to find the length c, so use the ratio containing c and the ratio with no unknowns.

> Cross multiply to solve for c.

Worked example 15.8

Q.   Find the size of angle BÂC.

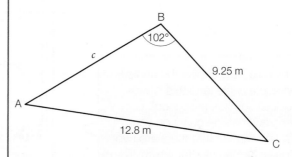

> There is no right angle, so you need to use the sine rule.

A. $\dfrac{\sin A}{a} = \dfrac{\sin B}{b} = \dfrac{\sin C}{c}$

$\dfrac{\sin A}{9.25} = \dfrac{\sin 102°}{12.8} = \dfrac{\sin C}{c}$

> Determine which pair of ratios you need.

$\dfrac{\sin A}{9.25} = \dfrac{\sin 102°}{12.8}$

> Cross multiply to solve for sin A.

$\sin A = \dfrac{\sin 102° \times 9.25}{12.8} = 0.70686\ldots$

> Use $\sin^{-1}$ key to get the angle in degrees.

$B\hat{A}C = 45.0°$

This is called the 'ambiguous case'. It only occurs when you are using the sine rule and have to find an angle larger than the one given. As the second angle can have two different values, the triangle can have two different shapes. The ambiguous case will not be examined.

Worked example 15.9

Q. Find the size of angle AB̂C.

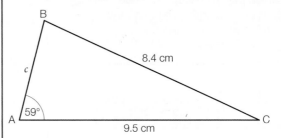

A.

$$\frac{\sin A}{a} = \frac{\sin B}{b} = \frac{\sin C}{c}$$

$$\frac{\sin 59°}{8.4} = \frac{\sin B}{9.5} = \frac{\sin C}{c}$$

$$\frac{\sin 59°}{8.4} = \frac{\sin B}{9.5}$$

$$\sin B = \frac{9.5 \times \sin 59°}{8.4} = 0.9694\ldots$$

$$A\hat{B}C = 75.8°$$

If $a > b$ then angle A > angle B. In this example, you are using the sine rule but have been given the size of an angle that is **smaller** than the angle you are trying to find, i.e. $a < b$. This has an interesting result, as you will see at the end.

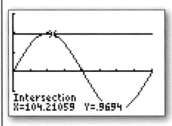

The triangle ABC shows the angle B as an acute angle (and this is what the calculation has produced). But if you draw the sine curve on your GDC, you will see that there are two alternative values of x for which $\sin x = 0.9694$; these are $x = 75.8°$ and $x = 104.2°$.

Triangle ABC could have angles of:

A = 59°, B = 75.8° and C = 45.2°

or

A = 59°, B = 104.2° and C = 16.8°

If you draw the diagram accurately, with the line AB at an angle of 59° to the line AC at A, then place your compass point at C and set it to 8.4 cm, you will find that it cuts the line AB in two places, hence the two possible solutions.

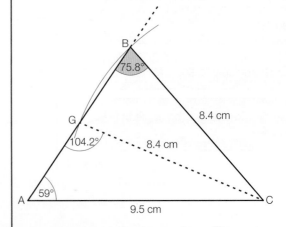

Exercise 15.4

1. Some of the dimensions of triangle ABC are given in the table below. The notation corresponds to that used for the sine rule, with the angles labelled as A, B and C. The corresponding opposite sides are labelled as *a*, *b* and *c*. Calculate the value of the missing values, *x* in each case.

hint

Sketch the diagrams.

	a	*b*	*c*	A	B	C
(a)		137.3	210.3		31.7	*x*
(b)	*x*		39.1	44.5		50.7
(c)		*x*	138.3		10.9	30.6
(d)	140.1	103.1		*x*	20.5	
(e)	135.1		*x*	59.9		74.8
(f)	90	71.1		88.6	*x*	

2. Calculate the length of side BC in each of the following triangles:

(a)
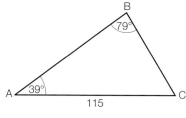

(b)
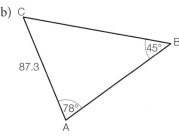

(c)
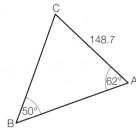

3. Find the size of the shaded angle in each of the following triangles:

(a)
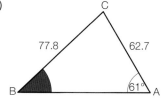

(b)
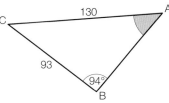

(c)
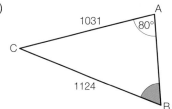

4. In each of the following triangles ABC you are given the lengths of AB and BC. You are also given the size of BÂC. Find the size of AĈB in each case.

	AB	BC	BÂC
(a)	78.1 cm	140 cm	108°
(b)	108 mm	130 mm	80°
(c)	51 m	65.2 m	62°
(d)	30 km	49.5 km	98°
(e)	42.72 cm	45.28 cm	83.5°

5. In each of the following triangles XYZ, you are given the sizes of YX̂Z and XŶZ and the length of side YZ. Find the length of XZ in each case.

	YX̂Z	XŶZ	YZ
(a)	85.7°	20.2°	105 cm
(b)	106.5°	35°	120.4 mm
(c)	64.8°	74.1°	50 m
(d)	49.6°	36.7°	30.4 m
(e)	41.8°	39°	42.7 km

hint

'Subtends an angle of 128°' means that the angle between AB and AC or the angle the chord makes at the centre of the circle is 128°.

6. A chord subtends an angle of 128° at the centre of a circle. Given that the length of the chord is 22 cm, find the radius of the circle.

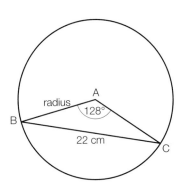

7. From the balcony on the 6th floor of a building, the angle of depression of the top of a tree is 38°. From the balcony on the 12th floor the angle of depression increases to 64°. Given that the distance between the two balconies is 18 m, find the distance between the 12th floor balcony and the top of the tree.

15.5 The cosine rule

If a problem gives you values for:

two sides and the angle between them,

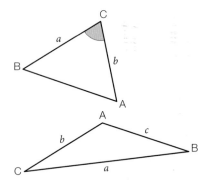

or three sides and no angle,

then you cannot use the sine rule, because you will not be able to fill in a complete ratio with values that you know.

Instead, you can use the cosine rule:

$$a^2 = b^2 + c^2 - 2bc \cos A$$
$$b^2 = a^2 + c^2 - 2ac \cos B$$
$$c^2 = a^2 + b^2 - 2ab \cos C$$

to find the length of a side,

$$\cos A = \frac{b^2 + c^2 - a^2}{2bc}$$ to find the size of an angle.

hint

Look for the pattern in all three formulae, and you will find it easy to remember them.

 Does this formula look familiar? What is the value of cos 90°?

Worked example 15.10

Q. Find the length AC.

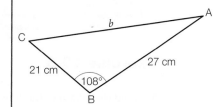

We have a known angle between two known lengths, so use the cosine rule.

A. $b^2 = a^2 + c^2 - 2ac \cos B$

$= 21^2 + 27^2 - 2 \times 21 \times 27 \cos 108°$

$= 1520.425\ldots$

Remember to use the square root key ($\sqrt{\ }$) to find b.

$b = \sqrt{1520.425}$

$b = 39.0 \, cm$

Worked example 15.11

Q. Find the size of angle A.

You know three lengths and need to find an angle, so use the cosine rule.

A. $\cos A = \frac{b^2 + c^2 - a^2}{2bc}$

$\cos A = \frac{9^2 + 6^2 - 8^2}{2 \times 9 \times 6}$

Use the cos⁻¹ key.

$\cos A = 0.4907\ldots$

$A = 60.6°$

Summary

This flow chart can help you to choose the correct trigonometric rule for any given problem.

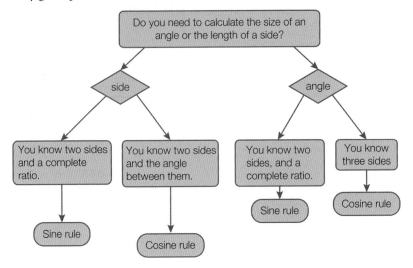

Exercise 15.5

1. Find the length of the side opposite the given angle in each of the following triangles:

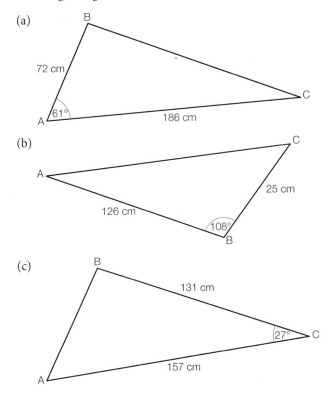

(a)

(b)

(c)

2. Calculate the size of the shaded angle in each of the following triangles:

(a)
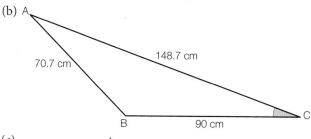

(b)
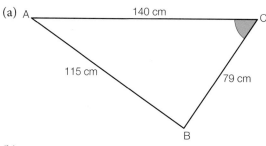

(c)
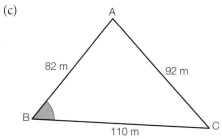

3. Use the cosine rule to find the lengths of all missing sides and the sizes of all missing angles in the following triangles:

(a)
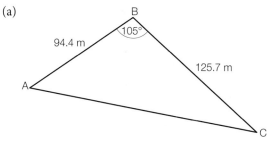

(b)
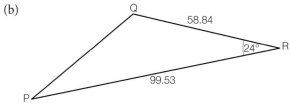

(c)
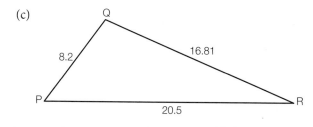

(d)

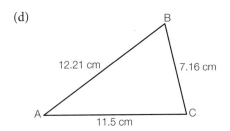

4. Three houses P, Q and R are located in the same neighbourhood. The distance of P from Q is 270 m and the distance of R from Q is 236 m. The angle PQ̂R is 111°. Find the distance between P and R.

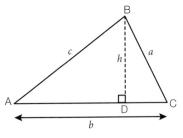

For an explanation about angles relative to 'North', see Learning links 15A on page 460.

5. Two ships are approaching the same port. Ship A is 27 km away from the port and its path makes an angle of 144° from North. Ship B is 19 km away from the port and its path makes an angle of 227° from North. Find the distance between the two ships.

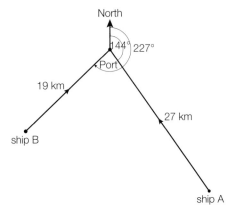

15.6 Area of a triangle

It is also possible to find the area of a triangle without first having to work out the height of the triangle.

We know that area of a triangle $= \frac{1}{2}$ base $(b) \times$ height (h).

But, using triangle BDC, $\sin C = \frac{h}{a}$ and so $h = a \times \sin C$,

so the formula can be re-written as: area $= \frac{1}{2}\, b \times a \times \sin C$.

hint

This formula always uses two sides and the angle that is between them. This angle is known as an **included angle**.

$a = \pi r^2$

Area of a triangle $= \frac{1}{2}ab\sin C$

Worked example 15.12

Q. Find the area of triangle ABC.

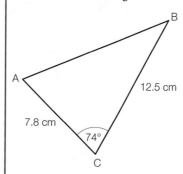

The perpendicular height of the triangle is not given, but we do have two lengths and an included angle so use the formula $\frac{1}{2}ab\sin c$.

A. $\text{Area} = \dfrac{1}{2}ab\sin C$

$\text{Area} = \dfrac{1}{2} \times 7.8 \times 12.5 \times \sin 74°$

$\text{Area} = 46.9\,\text{cm}^2$

Worked example 15.13

Q. This circle has a radius of 5 cm and the area of the triangle is 11 cm². Find the size of the acute angle BÂC.

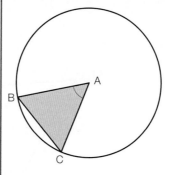

AB and AC are radii of the circle, so we know they are both 5 cm long. BÂC is the included angle between AB and AC, so we can use the formula $\text{Area} = \frac{1}{2}ab\sin c$ to calculate the value of BÂC.

A. $AB = AC = 5\,\text{cm}$

$\text{Area} = \dfrac{1}{2}bc\sin A$

$11 = \dfrac{1}{2} \times 5 \times 5 \times \sin A$

$22 = 25\sin A$

$\sin A = \dfrac{22}{25} = 0.88$

$\text{B}\hat{\text{A}}\text{C} = 61.6°$

Exercise 15.6

1. Calculate the area of the following triangles:

(a)

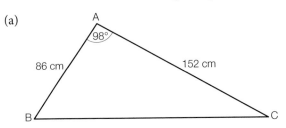

(b)

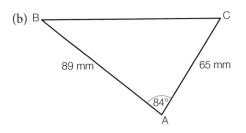

(c)

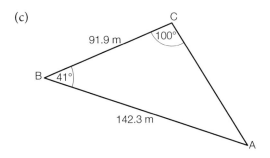

(d)

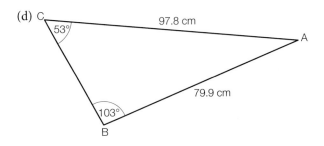

(e)

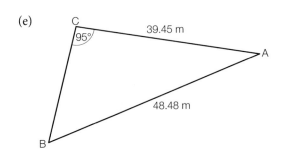

15.7 Constructing labelled diagrams

Practical problems are often expressed in words, which means you should sketch your own diagram and work out which formula you need to use.

When you draw the diagram for a problem, it is important that you:

- read the question more than once, and make sure that you understand it

- draw the diagram large enough; don't try to fit all the information into one small rough sketch

- draw the diagram in pencil; you may need to start again, change it or erase something

- label the diagram clearly and include all the information

- add any extra lines or angles that you are asked to find.

Practical problems set in the examinations are likely to use more than one of the triangle formulae. For every solution it is important to make sure that you have all the information written on your diagram so that you can make the correct decision about which formula to use.

Worked example 15.14

Q. Farmer Giles has a four-sided field, ABCD. He decides to divide the field into two triangles with a fence from A to C.

(a) What is the length of the fence from A to C?

(b) What is the area of field ACD?

(c) What is the size of angle DCA?

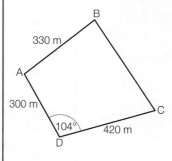

continued . . .

A. (a)

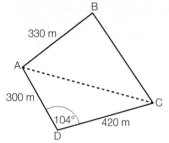

Draw in the line AC to break the shape into two triangles.

There is no right angle, but you are given two sides and the angle between them, so use the cosine rule.

$d^2 = a^2 + c^2 - 2ac \cos D$

$AC^2 = 300^2 + 420^2 - 2 \times 300 \times 420 \times \cos 104°$

$AC^2 = 327364.3\ldots$

$AC = 572 \text{ m}$

Use the area formula.

(b) $\text{Area} = \dfrac{1}{2} ac \sin D$

$\text{Area} = \dfrac{1}{2} \times 300 \times 420 \times \sin 104°$

$\text{Area} = 61129 \text{ m}^2$

$\text{Area} \approx 61100 \text{ m}^2$

(c)

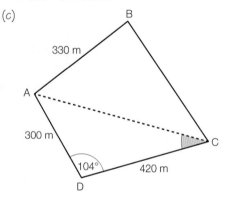

You know the size of one angle and the length opposite it, and need to find an unknown angle opposite a known length, so you can use the sine rule to calculate $D\hat{C}A$.

$\dfrac{\sin A}{a} = \dfrac{\sin B}{b} = \dfrac{\sin C}{c}$

$\dfrac{\sin C}{c} = \dfrac{\sin D}{d}$

The value of d is from part (a).

$\dfrac{\sin C}{300} = \dfrac{\sin 104°}{572}$

$\sin C = \dfrac{300 \times \sin 104°}{572}$

$\sin C = 0.5088\ldots$

$C = 30.6°$

For an explanation about angles 'from North', see Learning links 15A on the next page.

Worked example 15.15

Q. A small plane flies due west for 15 km, then turns through an angle of 148° *anticlockwise* from North and flies another 25 km.

(a) How far is the plane from its starting point?

(b) On the return journey, the plane flies on a straight path, direct to the starting point. What angle does its return flight make with the North line?

A. (a)

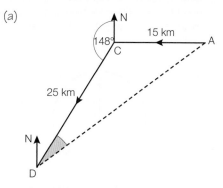

Sketch the diagram, making sure that you include all the information given in the question. You need to calculate the length of AD.

$$A\hat{C}D = 360 - 148 - 90 = 122°$$

Calculate angle A$\hat{C}$D using the angle relationship 'angles around a point add up to 360°'. The North line is perpendicular to the line AC, so makes an angle of 90°.

$$AD^2 = 15^2 + 25^2 - 2 \times 15 \times 25 \times \cos 122°$$
$$AD = 35.3 \text{ km}$$

You now know the length of two sides and the size of their included angle, so you can use the cosine rule.

(b)

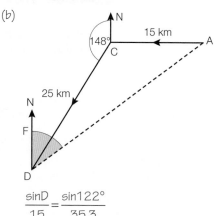

You can calculate angle A$\hat{D}$C, using the sine rule.

$$\frac{\sin D}{15} = \frac{\sin 122°}{35.3}$$

$$A\hat{D}C = 21.1°$$
$$\text{Angle} = 180° - 148° = 32°$$

So, angle F$\hat{D}$A = 32 + 21.1 = 53.1°

The return flight makes an angle of 53.1° with the North line.

If we label the North line at D with the letter F, we create the angle C$\hat{D}$F. The line CD is a transversal to two parallel lines (the two North lines) so we use the angle relationship 'co-interior angles add up to 180°' to calculate B$\hat{M}$C.

15A Angles 'from North'

Directions can be measured by reference to North, South, East or West, or by referring to the North only. When an angle is 'from North', it is measured clockwise from a vertical line denoted by North or N. When this happens, the term 'bearings' is used. Bearings are not included in the syllabus so you will not need to know them for the examinations. You **should** be aware however what is meant by 'clockwise from North' and 'anticlockwise from North'.

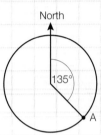

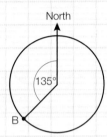

In this example, A is 135° *clockwise* from North.

In this example, B is 135° *anticlockwise* from North.

Exercise 15.7

1. ABCD is the plan of a school playground. It has two sections — a paved area and a grassed section.

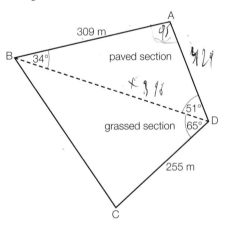

   (a) Calculate the length of the boundary line between the two sections of the playground.

   (b) Find the area of the paved section.

   (c) Calculate the area of the grassed section.

   (d) Find the **perimeter** of the playground.

2. When Amanda first sighted a plane at point A the angle of elevation was 53°. After flying a further 1600 m to point B the angle of elevation reduced to 32°. Calculate the distance between Amanda and the plane at point B.

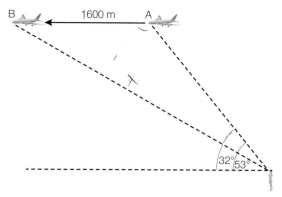

3. A lighthouse stands on a cliff. The angle of elevation of the bottom B of the lighthouse tower from a yacht is 46°. From the same yacht the angle of elevation of the top T of the lighthouse is 58°. Given that the height of the lighthouse is 35 metres, find the height of the cliff above sea level.

4. Three cities A, B and C form a triangle. The distances between the cities, AB, BC and AC, are 186.1 km, 208.6 km and 314 km respectively. Sketch a diagram to represent the above information and hence find the sizes of the three angles of the triangle.

5. Two towns, Silvagrad and Tinburgh, are 208 km apart. Tinburgh is located due east of Silvagrad. A third town, Westown, is located north-east of Tinburgh and 150 km away from Tinburgh. Find the distance of Westown from Silvagrad.

6. John is at the lighthouse. He sights a ship 15 km away at an angle of 41° east from North. At the same time he sights a boat 6 km away, at an angle of 36° east from South. How far away are the boat and the ship from each other?

hint

'36° east from South' would be:

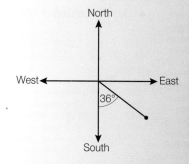

In other words, it is 36° to the right (east) of the 'South' direction.

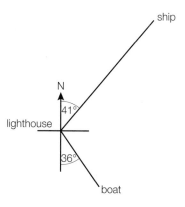

Summary

You should know:

- what the three different trigonometric ratios in right-angled triangles are:

    - $\sin(e)\theta = \dfrac{\text{opposite}}{\text{hypotenuse}}$

    - $\cos(ine)\theta = \dfrac{\text{adjacent}}{\text{hypotenuse}}$

    - $\tan(gent)\theta = \dfrac{\text{opposite}}{\text{adjacent}}$

- that the trigonometric ratios can be used to find the length of unknown sides and the size of unknown angles in right-angled triangles

- the definition of angles of elevation and depression

- that when a triangle is not right-angled, different trigonometric ratios are needed:

    - sine rule, $\dfrac{a}{\sin A} = \dfrac{b}{\sin B} = \dfrac{c}{\sin C}$ to find the length of a side or

      $\dfrac{\sin A}{a} = \dfrac{\sin B}{b} = \dfrac{\sin C}{c}$ to find the size of an angle

    - the cosine rule,
      $\left.\begin{array}{l} a^2 + b^2 + c^2 - 2bc\cos A \\ b^2 = a^2 + c^2 - 2ac\cos B \\ c^2 = a^2 + b^2 - 2ab\cos C \end{array}\right\}$ to find the length of a side, or

      $\cos A = \dfrac{b^2 + c^2 - a^2}{2bc}$ to find the size of an angle — this is useful when you have an included angle.

- the formula for the area of a triangle, when you do not know the perpendicular height, $A = \frac{1}{2}ab\sin C$

- how to construct labelled diagrams from verbal statements.

Mixed examination practice

Exam-style questions

1. Kitty and Betty are standing on the same side of a radio mast. The angle of elevation of the top of the mast from Kitty is 32°. From Betty's position the angle of elevation of the top of the mast is 43°. Given that the height of the mast is 198 m, find the distance between Kitty and Betty.

2. The horizontal distance between two buildings is 200 m. From the top of the taller building the angle of depression of the top of the shorter building is 28°. From the same point on the taller building the angle of depression of the bottom of the shorter building is 42°. Calculate the heights of both buildings.

3. Yuri and Yuko are trekking in the forest. They both set off due east. After walking a distance of 2000 m Yuri changes direction and heads due south for another 700 m and stops. Yuko continues to walk another 1000 m due east before she changes direction. She then walks due north for another 1600 m and stops.

   (a) Calculate the distance between the two girls.

   (b) Through what angle must Yuri turn in order to walk directly towards Yuko?

4. A motorcyclist is riding on a straight road towards a tower. From point A on the road, the angle of elevation of the top of the tower is 25°. After he has travelled a further 80 m towards the tower, the angle of elevation of the top of the tower increases to 40°. Find the distance between point A and the top of the tower.

5. A police helicopter departs from the police station, flying on a path 330° clockwise from North. After flying for 1600 m, it receives a message to divert to a crime scene. It then changes direction to fly to the crime scene and its new path is 260° clockwise from North. The crime scene is 1800 m in a diagonal straight line from the police station. The helicopter's route is illustrated below.

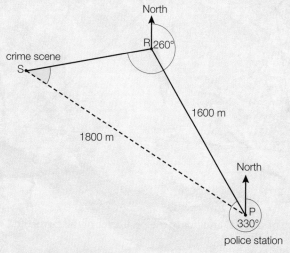

Calculate the size of angle $R\hat{S}P$.

6. Three friends, Pat, Queenie and Rahina, are picking wildflowers in a field. Pat is 56 m away from Queenie. Queenie (Q) is 83 m from Rahina(R) and Rahina is 102 m away from Pat (P).

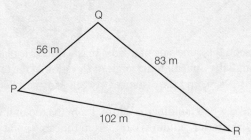

Given that the angle between PQ and North at P is 51°, calculate the value of the reflex angle between RQ and the North direction at R.

7. Jo has been offered a triangular shaped allotment. Two sides measure 9 m and 12.3 m. If the size of the included angle is 120°, calculate the area of the allotment.

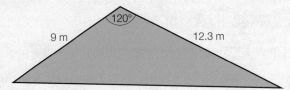

8. Mr Bonsu has a piece of farmland which he wants to sell. The land is in the shape of a quadrilateral ABCD. Three sides of the land, AB, AD and CD, have lengths 55 m, 155 m and 180 m respectively. Mr Bonsu wants to estimate the perimeter and the area of the farmland.

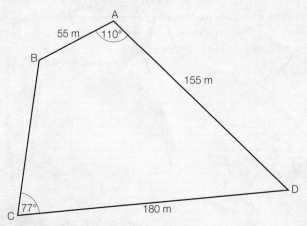

(a) Calculate the length of BD.

(b) Work out the magnitude of angle $C\hat{B}D$.

(c) Calculate the length of side BC and hence the perimeter of the farmland.

(d) Work out the area of the farmland.

9. A and B are two points on a level ground. They are located on opposite sides of a tall tree. From point A, the angle of elevation of the top of the tree is 20°. From point B, the angle of elevation of the top of the tree is 30°. The distance between the two points is 70 metres.

Calculate the height of the tree.

10. Three friends Darya, Maiya and Zeena are standing at three different positions on level ground. Maiya is standing 50 metres due east of Darya. Zeena is standing 30 metres due north of Darya. Maiya and Zeena are standing at two different positions along a straight river bank.

Darya decides to walk towards the river bank, taking the shortest route.

How far will Darya have to walk to get to the river?

Past paper questions

1. Points P(0,−4) and Q(0, 16) are shown on the diagram.

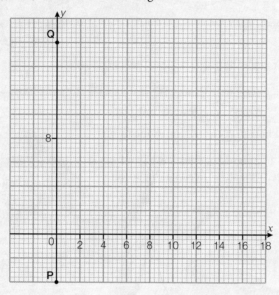

(a) Plot the point R(11, 16).

(b) Calculate angle QPR.

M is a point on the line PR. M is 9 units from P.

(c) Calculate the area of triangle PQM.   *[Total 6 marks]*

[May 2006, Paper 1, TZ0, Question 6] (© *IB Organization 2006*)

2. Triangle ABC is drawn such that angle ABC is 90°, angle ACB is 60° and AB is 7.3 cm.

(a) (i) Sketch a diagram to illustrate this information. Label the points A, B, C.

Show the angles 90°, 60° and the length 7.3 cm on your diagram.

(ii) Find the length of BC.   *[3 marks]*

Point D is on the straight line AC extended and is such that angle CDB is 20°.

(b) (i) Show the point D and the angle 20° on your diagram.

(ii) Find the size of angle CBD.   *[3 marks]*

[Total 6 marks]

[May 2008, Paper 1, TZ2, Question 3] (© *IB Organization 2008*)

3. An old tower (BT) leans at 10° away from the vertical (represented by line TG).

The base of the tower is at B so that $M\hat{B}T = 100°$.

Leonardo stands at L on flat ground 120 m away from B in the direction of the lean.

He measures the angle between the ground and the top of the tower T to be $B\hat{L}T = 26.5°$.

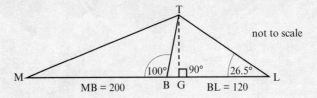

not to scale

(a) (i) Find the value of angle $B\hat{T}L$.

(ii) Use triangle BTL to calculate the sloping distance BT from the base, B to the top, T of the tower. *[5 marks]*

(b) Calculate the vertical height TG of the top of the tower. *[2 marks]*

(c) Leonardo now walks to point M, a distance 200 m from B on the opposite side of the tower. Calculate the distance from M to the top of the tower at T. *[3 marks]*

[Total 10 marks]

[May 2007, Paper 2, TZ0, Question 2(ii)] (© *IB Organization 2007*)

Chapter 16 Geometry of three-dimensional solids

Plato (429–347 BCE) is generally considered to have been a philosopher, but he also gave his name to the group of regular **solids** called the Platonic solids. These are three-dimensional shapes whose flat faces are regular polygons. In ancient Greece, science, mathematics and philosophy were not separate disciplines; it was considered the mark of an educated person that they were interested in all branches of knowledge.

The five Platonic solids are:

 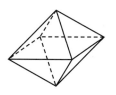

tetrahedron   **cube**   octahedron   dodecahedron   icosahedron

In Mathematics, the word 'solid' is used to describe any three-dimensional shape. A mathematical solid can even be hollow!

There are other solids that are not Platonic. These solids have faces of different shapes within the same solid. For example, a square-based pyramid has a square face as the base and the other four faces are triangles.

Some solids have edges that are straight lines:

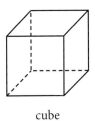
cube

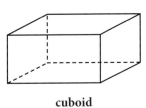
cuboid

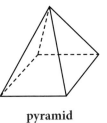
pyramid

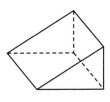
triangular **prism**

Some solids have curved edges, or a mix of curved and straight edges:

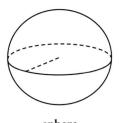
sphere

hemisphere

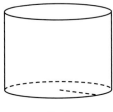
cylinder

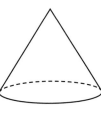
cone

Some solids are called prisms. A prism is a solid object that has two congruent ends and the cross-section is the same shape and area along its whole length.

cylinder

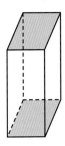
cuboid

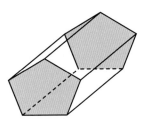
prism with a polygon as its base

The word 'right' is used to describe some solids in which the 'height' makes a right angle with the base.

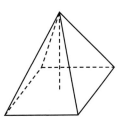

A **right pyramid** has its apex directly above the centre of its base.

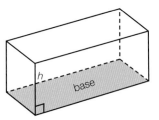

A **right prism** has its base directly below its top surface, and the height makes a right angle with the base.

16.1 Finding the length of a line within a three-dimensional solid

Trigonometry and Pythagoras' theorem can be used to solve problems that require you to find the lengths of lines within a solid. These lines may be inside or outside the shape. It can be helpful to think of the solid as being hollow, or to make a model so that you can move it around and understand it better.

In order to do the calculations involved in this sort of problem, you will need to find the triangles within the shape. This is easier to do if you draw these 'calculation' triangles outside the main diagram.

◄◄◄RR *You learned how to use trigonometry to solve problems in Chapter 15.*

exam tip

In examinations all questions on solids will be set so that you can answer them using right-angled triangles.

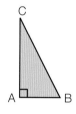
pyramid

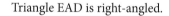
'calculation' triangle

These familiar shapes all contain unexpected right-angled triangles.

Cuboid

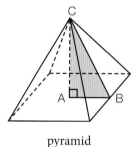

Triangle EAD is right-angled.

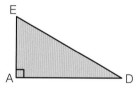

So is triangle FGD.

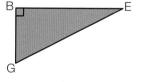

Triangular prism

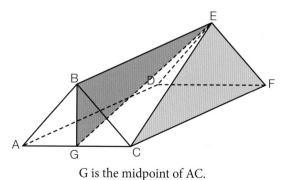

G is the midpoint of AC.

Triangle GBE is right-angled.

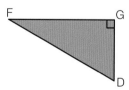

So is triangle CFE.

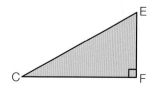

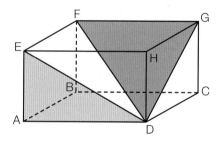

Pyramid

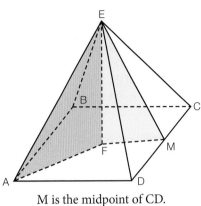

M is the midpoint of CD.

Triangle AFE is right-angled.

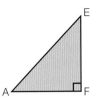

So is triangle EFM.

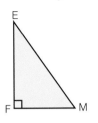

Worked example 16.1

Q. A shoe box is 32 cm long, 18 cm wide and 11 cm high. Calculate the length of the longest rod that will fit inside the box.

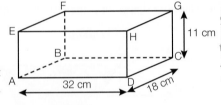

The longest length inside the box is the diagonal from one of the top vertices to the opposite bottom vertex. This is the triangle that you need to work with.

You need the triangle ACD to calculate the length of AC, and then the triangle AGC to calculate the length of AG.

A.

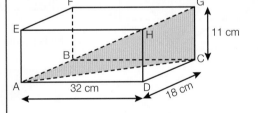

Draw triangle ACD separately first and use Pythagoras' theorem to calculate the length of AC.

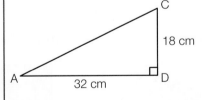

$$AC^2 = CD^2 + AD^2$$
$$AC^2 = 18^2 + 32^2$$
$$AC = \sqrt{1348}$$
$$AC = 36.7 \text{ cm}$$

Then draw triangle ACG and use Pythagoras' theorem to calculate the length of AG.

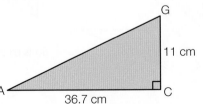

$$AG^2 = AC^2 + CG^2$$
$$AG^2 = 36.7^2 + 11^2$$
$$AG = \sqrt{1467.89}$$
$$AG = 38.3 \text{ cm}$$

Worked example 16.2

Q. EABCD is a square-based right pyramid, with sides of 12 cm. The height of the pyramid is 9.5 cm.

(a) Calculate the length of EC.

A point, M, is marked half way along one side of the base.

(b) Calculate the length of EM.

(c) Why is the length of EC not the same as EM?

A. (a)

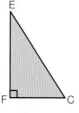

$CD = AD = AB = BC = 12\,cm$

$EF = 9.5\,cm.$

F is the midpoint of AC.

> Draw the solid and add in a helpful triangle.

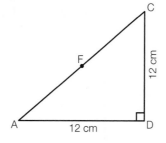

$AC^2 = AD^2 + DC^2$

$AC^2 = 12^2 + 12^2$

$AC^2 = 144 + 144 = 288$

$AC = \sqrt{288} = 16.97\ldots$

$FC = \dfrac{1}{2} \times AC$

$FC = 8.49\,cm$

> To find the length FC, you first need to use Pythagoras' theorem to find AC in triangle ACD.

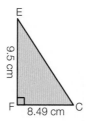

$EC^2 = EF^2 + FC^2$

$EC^2 = 9.5^2 + 8.49^2 = 162.25$

$EC = 12.7\,cm$

> To find the length EC, use the length FC and Pythagoras' theorem again.

(b)

> Add M to the diagram and draw another helpful triangle.

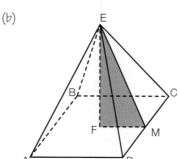

continued . . .

$$FM = \frac{1}{2} \text{ of } AD = \frac{1}{2} \times 12$$

$FM = 6\,cm$

$EM^2 = EF^2 + FM^2$

$EM^2 = 9.5^2 + 6^2 = 126.25$

$EM = \sqrt{126.25} = 11.2\,cm$

(c) $EM \neq EC$

The length EC is one of the slanted edges of the pyramid. The length EM is the vertical height of the triangle EDC.

> You can chose any edge to mark M on; as all edges are the same length, EM is the same for all four edges. We have chosen M to be the **midpoint** of CD.

Worked example 16.3

Q. If $AB = 11.3\,cm$ and $A\hat{B}C = 53°$, calculate the **radius** of the cone.

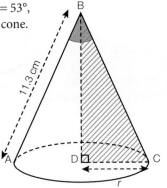

hint

Remember that the radius of a circle is the distance from the centre of the circle to the circumference. It is also half of the diameter.

A.

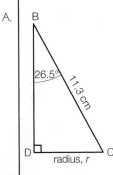

$A\hat{B}C = 53°$

$D\hat{B}C = 53° \div 2 = 26.5°$

$$\sin 26.5° = \frac{r}{11.3}$$

$r = 11.3 \times \sin 26.5°$

$r = 5.04\,cm$

> Sketch the right-angled triangle BDC. Use trigonometry to find the length r. You have the opposite and the hypotenuse, so use sin.

Exercise 16.1

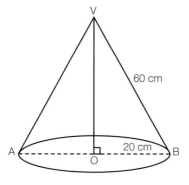

1. VAOB is a right circular cone with radius 20 cm and **slant height** 60 cm.

   Calculate the vertical height, VO.

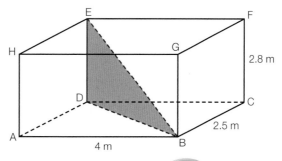

2. ABCDEFGH is a cuboid with dimensions 4 m by 2.5 m by 2.8 m.

   (a) Calculate the length of BD.

   (b) Find the length of the diagonal BE.

3. What is the longest rod that will fit inside a box 20 cm long, 12 cm wide and 16 cm high?

   hint

   A hemisphere is exactly half a sphere.

4. The diagram below shows a hemispherical bowl of radius 15 cm. Some liquid is poured into the bowl to a height of 8 cm with a circular surface of radius BC.

   (a) State the length of AC.

   (b) Write down the length AB.

   (c) Hence find the length of BC.

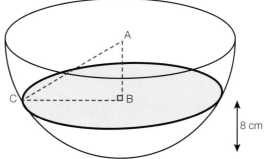

5. VABCD is a right pyramid on a square base. VO is the vertical height of the pyramid.

   The length of each side of the square base is 20 cm, and the slant height (VC) is 30 cm long.

   (a) Calculate the length of AC.

   (b) Calculate the vertical height of the pyramid, VO.

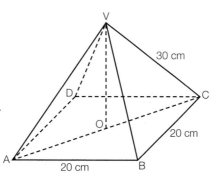

6. Liquid is poured into a spherical container to a height of h cm. The radius of the sphere is 22 cm. The top of the liquid is a circle of radius 10 cm.

Work out the height of the liquid, h.

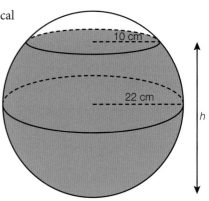

hint

Remember that a cross-section is a vertical slice through the length of a solid; and an isosceles triangle has two sides of equal length and two angles of equal size. The angle sum of all triangles is 180°.

7. The diagram shows farmer Neil's garden shed. The cross-section of the shed is a pentagon. BCD and IHG are **isosceles triangles**. AB = ED = 2 m. AE = BD = 3 m. EF = DG = 5 m. The vertical height of both C and H above the ground is 4.5 m.

(a) Calculate the length of AF.

K is the midpoint of JF.

(b) Calculate the length of AK.

Farmer Neil fits two straight wooden poles, AH and AG, into his shed.

(c) Which of the two poles is longer and by how much?

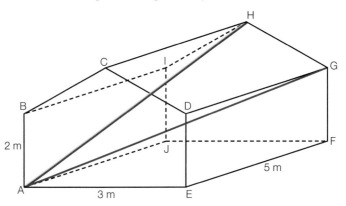

16.2 Finding the size of an angle in a three-dimensional solid

Finding angles in three dimensions uses similar techniques to finding lengths. You will need to identify a right-angled triangle within the solid and mark in the angle that you have been asked to find. Again, it will be easier to do the calculations if you sketch extra diagrams.

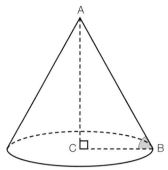

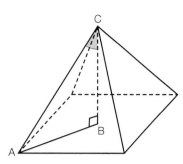

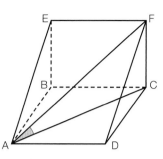

Angle AB̂C is the angle between the base of the cone and its slant edge, AB.

Angle AĈB is the angle between the height of the pyramid and the edge CA.

Angle FÂC is the angle between the line AF and the base of the prism, ABCD.

The angle between a line and a plane (a flat surface) is shown in this diagram. It is the angle between the line AB and the line BC that lies on the plane. The perpendicular line has been drawn to create a right-angled triangle.

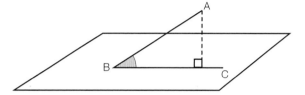

Worked example 16.4

> In every part of the question, the right-angled triangle has been identified and then sketched as a separate diagram. Make sure that you have copied all the letters from the three-dimensional diagram onto your new diagram correctly. Once you have done this, complete your calculations using Pythagoras' theorem or trigonometry.

> This is the base of the solid.

Q. For this triangular prism, calculate:

(a) the height EB

(b) the length of the line DB

(c) the length of the line DE

(d) the angle that the line DE makes with the base of the prism, ABCD.

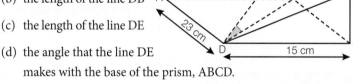

A. (a)

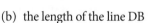

$$\tan 21° = \frac{EB}{15}$$

$$EB = 15 \times \tan 21°$$

$$EB = 5.76\,cm$$

(b)

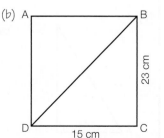

$$DB^2 = 15^2 + 23^2$$

$$= 754$$

$$DB = \sqrt{754}$$

$$DB = 27.5\,cm$$

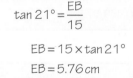

continued . . .

(c)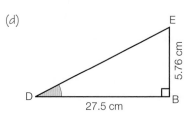

$DE^2 = 5.76^2 + 27.5^2$

$= \sqrt{789.42}$

$DE = 28.1 \, cm$

(d)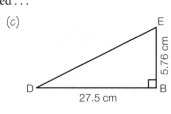

$\tan \hat{EDB} = \dfrac{5.76}{27.5}$

$\hat{EDB} = 11.8°$

Worked example 16.5

Q. A cylindrical drum contains a stick that fits the diagonal exactly. If the radius of the drum is 5.8 cm and the height is 15.8 cm, calculate:

(a) the length of the stick

(b) the angle that the stick makes with the side of the drum.

A. (a)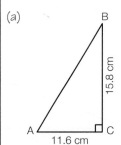

If the radius of the cylinder is 5.8 cm, the diameter of the cylinder is 11.6 cm.

$AB^2 = 15.8^2 + 11.6^2$

$= \sqrt{384.2}$

$AB = 19.6 \, cm$

> The length of the stick is given by the line AB.

> You now know all three sides of the triangle ABC, so you can use any trigonometric ratio to work out the angle AB̂C.
>
> It is more accurate to use the original measurements though.

(b)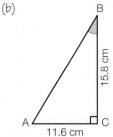

$\tan \hat{ABC} = \dfrac{11.6}{15.8}$

$\hat{ABC} = 36.3°$

Worked example 16.6

Q. A rescue helicopter is hovering 156 m above the sea. It is dark and the helicopter is shining a light down onto the surface of the sea. If the diameter of the cone formed by the beam of the light is 140 m, what is the angle at the apex of the cone?

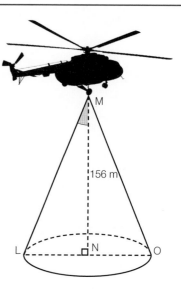

Use the right-angled triangle LMN. You need to find the angle LM̂N so use tan because you know the length of the opposite and the adjacent.

A.

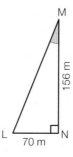

The diameter of the cone is 140 m.

The radius of the cone = 140 ÷ 2 = 70 m.

$$\tan L\hat{M}N = \frac{70}{156}$$

LM̂N is only half the angle at the apex of the cone, so multiply your answer by 2. Remember not to round your answer too soon.

LM̂N = 24.1666°

So the angle LM̂O = 2 × 24.1666°.

LM̂O = 48.3°

Exercise 16.2

1. VAOB is a right circular cone with radius 20 cm and slant height 60 cm.

   (a) What is the perpendicular height of the cone?

   (b) Calculate angle AV̂B.

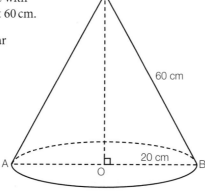

2. ABCDEFGH is a cuboid 12 cm long, 8 cm wide and 8 cm high.

   (a) Calculate the length of DF.

   (b) Find the length of the diagonal DG.

   (c) Calculate angle GD̂F.

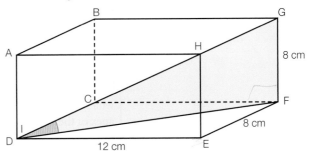

3. VABCD is a right pyramid on a square base. VO is the vertical height of the pyramid.

   The length of each side of the square base is 26 cm, and the slant height (VC) is 38 cm.

   Find the value of angle VÂC.

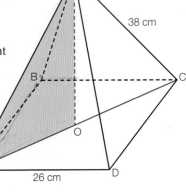

4. ABCDEF is a triangular prism.

   AB = ED = FC = 80 cm.

   BC = AF = 25 cm and DC = EF = 30 cm.

   Calculate:

   (a) the length of EC

   (b) the length of EB

   (c) the size of angle BÊC.

5. The diagram below shows a cylinder with radius 20 cm.

The height of the cylinder BD is 60 cm. C is the midpoint of BD.

Calculate the values of angles x and y.

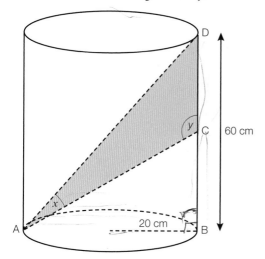

6. VABCD is a right pyramid. The base of the pyramid is a square of side 10 cm. The slant height of the pyramid is 18 cm. E and F are the midpoints of AD and DC respectively.

(a) Calculate the length of:

   (i) VE

   (ii) EF.

(b) Work out the size of angle x.

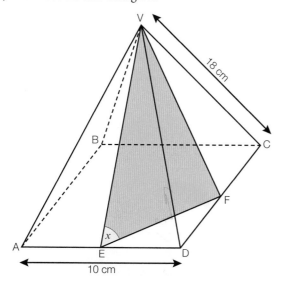

7. ABCDEFGH is a cuboid of length 80 cm, width 50 cm and height 60 cm. M is the midpoint of AB.

   (a) Calculate the lengths of MF and ME.

   (b) Work out the value of angle EM̂F.

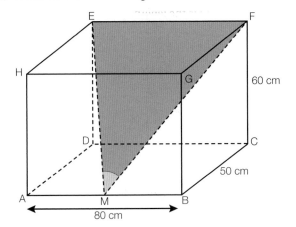

8. ABCDEF is a triangular prism. M is the midpoint of AC.

   CD = AF = BE = 100 cm,

   ED = EF = AB = CB = 40 cm, FD = AC = 30 cm.

   (a) Find the length of ME.

   (b) Calculate angle MÊB.

   (c) Calculate angle MD̂B.

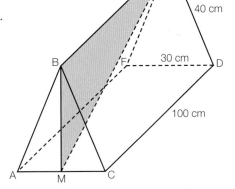

16.3 Calculating volumes and surface areas of three-dimensional solids

On the next page is a table listing some solids and the formula for calculating the volume and surface area. Not all of the formulae are in the Formula booklet, so make sure you know which ones you need to learn.

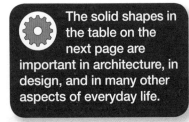

The solid shapes in the table on the next page are important in architecture, in design, and in many other aspects of everyday life.

The geometry of the surface of a sphere is not the same as that of a flat plane. Are you sure that the angles of a triangle add up to 180° on every surface, curved or flat? Do you know why the flight maps in airline magazines use curved lines to illustrate the different routes between airports?

Solid	Volume	Surface area	Notes
Cuboid 	$a = \pi r^2$ $V = l \times w \times h$ where: l is the length, w is the width, h is the height.	$A = 2(lw + lh + wh)$	A cuboid is a prism with a rectangular base.
Right pyramid 	$a = \pi r^2$ $V = \dfrac{1}{3}$ (area of base $\times$ vertical height)	A = area of base + area of all four triangles	The base can be either square or rectangular.
Cone 	$a = \pi r^2$ $V = \dfrac{1}{3}\pi r^2 h$ where: r is the radius, h is the vertical height.	For the curved surface area, $a = \pi r^2$ $A = \pi r l$ where: r is the radius, l is the slant height. For the total surface area, $A = \pi r l + \pi r^2$	A cone is a pyramid, but with a circular base.
Sphere 	$a = \pi r^2$ $V = \dfrac{4}{3}\pi r^3$ where: r is the radius.	$a = \pi r^2$ $A = 4\pi r^2$	A sphere is a solid in which all points on the surface are equidistant from the centre.
Hemisphere 	$V = \dfrac{2}{3}\pi r^3$	$A = 2\pi r^2$ (no base) $A = 2\pi r^2 + \pi r^2$ (with base)	A hemisphere is half a sphere; the base is circular.
Right prism 	$a = \pi r^2$ $V=$ area of cross-section $\times$ height or $V =$ area of cross-section $\times$ length	$A = 2$(area of the base) + area of all the rectangular sides	Prisms are solids with the same area of cross-section for their entire length.
Cylinder 	$a = \pi r^2$ $V = \pi r^2 h$ where: r is the radius, h is the height.	For the curved surface area, $a = \pi r^2$ $A = 2\pi r h$ For the total surface area, $A = 2\pi r h + 2(\pi r^2)$	A cylinder is a prism with a circular base.

If you have problems visualising in three dimensions, there are many clear diagrams and descriptions on the Internet that you might find helpful. Try making models of the solids and rotating them, or look for objects in your environment that have the same shape.

Your sketches do not have to be accurate – but do make sure that they are large enough and be prepared to erase them, start again, or adapt them in some way. You may not be right the first time!

Worked example 16.7

Q. Three tennis balls are packed in a cylindrical container, just touching the sides, top and bottom of the container. The diameter of a tennis ball is 6.7 cm.

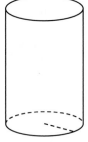

6.7 cm

(a) Write down:

    (i) the internal height of the container

    (ii) the diameter of the container.

(b) Calculate the volume of the container, giving your answer to the nearest whole number.

The curved surface of the cylinder is made of plastic, and the top and bottom are made of metal. Calculate:

(c) the area of plastic used

(d) the area of metal used.

The internal diameter of the container is the same as that of the tennis ball.

A. (a) (i) The internal height is: $h = 3 \times 6.7 = 20.1$ cm
     (ii) $d = 6.7$ cm

The radius is half the diameter.

(b) $V = \pi r^2 h$
    $V = \pi \times 3.35^2 \times 20.1 = 709$ cm^3

The formula for the curved surface area is $A = 2\pi rh$.

(c) Area of plastic:
    $2\pi rh = 2 \times \pi \times 3.35 \times 20.1 = 423$ cm^2

The top and bottom of the cylinder are circles, so use the formula for the area of a circle.

(d) Area of metal:
    $2 \times \pi r^2 = 2 \times \pi \times 3.35^2 = 70.5$ cm^2

Worked example 16.8

Q. The base of a prism is a regular hexagon with sides of 3.5 cm. The length of the prism is 19 cm.

(a) Calculate the volume of the prism.

(b) The prism is to be made of flexible plastic and sold as a pencil case. Calculate the area of material needed for each case.

> To calculate the volume, you must first calculate the area of cross-section of the prism. This may also be called the area of the base of the prism.

> In a regular polygon all the sides are the same length and all the angles are the same size. A regular hexagon consists of six **equilateral triangles**.

> The surface area of the prism has two hexagonal ends and six rectangular sides.

A. (a)

hint

Remember that an equilateral triangle has all three sides the same length and all three internal angles the same size.

Use the formula $A = \dfrac{1}{2} ab \sin C$ to find the area of one triangle.

Area of triangle $= \dfrac{1}{2} \times 3.5 \times 3.5 \times \sin 60° = 5.304\ldots$

Area of hexagon $= 6 \times 5.304\ldots = 31.8\,cm^2$

Volume of prism $= 19 \times 31.8 = 605\,cm^3$

(b)

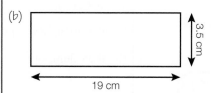

Area of one rectangle $= 19 \times 3.5 = 66.5\,cm^2$

Area of six rectangles $= 6 \times 66.5 = 399\,cm^2$

Area of the two hexagonal ends $= 2 \times 31.8 = 63.6\,cm^2$

Total area of plastic $= 399 + 63.6 = 463\,cm^2$

Using your GDC

For many of the problems you meet, your GDC will give answers to several decimal places. Even though the IB asks for all answers to be given to three significant figures, do not round your answers too early. Problems like the ones encountered in this chapter will require several stages of calculation, and if you round the first answer and then use the rounded figures, you will be building up inaccuracies as you continue to work. It is better to use the **Ans/ANS** key or store your first solution in one of the memories of the calculator. (See '*22.2C The Ans/ANS key*' and '*22.2D Using the GDC memory*' on page 643 of the GDC chapter for a reminder of how to use these features if you need to.)

The screens below show the calculation to find the volume of a cylinder with a radius of 5.6 cm and a length of 15 cm.

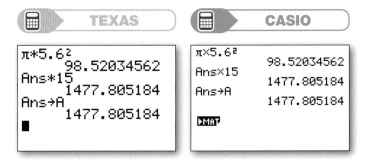

The area of the base is found; then the **Ans** key is used to substitute the area into the formula to find the volume.

Then the solution is stored in memory A.

The final answer, to three significant figures, is $V = 1480 \, \text{cm}^3$.

Worked example 16.9

Q. | A lampshade is made from a cone of glass, with a glass hemisphere as its base. The slant height of the cone is 29 cm, and the diameter of the hemisphere is 11 cm. Calculate:

(a) the surface area of the lampshade

(b) the volume of the lampshade.

> The diameter of the hemisphere is the same as the diameter of the cone.

A. | (a) The radius of the cone is $\dfrac{1}{2} \times 11 = 5.5$ cm.

Cone: curved surface area $= \pi r l$

$A = \pi \times 5.5 \times 29$

> Store 501.08... in memory A on your GDC.

$A = 501.08\ldots \, \text{cm}^2$

Hemisphere: surface area $= 2\pi r^2$

$A = 190.06\ldots \, \text{cm}^2$

Total area $= 691 \, \text{cm}^3$

continued . . .

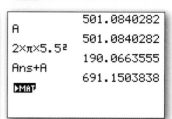

(b) $h^2 = 29^2 - 5.5^2$

$h = \sqrt{810.75}$

$h = 28.5\,cm$

Cone: volume $= \dfrac{1}{3}\pi r^2 h$

$V = \dfrac{1}{3} \times \pi \times 5.5^2 \times 28.5$

$V = 901.98\ldots cm^3$

Hemisphere: volume $= \dfrac{2}{3}\pi r^3$

$V = \dfrac{2}{3} \times \pi \times 5.5^3$

$V = 348.45\ldots$

Total volume $= 1250\,cm^3$

To find the volume of the cone, you need to know its height; use Pythagoras' theorem to do so.

Exercise 16.3

1. For each of the shapes in Exercise 16.1, questions 1–6, calculate:

   (a) the total surface area   (b) the volume.

   Give your answer to the nearest whole number. (Note: the solid in question 4 is an 'open' bowl so calculate the outside surface only.)

2. Calculate the volume of each of the following shapes, giving your answer to the nearest whole number:

   (a) a sphere with radius of 20 cm   (b) a hemisphere with radius of 24 cm

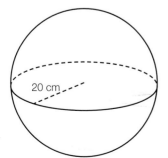

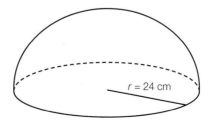

(c) a cylinder of radius 32 cm and length 120 cm

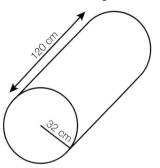

(d) a cylinder of radius 25 cm and height 80 cm

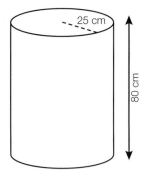

(e) a composite shape consisting of a hemisphere of radius 40 cm and a right cylinder of the same radius. The cylinder has a height of 140 cm.

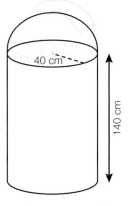

3. Work out the total surface area of each of the shapes in question 2 above, giving your answer to the nearest whole number.

4. Felix is designing a container for detergent. The container is to have a volume of one litre (1000 cm³). He is considering two options:

(a) a spherical container of radius r cm

(b) a cubical container of length x cm.

Find the values of r and x.

5. A garden shed has a cross-section in the form of a pentagon ABCDE.

   AB = ED = 2 m; BC = DC = 1.6 m; AE = BD = 2.3 m.

   (a) Calculate the volume of the shed.

   (b) Work out the total surface area of the roof of the shed BDGIHC.

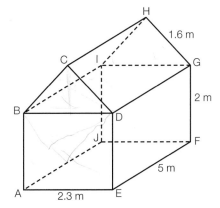

6. A pack of tennis balls contains 4 balls fitted into a cylindrical container. The radius of each of the balls is 3.2 cm.

   (a) Find the dimensions of the container if all 4 balls just fit into the container.

   (b) Calculate the volume of unoccupied space in the container.

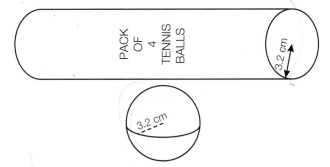

Summary

You should know:

- about the basic geometry of the following three-dimensional solids: cuboid, right prism, right pyramid, cylinder, sphere, hemisphere, cone and combinations of these solids

- how to calculate the distance between two points within a solid, such as the distance between two vertices, from a vertex to a midpoint, or from midpoint to midpoint

- how to calculate the size of an angle between two lines or between a line and a plane

- how to calculate the volume and surface area of the three-dimensional solids defined above.

Mixed examination practice

Exam-style questions

1. A cube ABCDEFGH has sides of length 8 cm.

   (a) Calculate the length of the diagonal AC.

   (b) Work out the length of the diagonal AF.

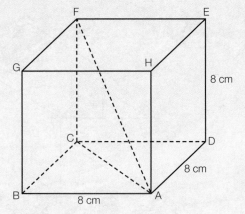

2. PQRSTUVW is a cuboid of length 200 cm, width 70 cm and height 90 cm.

   (a) Find the value of angle RP̂T.

   (b) Calculate angle TQ̂S.

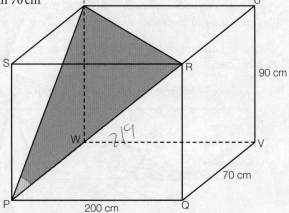

3. The diagram shows a cylindrical barrel of radius 1.2 metres and height 3.6 metres. A tube DEO is fixed into the cylinder. The tube consists of two straight parts OE and ED. O is at the centre of the base of the barrel and E lies along BC such that BE = 1.4 metres.

   Calculate the total length of the tube.

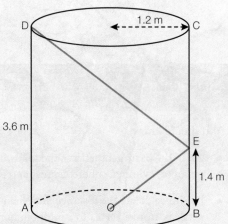

4. A composite shape consists of a hemisphere and a **right cone**, both of radius 28 cm. The height of the cone is 84 cm.

(a) Calculate the volume of the composite shape.

(b) Work out the total surface area of the shape.

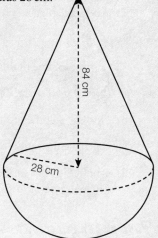

5. The following diagram shows a spherical ball of radius 10 cm, which just fits into a cylindrical container.

Calculate the volume of unoccupied space in the cylindrical container.

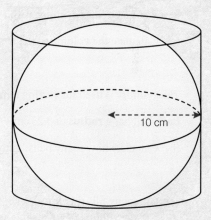

6. Each of the following three containers has a volume of 8000 cm³.

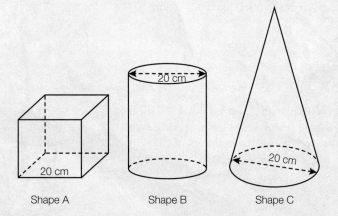

Shape A   Shape B   Shape C

Shape A is a cube of side 20 cm.

Shape B is a cylinder of diameter 20 cm.

Shape C is a right cone of diameter 20 cm.

Work out the heights of shapes B and C.

7. Loretta has moulded a sphere of radius 12 cm out of clay. Later she remoulds four smaller spheres out of the original, bigger sphere.

(a) Work out:

    (i)   the volume of the original sphere

    (ii) the total surface area of the original sphere.

(b) Find the volume of each of the smaller spheres.

(c) Calculate the radius of the smaller sphere.

(d) Would the total surface area of the four smaller spheres be the same as the surface area of the original sphere? Justify your answer.

Past paper questions

1. Jenny has a circular cylinder with a lid. The cylinder has height 39 cm and diameter 65 **mm**.

(a) Calculate the volume of the cylinder in cm³. Give your answer correct to **two** decimal places.

[3 marks]

The cylinder is used for storing tennis balls.

Each ball has a **radius** of 3.25 cm.

(b) Calculate how many balls Jenny can fit in the cylinder if it is filled to the top.

[1 mark]

(c) (i) Jenny fills the cylinder with the number of balls found in part (b) and puts the lid on. Calculate the volume of air inside the cylinder in the spaces between the tennis balls.

    (ii) Convert your answer to (c)(i) into cubic metres.

[4 marks]

[Total 8 marks]

[May 2007, Paper 2, TZ0, Question 2(i)] (© *IB Organization 2007*)

2. The triangular faces of a square based pyramid, ABCDE, are all inclined at 70° to the base. The edges of the base ABCD are all 10 cm and M is the centre. G is the midpoint of CD.

(Diagram not to scale)

(a) Using the letters on the diagram draw a triangle showing the position of a 70° angle.

[1 mark]

(b) Show that the height of the pyramid is 13.7 cm, to 3 significant figures.

[2 marks]

(c) Calculate:

  (i) the length of EG

  (ii) the size of angle DÊC.

[4 marks]

(d) Find the total surface area of the pyramid.

[2 marks]

(e) Find the volume of the pyramid.

[2 marks]

[Total 11 marks]

[May 2008, Paper 2, TZ1, Question 4(ii)] (© *IB Organization 2008*)

6 Mathematical models

Suppose you are given a problem — it may be a practical question that a friend asks you, or an issue that you have noticed yourself to which you want to find a solution; it may even be a mathematical problem that you are set in one of your classes. How do you solve it? If it is a practical problem, you might try out different approaches or talk it through with a friend. If it is a problem encountered in class, you might go back over your notes and textbooks, looking for a similar example to see how that was solved.

The mathematician George Pólya wrote a book called *How to Solve It*, which was published in 1945. In this book he describes several distinct steps taken by people who are good at problem-solving.

These steps are:

● understand the problem

● make a plan

● carry out your plan

● look back at your solution to see whether you can improve it or use it in another context.

This process of solving problems is called 'mathematical modelling', and the stages outlined by Pólya constitute what is known as the 'modelling cycle'.

Who uses mathematical modelling? It is the normal way for mathematicians to work, as well as designers, engineers, architects, doctors and many other professionals.

If you become good at problem-solving, you can reduce the number of things that you have to memorise: it is easier to remember formulae or concepts when you understand *how* they work.

Prior learning topics

It will be easier to study this topic if you have completed:

● Chapter 2
● Chapter 14.

Mathematical models allow us to use mathematics to solve practical problems, describe different aspects of the real world, test ideas, and make predictions about the future. A model may be a simplification of a real situation, but it is usually quick and cheap to work with and helps us to strengthen our understanding of the problem.

The concept of a function is fundamental to mathematical modelling. Before you can work with the more complex models in this topic, you need to be confident in your understanding and use of functions and function notation.

17.1 What is a function?

A **function** is like a **mapping** diagram between two sets, where each element of one set maps to a single element of the other set. A function can also be viewed as a machine where you feed numbers in at one end, it works on the numbers according to a certain rule, and then gives you the output at the other end.

For example:

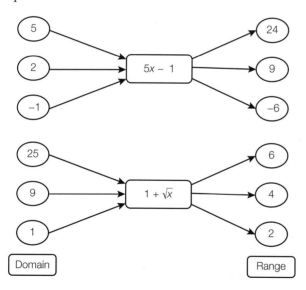

The set of numbers that go into the function is called the **domain**. Values in the domain are:

- the numbers chosen to describe that particular function

- values taken by the **independent** variable

- the numbers plotted on the horizontal axis when you draw a graph of that function.

In this chapter you will learn:

- what a function is and the definitions of domain and range
- about the graphs of some basic functions
- how to use function notation
- how to read and interpret a graph and use it to find the domain and range of a function
- about simple rational functions and asymptotes
- how to draw accurate graphs
- how to create a sketch from given information
- how to use your GDC to solve equations that involve combinations of the basic functions dealt with in this course.

Why can we use maths to describe real-world situations and make predictions? Are we imposing our own mathematical models on the world, or is it that we are discovering that the world runs according to the rules of mathematics?

You learned about dependent and independent variables in Chapter 12.

The numbers that come out of the function make up the **range** of that function. They are:

- values taken by the **dependent** variable

- the numbers plotted on the vertical axis when you draw a graph of the function.

Here are some alternative ways of thinking about a function:

- a mapping diagram

- a set of ordered pairs

- a graph

- an algebraic expression.

When representing a function by any of the above methods, you have to be careful because not all mapping diagrams, sets of ordered pairs, graphs or algebraic expressions describe a valid function. The important point to remember is that a valid function can have **only one output** for **each input value** that goes into the function.

	These are functions	These are not functions	Explanation
Mapping diagram			In the first diagram there is one output for every input. In the second diagram there are two different outputs for the input 6.
Set of ordered pairs	$\{(6, 8), (3, 2), (5, 9), (-1, 2)\}$ The domain consists of the x-coordinates: $\{6, 3, 5, -1\}$ The range consists of the y-coordinates: $\{8, 2, 9, 2\}$	$\{(6, 8)\ (3, 2)\ (6, 9)\ (-1, 2)\}$ The domain consists of the x-coordinates: $\{6, 3, 6, -1\}$ The range consists of the y-coordinates: $\{8, 2, 9, 2\}$	The first set of number pairs has one y-coordinate for every x-coordinate. The second set has two different y-coordinates for the x-coordinate 6.
Graph			The first graph has one y-value for every x-value. The second graph has two y-values for each positive x-value.

table continues on next page...

continued...

	These are functions	These are not functions	Explanation
			Graphs continued . . . This suggests the 'vertical line test': if a vertical line drawn at any x position in the domain crosses the graph only once, then the graph represents a valid function.
Algebraic expression	$f(x) = x^3 - x + 2$	$f(x) = \pm\sqrt{4 - x^2}$	The first expression will give the blue curve in the graph above. Plotting the second expression will give a circle, which fails the vertical line test.

FF⟩⟩ **The f(x) notation is explained further in section 17.2.**

Exercise 17.1

1. For each of the graphs below, indicate whether or not the graph represents a valid function.

(a)
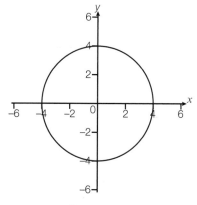

(b)
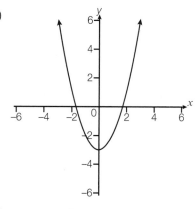

(c)
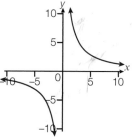

(d)
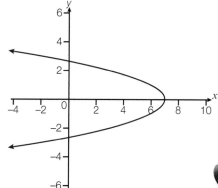

(e)

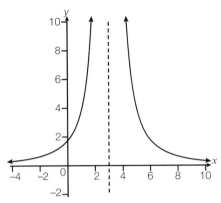

(f)

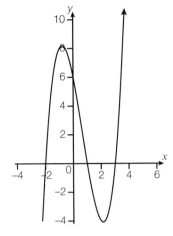

17.2 Functions in more detail

Function notation

If you are asked to draw a graph of $y = x^3 + x^2 - 5$, you know that this will be a curve because the powers of x are greater than 1, suggesting it is not linear. You can use the equation to calculate the values of y that correspond to particular values of x.

For instance, if $x = 3$, then:

$$y = 3^3 + 3^2 - 5 = 27 + 9 - 5 = 31$$

So the point (3, 31) lies on the curve.

The mathematical relationship $y = x^3 + x^2 - 5$ can also be written in function notation $f(x) = x^3 + x^2 - 5$. The second form gives you the same information — so why do we need this different notation for expressing the same thing?

The equation $y = x^3 + x^2 - 5$ tells you the link between the x- and y-coordinates of a graph, which enables you to draw that graph.

The function notation $f(x) = x^3 + x^2 - 5$ expresses the idea of a function as a 'machine':

So x represents the input, f is the 'machine', and $f(x)$ is the output (the result of applying f to x).

The function notation $f(x)$, pronounced as 'f of x', allows us to:

- distinguish between different functions by using different letters; for example, $f(x)$, $g(x)$, $h(x)$

- use an efficient shorthand for substituting values;
  for example, $f(3)$ means replace x by 3 so that
  $f(3) = 3^3 + 3^2 - 5 = 27 + 9 - 5 = 31$

- match a formula to a physical quantity in a meaningful way;
  for example, we can write $h(t) = -5t^2 + 3t - 1$ to show that this is a
  formula to find the height at a given time.

Worked example 17.1

Q. (a) If $f(x) = 5 - 3x$, find $f(4)$, $f(-2)$ and $f(0)$.

(b) If $V(r) = \dfrac{4}{3}\pi r^3$, find $V(2)$, $V(12)$ and $V(21)$ in terms of π.

(c) If $f(x) = x^2 - 3x + 2$, find x when $f(x) = 42$.

(d) If $f(x) = x^3 - 2x^2 + x + 5$, find a simplified expression for $f(2x)$.

> $f(4)$, $f(-2)$ and $f(0)$ mean to replace x in the expression $5 - 3x$ with 4, -2 and 0, respectively.

A. (a) $f(4) = 5 - 3 \times 4 = -7$

$f(-2) = 5 - 3 \times (-2) = 11$

$f(0) = 5 - 3 \times 0 = 5$

> $V(2)$, $V(12)$ and $V(21)$ mean to replace x in the expression $\frac{4}{3}\pi r^3$ by 2, 12 and 21, respectively.

(b) $V(2) = \dfrac{4}{3}\pi \times 2^3 = \dfrac{32\pi}{3}$

$V(12) = \dfrac{4}{3}\pi \times 12^3 = 2304\pi$

$V(21) = \dfrac{4}{3}\pi \times 21^3 = 12348\pi$

> $f(x) = 42$ is the same as $x^2 - 3x + 2 = 42$, which is a quadratic equation that you can solve using your chosen method from Chapter 2.

(c) $x^2 - 3x + 2 = 42$

$x^2 - 3x - 40 = 0$

 TEXAS   CASIO

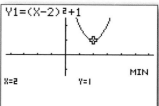

From GDC: $x = -5$ or $x = 8$

> $f(2x)$ means to replace every occurrence of x in the expression $x^3 - 2x^2 + x + 5$ by $2x$. It is best to put brackets around $2x$, so that you will remember to cube and square the 2 as well as x.

(d) $f(2x) = (2x)^3 - 2(2x)^2 + (2x) + 5$

$= (2x) \times (2x) \times (2x) - 2 \times (2x) \times (2x) + (2x) + 5$

$= 8x^3 - 8x^2 + 2x + 5$

Exercise 17.2

1. A function is defined as $f(x) = 3x - 8$. Find the following:

    (a) $f(4)$ (b) $f(-1)$ (c) $f\left(\dfrac{1}{3}\right)$ (d) $f(a)$

2. Given the function $g(x) = 11 - 5x$, find:

    (a) $g(6)$ (b) $2g(1)$ (c) $g(7) + 13$ (d) $g(2a)$

3. Given the function $f(x) = 2x^2 - 7x + 5$, find:

    (a) $f(-2)$ (b) $f(0)$ (c) $f(3) - 5$ (d) $f(c)$

4. Given that $g(x) = x^3 - 4x^2 + 3x - 7$, find:

    (a) $g(-4)$ (b) $g(-1)$ (c) $13g(5)$

5. For the function $h(t) = 14t - 4.9t^2$, find:

    (a) $h(1)$ (b) $h\left(\dfrac{1}{7}\right)$ (c) $h(3) - h(2)$ (d) $5h(10) + 200$

6. A function is defined as $f(x) = \dfrac{2+x}{x-2}$ for $x \neq 2$.

    (a) Work out $f(-7)$.

    (b) Find $f\left(\dfrac{3}{4}\right)$.

    (c) Calculate $f(6) - f(0)$.

    (d) Find a simplified expression for $f(x + 1)$.

Domain and range

If you are drawing a graph, the domain of a function consists of the values that are plotted along the x-axis; these are values of the independent variable. The domain may be all the real numbers on a number line, or it may be a restricted **interval** such as $-2 \leq x \leq 3$.

Suppose that a function is defined by $f(x) = 3 - 2x$.

If the domain is not specified, there are no values of x that cannot be used, and the graph looks like this:

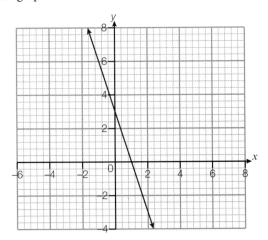

Note the arrows at both ends of the line.

If the domain is given as $x \in \mathbb{R}$, $x \geq 1$, the graph looks like this:

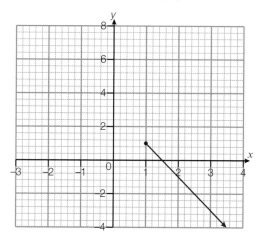

 You saw in Chapter 1 that $\mathbb{R}$ is the symbol for real numbers and in Chapter 8 that $\in$ is set notation for 'is a member of'; see Chapter 1 if you need to revise set notation for the various types of numbers and Chapter 8 if you need a reminder of set notation.

Note that there is an arrow at only one end of the line; the end at $x = 1$ is marked by a filled circle. '$x \in \mathbb{R}$, $x \geq 1$' indicates that the domain is all real numbers greater than or equal to 1.

If the domain is given as $-2 \leq x \leq 3$, the graph looks like this:

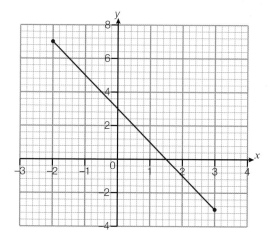

Now both ends, at $x = -2$ and $x = 3$, are marked by filled circles.

If the x value of one of the ends is not included in the domain, that end would be marked with an empty (non-filled) circle. For example, if the domain were $-2 < x \le 3$ (which means $x = -2$ is not included in the domain), then the graph would look like this:

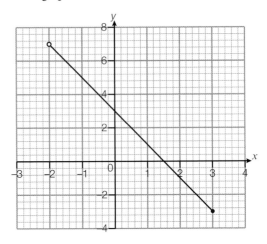

The range also changes depending on the domain:

• For $f(x) = 3 - 2x$, $x \in \mathbb{R}$, the range is also $f(x) \in \mathbb{R}$.

• For $f(x) = 3 - 2x$, $x \in \mathbb{R}$, $x \ge 1$, the range is $f(x) \le 1$, as you can see from the first graph on page 499.

• For $f(x) = 3 - 2x$, $x \in \mathbb{R}$, $-2 \le x \le 3$, the range is $-3 \le f(x) \le 7$, as you can see from the second graph on page 499.

Worked example 17.2

Q. Write down the domain and range for each of these functions:

(a)

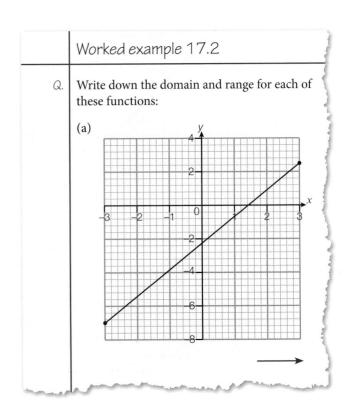

continued . . .

(b)

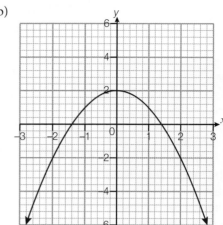

(c)

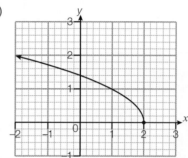

A.

The graph has filled circles at both ends, so the domain is restricted between, and also includes, the x-coordinates of these ends. The range is between the y-coordinates of these ends.

(a) The domain is $-3 \leq x \leq 3$.

The range is $-7 \leq f(x) \leq 2.5$.

The graph has arrows at both ends, so the domain is all real numbers. The curve has a maximum point at $(0, 2)$, so the range is all numbers less than or equal to 2.

(b) The domain is $x \in \mathbb{R}$.

The range is $f(x) \leq 2$.

There is an arrow at one end of the curve, which means that the domain (and range) is unrestricted in this direction; a filled circle at the other end means that the domain reaches up to $x = 2$ but no further. The minimum y-value on the curve is 0.

(c) The domain is $x \leq 2$.

The range is $f(x) \geq 0$.

If you use your GDC to draw the graph of a function, you can find the coordinates of important points on the curve, such as minimum and maximum points or the points at the beginning and end of the domain. See section '22.2G(e)' on page 648 or sections '22.3.17' and '22.3.18' on pages 678–683 of the GDC chapter for a reminder of the different methods.

Worked example 17.3

Q. Use your GDC to draw graphs of the following functions. State the domain and range in each case.

(a) $f(x) = (x - 2)^2 + 1$

(b) $f(x) = x^3 - x; -2 \leq x \leq 2$

(c) $f(x) = 2^{x-1}$

> Plot the graph on your GDC and find the coordinates of the minimum point on the parabola; this gives you the lowest value of the range. There is no restriction given on the domain, so it consists of all real numbers.

A. (a) TEXAS   CASIO

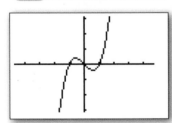   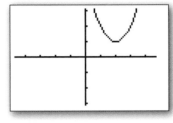

The minimum point on the parabola is at $(2, 1)$

The domain is $x \in \mathbb{R}$.

The range is $f(x) \geq 1$.

> In this case the domain is restricted to x values between, and including, -2 and 2. Use your GDC to find the coordinates of the points at the beginning and end of the domain.

(b) TEXAS   CASIO

   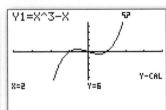

The domain is $-2 \leq x \leq 2$.

The range is $-6 \leq f(x) \leq 6$.

> The domain can take all real values, but the graph tells you that values in the range are always above zero.

(c) TEXAS   CASIO

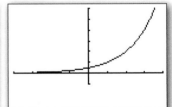   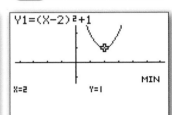

The domain is $x \in \mathbb{R}$.

The range is $f(x) > 0$.

The curve gets close to, but never touches, the x-axis, so there is a horizontal asymptote at $y = 0$.

 You will learn about horizontal and vertical asymptotes in section 17.3.

Exercise 17.3

1. Write down the domain and the range for each of the following functions.

(a)

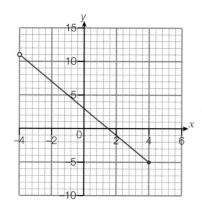

(b)

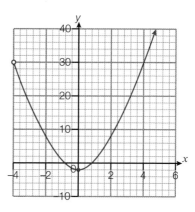

(c)

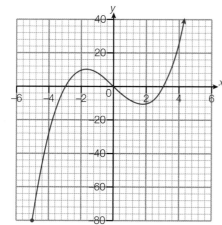

(d)

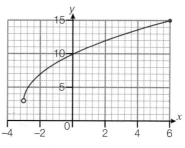

(e)

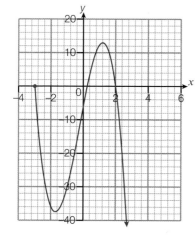

(f)

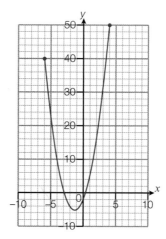

2. Use your GDC to draw the graphs of the following functions. State the range of each function.

    (a) $y = 4x - 7; -1 \leq x \leq 12$

    (b) $y = x^2 + 3; -7 \leq x < 7$

    (c) $y = x^3 - 4x; -5 \leq x \leq 4$

    (d) $y = (x + 5)(2x - 1); -6 < x < 6$

17.3 Rational functions

A rational function is a function whose algebraic expression looks like a fraction or ratio.

hint

Compare this with the term 'rational number' introduced in Chapter 1.

The simplest form of a rational function is $f(x) = \dfrac{a}{bx + c}$ where a, b and c are constants.

The graph of such a function has a distinctive shape, known as a **hyperbola**. In fact, the graph is made up of two curves; the values of a, b and c determine the positions of these curves.

By using a GDC or a maths software package on the computer, you can investigate how the constants a, b and c affect the basic shape of the graph. Be careful entering the function's formula: make sure to use brackets and division signs correctly.

For example, to enter $f(x) = \dfrac{3}{3x + 1}$, you need brackets to tell the GDC that it is dividing 3 by all of $(3x + 1)$. If you did not have the brackets around $3x + 1$, the GDC may draw the graph of $f(x) = \dfrac{3}{3x} + 1$, which is a different function, as you can see in the graph below.

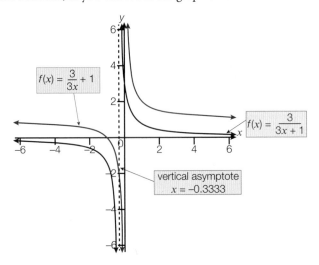

Try exploring hyperbola graphs yourself. Here are some suggestions:

- Start with the simplest rational function $f(x) = \dfrac{a}{x}$ and draw graphs for different values of a.

- Draw graphs of $f(x) = \dfrac{1}{x \pm c}$ for different positive numbers c.

- Draw graphs of $f(x) = \dfrac{1}{x \pm c} + d$ for various values of d.

You will find that each graph has both a vertical and a horizontal 'break'.

For example, the graph of $f(x) = \dfrac{2}{x-3} + 1$ looks like:

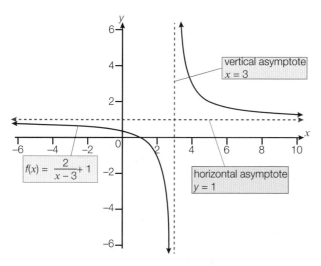

With your GDC, you can use a trace function or the table of coordinates to find the approximate location of the 'breaks' in the graph, which are called **asymptotes**. See sections '*17.2 Finding a vertical asymptote*' and '*17.3 Finding a horizontal asymptote*' on pages 679 and 680 of the GDC chapter if you need to.

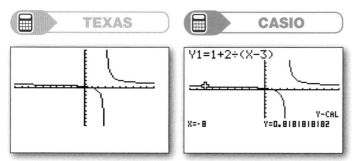

The horizontal break in the graph is called a **horizontal asymptote**. It occurs whenever a function's output (y) value approaches a certain number as x increases or decreases.

In the case of $f(x) = \dfrac{2}{x-3} + 1$, we can see that as x increases, $f(x)$ approaches 1. The fraction $\dfrac{2}{x-3}$ gets smaller and smaller because the denominator is getting larger and larger, so $f(x)$ approaches 1 but will never actually reach 1. Therefore, the equation of the horizontal asymptote is $y = 1$. You can draw $y = 1$ on your GDC to confirm that this is the location of the break.

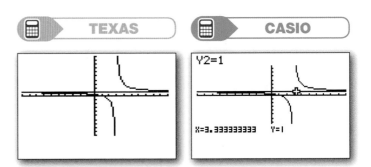

The vertical break in the graph is called a **vertical asymptote**. It occurs when a fraction's denominator becomes zero.

In general, the graph of $f(x) = \dfrac{a}{x \pm c}$ will have a vertical asymptote when $x \pm c = 0$. So:

- the graph of $f(x) = \dfrac{2}{x+3}$ will have a vertical asymptote when

  $x + 3 = 0$, i.e. at $x = -3$

- the graph of $g(x) = \dfrac{1}{2x-5}$ will have a vertical asymptote when

  $2x - 5 = 0$, i.e. at $x = 2.5$.

In both of the above cases, the horizontal asymptote is the line $y = 0$ (in other words, the x-axis).

To draw the graph of $h(x) = 2 + \dfrac{3}{x-1}$, note that there will be a vertical asymptote at $x = 1$ and a horizontal asymptote at $y = 2$.

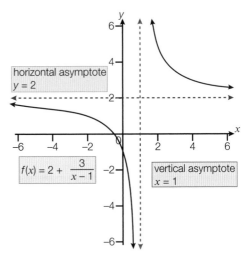

Asymptotes can sometimes be difficult to identify on the GDC screen. If you're having trouble locating the asymptotes on your GDC graph, check the 'table' function for the list of coordinates of the points on the graph. (See '*14.1 Accessing the table of coordinates from a plotted graph*' on page 678 of the GDC chapter if you need to.)

When identifying an asymptote from a table of coordinates:

• a horizontal asymptote is found by looking at what happens to the *y* values as the *x* values get larger:

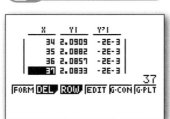

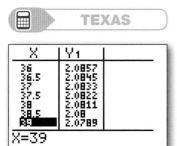

• a vertical asymptote occurs when the table shows an ERROR message:

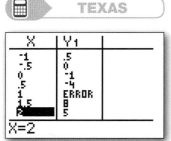

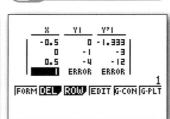

Worked example 17.4

Q. A function is defined by $g(x) = 3 - \dfrac{5}{x+2}$ for $-6 \le x \le 3$.

(a) Sketch its graph.

(b) Write down the equation of the vertical asymptote.

(c) What is the equation of the horizontal asymptote?

Use your GDC to sketch the graph. (See '22.2G Graphs' on page 645 of the GDC chapter if you need to.)

A. (a)

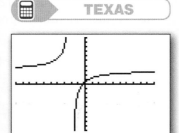

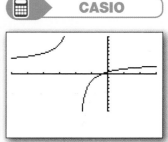

continued . . .

> The denominator of the fraction equals zero when $x + 2 = 0$.

(b) The vertical asymptote is $x = -2$.

(c)

> From the GDC graph, it looks as though the horizontal asymptote is at $y = 3$. Draw the line $y = 3$ on your GDC to check this, or use the table of coordinates to look at the y values as x increases. See '22.2G' and/or '17.3' of the GDC chapters as appropriate.

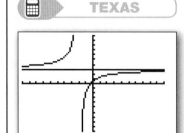

TEXAS

CASIO

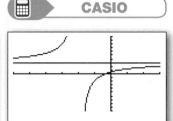

The horizontal asymptote is $y = 3$.

Exercise 17.4

1. By drawing the graphs of the following functions, in each case:

   (i) state the equation of the vertical asymptote

   (ii) find the horizontal asymptote.

   (a) $y = \dfrac{1}{x}$ (b) $y = \dfrac{3}{x}$ (c) $y = \dfrac{1}{x+1}$ (d) $y = \dfrac{2}{x+1}$

   (e) $y = \dfrac{1}{2x+1}$ (f) $y = \dfrac{4}{2x-3}$ (g) $y = 5 - \dfrac{7}{2x-3}$ (h) $y = \dfrac{1}{3x-2} + 4$

17.4 Drawing graphs and diagrams

As you have seen, graphs and diagrams are very powerful tools. They can help you to visualise and discover properties of the situation you are studying. Before moving on to mathematical models in the next few chapters, you need to:

- understand the difference between a sketch and an accurate graph

- be able to create a sketch from information that you have been given

- be able to transfer a graph from your GDC onto paper

- know how to draw an accurate graph

- be able to draw combinations of two or more graphs on one diagram

- know how to use your graphs to solve equations that involve combinations of functions that you have studied.

The difference between a sketch and an accurate graph

It is important to understand the difference between the instructions 'plot', 'sketch' and 'draw', and be able to choose the appropriate type of graph for a particular problem. Read any problem carefully and decide which kind of diagram will be the most useful initially; you can always draw another if the first does not give you sufficient clarity. It is also important to make sure that any diagram you draw is large enough! A tiny diagram, squashed into one corner of the paper, will not help you; nor will it be informative to the person who is checking or marking your work!

Sketch	A sketch represents a situation by means of a diagram or graph. It should be clearly labelled and give a general idea of the shape or relationship being described. All obvious and relevant features should be included, such as **turning points**, **intercepts** and **asymptotes**. The dimensions or points do not have to be drawn to an accurate scale/position.
Plot	To plot a graph, you need to calculate a set of accurate points and then mark them clearly, and accurately, on your diagram using a correct scale.
Draw	A drawing is a clearly labelled, accurate diagram or graph. It should be drawn to scale. Straight lines should be drawn with a ruler, and points that are known not to lie in a straight line should be joined by a smooth curve.

When you are drawing, plotting or sketching:

- Use a pencil — you may need to make changes, and using permanent ink would make this difficult.

- Mark the axes for the graph— and remember to label them. Not all graphs are x–y graphs; for example, you might be plotting height against time. Always use the correct labels.

Does a graph without labels or scales still have meaning?

- Follow any instructions relating to the scale, the domain or the range of a graph.

Creating a sketch

Draw the function $f(x) = x^4 - x^2 - \dfrac{1}{x}$ on your GDC. What do you notice?

What are the most important features to include in a sketch?

You should have obtained an image like this:

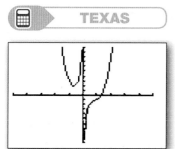
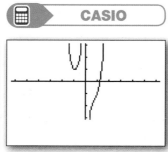

The points to notice are:

- This is an x–y graph, so the axes should be labelled x and y.

- The curve on the left of the y-axis has a minimum at approximately $(-1, 1)$.

- There is a vertical asymptote at $x = 0$ (the y-axis).

- There is an x-intercept between the points $(1, 0)$ and $(2, 0)$.

- There is no y-intercept.

Did you observe these features on your GDC graph?

Now you can make a sketch of the graph, by transferring these important features onto paper.

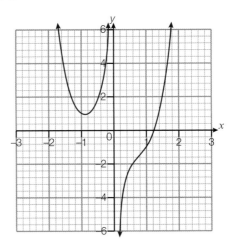

Worked example 17.5

Q. (a) Sketch the graph of $f(x) = 2 - \sqrt{x}$ for the domain $0 \leq x \leq 6$. Comment on the range of $f(x)$.

(b) Sketch the graph of $h(x) = \sqrt{2 - x}$ for the same domain as in (a). What do you notice about the range of this function?

A. (a)

> Draw the graph on your GDC. The curve is decreasing, so the value of the function at $x = 0$ is the maximum of the range, and the value at $x = 6$ is the minimum of the range; these values can be found with your GDC. See section '22.2G(e) The trace function' on page 648 of the GDC chapter if you need to.

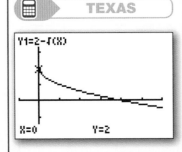

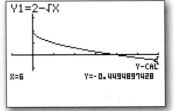

continued . . .

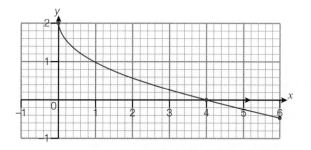

The range is $-0.449 \leq f(x) \leq 2$.

Transfer the sketch from your GDC onto paper; make sure you indicate the domain using filled circles at the ends of the curve.

(b)

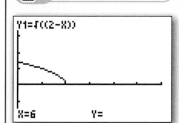

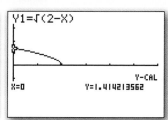

Draw the graph on your GDC. This graph has no values outside $0 \leq x \leq 2$, and it is decreasing over this interval, so the maximum and minimum values are the y values at $x = 0$ and $x = 2$.

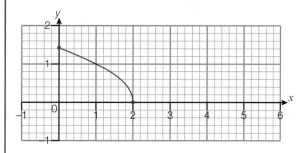

Transfer the sketch from your GDC onto paper. Even though the graph has no values outside $0 \leq x \leq 2$, you should still make the x-axis extend to $x = 6$, so that it includes all of the given domain.

The range is $0 \leq f(x) \leq 1.41$.

When x gets bigger than 2, the quantity inside the square root becomes negative. It is impossible to find the square root of a negative number, so this has restricted the domain and range of (x).

Plotting a graph

Worked example 17.6

Q. If $f(x) = 2x^3 - x + 2$ and $g(x) = 3x - 1$, plot $f(x)$ and $g(x)$ on the same graph. Use your graph to find the coordinates of the point where the two functions intersect. Take the domain to be $-2 \le x \le 2$.

A.

x	-2	-1	0	1	2
$f(x) = 2x^3 - x + 2$	-12	1	2	3	16

x	-2	-1	0	1	2
$g(x) = 3x - 1$	-7	-4	-1	2	5

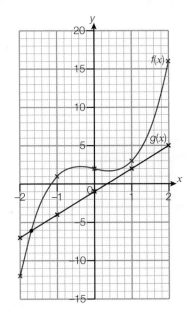

The two functions cross at the point $(-1.7, -6.1)$.

Exercise 17.5

1. Consider the function $f(x) = \sqrt{1-x}$.

   (a) Sketch $f(x)$ for the domain $-4 \le x \le 4$.

   (b) Comment on the range of $f(x)$.

   (c) Let $g(x) = 5 + f(x)$ for $-4 \le x \le 4$. Deduce the range of $g(x)$. Justify your answer.

2. (a) Sketch the graph of the function $f(x) = 3^x$ for the domain $-1 \le x \le 3$, and write down the range of $f(x)$.

(b) Sketch the graph of the function $g(x) = 3^x + \left(\dfrac{1}{3}\right)^x$ for the domain $-1 \le x \le 3$, and state the range of $g(x)$.

(c) Sketch the graph of the function $h(x) = 3^x - \left(\dfrac{1}{3}\right)^x$ for the same domain, and state the range of $h(x)$.

(d) Using your results from above, deduce the range of $g(x) + h(x)$. Justify your answer.

3. For each of the following functions, use your GDC to draw the graph, then look at the main features of the graph and hence sketch it on paper. Take the domain of each function to be $-3 \le x \le 3$.

(a) $f(x) = \dfrac{5x+1}{2x-3}$

(b) $f(x) = \dfrac{x+7}{x^2-4} + 5$

(c) $f(x) = 2 - \dfrac{x^2}{x+1}$

(d) $f(x) = x^2 + x - \dfrac{8}{x^2}$

4. Plot the graphs of the following pairs of functions for the domain $-3 \le x \le 3$. In each case give the coordinates of the points where the two functions intersect to 2 s.f.

(a) $f(x) = x^2 + x - \dfrac{1}{x}$, $g(x) = 2x - 1$

(b) $f(x) = 2^x - x^2$, $g(x) = 2x - 1$

(c) $f(x) = 3 \times 2^x + 1$, $g(x) = 1 - x$

(d) $f(x) = \dfrac{5x+1}{2x-1}$, $g(x) = x + 2$

Solving equations using graphs on your GDC

As you saw in Chapter 2, there are standard algebraic methods for solving linear, simultaneous and quadratic equations. However, many equations are very difficult to solve with algebra, and can often be solved much more easily by looking at a graph. Using a graph is also helpful because, as long as the domain and range are well chosen, it can show you **all** the solutions to an equation. If you use an equation solver on your GDC, you might find only one solution when there are several.

To solve equations with a graph, draw the function on the left-hand side of the equals sign as one line or curve, and the function on the right-hand side of the equation as another line or curve on the same graph; then look at where they intersect. The x-coordinate of each intersection will be a root of the equation.

For example, to solve the equation $x^3 - 3x^2 + 2x + 1 = \frac{1}{2}x - 1$, take the two functions $f(x) = x^3 - 3x^2 + 2x + 1$ and $g(x) = \frac{1}{2}x - 1$ and draw their graphs on the same axes.

The graph of $g(x)$ is a straight line, while the graph of $f(x)$ is a cubic curve with two turning points. You might expect that the equation will have three solutions, but by drawing the actual graphs on the same set of axes you will see that there is only one intersection.

You can use the intersection tool on your GDC to locate the point of intersection (see '19.2 (a) Solving unfamiliar equations using a graph' on page 684 of the GDC chapter for a reminder of how to use this tool if you need to).

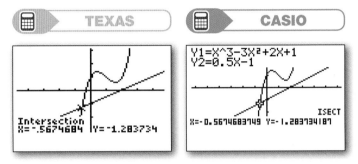

The GDC tells you that the curves intersect at $(-0.567, -1.28)$, so the solution to the equation $x^3 - 3x^2 + 2x + 1 = \frac{1}{2}x - 1$ is $x = -0.567$.

You can learn and practise this technique by plotting graphs on paper too.

Remember that you should round the answers given by the GDC to three significant figures if no other specific degree of accuracy has been requested.

Worked example 17.7

Q. The functions $f(x)$ and $h(x)$ are defined as $f(x) = 2^x + 1$ and $h(x) = 9 - x^2$ over the domain $-4 \le x \le 4$.

(a) Fill in the missing values in the following table.

x	−4	−3	−2	0	1	3	4
$f(x)$	1.0625		1.25	2		9	
$h(x)$	−7	0		9	8		−7

(b) Using a scale of 2 cm to represent one unit on the x-axis and 1 cm to represent two units on the y-axis, draw both functions on the same graph.

(c) Use your graph to find the solutions to the equation $2^x + 1 = 9 - x^2$. Give the answer to 1 d.p.

continued . . .

A. (a)

x	-4	-3	-2	0	1	3	4
$f(x)$	1.0625	1.125	1.25	2	3	9	17
$h(x)$	-7	0	5	9	8	0	-7

Substitute the given values of x into the algebraic expressions for $f(x)$ and $h(x)$. Label each curve.

(b)

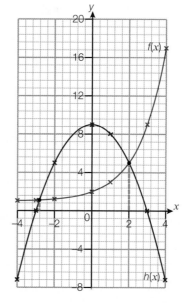

Plot the points from (a) on a set of axes drawn according to the given scale. Then draw a curve through each set of points. Label each curve.

Read off the x-coordinates of the two points of intersection. It can be helpful to draw dashed lines from the points of intersection to the x-axis.

(c) The solutions are $x = 2.0$ and $x = -2.8$.

Worked example 17.8

Plot the graphs of $y = \frac{2}{x+1}$ and $y = 1 - 2^{-x}$ on your GDC. Be careful when you enter the equations into your calculator. Use brackets for $(x + 1)$ and $2^{(-x)}$ to make sure that your GDC does the intended calculations.

Q. Find the solutions of the equation $\dfrac{2}{x+1} = 1 - 2^{-x}$.

A.

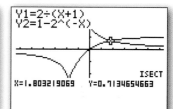

TEXAS

CASIO

Intersection
X=-1.803219   Y=-2.489981

Y1=2÷(X+1)
Y2=1-2^(-X)

ISECT
X=1.803219069   Y=0.7134654663

Find the x-coordinates of the two points of intersection. (See '19.2 (a) Solving unfamiliar equations using a graph' on page 684 of the GDC chapter for a reminder of how to use this tool if you need to).

The solutions are $x = -1.80$ and $x = 1.80$.

Exercise 17.6

1. The functions $f(x)$ and $g(x)$ are defined as $f(x) = x^2 - 2x$ and $g(x) = 2 - x$ for $-2 \leq x \leq 4$.

   (a) Copy the following table and fill in the missing values.

x	-2	-1	0	1	2	3	4
$f(x)$			0				8
$g(x)$			2				-2

   (b) Draw both functions on the same set of axes.

   (c) Use your graph to find the solutions to the equation
   $x^2 - 2x = 2 - x$.

2. The functions $f(x)$ and $g(x)$ are defined as $f(x) = 2x^3 - 1$ and $g(x) = 5x$ for $-2 \leq x \leq 2$.

   (a) Copy the following table and fill in the missing values.

x	-2	-1	0	1	2
$f(x)$					
$g(x)$					

   (b) Draw both functions on the same set of axes on graph paper.

   (c) Use your graph from (b) to find the solutions to the equation
   $2x^3 - 1 = 5x$. Give your answer to 1 d.p.

3. The functions $f(x)$ and $g(x)$ are defined as $f(x) = 3^x - 2$ and $g(x) = 1 - 2x - x^2$ for $-4 \leq x \leq 2$.

   (a) Copy the following table and fill in the missing values.

x	-4	-3	-2	-1	0	1	2
$f(x)$			-1.89				7
$g(x)$			1				-7

   (b) Draw both functions on the same set of axes on graph paper.

   (c) Use your graph to find the solutions to the equation
   $3^x - 2 = 1 - 2x - x^2$. If your answer is not exact, give it to 1 d.p.

4. Let $f(x) = x^3 - 3x^2 + 5x + 2$ and $g(x) = 7x - 5$.

   (a) Use your GDC to draw both functions on the same set of axes.

   (b) State the number of intersections of the two functions.

   (c) Hence find all the solutions of the equation $f(x) = g(x)$ to 1 d.p.

5. For each of the following pairs of functions, draw both functions on the same set of axes on your GDC, and hence:

   (i) state the number of intersections of the two functions

   (ii) find all the solutions to the equation $f(x) = g(x)$.

   (a) $f(x) = \sqrt{5x + 7}$ and $g(x) = x^3 + 2.451$

   (b) $f(x) = 2^{x+1}$ and $g(x) = 3^x$

   (c) $f(x) = 6.15 \times 9^x$ and $g(x) = 2.78 \times 10^{2x}$

   (d) $f(x) = 2^x - 4$ and $g(x) = \dfrac{3x}{x - 2}$

   (e) $f(x) = x^3 - 7x + 1$ and $g(x) = 8 - 5^x$

   (f) $f(x) = 3 - x^2$ and $g(x) = \dfrac{x - 1}{7 - 4x}$

6. Solve the following equations with your GDC, using the graphical method.

   (a) $x^2 = 3x + 6$

   (b) $-3x^3 + 2 = 8x^2 - 3x$

   (c) $1.5 - x^3 = 4x^2 + x - 3.142$

   (d) $x^4 - x^2 - 9 = x^2 + 6$

   (e) $x^4 + 5x^2 + 0.2 = 4x^3 + 3x - 1$

   (f) $1.7x^2 + 0.875x - 1.4 = 1.5x^4 + 4x^3 - 0.5$

   (g) $(x - 2)(x + 1)(x + 4) = 0.732x + 1.926$

7. Solve the following equations with your GDC, using the graphical method.

   (a) $1.02^t = 5$

   (b) $40^{0.0125x} = 25^{0.336x}$

   (c) $17 \times 2^{0.47t} = 23$

   (d) $28^{(5x + 0.336)} = 43^{0.127x}$

   (e) $2^x + 5^x = 7^x + 0.125$

   (f) $3.958^x = x^3 - 7x - 4$

   (g) $2.2 - \left(\dfrac{3}{4}\right)^x = 9.645 \times 10^x$

   (h) $\left(\dfrac{1}{3}\right)^x = 2.632 - 5^{2-x}$

Summary

You should know:

- the concept of a function and the definitions of domain and range

- how to recognise and use function notation

- how to interpret the graph of a function and use it to find the domain and range

- how to recognise and identify simple rational functions and asymptotes

- how to draw or plot accurate graphs

- how to sketch a graph from information given

- how to use a GDC and the hand-drawn graphical method to solve equations that involve combinations of the functions studied in this course.

Mixed examination practice

Exam-style questions

1. A function is defined as $f(x) = 7x - 13$.

   (a) Find $f(0)$.

   (b) State the value of $f(3)$.

   (c) Find an expression for:

       (i) $f(a)$

       (ii) $f(a - 2)$

2. The graph of the function $f(x)$ is shown below.

   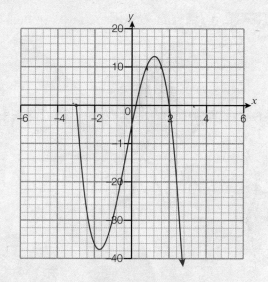

   (a) Write down the domain of the function.

   (b) State the range of $f(x)$.

   (c) Given that $f(k) = 0$, find all the possible values of k.

3. Sketch the graphs of the following functions for $-5 \leq x \leq 5$. In each case:

   (i) State the equation of the vertical asymptote.

   (ii) Find the horizontal asymptote.

   (a) $f(x) = \dfrac{3}{2 - x}$

   (b) $g(x) = 4 + \dfrac{5}{9x - 7}$

4. Use your GDC to draw the graph of the function $f(x) = \dfrac{7x-5}{1-8x} + 4$, with domain $-3 \le x \le 3$. Look at the main features of the graph and hence sketch the function on paper.

5. The functions $f(x)$ and $g(x)$ are defined as $f(x) = 1 - 4x - x^3$ and $g(x) = 7 - 2x$ for $-3 \le x \le 3$.

   (a) Copy the following table and fill in the missing values.

x	−3	−2	−1	0	1	2	3
$f(x)$							
$g(x)$							

   (b) Draw both functions on the same set of axes.

   (c) Use your graph from (b) to find the solutions to the equation $1 - 4x - x^3 = 7 - 2x$. Give your answer to 1 d.p.

6. Two functions are defined as $f(x) = 3 + 5^{x-1}$ and $g(x) = 4 + 3x + 6x^2 - x^4$. Both functions have the same domain, $-3 \le x \le 3$.

   (a) Use your GDC to draw both functions on the same set of axes.

   (b) State the number of intersections of the two functions.

   (c) Hence find all the solutions of the equation $f(x) = g(x)$ to 1 d.p.

Chapter 18 Linear and quadratic models

In the introduction to Topic 6, you saw an outline of the steps of **mathematical modelling** and problem-solving described by the mathematician George Pólya:

1. understand the problem

2. make a plan

3. carry out your plan

4. look back at your solution to see whether you can improve it or use it in another context.

Understanding the problem can take time. You need to clarify what you need to find or show, draw diagrams, and check that you have enough information. It may even be that you have too much information and need to decide what is relevant and what is not.

Making a plan can involve several different strategies. Your first idea may not give you a solution directly, but might suggest a better approach. You could look for patterns, draw more diagrams, or set up equations. You could also try to solve a similar, simpler version of the problem and see if that gives you some more insight.

If you have worked hard on the first two stages, **carrying out the plan** should be the most straightforward stage. Work out your solution according to the plan and test it. You may have to adjust the plan, but in doing so it will have given you further insights that may lead to a correct solution next time.

It is important to **look back at your solution** and reflect on what you have learned and why this plan worked when others did not. This will help you to become more confident in solving the next problem — and the one after that.

In this chapter and the next, you will learn how to solve problems using mathematical models that involve particular types of function, namely linear, quadratic, polynomial and exponential functions.

 It will be easier to study this chapter if you have already completed Chapters 2, 14 and 17.

> **In this chapter you will learn:**
> - about linear functions and their graphs
> - how to use linear models
> - about quadratic functions and their graphs (parabolae)
> - about the properties of a parabola: its symmetry, vertex and intercepts on the x-axis and y-axis
> - how to use quadratic models.

18.1 Linear models

In Chapter 2, the general equation of a straight line (known as a linear equation) was given as $y = mx + c$.

After meeting function notation in Chapter 17, you now know that the same relationship can be written as $f(x) = mx + c$, to express that the input x and the output y, or $f(x)$, are related through a **linear function** whose graph is a straight line with gradient m and y-intercept c.

Many practical situations may be modelled with linear functions. For example, monthly telephone costs typically include a fixed charge plus a charge per minute; a plumber's fee is usually made up of a fixed 'call-out' charge plus further costs depending on how long the job takes.

In Chapter 4 you studied currency conversions, where each currency is linked to another via a linear function. When you are travelling abroad and using a different currency on the metro or in shops and restaurants, a straight-line graph can help you to quickly get an idea of prices.

Imagine that Logan travels from Australia to India on holiday. He changes Australian dollars (AUD) into Indian rupees (INR), and the exchange rate at the time gives him 48 INR for 1 AUD. Using this exchange rate, he draws a conversion graph that plots the number of rupees against the number of Australian dollars:

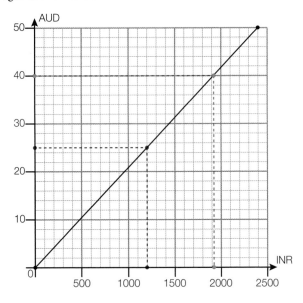

Now that Logan has this picture in his head, he can convert between INR and AUD with confidence. The graph quickly tells him, for instance, that:

- 1200 INR = 25 AUD

- 40 AUD ≈ 1900 INR.

The gradient of the graph is $m = \frac{1}{48}$ and, as 0 INR = 0 AUD, the y-axis intercept is at the origin. So the function can be written as $A(x) = \frac{1}{48}x$, where x represents the number of Indian rupees and $A(x)$ the number of Australian dollars.

Logan takes a taxi. The taxi company charges a fixed fee of 16 INR for all journeys, plus 10 INR for each kilometre travelled. The total cost of a journey is also a linear function.

If Logan travels x kilometres, he pays $10 \times x$ INR for this distance on top of the fixed charge of 16 INR, so the total cost function is $C(x) = 16 + 10x$.

Suppose Logan travels 8 km. How much will he pay?

$C(8) = 16 + 8 \times 10 = 96$ INR

If Logan pays 120 INR for a taxi ride, how far has he travelled?

$120 = 16 + 10x$

$120 - 16 = 10x$

$x = 10.4$ km

He visits a friend, and the friend recommends another taxi company, which has a lower initial charge but a higher charge per kilometre. This company's cost function is $D(x) = 4 + 14x$.

Logan needs to make a 20 km trip. He wants to know which of the two companies will be cheaper; he also wants to find out for what distance both companies will charge the same amount.

A graph can answer both questions. Drawing the two linear functions on a GDC makes it simple to find the **break-even point** where the charges of both companies will be the same — it is the point of intersection of the two lines:

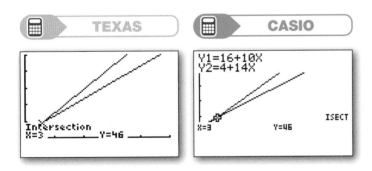

For $x = 20$:

$C(x) = 16 + 10 \times 20 = 216$ INR

$D(x) = 4 + 14 \times 20 = 284$ INR

so the first company will be cheaper.

Looking at the graph, the break-even point occurs at 3 km, for which the cost is 46 rupees. For journeys longer than 3 km Logan should use the first company, but for short journeys the second company would be cheaper.

Worked example 18.1

Q. Nimmi and her Theatre Studies group are presenting a show at the Iowa Festival Fringe. Nimmi is in charge of publicity and needs to order leaflets to advertise their show. A local printer quotes her '$40 to set up and 2 cents for every leaflet'.

(a) Write down the cost function in the form $C(p) = mp + c$, where p is the number of leaflets and $C(p)$ is total cost of printing them.

(b) What is the cost of 600 leaflets?

She finds a printer on the Internet who will charge her $32 as an initial cost, then 3 cents for every leaflet.

(c) Write down the cost function for the second printer in the form $D(p) = mp + c$.

(d) If the bill from the online printer is $77, how many leaflets did Nimmi order?

(e) What is the break-even point where the two printers charge the same?

First, make sure you are working with consistent units. There are 100 cents in a dollar, so 2 cents = $0.02.

A. (a) $C(p) = 40 + 0.02p$

To find the cost of 600 leaflets, substitute 600 for p in the function's formula.

(b) $C(600) = 40 + 600 \times 0.02 = 52$

so the cost is $52.

This is similar to part (a), but with different values of m and c.

(c) $D(p) = 32 + 0.03p$

The bill from the online printer is $D(p)$, so we need to solve $D(p) = 77$.

(d) $77 = 32 + 0.03p$

$45 = 0.03p$

$p = 1500$

$\longrightarrow$

continued . . .

continued . . .

(e)

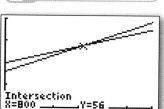

The break-even point is at 800 leaflets.

The break-even point is where $C(p) = D(p)$. Plot both functions on your GDC and look for their intersection (see '2.1 (a) Solving linear equations using a graph' on page 652 of the GDC chapter if you need a reminder of how to use your GDC here).

Worked example 18.2

Q. A company that makes hinges has fixed costs of €10,000. Each hinge costs €5 to make and is sold for €12.50.

(a) Write down the cost function.

(b) Write down the revenue function.

(c) Find the point at which the company starts to make a profit.

(d) What is the profit when the company makes 2400 hinges?

The cost function is made up of the fixed cost plus the cost of making the hinges at €5 per hinge.

A. (a) Let H be the number of hinges made; then they will cost €$5H$ in total to make.
$$C(H) = 10000 + 5H$$

The revenue is the amount earned from selling the hinges.

(b) $R(H) = 12.5H$

The company will start to make a profit when the revenue first becomes greater than the cost, so we need to look for the point where $C(H) = R(H)$, i.e. the break-even point. You can solve this equation with algebra or by plotting graphs on your GDC.

(c)

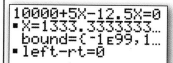

continued . . .

$$10000 + 5H = 12.5H$$
$$10000 = 7.5H$$
$$H = 1333.33\ldots$$

The company starts to make a profit when it manufactures more than 1333 hinges.

> The profit is the revenue minus the cost.

> To find the profit from 2400 hinges, substitute 2400 for *p* in the profit function.

(d) $P(H) = R(H) - C(H) = 12.5H - (10000 + 5H)$
$P(2400) = 30000 - 22000 = 8000$
so the profit is €8000.

Exercise 18.1

1. The Thompsons are planning a holiday. They want to rent a family car and see the following two advertisements in a newspaper:

ZOOM CAR RENTALS

Flat fee: $30

plus

$0.20 per mile

SAFE RIDE RENTALS

Flat fee: $50

plus

$0.15 per mile

The cost of renting a car from Zoom can be expressed as:

$$C = 30 + 0.2m$$

where *C* is the total cost in dollars and *m* is the number of miles driven.

(a) Write a similar equation for the cost of renting a car from Safe Ride.

(b) What is the total number of miles that would make rental costs the same for both companies?

(c) Which of the two companies should the Thompsons use if they plan to drive at least 1000 miles? Justify your answer.

2. The Martins have switched their natural gas supply to a company called De GAS. The monthly bill consists of a standing charge of £6.50 and an additional charge of £0.035 per unit of gas used.

(a) If the Martins use *n* units of gas in a month, write an equation to represent the total monthly charge, $C(n)$, in pounds.

(b) Calculate their bill when the Martins use 1300 units in a calendar month.

(c) The Martins were charged £70.90 in one month. Calculate the number of units of gas they used that month.

3. The Browns are reviewing their electricity consumption. Their monthly bill includes a standing charge of £5.18 and an additional charge of £0.13 per kWh of electricity used.

(a) Assuming the Browns use n units (kWh) of energy per month, write an equation to represent the total monthly cost of electricity, $C(n)$, in pounds.

(b) In one month the Browns used 500 units of electricity. Calculate the total cost of the energy used.

(c) The electricity bill for the Browns was £89.68 in one calendar month. Determine the number of units used in that month.

4. Emma is considering the following two advertisements in the local newspaper:

GYM BUDDIES

$120 annual subscription

plus

$5 per visit

FIT MATES

$300 annual subscription

plus

$2 per visit

(a) For how many visits in a year will the cost of the two gym services be the same?

(b) Which of the two gyms should Emma use if she plans to make:

(i) no more than 52 visits a year?

(ii) at least 70 visits a year?

(c) Work out the difference in cost for (i) and (ii) in part (b).

5. Larisa and her friends are setting up a Young Enterprise company in their school to design and sell birthday cards. Initial set-up costs amount to £120. The cost of producing each card is 90 pence.

(a) Work out how many cards they have to sell to break even if each card is sold for:

(i) £1.70   (ii) £1.90   (iii) £2.10

(b) How much profit can they expect to make if they sell 300 cards at £1.90 each?

(c) How much profit would be made if they sold the first 100 cards at £1.70 each and the next 200 cards at £2.10 each?

(d) What would the estimated profit be if they sold the first 200 cards at £1.70 each and the next 100 cards at £2.10 each?

In Chapter 2 you learned that a **quadratic equation**:

- is an equation of the general form $ax^2 + bx + c = 0$ where $a \neq 0$

- can have no solution, one solution or two possible solutions.

The concept of a **quadratic function** is broader. A quadratic function is a function having the general form:

$$f(x) = ax^2 + bx + c \text{ where } a \neq 0$$

Rather than concentrating on solutions to the equation $ax^2 + bx + c = 0$, as we did in Chapter 2, we will now look at other properties of the function $f(x) = ax^2 + bx + c$, and discuss how to use such a function in mathematical modelling.

Using your GDC, draw graphs of $f(x) = ax^2$ for different values of a. Try both positive and negative values. (See '22.2G Graphs' on page 645 of the GDC chapter for a reminder of how to plot graphs if you need to.)

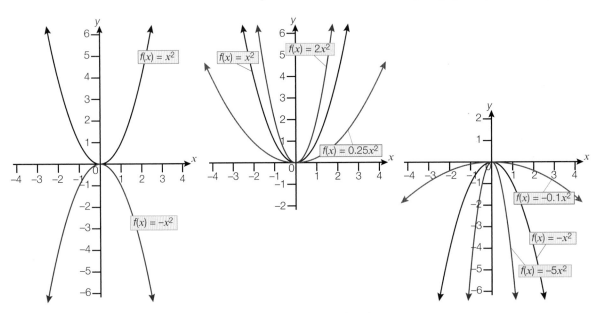

Compare your graphs. What do you notice?

You should see that:

- If a is positive, the function has a minimum point.

- If a is negative, the function has a maximum point.

- As the magnitude of a increases (whether it is positive or negative), the parabola becomes steeper.

- As the magnitude of a decreases, the parabola becomes shallower.

You should also have observed that the graph is symmetrical: there is a **line of symmetry** (also called an axis of symmetry) that cuts the curve in half so that each side is the mirror image of the other. The line of symmetry runs through the maximum or minimum point. This turning point, where the curve changes direction, is called the **vertex** of the parabola.

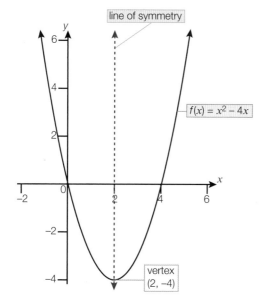

Equation of the line of symmetry

Using your GDC, draw graphs of $f(x) = ax^2 + bx + c$ with different values of a and b. See if you can find a link between the values of a and b that will give you an equation for the line of symmetry.

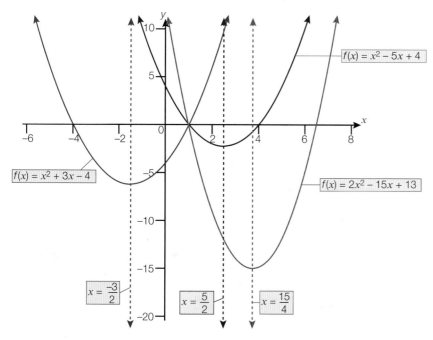

Function	$f(x) = x^2 - 5x + 4$	$f(x) = x^2 + 3x - 4$	$f(x) = 2x^2 - 15x + 13$
Location of line of symmetry	$x = \dfrac{5}{2}$	$x = \dfrac{-3}{2}$	$x = \dfrac{15}{4}$

 hint

Remember that the coefficient is the number that multiplies a variable.

In the examples above, look at the **coefficient** of the x^2 term and the coefficient of the x term.

In each case, if you take the coefficient of the x term (e.g. -5), change its sign (e.g. 5), divide by the coefficient of the x^2 term (e.g. 1) and then divide again by 2, you get the location of the line of symmetry (e.g. $x = \frac{5}{2}$).

This gives us a general formula for the line of symmetry of a quadratic function.

 $a = \pi r^2$ For the quadratic function $f(x) = ax^2 + bx + c$, the equation of the line of symmetry is $x = \dfrac{-b}{2a}$.

The vertex of a parabola

As the vertex of the parabola lies on the line of symmetry, you can use the line of symmetry as the x-coordinate to calculate the corresponding y-coordinate of the vertex.

For example, $f(x) = x^2 - 5x + 4$ has line of symmetry $x = \frac{5}{2}$.

Substituting this value of x into the function, we get:

$$y = f\left(\frac{5}{2}\right) = \left(\frac{5}{2}\right)^2 - 5\left(\frac{5}{2}\right) + 4 = -\frac{9}{4}$$

So the vertex is the point $\left(\frac{5}{2}, -\frac{9}{4}\right)$.

You could also find the vertex and line of symmetry of a parabola using your GDC, but in that case you would work the other way round, locating first the vertex and then the line of symmetry. See '*18.1 Using a graph to find the vertex and line of symmetry of a parabola*' on page 680 of the GDC chapter if you need a reminder of how.

For example, to find the vertex of $f(x) = 4 + 6x - x^2$, draw the graph of $y = 4 + 6x - x^2$ on your GDC, and find the coordinates of the maximum point.

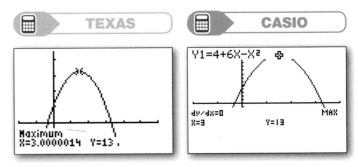

The maximum point is at $(3, 13)$, so the equation of the line of symmetry is $x = 3$.

Worked example 18.3

Q. Draw the function $f(x) = 2x^2 - 7x + 8$ on your GDC.

(a) Write down the coordinates of the vertex.

(b) Write down the equation of the line of symmetry.

(c) Write down the range of the function.

 RR *If you need a reminder of what the range is, look back at section 17.1.*

(d) What is the range of the function $-f(x)$?

A.

TEXAS	CASIO

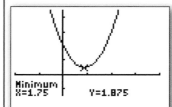 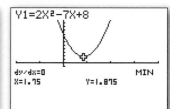

Enter $y = 2x^2 - 7x + 8$ into your GDC and draw its graph.

Use your GDC to find the coordinates of the minimum point. See section '18.1' on page 680 of the GDC chapter if you need to.

(a) The vertex is at $(1.75, 1.875)$.

The equation of the line of symmetry is given by the x-coordinate of the vertex.

(b) The line of symmetry is $x = 1.75$.

Check using the formula $x = \dfrac{-b}{2a}$.

$$x = \frac{-(-7)}{2 \times 2} = 1.75$$

As the minimum is at (1.75, 1.875), the graph never has a y-value less than 1.875, though it can extend arbitrarily far upwards.

(c) The range is $f(x) \geq 1.875$.

continued . . .

(d)

TEXAS

CASIO

Draw the graph of $-f(x)$ on your GDC by entering $y = -(2x^2 - 7x + 8)$. You can see that this is just the graph of $f(x)$ reflected in the x-axis, so the minimum has now become a maximum.

Maximum
X=1.75   Y=-1.875

Y1=-(2X²-7X+8)

dy/dx=0
X=1.75   Y=-1.875   MAX

$-f(x) \leq -1.875$

Exercise 18.2A

1. Draw the following functions on your GDC. In each case:

   (i) Write down the coordinates of the vertex.

   (ii) State the equation of the line of symmetry.

   (iii) Write down the range of the function.

   (a) $f(x) = x^2 + 3x$
   (b) $f(x) = x^2 - 7x + 2$

   (c) $f(x) = -2x^2 + x - 6$
   (d) $g(x) = 9 - 4x + 3x^2$

   (e) $g(x) = (x - 3)(x + 5)$
   (f) $g(x) = 1 - (x + 1)(2 - x)$

   (g) $h(x) = \dfrac{1}{2}x^2 - \dfrac{3}{4}x + \dfrac{5}{2}$
   (h) $f(x) = 5.3 + 4.9x - 0.7x^2$

2. By sketching the graph of each of the following quadratic functions, find the coordinates of the vertex and hence:

   (i) state the maximum or minimum value of the function

   (ii) determine the equation of the line of symmetry

   (iii) state the range of the function.

   (a) $f(x) = 1.44 - 0.1x^2$

   (b) $g(x) = 10 - (5 - 2x)^2$

   (c) $h(x) = 3(x + 1.7)^2 + 8$

Intercepts on the x and y axes

The quadratic function $f(x) = ax^2 + bx + c$ will always have **one** *y*-**intercept** — it is the value of $f(x)$ when $x = 0$, which is just the number c.

With *x*-**intercepts**, there are three different situations that can arise.

(a)	(b)	(c)
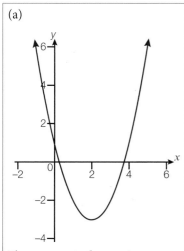	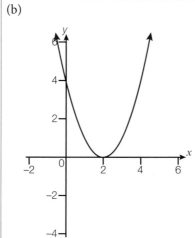	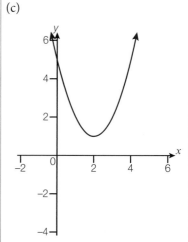
The curve cuts the *x*-axis at two points.	The curve touches the *x*-axis at one point.	The curve does not touch or cross the *x*-axis.

In (a), there are two places where the function crosses the *x*-axis; so there are two *x*-intercepts. If you are using the graph to solve a quadratic equation, you can say that there are two solutions to the equation, or two real **roots**.

In (b), the parabola just touches the *x*-axis tangentially at one point, so there is only one solution to the equation $ax^2 + bx + c = 0$.

 Tangentially means that the curve only touches the axis at a single point and does not cross the axis. You will learn about tangents in Chapter 20.

 GDC

Some calculators use the word 'zero' instead of 'solution' or 'root'.

In (c), the curve does not meet the *x*-axis at all, so there are no *x*-intercepts and thus no solutions to the equation $ax^2 + bx + c = 0$.

After drawing the graph of a quadratic function $f(x) = ax^2 + bx + c$ on your GDC, you can easily use it to locate the solutions of $ax^2 + bx + c = 0$ (i.e. the *x*-intercepts); see '*18.2 Using a graph to find the zeros (roots) of a quadratic equation*' on page 681 of the GDC chapter if you need a reminder of how to do this.

Worked example 18.4

Q. Use your GDC to draw the following functions:

$$f(x) = 3x^2 - 2x + 1, \qquad g(x) = 5 + x - 2x^2, \qquad h(x) = x^2 + 4x$$

(a) Write down the y-intercept of $h(x)$.

(b) Which function(s) has/have two x-intercepts?

(c) Which function has no x-intercept?

(d) Consider the function $j(x) = x^2 + 4x + 4$. How many x-intercepts does this function have? Write down the value(s) of x at the intercept(s).

A.

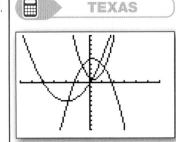
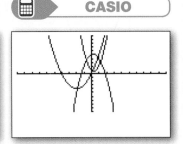

> If all three graphs are plotted on the same axes, you can tell them apart by observing that $g(x)$ is the curve with a maximum point, and $h(x)$ is the curve that goes through $(0, 0)$.

> The y-intercept is the point on the graph where $x = 0$.

(a) The y-intercept of $h(x)$ is $(0, 0)$.

(b) $g(x)$ and $h(x)$ have two x-intercepts.

> The minimum point of $f(x)$ is above the x-axis, so the curve will never touch or cross the x-axis.

(c) $f(x)$ has no x-intercept.

(d)

> Draw the graph of $j(x)$. It touches the x-axis at the point $(-2, 0)$. Alternatively, note that $j(x) = h(x) + 4$, so the graph of $j(x)$ is just the graph of $h(x)$ shifted up by 4 units; the vertex $(-2, -4)$ of $h(x)$ becomes the vertex $(-2, 0)$ of $j(x)$ on the x-axis.

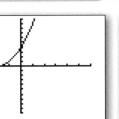
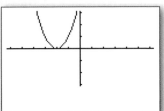

$j(x)$ has one x-intercept at $x = -2$.

Exercise 18.2B

1. Find the coordinates of the points where the graph $y = x^2 - 2x - 7$ intersects the x-axis.

2. Consider the following functions:

$$f(x)= 6x^2 - 13x - 5, \quad g(x) = x^2 + 3x + 5, \quad h(x) = \frac{16}{9}x^2 - \frac{20x}{3} + \frac{25}{4}$$

   (a) Which of the three functions from above has:

   (i) two x intercepts?   (ii) no x intercepts?   (iii) one x intercept?

   (b) State the y-intercept of each of the three functions.

3. Draw the graphs of the following quadratic functions on your GDC, and in each case state the coordinates of:

   (i) the x-intercepts   (ii) the y-intercept

   (a) $y = 3x^2 - 12$ (b) $y = 16 - 9x^2$

   (c) $y = 8 - x(x - 5)$ (d) $y = (x - 3)^2 - (1 - 2x)^2$

   (e) $y = 1 + (2x - 7)(x + 3)$ (f) $f(x) = 3.144 - 1.07(2x - 5)^2$

If you are taking values from a sketch on your GDC, look carefully at the scale used for the window. If you set a scale of 1, you can count along the axes to get the x and y values. However, if you have used ZOOM FIT (TEXAS) or AUTO (CASIO), the GDC will set the scale, which is often diverse and complicated, with fractional scales, giving you a very different picture.

4. Consider the function $f(x) = 7x - 1.4x^2, -1 \le x \le 5.5$.

   (a) State the x-intercepts.

   (b) Write down the equation of the line of symmetry.

   (c) State the range of $f(x)$.

5. The diagram shows the graph of the function $f(x) = 18 - 11x - 2x^2$. Q is the vertex of the parabola; P, R and S are the intercepts with the axes.

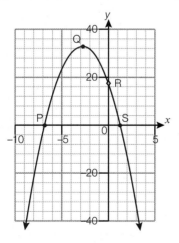

   (a) Use your GDC to find the coordinates of points P, Q, R and S.

   (b) State the range of the parabola.

   (c) Write down the equation of the line of symmetry.

Look around you. How many parabolas have you encountered today? Have you walked past a fountain or travelled over a suspension bridge? A quadratic function can be used to model all of these shapes.

Ask two friends to throw a ball to each other, and watch the path of the ball or, if you can, take a video of the ball-throwing and play it back frame by frame. The path of the ball looks like a parabola.

Galileo Galilei (1564–1642) was born in Pisa, Italy. He began to study medicine at the University of Pisa when he was 17, but did not complete his studies there, leaving in order to concentrate on philosophy and mathematics. In 1589, the university appointed him professor of mathematics, and a year later he wrote his book *De Moto* on the study of motion. At the time, with the development of guns and cannons, there was much interest in understanding the motion of projectiles. Galileo used a combination of experiments and mathematics to investigate how horizontal and vertical forces determine the path of a projectile; he showed that the path of a projectile can be modelled by a quadratic equation.

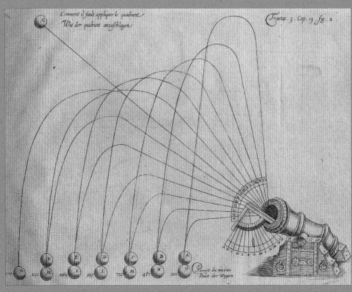

Quadratic functions can be used to solve problems in many real-life situations. Using a quadratic function to solve a problem is quite straightforward if you are given the function.

You learned about solving quadratic equations in Chapter 2.

Worked example 18.5

Q. The height of a ball that has been thrown up into the air can be modelled by the quadratic function $H(t) = a + bt - 4.9t^2$ where t is the time in seconds after the ball is thrown, a is the initial height of the ball in metres and b is the initial velocity of the ball.

(a) Amy is playing with a tennis ball. When the ball is at a height of 1.2 m above the ground she hits it vertically upwards with an initial velocity of 22 m s^{-1}. What is the ball's height after 2 seconds?

(b) Catherine can hit the ball harder. She hits the ball vertically upwards with an initial velocity of 26 m s^{-1} from a height of 1.5 m. When the ball reaches a height of 35.9 m, how long has it been in the air?

Substitute given values of a and b into the expression for $H(t)$.

To find the height after 2 seconds, substitute $t = 2$ in the function $H(t)$.

Find the function for Catherine in the same way.

If the height is 35.9 m, then $H(t) = 35.9$, and we need to solve this equation for t.

Use any method you like, for example the equation solver on your GDC; see '2.3 Solving quadratic equations' on page 656 of the GDC chapter if you need a reminder.

A. (a) For Amy, $a = 1.2$ and $b = 22$
$$H(t) = 1.2 + 22t - 4.9t^2$$

$$H(2) = 1.2 + 22 \times 2 - 4.9 \times 2^2 = 25.6\,\text{m}$$

(b) For Catherine, $a = 1.5$ and $b = 26$
$$H(t) = 1.5 + 26t - 4.9t^2$$

$$1.5 + 26t - 4.9t^2 = 35.9$$

From GDC: $t = 2.79$ seconds

Using a quadratic function to solve a problem is more complicated if you have to find an expression for the function first.

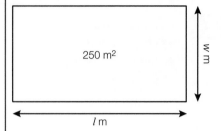

Worked example 18.6

Q. The area of a rectangular vegetable garden is 250 m². The perimeter of the plot is 65 m. What are the dimensions of the garden?

250 m²

w m

l m

> First, express the given information using algebra. The perimeter is made up of two lengths plus two widths.

A. $P = 2w + 2l = 65$

$w + l = 32.5$

so $l = 32.5 - w$

> The area of the garden is length times width. We now have a quadratic equation.

$A = l \times w = 250$

$(32.5 - w)w = 250$

$32.5w - w^2 = 250$

> Now we can find w by solving this quadratic equation. First rearrange it into the general form.

$w^2 - 32.5w + 250 = 0$

> Use your GDC to solve (see Section '*2.3 Solving quadratic equations*' on page 656 if you need to.)

From GDC: $w = 12.5$ or $w = 20$

> Calculate the corresponding values of l.

If $w = 12.5$, then $l = 32.5 - 12.5 = 20$

If $w = 20$, then $l = 32.5 - 20 = 12.5$

> Notice that either of the two solutions for w will give the same overall set of dimensions.

The dimensions are 12.5 m × 20 m.

There is another way that you can investigate quadratic functions to model parabolas that you see in everyday life. Your GDC can fit a curve to any coordinates that you give it, and find the equation that fits your data the closest. It can also give you the product moment correlation coefficient, so that you know how accurate the equation is as a model for your data. See '*18.3 Using the statistics menu to find an equation*' on page 682 of the GDC chapter for a reminder if you need to.

《《RR *You learned about product moment correlation coefficients in Chapter 12.*

Worked example 18.7

Q. Kitty sees an arch that she thinks is in the shape of a parabola. She takes a photograph, and then lays a grid over the picture to read off some coordinates. She finds the following coordinates:

x	0	2	4	5	6
y	0.4	1.2	2.8	4.2	7.0

Use this table of coordinates to determine if Kitty is correct; is the arch is in the shape of a parabola?

> Enter the coordinates into your GDC and draw a scatter graph. (See '*12.1 Drawing a scatter diagram of bivariate data*' on page 672 of the GDC chapter if you need a reminder of how to draw a scatter diagram on your GDC.)

A.

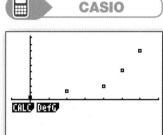

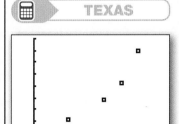

> The scatter graph confirms Kitty's idea because it shows a positive correlation between the x and y coordinates; use your GDC to fit a curve to the points and find an equation of the curve. (See '*18.3 Using the statistics menu to find an equation*' on page 682 of the GDC if you need to.)

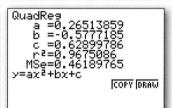

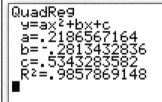

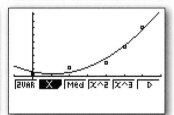

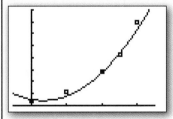

Equation of the curve:

$y = 0.22x^2 - 0.28x + 0.53$

$r = 0.99$ (2 d.p.)

Equation of the curve:

$y = 0.27x^2 - 0.58x + 0.63$

$r = 0.98$ (2 d.p.)

The value of r suggests there is a strong positive correlation between the x- and y-coordinates and the equation of the curve calculated by the GDC. The equation of the curve contains x^2 and is therefore a quadratic, which suggests that Kitty was correct in thinking the arch is in the shape of a parabola.

hint

You will see that the two GDCs have given different results for the coefficients of the quadratic function, even though both curves seem to fit quite well; this is because they are using different formulae to calculate the quadratic curve of best fit. If you use this curve-fitting technique in a project, it might be an issue to discuss when you are assessing the validity of your results.

Using the same method, you could fit a quadratic function to the path of the ball thrown between two people that we mentioned at the beginning of this section.

Exercise 18.3

1. Sabina hits a tennis ball vertically upwards from an initial height of 1.4 metres giving the ball an initial velocity of $20\,\mathrm{m\,s^{-1}}$.

   The flight of the ball can be modelled with the equation:

   $$h(t) = 1.4 + 20t - 4.9t^2$$

   where $h(t)$ is the height of the ball above the ground, t seconds after Sabina hit it.

   (a) Find the height of the ball after 1.5 seconds.

   (b) Use your GDC to draw the graph of $h(t)$ and hence find the maximum height of the ball above the ground during its flight.

   (c) Sabina catches the ball when it falls back to a height of 1.4 metres. Find the total time that the ball was in flight.

2. Joey reckons that the approximate distance it takes to stop a car, depending on the speed at which the car is travelling, can be modelled by the equation:

   $$y = 0.0555x^2 + 1.112x - 0.6494$$

   where y is the stopping distance in feet and x is the speed of the car in miles per hour.

   Use the model to predict estimates of the stopping distances in the following table to 1 d.p.

Speed, x (mph)	20	30	40	50	60	70
Stopping distance, y (feet)						

3. The profit made by a large Slovenian company can be modelled as a function of the expenditure on advertising:

   $$P(x) = 40.8 + 3.6x - 0.2x^2$$

   where P is the profit in millions of euros and x is the expenditure on advertising in millions of euros.

   (a) Use your GDC to sketch the graph of $P(x)$ for $0 \le x \le 30$.

   (b) Hence find the expenditure on advertising that will maximise the profit.

   (c) Calculate the estimated profit when the company spends €5 million on advertising.

4. Tom hits a golf ball. The height of the ball can be modelled by the equation:

$$h(t) = 7t - t^2$$

where $h(t)$ is the height of the ball in metres, t seconds after Tom hit it.

(a) What was the height of the ball after 3 seconds?

(b) After how long did the ball reach a height of 10 metres for the first time?

(c) What was the maximum height of the ball?

(d) For how long was the ball more than 8 metres above the ground?

5. In a game of cricket, the batsman hits the ball from ground level. The flight of the ball can be modelled by a parabola. The path of the ball is expressed as:

$$y = 1.732x - 0.049x^2$$

where y is the height of the ball in metres above the ground and x is the horizontal distance in metres travelled by the ball.

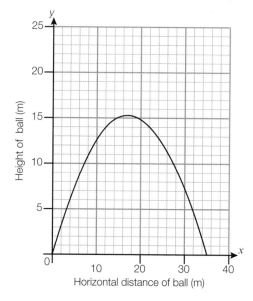

(a) Use your GDC to find:

(i) the maximum height reached by the ball

(ii) the horizontal distance travelled by the ball before it falls to the ground.

(b) Work out the height of the ball when:

(i) $x = 12$ m   (ii) $x = 20$ m.

(c) Find the horizontal distance of the ball from the batsman when the ball first reaches a height of 13 metres.

Summary

You should know:

- how to identify linear functions, $f(x) = mx + c$, and their graphs

- how to use linear models for solving practical problems

- how to identify quadratic functions, $f(x) = ax^2 + bx + c$, and their graphs (parabolae)

- about the various properties of a parabola:

  - the equation of its line of symmetry, $x = \dfrac{-b}{2a}$

  - how to find the coordinates of its vertex

  - how to find its intercepts on the x-axis and y-axis

- how to use quadratic models to solve practical problems.

Mixed examination practice

Exam-style questions

1. Draw the graph of the following functions on your GDC. In each case:

   (i) Write down the coordinates of the vertex.

   (ii) State the equation of the line of symmetry.

   (iii) Write down the range of the function.

   (a) $y = x(5x - 9)$ (b) $y = 7 - 2x^2$ (c) $y = x^2 - 3x - 28$

2. Sketch the graph of $f(x) = 11 - 4x - 6x^2$ on your GDC.

   (a) Find the maximum or minimum value of the function.

   (b) Determine the equation of the line of symmetry.

   (c) State the range of the function.

3. The Smiths are looking for a plumber. They find this advert in the local paper.

   > Sydner Plumber
   > $140 call out + $98 per hour

   The total charge, C, for plumbing services can be written as:

   $$C = a + bx$$

   where x is the number of hours taken to finish the work.

   (a) State the values of a and b.

   (b) How much will it cost the Smiths if it takes 5 hours to complete the work?

   (c) In his next call out, the plumber charged Mr Jones $826. How long did the plumber work on this job?

4. The area of a rectangular soccer pitch is $4050\,\text{m}^2$. The perimeter of the pitch is $270\,\text{m}$.

   (a) Taking the length of the pitch to be $x\,\text{m}$, find an expression for the width of the pitch in terms of x.

   (b) Hence show that x satisfies the equation $x^2 - 135x + 4050 = 0$.

   (c) Solve the equation to find the dimensions of the pitch.

5. The trajectory of a golf ball is in the form of a parabola. The path of the ball can be modelled by the equation:

   $$y = 0.57x - 0.002375x^2$$

   where x is the distance in metres from where the ball was hit and y is the height of the ball in metres above the ground.

   (a) Find the maximum height reached by the ball.

   (b) How far does the ball travel before it hits the ground for the first time?

   (c) What was the horizontal distance of the ball from where it was hit when its height was $19\,\text{m}$?

6. The subscription to a mathematics revision website MATHSMANAGER is £5 per month. There is an additional charge of 60p per visit. The total monthly cost of using the site can be represented as:

$$C = C_0 + n \times t$$

where: C is the total monthly cost

C_0 is the fixed monthly subscription fee

n is the number of visits in a month

t is the charge per visit.

(a) Calculate the total cost for:

(i) Saif, who visited the site 11 times last month

(ii) Jeevan, who made 40 visits to the site last month.

A second website MATHS-PLUS-U charges a £3.20 monthly subscription and 65p per visit.

(b) How much would it have cost Saif and Jeevan individually if they had used MATHS-PLUS-U instead?

(c) Jack intends to revise intensely over the two months preceding his mock examinations. He is planning to visit one of the revision websites at least 100 times.

(i) Which of the two sites will be cheaper for him to use?

(ii) What is the difference in cost between using these sites?

Past paper questions

1. The function $Q(t) = 0.003t^2 - 0.625t + 25$ represents the amount of energy in a battery after t minutes of use.

(a) State the amount of energy held by the battery immediately before it was used.

(b) Calculate the amount of energy available after 20 minutes.

(c) Given that $Q(10) = 19.05$, find the average amount of energy produced per minute for the interval $10 \leq t \leq 20$.

(d) Calculate the number of minutes it takes for the energy to reach zero.

[Total 6 marks]

[May 2006, Paper 1, TZ0, Question 7] *(© IB Organization 2006)*

See also the past paper questions at the end of Chapter 2.

Chapter 19 Exponential and polynomial functions

'Exponential growth' is a phrase we hear every day on the news and in general life. But what does exponential mean? And what is exponential growth? The graph below shows the increase (in millions) in number of users of the social network site *Facebook* over a five and a half year period. It demonstrates the typical shape of an exponential function: the increase in the vertical axis starts off very small and gradual and then increases in massive jumps of size despite the changes in the horizontal axis maintaining the same size. The graph below demonstrates that *Facebook* has seen an exponential growth in its number of users from 2004 to 2010.

In this chapter you will learn:

- about exponential functions and their graphs
- how to find horizontal asymptotes for exponential functions
- how to use exponential models
- about functions of the form $f(x) = ax^n + bx^m + \ldots$, where n and m are positive integers, and their graphs
- how to use models of the form $f(x) = ax^n + bx^m + \ldots$ where $n, m \in \mathbb{Z}^+$
- how to use graphs to interpret and solve modelling problems.

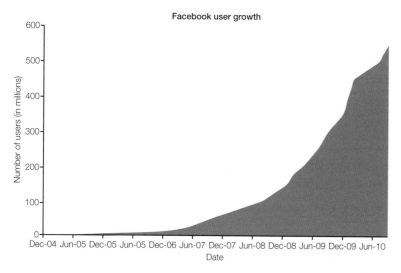

Facebook user growth

An exponential function gets its name from the fact that the independent variable is an exponent in the equation and this causes the dependent variable to change in very large jumps.

 It will be easier to study this chapter if you have already completed Chapters 2, 14, 17 and 18.

19.1 Exponential functions and their graphs

Living organisms that reproduce sexually have two biological parents, four biological grandparents and eight great-grandparents. So the number of forebears (ancestors) doubles with each generation.

You can demonstrate this example using a table:

Generation	1	2	3	4	5	6	x
Number of forebears	2	4	8	16	32	64	2^x
Power of 2	2^1	2^2	2^3	2^4	2^5	2^6	2^x

You can show the same information using a graph:

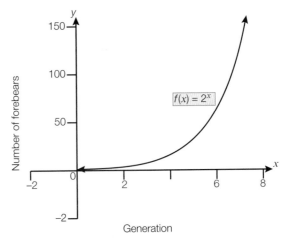

You can see from the graph that the growth in the number of forebears is very fast. Human genealogists use an estimate of four generations per century, so if you try to trace your family back 200 years, you could be looking for $2^8 = 256$ different people!

Some organisms reproduce very fast, such as bacteria; they can achieve a population of millions in a very short time.

The type of growth described by the table and graph above is called **exponential growth**, and it is based on the function $f(x) = a^x$ where a is a number greater than 1.

The general form of an **exponential function** is:

$$f(x) = ka^x + c$$

where $a > 0$, x is a variable that can be positive or negative, and k and c are constants (which can be positive or negative).

The exponential function is very interesting to explore using a computer graphing package or a GDC. Start with the simplest case and draw graphs of $f(x) = a^x$ for different values of $a > 1$:

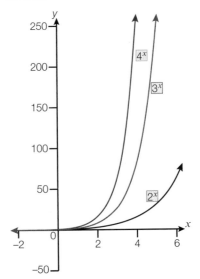

Next, draw the $f(x) = a^{-x}$ (note the negative sign in the exponent) for different values of $a > 1$:

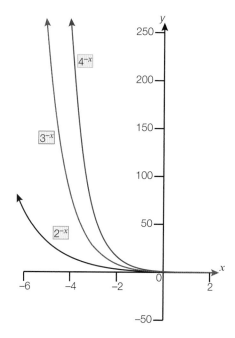

Note that this is the same as drawing graphs of $f(x) = a^x$ for positive values of $a < 1$. Try it: draw the graphs of a^x for $a = 0.5, 0.333, 0.25$. Can you see why this is the case?

You can also draw a set of graphs of $f(x) = ka^x$ and $f(x) = ka^{-x}$ for the same value of a but different values of k:

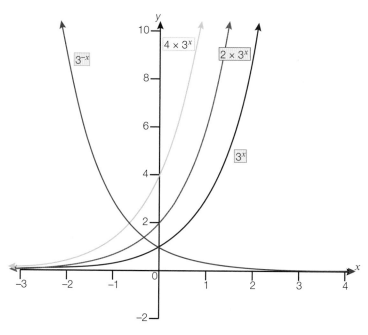

Now try drawing the graphs of $f(x) = a^x \pm c$ with the same value of a but different values of c.

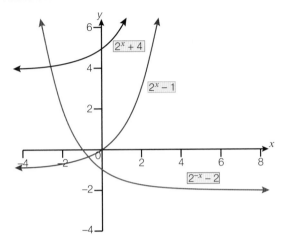

After these explorations, you should find that:

- The curve always has a similar shape.

 You learned about asymptotes in Chapter 17.

- The curve levels off to a particular value. The horizontal line at this y-value is called a **horizontal asymptote**; the curve approaches this line very closely but never actually reaches it.

- The graph of $f(x) = a^x$ or a^{-x} passes through the point $(0, 1)$.

- The graph of $f(x) = ka^x$ or ka^{-x} passes through the point $(0, k)$.

- The constant $\pm c$ moves the curve of ka^x up or down by c units, giving the graph a horizontal asymptote at c or $-c$.

Worked example 19.1

See '17.3 Finding the horizontal asymptote' on page 680 of the GDC chapter if you need a reminder of how to find horizontal asymptotes with your GDC.

Q. Draw the following functions on your GDC and find the equation of the asymptote for each function.

(a) $f(x) = 1.5^x$ (b) $g(x) = 3^x - 2$ (c) $h(x) = 3 + 2^{-x}$

A. (a)

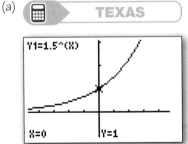

The asymptote is $y = 0$ (the x-axis).

continued . . .

(b)

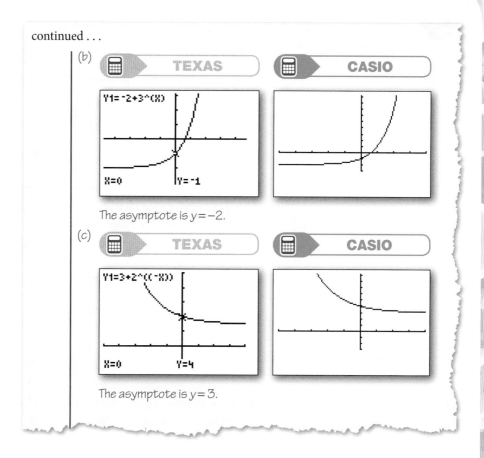

The asymptote is $y = -2$.

(c)

The asymptote is $y = 3$.

Evaluating exponential functions

Recall from section 17.2 that function notation provides an efficient shorthand for substituting values into a function. For example, to find the value of $f(x) = 6 + 3^{-x}$ when $x = 2$, you write $f(2)$ to mean 'replace x by 2 in the expression $6 + 3^{-x}$'. This is called '**evaluating** the function $f(x)$ at $x = 2$'.

You can evaluate any function at a given value using either algebra or your GDC. If you use your GDC, be careful to enter brackets where needed, especially with negative values.

Let's look at how to evaluate $f(x) = 6 + 3^{-x}$ at $x = 2$ with three different methods.

Using algebra:

Replace x with 2.

$$f(2) = 6 + 3^{-2} = 6 + \frac{1}{3^2} = 6\frac{1}{9} = \frac{55}{9}$$

 See Learning links 1B on page 24 for a reminder about negative indices if you need to.

exam tip

Using algebra is sometimes quicker and more accurate than using a GDC. If you give your answer as a fraction, the answer is exact, whereas a recurring decimal is not.

Using your GDC to evaluate directly:

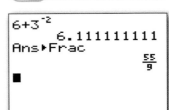 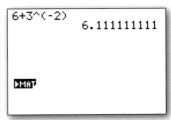

 Using a graph on your GDC (see '*19.2 Solving unfamiliar equations*' on page 684 of the GDC chapter, if you need a reminder).

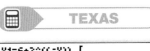 

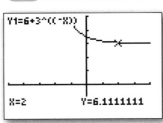 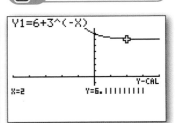

If you are drawing an exponential graph on a GDC, you need to be particularly careful in your choice of scale for the axes. In this example, $f(x) \geq 6$ always, so there is no need for a negative scale on the y-axis; however, you will only get a good view of the shape of the graph if you allow a wide enough domain for the x-axis.

Check that the same methods give $f(-1) = 9$ and $f(-3) = 33$.

Worked example 19.2

Q. Let $f(x) = -1 - 2^{-x}$, $g(x) = 1 + 3^x$ and $h(x) = 2 \times 1.5^{-0.5x}$. Find:

(a) $f(2)$ (b) $g(5)$ (c) $h(-4)$

> Let's calculate these using algebra first.

A. (a) $f(2) = -1 - 2^{-2} = -1 - \dfrac{1}{2^2} = -1 - \dfrac{1}{4} = -\dfrac{5}{4}$

(b) $g(5) = 1 + 3^5 = 1 + 243 = 244$

(c) $h(-4) = 2 \times 1.5^{-0.5 \times (-4)} = 2 \times 1.5^2 = 2 \times 2.25 = 4.5$

> Now check the answers using your GDC.

 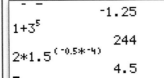

Exercise 19.1

1. Draw the following functions on your GDC, and find the equation of the asymptote in each case:

   (a) $f(x) = 3^x$

   (b) $f(x) = 3^{2x}$

   (c) $f(x) = 3^x + 5$

   (d) $f(x) = 3^x - 4$

   (e) $f(x) = 2 \times 3^x - 4$

2. Draw the following functions on your GDC for the given domain, and in each case state the coordinates of the y-intercept and the range.

   (a) $g(x) = 5^x$ for $-3 \leq x \leq 6$

   (b) $g(x) = 5^{3x}$ for $-4 \leq x \leq 4$

   (c) $g(x) = 5^{3x+2}$ for $-2 \leq x \leq 5$

   (d) $g(x) = 5^{x+7}$ for $-10 \leq x \leq 0$

   (e) $g(x) = 5^{x-4}$ for $0 \leq x \leq 9$

3. Draw the following functions on your GDC. In each case state:

   (i) the equation of the asymptote

   (ii) the coordinates of the y-intercept

   (iii) the range.

   (a) $f(x) = 2^{-x}$ for $x \geq -4$

   (b) $f(x) = 3^{-x}$ for $x \geq -6$

   (c) $f(x) = \left(\dfrac{1}{2}\right)^x$ for $x \geq -8$

   (d) $f(x) = \left(\dfrac{1}{3}\right)^x$ for $x \geq -3$

   (e) $f(x) = 6^{-x} + 5$ for $x \geq -5$

   (f) $f(x) = 6^{-x} - 4$ for $x \geq 0$

   (g) $f(x) = 2 \times 5^x$ for $x \leq 6$

   (h) $f(x) = 4 \times 5^x$ for $x \leq 10$

4. For each of the following functions calculate:

   (i) $f(0)$

   (ii) $f(3)$

   (iii) $f(-1)$

   (iv) $f\left(\dfrac{1}{2}\right)$

   (a) $f(x) = 5^x$

   (b) $f(x) = 5^{2x}$

   (c) $f(x) = 5^{2x+3}$

   (d) $f(x) = 5^{2x-7}$

   (e) $f(x) = 1.608 \times 5^x$

   (f) $f(x) = 3.264 \times 10^{2x+4}$

   (g) $f(x) = 5.27 \times 10^{3x-8}$

   (h) $f(x) = 4.376^x$

   (i) $f(x) = 34 \times 2^{1.45x}$

   (j) $f(x) = 90 \times 10^{1.25x-3.578}$

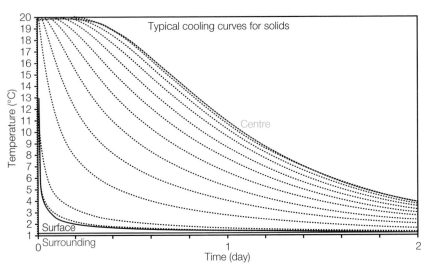

Typical cooling curves for solids

Powered by AKTSAG.

Exponential functions can be used to model both 'growth' and 'decay'; in the modelling context these phenomena are interpreted very broadly.

You already encountered a particular form of exponential function when you were studying compound interest, inflation and depreciation. For example, the formula for compound interest: $FV = PV(1+r)^n$.

«RR *Look back at Chapter 4 to refresh your memory on compound interest, inflation and depreciation.*

Compare $f(x) = ka^x$ with the formula $FV = PV(1+r)^n$. If you replace PV by k, n by x, and $(1+r)$ by a, then you can see that the compound interest formula is just an exponential function.

In this section we will look at some other, non-financial, models, such as cooling and the growth or decay of populations.

In a laboratory that studies bacteria, the researchers are interested in the pattern of growth or decline of the bacterial populations. Suppose Jin has 30 g of bacteria originally and has established that the colony will grow according to the function:

$$W(t) = 30 \times 1.008^t$$

where $W(t)$ represents the mass of the colony at time t, measured in hours.

Exponential curves can be used as efficient models for a wide range of scientific and economic phenomena, such as the spread of a new technology or the way a virus infects a population. Although you often hear the term 'exponential' used to describe any growth pattern that shows a rapid increase (or decrease), it is important to be aware that exponential models will not always fit data outside a certain range; for instance, realistically populations do not increase forever without limit. So, while exponential models are very convenient, to make the best use of them we also need to understand their limitations.

She draws a graph of the growth she expects to see in the first week. Plotting the mass of the bacteria colony against time, she gets the following graph:

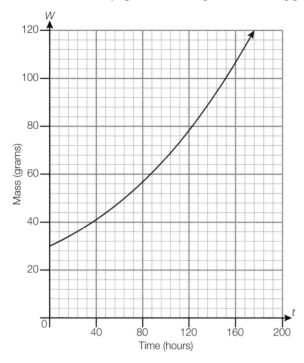

What is the mass of bacteria that she can expect to find at the end of the first week?

At the end of the week, $t = 7 \times 24 = 168$ hours, so the mass should be:

$$W(168) = 30 \times 1.008^{168} = 114\,\text{g}$$

At the end of the week, something contaminates Jin's sample and the bacteria start dying. There are 50 g left after five days, and Jin wants to find a function that will model the decay of the population.

Let the new function for modelling the decay of the bacterial population be called $H(t)$, which represents the mass of the colony t hours **after the contamination**. (Note that this 't' has a different meaning from the 't' in $W(t)$.)

Jin immediately writes $H(t) = 114 \times a^t$, so that $H(0) = 114$, and needs to find a value for a.

She knows that $H(5) = 50$ or, in other words, $50 = 114 \times a^{5 \times 24}$. So:

$$50 = 114 \times a^{120}$$

$$a^{120} = \frac{50}{114}$$

$$a^{120} = 0.4386$$

hint

The 114 in the expression for $H(t)$ comes from the mass of the colony at the end of the first week, when the contamination occurred.

One method to find the value of a from the above equation is to draw the graph of the left-hand side of the equation on the same axes as the graph of the right-hand side of the equation, and see where they intersect. So Jin would enter $y_1 = x^{120}$ and $y_2 = 0.4386$ into her GDC and plot their

graphs (see '*19.1 Solving growth and decay problems*' on page 683 of the GDC chapter for a reminder of how to solve exponential equations using your GDC):

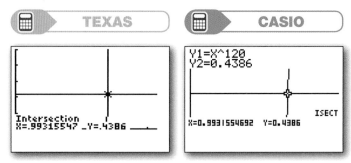

Alternatively, she could take the 120th root of 0.4396 to get the same answer:

$$a = \sqrt[120]{0.4386} = 0.993$$

Therefore, the population decay function is $H(t) = 114 \times 0.993^t$.

With this function, it is possible to answer questions such as 'how long will it take for the mass of the colony to decrease to the original 30 g?' All we need to do is solve the equation $H(t) = 30$ for the value of t:

$$H(t) = 30$$

$$114 \times 0.993^t = 30$$

By drawing the graphs of $y_1 = 114 \times 0.993^x$ and $y_2 = 30$, we see that $t = 190$ hours.

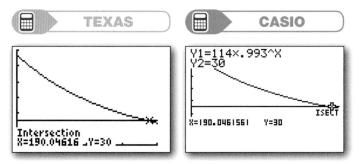

Worked example 19.3

Q. The population of Inverness was 12 000 in 2010. The town council estimates that the population is growing by 3% each year.

The growth can be modelled by the function $P(t) = 12000 \times 1.03^t$, where t is the number of years after 2010.

(a) Estimate the population of Inverness in 2020. Give your answer to the nearest ten people.

(b) In which year will the population be double that in 2010?

continued . . .

2020 is ten years after 2010, so take $t = 10$ and evaluate $P(10)$.

A. (a) $P(10) = 12000 \times 1.03^{10} = 16100 \, (3 \text{ s.f.})$

If the population doubles, that means $P(t) = 2 \times 12000$. So solve this equation for t.

(b) $2 \times 12000 = 12000 \times 1.03^t$

Dividing through by 12000,

$2 = 1.03^t$

Draw the graphs of $y_1 = 1.03^x$ and $y_2 = 2$. Find their point of intersection; see section '19.1' in the GDC chapter if you need to

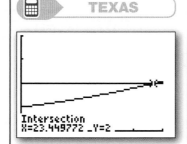

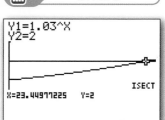

Remember that t is not the final answer; you need to add this value to 2010.

$t = 23.4$, so the population will have doubled in 2033.

hint

The number e is a mathematical constant that often appears in growth or decay functions. It is an irrational number, $e = 2.71828\ldots$, with an infinite number of decimals that do not show any repeating pattern. The concept of e is not in the syllabus for this course, but you may meet it in other contexts.

Worked example 19.4

Q. A cup of coffee is left to cool. It is estimated that its temperature decreases according to the model $T(t) = 90e^{-0.11t}$, where e is a constant with value approximately 2.718, and time t is measured in minutes.

(a) What is the initial temperature of the coffee?

(b) Calculate the temperature after 5 minutes.

(c) How long will it take for the coffee to cool to a room temperature of 21°C?

'Initial' means at $t = 0$, so the initial temperature is found by evaluating $T(0)$.

A. (a) $T(0) = 90 \times 2.718^0 = 90 \times 1 = 90°C$

Substitute $t = 5$ into the exponential function.

(b) $T(5) = 90 \times 2.718^{-0.11 \times 5} = 51.9°C$

continued . . .

Now we want to find the value of t for which $T(t) = 21$. In other words, we need to solve this equation for t.

(c) $90 \times 2.718^{-0.11t} = 21$

 TEXAS

 CASIO

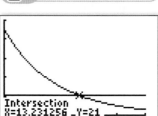

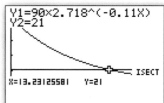

On your GDC, draw the graphs of $y_1 = 90 \times 2.718^x$ and $y_2 = 21$.

Find the point of intersection.

$t = 13.2$ minutes

GDC

On the GDC you use 'x' as the variable, but when writing down your answer, remember to use the correct letter given in the question, which is 't' in Worked example 19.4.

Exercise 19.2

1. The population of a town is growing at a constant rate of 2% per year. The present population is 48 000. The population P after t years can be modelled as:

   $P = 48000 \times 1.02^t$

   (a) Calculate the population of the town:

      (i) after 5 years

      (ii) after 12 years

      (iii) after 14.5 years.

   (b) Find how long it will take for the population of the town to reach:

      (i) 60 000   (ii) 100 000.

   (c) Find how long it will take for the population of the town to:

      (i) double   (ii) treble.

2. The population of a large city was 5.5 million in the year 2000. Assume that the population of the city can be modelled by the function:

   $P(t) = 5.5 \times 1.0225^t$

   where $P(t)$ is the population in millions and t is the number of years after 2000.

   (a) Calculate an estimate of the city's population in:

      (i) 2010   (ii) 2018.

(b) In what year does the population of the city become double that in 2000?

The population of another city can be modelled as:

$$P(t) = 6.05 \times 1.01^t$$

where t is the number of years after the year 2000.

(c) In which year will the two cities have the same population?

3. Ali has been prescribed medication by his doctor. He takes a 200 mg dose of the drug. The amount of the drug in his bloodstream t hours after the initial dose is modelled by:

$$C = C_0 \times 0.875^t$$

(a) State the value of C_0.

(b) Find the amount of the drug in Ali's bloodstream after:

  (i) 4 hours   (ii) 8 hours.

(c) How long does it take for the amount of drug in the bloodstream to fall below 40 mg?

4. The population of bacteria in a culture is known to grow exponentially. The growth can be modelled by the equation:

$$N(t) = 420e^{0.0375t} \qquad \text{(where e} = 2.718282)$$

Here $N(t)$ represents the population of the bacteria t hours after the culture was initially monitored.

(a) What was the population of the bacteria when monitoring started?

(b) Calculate $N(4)$.

(c) Work out $N(48)$.

(d) Calculate $N(72)$.

(e) How long does it take for the population of the bacteria to exceed 1000?

(f) How long does it take for the population of the bacteria to treble?

5. A liquid is heated to 100°C and then left to cool. The temperature θ after t minutes can be modelled as:

$$\theta = 100 \times e^{-0.0024t} \qquad \text{(where e} = 2.718282)$$

(a) Calculate the temperature of the liquid after:

  (i) 20 minutes   (ii) 50 minutes   (iii) 2 hours.

(b) How long does it take for the temperature of the liquid to drop to 80°C?

(c) Work out the time taken for the temperature of the liquid to drop to 40°C.

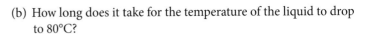

19.3 Polynomial functions

The function $f(x) = ax^n + bx^m + \dots$, where the powers of x (the n and m in the expression) are **positive integers**, is called a **polynomial**.

You have already studied two types of polynomial: linear functions, where the highest power of x is 1, and quadratic functions, where the highest power of x is 2. Now you will meet some others. The **degree** of the polynomial is the highest power (or exponent, or index) that appears in the function's expression; so a linear function is of degree 1, and a quadratic function is of degree 2.

The simplest polynomial of degree n is the function $f(x) = x^n$. Draw some graphs of $f(x) = x^n$ for various values of n:

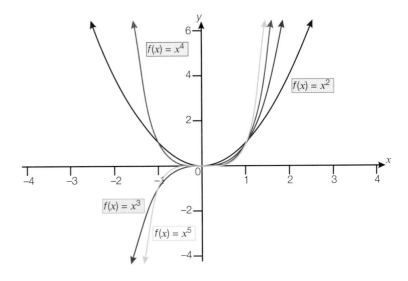

You can see that:

- The curves are all centred at the origin.

- If the power of x is even, the curve is symmetrical about the y-axis.

- If the power of x is odd, the curve has 180° rotational symmetry about $(0, 0)$.

As you add more terms to the function, the graph becomes more interesting and develops more curves.

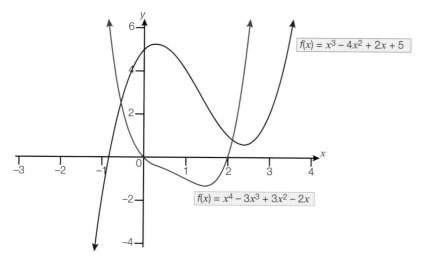

$f(x) = x^3 - 4x^2 + 2x + 5$

$f(x) = x^4 - 3x^3 + 3x^2 - 2x$

Name of function	General algebraic expression	Degree of polynomial	Maximum number of turning points
Linear	$f(x) = ax + b$	1	0
Quadratic	$f(x) = ax^2 + bx + c$	2	1
Cubic	$f(x) = ax^3 + bx^2 + cx + d$	3	2
Quartic	$f(x) = ax^4 + bx^3 + cx^2 + dx + e$	4	3
Quintic	$f(x) = ax^5 + bx^4 + cx^3 + dx^2 + ex + f$	5	4

For each degree of polynomial, there is a maximum number of **turning points** that the graph can have. But some polynomials of that degree will have fewer turning points; for example, not all polynomials of degree 4 will have 3 turning points. It is best to draw any given polynomial function on your GDC to get an idea of what shape to expect.

Worked example 19.5

Q. Look at the following functions and write down the degree in each case:

(a) $f(x) = 5x^4 - 6x^5 + 4x - 3$

(b) $g(x) = 3 + x - x^3 - \dfrac{1}{x}$

(c) $h(x) = 7x + 2$

(d) $j(x) = 1 - x - x^3 + x^2$

The term with the highest power is $-6x^5$.

A. (a) The degree is 5.

This has a rational term $\dfrac{1}{x}$ (which is a negative power of x).

Remember that in a polynomial all exponents of x should be positive integers.

(b) It is not a polynomial.

continued . . .

The term with the highest power is $7x$; this is a linear function.

(c) The degree is 1.

The term with the highest power is $-x^3$.

(d) The degree is 3.

As polynomial functions become more complicated, they may also have more intercepts on the x-axis. Finding these intercepts is very similar to finding the solutions (or roots) of a quadratic equation, and you can use your GDC to do this. (See '19.3 Solving polynomial equations (a) using a graph' and '(b) using an equation solver' on page 685 of the GDC chapter if you need a reminder.)

See section '19.3 Solving polynomial equations' on page 685 of the GDC chapter if you need to.

Worked example 19.6

Q. Sketch the following curves with your GDC. In each case write down the y-intercept and use your GDC to find any x-intercepts.

(a) $f(x) = 2x^4 - 5x^2 + x$

(b) $g(x) = 2 - 5x^2 + 2x^3$

(c) $h(x) = x^4 + x^3 - 6$

A. (a)

TEXAS

CASIO

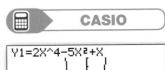

```
Zero
X=-1.672982   Y=0
```

```
Y1=2X^4-5X²+X

                    ROOT
X=-1.672981648   Y=0
```

For the y-intercept, look at the graph or evaluate $f(0)$.

If you zoom in near the origin, you should see that there are two x-intercepts there; be careful not to miss one.

y-intercept: $(0, 0)$

x-intercepts: $(-1.67, 0), (0, 0), (0.203, 0), (1.47, 0)$

continued . . .

(b)

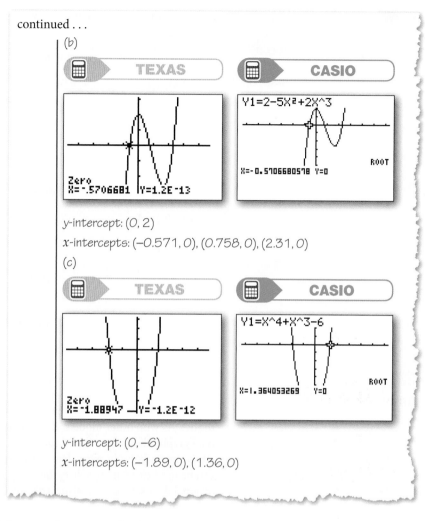

y-intercept: $(0, 2)$

x-intercepts: $(-0.571, 0)$, $(0.758, 0)$, $(2.31, 0)$

(c)

y-intercept: $(0, -6)$

x-intercepts: $(-1.89, 0)$, $(1.36, 0)$

Remember that in a polynomial function the powers of x should all be positive integers. If a function of the form $f(x) = ax^n + bx^m + \ldots$ contains one or more powers of x that are **negative** integers, then $f(x)$ is not a polynomial. Instead, it is a **rational function**. For example, $f(x) = 5x^2 + \frac{4}{x}$ contains a negative power of x (because $\frac{4}{x} = 4x^{-1}$) and can be written as $f(x) = \frac{5x^3 + 4}{x}$, which is a ratio of two polynomials. The graphs of such rational functions will have $x = 0$ (the y-axis) as a vertical asymptote.

 Rational functions and their graphs were covered in section 17.3.

Exercise 19.3

1. Sketch the following curves on your GDC. In each case:

    (i) Write down the y-intercept.   (ii) Find any x-intercepts.

    (a) $f(x) = x^3 - 7x + 6$ (b) $f(x) = x^3 + x^2 - 5x + 3$

    (c) $f(x) = 8 - 2x - 5x^2 - x^3$ (d) $f(x) = 6 - 7x - 18x^2 - 5x^3$

    (e) $f(x) = x^3 + 3x^2 - 4$ (f) $f(x) = x^3 + 5x^2 - 6x$

    (g) $f(x) = 2x^3 + x^2 - 13x + 6$ (h) $g(x) = x^4 - 6x^2 - 8$

    (i) $g(x) = 2x^4 + 7x^3 - 6x^2 - 7x + 4$ (j) $g(x) = x^5 - 9x^3 + x^2 - 9$

‹‹RR *You learned about the domain and range in Chapter 17.*

2. Sketch the following curves on your GDC for the stated domains. In each case:

(i) write down the coordinates of the intercepts with the axes

(ii) state the range of the function.

(a) $f(x) = x^2 - x - 12$ for $-4 \le x \le 5$

(b) $f(x) = 1 + 7x - x^2$ for $-1 \le x \le 7$

(c) $f(x) = 8x + 2x^2 - x^3$ for $-4 \le x \le 6$

(d) $f(x) = x^3 - 2x^2 - 5x + 6$ for $-2 \le x \le 4$

(e) $g(x) = 3 + 7x^3 - 6x^2 - 2x^4$ for $-1 \le x \le 3$

(f) $g(x) = x^3 + x^2 - 5x + 4$ for $-4 \le x \le 6$

(g) $f(x) = \dfrac{1}{4}x^3 - 7x^2 - \dfrac{1}{3}x + 10$ for $-2 \le x \le 2$

(h) $f(x) = x^4 - \dfrac{1}{2}x^3 + x^2 - x + 6$ for $0 \le x \le 2$

19.4 Modelling with polynomial functions

Some practical situations can be described fairly well by a polynomial model. As with other models, the first step is to collect data and plot it on a graph. Then try to find a curve that fits the data and helps you to study the problem in more depth. The function represented by the curve can be used to estimate values that were not collected as part of the original data set. You can also work out when that function will reach certain values of interest.

Worked example 19.7

Q. Bram is working in a laboratory, measuring the speed (in metres per second) at which a particle drops through a certain liquid. He draws a graph of velocity against time, and thinks that it will fit a cubic model. After a bit more work, he decides that the equation $v(t) = 34.3t^3 - 25.0t^2 + 6.28t + 0.16$ would describe the data well during the first second.

(a) Use this equation to estimate the velocity of the particle when $t = 0.5$ seconds.

(b) Calculate the time at which the velocity of the particle is $0.6 \, \text{m s}^{-1}$.

> Finding the velocity at $t = 0.5$ means to replace t by 0.5 in the equation for $v(t)$, i.e. to evaluate $v(0.5)$.

A. (a) $v(0.5) = 34.3(0.5)^3 - 25.0(0.5)^2 + 6.28(0.5) + 0.16 = 1.34 \, \text{m s}^{-1}$

$\longrightarrow$

continued . . .

continued . . .

(b) $34.3t^3 - 25.0t^2 + 6.28t + 0.160 = 0.6$

We want to find the value of t for which $v(t) = 0.6$. This involves solving a polynomial equation.

You can use the equation solver on your GDC (or you could plot graphs and find the point of intersection). See '19.3 (b) Solving polynomial equations using an equation solver' on page 685 of the GDC chapter if you need to.

 TEXAS

 CASIO

```
34.3X^3-25X²+…=0
■X=.11304818277…
  bound={-1ᴇ99,1…
■left-rt=0
```

```
Eq:34.3X^3-25X²+6.28X
    X=0.1130481828
Lft=0.6
Rgt=0.6

REPT
```

The velocity of the particle is $0.6\ \text{m s}^{-1}$ after 0.113 seconds.

Worked example 19.8

Q. Risha has been monitoring the level of water in a local reservoir over the past three months. She finds that the depth of the water can be modelled by the function:

$$D(t) = 0.024t^3 - 0.87t^2 + 4.9t + 39$$

where t is measured in weeks.

(a) Find the depth of water in the reservoir when Risha begins her study.

(b) After how many weeks is the depth of water in the reservoir at $25\ \text{m}$?

The beginning of the study corresponds to $t = 0$, so evaluate $D(0)$.

(c) During Risha's study, the water level first rises and then falls. What is the maximum depth of water that Risha measures?

A. (a) $D(0) = 39\ \text{m}$

(b) $0.024t^3 - 0.87t^2 + 4.9t + 39 = 25$

We want to find the value of t for which $D(t) = 25$. This involves solving a cubic equation, which you can do by drawing graphs on your GDC and finding the points of intersection (or using the equation solver program). See '19.3 Solving polynomial equations' on page 685 of the GDC chapter if you need to.

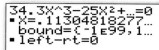 TEXAS

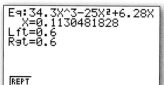 CASIO

```
Intersection
X=10        Y=25
```

```
Y1=0.024X^3-0.87X²+4.
Y2=25

                      ISECT
X=10        Y=25
```

From GDC: $t = 10$ weeks

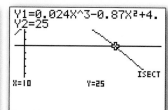

continued . . .

(c)

The maximum depth is 46.6 m, which occurs 3.25 weeks after Risha starts her study.

Draw the graph of $D(t)$ and find the coordinates of the maximum point on the curve. (See '18.1 Using a graph to find the vertex and line of symmetry of a parabola' on page 680 of the GDC chapter for a reminder of how to find the minimum and maximum points, if you need to.)

Exercise 19.4

1. Jana has been studying trends in the exchange rate between the US dollar and the euro over the 12 months in 2011. She has suggested an approximate cubic model; the equation of the modelling function is:

$$f(x) = 0.0003x^3 - 0.0088x^2 + 0.0748x + 1.2582$$

where $f(x)$ is the number of US dollars per euro, x months after 1 January 2011.

(a) Using this model, estimate the exchange rate of USD to EUR on:

   (i) 1 April 2011   (ii) 1 August 2011   (iii) 1 November 2011.

(b) Use your GDC to sketch the graph of $f(x)$, and hence estimate the peak value of the exchange rate over the 12-month period.

2. The total population of the world in billions between 1950 and 2010 can be modelled by the following function:

$$p(x) = 2.557 + 0.3554x + 0.145x^2 - 0.0207x^3 + 0.001316x^4 - 0.00003718x^5$$

where $p(x)$ is the mid-year population of the world in billions, x decades after 1950.

(a) The actual mid-year populations are given in the following table. Use the model to calculate the estimated populations. Work out the percentage error in using the model to estimate the population of the world.

Decade		1970	1990	2010
Population (billions)	Actual	3.706618	5.278640	6.848933
	Estimated from model			
Percentage error				

(b) Use the model to estimate the projected mid-year population of the world in:

  (i) 2020   (ii) 2030   (iii) 2040.

3. Marko has studied trends in the price of silver on the commodities market over a six-year period. He has suggested a model for the price per ounce of silver, in US dollars, over the six years since 2000.

  According to Marko, the price of silver can be modelled by the function

  $$f(x) = -0.0669x^5 + 1.0383x^4 - 5.9871x^3 + 16.817x^2 - 22.471x + 15.78$$

  where $f(x)$ is the price in USD per ounce of silver and x is the number of years after 1 January 2000.

  (a) Use Marko's model to complete the following table:

Year	2000	2002	2004	2006
Price of silver on 1 January				

  (b) Use Marko's model to predict the price of silver on 1 January 2005.

  The actual price of silver on the commodities market on 1 January 2004 was US$9.08 per ounce.

  (c) Calculate the percentage error in using Marko's model to determine the price of silver on 1 January 2004.

4. Martha found the following diagram in an Economics journal. The diagram shows the price of gold per ounce, in US dollars, over a ten-year period. However, the numbers on one of the axes are missing.

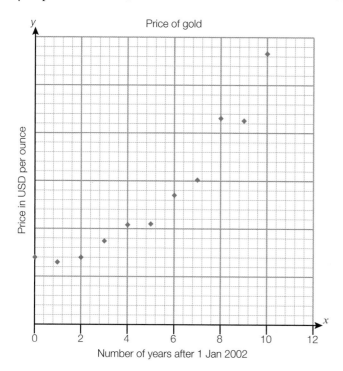

Price of gold

Price in USD per ounce

Number of years after 1 Jan 2002

After some effort, Martha managed to find an approximate function $g(x)$ to fit the trend of prices. Her function $g(x)$ is:

$$g(x) = -0.007x^5 + 0.2527x^4 - 2.7818x^3 + 20.306x^2 - 23.773x + 278$$

where $g(x)$ is the price in USD per ounce of gold x years after 1 January 2002.

(a) Use Martha's model to complete the following table:

Year	2002	2004	2006	2008	2010	2012
Price of gold on 1 January						

(b) Use Martha's model to estimate the price of gold on 1 January 2011.

(c) If the actual price of gold on 1 January 2011 was US$853.60 per ounce, calculate the percentage error in using Martha's model to estimate the price on 1 January 2011.

Summary

You should know:

- what an exponential function is, and how to recognise one and its graph:

  $f(x) = ka^x + c$

  or $f(x) = ka^{-x} + c$

  (where $a \in \mathbb{Q}^+$, $a \neq 1$, $k \neq 0$)

 Recall from Chapter 1 that $\mathbb{Q}$ denotes 'rational numbers'; the superscript '+' means all positive rational numbers.

- how to find the horizontal asymptote of an exponential function

- how to use exponential models

- what a polynomial function is, and how to recognise one and its graph:

  $f(x) = ax^n + bx^m + \dots$ (where the powers of x are positive integers)

- how to use polynomial functions as mathematical models.

Mixed examination practice

Exam-style questions

1. A function is defined as $g(x) = -2x^4 + 5x^3 + 6x^2 - 7x - 4$. Sketch the graph of the function on your GDC, with the domain $-2 \leq x \leq 4$, and use it to answer the following questions.

   (a) State the coordinates of the y-intercept.

   (b) Find all intercepts with the x-axis.

   (c) Determine the range of the function.

2. Use your GDC to draw the graph of the function $f(x) = 8^{-x}$.

   (a) State the coordinates of the y-intercept.

   (b) Write down the equation of the asymptote.

   (c) State the range of the function.

3. The curve with equation $y = A \times 2^x + 5$ passes through the point B with coordinates $(0, 8)$.

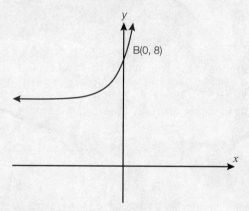

   (a) Find the value of A.

   (b) Write down the equation of the asymptote.

4. The temperature of a bowl of soup left to cool outside can be modelled by an exponential function. The temperature θ in degrees Celsius after t hours is:

   $\theta = 24 + 56e^{-1.754t}$ (where e $= 2.718282$)

   (a) Calculate the temperature of the soup after:

   (i) half an hour   (ii) 48 minutes   (iii) two hours   (iv) 156 minutes.

   (b) Find how long it takes for the temperature of the soup to drop to:

   (i) 70°C   (ii) 34°C   (iii) 28°C.

5. The diagram below illustrates the trend in the debt of a major western country as a percentage of its GDP from 1999 to 2011.

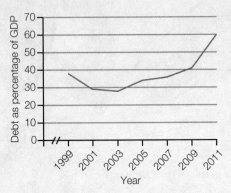

The curve can be modelled approximately by a polynomial with equation:

$$p(x) = 0.017045x^4 - 0.402146x^3 + 3.38636x^2 - 10.37626x + 38.2121$$

where $p(x)$ is the national debt as a percentage of GDP and x is the number of years after 1999.

Use the model to complete the following table.

Year	2000	2002	2004	2006	2008	2010
Debt (% of GDP)						

6. After a person took a dose of a drug, the initial concentration of the drug in their bloodstream was 8 mg/ml. Six hours later, the concentration of the drug in the bloodstream had dropped to 4.8 mg/ml.

Suppose that the concentration C, in mg/ml, of the drug in the bloodstream t hours after the initial dose can be modelled by:

$$C = C_0 \times e^{kt}$$

(you may assume that $e = 2.718282$). Find the values of C_0 and k.

7. Pauli is modelling the electricity demand curve of a major country on a typical day. He has fitted a curve to approximate the original demand curve:

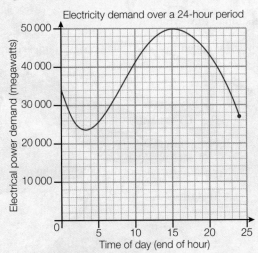

Electricity demand over a 24-hour period

The equation of his polynomial modelling function is:

$$p(x) = -0.0037x^6 + 0.2351x^5 - 4.177x^4 - 22.112x^3 + 1178.7x^2 - 6637.9x + 33969$$

where $p(x)$ is the demand in megawatts x hours after midnight.

(a) Use Pauli's model to estimate the electricity demand at:

   (i) 6.00 a.m.   (ii) 12 noon   (iii) 6.00 p.m.   (iv) 9.00 p.m.

   Give your answers to the nearest 10 megawatts.

(b) Use your GDC to find the times of the day when electricity demand is estimated to be:

   (i) 38 000 megawatts   (ii) 43 000 megawatts.

Past paper questions

1. (a) Sketch the graph of the function $f(x) = \dfrac{2x+3}{x+4}$ for $-10 \le x \le 10$, indicating clearly the axis intercepts and any asymptotes. *[6 marks]*

   (b) Write down the equation of the vertical asymptote. *[2 marks]*

   (c) On the same diagram sketch the graph of $g(x) = x + 0.5$. *[2 marks]*

   (d) Using your graphical display calculator write down the coordinates of **one** of the points of intersection on the graphs of f and g, **giving your answer correct to five decimal places**. *[3 marks]*

   (e) Write down the gradient of the line $g(x) = x + 0.5$. *[1 mark]*

   (f) The line L passes through the point with coordinates $(-2, -3)$ and is perpendicular to the line $g(x)$. Find the equation of L. *[3 marks]*

   [Total 17 marks]

   [May 2008, Paper 2, TZ1, Question 1] (© *IB Organization 2008*)

2. In an experiment it is found that a culture of bacteria triples in number every four hours.

   There are 200 bacteria at the start of the experiment.

Hours	0	4	8	12	16
No. of bacteria	200	600	a	5400	16200

   (a) Find the value of a. *[1 mark]*

   (b) Calculate how many bacteria there will be after one day. *[2 marks]*

   (c) Find how long it will take for there to be two million bacteria. *[3 marks]*

   [Total 6 marks]

   [May 2008, Paper 1, TZ1, Question 15] (© *IB Organization 2008*)

3. The following graph shows the temperature in degrees Celsius of Robert's cup of coffee, t minutes after pouring it out. The equation of the cooling graph is $f(t) = 16 + 74 \times 2.8^{-0.2t}$ where $f(t)$ is the temperature and t is the time in minutes after pouring the coffee out.

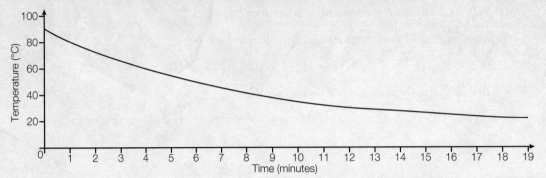

(a) Find the initial temperature of the coffee. [1 mark]

(b) Write down the equation of the horizontal asymptote. [1 mark]

(c) Find the room temperature. [1 mark]

(d) Find the temperature of the coffee after 10 minutes. [1 mark]

If the coffee is not hot enough it is reheated in a microwave oven. The liquid increases in temperature according to the formula

$$T = A \times 2^{1.5t}$$

where T is the final temperature of the liquid, A is the initial temperature of coffee in the microwave and t is the time in minutes after switching the microwave on.

(e) Find the temperature of Robert's coffee after being heated in the microwave for 30 **seconds** after it has reached the temperature in part (d). [3 marks]

(f) Calculate the length of time it would take a similar cup of coffee, initially at 20°C, to be heated in the microwave to reach 100°C. [4 marks]

[Total 11 marks]

[**Nov 2007, Paper 2, TZ0, Question 3(i)**] (© *IB Organization 2007*)

Introduction to differential calculus

Surfing and snowboarding are among the many sports that use a flat board in contact with a curved surface. The skill lies in how the surfer or snowboarder manipulates the board against the curve to effect changes in velocity and acceleration.

Velocity and acceleration are variables that are described in terms of the rate of change of one physical quantity in relation to another; velocity is the rate of change of displacement with respect to time, and acceleration is the rate of change of velocity with respect to time.

Calculus is the mathematics of change — the study of quantities that do not stay the same and whose rate of change is important in a particular context. It is used in fields as varied as physics and finance, architecture and engineering, the setting of credit card payments and the science behind computer games.

The development of calculus is one of the major achievements of mathematics. It stimulated the flowering of mathematics and science that sparked the industrial revolution and led to the growth of the technology that we know today.

Prior learning topics

It will be easier to study this topic if you have completed:

- Chapter 2
- Chapter 14
- Topic 6 (Chapters 17–19)

Chapter 20 Introduction to differential calculus

In this chapter you will learn:

- the two concepts of the derivative
  - as a rate of change of a function
  - as a gradient of a graph
- about the concept of the gradient of a curve as the gradient of a tangent line
- that if $f(x) = ax^n$, then $f'(x) = nx^{n-1}$
- how to find the derivative of functions of the form $f(x) = ax^n + bx^m + \ldots$ where all exponents are integers
- how to find the gradient of a curve at given values of x
- how to find the values of x at which a curve has a given gradient
- how to find the equation of the tangent at a given point on a curve
- how to find the equation of the line perpendicular to the tangent at a given point (the normal).

In the seventeenth century, two historical figures approached the theory of differential calculus from two very different directions. The English scientist Sir Isaac Newton viewed differential calculus in terms of physics, as the rate of change of a quantity over time. The German mathematician Gottfried Leibniz viewed differential calculus in terms of geometry, as the way in which the gradient of a curve changes over distance.

Newton developed his ideas before Leibniz, but Leibniz published his results earlier; the two men had a long feud over plagiarism. Today, both Newton and Leibniz are credited with the modern development of calculus, and it is generally accepted that they worked independently from different directions and that there was no evidence of plagiarism.

Isaac Newton (1642–1727) was an English scientist and mathematician, who worked in Cambridge and became President of the Royal Society. He made influential contributions to optics and mechanics, and his work on the paths of planets led to his formulation of calculus. He also pursued many other interests, ranging from alchemy to the study of religion. His final post was as Master of the Royal Mint in London, where he introduced the idea of a milled edge to coins.

Gottfried Leibniz (1646–1716) was born in Germany. He worked as a lawyer and librarian, but is described as a polymath — a universal genius who contributed ideas to a wide range of fields. He also travelled widely, and is said to have corresponded with more than 600 people, including many influential mathematicians and scientists of the day. Leibniz invented an early calculating machine, and worked on the mathematics of zero and one; this is now called binary mathematics and forms the basis of modern computer systems.

Mathematical concepts can take centuries to grow and yet be based on fundamentally the same idea. Archimedes proposed finding the area of a circle by looking at polygons with more and more sides; Johannes Kepler found a formula for the volume of barrels by splitting them into thinner and thinner slices. The same idea (of dividing into more and more smaller and smaller pieces) lies behind the development of 'integral calculus'. Two hundred years before Newton and Leibniz, Madhava of Sangamagrama (in present day Kerala, India) worked on the idea of infinite series and found a value for π that was accurate to 13 decimal places. Owing to his work on the links between finite algebra and infinite series, he is now also considered to be an important figure in the history of calculus.

How is it possible to reach the same conclusion from different directions? Can the development of mathematics be thought of as a straight line, or is it more like a tree diagram? (You learned about tree diagrams in Chapter 10.)

 20.1 The derivative

A straight line has constant **gradient**. For a straight line plotted on (x, y) axes, the gradient is defined as:

$$m = \frac{\text{change in vertical distance}}{\text{change in horizontal distance}} = \frac{\text{change in } y}{\text{change in } x}$$

 RR *You met this formula in Chapter 14.*

So a constant gradient means that the rate at which y changes with x is always the same.

How can we adapt this idea to define the gradient of a **curve**?

Using a GDC or maths software on a computer, you can graph a curve and 'zoom in' on it to look more closely at a small section, as shown in the following three diagrams. The more you zoom in, the more the curve looks like a straight line.

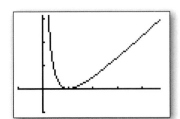 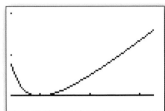 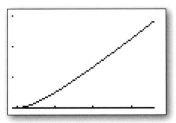

If we use the definition of the gradient of a straight line given above for a very short section of curve, we can get a good **approximation** of the 'gradient' of the curve in that region. By taking shorter and shorter sections around a particular point on the curve and calculating the gradient over them, you can obtain better and better estimates of the **gradient of the curve at that point**.

Finding the gradient of a curve at a point

Look at the graph of $y = x^2$:

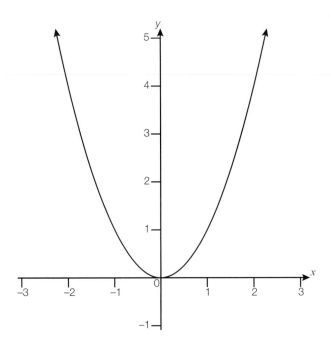

The gradient is different at every point on the curve. For example:

- when $x = -2.5$, the curve is decreasing steeply — the gradient is negative and large

- as x increases towards zero, the gradient remains negative but becomes smaller in magnitude (the curve becomes less steep)

- the curve is 'flat' at $(0, 0)$, which means here the gradient is zero

- as x increases from 0, the curve slopes upward and gets steeper — the gradient is positive and getting larger.

The rate of change of y against x is different at every point on the curve.

To find the gradient at any particular point P on the curve $y = x^2$, start by considering a **chord** PQ across a segment of the curve.

For example, to find the gradient at $(2, 4)$, plot the points P$(2, 4)$ and Q$(3, 9)$ on the curve and join them with a straight line.

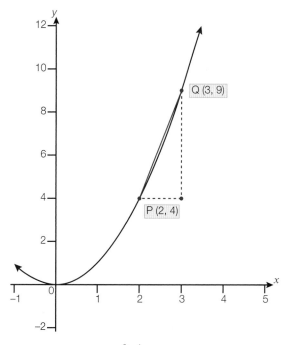

The gradient of the chord PQ is $\frac{9-4}{3-2} = 5$.

Now move Q closer to P. The chord PQ becomes shorter and also lies closer to the section of curve between P and Q. For instance, taking Q to be $(2.5, 6.25)$:

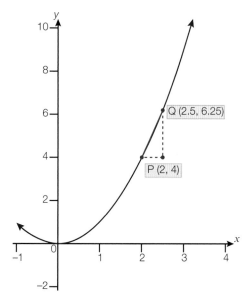

This time, the gradient of PQ is $\frac{6.25-4}{2.5-2} = 4.5$.

If we continue to push Q towards P, the values of the gradient of PQ are as follows:

P	Q	Gradient of PQ
2	3	$\frac{9-4}{3-2} = 5$
2	2.5	$\frac{6.25-4}{2.5-2} = 4.5$
2	2.25	$\frac{5.0625-4}{2.25-2} = 4.25$
2	2.1	$\frac{4.41-4}{2.1-2} = 4.1$
2	2.01	$\frac{4.0401-4}{2.01-2} = 4.01$

You can see that as Q moves closer to P, the gradient of the line PQ gets closer to 4.

When P and Q are so close that they are effectively the same point, the line PQ becomes the **tangent** to the curve at the point (2, 4).

The tangent to a curve is a straight line that touches the curve at one single point. The gradient of the curve at a point will be the same as the gradient of the tangent at that point.

We can use the same technique as above to find the gradient of the $y = x^2$ curve at other points.

If you repeat the calculations you did for the point (2, 4) at different points on the curve, you will get results like the following:

P	Gradient of curve at P	Pattern observed
$(-3, 9)$	-6	$-3 \times 2 = -6$
$(-2, 4)$	-4	$-2 \times 2 = -4$
$(-1, 1)$	-2	$-1 \times 2 = -2$
$(0, 0)$	0	$0 \times 2 = 0$
$(2, 4)$	4	$2 \times 2 = 4$
$(4, 16)$	8	$4 \times 2 = 8$
(x, x^2)	$2x$	$x \times 2 = 2x$

These results suggest that the gradient of $y = x^2$ at any point on the curve can be calculated by multiplying the x-coordinate of that point by 2. Note that the gradient of a curve depends on the position at which you are calculating it; in other words, the gradient is itself a function of x. It is often referred to as the **gradient function** of a curve.

 You learned about functions in Chapter 17.

Using more compact notation makes it easier to list results and conclusions. There are two types of notation that are commonly used. You should be familiar with both as you might meet either of them in the examinations.

The notation introduced by Leibniz is generally considered more convenient than that formulated by Newton, and is often the one that is used by teachers when they first introduce students to calculus.

	Leibniz notation	Newton's notation
Equation of curve or function	$y = x^2$	$f(x) = x^2$
Equation for the gradient	$\dfrac{dy}{dx} = 2x$	$f'(x) = 2x$

> **hint**
>
> Some people remember Leibniz notation as $\dfrac{dy}{dx} = \dfrac{\text{difference in } y}{\text{difference in } x}$
> $\dfrac{dy}{dx}$ is pronounced 'DY by DX'.

In applications, often the independent variable is called t (for time) instead of x, in which case we would write, for example:

- in Leibniz notation, if $y = t^2$ then $\dfrac{dy}{dt} = 2t$
- in Newton's notation, if $f(t) = t^2$ then $f'(t) = 2t$.

20.2 Differentiation

The process of finding the gradient function of a curve is called **differentiation**. To 'differentiate' a function or the equation of a curve means to find its derivative or gradient. Both numerical differentiation and differentiation from first principles will give the following results for these curves. (See Learning links 20A on page 581 if you are interested in differentiation from first principles.)

Function $y = f(x)$	Derivative $\dfrac{dy}{dx}$	Graph of function
$y = x^2$	$2x$	

continued . . .

Function $y = f(x)$	Derivative $\dfrac{dy}{dx}$	Graph of function
$y = x^3$	$3x^2$	
$y = x^2 + x$	$2x + 1$	
$y = 6x$	6	

$\longrightarrow$

continued . . .

Function $y = f(x)$	Derivative $\dfrac{dy}{dx}$	Graph of function
$y = 5x^3 - 2x$	$15x^2 - 2$	

In each case:

- $y = f(x)$ gives the rule for plotting the original curve

- $\dfrac{dy}{dx}$ gives the formula for finding the gradient at any point on the curve.

If you look carefully at the results in the table above, you can see that there is a general rule relating the formula for the function and the formula for the gradient.

- If $y = x^n$, then $\dfrac{dy}{dx} = n \times x^{n-1}$ or, equivalently, $f(x) = x^n \Rightarrow f'(x) = nx^{n-1}$
  in Newton's notation

- If $y = a \times x^n$, then $\dfrac{dy}{dx} = n \times a \times x^{n-1} = nax^{n-1}$ or, equivalently,
  $f(x) = ax^n \Rightarrow f'(x) = nax^{n-1}$

The formula that you are given in the Formula booklet is in Newton's notation:

$a = \pi r^2$ $\quad f(x) = ax^n \Rightarrow f'(x) = nax^{n-1}$

In words we say: 'to differentiate a power of x, multiply by the power and then reduce the power by one. If there is a coefficient (or constant factor), multiply the coefficient by the power'.

The following example uses both styles of notation.

Differentiate:

(a) $y = x^4$

(b) $f(x) = 3x^2$

(c) $y = 6x^3 + 2x^2$

(d) $f(x) = \dfrac{1}{2} x^3 - 6x$

The power is 4, so multiply by 4 and then reduce the power by 1.

(a) $\dfrac{dy}{dx} = 4 \times x^{4-1} = 4x^3$

The power is 2, and there is also a coefficient 3, so multiply the coefficient by 2 and reduce the power.

(b) $f'(x) = 2 \times 3x^{2-1} = 6x^1 = 6x$

Now we have a sum of two powers of x, both with coefficients. Differentiate each term separately; first differentiate $6x^3$ and then $2x^2$. Then add the results together.

(c) $\dfrac{dy}{dx} = 3 \times 6x^{3-1} + 2 \times 2x^{2-1}$

$= 18x^2 + 4x$

Follow the same procedure as in (c). Remember that $x = x^1$ and reducing the power by 1 gives $x^0 = 1$.

(d) $f'(x) = 3 \times \dfrac{1}{2} x^{3-1} - 1 \times 6x^{1-1}$

$= \dfrac{3}{2} x^2 - 6x^0$

$= 1.5x^2 - 6$

In parts (c) and (d) of Worked example 20.1, each term has been differentiated separately.

This is the procedure to follow for all curves whose equations are made up of more than one term:

If $y = ax^n + bx^m + \ldots$, then $\dfrac{dy}{dx} = anx^{n-1} + bmx^{m-1} + \ldots$

This is called the 'derivative of a sum' in the Formula booklet:

 $f(x) = ax^n, g(x) = bx^m \Rightarrow f'(x) + g'(x) = nax^{n-1} + mbx^{m-1}$ (in Newton's notation)

hint

Remember that each term of an equation is separated by either a '+' or '−' operator or the '=' sign. The '×' and '÷' operators do not separate terms; they form part of the term.

Exercise 20.1

1. Find $\dfrac{dy}{dx}$ for each of the following functions.

   (a) $y = x^5$

   (b) $y = 6x^3$

   (c) $y = -7x^4$

   (d) $y = \dfrac{4}{3}x^6$

   (e) $y = x^2 - 4x$

   (f) $y = 8x^9 - 15x^2$

   (g) $y = 19x + 11x^2$

   (h) $y = 3x^2 + 5x - 7x^3$

2. Find $f'(x)$ for each of the following functions.

   (a) $f(x) = x - x^7$

   (b) $f(x) = 20x^2 - x^9$

   (c) $f(x) = 11x^3 - 9x^2 - 7x$

   (d) $f(x) = 6x^5 - x^3 - 13x$

   (e) $f(x) = 10x - 9x^2 - x^4$

   (f) $f(x) = 8x^4 - 5x^3 + 2x^2 + 7x$

   (g) $f(x) = \dfrac{1}{2}x^2 + x^3 - \dfrac{2}{3}x^5$

   (h) $f(x) = 0.3x^3 + 0.12x^2 - x$

Learning links

20A Differentiation from first principles

As shown above, the gradient function of a curve can be found by taking different points on the curve (corresponding to different values of x) and calculating the gradients of shorter and shorter chords starting from each point. This method is called 'numerical differentiation', because you use actual numbers in the calculations.

You can follow a similar procedure but put letters in place of the numbers, by using algebra. This method is referred to as **differentiation from first principles**.

For example, on the curve $y = x^2$, take a general point P(x, x^2) and another point which is a distance h from P in the horizontal direction; it will be the point Q($(x + h)$, $(x + h)^2$):

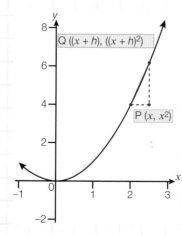

continued . . .

The gradient of PQ is:

$$\frac{(x+h)^2 - x^2}{x+h-x}$$

$$= \frac{x^2 + 2xh + h^2 - x^2}{h}$$

$$= \frac{2xh + h^2}{h}$$

$$= 2x + h$$

Moving Q closer to P is the same as letting h get smaller and smaller. This is written as '$h \to 0$' in mathematical notation (pronounced as 'h tends to zero'). So, when $h \to 0$, $2x + h$ approaches $2x$. Therefore we can say that the gradient of the curve $y = x^2$ at the point (x, x^2) is $2x$, or $\frac{dy}{dx} = 2x$.

This is not covered in the syllabus, but you might see in other books the notation $\frac{dy}{dx} = \lim_{h \to 0}(2x + h) = 2x$ this just means that the derivative has been calculated using first principles, i.e. 'as h tends to zero'.

 exam tip

Differentiation from first principles will not be examined, but it helps to understand the basic idea, which is very important in the development of calculus.

The number h is brought closer and closer to zero but can never equal zero, because when $h = 0$ the expression for the gradient of PQ, which is $\frac{f(x+h) - f(x)}{h}$, will have a zero in the denominator. This is an important issue, referred to as the understanding of **limits**, which neither Newton nor Leibniz addressed in their work.

1. The diagram shows a curve with two points P(2, 8) and Q(4, 64) marked on it.

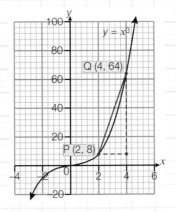

Complete the table below by following these steps:

- Find the gradient of the chord PQ.

- Keeping P fixed at (2, 8), change the coordinates of Q progressively by reducing the x-coordinate from $x = 4$ down to $x = 2.001$.

continued . . .

- Find the gradient of each chord PQ as Q gets closer to P.

P	Q	Gradient of PQ
2	4	$\dfrac{64-8}{4-2} = 28$
2	3.5	$\dfrac{42.875-8}{3.5-2} = 23.25$
2	3	$\dfrac{27-8}{3-2} = 19$
2	2.5	
2	2.3	
2	2.1	
2	2.01	
2	2.001	
2	2.0001	

(a) As Q moves closer to P, the gradient of the line PQ becomes closer to the value _____.

(b) The gradient of the tangent to the curve at $x = 2$ is _____.

2. Repeat the process in question 1 for the function $y = x^2 + x$, using the initial coordinates P(3, 12) and Q(4, 20).

(a) Draw a sketch of the graph $y = x^2 + x$.

(b) Copy and complete the table below.

P	Q	Gradient of PQ
3	4	$\dfrac{20-12}{4-3} = 8$
3	3.5	$\dfrac{15.75-12}{3.5-3} = 7.5$
3	3.4	$\dfrac{14.96-12}{3.4-3} = 7.4$
3	3.2	
3	3.1	
3	3.01	
3	3.001	
3	3.0001	

(c) As Q moves closer to P, the gradient of the line PQ becomes closer to the value _____.

(d) The gradient of the tangent to the curve at $x = 3$ is _____.

Differentiation in more detail

So far, we have seen the general rule for differentiating powers of x by looking at positive integer powers. However, the rule can be proved to hold for all power functions x^p where p can be zero, negative, a rational number, or even an irrational number.

Differentiation should also confirm some geometrical facts that you already know.

Differentiating constants

To differentiate $y = 5$, note that since $x^0 = 1$, we can rewrite the function as $y = 5x^0$.

Then, using the general rule gives $\dfrac{dy}{dx} = 0 \times 5x^{0-1} = 0$.

Let's look at the graph of $y = 5$:

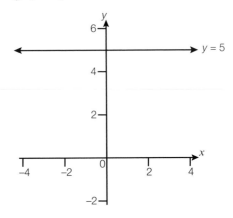

A horizontal line has a gradient of zero, so differentiation has confirmed something that you already know, that $y = 5$ is a horizontal line.

The graph of $y = c$, where c is any constant, will be a horizontal line with gradient zero. So whenever you differentiate a constant, you get zero:

If $y = c$, then $\dfrac{dy}{dx} = 0$.

Differentiating a straight line

To differentiate $y = 3x$, note that since $x = x^1$, we can rewrite the function as $y = 3x^1$.

Then, using the general rule gives $\dfrac{dy}{dx} = 1 \times 3x^{1-1} = 3x^0 = 3$.

So $y = 3x$ is a line with a gradient of 3.

Compare this with the equation $y = mx + c$ which you are already familiar with, where the coefficient of 'x' gives the gradient of the line.

You learned about $y = mx + c$ **in Chapter 14.**

Now let's differentiate $y = 3x + 2$. If we rewrite it as $y = 3x^1 + 2x^0$, then applying the general rule gives $\dfrac{dy}{dx} = 1 \times 3x^{1-1} + 0 \times 2x^{0-1} = 3 + 0 = 3$.

Again, comparing this with $y = mx + c$ confirms that $m = 3$ is the gradient of the line. It also tells us that the y-intercept, 2 in this case, has no effect on the gradient; it simply positions the line relative to the coordinate axes.

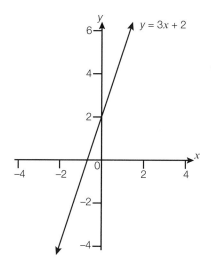

Differentiating a rational function

To differentiate the rational function $y = \frac{2}{x}$, rewrite it as a power function with a negative power: $y = \frac{2}{x} = 2x^{-1}$.

The general rule then gives $\frac{dy}{dx} = -1 \times 2x^{-1-1} = -2x^{-2} = \frac{-2}{x^2}$.

The general rule is used in exactly the same way for a negative index as it is for a positive index.

The gradient function $\frac{-2}{x^2}$ shows that the gradient of the curve will always be negative. If you look at the graph, notice that both of the curves that make up the graph are always sloping downwards.

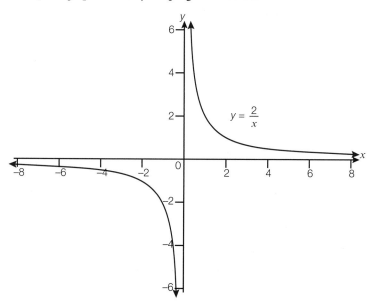

Worked example 20.2

Q. The function $f(x)$ is given by $f(x) = x^4 - 3x^3 + 5x + 7$.

(a) Find $f'(x)$.

(b) Calculate the value of $f'(x)$ when $x = -1$.

> Differentiate each term separately according to the general formula on page 580. Differentiating the constant 7 gives 0.

A. (a) $f'(x) = 4x^3 - 9x^2 + 5$

> The derivative $f'(x)$ is itself a function of x, so you can evaluate it at any given x value. Substitute in $x = -1$.

(b) When $x = -1$,

$$f'(-1) = 4(-1)^3 - 9(-1)^2 + 5$$
$$= -4 - 9 + 5 = -8$$

In examinations, several different instructions may be used that all mean 'find $\frac{dy}{dx}$':

Instruction	Example function given	Example answer
Find $f'(x)$	$f(x) = 3x^3 - x + 2$	$f'(x) = 9x^2 - 1$
Differentiate with respect to x	$y = 5 - x^2$	$\frac{dy}{dx} = -2x$
Find the gradient function	$g(t) = 4t^2 + 3t$	$g'(t) = 8t + 3$
Find the derivative of the function	$h(x) = 9x - 2x^4$	$h'(x) = 9 - 8x^3$

Worked example 20.3

Q. The equation of a curve is given as $y = 2x^3 - 5x^2 + 4$

(a) Find $\frac{dy}{dx}$.

(b) Copy and complete the table below.

x	-1	0	1	2	3
y	-3	4		0	13
$\frac{dy}{dx}$		0	-4		24

(c) What is the gradient of the curve when $x = 2$?

(d) Use the table to sketch the graph of the curve.

continued . . .

Callout box 1:
Differentiate term by term using the general formula on page 580.

A. (a) $\dfrac{dy}{dx} = 6x^2 - 10x$

To find the missing entry in the second row, substitute that value of x into the equation for the curve.

To find the missing entries in the third row, substitute the corresponding values of x into the equation for $\dfrac{dy}{dx}$.

(b)

x	-1	0	1	2	3
y	-3	4	1	0	13
$\dfrac{dy}{dx}$	16	0	-4	4	24

The gradient of the curve when $x = 2$ is the value of $\dfrac{dy}{dx}$ at $x = 2$. You can read this off from the table in part (b).

(c) When $x = 2$, $\dfrac{dy}{dx} = 4$

Use the first two rows of the table to plot points on the curve; the third row tells you how steep the curve should be at those points.

(d)

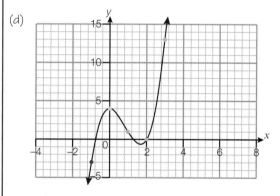

Worked example 20.4

Q. (a) Write $f(x) = \dfrac{3}{x^2}$ in the form $f(x) = 3x^n$.

Use this form to differentiate $f(x)$.

(b) Write $f(x) = \dfrac{1}{2x^3}$ in the form $f(x) = \dfrac{1}{2}x^n$.

Use this form to differentiate $f(x)$.

continued . . .

A power of x in the denominator can be written as a negative power and then differentiated using the formula on page 580.

→A. (a) $f(x) = \dfrac{3}{x^2} = 3x^{-2}$

$f'(x) = -2 \times 3x^{-2-1} = -6x^{-3}$

or $f'(x) = \dfrac{-6}{x^3}$

The power can be treated in the same way as in part (a), but in (a) the constant 3 was in the numerator, and here we have a coefficient 2 in the denominator instead.

Take extra care when working with coefficients and constants in the denominator. When differentiating, the value of the power has to multiply the fraction $\frac{1}{2}$, not the 2 in the denominator. Also be careful not to accidentally switch the numerator and denominator, which is a common mistake.

(b) $f(x) = \dfrac{1}{2x^3} = \dfrac{1}{2}x^{-3}$

$f'(x) = -3 \times \dfrac{1}{2}x^{-3-1}$

$= -\dfrac{3}{2}x^{-4}$

$= -\dfrac{3}{2} \times \dfrac{1}{x^4}$

$= \dfrac{-3}{2x^4}$

Exercise 20.2

1. Find $\dfrac{dy}{dx}$ for each of the following functions.

   (a) $y = \dfrac{5}{7x}$

   (b) $y = 2x^5 - x^{-2}$

   (c) $y = x^3 - \dfrac{9}{8x^2}$

   (d) $y = x - \dfrac{3}{4x^2}$

   (e) $y = 3x^{-5} - 11x^2$

2. Find $f'(x)$ for each of the following functions.

   (a) $f(x) = x^8 + x^{-5} + 6$

   (b) $f(x) = 8x^4 - 2x^3 + x^{-4} + 13x$

   (c) $f(x) = \dfrac{1}{x^3} - 10x + 2$

   (d) $f(x) = \dfrac{5}{x^7} + 4x - 13$

   (e) $f(x) = 9x - \dfrac{3}{5x}$

3. Differentiate the following with respect to x.

   (a) $1 + x - 3x^3 + 5x^5 - 7x^7$

   (b) $3 - 4x^{-2}$

   (c) $10x + 9x^{-3} + \dfrac{2}{x}$

   (d) $\dfrac{3}{7}x^2 + \dfrac{5}{x^2}$

   (e) $\dfrac{1}{x^3} - 4x^{-5}$

4. A function is defined as $f(x) = 2x^3 - 7x^2 - 4x + 9$

   (a) Find the gradient function $f'(x)$.

   (b) Find the gradient of the function when:

       (i) $x = 1$

       (ii) $x = -2$

       (iii) $x = 0$

   (c) Find the value of $f'(-1)$ and explain what your answer represents.

5. The equation of a curve is defined as $y = 10 + 8x - 2x^3$

   (a) Find $\dfrac{\mathrm{d}y}{\mathrm{d}x}$.

   (b) Calculate the gradient of the function when:

       (i) $x = 0$

       (ii) $x = -2$

       (iii) $x = 3$

20.3 Rates of change

Leibniz defined the derivative by calculating how the gradient of a curve changes. He took a graphical approach that was based on the rate at which 'y' changed in relation to a small change in 'x'. Newton's development of calculus was built on his work with rates of change in physics; he used variables other than 'x' and 'y'.

As you have seen in Chapter 18, the height of a ball that has been thrown can be modelled by a quadratic function of time. Here is an example of a graph of height plotted against time:

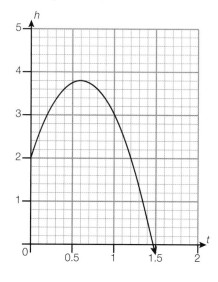

The curve gets flatter near the top, showing that the ball slows (decelerates) as it goes higher; it stops for an instant at the maximum height, where the derivative (gradient of the curve) is zero, and then descends, gaining speed (accelerating) as it does so, which is shown by the curve getting steeper.

If the height of the ball is described by the equation $h = 2 + 6t - 5t^2$, then the rate at which the height is changing is given by $\frac{dh}{dt}$. So

$h = 2 + 6t - 5t^2$ gives the height of the ball at time t;

$\frac{dh}{dt} = 6 - 10t$ gives the rate at which the height is changing at time t.

Other variables are used in economics. For example, an equation can be used to describe the total cost (C_T) of manufacturing a certain quantity q of a product.

The **marginal cost** (C_M) is the change in total cost resulting from a small change in output.

If $C_T = 6q^2 - 7q + 10$

then $C_M = \frac{dC_T}{dq} = 12q - 7$

Whenever you want to find the rate of change of one quantity against another, you can use calculus. In any context, it is important to know what is the independent variable (x, t, q in our examples, or something else) and what is the dependent variable (y, h, C_T in our examples, or something else).

For instance, if you are studying the rate at which a plant grows, the height of the plant might be the dependent variable, and time will be the independent variable.

Worked example 20.5

Q. Ped throws a stone into a pond and watches the circular ripples spread out from the centre. The area of a circular ripple is given by the formula $A = \pi r^2$.

(a) What is the average change in ripple area as the radius changes from 3 m to 6 m?

(b) What is the rate of change of the ripple area when the radius is exactly 4 m?

→

continued . . .

Sketch the graph of A against r.

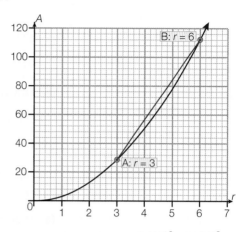

A. (a) Average change in area $= \dfrac{\pi \times 6^2 - \pi \times 3^2}{6-3}$

$= 9\pi$

The average change in area as the radius changes is given by $\dfrac{\text{change in area}}{\text{change in radius}}$. On the graph, this is the gradient of the **chord** AB.

(b)

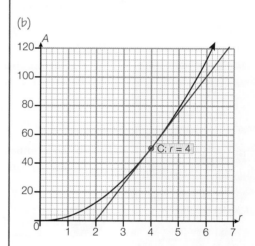

The rate of change when r is exactly 4 is given by the gradient of the **tangent** at point C.

$\dfrac{dA}{dr} = 2\pi r$

This is just the derivative $\dfrac{dA}{dr}$, evaluated at $r = 4$.

When $r = 4$, $\dfrac{dA}{dr} = 2\pi \times 4 = 8\pi$

exam tip

The rate of change in part (b) of Worked example 20.5, i.e., the gradient of the tangent at a point, can also be called the '**instantaneous** rate of change'.

Exercise 20.3

1. The displacement s, in metres, of a particle t seconds after leaving point O is given by:

   $$s(t) = 3t^2 - 5t + 6$$

   (a) Find the average change in displacement between $t = 1$ and $t = 4$.

   (b) What is the rate of change of displacement when $t = 5$?

   (c) Calculate $s'(3)$ and explain what your answer represents.

2. A football is kicked vertically upwards. Its height h above the ground after t seconds is described by $h = 14t - 10t^2$.

   (a) Differentiate h with respect to t to find $\dfrac{dh}{dt}$.

   (b) Given that $\dfrac{dh}{dt}$ represents the velocity of the ball at a given instant, find the velocity of the ball when:

   (i) $t = 0.5$

   (ii) $t = 0.7$

3. The surface area of a circular pool of water is spreading uniformly. The area is $A = \pi r^2$, where r is the radius of the circle in metres.

   (a) Find the average rate of change of the area as the radius changes from 2 m to 4 m.

   (b) Determine the rate of change of the area when the radius is exactly 5 m.

20.4 The second derivative

We have seen that the derivative, or gradient, of a curve is itself a function of the independent variable. As it is a function, it too can be differentiated. The method is exactly the same as for finding the first derivative, but the result has a different meaning and is called a 'second derivative'.

In physics, **velocity** is the rate of change of the distance moved in a certain direction, i.e. the **displacement**; in other words, velocity is the derivative of displacement with respect to time. The rate of change of velocity is called **acceleration**, so acceleration is the second derivative of displacement with respect to time.

For example, if the distance travelled by an object is given by the function:

$$s = 3t^2 - 2t^3 + 1$$

then the velocity is:

$$v = \frac{\mathrm{d}s}{\mathrm{d}t} = 6t - 6t^2$$

and the acceleration is:

$$a = \frac{\mathrm{d}^2 s}{\mathrm{d}t^2} = 6 - 12t$$

(the expression $\frac{\mathrm{d}^2 s}{\mathrm{d}t^2}$ is pronounced as 'D two S by D T squared').

If distance is measured in metres and time in seconds, then velocity is measured in metres per second ($\mathrm{m\,s^{-1}}$) and acceleration is measured in metres per second per second ($\mathrm{m\,s^{-2}}$).

Using Newton's notation, we have the displacement $s = f(t)$, the velocity $v = f'(t)$ and the acceleration $a = f''(t)$.

exam tip

Examiners will not assume that students have knowledge of the second derivative. You may use the second derivative to answer examination questions though, as long as your working makes it clear that you understand why you are using the second derivative and you have given a clear result.

Worked example 20.6

Q. A ball is thrown from the top of a cliff. Its height in metres above the cliff-top t seconds after being thrown is given by $h = 1.5 + 3t - 5t^2$. Find the equations for the velocity and acceleration of the ball, and interpret their meaning.

Differentiate the height function to get the velocity.

A. $h = 1.5 + 3t - 5t^2$

$$\text{Velocity} = \frac{\mathrm{d}h}{\mathrm{d}t} = 3 - 10t$$

When t is very small, the velocity is positive, which means that the ball is initially moving upwards. When t gets bigger than 0.3, the velocity becomes negative, which means that after 0.3 seconds the ball is falling downwards.

Differentiate the velocity to get acceleration.

$$\text{Acceleration} = \frac{\mathrm{d}^2 h}{\mathrm{d}t^2} = -10$$

The acceleration has a constant magnitude of $10\,\mathrm{m\,s^{-2}}$, and the negative sign tells us that its direction is downward. This is the acceleration due to gravity.

Differentiation can give you the gradient function for any curve.

By using the formula given in section 20.2, you can find the gradient function of any curve with an equation of the form $f(x) = ax^n + bx^m + \ldots$.

It is possible to differentiate far more complex curves, but those methods are not in the syllabus for this course.

The following curve is the graph of $f(x) = 6 - x - x^2$.

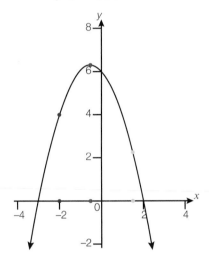

Differentiate to find the equation of the gradient function:

$$f'(x) = -1 - 2x$$

Using this equation you can calculate the gradient at any particular point on the curve. For instance:

When $x = -2$, $f'(x) = -1 - 2 \times (-2) = -1 + 4 = 3$; the gradient is positive.

When $x = -\frac{1}{2}$, $f'(x) = -1 - 2 \times (-\frac{1}{2}) = -1 + 1 = 0$; the gradient is zero.

When $x = 1.5$, $f'(x) = -1 - 2 \times 1.5 = -1 - 3 = -4$; the gradient is negative.

Compare these results with the graph. Notice that as x increases, the gradient changes from positive values, through zero, to negative values.

Finding x- and y-coordinates from the gradient

It is also possible to work backwards: if you are given a specific value of the gradient, you can use the gradient function to find the x-coordinate(s) of the point(s) on the curve with that gradient. Once you know the x-coordinate, you can use the equation of the curve to calculate the corresponding value of y.

Consider the function $f(x) = 6 - x - x^2$ again. What are the coordinates of the point where the curve has a gradient of 4?

The gradient function is $f'(x) = -1 - 2x$, so you are looking for the x value that makes this equal to 4:

$$-1 - 2x = 4$$

so $\qquad x = -2.5$

For $x = -2.5$, use the equation $f(x) = 6 - x - x^2$ to find the corresponding y-coordinate:

$$f(-2.5) = 6 - (-2.5) - (-2.5)^2 = 6 + 2.5 - 6.25 = 2.25$$

The curve $f(x) = 6 - x - x^2$ has a gradient of 4 at the point $(-2.5, 2.25)$.

Worked example 20.7

Q. Consider the function $f(x) = x^3 + 2x^2 - 12x + 8$. Find:

(a) $f'(x)$

(b) $f'(2)$ (the value of $f'(x)$ when $x = 2$)

(c) the coordinates of the point where the gradient is 27.

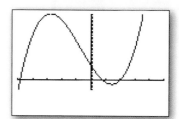

> Sketch the curve using either your GDC or a computer, it will help you to understand the rest of the question. (See '22.2G Graphs' on page 645 of the GDC chapter if you need a reminder.)

> Differentiate term by term using the formula on page 580.

A. (a) $f'(x) = 3x^2 + 4x - 12$

> Substitute $x = 2$ into the gradient function.

(b) $f'(2) = 3 \times 2^2 + 4 \times 2 - 12 = 12 + 8 - 12 = 8$

> You want to find the value of x for which $f'(x) = 27$.

(c) $3x^2 + 4x - 12 = 27$

> Rearrange into the general form of a quadratic equation ($ax^2 + bx + c = 0$).

$3x^2 + 4x - 39 = 0$

continued . . .

> Use your GDC (or other method) to solve the equation. (See Chapter 2 for a reminder of methods.)

From GDC: $x = 3$ or $x = -4.33$

> The question asks for the **coordinates** of the points, so use $f(x) = x^3 + 2x^2 - 12x + 8$ to find the y-coordinate corresponding to each x value.

When $x = 3$, $y = 3^3 + 2 \times 3^2 - 12 \times 3 + 8 = 17$

When $x = -4.33$, $y = (-4.33)^3 + 2 \times (-4.33)^2 - 12 \times (-4.33) + 8 = 16.2$

The points are $(3, 17)$ and $(-4.33, 16.2)$.

Worked example 20.8

Q. As part of their Business Studies course, Myra and Salim have set up a company to manufacture scarves. They calculate that the total cost of production (C_T), in US dollars, is given by the function:

$$C_T = 2q^2 - 6q + 5$$

where q is the number of scarves produced.

(a) Find the value of the marginal cost, $\dfrac{dC_T}{dq}$, when $q = 25$. (The marginal cost can be thought of as the additional cost of making one extra scarf above the current quantity.)

(b) If the marginal cost is \$42, how many scarves are they producing?

> Differentiate C_T to get the marginal cost function.

A. (a) $\dfrac{dC_T}{dq} = 4q - 6$

When $q = 25$, the marginal cost is $4 \times 25 - 6 = \$94$

> Now we want to find the value of q for which $\dfrac{dC_T}{dq} = 42$.

(b) $4q - 6 = 42$

$4q = 48$

$q = 12$

They are making 12 scarves.

Using your GDC for differential calculus

Your GDC cannot differentiate a function for you, but there are many ways in which your GDC can help you with questions involving gradients. Here are some ideas.

Your GDC can:

- draw the curve, so that you can see how the gradient changes
- get the **value** of $\dfrac{dy}{dx}$ for a given value of x
- find the y-coordinate corresponding to any given x-coordinate
- solve any equations that arise in the problem.

Worked example 20.9

Q. (a) Differentiate the following function with respect to x:
$$f(x) = 2x^2 - x + \frac{1}{x}$$

(b) Calculate $f'(3)$.

(c) Find the value of x at the point where the gradient of the curve is 2.

Draw the curve on your GDC to get an idea of what you're dealing with. (See '22.2G Graphs' on page 645 of the GDC chapter if you need a reminder of how.)

 TEXAS    CASIO

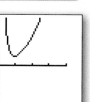 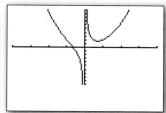

Rewrite $f(x)$ as a sum of powers of x.

A. (a) $f(x) = 2x^2 - x + x^{-1}$

Differentiate term by term using the formula on page 580.

Your calculator can't help you with this!

$$f'(x) = 4x - 1 - x^{-2}$$
$$= 4x - 1 - \frac{1}{x^2}$$

$\longrightarrow$

continued . . .

Calculating $f'(3)$ is the same as finding $\dfrac{dy}{dx}$ when $x = 3$. You can substitute $x = 3$ into the derivative function found in part (a) or use your GDC. See *'20.1 (a) Finding the numerical value of $\dfrac{dy}{dx}$ using a graph'* on page 686 of the GDC chapter if you need to.

(b)

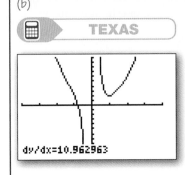

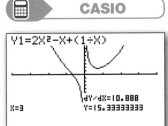

When $x = 3$, $\dfrac{dy}{dx} = 10.9$

To find the value of x where the gradient is 2, you need to solve the equation $f'(x) = 2$.

(c) $4x - 1 - \dfrac{1}{x^2} = 2$

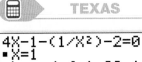

You can use the equation solver on your GDC. *See '19.2 (b) Solving unfamiliar equations using the equation solver'* on page 685 of the GDC chapter if you need to.

The gradient of the curve is 2 at the point where $x = 1$.

If you are asked for the coordinates of the point where the gradient has a particular value, you can find this information using the table function on your GDC (see *'20.1 (b) Finding the numerical value of the derivative $(\frac{dy}{dx})$ using the table'* on page 687 of the GDC chapter of you need a reminder of how to do this). For part (c) of Worked example 20.9, the table on a CASIO calculator would look like this:

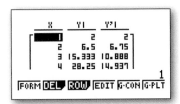

From the table you can see that when the gradient (third column) is 2, the x-coordinate is 1 (first column) and the y-coordinate is 2 (second column). So (1, 2) is the point on the curve where the gradient is 2.

Note that on a TEXAS GDC, the table will not show values of the gradient in the third column. In this case, you would need to find the value of x for a given gradient, and then look up the corresponding y value in the table.

Exercise 20.4

1. Find the gradient of the following curves at the points with the specified x-coordinates:

    (a) $f(x) = 3x^4$, when $x = 5$

    (b) $g(x) = -12x^3$, when $x = 1$

    (c) $h(x) = x^2 - 13x$, when $x = 0$

    (d) $y = 8x - \dfrac{5}{6}x^2$, when $x = -6$

    (e) $y = x^2 - 10x + 7$, when $x = 3$

    (f) $y = 5 + 6x - 4x^3$, when $x = -2$

    (g) $f(x) = 7 - 8x^2 - 2x^3$, when $x = -1$

    (h) $f(x) = 11 - 2x^2 + 3x^4$, when $x = \dfrac{1}{2}$

    (i) $y = 9 - 8x^2 + \dfrac{2}{3}x^3$, when $x = 4$

    (j) $y = \dfrac{5}{x^2}$, when $x = 1$

    (k) $f(x) = 3x + \dfrac{12}{x^4}$, when $x = -3$

    (l) $y = \dfrac{5}{x^3} + \dfrac{1}{4x}$, when $x = 2$

2. In the following questions you are given the equation for the total cost of production, C, for a quantity of items, q.

    In each case:

    (i) Work out an equation for the marginal cost by differentiating the total cost with respect to q; that is, find $\dfrac{dC}{dq}$.

    (ii) Determine the marginal cost for the stated value of q.

    (a) $C(q) = 8q^2 - 9$, when $q = 10$

    (b) $C(q) = 300 + 5q^2$, when $q = 120$

    (c) $C(q) = 70 + 5q + 3q^2$, when $q = 80$

    (d) $C(q) = 3q^2 - 10q + 64$, when $q = 14$

    (e) $C(q) = 2q^3 - 9q^2 + 45q + 7$, when $q = 200$

3. The equation defining a function is $y = x^2 - 4x - 12$.

    (a) Differentiate the equation to find the gradient function, $\dfrac{dy}{dx}$.

    (b) Find the gradient of the curve at the point where the x-coordinate is 3.

    (c) Find the value of x where the gradient of the curve is 8.

4. A function f is defined as $f(x) = x^3 - 4x^2 + 8$.

   (a) Work out $f'(x)$ in terms of x.

   (b) Find $f'(-2)$.

   (c) Find the coordinates of the points on the curve where the gradient is -4.

5. The equation of a curve is $y = 2x + \dfrac{1}{x}$.

   (a) Find $\dfrac{dy}{dx}$.

   (b) Find the gradient of the curve at the point where the x-coordinate is -1.

   (c) Find the coordinates of the points on the curve where the gradient is -7.

6. The total cost (in dollars) of manufacturing q items of a certain product is given by:

   $$C_{\text{T}} = 800 - 5q + \frac{2}{3}q^2$$

   (a) Find the marginal cost, $\dfrac{dC_{\text{T}}}{dq}$, when 90 items are being produced.

   (b) Find the number of items being produced when the marginal cost is \$55.

7. Given that $s = 28t - 10t^2$, where s is the displacement in metres and t is the time in seconds, find an expression for:

   (a) the velocity of the particle $(v = \dfrac{ds}{dt})$

   (b) the acceleration of the particle $(a = \dfrac{d^2s}{dt^2})$.

20.6 Equation of the tangent at a given point

The tangent to a curve at a particular point has been defined as a straight line that touches the curve at that point.

It is possible to find the equation of any line provided that you know its **gradient** and the **coordinates of one point** that it passes through. So, you can find the equation of the tangent to a curve at a given point using methods that are already familiar.

If you are given the x-coordinate of the point, you can use the equation of the curve to find the y-coordinate. The gradient of the tangent is just the gradient of the curve at that point; so to find the gradient, differentiate the equation of the curve and calculate the value of the derivative at the given x value.

For example, to find the equation of the tangent to the curve $y = 2x - x^3$ at the point where $x = 2$:

- Calculate the y-coordinate. If $x = 2$, then $y = 2 \times 2 - 2^3 = 4 - 8 = -4$

- Differentiate to get the gradient function. $\dfrac{dy}{dx} = 2 - 3x^2$

- Find the gradient when $x = 2$. When $x = 2$, $\dfrac{dy}{dx} = 2 - 3 \times 2^2 = 2 - 12 = -10$

- Taking the general equation of a line, $y = mx + c$, put in the x- and y-coordinates and the value of the gradient (m) and solve for c:
  $-4 = -10 \times 2 + c$
  $c = 16$

- Hence the equation of the tangent is $y = -10x + 16$.

Alternatively, you can use your GDC:

📱 TEXAS	📱 CASIO

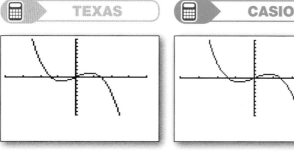

Draw the curve (see '22.2G Graphs' on page 645 of the GDC chapter if you need to).

📱 TEXAS	📱 CASIO

There is not a column for y'_1 in the TEXAS table of coordinates, so substitute $x = 2$ into the gradient function to find y'_1.

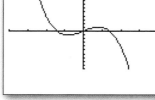

Look at the table of coordinates for the graph (see '20.1 (b) Finding the numerical value of the derivative using a table.' on page 686 of the GDC chapter if you need to), and find the value of y corresponding to $x = 2$. If you are using a CASIO calculator you will also be able to see that the gradient at $x = 2$ is -10.

When $x = 2$, $y = -4$

📱 TEXAS	📱 CASIO

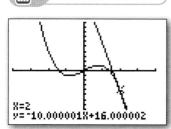

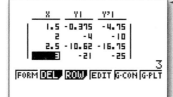

Draw the tangent to the curve at the point $(2, -4)$. See '20.2 Finding the equation of tangents at a point' on page 687 of the GDC chapter if you need to.

The equation of the tangent is $y = -10x + 16$.

Read off the equation of the tangent from the screen. Note that you should round the figures on the screen to whole numbers.

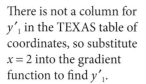

We will solve this problem first using algebra and then using the GDC in two ways.

Q. Find the equation of the tangent to the curve $y = \dfrac{3}{x^2} - 2x$ at the point where $x = -2$.

A. Method 1:

Using algebra: rewrite the function as a sum of powers of x, and differentiate term by term using the formula on page 580.

$$y = \frac{3}{x^2} - 2x$$

$$y = 3x^{-2} - 2x$$

$$\frac{dy}{dx} = -6x^{-3} - 2$$

$$= \frac{-6}{x^3} - 2$$

Find the y-coordinate and the gradient at $x = -2$.

At $x = -2$,

$$y = \frac{3}{(-2)^2} - 2 \times (-2) = 4\frac{3}{4} = \frac{19}{4}$$

$$\frac{dy}{dx} = \frac{-6}{(-2)^3} - 2 = \frac{6}{8} - 2 = -\frac{5}{4}$$

Put these values into $y = mx + c$ and solve for c.

$$y = mx + c$$

$$\frac{19}{4} = -\frac{5}{4} \times (-2) + c$$

$$\frac{19}{4} = \frac{10}{4} + c$$

$$c = \frac{9}{4}$$

Write down the equation of the tangent.

Equation of the tangent is

$$y = -\frac{5}{4}x + \frac{9}{4}$$

Method 2(a):

 TEXAS

 CASIO

Using your GDC: draw the curve (see '22.2G Graphs' on page 645 of the GDC chapter if you need to).

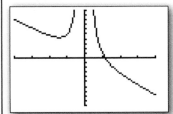

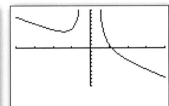

continued . . .

  TEXAS   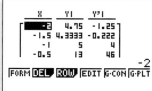 CASIO

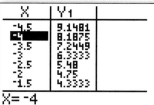

When $x = -2$, $y = 4.75$

Look at the table of coordinates to find the y-coordinate corresponding to $x = -2$. (See '14.1' on page 678 of the GDC chapter if you need to.)

From the graph, find the value of $\dfrac{dy}{dx}$ when $x = -2$. (See '20.1 (a) Finding the numerical value of the derivative using a graph' on page 686 of the GDC chapter if you need to.)

 TEXAS   CASIO

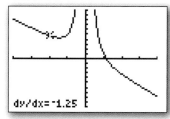   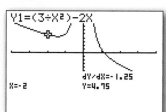

$$\frac{dy}{dx} = -1.25$$

Substitute the values into $y = mx + c$ and solve for c.

$y = mx + c$

$4.75 = -1.25 \times (-2) + c$

$c = 4.75 - 2.5 = 2.25$

Equation of the tangent is

$y = -1.25x + 2.25$

<u>Method 2(b):</u>

Using your GDC: on the graph, draw the tangent to the curve at $x = -2$. (See '20.2 Finding the equation of a tangent at a point' on page 687 of the GDC chapter if you need to.)

 TEXAS   CASIO

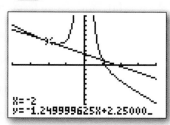   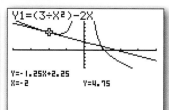

Read off the equation of the tangent from the screen.

$y = -1.25x + 2.25$

Exercise 20.5

1. For each of the following curves, use your GDC to find the equation of the tangent at the point with the given x-coordinate.

(a) $y = 3x^2 - 10$, at $x = 4$

(b) $y = 4 - x^2$, at $x = -3$

(c) $f(x) = 9 - x^4$, at $x = -1$

(d) $f(x) = x - x^3$, at $x = \dfrac{1}{2}$

(e) $y = 2x^3 + 7x^2 - 3x + 4$, at $x = 1$

(f) $y = 2 + \dfrac{1}{x}$, at $x = -2$

(g) $g(x) = 8 - \dfrac{3}{x^2}$, at $x = 2$

(h) $y = \dfrac{7}{x^3} - \dfrac{1}{x^2}$, at $x = 1.5$

2. For each of the following curves, find the equation of the tangent to the curve at the given point.

(a) $y = x^2 - x - 12$ at $(-3, 0)$

(b) $y = 2x^3 + 3x^2 - 23x - 12$ at $(2, -30)$

(c) $y = 6x^3 - 19x^2 + 19x - 6$ at $(-\dfrac{1}{2}, -21)$

(d) $f(x) = 11 - 2x^2$ at $(3, -7)$

(e) $f(x) = \dfrac{3}{x^2} - x$ at $(\dfrac{1}{2}, \dfrac{23}{2})$

(f) $y = 1 - 2x - \dfrac{2}{x}$ at $(-1, 5)$

3. A function is defined as $y = 2x^3 - x^2 + 4x + 1$.

(a) Find $\dfrac{dy}{dx}$ in terms of x.

The point P lies on the curve. The x-coordinate at P is 2.

(b) Find the gradient of the curve at P.

(c) State the y-coordinate of P.

(d) Write down the equation of the tangent to the curve at P.

4. A function is defined as $y = 9 - \dfrac{x^2}{16}$.

(a) Find $\dfrac{dy}{dx}$ in terms of x.

The point P lies on the curve. The x-coordinate at point P is -1.

(b) Find the gradient of the curve at P.

(c) State the y-coordinate of P.

(d) Write down the equation of the tangent to the curve at P in the form $ax + by + d = 0$ where a, b and d are integers.

20.7 Equation of the normal at a given point

A straight line that makes a right angle with the tangent to a curve at a particular point is called the **normal** to the curve at that point. As the normal is perpendicular to the tangent, the rule for two perpendicular gradients can be used:

If two lines are perpendicular, their gradients multiply to give −1.

$$m_1 \times m_2 = -1$$

«RR *This relationship was covered Chapter 14.*

So if the tangent at a point on the curve has gradient 4, the gradient of the normal will be $-\frac{1}{4}$, because $4 \times \left(-\frac{1}{4}\right) = -1$.

A quick way of finding the gradient of the normal is to **turn the gradient of the tangent upside down, and change the sign.**

For the example above, the gradient of the tangent, which is 4, can be written as the fraction $\frac{4}{1}$. Turning it upside down gives $\frac{1}{4}$, and then switching the sign gives $-\frac{1}{4}$.

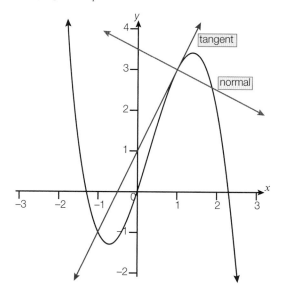

The curve illustrated in the diagram above is the function $f(x) = 3x + x^2 - x^3$. The tangent and normal have been drawn at the point (1, 3).

To find the equation of the normal, first differentiate the equation of the curve to find the gradient function:

$$f'(x) = 3 + 2x - 3x^2$$

Replace x by 1 to get:

$$f'(1) = 3 + 2 \times 1 - 3 \times 1^2 = 3 + 2 - 3 = 2$$

This means that the gradient of the tangent at (1, 3) is 2.

So the gradient of the normal is $-\frac{1}{2}$.

Now we can substitute the coordinates (1, 3) and the gradient $-\frac{1}{2}$ into the equation $y = mx + c$ and solve for c:

$$3 = -\frac{1}{2} \times 1 + c$$
$$c = 3 + \frac{1}{2} = 3\frac{1}{2}$$

Therefore the equation of the normal is $y = -\frac{1}{2}x + 3\frac{1}{2}$.

You can also use your GDC to help you find the equation of the normal. Some calculators have this facility built into them (most CASIO models), in which case you would just tell it to draw the normal to the curve at a specified point, and it will display the equation of the normal.

Other models of calculator (most TEXAS models) may not be able to give you the equation of the normal directly. In this case, you could still use your GDC to find the coordinates of the point and the gradient of the tangent; then follow the procedure above to calculate the gradient of the normal and the constant c in $y = mx + c$.

Worked example 20.11

Q. If $f(x) = \dfrac{2}{x^2} + x$, find the equation of the normal at $x = -1$.

A.

🖩 ▶ **TEXAS**	🖩 ▶ **CASIO**

Draw the curve to get an idea of its shape.

🖩 ▶ **TEXAS**	🖩 ▶ **CASIO**

Look at the table of coordinates to find the value of the *y*-coordinate.

(See '14.1 Accessing the table of coordinates from a plotted graph' on page 678 of the GDC chapter if you need to.) 🖩

When $x = -1$, $y = 1$

→

Find the value of $\dfrac{dy}{dx}$ when $x = -1$. This is the gradient of the tangent. (See '20.2 Finding the equation of the tangent at a point' on page 687 of the GDC chapter if you need to.)

continued . . .

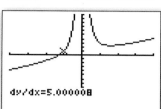

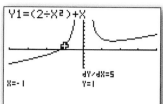

dy/dx=5.000008

X=-1   dY/dX=5
         Y=1

$$\dfrac{dy}{dx} = 5$$

Now calculate the gradient of the normal. $\dfrac{dy}{dx} = 5$, and $5 = \dfrac{5}{1}$; turn it upside down to get $\dfrac{1}{5}$, and then change the sign from positive to negative.

So the gradient of the normal is $-\dfrac{1}{5}$.

Substitute the coordinates and the gradient into the equation for a straight line.

$y = mx + c$

$1 = -\dfrac{1}{5} \times (-1) + c$

$c = 1 - \dfrac{1}{5} = \dfrac{4}{5}$

Finally, write down the equation of the normal.

The equation of the normal is $y = -\dfrac{1}{5}x + \dfrac{4}{5}$.

CASIO

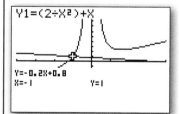

Y=-0.2X+0.8
X=-1   Y=1

If your GDC is able to give you the equation of the normal directly, then you can read it off directly from the screen. (See '20.2 Finding the equation of the tangent at a point' on page 687 of the GDC chapter if you need to.)

(TEXAS calculators do not have a direct function for this.)

The equation of the normal is
$y = -0.2x + 0.8$

Exercise 20.6

GDC

1. For each of the following curves, use your GDC to find the equation of the normal to the point with the given x-coordinate.

   (a) $y = 3x^2 - 10$, at $x = 4$

   (b) $y = 4 - x^2$, at $x = -3$

   (c) $f(x) = 9 - x^4$, at $x = -1$

   (d) $f(x) = x - x^3$, at $x = \dfrac{1}{2}$

A normal line drawn by a GDC is likely to look distorted, and may not appear to be at right angles to the curve.

(e) $y = 2x^3 + 7x^2 - 3x + 4$, at $x = 1$ (f) $y = 2 + \dfrac{1}{x}$, at $x = -2$

(g) $g(x) = 8 - \dfrac{3}{x^2}$, at $x = 2$ (h) $y = \dfrac{7}{x^3} - \dfrac{1}{x^2}$, at $x = 1.5$

2. Find the equation of the normal to the curve at the given point.

(a) $y = x^2 - x - 12$, at $(-3, 0)$

(b) $y = 2x^3 + 3x^2 - 23x - 12$, at $(2, -30)$

(c) $y = 6x^3 - 19x^2 + 19x - 6$, at $(-\dfrac{1}{2}, -21)$

(d) $f(x) = 11 - 2x^2$, at $(3, -7)$

(e) $f(x) = \dfrac{3}{x^2} - x$, at $(\dfrac{1}{2}, \dfrac{23}{2})$

(f) $y = 1 - 2x - \dfrac{2}{x}$, at $(-1, 5)$

3. Find the equation of the normal to the curve with equation $y = 1 - 3x^2 - x^3$ at the point where $x = -1$.

4. A curve is the graph of the function $f(x) = x^3 + 5x^2 - 2$. A point N lies on the curve. The x-coordinate of N is -4. Find the equation of the normal to the curve at the point N.

Summary

You should know:

- the two concepts of a derivative
  - as a rate of change
  - as the gradient of a graph

- how to obtain a tangent to a curve at a particular point on the curve, and how to use the gradient of the tangent to define the gradient of a curve

- the general differentiation formula $f(x) = ax^n \Rightarrow f'(x) = nax^{n-1}$

- how to calculate the derivative of a function of the form $f(x) = ax^n + bx^m + \dots$ where all exponents are integers (positive or negative)

- how to find the gradient of a curve at a given value of x

- how to find the value(s) of x on a curve that has a given value of $f'(x)$

- how to calculate the equation of the tangent to a curve at a given point

- that the normal is the line perpendicular to the tangent at a given point

- how to calculate the equation of the normal at a given point.

Mixed examination practice

Exam-style questions

1. The equation of a curve is defined as $y = x^4 - 7x^3 - 9x + 6$. Find $\dfrac{dy}{dx}$.

2. The equation of a function is $y = x^2 - 8x + 7$.

   (a) Differentiate the equation to find the gradient function $\dfrac{dy}{dx}$.

   (b) Find the gradient of the curve at the point where the x-coordinate is 3.

   (c) Find the value of x at which the gradient of the curve is 6.

3. The equation for the total cost of production, C_T, for a quantity of items, q, is given by:

   $$C(q) = 120q - q^2 - 0.005q^3$$

   (a) Find an equation for the marginal cost by differentiating the total cost with respect to q; that is, find $\dfrac{dC_T}{dq}$.

   (b) Determine the marginal cost $\dfrac{dC_T}{dq}$ when $q = 40$.

4. The displacement, s, of a particle t seconds after leaving point O is described by:

   $$s(t) = 12 + t - t^2$$

   (a) Find the average change in displacement between $t = 1$ and $t = 2$.

   (b) What is the rate of change of displacement when $t = 3$?

   (c) Calculate $s'(3.5)$ and explain what your answer represents.

5. A particle moves such that its displacement, s metres, at time t seconds is given by:

   $$s = 2t^3 - 4t^2 + 4t - 7$$

   (a) Find an expression for:

      (i) the velocity of the particle, v

      (ii) the acceleration of the particle, a

   (b) Calculate the velocity of the particle when:

      (i) $t = 2$ (ii) $t = 4$.

   (c) Determine the acceleration of the particle when:

      (i) $t = 1$ (ii) $t = 4$.

   (d) Find the time t when the acceleration is zero.

6. A curve has equation $f(x) = 5x^2 - 4x - \dfrac{3}{x}$.

   (a) State the value of $f(1)$. What does $f(1)$ represent?

(b) Find the value of $f'(1)$. What does your answer represent?

The point Q lies on the curve. At Q, $x = 1$.

(c) Write down the equation of the tangent to the curve at Q.

7. A curve has equation $y = x^3 - 4x^2 - x + 5$.

   (a) Find the gradient of the tangent to the curve at $x = 1$.

   (b) State the gradient of the normal to the curve at $x = 1$.

   The point P lies on the curve and has x-coordinate equal to 1.

   (c) Find the y-coordinate of P.

   (d) Write down the equation of the tangent to the curve at P.

   (e) Work out the equation of the normal to the curve at P.

8. A curve has equation $y = x^2(3x - 5)$.

   (a) Expand the expression $x^2(3x - 5)$.

   (b) Use your answer from part (a) to find the gradient function of the curve in terms of x.

   (c) Find the gradient of:

       (i)   the tangent   (ii)   the normal

   to the curve at the point Q whose x-coordinate is -2.

   (d) Write down the equation of:

       (i)   the tangent   (ii)   the normal

   to the curve at point Q.

Past paper questions

1. The figure below shows the graphs of functions $f_1(x) = x$ and $f_2(x) = 5 - x^2$.

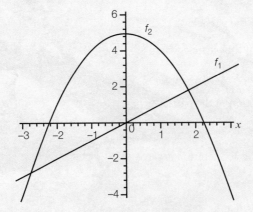

(a) (i) Differentiate $f_1(x)$ with respect to x.

    (ii) Differentiate $f_2(x)$ with respect to x.

(b) Calculate the value of x for which the gradient of the two graphs is the same.

(c) Draw the tangent to the **curved** graph for this value of x on the figure, showing clearly the property in part (b).

[Total 6 marks]

[**May 2007, Paper 1, Question 11**] (© *IB Organization 2007*)

2. Consider the function $f(x) = 2x^3 - 5x^2 + 3x + 1$.

(a) Find $f'(x)$.   *[3 marks]*

(b) Write down the value of $f'(2)$.   *[1 mark]*

(c) Find the equation of the tangent to the curve $y = f(x)$ at the point $(2, 3)$.   *[2 marks]*

[Total 6 marks]

[**May 2008, Paper 1, TZ1, Question 3**] (© *IB Organization 2008*)

3. The diagram below shows the graph of a line L passing through $(1, 1)$ and $(2, 3)$ and the graph P of the function $f(x) = x^2 - 3x - 4$.

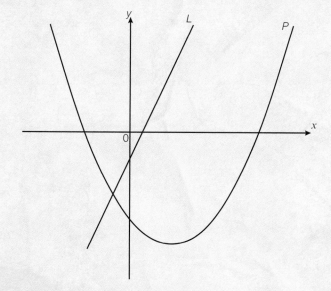

(a) Find the gradient of the line L.   *[2 marks]*

(b) Differentiate $f(x)$.   *[2 marks]*

(c) Find the coordinates of the point where the tangent to P is parallel to the line L.   *[3 marks]*

(d) Find the coordinates of the point where the tangent to P is perpendicular to the line L.   *[4 marks]*

(e) Find:

    (i) the gradient of the tangent to P at the point with coordinates $(2, -6)$;

    (ii) the equation of the tangent to P at this point.   *[3 marks]*

(f) State the equation of the axis of symmetry of P.   *[1 mark]*

(g) Find the coordinates of the vertex of P and state the gradient of the curve
at this point.   *[3 marks]*

[Total 18 marks]

[Nov 2007, Paper 2, TZ0, Question 5] (© *IB Organization 2007*)

Chapter 21 Stationary points and optimisation

Differential calculus provides mathematicians, scientists, economists and other technical professionals with a powerful technique for solving practical problems.

If an equation can be found that models a situation and connects some of the variables that are being studied, then the rates at which those variables change relative to each other can be analysed.

For instance:

- In medicine: What is the most efficient way of administering a drug? When is the concentration of that drug in the patient's bloodstream at its highest or lowest?

- In engineering: Where are the greatest stresses on a beam? What is the maximum load that a bridge can bear?

- In commerce: How can a company maximise its use of resources? What is the minimum quantity of material that could be ordered and still get the job done?

In Ian Stewart's book *Seventeen Equations that Changed the World*, he says:

'… calculus is simply an indispensible tool in the engineer's and scientist's tool kit. More than any other mathematical technique, it has created the modern world.'

Source: Ian Stewart, *Seventeen Equations that Changed the World* (Profile Books, 2012).

21.1 Increasing and decreasing functions

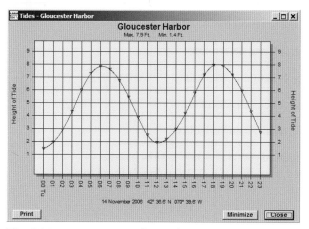

The CAPN navigation software (www.thecapn.com)

The graph shows the height of tides at Gloucester Harbor, Massachusetts, over a period of one day.

From midday to 6 p.m. the height of the water is increasing; high tide occurs at around 6 p.m., and after that the height of the water decreases until about midnight. The same pattern continues into the next day.

For any curve or function, you can give a similar description of which sections of it are 'increasing' and which sections are 'decreasing'.

Calculus allows you to add more detail and precision to such a description of functions.

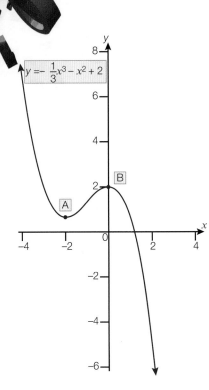

$y = -\frac{1}{3}x^3 - x^2 + 2$

Look at the graph of $f(x) = -\frac{1}{3}x^3 - x^2 + 2$.

The curve is decreasing from left to right up to the point $A(-2, \frac{2}{3})$. It is then increasing from A to B(0, 2), and on the right of B it is decreasing.

Using calculus, we can calculate the gradient at various points along the curve. Differentiating gives $f'(x) = -x^2 - 2x$, so:

$$f'(-3) = -(-3)^2 - 2(-3) = -3$$

$$f'(-1) = -(-1)^2 - 2(-1) = 1$$

$$f'(2) = -2^2 - 2 \times 2 = -8$$

《RR *You learned how to differentiate in Chapter 20.*

From these results, you can see that:

- At points where the function is **decreasing**, the gradient is negative: $f'(x) < 0$

- At points where the function is **increasing**, the gradient is positive: $f'(x) > 0$

A point where $f'(x) = 0$ is called a **stationary point**. The points A and B on the above graph are stationary points; the tangent to the curve at each of these points is a horizontal line, and the rate of change of y against x is instantaneously zero at those points. You can think of the curve as 'pausing' for an instant before changing direction. Another name for points like A and B is **turning points**.

Worked example 21.1

Q. Draw a graph of the function $f(x) = x^3 + 3x - 2$.

(a) Look at the graph and determine:

    (i) where the function is increasing

    (ii) where the function is decreasing.

(b) Confirm your results using calculus.

(c) Graph the function $g(x) = x^3 - 3x - 2$. How has the graph changed from that of $f(x)$? Why do you think this has happened?

continued . . .

A. (a)

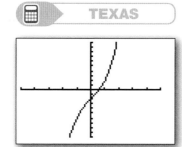

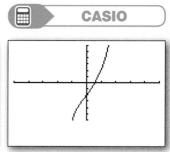

> Use your GDC to draw the graph of $y = x^3 + 3x - 2$. (See '224.2G Graphs' on page 645 of the GDC chapter if you need to.)

> The curve seems to be sloping upwards throughout.

(i) The function is increasing at every point.

(ii) There is no part of the curve that is decreasing.

(b) $f(x) = x^3 + 3x - 2$

$f'(x) = 3x^2 + 3$

As $x^2 \geq 0$ for all values of x, it means that $3x^2 + 3 > 0$ for all values of x. This tells us that the gradient is always positive and hence there is no part of the curve that is decreasing.

> Differentiate $f(x)$ one term at a time using the formula on page 580. So for each term, multiply the term by the power, and reduce the power of x by 1.

(c)

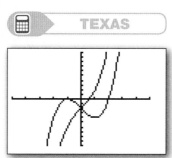

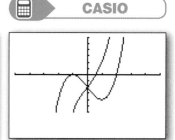

> Use your GDC to draw the graph of $y = x^3 - 3x - 2$ on the same axes as the graph from part (a). Just by looking at the shape of the graph of $g(x)$ you can see that the gradient is negative in some places. Use the derivative $g'(x)$ to look for clues to the different shapes of the $f(x)$ and $g(x)$ curves.

$g'(x) = 3x^2 - 3$

In contrast to $f(x)$, the gradient of $g(x)$ can be negative; this occurs for x between -1 and 1, so the graph is decreasing between the points $(-1, 0)$ and $(1, -4)$. This is confirmed by looking at the derivative $g'(x) = 3x^2 - 3$; although $x^2 \geq 0$ for all values of x, for some values of x subtracting 3 from $3x^2$ will lead to a negative value.

Exercise 21.1

exam tip

Questions in IB examinations often ask for the values of x for which $f(x)$ is increasing or decreasing — the y value doesn't matter.

1. The graph of the function $f(x) = 1 + 3x^2 - x^3$ is shown. State the values of x between which the function is increasing and decreasing.

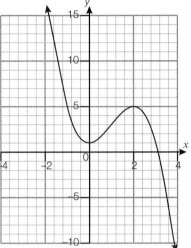

2. The graph of the curve $y = (2x + 1)(x - 2)(x + 3)$ is shown.

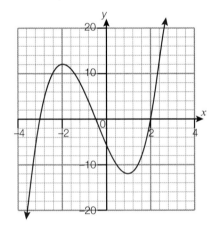

   State the interval of x values for which the function is:

   (a) increasing   (b) decreasing.

3. Draw the graph of each of the following functions on your GDC and, by looking at the graph, determine the interval(s) of x values for which the function is:

   (i) increasing   (ii) decreasing

   (a) $f(x) = 3x(x - 8)$ (b) $f(x) = x(2x + 9)$

   (c) $y = x^2 - x - 56$ (d) $y = x^3 + 8x - 2$

   (e) $y = x^3 - 12x + 3$ (f) $y = 2x^3 - 3x^2 - 12x + 6$

   (g) $g(x) = \dfrac{x^3}{3} - 3x^2 + 5$ (h) $y = \dfrac{x^3}{3} + \dfrac{x^2}{2} - 4x + 1$

4. Find the range of values of x for which $f(x) = x^3 - 6x^2 + 3x + 10$ is an increasing function.

5. A function has equation $f(x) = 2 + 9x + 3x^2 - x^3$.

    (a) Find $f'(x)$.

    (b) Calculate $f'(-2)$.

    (c) Determine whether $f(x)$ is increasing or decreasing at $x = -2$.

6. A curve is defined by the equation $f(x) = \dfrac{x^3}{3} - x^2 - 3x + 1$.

    (a) Find $f'(x)$.

    (b) Calculate:

        (i) $f'(-4)$ (ii) $f'(1)$.

    (c) State whether the function is increasing or decreasing at:

        (i) $x = -4$ (ii) $x = 1$.

21.2 Stationary points, maxima and minima

In the previous section, stationary points were defined as points where a curve has a gradient equal to zero. In this section, you will learn how to determine whether a stationary point is a maximum, minimum or inflexion point. A point of inflexion is a place where the curve 'pauses' but then continues in the same direction.

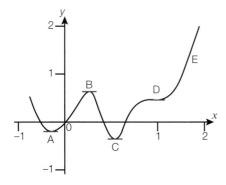

In the diagram, A, B, C and D are all stationary points.

- A, B and C are **turning points**, places where the curve changes direction.

- A and C are local **minimum points**, or local **minima** (plural of minimum), where the curve changes from decreasing to increasing.

- B is a local **maximum point** (plural: **maxima**), where the curve changes from increasing to decreasing.

Although a local maximum or local minimum is always a turning point, it is not necessarily the highest or lowest point on the entire graph; this is why the term 'local' is used. For instance, the point E has a greater y value than the local maximum B; but because the curve does not change direction at E, it is not a maximum.

D is a point of **inflexion**; the curve is increasing before it reaches D, then it 'pauses' at this point and the gradient is instantaneously zero, and then it starts increasing again. There are also points of inflexion where the curve is decreasing on both sides. The important thing to remember is that inflexion points are stationary points which are **not** turning points.

To find the stationary points on a given curve, and to classify each of them as a local maximum or minimum, there are several steps that you need to work through.

For example, consider the function $f(x) = x^3 + 3x^2 - 9x - 10$.

1. It is a good idea to sketch the curve first. Using calculus, you can find stationary points without a diagram, but you are less likely to make mistakes if you start by drawing the curve on your GDC or computer.

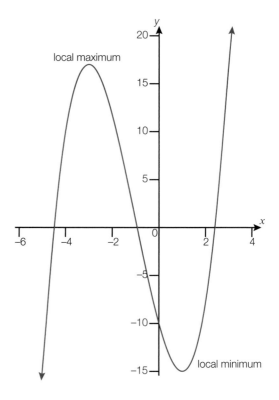

2. Differentiate $f(x)$ to find the gradient function:

$$\frac{dy}{dx} = 3x^2 + 6x - 9$$

3. Stationary points occur where $\frac{dy}{dx} = 0$, so solve this equation to find the x-coordinates of any stationary points.

$3x^2 + 6x - 9 = 0$

From the GDC: $x = -3$ or $x = 1$

> This is the equation $\frac{dy}{dx} = 0$.
> This is a quadratic equation, so solve using one of the methods you met in Chapter 2.

4. Now that you know the x-coordinates of the stationary points, you can find the corresponding y-coordinates using the equation of the curve.

$f(x) = x^3 + 3x^2 - 9x - 10$

$f(-3) = (-3)^3 + 3(-3)^2 - 9(-3) - 10 = -27 + 27 + 27 - 10 = 17$

$f(1) = 1^3 + 3 \times 1^2 - 9 \times 1 - 10 = 1 + 3 - 9 - 10 = -15$

So the stationary points of the curve are at $(-3, 17)$ and $(1, -15)$.

> Substitute $x = -3$ and $x = 1$ into the original equation.

5. To determine whether a stationary point is a maximum or a minimum (or neither), look at the gradient on either side of the stationary point.

$f'(0.5) = 3(0.5)^2 + 6(0.5) - 9 = -5.25 < 0$

$f'(1.5) = 3(1.5)^2 + 6(1.5) - 9 = 6.75 > 0$

A table/diagram like the following makes it easy to see whether you have a maximum or a minimum.

> For the point $(1, -15)$, check the gradient at $x = 0.5$ and $x = 1.5$ by substituting these values of x into the equation of the derivative.

Value of x	0.5	1	1.5
Value of $\frac{dy}{dx}$	−5.25	0	6.75
	↘	—	↗

The point $(1, -15)$ is a local minimum because the curve changes from decreasing to increasing.

$f'(-3.5) = 3(-3.5)^2 + 6(-3.5) - 9 = 6.75 > 0$

$f'(-2.5) = 3(-2.5)^2 + 6(-2.5) - 9 = -5.25 < 0$

Make a similar diagram as before:

> For the point $(-3, 17)$, check the gradient at $x = -3.5$ and $x = -2.5$ by substituting these values of x into the equation of the derivative.

Value of x	−3.5	−3	−2.5
Value of $\frac{dy}{dx}$	6.75	0	−5.25
	↗	—	↘

The point $(-3, 17)$ is a local maximum because the curve changes from increasing to decreasing.

For some types of function, you can use the shape of the general graph to help you decide whether a stationary point is a maximum or a minimum. For example,

- From left to right on the graph below, a cubic function whose x^3 term has positive sign will have a maximum followed by a minimum:

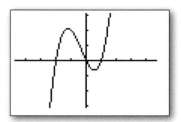

- From left to right on the graph below, a cubic function whose x^3 term has negative sign will have a minimum followed by a maximum.

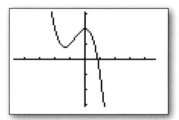

So, for $f(x) = x^3 + 3x^2 - 9x - 10$, since the x^3 term has positive sign, you know immediately that the stationary point on the left, $(-3, 17)$, is a local maximum, while the stationary point on the right, $(1, -15)$, is a local minimum.

Summary

To find and classify the stationary points of a function:

1. Sketch the curve on your GDC.

2. Differentiate to find the gradient function.

3. Put $\frac{dy}{dx} = 0$ and solve the equation for the x-coordinate(s) of any stationary points.

4. Use the equation of the curve to find the y-coordinate for each stationary point.

5. Check the sign of $\frac{dy}{dx}$ on either side of each stationary point, to determine whether it is a local maximum or minimum.

Using your GDC

It is possible to use your calculator to a greater extent than in the example above to find and classify stationary points. See '*21.2 Finding local maximum and minimum points*' on page 690 of the GDC chapter for a reminder if you need to. However, to gain a better understanding of the mathematics, it is a good idea to practise the traditional calculus method described above before relying more heavily on your GDC.

Let's look at how you could use a GDC to find the stationary points of $f(x) = x^3 + 3x^2 - 9x - 10$.

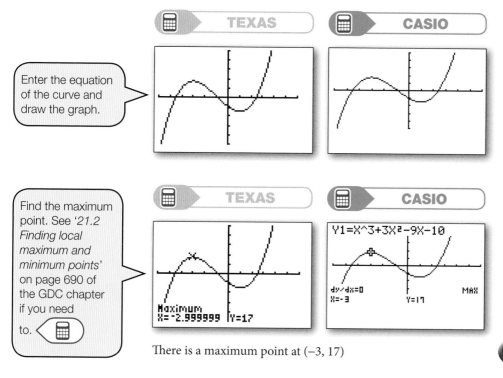

Enter the equation of the curve and draw the graph.

Find the maximum point. See '21.2 Finding local maximum and minimum points' on page 690 of the GDC chapter if you need to.

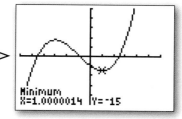

There is a maximum point at $(-3, 17)$

Find the minimum point.

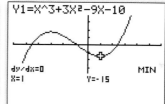

There is a minimum point at $(1, -15)$

exam tip

Remember that your GDC cannot differentiate functions; so if a question asks you to find a derivative, that is a calculation you will **always** have to do for yourself.

	Worked example 21.2
Q.	Consider the function $f(x) = x^4 - x^3 - 12x + 1$.
	(a) Find $f'(x)$.
	(b) Evaluate $f(x)$ and $f'(x)$ at the point where $x = 2$. Is the function increasing or decreasing at this point?
	(c) Calculate the coordinates of the turning points on the curve and determine the nature of the points.

continued ...

Differentiate each term separately by multiplying the term by the power of x, then reducing the power of x by 1.

A. (a) $f'(x) = 4x^3 - 3x^2 - 12$

Using algebra and your GDC: for parts (b) and (c), we will show two ways of answering the question.

Substitute the value of $x = 2$ into the original function, and then into the derivative.

Method 1:

(b) When $x = 2$,

$$f(2) = 2^4 - 2^3 - 12 \times 2 + 1 = -15$$
$$f'(2) = 4 \times 2^3 - 3 \times 2^2 - 12 = 8$$

To see whether the function is increasing or decreasing, look at whether the gradient is positive or negative.

As $f'(2) > 0$, the function is increasing at the point $(2, -15)$.

At stationary points, $f'(x) = 0$.

(c) $4x^3 - 3x^2 - 12 = 0$

TEXAS

```
4X^3-3X2-12=0
■X=1.7404133043...
 bound={-1E99,1...
■left-rt=0
```

CASIO

```
Eq:4X^3-3X2-12=0
  X=1.740413304
Lft=0
Rgt=0

REPT
```

This is a complicated equation to solve, so use your GDC. (See '19.3 (b) Solving polynomial equations using an equation solver' on page 685 of your GDC if you need to, and apply the principles to solving this cubic equation).

There is only one solution, $x = 1.74$

Find the corresponding y value by substituting $x = 1.74$ into the original equation.

$$f(x) = x^4 - x^3 - 12x + 1$$
$$f(1.74) = (1.74)^4 - (1.74)^3 - 12 \times 1.74 + 1$$

When $x = 1.74$, $y = -16.0$ (3 s.f.), so there is a stationary point at $(1.74, -16.0)$.

continued . . .

Value of x	1.5	1.74	2
Value of $f'(x)$	−5.25	0	8
	↘	———	↗

$(1.74, -16.0)$ is a minimum point.

(b) <u>Method 2:</u> (mostly your GDC)

> To determine the nature of the stationary point, check the sign of the gradient on either side of it, and make a diagram to show this.

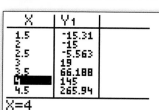 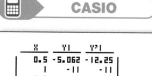

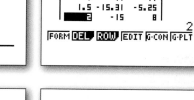

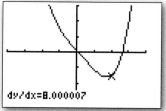 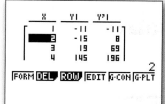

> Using some algebra and your GDC: use the table of coordinates on your GDC to find the y-coordinate, and the table or graph to find the value of $\frac{dy}{dx}$. (If you need a reminder, see '14.1 Accessing the table of coordinates from a plotted graph' on page 678 and '20.1 Finding the numerical value of the derivative' on page 686 and '21.1 Finding increasing and decreasing functions' on page 689 of the GDC chapter.)

From the GDC:

$f(2) = -15$, $f'(2) = 8$

As $f'(2) > 0$, the function is increasing at the point $(2, -15)$.

(c)

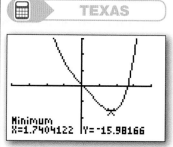 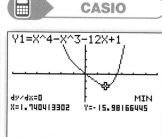

> Use the GDC to locate the turning point. (See '21.2 Finding local maximum and minimum points' on page 690 of the GDC chapter if you need to.)

There is a minimum point at $(1.74, -16.0)$.

Exercise 21.2

1. For each of the following functions, draw the graph on your GDC and find all the stationary points on the curve, classifying them as minimum or maximum points.

   (a) $y = x^2 + 4x$

   (b) $y = 8x - x^2$

   (c) $y = x^2 - 6x + 5$

   (d) $f(x) = 4 + 3x - x^2$

   (e) $g(x) = x^3 - x^2 - x$

   (f) $h(x) = x^3 - 3x - 1$

   (g) $y = 4 + 3x - x^3$

   (h) $y = 4x^3 - 3x + 5$

   (i) $y = x^3 - 4x^2 + 4x + 3$

   (j) $f(x) = x^5 - 5x - 1$

2. Use calculus to find and classify the stationary points for all the functions in question 1. So, in each case:

   • Find the gradient function.

   • Equate the gradient function to zero and solve for the x values of stationary points.

   • Find the corresponding y-coordinates.

   • Determine the nature of the stationary points (i.e. whether they are maximum or minimum points).

3. A curve has equation $y = x^3 - 3x^2 - 8x - 11$.

   (a) Find $\dfrac{dy}{dx}$.

   The points P and Q are the stationary points on the curve.

   (b) Find the coordinates of P and Q.

   (c) Determine the nature of each of the stationary points.

4. A curve with equation $y = 2x^5 + 5x^2 - 3$ passes through the points R and S with coordinates $(-1, 0)$ and $(0, -3)$, respectively.

   (a) Verify that the points R and S are stationary points on the curve.

   (b) Determine the nature of the stationary points.

5. The equation of a curve is $y = x^3 - 4x$.

   (a) Find $\dfrac{dy}{dx}$.

   (b) Hence find the two values of x for which $\dfrac{dy}{dx} = 0$.

   (c) Find the coordinates of the stationary points on the curve.

   (d) Determine the nature of each stationary point.

6. If $f(x) = x^3 - 6x^2$, find the coordinates of the stationary points and determine whether they are maxima or minima.

7. Find the coordinates of the two stationary points on the curve with equation $y = x^3 - 3x$. Classify each of the points as a maximum or a minimum.

21A Using the second derivative to classify stationary points

You can use the second derivative of a function to distinguish between local maxima and local minima.

- If $f''(x) > 0$ at a stationary point, then the stationary point is a local minimum.

- If $f''(x) < 0$ at a stationary point, then the stationary point is a local maximum.

Take the function $f(x) = x^3 + 3x^2 - 9x - 10$ that we investigated in section 21.2.

We saw that there are two stationary points, $(-3, 17)$ and $(1, -15)$.

Differentiating the derivative $f'(x) = 3x^2 + 6x - 9$ gives the second derivative:

$$f''(x) = 6x + 6$$

Now check:

$$f''(-3) = 6 \times (-3) + 6 = -12$$

As $-12 < 0$, the point $(-3, 17)$ is a maximum.

$$f''(1) = 6 \times 1 + 6 = 12$$

As $12 > 0$, the point $(1, -15)$ is a minimum.

The following table shows how the gradient of a function's graph changes around a maximum or minimum point, and what this means for the second derivative.

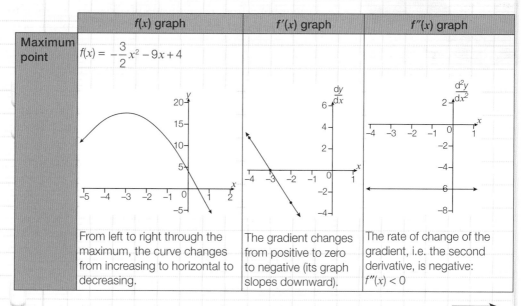

	$f(x)$ graph	$f'(x)$ graph	$f''(x)$ graph
Maximum point	$f(x) = -\dfrac{3}{2}x^2 - 9x + 4$		
	From left to right through the maximum, the curve changes from increasing to horizontal to decreasing.	The gradient changes from positive to zero to negative (its graph slopes downward).	The rate of change of the gradient, i.e. the second derivative, is negative: $f''(x) < 0$

continued . . .

	$f(x)$ graph	$f'(x)$ graph	$f''(x)$ graph
Minimum point	$f(x) = \dfrac{3}{2}x^2 - 3x - 16$ 	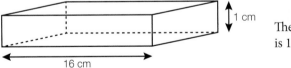	
	From left to right through the minimum, the curve changes from decreasing to horizontal to increasing.	The gradient changes from negative to zero to positive (its graph slopes upward).	The rate of change of the gradient, i.e. the second derivative, is positive: $f''(x) > 0$

21.3 Optimisation

A group of friends are preparing for a party. Some of them are making candy boxes from 18 cm squares of coloured card. The boxes all have square bases but different depths. What is the volume of the boxes that they are making?

Zaira makes a shallow box, 1 cm deep, like this:

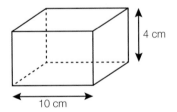

The volume of Zaira's box is $1 \times 16 \times 16 = 256\,cm^3$.

Mike makes a box that is deeper, with a depth of 4 cm:

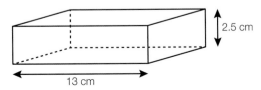

The volume of Mike's box is $4 \times 10 \times 10 = 400\,cm^3$.

Polli makes her box like this; it has a volume of $422.5\,cm^3$.

Even though the size of the card used stays the same, the volume of the box seems to change depending on the depth of the box. How can the friends design a box made from an 18 cm by 18 cm piece of card with the greatest possible volume?

This is an **optimisation** problem, where you want to find the most efficient use of the resources that you have. In these circumstances we need to create a function to represent the situation and then plot the graph of this function to find the local maximum. In other examples, you might want to find the *smallest* value and you would plot a graph of the function and locate the local minimum.

Worked example 21.3

Q. How can the friends design a box made from an 18 cm by 18 cm piece of card with the greatest possible volume?

To find the box with the largest volume, visualise the box as in the diagram, and then use algebra to generalise the problem.

By cutting out or folding an x cm square piece at each corner of the 18 cm square card, you can make a box that is x cm high, with a square base of side length $(18 - 2x)$ cm.

A.

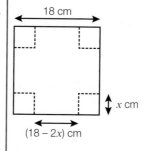

We know that the volume of a box = length × width × height.

In this case, the height (depth) is x cm and the length and width are both $(18 - 2x)$ cm.

$V = (18 - 2x)(18 - 2x)x$

To find the value of x that will give the maximum volume, graph this equation on a GDC (see '21.2 *Finding local maximum and minimum points*' on page 690 of the GDC chapter if you need to.)

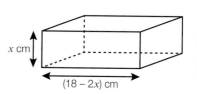

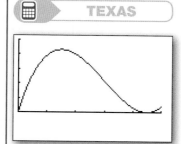

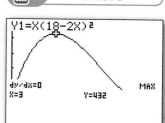

There is a clear maximum point on the curve. Use your GDC to find the coordinates of the point.

continued . . .

From GDC: coordinate of local maximum is (3, 432). So, x = 3, y = 432. So the box with the greatest volume, made from an 18 cm square of card, is one that has a depth of 3 cm and a length and width of 12 cm, giving a volume of 432 cm².

Exercise 21.3

1. Sierra has a 20 cm by 20 cm square piece of card. She wants to make an open-top box out of the card. If she wants her box to have the maximum possible volume, find the dimensions of this box.

2. The sum of two positive integers is 13. Find the maximum product you can get from the pair of integers.

3. A rectangle has a perimeter of 24 cm. Calculate the dimensions of the rectangle which will result in the maximum area. You may assume that the lengths of the sides of the rectangle can be integer values only.

4. The area of a rectangle is 18 cm². Calculate the dimensions which will result in the minimum perimeter. You may assume that the lengths of the sides of the rectangle can be integer values only.

Using calculus to solve optimisation problems

Problems asking for maximum or minimum solutions occur in many different contexts. For instance, the Laffer curve, first proposed by the American economics professor Arthur Laffer, suggests that there is a maximum amount of tax that can be imposed on the citizens of a country. If a government asks its citizens for more than 60% of their income in tax, the government will lose revenue rather than gain it.

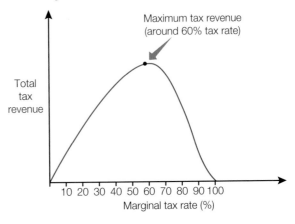

- In business, it is useful to be able to predict whether you can make more profit by selling many things cheaply or fewer things at a higher price.

- In manufacturing, optimisation can help a company find the break-even price of an item, that is, the point where production costs and revenue would be equal.

- Packaging companies need to calculate the most economical dimensions for different shapes and styles of package.

- Doctors want to find out the most effective dosage for a medicine, and when the drug would be at its highest concentration in a patient's bloodstream.

Problems like these can all be solved by:

- finding an equation that describes the problem

- using calculus to look for a maximum or minimum point.

To solve an optimisation problem, work through the following steps:

1. Read the question carefully and make sure you understand it. You may need to read it more than once to absorb all the information.

2. Draw a diagram if possible.

3. Formulate an equation that links the variables of interest. With the techniques we have learned so far, you can use only two variables.

4. Differentiate the equation to find the gradient function.

5. Set the gradient function equal to zero to find the stationary points.

6. Solve the equation for the stationary points and check whether you have a stationary point of the type you are seeking (maximum or minimum).

7. Use your results to give your answer to the original problem.

hint

Not every step will be needed for every problem, but the sequence of steps is always the same.

Let's use the steps above to solve the following problem.

A zoo needs a rectangular enclosure for some small animals. The enclosure can use one wall of an existing building, and there are 80 metres of fencing panels available for the remaining three sides. Find the maximum area of the enclosure and its dimensions.

1. Read the question. Why does it mention the 'remaining three sides'?

2. Draw a diagram and mark in the information from the question:

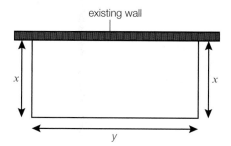

existing wall

x

x

y

3. The question asks for an area. The area of the enclosure is $A = x \times y$.

   This equation has three variables, A, x and y; however, the question gives you enough information to make a link between x and y, which would allow the equation to be simplified.

   Since there is 80 m of fencing available, the diagram shows that $x + y + x = 80$. So you can write $y = 80 - 2x$, and now,

   $$A = x \times (80 - 2x)$$
   $$= 80x - 2x^2$$

4. Differentiating gives $\dfrac{dA}{dx} = 80 - 4x$.

5. For stationary points, $\dfrac{dA}{dx} = 0$, that is, $80 - 4x = 0$.

6. Solving $80 - 4x = 0$ gives $x = 20$.

   If $x = 20$, then $y = 80 - 2 \times 20 = 40$.

7. The maximum area of the enclosure is $40 \times 20 = 800\,\text{m}^2$, and its dimensions are $40\,\text{m} \times 20\,\text{m}$.

Using your GDC, you could follow steps 1 to 3 as before, and then graph the equation $A = 80x - 2x^2$ on your GDC and find the coordinates of the maximum point directly:

See '21.2 Finding local maximum and minimum points' on page 690 of the GDC chapter if you need a reminder.

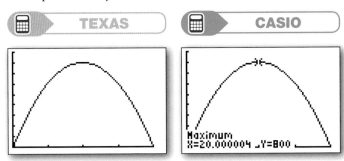

TEXAS   CASIO

Maximum
X=20.000004   Y=800

Worked example 21.4

Q. Myra and Salim (from Worked example 20.8) are looking again at their Business Studies project of scarf manufacturing. They now calculate that their fixed costs are $25, which will remain the same regardless of how many scarves they make. The material for each scarf costs $8, but this will decrease by $0.20 for each additional item made, as their supplier will give them a discount if they buy more material. At what production level will the total costs reach a maximum, and what is this maximum cost?

continued...

> Total cost = fixed costs + variable costs, where the variable costs depend on the number of items produced.

A. Let x be the number of scarves made; then
$$C(x) = 25 + x(8 - 0.2x)$$
$$C(x) = 25 + 8x - 0.2x^2$$

> Differentiate to find the rate of change of total cost with respect to number of items.

$$C'(x) = 8 - 0.4x$$

> Solve the equation $\frac{dC}{dx} = 0$ to find stationary points.

$$8 - 0.4x = 0$$
$$x = 20$$

> Check that the stationary point is a maximum, and find its y-coordinate. You can use the GDC for this. (See '21.2 Finding local maximum and minimum points' on page 690 of the GDC chapter if you need to.)

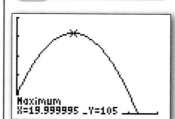 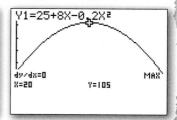

When $x = 20$, $C(x) = 105$.

The maximum cost, $105, occurs when they make 20 scarves.

Worked example 21.5

Q. The formula for the rate P at which a car's engine is working is:
$$P = 12v + \frac{5000}{v}$$
where v is the speed of the car in $m\,s^{-1}$.

(a) Find $\dfrac{dP}{dv}$.

(b) Use your expression in (a) to calculate the speed of the car when the engine is working at its most efficient.

(c) Confirm your result in (b) with a graph.

continued . . .

Rewrite the equation as a sum of powers of v.

A. (a) $P = 12v + 5000v^{-1}$

Differentiate with respect to v.

$$\frac{dP}{dv} = 12 - 5000v^{-2} = 12 - \frac{5000}{v^2}$$

'Most efficient' tells you that this is an optimisation problem, so look for stationary points.

(b) $\dfrac{dP}{dv} = 0$

$$12 - \frac{5000}{v^2} = 0$$

$$12 = \frac{5000}{v^2}$$

Use your GDC to solve the equation, (see '19.2 Solving unfamiliar equations' on page 684 of the GDC chapter if you need to.) ▦

From GDC: $v = 20.4$

The engine is at its most efficient when the car's speed is $20.4\,\mathrm{m\,s^{-1}}$.

Drawing the graph confirms that $v = 20.4$ is a local minimum; that is, the engine uses the least effort at this speed.

(c)

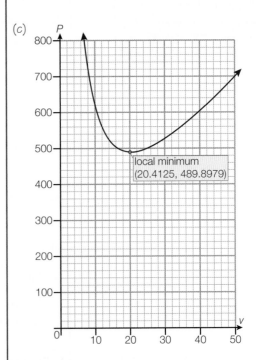

local minimum
(20.4125, 489.8979)

Exercise 21.4

1. The profit function of a certain manufacturing company is:

   $$P = 25 + 120q - 4q^2,$$

   where P is the profit in thousands of pounds and q is the output level in number of units produced.

   (a) Find $\dfrac{dP}{dq}$.

   (b) Determine the value of q for which $\dfrac{dP}{dq} = 0$.

   (c) Hence find the maximum profit, P_{max}.

2. The total cost function of a certain manufacturing company is given by:

   $$C = 3800 - 240n + 1.5n^2$$

   where C is the total cost in thousands of dollars and n is the number of items produced.

   (a) Determine the value of n which minimises the total cost.

   (b) Use calculus to justify your reason for deciding that your answer is the minimum rather than the maximum value.

3. The diagram shows a 20 cm by 20 cm square piece of card. A square of side x cm is cut from each corner of the card to make an open box with a square base and a height of x cm.

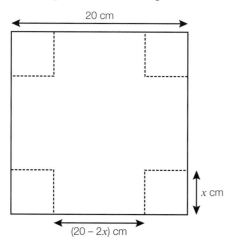
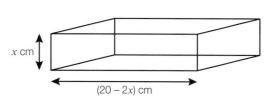

   (a) Show that the volume, V cm³, of the box can be written as

   $$V = 4x^3 - 80x^2 + 400x$$

   (b) Find $\dfrac{dV}{dx}$.

   (c) Determine the value of x for which the volume of the box is maximum.

   (d) Hence find the dimensions of the box that give the maximum volume. Calculate the corresponding volume.

4. Melissa is designing an open-topped toy box out of cardboard. The base of the box is rectangular with length three times as long as the width. The total surface area of the five faces of the box is 7488 cm².

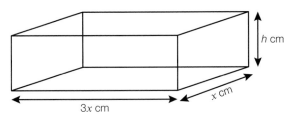

h cm

3x cm

x cm

(a) Taking the width of the box to be x cm and the height to be h cm, show that:

$$3x^2 + 8xh = 7488$$

(b) By expressing h in terms of x, show that the volume, V, of the box can be written as:

$$V = 2808x - \frac{9x^3}{8}$$

(c) Find $\dfrac{\mathrm{d}V}{\mathrm{d}x}$.

(d) Hence determine the value of x corresponding to the maximum volume of the box.

(e) Find the dimensions of the box that give the maximum volume.

(f) State the maximum volume of the box.

5. The total revenue function of a company is:

$$R = 320n - 4n^2$$

where R is the total revenue in thousands of dollars and n is the number of items produced.

(a) Find $\dfrac{\mathrm{d}R}{\mathrm{d}n}$.

(b) Hence find the value of n which maximises the total revenue. Justify your reason for deciding it is the maximum.

(c) Calculate the maximum total revenue.

6. Josephine has bought a piece of rectangular card with a **perimeter** of 120 cm. She wants to roll the rectangle into a cylinder with the largest possible volume.

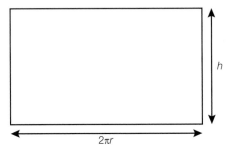

h

h

r

$2\pi r$

(a) If she labels the piece of card as shown in the diagram, show that $h + 2\pi r = 60$.

(b) The volume of a cylinder is given by $V = \pi r^2 h$. Use your result from (a) to show that V can also be written as $V = \pi r^2(60 - 2\pi r)$.

(c) Find $\dfrac{dV}{dr}$.

(d) Calculate the value of r that will give Josephine the greatest volume for her cylinder.

(e) Find the volume of this largest cylinder.

Summary

You should know:

- how to identify increasing and decreasing functions

- how to interpret graphically the gradient $f'(x)$

    - at points where the function is decreasing, the gradient is negative, $f'(x) < 0$

    - at points where the function is increasing, the gradient is positive, $f'(x) > 0$

    - at points where the gradient is equal to zero, $f'(x) = 0$, the point is a stationary point

- how to find values of x where the gradient of a curve is zero

- that a stationary point can be

    - a turning point

        ▪ that is a local minimum (the curve changes from decreasing to increasing)

        ▪ that is a local maximum (the curve changes from increasing to decreasing)

    - a point of inflexion (where the curve continues in the same direction, i.e. points of inflexion are stationary points that are **not** turning points)

- how to find a stationary point and identify what type of stationary point it is

- that optimisation problems require you to construct an equation, the local maximum or minimum of which is the solution to the optimisation problem

- that the solution of the equation $f'(x) = 0$ is important because you can use it to solve optimisation problems by finding a local maximum or minimum

- how to use calculus to solve optimisation problems that involve maximising or minimising a certain quantity.

Mixed examination practice

Exam-style questions

1. The following graph shows the function with equation $y = x^3 - 6x^2 + 3x + 10$.

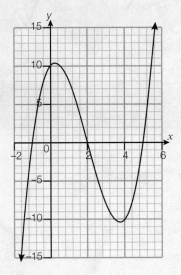

State the values of x for which the function is:

(a) increasing

(b) decreasing.

2. A function is defined as $f(x) = 7x^3 - 12x + 3$.

(a) Find $f'(x)$.

(b) Calculate $f'(4)$.

(c) Determine whether $f(x)$ is increasing or decreasing at $x = 4$.

3. The curve C with equation $y = 3 + 6x^2 - 4x^3$ passes through the points P(0, 3) and Q(1, 5).

(a) Find $\dfrac{dy}{dx}$.

(b) Verify that the points P and Q are stationary points on the curve.

(c) Determine the nature of each stationary point.

4. The equation of a curve is $y = 2x^3 - 9x^2 - 24x + 3$.

(a) Find $\dfrac{dy}{dx}$.

(b) Hence find the two values of x for which $\dfrac{dy}{dx} = 0$.

(c) Find the coordinates of the stationary points on the curve.

(d) Determine the nature of each stationary point.

5. The equation of a curve is given by $f(x) = 5 + 6x^2 - x^3$.
   The points R and S on the curve are the minimum and maximum points, respectively.
   Find the coordinates of R and S. Justify your answer using calculus.

6. Francis the farmer plans to section off part of a field to form a rectangular enclosure. He has 200 m of fencing material. The enclosure will use one wall of an existing building, and the remaining three sides will be fenced. Find the maximum area of the enclosure and its corresponding dimensions.

7. Liam is designing a drinks can for his Technology project. The cylindrical can should hold 330 cm³ of fluid. Liam wants to minimise the material needed for producing the can.

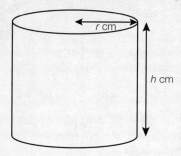

   Use calculus to determine the dimensions of the can (radius r and height h) that will minimise the surface area.

8. A farmer has 800 m of fencing material. Determine the dimensions of the rectangular enclosure that will maximise the fenced area. Work out the maximum area of the enclosure.

9. A box with a square base is to be designed to have a volume of 8000 cm³.

   (a) Find the dimensions of the box which will minimise the amount of material used.

   (b) Determine the minimum surface area of the box.

10. Repeat question 9 for an open-topped, square-based box of the same volume.

Past paper questions

1. A function is represented by the equation:

   $$f(x) = ax^2 + \frac{4}{x} - 3$$

   (a) Find $f'(x)$.   [3 marks]

   The function $f(x)$ has a local maximum at the point where $x = -1$.

   (b) Find the value of a.   [3 marks]

                                                                              [Total 6 marks]

[Nov 2007, Paper 1, Question 15] (© IB Organization 2007)

2. A football is kicked from a point A(a, 0), $0 < a < 10$, on the ground towards a goal to the right of A.

The ball follows a path that can be modelled by **part** of the graph:

$$y = -0.021x^2 + 1.245x - 6.01, \ x \in \mathbb{R}, \ y \geq 0.$$

x is the horizontal distance of the ball from the origin
y is the height above the ground
Both x and y are measured in metres.

(a) Using your graphic display calculator or otherwise, find the value of a.   *[1 mark]*

(b) Find $\dfrac{dy}{dx}$.   *[2 marks]*

(c) (i) Use your answer to part (b) to calculate the horizontal distance the ball has travelled from A when its height is a maximum.

    (ii) Find the maximum vertical height reached by the football.   *[4 marks]*

(d) Draw a graph showing the path of the football from the point where it is kicked to the point where it hits the ground again. Use 1 cm to represent 5 m on the horizontal axis and 1 cm to represent 2 m on the vertical scale.   *[4 marks]*

The goal posts are 35 m from **the point where the ball is kicked**.

(e) At what height does the ball pass over the goal posts?   *[2 marks]*

[Total 13 marks]

[May 2007, Paper 2, Question 3 (ii)] (© *IB Organization 2007*)

3. A farmer has a rectangular enclosure with a straight hedge running down one side. The area of the enclosure is 162 m². He encloses this area using x metres of the hedge on one side as shown on the diagram below.

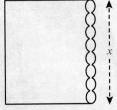

diagram not to scale

(a) If he uses y metres of fencing to complete the enclosure, show that $y = x + \dfrac{324}{x}$.   *[3 marks]*

The farmer wishes to use the least amount of fencing.

(b) Find $\dfrac{dy}{dx}$.   *[3 marks]*

(c) Find the value of x which makes y a minimum.   *[3 marks]*

(d) Calculate this minimum value of y.   *[2 marks]*

(e) Using $y = x + \dfrac{324}{x}$ find the values of a and b in the following table.

x	6	9	12	18	24	27	36
y	60	45	39	a	37.5	b	45

[2 marks]

(f) Draw an accurate graph of this function using a horizontal scale starting at 0 and taking 2 cm to represent 10 metres, and a vertical scale **starting at 30** with 4 cm to represent 10 metres.

[5 marks]

(g) Write down the values of x for which y increases.

[2 marks]

[Total 20 marks]

[Nov 2006, Paper 2, Question 5] (© IB Organization 2006)

4. A closed rectangular box has a height y cm and width x cm. Its length is twice its width. It has a fixed outer surface area of 300 cm².

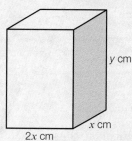

(a) Show that $4x^2 + 6xy = 300$.

[2 marks]

(b) Find an expression for y in terms of x.

[2 marks]

(c) Hence show that the volume V of the box is given by $V = 100x - \dfrac{4}{3}x^3$.

[2 marks]

(d) Find $\dfrac{dV}{dx}$.

[2 marks]

(e) (i) Hence find the value of x and of y required to make the volume of the box a maximum.

(ii) Calculate the maximum volume.

[5 marks]

[Total 13 marks]

[May 2008, Paper 2, TZ1, Question 5(ii)] (© IB Organization 2008)

5. The function $f(x)$ is such that $f'(x) < 0$ for $1 < x < 4$. At the point P(4, 2) on the graph of $f(x)$ the gradient is zero.

(a) Write down the equation of the tangent to the graph of $f(x)$ at P.

[2 marks]

(b) State whether $f(4)$ is greater than, equal to or less than $f(2)$.

[2 marks]

(c) Given that $f(x)$ is increasing for $4 \leq x < 7$, what can you say about the point P?

[2 marks]

[Total 6 marks]

[May 2008, Paper 1, TZ2, Question 15] (© IB Organization 2008)

Chapter 22 How to use your graphical calculator

In the *Mathematical Studies for the IB Diploma* course, you are expected to use a graphical display calculator (GDC) at all times. It is a vital tool to use while you are learning, as well as during **both** the examinations.

If you learn to use your calculator quickly and efficiently you will find it invaluable. But be careful, not all calculators are the same. If you borrow someone else's, the required key sequences and menus may be different and you will have to relearn some processes. So, always take **your own** calculator to lessons.

When you choose your graphical calculator you need to make sure that it can:

- draw graphs
- change the scale of the screen
- solve equations numerically
- display matrices
- find a numerical derivative at any point
- give the results of normal distribution, chi-squared tests and correlation coefficients
- find *p*-values.

You are also allowed to use the following Apps:

- finance
- programs to solve simultaneous and quadratic equations
- language programs that translate prompts and error messages.

If you do not have any of the Apps, download them from the website that has been set up by the manufacturer:

Texas Instruments	*http://education.ti.com/educationportal/sites/US/productCategory/us_graphing.html*
Casio calculators	*http://www.casio.com/products/Calculators_%26_Dictionaries/Graphing/*

You are **not** allowed to use a calculator that has:

- a QWERTY keyboard (with letter keys like that of a computer keyboard)
- computer algebra systems installed
- Apps that give facts or formulae that you are expected to know.

The processes and key sequences in this chapter will be useful throughout the course. They have been written based on the following models of GDC because these are the ones the authors have, but this is in no way an endorsement of these specific models, and you should use a model of your choice:

- CASIO fx-9750GII
- TEXAS INSTRUMENTS TI-84 Plus Silver Edition. Please note that all instructions also apply to the TI-84 Plus, unless otherwise stated.

The instructions provided in this chapter will be very similar for many of the different models from the same manufacturers. If your model of GDC is not exactly the same as one of those used in this coursebook, you might find that despite some differences in the locations of keys and menus, you can still determine what you need to do. However, you might find that the keys, menus and entire processes are different and you will need to refer to the manufacturer's instruction booklet for support instead. Therefore, it is very important that you **don't throw the manufacturer's instruction booklet away or lose it**! You will almost definitely need it at some point.

Throughout this chapter, the left-hand column details the key sequences for the TI-84 Plus and the right-hand column details the key sequences for the Casio fx-9750GII. This is the convention used throughout this book for GDC screenshots.

 TEXAS   CASIO

22.2 Getting started

A. Setting your calculator to degree mode

TEXAS	METHOD	CASIO
Press the [ON] button.	**1** Turn the calculator on.	Press the [AC/ON] button.
[MODE]	**2** Access the required menu.	[MENU]
		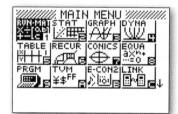
[▼] [▼] [▶] (DEGREE) [ENTER]	**3** Choose the required settings menu to change from radians to degree mode (new GDCs are set to radian by default).	[1] (RUN MAT) [SHIFT] [MENU] (SET UP) [▼] [▼] [▼] [▼] [▼] [F1] (Deg)

[2nd] [MODE] (QUIT)	**4** To exit the menu.	[EXE]

B. The second and third functions of a calculator key

Some GDC keys have more than one function: the function written directly on the key and the function(s) written above it. This means that some keys can 'do' and 'undo' (inverse) the same operation. For example, the key used for the function 'sin' can also be used for the inverse function 'sin⁻¹'. Be aware, not all second or third functions are inverse functions; sometimes they are just different functions. Here we show an example where the x^2 key has the inverse function $\sqrt{x}$, and where the sin key has the inverse function $\sin^{-1}$.

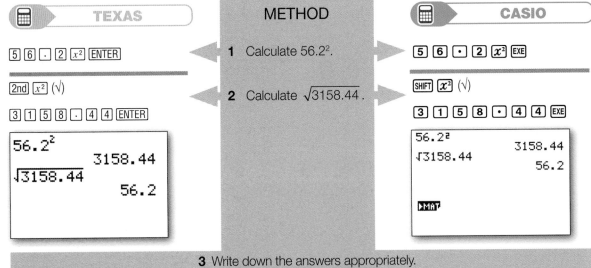

TEXAS

$\boxed{5}\,\boxed{6}\,\boxed{.}\,\boxed{2}\,\boxed{x^2}\,\boxed{ENTER}$

$\boxed{2nd}\,\boxed{x^2}\,(\sqrt{})$

$\boxed{3}\,\boxed{1}\,\boxed{5}\,\boxed{8}\,\boxed{.}\,\boxed{4}\,\boxed{4}\,\boxed{ENTER}$

METHOD

1 Calculate 56.2^2.

2 Calculate $\sqrt{3158.44}$.

CASIO

$\boxed{5}\,\boxed{6}\,\boxed{.}\,\boxed{2}\,\boxed{x^2}\,\boxed{EXE}$

$\boxed{SHIFT}\,\boxed{x^2}\,(\sqrt{})$

$\boxed{3}\,\boxed{1}\,\boxed{5}\,\boxed{8}\,\boxed{.}\,\boxed{4}\,\boxed{4}\,\boxed{EXE}$

3 Write down the answers appropriately.
1. 3158.44
2. 56.2

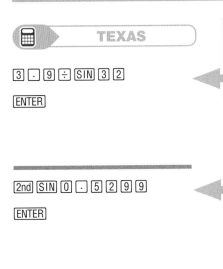

TEXAS

$\boxed{3}\,\boxed{.}\,\boxed{9}\,\boxed{\div}\,\boxed{SIN}\,\boxed{3}\,\boxed{2}$

$\boxed{ENTER}$

$\boxed{2nd}\,\boxed{SIN}\,\boxed{0}\,\boxed{.}\,\boxed{5}\,\boxed{2}\,\boxed{9}\,\boxed{9}$

$\boxed{ENTER}$

METHOD

1 Calculate $3.9 \div \sin(32)°$ (a calculation like this might be used in trigonometry to calculate an unknown length).

2 Calculate the angle in degrees equivalent to $\sin(x) = 0.5299192642$ (a conversion such as this might be required in a trigonometry question that asks for the size of an unknown angle).

CASIO

$\boxed{3}\,\boxed{.}\,\boxed{9}\,\boxed{\div}\,\boxed{sin}\,\boxed{3}\,\boxed{2}$

$\boxed{EXE}$

$\boxed{SHIFT}\,\boxed{sin}\,\boxed{0}\,\boxed{.}\,\boxed{5}\,\boxed{2}\,\boxed{9}\,\boxed{9}$

$\boxed{EXE}$

3 Write down the answer appropriately.
1. 7.36 (3 s.f.)
2. 32.0° (3 s.f.)

C. The Ans/ANS key

The Ans/ANS key automatically stores the answer to the last calculation you completed (it only works if you have pressed ENTER for TEXAS or EXE for CASIO at the end of the calculation). This means you can simply press this key to use the answer in the next calculation. So, if you have a calculation where you need to apply a function to the answer of the previous part of the calculation, don't delete the answer and rekey it; use the Ans/ANS key instead.

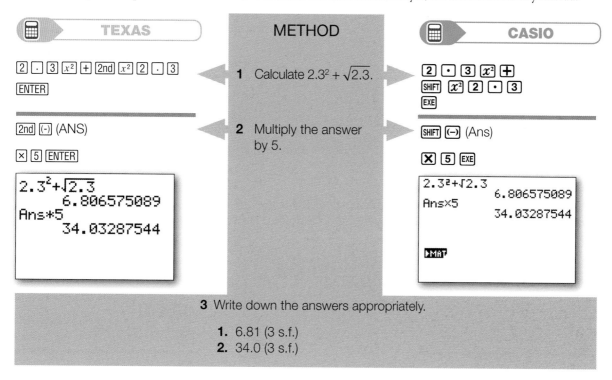

METHOD

1 Calculate $2.3^2 + \sqrt{2.3}$.

2 Multiply the answer by 5.

3 Write down the answers appropriately.

    1. 6.81 (3 s.f.)
    2. 34.0 (3 s.f.)

D. Using the GDC memory

GDCs have 26 memories, labelled using the letters of the alphabet. These are an example of a third function of a key, as the letter of the alphabet is printed above the relevant key.

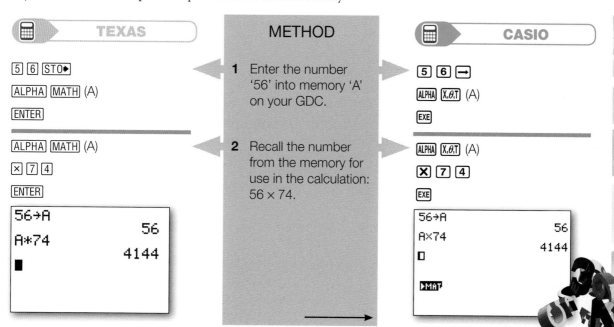

METHOD

1 Enter the number '56' into memory 'A' on your GDC.

2 Recall the number from the memory for use in the calculation: 56×74.

If you are doing a long calculation and using several memories, it is a good idea to write the letter of the memory that you use beside the relevant number.

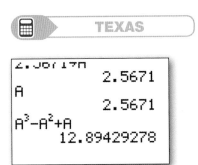

TEXAS

```
2.5671→A
            2.5671
A
            2.5671
A³-A²+A
        12.89429278
```

METHOD

Given the calculation:
$x^3 - x^2 + x$, where
$x = 2.5671$, you can
store x as A, so that the
calculation becomes
$A^3 - A^2 + A$.

CASIO

```
2.5671→A
            2.5671
A
            2.5671
A^3-A²+A
        12.89429278
▶MAT
```

E. Entering fractions

In some calculations it is more accurate to use fractions and to give the answer as a fraction. You can enter a fraction directly into your GDC. You can also convert a decimal answer into a fraction or a fraction into a decimal.

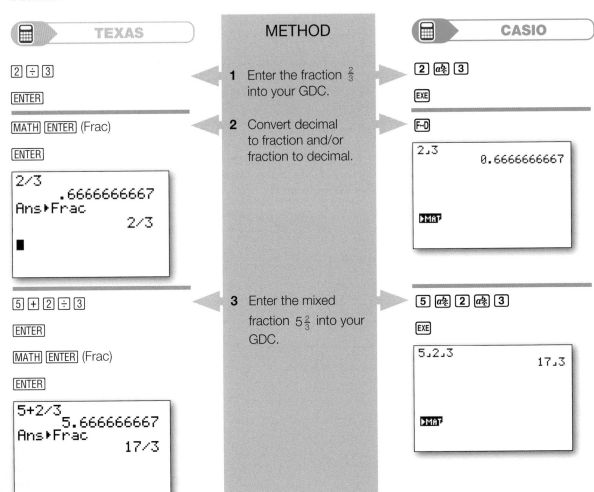

TEXAS

2 ÷ 3

ENTER

MATH ENTER (Frac)

ENTER

```
2/3
    .6666666667
Ans▶Frac
            2/3
■
```

5 + 2 ÷ 3

ENTER

MATH ENTER (Frac)

ENTER

```
5+2/3
    5.666666667
Ans▶Frac
            17/3
```

METHOD

1 Enter the fraction $\frac{2}{3}$ into your GDC.

2 Convert decimal to fraction and/or fraction to decimal.

3 Enter the mixed fraction $5\frac{2}{3}$ into your GDC.

CASIO

2 $a\frac{b}{c}$ 3

EXE

F↔D

```
2⌐3
        0.6666666667
▶MAT
```

5 $a\frac{b}{c}$ 2 $a\frac{b}{c}$ 3

EXE

```
5⌐2⌐3
            17⌐3
▶MAT
```

F. The subtract (–) and negative ((–)) keys

The ((–)) key (where the '–' symbol is inside a pair of brackets) is used to make a number negative. The (–) key is the subtraction operator.

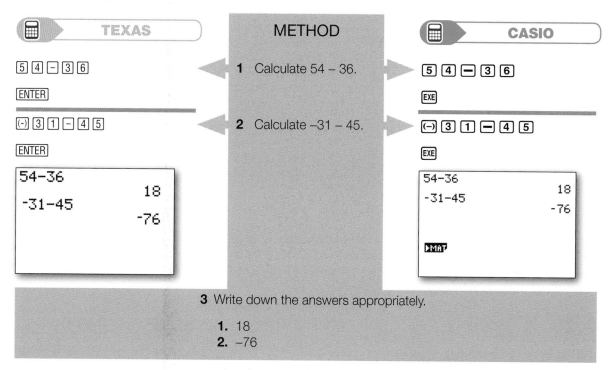

TEXAS	METHOD	CASIO
5 4 − 3 6	**1** Calculate 54 – 36.	5 4 − 3 6
ENTER		EXE
(-) 3 1 − 4 5	**2** Calculate –31 – 45.	(-) 3 1 − 4 5
ENTER		EXE

```
54-36
          18
-31-45
         -76
```

```
54-36
          18
-31-45
         -76

▶MAT
```

3 Write down the answers appropriately.

1. 18
2. –76

G. Graphs

(a) Drawing a graph

You can use your GDC to plot and draw a graph by entering its equation.

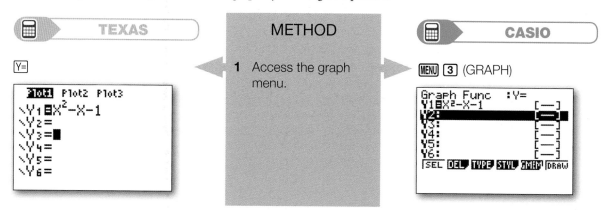

TEXAS	METHOD	CASIO
Y=	**1** Access the graph menu.	MENU 3 (GRAPH)

```
Plot1 Plot2 Plot3
\Y1◼X²-X-1
\Y2=
\Y3=◼
\Y4=
\Y5=
\Y6=
```

```
Graph Func  :Y=
Y1◼X²-X-1       [—]
Y2:             [—]
Y3:             [—]
Y4:             [—]
Y5:             [—]
Y6:             [—]
SEL DEL TYPE STYL GMEM DRAW
```

METHOD

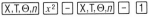

2 Enter the equation of the graph you want to plot:

$$y_1 = x^2 - x - 1$$

X,T,Θ,n x^2 − X,T,Θ,n − 1

GRAPH

X,θ,T $\mathbf{x^2}$ − X,θ,T − 1

EXE

F6 (DRAW)

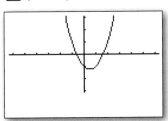

(b) Setting a window

You can use the default scale and window set by the manufacturer or you can set up your own window to suit the graph that you are investigating. The best graphs are drawn using a window that you have set yourself but the programmed ones can be a useful starting point. If you plot a graph and you cannot see it on the screen, check the scale and window as this might be the problem.

 TEXAS

METHOD

 CASIO

1 Plot the graphs of $y = 2^x$ *and* $y = 25$ as per section '*22.G Graphs*'.

WINDOW

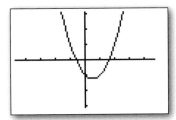

2 Set the window so that you can view the *x*-axis from −5 to 8, and the *y*-axis from −1 to 30. To fit these axes on your GDC screen, use a scale of 1 for the *x*-axis and a scale of 10 for the *y*-axis. (Note that on the CASIO, you press F3 from the graph screen; if you are on the 'Graph func' screen where you enter the equation, you will need to press SHIFT F3 .)

F3 (V-window)

View Window
 max :8
 scale:1
 dot :0.09523809
Ymin :-1
 max :30
 scale:10

(-) 5 ENTER (Xmin)

8 ENTER (Xmax)

1 ENTER (Xsc1)

(-) 1 ENTER (Ymin)

3 0 ENTER (Ymax)

1 0 ENTER (Yscl)

(−) 5 EXE (Xmin)

8 EXE (max)

1 (scale)

⌄

(−) 1 EXE (Ymin)

3 0 EXE (max)

1 0 EXE (scale)

EXE

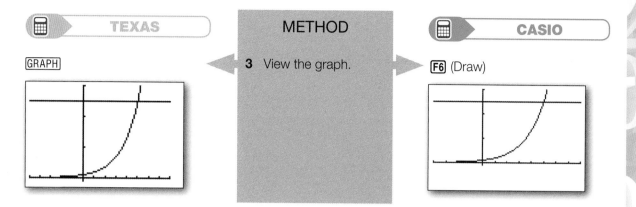

TEXAS

GRAPH

3 View the graph.

CASIO

[F6] (Draw)

(c) Windows set by the manufacturer

These are windows that you can access quickly, and make good starting points.

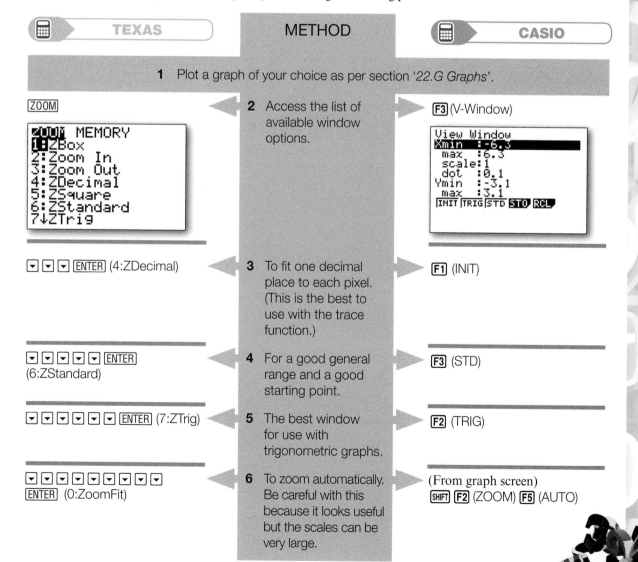

TEXAS	METHOD	CASIO
	1 Plot a graph of your choice as per section '*22.G Graphs*'.	

TEXAS

ZOOM

```
ZOOM MEMORY
1:ZBox
2:Zoom In
3:Zoom Out
4:ZDecimal
5:ZSquare
6:ZStandard
7↓ZTrig
```

METHOD

2 Access the list of available window options.

CASIO

[F3] (V-Window)

```
View Window
Xmin :-6.3
 max :6.3
 scale:1
 dot :0.1
Ymin :-3.1
 max :3.1
INIT TRIG STD STO RCL
```

[▼] [▼] [▼] [ENTER] (4:ZDecimal)

3 To fit one decimal place to each pixel. (This is the best to use with the trace function.)

[F1] (INIT)

[▼] [▼] [▼] [▼] [▼] [ENTER] (6:ZStandard)

4 For a good general range and a good starting point.

[F3] (STD)

[▼] [▼] [▼] [▼] [▼] [▼] [ENTER] (7:ZTrig)

5 The best window for use with trigonometric graphs.

[F2] (TRIG)

[▼] [▼] [▼] [▼] [▼] [▼] [▼] [▼] [▼] [ENTER] (0:ZoomFit)

6 To zoom automatically. Be careful with this because it looks useful but the scales can be very large.

(From graph screen)
[SHIFT] [F2] (ZOOM) [F5] (AUTO)

(d) Zooming in

Using ZOOM allows you to:

- zoom in and look at a graph more closely

- zoom out to see more of a graph.

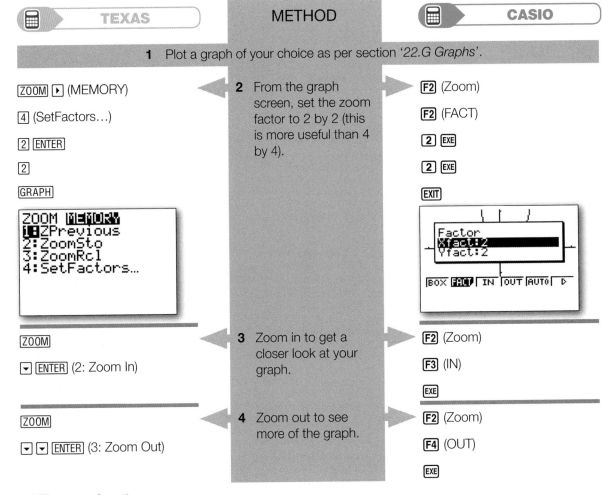

TEXAS	METHOD	CASIO
	1 Plot a graph of your choice as per section '22.G Graphs'.	

TEXAS

ZOOM ▶ (MEMORY)

4 (SetFactors…)

2 ENTER

2

GRAPH

```
ZOOM MEMORY
1:ZPrevious
2:ZoomSto
3:ZoomRcl
4:SetFactors…
```

METHOD

2 From the graph screen, set the zoom factor to 2 by 2 (this is more useful than 4 by 4).

CASIO

F2 (Zoom)

F2 (FACT)

2 EXE

2 EXE

EXIT

```
Factor
Xfact:2
Yfact:2

BOX FACT IN OUT AUTO ▷
```

TEXAS

ZOOM

▼ ENTER (2: Zoom In)

METHOD

3 Zoom in to get a closer look at your graph.

CASIO

F2 (Zoom)

F3 (IN)

EXE

TEXAS

ZOOM

▼ ▼ ENTER (3: Zoom Out)

METHOD

4 Zoom out to see more of the graph.

CASIO

F2 (Zoom)

F4 (OUT)

EXE

(e) The trace function

Use the trace function to find where the graph of $y = x^2 - 1$ crosses the x-axis.

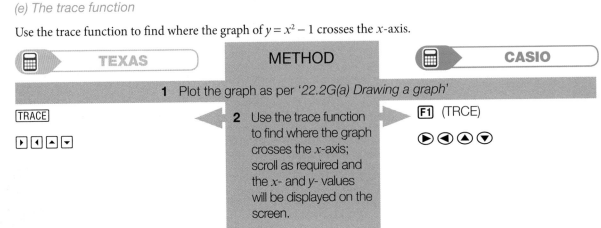

TEXAS	METHOD	CASIO
	1 Plot the graph as per '22.2G(a) Drawing a graph'	

TEXAS

TRACE

▶ ◀ ▲ ▼

METHOD

2 Use the trace function to find where the graph crosses the x-axis; scroll as required and the x- and y- values will be displayed on the screen.

CASIO

F1 (TRCE)

▶ ◀ ▲ ▼

22.3 GDC support by chapter

22.3.1 Chapter 1 Number

1.1 Rounding

You can use your GDC to round answers to a specific number of decimal places. (Note, however, that not every model allows you to round to a specific number of significant figures.)

The model of TEXAS used in this book does not set to 3 s.f.; therefore, it is best to work in equivalent decimal places (using FLOAT), or leave the GDC in its default setting and round the answer yourself.

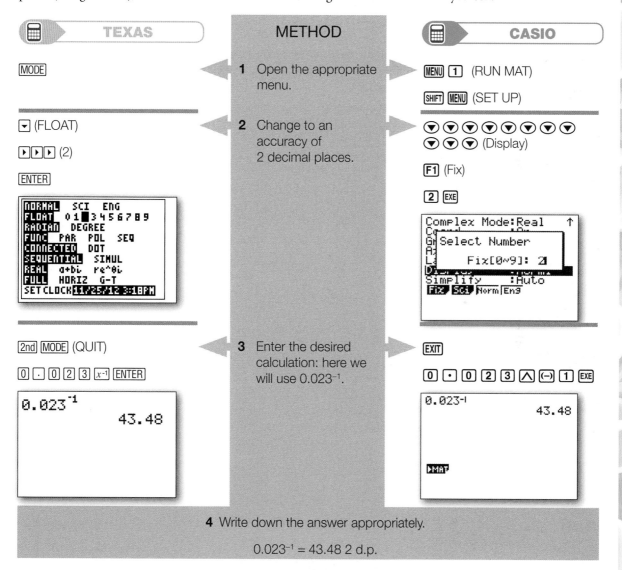

TEXAS

MODE

⏷ (FLOAT)

▶ ▶ ▶ (2)

ENTER

METHOD

1 Open the appropriate menu.

2 Change to an accuracy of 2 decimal places.

CASIO

MENU 1 (RUN MAT)

SHIFT MENU (SET UP)

⏷ ⏷ ⏷ ⏷ ⏷ ⏷ ⏷ ⏷
⏷ ⏷ ⏷ (Display)

F1 (Fix)

2 EXE

2nd MODE (QUIT)

0 . 0 2 3 x^{-1} ENTER

3 Enter the desired calculation: here we will use 0.023^{-1}.

EXIT

0 . 0 2 3 ^ (−) 1 EXE

0.023^{-1}

43.48

0.023^{-1}

43.48

4 Write down the answer appropriately.

$0.023^{-1} = 43.48$ 2 d.p.

If you are confident in rounding you can leave your calculator in the default setting. To return to the default setting after you have changed the degree of accuracy, follow step 1 above and then proceed as follows:

TEXAS	METHOD	CASIO
▼ (FLOAT) [ENTER]	Return your GDC to the default degree of accuracy setting.	[F3] (Norm) [EXE]

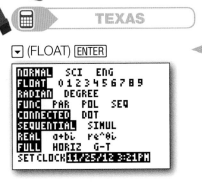

1.2 Answers in standard form

You can set your GDC to give all answers in the form $a \times 10^k$ where $1 \leq a < 10$ and k is an integer (i.e. in standard form) to a given number of significant figures. **Be careful**: make sure that you write the answers in the correct mathematical form – not in calculator language!

TEXAS	METHOD	CASIO
[MODE] ▶ (SCI) [ENTER]	**1** Open the appropriate menu and set to standard form (also known as scientific notation).	[MENU] [1] (RUN MAT) [SHIFT] [MENU] (SET UP) ▼ ▼ ▼ ▼ ▼ ▼ ▼ ▼ ▼ ▼ ▼ (Display) [F2] (Sci)

TEXAS	METHOD	CASIO
▼ (FLOAT) ▶ ▶ ▶ (2) [2nd] [MODE] (QUIT)	**2** Choose the degree of accuracy to be 3 significant figures. Note that because the TEXAS GDC does not work to significant figures, here we have set it to 2 decimal places instead. You do not have to do this step, you could just round the final answer to 3 s.f. yourself.	[3] [EXE] [EXIT]

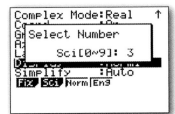

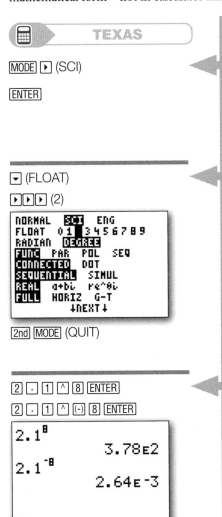

3 Calculate:

(a) 2.1^8

(b) 2.1^{-8}

TEXAS:
[2] [.] [1] [^] [8] [ENTER]
[2] [.] [1] [^] [(-)] [8] [ENTER]

CASIO:
[2] [·] [1] [∧] [8] [EXE]
[2] [·] [1] [∧] [(-)] [8] [EXE]

4 Write down the answers appropriately.
(a) 3.78×10^2
(b) 2.64×10^{-3}

1.3 Time in hours, minutes and seconds

Converting decimal time to a value given in hours, minutes and seconds is a very useful tool of your GDC.

TEXAS	METHOD	CASIO

TEXAS

4 6 3 . 7 ÷ 6 0 ENTER

2nd APPS (ANGLE)

4 (DMS)

ENTER

```
463.7/60
        7.728333333
Ans▸DMS
          7°43'42"
```

METHOD

1 Change 463.7 minutes into hours, minutes and seconds.

CASIO

4 6 3 · 7 ÷ 6 0 EXE

OPTN F6 (>)

F5 (ANGL)

F5

(or F6 (>) F3 (DMS) EXE)

```
463.7÷60
              7°43'42"
```

2 Write down the answer appropriately.

463.7 minutes = 7 hours, 43 minutes and 42 seconds

TEXAS

5 6 2nd APPS (ANGLE) 1 (°)

3 1 2nd APPS (ANGLE) 2 (')

ENTER

3 (a) Change 56 minutes and 31 seconds into a decimal.

CASIO

5 6 OPTN F6 (>)

F5 (ANGL)

F4 (°′″)

3 1 F4 (°′″) EXE

÷ 6 0 ENTER

(b) Divide the answer by 60 to change the answer into hours.

÷ 6 0 EXE

2nd APPS (ANGLE)

4 (DMS)

ENTER

```
56°31'
       56.51666667
Ans/60
       .9419444444
Ans▸DMS
         0°56'31"
```

(c) Convert to hours, minutes and seconds.

F5

```
56°31°
              56.51666667
Ans÷60
               0°56'31"
▯
```

TEXAS | METHOD |  CASIO

4 Write down the answers appropriately.

(a) 56.52 minutes (2 d.p.)
(b) 0.94 hours (2 d.p.)
(c) 0 hours, 56 minutes and 31 seconds.

5 On the CASIO, it is also possible to convert to other units such as area, length, volume, etc.

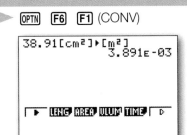

OPTN F6 F1 (CONV)

22.3.2 Chapter 2 Solving equations

2.1 Solving linear equations

(a) using a graph

Solve the equation $2x + 3 = 25$

TEXAS | METHOD | CASIO

1 Plot the graphs of $y = 2x + 3$ and $y = 25$ as per section '**22.2G Graphs**'.

2nd TRACE (CALC)

5 (intersect)

(First curve?) ENTER

(Second curve?) ENTER

(Guess?) ▶ ▶ ▶ (use cursor to move to point of intersection)

ENTER

2 Find the point where the two lines intersect.

SHIFT F5 (G-SLV)

F5 (ISCT)

3 Write down the answer appropriately.

$$x = 11$$

(b) using an equation solver

 TEXAS

METHOD

 CASIO

MATH 0 (0: Solver)*

(Or, MATH ▾ until '0: Solver ...'
then ENTER)

1 Access the linear
equation solver
program on your
GDC.

Please note that on
the TI-84 Plus and some
operating systems on
the Silver Edition it is:
MATH ALPHA APPS
(B: Solver ...)
(Or, MATH ▾ until 'B:
Solver ...' then ENTER)

MENU 8 (EQUA)

F3 (Solver)

```
Equation

Select Type
F1:Simultaneous
F2:Polynomial
F3:Solver
SIML POLY SOLV
```

▲ (to get onto the correct line)

CLEAR

2 0 × 1 . 3 X,T,Θ,n

– 5 0 0

ENTER

ALPHA ENTER (Solve)

```
20*1.3X–500=0
•X=■9.230769230…
 bound=(-1E99,1…
•left-rt=0
```

2 Enter the linear
equation,
$20 \times 1.3x = 500$, into
your GDC and solve.

For the TEXAS GDC you
will need to rearrange
the equation so that it is
equal to zero before you
enter it into your GDC:

$20 \times 1.3x - 500 = 0$.

2 0 × 1 . 3 X,θ,T

SHIFT . (=)

5 0 0 EXE

F6 (Solve)

```
Eq:20×1.3X=500
  X=19.23076923
Lft=500
R9t=500


REPT
```

3 Write down the answer appropriately.

$x = 19.2$ (3 s.f.)

2.2 Solving pairs of linear equations

(a) using a graph

Solve $2x - y = 5$ and $x + y = 1$ by drawing a graph on your GDC.

 TEXAS

METHOD

 CASIO

1 Rearrange each equation into the form $y = mx + c$:

$y = 2x - 5$ and $y = -x + 1$

TEXAS	METHOD	CASIO

TEXAS

Y=

CLEAR (to remove any existing equations)

2 X,T,Θ,n (-) 5 ENTER

1 – X,T,Θ,n

METHOD

2 Access the graph menu and enter the equations as per '22.2G Graphs':

Y1 ($2x - 5$)

Y2 ($-x + 1$)

CASIO

MENU 3 (GRAPH)

F2 (Del)

F1 (Yes) (to remove any existing equations)

2 X,θ,T – 5 EXE

– X,θ,T + 1 EXE

ZOOM 4 (Z:Decimal)

3 Set to an appropriate window (as per '22.2G (b) Setting a window'), in this case one that shows one decimal place as a pixel, and then plot the graph.

SHIFT F3 (INIT)

F6 (DRAW)

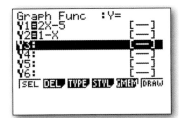

2nd TRACE (CALC)

5 (intersect)

(First curve?) ENTER

(Second curve?) ENTER

(Guess?) ▶ ▶ ▶ (use cursor to move to point of intersection)

ENTER

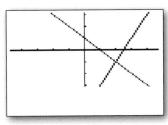

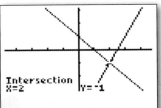

4 Find the point where the two lines intersect.

SHIFT F5 (G-SLV)

F5 (ISCT)

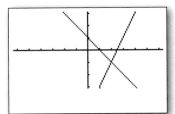

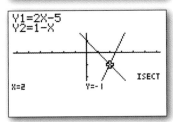

---

5 Write down the answer appropriately.

$x = 2, y = -1$

(b) using an equation solver

Solve $2x - y = 5$ and $x + y = 1$ using a simultaneous equation solver on your GDC.

TEXAS	METHOD	CASIO

TEXAS

APPS ▼ until (PlySmlt2) ENTER *

2 (SIMULT EQN SOLVER)

ENTER (Equations 2)

▼ 2 (Unknowns 2) ENTER

METHOD

1 Access the equation solver for simultaneous equations, and enter the number of unknowns (2). *****Please note** on the TI-84 Plus and some Silver Editions, the PlySmlt2 function is accessed by: APPS 9, or APPS ▼ until '9:PlySmlt2' ENTER.

CASIO

MENU 8 (EQUA)

F1 (Simultaneous)

F1 (2 unknowns)

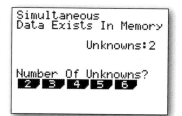

TEXAS

GRAPH (NEXT)

2 ENTER (*x*-coefficient)

(-) 1 ENTER (*y*-coefficient)

5 ENTER (constant)

1 ENTER (*x*-coefficient)

1 ENTER (*y*-coefficient)

1 ENTER (constant)

METHOD

2 Enter the coefficient of *x*, the coefficient of *y*, and the constant for each equation.

CASIO

2 EXE] (*x*-coefficient)

− 1 EXE (*y*-coefficient)

5 EXE (constant)

1 EXE (*x*-coefficient)

1 EXE (*y*-coefficient)

1 EXE (constant)

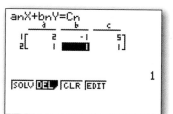

TEXAS

GRAPH (SOLVE)

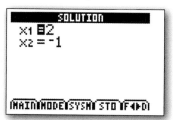

METHOD

3 Solve.

CASIO

F1 (SOLVE)

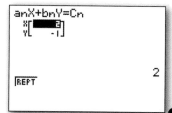

---

4 Write down the answers appropriately.

$x = 2$ and $y = -1$

(a) using a graph

Solve $2x^2 - 5x + 2 = 0$ by drawing a graph on your GDC.

TEXAS	METHOD	CASIO
2 $\boxed{X,T,\Theta,n}$ $\boxed{x^2}$ $\boxed{-}$ 5 $\boxed{X,T,\Theta,n}$ $\boxed{+}$ 2 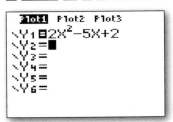	**1** Plot the graph of $2x^2 - 5x + 2 = 0$ as per the methods in '*22.2G Graphs*'.	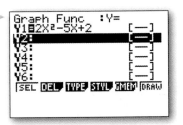 
$\boxed{ZOOM}$ 4 (ZDecimal)	**2** Set the window so that each decimal place is represented by a pixel, as per '*22.2G (b) Setting a window*'.	$\boxed{SHIFT}$ $\boxed{F3}$ (V-Window) [INIT] $\boxed{EXIT}$ [DRAW]
$\boxed{2nd}$ $\boxed{TRACE}$ 2 (ZERO) (Move cursor to the left of the zero you need) $\boxed{ENTER}$ (Move cursor to the right) $\boxed{ENTER}$ (Move cursor to approximately the correct place) $\boxed{ENTER}$ (Guess?) 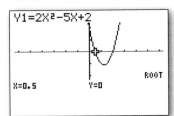	**3** The solutions are where the graph crosses the x-axis. To find the first solution …	$\boxed{SHIFT}$ $\boxed{F5}$ (G-SOLV) $\boxed{F1}$ (ROOT) 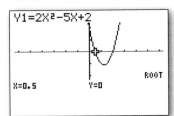
Repeat as per step 3 above. 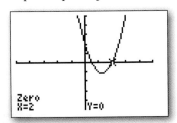	**4** To find the next solution …	$\blacktriangleright$ 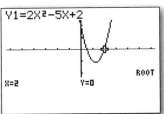

5 Write down the answer appropriately.

$x = 0.5$ or $x = 2$

(b) using an equation solver

Solve $2x^2 - 5x + 2 = 0$ using a quadratic equation solver on your GDC.

TEXAS	METHOD	CASIO
[APPS] [▼] until (PlySmlt2) [ENTER] *	**1** Access the equation solver for quadratic equations. ***Please note** on the TI-84 Plus and some Silver Editions, the PlySmlt2 function is accessed by [APPS] [9], or [APPS] [▼] until 9:PlySmlt2 [ENTER].	[MENU] [8] (EQUA)
[1] (POLY ROOT FINDER)		[F2] (Polynomial)
[2] (ORDER 2)		[F1] (2 Degree)
[ENTER]		
		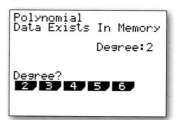
[GRAPH] (NEXT)	**2** Enter the coefficient of x^2, the coefficient of x, and the constant.	[2] [EXE]
[2] [ENTER]		[–] [5] [EXE]
[(-)] [5] [ENTER]		[2] [EXE]
[2] [ENTER]		
		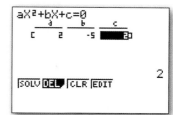
[GRAPH] (SOLVE)	**3** Solve.	[F1] (SOLV)

4 Write down the answer appropriately.

$x = 0.5$ or $x = 2$

3.1 Finding the number of terms in an arithmetic sequence

(a) using the recursion mode to enter the common difference repeatedly

Find the number of terms in the sequence 49, 43, 37, …, 1

TEXAS	METHOD	CASIO
④ ⑨ ⊟ ④ ③ ENTER	**1** Work out the common difference by subtracting the second term from the first.	④ ⑨ ⊟ ④ ③ EXE
④ ⑨ ENTER ⊟ ⑥ ENTER	**2** Enter the first term of the sequence into your GDC and press ENTER / EXE, then enter the common difference (–6).	④ ⑨ EXE ⊟ ⑥ EXE
ENTER	**3** Keep count of how many times you press ENTER / EXE until you reach the last term of the sequence (1).	EXE

```
49
            49
Ans-6
            43
Ans-6
            37
```

```
49
            49
Ans-6
            43
            37
            31
            25
■
```

4 Write down the answer appropriately.
There are 9 terms in the sequence.

(b) using the linear equation solver

Find the number of terms in the sequence 49, 43, 37, …, 1

TEXAS	METHOD	CASIO

1 Use the formula for the general term of an arithmetic sequence, $u_n = u_1 + (n-1)d$, and substitute in the known values, for example: $1 = 49 + (n-1) \times (-6)$
2 Rearrange the formula so that it is equal to zero:
$$6(n-1) - 48 = 0$$

TEXAS	METHOD	CASIO
[MATH] [0] * (Or [MATH] [▼] until '0: Solver') [▲] [CLEAR] [6] [(] [X,T,Θ,n] [−] [1] [)] [−] [4] [8] [ENTER]	**3** Access the linear equation solver on your GDC and enter the equation from (2). *Please note on the TI-84 and some Silver Editions, this is [MATH] [ALPHA] [APPS] (B: Solver), (Or [MATH] [▼], until 'B: Solver' then [ENTER]).	[MENU] [8] (EQUA) [F3] (Solver) [6] [(] [X,θ,T] [−] [1] [)] [−] [4] [8] [SHIFT] [.] [0] [EXE]
[1] [ALPHA] [ENTER] (SOLVE) ```6(X−1)−48=0 •X=9 bound={-1E99, 1… •left−rt=0 ```	**4** Enter the 'target' value of 1 and solve.	[1] [EXE] [F6] (SOLV) ```Eq:6(X−1)=48 X=9 Lft=48 Rgt=48 REPT ```

5 Write down the answer appropriately.
There are 9 terms in the sequence.

3.2 Finding the sum of an arithmetic series using the 'sum' and 'seq' functions

The GDC has a function called 'seq' that can calculate the terms in an arithmetic series when given the first term, the common difference and the formula for the nth term. GDCs also have a function that can calculate the sum of an arithmetic series, this is called 'sum'. You can use the 'sum' and 'seq' functions together to find the sum of a series.

This is not a substitute for using the correct formulae but does allow you to quickly check your answer and to calculate sums to different numbers of terms.

Calculate the sum of the arithmetic series with the formula for the nth term of $u_n = 2x + 1$, when $n = 15$, $u = 3$ and $d = 2$.

TEXAS	METHOD	CASIO
[2nd] [STAT] (LIST) [▶] [▶] (MATH) [5] (sum)	**1** Access the 'sum' function first. (Your GDC screen should just have the text 'sum' on it with a flashing cursor; your GDC will sum whatever you type in place of the cursor.)	[MENU] [1] (RUNMAT) [OPTN] [F1] (LIST) [F6] (>) [F6] (>) [F1] (Sum)
[2nd] [STAT] (LIST) [▶] (OPS) [5] (seq)	**2** Now you need to tell your GDC about the sequence you want to sum. Access the 'seq' function...	[OPTN] [F1] (LIST) [F5] (Seq)
[2] [X,T,Θ,n] [+] [1] (Expr) [ENTER]* [X,T,Θ,n] (Variable) [ENTER] [1] (Start) [ENTER] [1] [5] (End) [ENTER] [1] (Step) [ENTER] (until see answer) sum(seq(2X+1,X, ▶ 　　　　　　 255	**3** ... and enter the parameters that allow your GDC to generate the sequence and then activate the 'sum' function: ● the variable (x) ● the starting position is term 1, so enter 1 ● number of terms (15) ● the increase in position from term to term (1). *Please note** that if you get an error you should replace [ENTER] with [,].	[2] [X,θ,T] [+] [1] [,] [X,θ,T] [,] [1] [,] [1] [5] [,] [1] [EXE] Sum Seq(2X+1,X,1,15,1 　　　　　　　　 255 **List** **L→M** **Dim** **Fill** **Seq** ▷

4 Write down the answer appropriately.

$$S_n = 255$$

3.3 Finding the sum of a geometric series using the list function

Calculate the sum of the first ten terms in the sequence with the formula $u_n = -1 \times -2^{n-1}$.

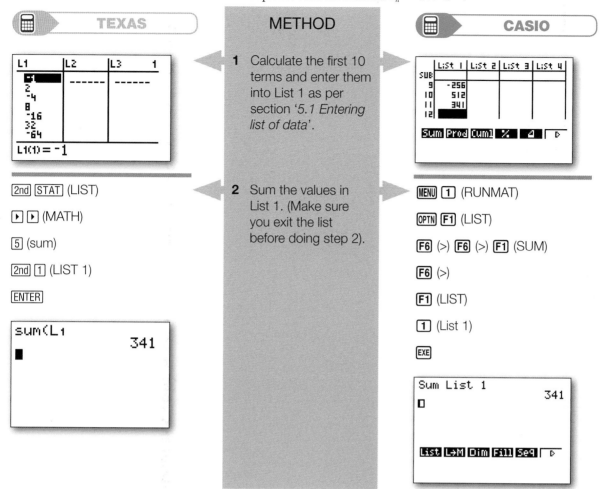

22.3.4 Chapter 4 Financial mathematics

4.1 The financial App, TVM

This is the financial App allowed by the IB. It is built into the CASIO calculator and *some* TEXAS models. If it is not on your GDC you can download it from the TI website.

Siva invests 15,000 INR at a rate of 4.3% per annum. How long does it take for his investment to double?

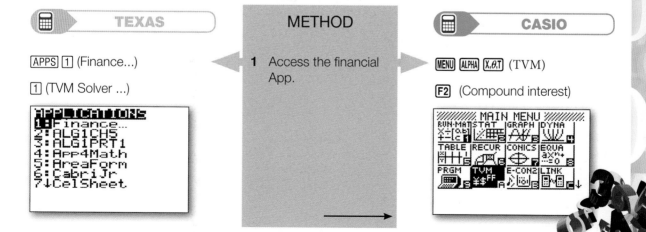

```
CALC VARS
1:TVM Solver…
2:tvm_Pmt
3:tvm_I%
4:tvm_PV
5:tvm_N
6:tvm_FV
7↓npv(
```

```
N=0
I%=0
PV=0
PMT=0
FV=0
P/Y=1
C/Y=1
PMT:END BEGIN
```

```
Financial(1/2)
F1:Simple Interest
F2:Compound Interest
F3:Cash Flow
F4:Amortization
F5:Conversion
F6:Next Page
SMPL CMPD CASH AMT CNVT ▷
```

2 Enter the parameters appropriate for your example. (We want to calculate N so we can enter any placeholder value for N.)

N = number of time periods.

I% = rate of interest given (4.3)

PV = Present Value. (–15000 as investments are negative)

PMT = extra payments to the account (0)

FV = Final Value (30 000)

P/Y = number of interest payments made to the account each year (1)

C/Y = number of compounding periods each year (1)

```
Compound Interest:End
n  =1
I%  =1
PV =-100
PMT=0
FV =101
P/Y=1
 n  I%  PV PMT FV AMT
```

▲ until N, then

ALPHA ENTER (SOLVE)

3 Select the value you want to calculate (in this example it is N).

 (n)

```
N=■
I%=4.3
PV=-15000
PMT=0
FV=30000
P/Y=1
C/Y=1
PMT:END BEGIN
```

```
•N=16.46384368
 I%=4.3
 PV=-15000
 PMT=0
 FV=30000
 P/Y=1
 C/Y=1
PMT:END BEGIN
```

```
Compound Interest:End
n  =1
I%  =4.3
PV =-15000
PMT=0
FV =30000
P/Y=1
 n  I%  PV PMT FV AMT
```

```
Compound Interest
n  =16.46384368



REPT        AMT      GRPH
```

4 Write down the answer appropriately.

$N = 16.46\ldots$ Siva's investment will not double until year 17.

22.3.5 Chapter 5 Classification and display of data

5.1 Entering lists of data

 TEXAS | METHOD | CASIO

[STAT]

[1] (Edit...)

1 Access the statistics menu.

[MENU] [2] (STAT)

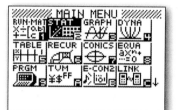

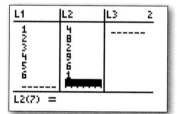

2 Enter data values individually. Press [ENTER]/[EXE] as appropriate after each entry. Use [▶] [◀] to scroll between lists.

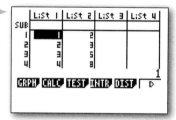

[STAT] [4] (ClrList)

[2nd] [1] (L_1)

[ENTER]

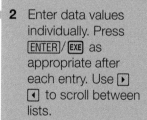

3 To delete a list, for example List 1 (L_1).

(Make sure the cursor is in the list you want to delete, e.g. List 1.)

[F6] (▷)

[F4] (DEL A)

[F1] (Yes)

| TEXAS | METHOD | CASIO |

1 Enter your data into a list as per the instructions in section '*5.1 Entering lists of data*':

List 1: 1, 2, 3, 4, 5, 6, 7

List 2: 2, 3, 5, 8, 4, 2, 1

(If there is already data stored in lists, you might need to delete it.)

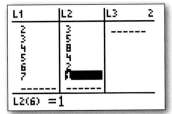

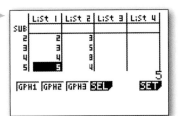

2 Access the graph menu and set to histogram.

TEXAS:

2nd Y= (STAT PLOTS)

ENTER (1: Plot 1 ... off)

ENTER (ON)

▼ ▶ ▶ (histogram) ENTER

CASIO:

F1 (GRPH)

F6 (SET)

▼ (Graph Type)

F6 (>)

F1 (Hist)

3 Make sure that you have the correct data set as Xlist (variable), e.g. List 1, and Frequency, e.g. List 2.

TEXAS:

▼ (Xlist); 2nd 1 (L₁)

▼ (Freq); 2nd 2 (L₂)

CASIO:

▼ (Xlist); F1 (LIST) 1 EXE

▼ (Frequency);

F2 (LIST) 2 EXE

4 Display the histogram and set the window so that you can view your histogram appropriately.

TEXAS:

GRAPH

WINDOW

0 ENTER (Xmin)

1 0 ENTER (Xmax)

1 ENTER (Xsc1)

CASIO:

EXIT EXIT

F1 (GRPH)

F1 (GPH1)

0 EXE (initial point)

→

TEXAS

0 ENTER (Ymin)

1 0 ENTER (Ymax)

1 ENTER (Ysc1)

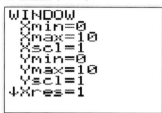

GRAPH *

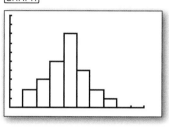

METHOD

* If the graph does not plot, clear graphs in Y=.

CASIO

1 (width of bar)

EXE

EXE (Draw)

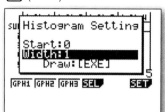

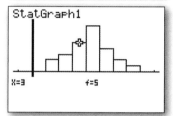

TRACE

▶ / ◀ (as often as required)

5 Find the frequency value of a bar using trace.

SHIFT F1 (TRCE)

▶ / ◀ (as often as required)

5.3 Drawing a box and whisker diagram

| TEXAS | METHOD | CASIO |

1 Enter your data into a list as per the instructions in section '*5.1 Entering lists of data*'. Use:

List 1: 1, 2, 3, 4, 5

List 2: 2, 3, 5, 8, 4

(If there is already data stored in lists, you might need to delete it.)

2nd Y= (STAT PLOT)

ENTER (1: Plot 1 ... off)

ENTER (ON)

▼ ▶ ▶ ▶ ▶ (icon of a box and whisker with median)

ENTER

2 Access the graph menu and set to box and whisker diagram. (Make sure you have the correct data as Xlist (variable), e.g. List 1, and Frequency, e.g. List 2.

F1 (GRPH)

F6 (SET)

⊙ (Graph Type)

F6 (>)

F2 (Box)

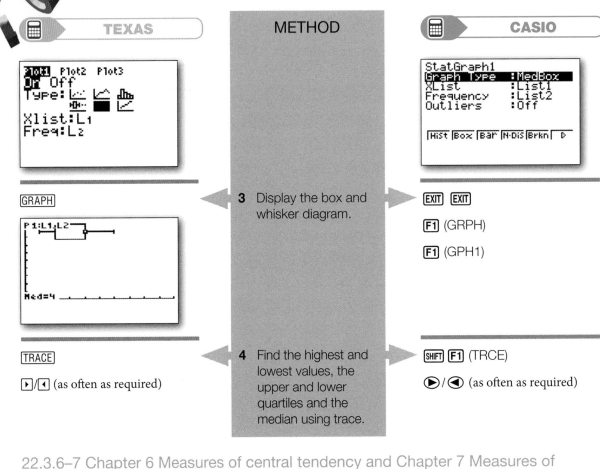

TEXAS	METHOD	CASIO
GRAPH	**3** Display the box and whisker diagram.	EXIT EXIT F1 (GRPH) F1 (GPH1)
TRACE ▶/◀ (as often as required)	**4** Find the highest and lowest values, the upper and lower quartiles and the median using trace.	SHIFT F1 (TRCE) ▶/◀ (as often as required)

22.3.6–7 Chapter 6 Measures of central tendency and Chapter 7 Measures of dispersion

6.1 Finding the mean, median, quartiles and standard deviation

(a) for a simple list of data (single variable, no frequency)

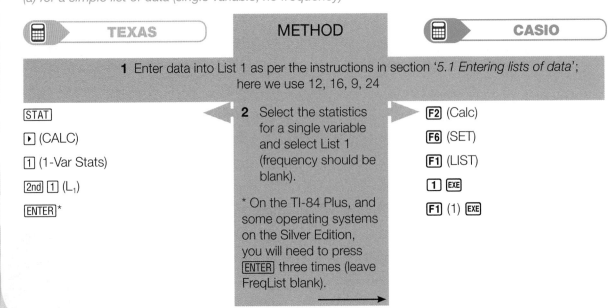

TEXAS	METHOD	CASIO
	1 Enter data into List 1 as per the instructions in section '*5.1 Entering lists of data*'; here we use 12, 16, 9, 24	
STAT ▶ (CALC) 1 (1-Var Stats) 2nd 1 (L₁) ENTER*	**2** Select the statistics for a single variable and select List 1 (frequency should be blank). * On the TI-84 Plus, and some operating systems on the Silver Edition, you will need to press ENTER three times (leave FreqList blank).	F2 (Calc) F6 (SET) F1 (LIST) 1 EXE F1 (1) EXE

TEXAS

```
EDIT CALC TESTS
1:1-Var Stats
2:2-Var Stats
3:Med-Med
4:LinReg(ax+b)
5:QuadReg
6:CubicReg
7↓QuartReg
```

```
1-Var Stats
 x̄=15.25
 Σx=61
 Σx²=1057
 Sx=6.5
 σx=5.629165125
↓n=4
 ■
```

```
1-Var Stats
↑n=4
 minX=9
 Q₁=10.5
 Med=14
 Q₃=20
 maxX=24
```

METHOD

3 To find values of:

- $\bar{x}$ (the mean)

- σ_x (the standard deviation)

- n (the number of entries)

- Q1 (lower quartile)

- Med (median)

- Q3 (upper quartile)

scroll as required.

CASIO

F1 (1Var)

```
1Var XList :List1
1Var Freq  :1
2Var XList :List1
2Var YList :List2
2Var Freq  :1

LIST
```

```
1-Variable
x̄     =15.25
Σx    =61
Σx²   =1057
xσn   =5.62916512
xσn-1 =6.5
n     =4          ↓
```

```
1-Variable
n     =4          ↑
minX  =9
Q1    =10.5
Med   =14
Q3    =20
maxX  =24         ↓
```

⊙ ⊙

(b) for grouped data (single variable with frequency)

TEXAS

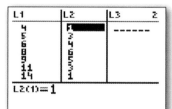

METHOD

1 Enter the variable into List 1 and the frequency into List 2, as per the instructions in section '5.1 Entering lists of data'; here we use:

x	Freq
4	1
5	3
6	4
8	6
9	5
11	3
14	1

CASIO

```
     List 1 List 2 List 3 List 4
SUB
 1      4      1
 2      5      3
 3      6      4
 4      8      6
                           1
TOOL EDIT DEL DEL-A INS  ▷
```

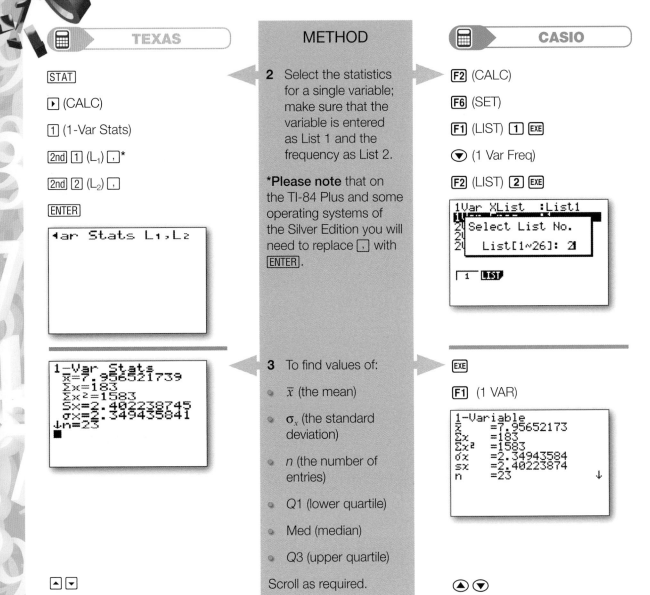

TEXAS	METHOD	CASIO
[STAT]	**2** Select the statistics for a single variable; make sure that the variable is entered as List 1 and the frequency as List 2.	[F2] (CALC)
[▶] (CALC)		[F6] (SET)
[1] (1-Var Stats)		[F1] (LIST) [1] [EXE]
[2nd] [1] (L₁) [,]*		[⊙] (1 Var Freq)
[2nd] [2] (L₂) [,]	***Please note** that on the TI-84 Plus and some operating systems of the Silver Edition you will need to replace [,] with [ENTER].	[F2] (LIST) [2] [EXE]
[ENTER]		

Texas screen shows: `1ar Stats L₁,L₂`

Casio screen shows:
```
1Var XList  :List1
  Select List No.
   List[1~26]: 2
   1  LIST
```

	3 To find values of:	[EXE]
Texas screen: `1-Var Stats` `x̄=7.956521739` `Σx=183` `Σx²=1583` `Sx=2.402238745` `σx=2.349435841` `↓n=23`	• $\bar{x}$ (the mean)	[F1] (1 VAR)
	• σ_x (the standard deviation)	Casio screen: `1-Variable` `x̄ =7.95652173` `Σx =183` `Σx² =1583` `σx =2.34943584` `sx =2.40223874` `n =23  ↓`
	• n (the number of entries)	
	• Q1 (lower quartile)	
	• Med (median)	
	• Q3 (upper quartile)	
[▲][▼]	Scroll as required.	[▲][▼]

Be careful! You are expected to use the σ_x value as the standard deviation even though this is not the symbol used elsewhere for the *sample* standard deviation. On GDCs, s_x represents the standard deviation of the population, so you do not have to look at that value.

22.3.8–10 Chapters 8–10 (Topic 3: Logic, sets and probability)

Your calculator is useful for general calculations and for working with fractions, but not for any specific techniques in this topic.

22.3.11 Chapter 11 The normal distribution

11.1 Finding the area under a normal distribution curve

(a) using a graph

 TEXAS   **METHOD**   **CASIO**

---

1 Make sure you know the parameters of your normal distribution N (μ, σ^2). Make sure you know what the lower and upper bounds are. For this example:

X~N (0, 1^2) so $\mu = 0$, $\sigma = 1$, Upper = 1.4, Lower = -1E$+99$

[2nd] [VARS] (DISTR)

[▼] (2: normal cdf) (do not press enter yet)

```
DISTR DRAW
1:normalpdf(
2:normalcdf(
3:invNorm(
4:invT(
5:tpdf(
6:tcdf(
7↓X²pdf(
```

[▶] (DRAW)

```
DISTR DRAW
1:ShadeNorm(
2:Shade_t(
3:ShadeX²(
4:ShadeF(
```

[1] (ShadeNorm)

2 Select the normal distribution statistics for drawing a normal distribution curve.

[MENU] [2] (STATS)

[F5] (DIST)

[F1] (NORM)

[F2] (Ncd)

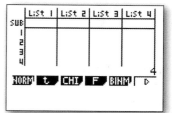

---

3 Enter the parameters and draw the graph.

⟶

TEXAS	METHOD	CASIO

TEXAS

[(-)] [1] [2nd] [,] (EE) [9] [9]

[,]*

[1] [.] [4] [,]

[0] [,] (mean)

[1] (standard deviation)

[ENTER] (Draw)

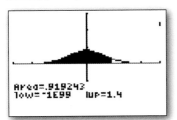

METHOD

* **Please note** on the TI-84 Plus, and some operating systems on the Silver Edition, replace [,] with [ENTER] (except when selecting EE).

CASIO

(Make sure 'Data' is set to variable.)

[F2] (Var)

[⌄] [(-)] [1] [EXP] [9] [9] [EXE]

[1] [.] [4] [EXE]

[1] [EXE] (standard deviation)

[0] [EXE] (mean)

[⌄]

[F6] (DRAW)

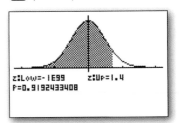

4 Write down the answer appropriately.

$p = 0.919$ (3 s.f.)

(b) without a graph

TEXAS	METHOD	CASIO

In this example, $X \sim N(5, 1.6^2)$, the lower bound is 6 and the upper bound is 8.

TEXAS

[2nd] [VARS] (DISTR)

[2] (normal cdf)

METHOD

1 Select the normal distribution statistics.

CASIO

[MENU] [2] (STATS)

[F5] (DIST)

[F1] (NORM)

[F2] (Ncd)

6 $,$ *

8 $,$

5 $,$

1 $.$ 6

ENTER

2 Enter the parameters.

* Please note on the TI-84 Plus, and some operating systems on the Silver Edition, replace $,$ with ENTER.

(Make sure 'Data' is set to variable.)

F2 (Var)

▼ 6 EXE

8 EXE

1 $.$ 6 EXE

5 EXE

EXE

```
normalcdf(6,8,5▸
        .2355891706
```

3 Write down the appropriate answer.

$p = 0.236$ (3 s.f.)

```
Normal C.D
P   =0.23558916
z:Low=0.625
z:Up =1.875
```

11.2 Inverse normal calculations

2nd VARS (DISTR)

3 (invNorm)

1 Select the inverse normal distribution from the statistics menu.

MENU 2 (STATS)

F5 (DIST)

F1 (NORM)

F3 (InvN)

```
Inverse Normal
Data    :List
Tail    :Left
List    :List1
σ       :1
μ       :0
Save Res:None    ↓
List Var
```

TEXAS	**METHOD**	CASIO

0 . 5 5 . * (area)

0 . (mean)

1 (standard deviation)

ENTER

2 Enter the parameters. In this example: the data is a variable and we have a left tail; area is 0.55, standard deviation is 1 and mean is 0.

* Please note on the TI-84 Plus, and some operating systems on the Silver Edition, replace . with ENTER.

F2 (VAR)

⊙ (Tail)

F1 (LEFT)

⊙ (Area)

0 . 5 5 EXE

1 EXE (standard deviation)

0 (mean)

EXE EXE

```
Inverse Normal
Data    :Variable
Tail    :Left
Area    :0.55
σ       :1
μ       :0
Save Res:None        ↓
```

```
invNorm(0.55
        .1256613375
■
```

3 Write down the appropriate answer.

For $X \sim (0,1)$,
$P(X \le a) = 0.55$

$a = 0.126$ (3 s.f.)

```
Inverse Normal
 xInv=0.12566134
```

22.3.12 Chapter 12 Correlation

12.1 Drawing a scatter diagram of bivariate data

TEXAS	**METHOD**	CASIO

```
L1      L2      L3      2
0       4.1     ------
1       5.5
2       7.2
3       8.7
4       ■
------
L2(6) =
```

1 Enter your data into lists as per '*5.1 Entering lists of data*'.

Make sure you enter the independent x-variable in List 1 and the dependent y-variable in List 2.

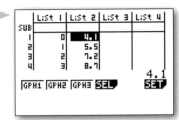

METHOD

2nd Y= (STAT PLOT)

1 ENTER

ENTER (ON)

⏷ (Type)

ENTER (highlight the scatter graph, the first icon)

⏷ 2nd 1 (L₁) ENTER

2nd 2 (L₂) ENTER

2 Select a scatter diagram from the graph menu and make sure that 'Xlist' is your list of x-variables (L₁) and 'Ylist' is your list of y-variables (L₂).

MENU 2 (STATS)

F1 (GRPH)

F6 (SET)

⏷ (Graph Type)

F1 (Scat)

⏷ (XList)

F1 (LIST)

1 EXE (L₁)

⏷ (YList)

F1 (LIST)

2 EXE (L₂)

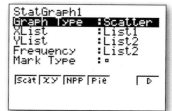

GRAPH

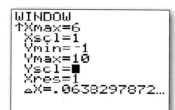

3 Display the graph and set the window if you need to.

EXIT

F1 (GPH1)

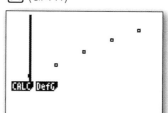

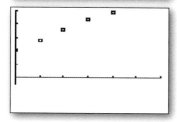

TEXAS | METHOD | CASIO

1 Enter your data into lists as per step (1) in '*12.1 Drawing a scatter diagram of bivariate data*'.

2nd 0 (CATALOG)

⊡ scroll down to
'DiagnosticOn' ENTER ENTER

```
CATALOG       ▣
  Degree
  DelVar
  DependAsk
  DependAuto
  det(
  DiagnosticOff
 ▶DiagnosticOn
```

2 Set up your calculator appropriately.

Plot a scatter graph as per steps (2) and (3) in '*12.1 Drawing a scatter diagram of bivariate data*'

STAT

▶ (CALC)

4 (LinReg (ax + b))

2nd 1 (L₁)

, *

2nd 2 (L₂)

ENTER

```
LinReg
  y=ax+b
  a=1.48
  b=4.12
  r²=.9970866715
  r=.9985422733
■
```

3 Access the linear regression function on your GDC. Make sure that Xlist is your list of x-variables (List 1) and Ylist is your list of y-variables (List 2).

* Please note on the TI-84 Plus, and some operating systems on the Silver Edition, replace , with ENTER, CLEAR the FreqList, and press ENTER three times after 2nd 2 (L₂).

(With the scatter diagram on the screen.)

F1 (CALC)

F2 (X)

F1 (ax + b)

(Using F2 (X) assumed that the scatter graph was linear. You can also test for curves.)

```
LinearReg(ax+b)
  a =1.46645955
  b =4.15454978
  r =0.99814179
  r²=0.99628703
  MSe=0.01536012
 y=ax+b
            COPY DRAW
```

	TEXAS		METHOD			CASIO

TEXAS

$Y=$ 1 $.$ 4 8 X,T,Θ,n $+$

4 $.$ 1 2 $\boxed{GRAPH}$

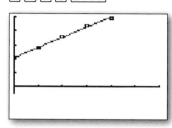

METHOD

4 Display the regression line.

5 Write down the information appropriately. Note that *a* and *b* will vary according to GDCs.
CASIO:
$y = 1.47x + 4.15$ (3s.f.)
TEXAS:
$y = 1.48x + 4.12$ (3s.f.)

CASIO

$\boxed{F6}$ (DRAW)

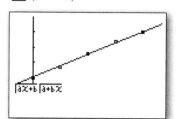

22.3.13 Chapter 13 Chi-squared hypothesis testing

13.1 The χ^2 test for independence

This is broken down into two parts: entering the data into a matrix (steps 1–3) and calculating the χ^2 statistic (steps 4–6).

TEXAS

$\boxed{2nd}$ $\boxed{x^{-1}}$ (MATRIX)

$\boxed{\triangleright}$ $\boxed{\triangleright}$ (EDIT)

$\boxed{1}$ (Matrix A) (You can select other blank matrices.)

$\boxed{3}$ $\boxed{\triangleright}$ $\boxed{3}$ $\boxed{ENTER}$

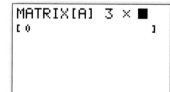

METHOD

1 Access the matrix menu and select a matrix (some GDCs might have one already entered so you can delete the data in this matrix, or select a different matrix).

2 Enter the number of rows and the number of columns. In this example, we use the following data:

	BH	BrH	BlH
BE	5	7	12
BrE	15	10	2
GE	3	4	5

There are 3 rows of data and 3 columns of data.

CASIO

$\boxed{MENU}$ $\boxed{1}$ (RUN MAT)

$\boxed{F1}$ (MAT)

$\boxed{EXE}$ (Matrix A) (You can select other blank matrices.)

$\boxed{3}$ $\boxed{EXE}$

$\boxed{3}$ $\boxed{EXE}$

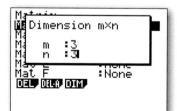

TEXAS	METHOD	CASIO

5 ENTER 7 ENTER
1 2 ENTER 1 5 ENTER
1 0 ENTER
2 ENTER 3 ENTER
4 ENTER 5 ENTER

2nd MODE (QUIT)

3 Enter the observed data.

5 EXE 7 EXE
1 2 EXE 1 5 EXE
1 0 EXE 2 EXE
3 EXE 4 EXE 5 EXE

EXIT EXIT

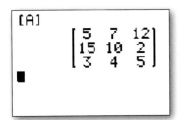

$$[A] \begin{bmatrix} 5 & 7 & 12 \\ 15 & 10 & 2 \\ 3 & 4 & 5 \end{bmatrix}$$

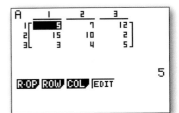

STAT

◄ ► ► (TESTS)

ALPHA PRGM (C: χ^2-test)

(or scroll ▼ until you reach 'C: χ^2 test' and then ENTER)

4 Select the χ^2 statistic function.

MENU 2 (STAT)

F3 (TEST)

F3 (CHI)

F2 (2WAY)

```
EDIT CALC TESTS
B↑2-PropZInt…
  C:χ²-Test…
D:χ²GOF-Test…
E:2-SampFTest…
F:LinRegTTest…
G:LinRegTInt…
H:ANOVA(
```

```
χ² Test
Observed:Mat A
Expected:Mat B
Save Res:None
Execute

Mat ►MAT
```

```
χ²-Test
 Observed:[A]
 Expected:[B]
 Calculate  Draw
```

5 Confirm that observed data is in matrix A. Matrix B will fill automatically (you can change the degree of accuracy as required).

```
χ² Test
Observed:Mat A
Expected:Mat B
Save Res:None
Execute

CALC                    DRAW
```

▼ ▼ ► (DRAW)

ENTER

6a Draw the graph or go to step 6b.

▼ ▼ ▼ (Execute)

F6 (DRAW)

F1 (CH1)

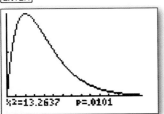

χ²=13.2637   p=.0101

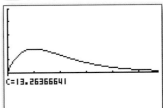

C=13.26366641

METHOD

⊡ ⊡ (CALCULATE)

6b Get the statistics as a
list on screen.

Press EXE immediately after doing
point 4.

[ENTER]

```
X²-Test
 X²=13.26366641
 P=.0100568114
 df=4

■
```

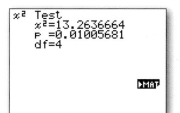

13.2 Viewing the contents of a matrix

METHOD

[2nd] [x⁻¹] (MATRIX)

Access the matrix
menu and view
matrix B.

[MENU] [1] (RUN MAT)

[2] (B)

[F1] (MAT)

[ENTER]

⊡ (Mat B)

```
NAMES MATH EDIT
1:[A]  3×3
2:[B]  3×3
3:[C]
4:[D]
5:[E]  3×3
6:[F]
7↓[G]
```

[EXE]

```
[B]
 [[8.8 8.0 7.2]
  [9.9 9.0 8.1]
  [4.4 4.0 3.6]]
```

```
B    1      2      3
1┌3.7619   8  7.238┐
2│9.8571   9  8.1428│
3└4.3809   4  3.619┘

                        8.8

R·OP ROW COL EDIT
```

22.3.14 Chapter 14 Equation of a line in two dimensions

14.1 Accessing the table of coordinates from a plotted graph

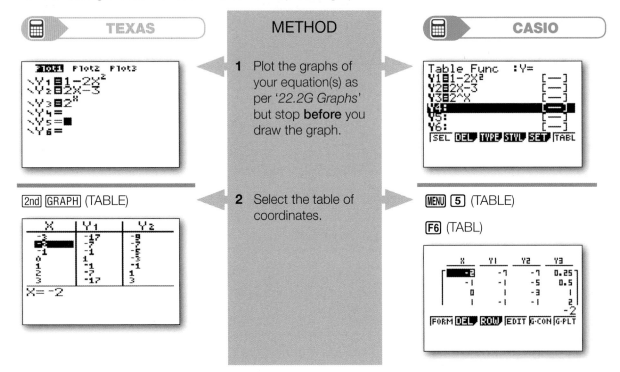

TEXAS	METHOD	CASIO
	1 Plot the graphs of your equation(s) as per '*22.2G Graphs*' but stop **before** you draw the graph.	
[2nd] [GRAPH] (TABLE)	**2** Select the table of coordinates.	[MENU] [5] (TABLE) [F6] (TABL)

22.3.15–16 Chapter 15 Trigonometry and Chapter 16 Geometry of three-dimensional solids

Your calculator is useful for finding the values of the sine, tangent and cosine for a given angle, and the inverses, $\sin^{-1}$, $\cos^{-1}$ and $\tan^{-1}$. Remember to make sure that your GDC is **ALWAYS** set in **degree mode**.

22.3.17 Chapter 17 Functions and graphs

17.1 Finding the range for a given domain

Find the range for $f(x) = \sqrt{(3+2x)}$, $x \geq -1.5$.

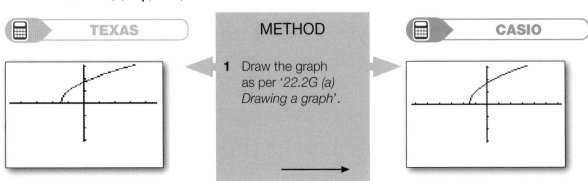

TEXAS	METHOD	CASIO
	1 Draw the graph as per '*22.2G (a) Drawing a graph*'.	

TEXAS	METHOD	CASIO
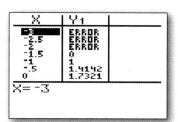	**2** Access the table of coordinates as per '*14.1 Accessing the table of coordinates from a plotted graph*'. Use this table to work out the range.	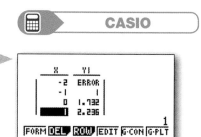

3 Write down the answer appropriately.

The range is $f(x) \geq 0$

17.2 Finding the vertical asymptote

Find the vertical asymptote of the graph $y = \dfrac{3}{2 - x}$.

TEXAS	METHOD	CASIO
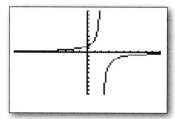	**1** Draw the graph as per '*22.2G (a) Drawing a graph*'. Find the asymptote by looking for the break in the graph along the x-axis. In this example, we can see a break at $x = 2$.	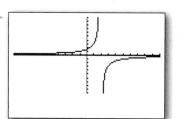
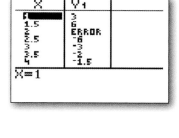	**2** Access the table of coordinates per '*14.1 Accessing the table of coordinates from a plotted graph*'. Use this table to confirm the asymptote from step 1. The error message confirms that the vertical asymptote occurs when $x = 2$.	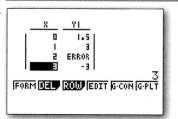

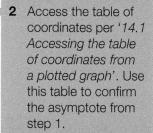

17.3 Finding the horizontal asymptote

Find the horizontal asymptote of the graph $y = 1.5^x - 3$.

 TEXAS **METHOD**   **CASIO**

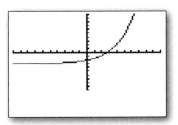

1 Draw the graph as per '22.2G (a) Drawing a graph'.

Find the asymptote by looking for what value of y the graph approaches.

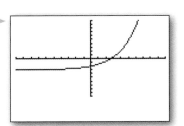

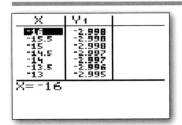

2 Access the table of coordinates as per '14.1 Accessing the table of coordinates from a plotted graph'. Scroll through the table to confirm the asymptote from step 1.

You can see that the value of Y_1 approaches -3. This confirms that the asymptote is $y = -3$.

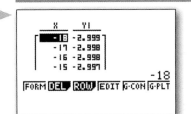

22.3.18 Chapter 18 Linear and quadratic models

18.1 Using a graph to find the vertex and line of symmetry of a parabola

Find the vertex and line of symmetry of the graph $y = 7 - 5x - 2x^2$

 TEXAS **METHOD**   **CASIO**

1 Draw the graph as per '22.2G (a) Drawing a graph'.

⟶

2nd TRACE (CALC)

4 (maximum)

Move the cursor to the left of the vertex:
ENTER (confirm left bound).

Move cursor to the right of the vertex:
ENTER (confirm right bound).

Move cursor over the vertex:
ENTER (confirm position of vertex).

2 Decide if the graph has a minimum or a maximum and select appropriately. In this example, the parabola has a maximum.

SHIFT F5 (G-Solv)

F2 (MAX)

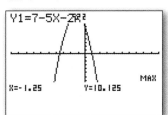

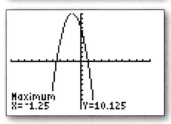

3 (minimum)

To find the minimum, you would do as above but select 'minimum' instead of 'maximum'.

F3 (minimum)

3 Write down the answer appropriately.

The vertex is at $(-1.25, 10.125)$ and the line of symmetry is $x = -1.25$

18.2 Finding the zeros (roots) of a quadratic equation using a graph

Solve $y = 7 - 5x - 2x^2$.

1 Draw the graph as per '*22.2G (a) Drawing a graph*'.

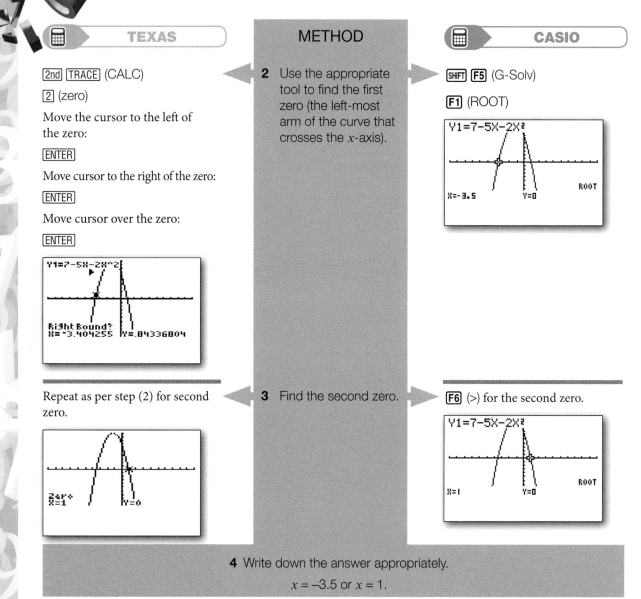

TEXAS	METHOD	CASIO
2nd TRACE (CALC) 2 (zero) Move the cursor to the left of the zero: ENTER Move cursor to the right of the zero: ENTER Move cursor over the zero: ENTER	**2** Use the appropriate tool to find the first zero (the left-most arm of the curve that crosses the x-axis).	SHIFT F5 (G-Solv) F1 (ROOT)
Repeat as per step (2) for second zero.	**3** Find the second zero.	F6 (>) for the second zero.

4 Write down the answer appropriately.

$$x = -3.5 \text{ or } x = 1.$$

18.3 Using the statistics menu to find an equation

You might have a set of data plotted on a graph and want to find the equation of the curve or line without having to use the methods learned in Chapter 14. You can use the statistics menu to find the equation of different curves, or of a line.

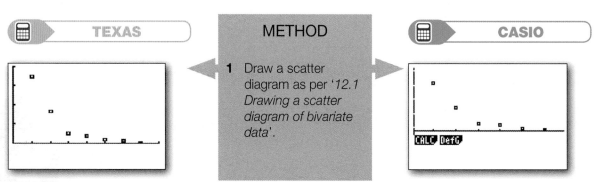

TEXAS	METHOD	CASIO
	1 Draw a scatter diagram as per '*12.1 Drawing a scatter diagram of bivariate data*'.	

STAT

▶ (CALC)

0 (ExpReg)

2 Look at the shape of the graph to decide what type of graph it is (linear, parabola, hyperbola, exponential). In this example, the shape of the graph suggests it is an exponential graph: $y = a \times b^x$. Select this type of graph from the list.

F1 (CALC)

F6 (>)

F3 (EXP)

F2 (ab^x)

ExpReg(a·b^x)
 a =73.2267653
 b =0.47152261
 r =-0.9891428
 r²=0.97840351
 MSe=0.01765677
y=a·b^x
                    COPY DRAW

(Make sure the Xlist and Ylist are the correct lists according to where you entered the data in step 1, e.g. Xlist should be the x-variable in L_1 and Ylist should be the y-variable in L_2)

▼ (CALCULATE)

ENTER

ExpReg
 y=a*b^x
 a=61.65668827
 b=.497720483
 r²=.9753614326
 r=-.9876038845

22.3.19 Chapter 19 Exponential and polynomial functions

19.1 Solving growth and decay problems

Growth and decay problems often involve finding the variable when it is the exponent, e.g. $y = a \times b^x$. In many cases you will have a value of y and want to know what value of x gives this value of y, e.g. if $y = 10$, you would get the equation $10 = a \times b^x$, where the values of a and b are known. A simple way to solve an equation involving x in the exponent is to plot the exponential graph ($y = a \times b^x$) and the line of the target value of y, e.g. $y = 10$. At the point where the line intersects with the exponential curve, you will find the value of x that makes the equation $10 = a \times b^x$ true. This is the solution to the equation.

Solve $0.3 \times 1.7^x = 35$.

The value of x that makes this equation true can be found at the point of intersection between the two graphs:

$$y = 0.3 \times 1.7^x \text{ and } y = 35.$$

 TEXAS	METHOD	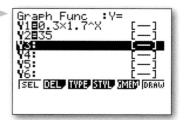 CASIO
	1 Plot the graphs as per '22.2G (a) Drawing a graph'. Adjust the window as required.	

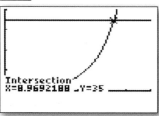	METHOD	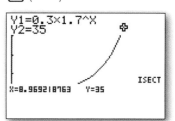
2nd TRACE (CALC) 5 (intersect) (First curve?) ENTER (Second curve?) ENTER (Guess?) ▶ ▶ ▶ (use cursor to move to point of intersection) ENTER	**2** Find the point of intersection of the line with the exponential equation.	SHIFT F5 (G-Solv) F5 (ISCT)

3 Write down the answer appropriately.

$$x = 9.00 \text{ (3 s.f.)}$$

19.2 Solving unfamiliar equations

Your GDC can be particularly useful when you have equations whose graph would be quite complicated to plot by hand. Examples of such graphs are those where the variable is the exponent, e.g. $y = 1 - 2^x$. Other more complicated equations include those in the form $y = \sqrt{(2 + x)}$, where the variable is inside a root function.

(a) using a graph

Solve $1 - 2^x = \sqrt{(2 + x)}$.

TEXAS	METHOD	CASIO
Draw the equation each side of the '=' sign as a separate graph and find the point of intersection. At this point, the value of x makes both equations true such that $1 - 2^x = \sqrt{(2 + x)}$.		
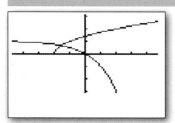	**1** Draw each graph as per '22.2G (a) Drawing a graph'.	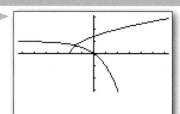

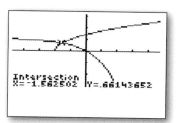
METHOD

2 Find the point of intersection as per step (2) in '*19.1 Solving growth and decay problems*'.

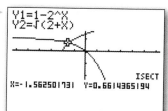

Intersection
X=-1.562502   Y=.66143652

```
Y1=1-2^X
Y2=√(2+X)
```

                                    ISECT
X=-1.562501731   Y=0.6614365194

3 Write down the appropriate answer.

$$x = -1.56 \text{ (3 s.f.)}$$

(b) using an equation solver

Solve $1 - 2^x = \sqrt{(2+x)}$.

METHOD

[MATH] [0] * (0: Solver…)

(Or, [MATH] [▼] until '0: Solver...' [ENTER])

(You will need to rearrange the equal to equal zero.)

[2nd] [x²] (√) [2] [+] [X,T,Θ,n] [ )]

[−] [( ] [1] [−] [2] [^] [X,T,Θ,n] [ )]

[ALPHA] [ENTER] (Solve)

1 Use the equation solver and key in the equation.

* Please note on the TI-84 Plus, and some OS on other Silver Editions, it is: [MATH] [ALPHA] [APPS] (B: Solver...) or [MATH] [▼] until 'B: Solver' [ENTER].

[MENU] [8] (EQUA)

[F3] (Solver)

[1] [−] [2] [^] [X,θ,T] [SHIFT] [•] (=)

[SHIFT] [x²] (√) [( ] [2] [+] [X,θ,T] [EXE]

[F6] (SOLV)

2 Write down the appropriate answer.
$$x = 14.5.$$

19.3 Solving polynomial equations

(a) using a graph

Use the methods as per section '*18.2 Finding the zeros (roots) of a quadratic equation using a graph*', repeating the methods to find all the roots as required.

(b) using an equation solver

Use the methods as per section '*2.3 (b) Solving quadratic equations using an equation solver*', but in step 1 you would enter the appropriate order/degree to suit the polynomial that you have. So, if you wanted to solve a cubic equation, the order/degree would be '3'; if you wanted to solve a quadratic equation, the order/degree would be '2' and so on. In step 2, you enter the appropriate coefficients in decreasing order/degree of x terms. So, for a cubic graph you would enter the coefficient of the x^3 term first, then the coefficient of the x^2 term, then the coefficient of the x term and finally the constant.

22.3.20 Chapter 20 Introduction to differential calculus

20.1 Finding the numerical value of the derivative $\left(\dfrac{dy}{dx}\right)$

(a) using a graph

TEXAS	METHOD	CASIO
(Not required)	**1** Set up your calculator appropriately.	[MENU] [3] (GRAPH) [SHIFT] [MENU] (SET UP) ⊙ ⊙ ⊙ ⊙ ⊙ (Derivative) [F1] (ON) 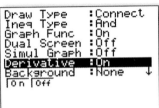

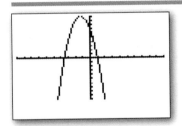

2 Draw a graph as per '22.2G (a) Drawing a graph'.

We will use the following graph in this example:

$y = 7 - 5x - 2x^2$

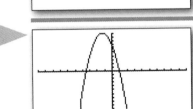

[2nd] [TRACE] (CALC)

[6] $\left(\dfrac{dy}{dx}\right)$

[2]

[ENTER]

3 Select the tangent tool and choose an x-coordinate from which it can be drawn. In this example we will use $x = 2$.

[SHIFT] [F1] (TRACE)

[2] [EXE]

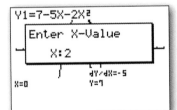

```
CALCULATE
1:value
2:zero
3:minimum
4:maximum
5:intersect
6:dy/dx
7:∫f(x)dx
```

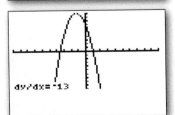

dy/dx=-13

(b) using the table

TEXAS

The table function does not give values of the derivative at a point on this calculator.

METHOD

1. Access the table menu and enter the equation whose derivative you want to find. In this example we will use $y = 7 - 5x - 2x^2$

CASIO

MENU 5 (TABLE)

7 − 5 X,θ,T − 2

X,θ,T x²

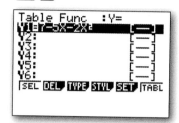

```
Table Func  :Y=
Y1=7-5X-2X²
Y2:
Y3:
Y4:
Y5:
Y6:
[SEL][DEL][TYPE][STYL][SET][TABL]
```

2. Use the table to read off the x-coordinate, y-coordinate and value of $\dfrac{dy}{dx}$ ($y'1$), at each point.

F6 (TABL)

```
  X    Y1    Y'1
 -3     4      7
 -2     9      3
 -1    10     -1
  0     7     -5
                    0
[FORM][DEL][ROW][EDIT][G·CON][G·PLT]
```

20.2 Finding the equation of the tangent at a point

TEXAS

(Not possible)

METHOD

1. Set up your calculator appropriately.

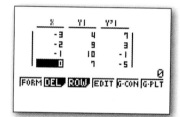

CASIO

MENU 3 (GRAPH)

SHIFT MENU (SET UP)

▽ ▽ ▽ ▽ ▽ (Derivative)

F1 (ON)

```
Draw Type    :Connect
Ineq Type    :And
Graph Func   :On
Dual Screen  :Off
Simul Graph  :Off
Derivative   :On
Background   :None    ↓
[On][Off]
```

2. Draw a graph as per '22.2G (a) Drawing a graph'.
We will use the following graph in this example:
$$y = 7 - 5x - 2x^2$$

2nd PRGM (Draw)

5 (Tangent)

(-) 3 ENTER

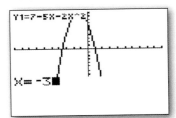

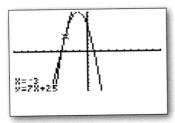

3 Once you have the graph on screen, select the tangent function and enter the value of x at the coordinate of choice. This will give you the tangent and tell you its equation.

SHIFT F4 (Sketch)

F2 (Tang)

(-) 3 EXE

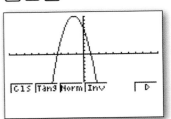

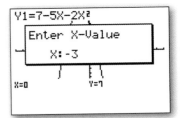

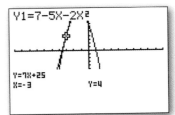

There is no program for finding the equation of the normal on this calculator.

4 To find the equation of the normal.

Repeat as per steps (2) and (3) above but replace:

F2 (Tang) with:

F3 (Norm)

(-) 3 EXE

21.1 Finding increasing and decreasing functions

Describe the function $f(x) = 3x^2 - x^2 - 2$ in terms of when it is increasing and decreasing.

(a) using a graph

TEXAS	METHOD	CASIO
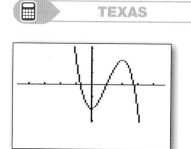	**1** Plot the graph as per '*22.2G (a) Drawing a graph*'.	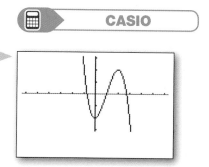

2 Look at the graph and determine for what values of x:

- the gradient is negative, $f'(x) < 0$; this is where the function is decreasing
- the gradient is positive, $f'(x) > 0$; this is where the function is increasing
- the gradient is zero, $f'(x) = 0$; this is a stationary point.

3 Write down the answer appropriately.

The function is decreasing when $x < 0$.

The function is increasing when $0 < x < 2$.

The function is decreasing when $x > 2$.

(b) using a table

METHOD

The table function does not give values of the derivative at a point.

1 Access the table of values as per the instructions in '*20.1 (b) Finding the numerical value of the derivative* $\left(\dfrac{dy}{dx}\right)$ *using a table*'.

MENU 5 (TABLE)

F6 (TABL)

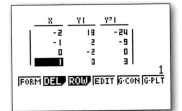

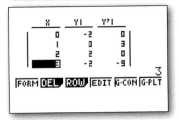

If Y'1 is negative, the function is decreasing.

If Y'1 is positive, the function is increasing.

2 Write down the answer appropriately.
When $x < 0$ the function is decreasing.
When $0 < x < 2$ the function is increasing.
When $x = 3$, the function is decreasing.

21.2 Finding local maximum and minimum points

Find the local maximum and minimum points of the graph $y = 3x^2 - x^2 - 2$.

METHOD

1 Draw a graph as per '*22.2G (a) Drawing a graph*'.

2nd TRACE (CALC)

3 (minimum)

Move the cursor to the left of vertex:
ENTER (confirm left bound)

Move cursor to the right of vertex:
ENTER (confirm right bound)

2 Use the appropriate tool to locate the minimum.

SHIFT F5 (G-Solv)

F3 (MIN)

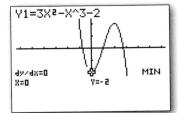

TEXAS

Move cursor over the vertex: ENTER (confirm position of vertex)

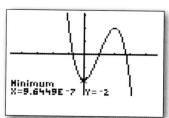

In this example, $x = 0$ even though the GDC has actually given a value very close to zero.

2nd TRACE (CALC)

4 (maximum)

Move the cursor to the left of the vertex ENTER (confirm left bound).

Move cursor to the right of the vertex ENTER (confirm right bound).

Move cursor over the vertex ENTER (confirm position of vertex).

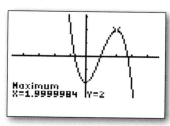

METHOD

3 Use the appropriate tool to locate the maximum.

CASIO

SHIFT F5 (G-Solv)

F2 (MAX)

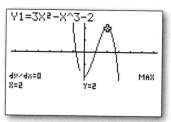

4 Write down the answer appropriately.
The local minimum is $x = 0$ and the local maximum is $x = 2$.

Chapter 23 Internal assessment

23.1 Why is there a project in this course?

The project is intended to give you the experience of doing an extended piece of mathematics. A good project should help to convince you that mathematics is not a list of 'sums' with right or wrong answers but, instead is, a useful skill that will continue to be relevant to you after you have completed your diploma. A successful project will show you that mathematics is a valuable analytical tool that can assist you in future studies as well as in your career.

As part of the course:

- Your project accounts for 20% of your final mark.

- There are a total of 20 possible marks for your project (with no partial marks).

- The syllabus allocates 25 teaching hours for the project. This includes time for you to look at examples of past projects, study the marking criteria and discuss a suitable focus of study with your teacher.

- The project should be approximately 2000 words in length, excluding diagrams, appendices and bibliography.

- If you do not submit a project, you will not receive an overall grade for this course.

23.2 How do I start?

You should start thinking about your project during the first year of your course, even if you do not expect to complete the work until you are in your second year.

To help you get started:

- Ask your teacher to show you some past projects. If you look at them in class, you can also discuss them with your teacher and fellow students.

- Study the marking criteria and make sure you understand what is expected. Try marking some past projects according to the assessment criteria. You could do this together with a few other students so that you can discuss the projects you are reviewing and whether or not you think they have met the criteria.

- Re-examine past projects and make a note of anything that impresses you, or anything that you think could have been improved.

- Think about an aspect of mathematics that you particularly enjoy and feel comfortable with, or do you have a favourite sport or hobby that you could use as a basis for your project?

23.3 Is my topic a good one?

Finding a good topic is the hardest part of the project. Once you have an idea, discuss it with your teacher, who can advise and guide you through the process of formulating a theme for your project. The International Baccalaureate Organization publishes a list of titles of successful past projects, which you can look at to get some ideas.

Make sure that:

- your chosen project will involve enough mathematics to demonstrate your level of skill; an idea may seem really interesting, but consider whether its interest is more artistic or historical than mathematical

- you can clearly identify a 'research question' within your chosen topic and that you will have enough mathematical knowledge to explore it in depth

- the topic actually interests you — you will not feel motivated to spend time on something that bores you or seems pointless.

23.4 What is the structure of the project?

Your project should have a logical structure so that your analysis and conclusions are easy to understand.

Make sure that your project contains:

- an appropriate title

- a clear statement of your task and a plan for how you are going to approach it

- the information or data that you have collected and have analysed mathematically

- your analysis of the information or data collected; there are many ways in which you can present this — just be careful to always use the correct mathematical notation

- your interpretation of the results and a discussion about their validity or whether you suspect bias or other faults

- your conclusion — have you answered the question that you started out with? Have you discovered anything that surprises you?

23.5 What are the assessment criteria?

Your project will be marked by your teacher according to a set of official criteria.

	Criterion	Maximum mark
A	Introduction	3
B	Information and/or measurements	3
C	Mathematical processes	5
D	Interpretation of results	3
E	Validity	1
F	Structure and communication	3
G	Notation and terminology	2

After your teacher has marked all the projects for his/her class, a sample of the projects will be sent to an IB moderator. This means that someone who does not know the students in person will mark the projects again. This checking procedure is intended to ensure that all projects, from all over the world, are marked to the same standard.

Criterion A. Introduction

You should aim to get top marks for this criterion. To achieve the full 3 marks, you need to give the project a suitable title, provide a clear statement of the task you are undertaking, and write a detailed plan of how you will approach the task, the techniques you will use and the reasons for choosing them. If your work is based on a specific research question or null hypothesis, this is where you should state it.

Although it's a good idea to start with a detailed plan, some projects change considerably during the course of the investigation. It is fine to adapt your plan while you are working on the project, but when you have finished, remember to go back and make sure that your introduction still fits.

Criterion B. Information and/or measurements

It is important that you collect enough information but not too much. It is as easy to be overwhelmed by too much material as it is to be stuck because you have not collected enough. How much is enough? This is a difficult question as it depends on the individual project, so don't be hesitant to check with your teacher.

If you collect your own information, make sure that all of it is relevant and that you are aware of any bias or faults in your selection methods. If you have used a questionnaire to collect data for statistical analysis, include a copy of it with your project, but do not attach all the completed questionnaires.

If you are using secondary data, make sure that you have explained where you found it, and give the references to any books, periodicals or websites that you used. You may have so much secondary data that you have to work with samples, in which case you need to describe any sampling techniques that you have used.

Once you have assembled all your information or measurements, organise it in a form that is straightforward to understand and analyse. Remember that your project may be sent to the IB moderator, so you, your teacher and the moderator must all be able to make sense of your material easily.

Criterion C. Mathematical processes

This is the core of your project and the section on which you will spend the most time. Think of your mathematics as something that will develop as you work, so don't be tempted to begin your project with a complicated technique. The key word in this criterion is 'relevant': the mathematical processes that you use must be directly related to and appropriate for your project.

Here are some tips to guide you in this part of the project:

- Start with simple processes that you are confident about — and keep checking at each stage that your working is correct.

- Draw diagrams or graphs where they can illustrate and explain your methods.

- If you are using formulae, quote them and show how, and why, you have used them.

- Don't keep repeating the same process. Some projects may require repetition, but after you have worked through a process once and explained it clearly, any further applications of the same procedure should be presented concisely, for example using technology, with the results summarised in tables.

- Once you have a solid foundation for your work, you can move on to other, more complicated, techniques; but still make sure that these are relevant and that you have explained why you are using them. There is no merit in doing something complicated just because you can.

- If something unexpected happens, do not ignore it. For instance, if a scatter graph shows little correlation, or a correlation coefficient turns out to be very small, there is no point in continuing with your original plan to calculate a regression line. Instead, explain why you have not obtained a line of best fit; this demonstrates that you actually understand the concepts behind a technique. In fact, it can be really useful when things do not go as you expect, since it gives you plenty of scope to discuss why that might have happened.

- To gain the highest possible mark for this criterion, you are expected to build on the simple processes that you started with by using at least one further, more complex, process. This further process must, as always, be relevant and correctly applied.

Criterion D. Interpretation of results

To satisfy this criterion, you need to discuss the mathematics that you used to obtain your results, why you used it, and what the results tell you.

You can include here a discussion of anything unexpected that you found. The recognition that your calculations produced an unexpected result is already valuable, but you also need to discuss possible reasons for why this could have happened.

To gain the highest mark for this criterion, you must discuss your results in a meaningful way, making sure that your conclusions are consistent with the mathematics that you used and are interpreted in the context of the question or task stated in the introduction. If your project is too simple, you will find this difficult to do.

Criterion E. Validity

This criterion is easy to miss; some students think that it is irrelevant to their project and that they can ignore it.

For most projects you can discuss the accuracy of the measurements, or any bias that may be present in your data.

Assessing the validity of your information or methods is also an opportunity to examine anything that went wrong and to show what you learned from any mistakes.

If you are quite sure that the validity of information and techniques is not relevant to your project, make sure that you state this and give your reasons for believing so.

As part of this criterion you can also discuss whether and how your project could be improved or extended. However, be sure that you give clear reasons; 'I could improve this project if I had more time' will not be considered sufficient!

Criterion F. Structure and communication

This criterion follows on from criteria A, D and E. If you started with a clear, detailed plan and have been able to follow it, then the structure of your project should be good. If you have given a coherent discussion of your results and their validity, then you have communicated well.

Look at any graphs or diagrams: have you given each one a title and labelled them correctly? Is it clear why they are included in that place and what they are meant to illustrate? Are your calculations correct and is it obvious how you did them? If you used a computer or GDC for most of your calculations, make sure you have explained clearly how, and why, you used that technology.

Reread your project and make sure that it flows well and that your discussions are in the right place and are easy to follow. It is a good idea to ask a non-mathematician to read your project. They should be able to see clearly why you did the project and what you found out by doing it. They may not understand the maths you used, but your project should give them confidence that you do know what you're doing; they should not drop to sleep with boredom trying to read through 20 pages of data or endless repeats of similar calculations!

Have you cited properly any resources that you used? Remember that if you need to add an appendix containing references, it will not be included in your word count.

When you are sure that your project is complete, ask other people to read it. If you can convince someone (other than your teacher or your best friend) that your project is well-structured and interesting, well done!

Criterion G. Notation and terminology

If you are very skilled with your GDC or computer, it is quite easy to lose marks by using incorrect notation. Any variables you use should be defined clearly. Remember that calculator notation is not acceptable in either the examinations or the project. Technology can be an important tool while you are working on your project, but you are still expected to use correct notation and mathematical vocabulary when writing up your results.

23.6 What do I do when I have finished my project?

If you have done your entire project on a computer, ensure that you have made a back-up copy before you submit it to your teacher.

If you have used a combination of computer-generated and hand-drawn charts or diagrams, save back-up copies of the electronic ones and scan or keep photocopies of anything that you drew on paper.

Your teacher will give you a form to sign. This requires you to verify that the work is entirely your own and that you have acknowledged the use of any material, whether written or visual, that belongs to another person. Plagiarism is taken very seriously by the IB. The unauthorised use of another person's material will result in your project being disqualified.

After you have submitted your project, it will be marked by your teacher according to the criteria described above, and it may be included in the sample sent to an IB moderator for re-marking.

You can now move on to the rest of your course!

Answers

Answers are given to 3 s.f. unless the question specifies otherwise.

Chapter 1

Exercise 1.1

1. (a) T
   (b) T
   (c) F; $\sqrt{17}$ is irrational
   (d) F; 1.51 can be written as 151/100
   (e) T
   (f) F; all irrational numbers are real numbers
   (g) F; the sum of two integers is always an integer
   (h) T

2. Answers may vary, for example:
   (a) -6
   (b) $\frac{25}{4}$
   (c) $\sqrt{5}$
   (d) 8

3.

4. (a) $-5.1, -2.5, -2, 0, \frac{6}{7}, \sqrt{2}, \sqrt{3}, 12$
   (b) 12, 0
   (c) 12, -2, 0
   (d) 12, -5.1, -2, 0, $\frac{6}{7}$, -2.5
   (e) $\sqrt{2}, \sqrt{3}$; irrational numbers

5. (a) Natural
   (b) Natural, integer, rational
   (c) Negative integer
   (d) Irrational
   (e) Natural number

Exercise 1.2

1. (a) 169 cm
   (b) 1 h 45 min
   (c) 3200
   (d) 220 AUD
   (e) 628 m²
   (f) 75 kg

2. (a) 50
   (b) 200
   (c) 320
   (d) 2150
   (e) 20 460

3. (a) 300
   (b) 2000
   (c) 100
   (d) 67 900
   (e) 708 500

4. (a) 2
   (b) 32
   (c) 13
   (d) 113

6. (a) Answers may vary, e.g. $1\frac{1}{4}$
   (b) Answers may vary, e.g. $3\frac{1}{4}$

7. (a) 43, 2, 17, 13
   (b) 21, 15, -6, 6
   (c) 2, -6, 6, -4
   (d) 2

Exercise 1.3

1. (a) (i) 6.8   (ii) 6.82
   (b) (i) 153.8   (ii) 153.81
   (c) (i) 18.0   (ii) 17.97
   (d) (i) 0.2   (ii) 0.16

2. (a) 41.9
   (b) 45.6
   (c) 7.1

3. (a) 145.27 cm²
   (b) 93.29 cm³
   (c) 72.97 cm³

Exercise 1.4

1. (a) 93.5
   (b) 108
   (c) 0.00784
   (d) 8.56
   (e) 0.0626

2. (a) 3.08
   (b) 1080
   (c) 8.77
   (d) 6.69

3. (a) 43.5 cm²
   (b) 3.18 cm
   (c) 8.60 cm

4. 132 cm³

Exercise 1.5

1. (a) 72; 75.69
   (b) 60; 72.513…
   (c) 8; 7.34496…

2. (a) (i) 138.18 cm²;
      (ii) 138.2 cm²;
      (iii) 138 cm²
   (b) 3.18 cm²

3. (a) $m = 30$, $n = 10$, $p = 100$ (to 1 s.f.)
   (b) 6.82
   (c) 5.573868149
   (d) 1.25

4. (a) 110 304 m²
   (b) When rounding either of the values to 1 s.f., he probably dropped a zero from the rounded value.

Exercise 1.6

1. (a) 2.65%
(b) 7.32%
(c) 6.11%
(d) 31.8%

2. (a) 354.78 cm³
(b) 3.52%

Exercise 1.7

1. (a) 6   (b) 4   (c) −3
(d) 6   (e) 0

2. (a) 12 500   (b) 3080
(c) 288 000 000 (d) 0.0421
(e) 0.00972   (f) 0.00000838

3. (a) 6.21×10^4 (b) 2.1×10^3
(c) 9.84×10^7 (d) 5.2×10^1

4. (a) 7.27×10^{-1} (b) 3.19×10^{-2}
(c) 2.57×10^{-6} (d) 4.08×10^{-4}

5. (a) 398×10^1, 0.17×10^3,
370×10^2, 0.02×10^2
(b) 3.98×10^3, 1.7×10^2,
3.70×10^4, 2×10^0
(c) 3.8×10^{-5}, 2.4×10^{-3},
2×10^0, 1.2×10^2, 1.7×10^2,
3.98×10^3, 3.70×10^4

6. (a) 3.17×10^{10} (b) 9.89×10^{-2}
(c) 4.56×10^{-9} (d) 1.54×10^{-6}
(e) 8.12×10^4 (f) 3.44×10^{-7}

7. (a) 3.90×10^3 (b) 3.90×10^3
(c) 2.65×10^0 (d) 5.74×10^6

8. (a) 33 min
(b) 12 min
(c) 79 min

9. 1270 times (to 3 s.f.)

Exercise 1.8

1. (a) 395 s
(b) 9 min 22 s
(c) 3 d 6 h
(d) 1 h 48 min 20 s
(e) 17 595 min
(f) 22 030 s

Exercise 1.9

1.

City	Miami	Riga	Milan	Bahrain	Lima	Perth	Moscow
Celsius (°C)	27.8	−2	7	18.3	25	32.2	−12
Fahrenheit (°F)	82	28.4	44.6	65	77	90	10.4

Exercise 1.10

1. (a) 38 km h⁻¹
(b) 7.19 h
(c) 29.3 km

2. (a) 2.625 km h⁻¹
(b) 2.64 km h⁻¹; faster
(c) 2.63 km h⁻¹

Exercise 1.11

1. (a) 3.5 m   (b) 2760 mm
(c) 4.8 km   (d) 35 200 cm

2. (a) 5800 g
(b) 0.03 kg
(c) 1.26 g
(d) 1 000 000 mg

3. (a) 45 000 cm²
(b) 0.0685 m²
(c) 1.4×10^6 m²
(d) 1.2 cm²

4. (a) 1.2×10^7 cm³
(b) 0.024 m³
(c) 1300 mm³
(d) 5×10^5 cm³

5. (a) 7.9 l   (b) 3950 ml
(c) 83 300 cm³ (d) 687 cm³

6. (a) (i) 70 000 cm²
(ii) 7 m²
(b) (i) 8.21×10^5 cm³
(ii) 0.821 m³
(c) 33.1 cm²

7. (a) 38   (b) 16 cm

8. 1250

9. (a) 53   (b) 20 cm³

10. (a) 255 m²   (b) 20.4 m³

Mixed examination practice 1

Exam-style questions 1

1.

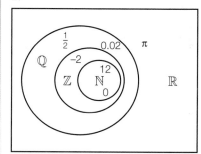

2.

3. (a) 2, natural number
(b) $4\dfrac{8}{9} = 4.8$, rational number
(c) 2, natural number
(d) 42.7256… , irrational number
(e) 10, natural number
(f) −36, integer
(g) $-\dfrac{101}{3}$, rational number
(h) −4, integer

4. (a) 40.0 cm²   (b) 8.4 cm²
(c) 6.4 m

5. (a) $R = 20$, $r = 10$, $\pi = 3$ (1 s.f.)
(b) $A \approx 900$
(c) 788

6. (i) 2.7   (ii) 2.66

7. 9.09×10^6

8. (a) $958 \, \text{kg} \, \text{m}^{-3}$ (b) $10^6 \, \text{cm}^3$
    (c) $9.58 \, \text{g}$

9. (a) $11\,305 \, \text{kg}$
    (b) $4.42 \times 10^{-6} \, \text{m}^3 = 4.42 \, \text{cm}^3$

Past paper questions 1

1. (a) 1.265×10^{-1}
    (b) 0.13
    (c) 2.77%

2. (a) 144.75
    (b) 1.4475×10^2
    (c) (i) $96 \, \text{m}^2$ (ii) 6.67%

Chapter 2

Exercise 2.1

1. (a), (d), (e) and (f) are linear;
    (b) and (c) are not

2. B and D

Exercise 2.2

1. (a) $y = x + 4$
    (b) $y = -3x + 7$
    (c) $y = \frac{1}{9}x - \frac{15}{9}$
    (d) $y = -\frac{5}{2}x + \frac{15}{2}$
    (e) $y = x - \frac{10}{11}$
    (f) $y = \frac{1}{3}x - \frac{13}{6}$
    (g) $y = -\frac{3}{4}x + \frac{27}{2}$
    (h) $y = \frac{15}{4}x + 1$
    (i) $y = \frac{2}{9}x + 7$

2. (a) $5x - y + 4 = 0$
    (b) $x - 2y - 5 = 0$
    (c) $3x + 2y - 6 = 0$
    (d) $3x - 4y - 10 = 0$
    (e) $9x - 2y = 0$
    (f) $5x + 2y - 1 = 0$

Exercise 2.3

1. (a) $m = 1$
    (b) $z = 70$
    (c) $y = -1$
    (d) $x = 16$

2. (a) $m = \frac{10}{3}$
    (b) $f = 0.2$
    (c) $x = 2.8$

3. (a) $x = \frac{1}{8}$
    (b) $z = 4.25$
    (c) $y = 19$

4. (a) $x = 13$
    (b) $y = 5$
    (c) $m = 2$
    (d) $x = -\frac{1}{16}$

Exercise 2.4

1. (a) $x = 8, y = 13$
    (b) $x = 3, y = 4$
    (c) $x = 0.5, y = 4$
    (d) $x = 9, y = 8$
    (e) $x = -0.538, y = -2.77$
    (f) $x = 2.81, y = 0.484$
    (g) $x = 3.6, y = 1.6$
    (h) $x = 0.4, y = 2.47$

2. (a) $s = 5.14, t = -3.79$
    (b) $s = 2.83, t = -1.16$
    (c) $s = -1.60, t = -3.49$
    (d) $s = 197, t = 33.3$

Exercise 2.5

1. (a) $3m + b = 85$
    (b) $m = 22, b = 19$

2. (a) $6s + 2t = 100$
    (b) Snickers: 6 AED; Twix:
        32 AED

3. $x + y = 97$ and $x - y = 23$; 60
    and 37

4. (a) $2c + 7d = 128.91$
    (b) CDs: £11.99; DVDs: £14.99

5. Batteries: £2.99; calculators:
    £14.50

6. (a) $3x + 4y = 2987, 2x + 5y = 3123$ (where x is the price
    of an easy-click laptop and
    y is the price of a smooth-
    tab laptop)
    (b) Easy-click: $349; smooth-
        tab: $485

7. $345

8. 9 shorter and 6 longer
    questions

9. (a) $S\left(-\frac{7}{3}, 0\right)$, and T (0, 7)
    (b) R (−2, 1)

Exercise 2.6

1. (a), (b), (d), (f) , (h) and (i)

2. A and D

3. (a) Max   (b) Min
    (c) Min   (d) Max

4. (a) $x^2 + x = 0$
    (b) $x^2 - 2x - 3 = 0$
    (c) $4x^2 + x - 4 = 0$
    (d) $x^2 - 5x - 6 = 0$
    (e) $x^2 + 5x - 15 = 0$
    (f) $x^2 - 6x - 7 = 0$

Exercise 2.7

1. (a) $1, -1.33$
    (b) $2, 0.571$
    (c) $-2.5, 0.667$
    (d) $-1.12, 10.7$
    (e) $14.8, 0.203$
    (f) $-0.805, 1.74$

2. (a) $2x^2 + 3x - 2 = 0$; 0.5, −2
    (b) $3x^2 + 11x - 9 = 0$; 0.689,
        −4.36
    (c) $x^2 + 7x - 13 = 0$; 1.52, −8.52
    (d) $6x^2 + 7x - 3 = 0$; 0.333, −1.5
    (e) $4x^2 - 5x - 8 = 0$; 2.17, −0.921
    (f) $9x^2 + x - 4 = 0$; −0.724,
        0.613

3. (a) 2.70, −1.16
(b) 0.614, −2.24
(c) 4.11, −0.608
(d) 3.95, 0.198
(e) 0.414, −2.41
(f) 1.26, −1.59

Exercise 2.8

1. $n^2 + n − 306 = 0$; 17 and 18

2. (a) $x^2 + 7x − 60 = 0$
(b) 5 cm and 12 cm

3. (a) $x^2 + x − 156 = 0$
(b) $x = 12$
(c) Parallel sides 12 cm and 18 cm, height 10 cm

4. (a) 1.24 s and 2.97 s
(b) 5.46 s

Mixed examination practice 2

Exam-style questions 2

1. $x = 6$

2. (a) $x = −1, y = 2$
(b) $x = 1.24, y = 2.33$
(c) $x = −2.91, y = 1.57$

3. (a) 0.286, 0.333
(b) 4.85, −1.85
(c) 4.92, −6.92
(d) 8.72, −1.72
(e) 1.61, −0.811

4. (a) $4x + 3y = 5529, 2x + 5y = 6751$
(b) Bracelet: 528 INR; pendant: 1139 INR

5. (a) $m + c = −5, 4m + c = 4$
(b) $m = 3, c = −8$
(c) No

6. (a) $a + 820b = 106.24,$
$a + 650b = 85.84$
(b) $a = 7.84, b = 0.12$
(c) £97.24

7. 20 m by 38 m

8. (a) 1.22 s, 3.56 s
(b) 4.78 s

1. (a) $6b + 9m = 23.40$
(b) $b = 1.80, m = 1.40$
(c)

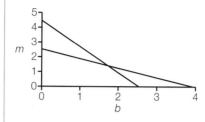

2. (a)

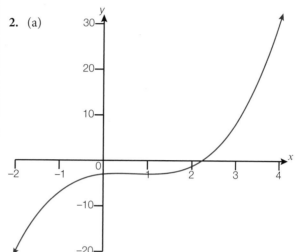

y-intercept = −3;
x-intercept = 2.2

(b)

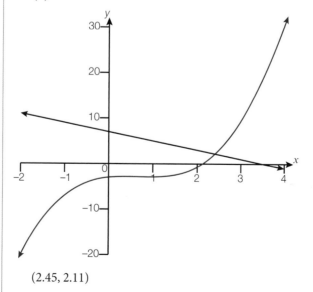

(2.45, 2.11)

Chapter 3

Exercise 3.1

1. (c), (d) and (f)

2. (a) 3; 14, 17, 20
   (b) −3; −7, −10, −13
   (c) −33; 251, 218, 185
   (d) 21; 252, 273, 294
   (e) 4.2; 41.3, 45.5, 49.7
   (f) $\frac{3}{4}; \frac{11}{4}, \frac{7}{2}, \frac{17}{4}$

   (g) $\frac{2}{3}; \frac{18}{7}, \frac{68}{21}, \frac{82}{21}$

   (h) $-x - 9; -x - 20, -2x - 29,$
   $-3x - 38$

Exercise 3.2

1. (a) 115, 163   (b) 435, 855
   (c) 58, −124   (d) 142, 340
   (e) 105, 337   (f) 970.8, 768
   (g) −372, −820 (h) 428.4, 723.6
   (i) $\frac{134}{35}, \frac{197}{35}$

2. (a) 20, 32   (b) 149, 226
   (c) 67, 191   (d) −88, −116
   (e) −88, −250 (f) −267, −998
   (g) 3.51, 6.4 (h) $\frac{37}{18}, \frac{50}{9}$

   (i) $17x + 62, 24x + 97$

Exercise 3.3

1. (a) 3   (b) 8
   (c) 11   (d) −2.3
   (e) −13.65 (f) 8
   (g) 26   (h) −2.1
   (i) −1.9   (j) 0.563

2. (a) 36   (b) 27
   (c) 46   (d) 39
   (e) 55   (f) 100
   (g) 46   (h) 75
   (i) 46   (j) 58

3. (a) 12   (b) 19
   (c) 400 (d) 198
   (e) 56   (f) 188
   (g) 1990 (h) 88
   (i) 205 (j) 60

4. (a) $u_1 + 4d = 9, u_1 + 10d = 45$
   (b) $u_1 = -15, d = 6$
   (c) 279

5. (a) $u_1 = 64, d = 18$
   (b) 406

6. (a) $u_1 = 172, d = -17$
   (b) −440

7. (a) $d = -6, u_1 = -34.93$
   (b) −268.93
   (c) No

Exercise 3.4

1. (a) 47
   (b) 13 months

2. (a) 100
   (b) In the 20th week

3. (a) 97 minutes
   (b) After the 19th week
   (c) 161 minutes

4. (a) 132 tonnes
   (b) In the 16th year

5. (a) 800 rupees
   (b) In the 36th month

Exercise 3.5

1. (a) 710   (b) 6576
   (c) −696   (d) −2300
   (e) 3259.2 (f) −3438

2. (a) 32   (b) 24
   (c) 28   (d) 24
   (e) 80   (f) 310

Exercise 3.6

1. (a) 500   (b) 3042
   (c) 5565 (d) −3010
   (e) 50   (f) 500
   (g) −1305 (h) −3565.65

2. (a) 558   (b) 2270
   (c) 6006 (d) −14840
   (e) −1260 (f) 1372.5
   (g) −341.25 (h) 794.592

Exercise 3.7

1. (a) 2376   (b) 2168
   (c) −11940 (d) 2207.52
   (e) $\frac{129}{4} = 32.25$

2. (a) 20, 2750   (b) 32, 17136
   (c) 19, 363.85 (d) 30, −4605
   (e) 31, 1666.25

3. (a) 3240   (b) 14630
   (c) 14850 (d) 4215
   (e) 16830

4. (a) 97   (b) 17
   (c) 17140

5. (a) 1700
   (b)
   $S_n = \frac{n}{2}(2u_1 + (n-1)d);$
   i.e. $5800 = \frac{n}{2}(2 \times 28 + 6(n-1))$
   $= 28n + 3n(n-1)$
   $= 25n + 3n^2$
   (c) 40

Exercise 3.8

1. (a) €1000   (b) €5950
   (c) €12,650

2. (a) $u_{10} = u_1 + (n-1)d$
   $= 3 + (10-1) \times 2$
   (b) 440
   (c) 9th week

3. (a) $103   (b) $10,816

4. (a) 40,500 nairas
   (b) 169,500 nairas

Exercise 3.9

1. (b), (d), (e), (g) and (h)

2. (a) 32, 64, 128
   (b) 43.2, 25.92, 15.552
   (c) 27, 9, 3
   (d) 52.704, 63.2448, 75.89376

3. (a) 270, 151.875
   (b) 3.125, 6.25
   (c) −18, −54
   (d) $\frac{1}{25}, \frac{1}{125}, \frac{1}{625}$

Exercise 3.10

1. (a) $15/10 = 22.5/15 = 1.5$

   (b) $u_1 = 10$, $r = 1.5$
   (c) 384.4

2. (a) $r = 2$, $u_1 = 0.75$, $u_{10} = 384$
   (b) $r = 3$, $u_1 = \frac{1}{3}$, $u_{10} = 6561$

3. (a) $u_1 = 2.5$ and $r = 2$, or
      $u_1 = -2.5$ and $r = -2$
   (b) 5120

4. (a) 4, 786 432
   (b) 1.5, 1.42×10^5 (3 s.f.)
   (c) 3.2, 3.48×10^{10} (3 s.f.)
   (d) 1.5, 438 (3 s.f.)
   (e) −1.1, −514 (3 s.f.)
   (f) 2.2, -3.17×10^8 (3 s.f.)

5. (a) 1.5; 4.5, 6.75, 10.125
   (b) −2; −4, 8, −16
   (c) 0.5; 25, 12.5, 6.25
   (d) 1.1; 1.21, 1.331, 1.4641

Exercise 3.11

1. (a) 9   (b) 4
   (c) 6   (d) 8
   (e) 6   (f) 7

2. (a) 5   (b) 7
   (c) 11   (d) 11
   (e) 13   (f) 11

3. 5

4. (a) 12   (b) 8
   (c) 7   (d) 8
   (e) 8   (f) 6

Exercise 3.12

1. (a) 2046
   (b) 29 296.8
   (c) 4.83×10^8 (3 s.f.)
   (d) 54 613.125
   (e) 39.6 (3 s.f.)
   (f) 1.32×10^7 (3 s.f.)

2. (a) 625
   (b) 1600
   (c) 2.28 (3 s.f.)
   (d) 56.0 (3 s.f.)
   (e) 47.4 (3 s.f.)
   (f) 808 (3 s.f.)

3. (a) 4092
   (b) 47300 (3 s.f.)
   (c) −712 (3 s.f.)
   (d) 1.96×10^{10} (3 s.f.)
   (e) 5620 (3 s.f.)

4. (a) 2; 10 485 750
   (b) 3; 4.24×10^{11} (3 s.f.)
   (c) 0.5; 256 (3 s.f.)
   (d) 1.2; 350 (3 s.f.)
   (e) 0.2; 7.81 (3 s.f.)
   (f) 2; 8 388 600
   (g) 343; 7.05×10^{60} (3 s.f.)

5. (a) 0.4
   (b) 1500 (3 s.f.)

6. (a) $u_1 = 1000$, $r = 0.5$
   (b) 2000 (3 s.f.)

7. 63.996

8. (a) $u_1 = 5$, $r = 3$
   (b) 107 616 800
   (c) 108 000 000 (3 s.f.)
   (d) 1.08×10^8 (3 s.f.)

Exercise 3.13

1. 9430 (3 s.f.)

2. 124,000 AUD

3. (a) 9353.60, 9540.88, 9731.91,
      9926.77, 10125.53,
      10328.26, 10535.06,
      10745.99
   (b) £98,448.00

4. (a) £817.59   (b) £4457.36

Mixed examination practice 3

Exam-style questions 3

1. (a) 17   (b) 347   (c) 3710

2. (a) $u_1 + 4d = 42$, $u_1 + 8d = 64$
   (b) $u_1 = 20$, $d = 5.5$

3. (a) 51   (b) 1272
   (c) 576   (d) 15

4. (a) 0.8   (b) 1960 (3 s.f.)

5. 0.754 m (3 s.f.)

6. (b) €145.86, €186.16
   (c) €1509.35

7. (b) 7.32 h (3 s.f.)
   (c) 107 h (3 s.f.)

8. Option 2

9. (i) (a) $305
        (b) $13,050
   (ii) (a) $16,560
        (b) 51st month

10. (a) 326 000 bricks (3 s.f.)
    (b) 2 600 000 bricks (3 s.f.)

Past paper questions 3

1. (b) 11, 18, 25   (c) 7
   (d) 144   (e) 900

2. (a) 10
   (b) $\frac{1}{3}$

   (c) 1.50 (3 s.f.)

   (d) Both $\left(\frac{1}{3}\right)^{10}$ and $\left(\frac{1}{3}\right)^{1000}$

      (or those numbers divided
      by $\frac{2}{3}$) are 0 when corrected
      to 3 s.f.

   (e) 29 525.5

3. (a) 1140
   (b) $6r^5 = 16 \times 12$
   (c) 2

4. (a) (i) $2050   (ii) $5120
   (b) $11,500
   (c) Total value after 10 weeks:
      option one $10,000; option
      two $11,500; option three
      $10,230. Therefore, option
      two would be best.

Chapter 4

Exercise 4.1

1. (a) 1175.88 CAD
   (b) 967.74 GBP
   (c) 805.30 AUD
   (d) 902.00 EUR
   (e) 3201.07 USD

2. (a) 1446 CAD
   (b) $561
   (c) ¥46 556

3. (a) €728.79
   (b) 152.15 CHF

Exercise 4.2

1. (a) 37,490.88 THB
   (b) 3.55 SGD

2. (a) £147 (b) €171.99
   (c) £8.21

3. (a) €653.36 (b) $861.24
   (c) $38.76

4. (a) £1005.43 (b) £1004.83
   (c) Bank A

5. (a) 2842.51 HKD (b) £63.02

Exercise 4.3

1. (a) €53,529.02
   (b) €53,874.20
   (c) €53,954.01

2. (a) 520,302.00 AUD
   (b) 520,370.77 AUD
   (c) 520,397.39 AUD

3. 5.64% (3 s.f.)

4. 15.7% (3 s.f.)

5. (a) 16.8 years (b) 26.7

6. (a) £76,379.84
   (b) No; investment is worth
   £91,154.38 after 10 years.

Exercise 4.4

1. (a) £64 (b) £46,620

2. (a) £832 (b) £49,920
   (c) £592
   (d) Arthur; Ken repaid a total
   of £53,280, which is greater
   than Arthur's total by
   £3360.

3. (a) £2500 (b) £22,500
   (c) £549 (d) £3852

4. (a) €86.32 (b) €5179.20
   (c) €799.20
   (d) Yes; they would have saved
   about €296.

5. (a) Monthly payments:
   £387.72; customer deposit
   £17,108
   (b) Total amount of credit:
   £19,404; total amount
   payable: £36,428

6. (a) $160.32 (b) $9619.20
   (c) $1619.20

7. (a) $56,346.36
   (b) $16,843.36
   (c) No; option 3 would make
   them worse off by $1165.44

Exercise 4.5

1. £433,842.38

2. €54112.55

3. ¥4.30 million (3 s.f.)

4.

Commodity	Overall rate of inflation, %	Annual % rate of inflation
Rump steak, British	10.3	0.702
Cod fillets	50.5	2.96
Sugar, granulated	19.4	1.27
Cheese, Cheddar	71.8	3.94
Apples, eating	21.4	1.39
Carrots	−3.39	−0.246

5. 20 years 6. 10

Exercise 4.6

1. (a) £250.76 (b) £286.19

2. (a) $15,383.74
   (b) $34,611.26
   (c) Yes; he would be better off
   by $399.01.

Mixed examination practice 4

Exam-style questions 4

1. (a) 23,763.52 RUB
   (b) 235.66 CAD

2. (a) $10,463.23
   (b) $3800.39

3. (a) £12,957.15
   (b) 44.9% (3 s.f.)

4. (a) 207,184.07 ZAR
   (b) 14.8 years (3 s.f.)
   (c) 23.4 (3 s.f.)

5. (a) 25 months (b) $184.73

8. (a) ¥1234.82 (b) ¥44,453.52
   (c) ¥1453.52

3. 2.84 (3 s.f.)

4. 10.4 years (3 s.f.)

5. (a) $179,200
   (b) 32.0 (3 s.f.)
   (c) 3.06 years (3 s.f.)

6. (a) 7.26
   (b) (i) $34,768.38
   (ii) $30,221.00

7. (a) Monthly payment £700;
   (b) total interest £2151.76;
   (c) total amount payable
   £25,151.76

8. (a) £19,071.50
   (b) 11.2%
   (c) £4062.10
   (d) 11.7%
   (e) Yes; if the annual rate of
   depreciation stayed at 14%
   (value based on salesman's
   claim), the car would be
   worth less than £20,000
   after 3 years.

Past paper questions 4

1. (a) A: $1200; B: $1239.51;
   C: $1230; D: $1273.37
   (b) D; the total allowance is the
   highest (or grows the fastest).
   (c) 10%

2. (a) $29,263.23
   (b) (i) In the 4th year
         (3.46 years)
      (ii) $298.20

3. (a) (i) $2700, $2900
      (ii) $6300
   (b) (i) $2160
   (c) 6%   (d) $3523.93

4. (a) €612.80   (b) $780.64
   (c) $19.36, 2.42%

5. (a) €16,857.45   (b) 30.6

Chapter 5

Exercise 5.1

1. (a) Continuous
   (b) Discrete
   (c) Continuous
   (d) Discrete
   (e) Discrete
   (f) Continuous
   (g) Continuous
   (h) Discrete
   (i) Discrete
   (j) Continuous

Exercise 5.2

1.

Mark	Frequency
5	4
6	4
7	6
8	4
9	4
10	3

2.

Number of rejects	Frequency
0	10
1	6
2	7
3	7
4	4
5	2

3.

Home runs	Frequency
23	1
24	2
25	1
26	2
27	4
28	4
29	0
30	0
31	2
32	0
33	0
34	1

Exercise 5.3

1.

Number of students	Frequency
0–4	4
5–9	6
10–14	16
15–19	7
20–24	7

2.

Number of CDs	Frequency
45–49	2
50–54	7
55–59	4
60–64	2
65–69	11
70–74	4

3.

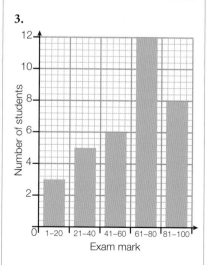

4.

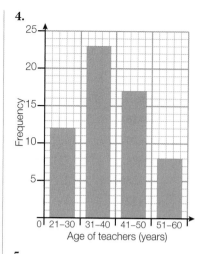

5.

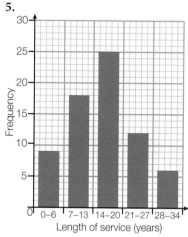

6.

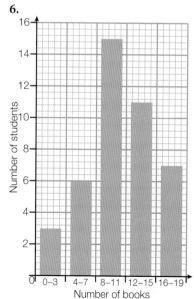

Exercise 5.4

Answers may vary, depending on how the classes are defined in each case.

1.

Time (s)	Frequency
12–16	5
16–20	13
20–24	9
24–28	2
28–32	1

2.

Distance (m)	Frequency
5–7	8
7–9	8
9–11	7
11–13	5
13–15	2

3.

Distance (m)	Frequency
1.5–2.5	2
2.5–3.5	2
3.5–4.5	12
4.5–5.5	8
5.5–6.5	6

4.

Time (s)	Frequency
60–64	1
64–68	6
68–72	6
72–76	12
76–80	3
80–84	2

5.

Distance (m)	Frequency
25–30	5
30–35	9
35–40	9
40–45	5
45–50	2

Exercise 5.5

1.

Time (s)	Class boundaries	Frequency	Class width	Mid-interval value
$18 \leq t < 20$	18–20	3	2	$(18 + 20) \div 2 = 19$
$20 \leq t < 22$	20–22	4	2	21
$22 \leq t < 24$	22–24	6	2	23
$24 \leq t < 26$	24–26	10	2	25
$26 \leq t < 28$	26–28	3	2	27
$28 \leq t < 30$	28–30	2	2	29

2. (Exercise 5.3 question 3)
Class boundaries: 1–20, 21–40, 41–60, 61–80, 81–100
Class widths: all 19
Mid-interval values: 10.5, 30.5, 50.5, 70.5, 90.5

(Exercise 5.3 question 4)
Class boundaries: 21–30, 31–40, 41–50, 51–60
Class widths: all 9
Mid-interval values: 25.5, 35.5, 45.5, 55.5

(Exercise 5.3 question 5)
Class boundaries: 0–6, 7–13, 14–20, 21–27, 28–35
Class widths: all 6
Mid-interval values: 3, 10, 17, 24, 31

(Exercise 5.3 question 6)
Class boundaries: 0–3, 4–7, 8–11, 12–15, 16–19
Class widths: all 3
Mid-interval values: 1.5, 5.5, 9.5, 13.5, 17.5

3. Answers may vary depending on how the classes were defined in Exercise 5.4.

(Exercise 5.4 question 1)
Class boundaries: 12–16, 16–20, 20–24, 24–28, 28–32
Class widths: 4
Mid-interval values: 14, 18, 22, 26, 30

(Exercise 5.4 question 2)
Class boundaries, 5–7, 7–9, 9–11, 11–13, 13–15
Class widths: 2
Mid-interval values: 6, 8, 10, 12, 14

(Exercise 5.4 question 3)
Class boundaries: 1.5–2.5, 2.5–3.5, 3.5–4.5, 4.5–5.5, 5.5–6.5
Class widths: 1
Mid-interval values: 2, 3, 4, 5, 6

(Exercise 5.4 question 4)
Class boundaries: 60–64, 64–68, 68–72, 72–76, 76–80, 80–84
Class widths: 4
Mid-interval values: 62, 66, 70, 74, 78, 82

(Exercise 5.4 question 5)
Class boundaries: 25–30, 30–35, 35–40, 40–45, 45–50
Class widths: 5
Mid-interval values: 27.5, 32.5, 37.5, 42.5, 47.5

Exercise 5.6

1. Frequencies: 7, 6, 2, 3, 8, 4

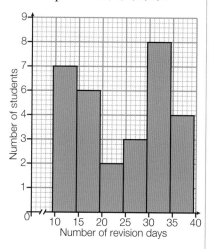

2. Frequencies: 4, 10, 4, 9, 8, 5

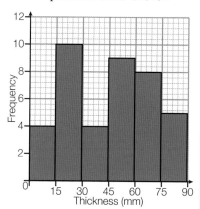

3. Frequencies: 2, 6, 10, 12, 11, 4

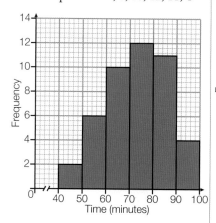

4. Class boundaries: 150.5–190.5, 190.5–230.5, 230.5–270.5, 270.5–310.5, 310.5–350.5
   Class widths: 40
   Mid-interval values: 170.5, 210.5, 250.5, 290.5, 330.5
   Frequencies: 2, 12, 17, 6, 3

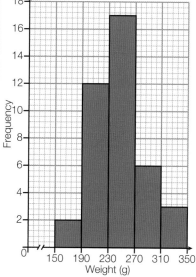

5. Class boundaries: 19.5–39.5, 39.5–59.5, 59.5–79.5, 79.5–99.5, 99.5–119.5
   Class widths: 20
   Mid-interval values: 29.5, 49.5, 69.5, 89.5, 109.5
   Frequencies: 5, 12, 20, 9, 4

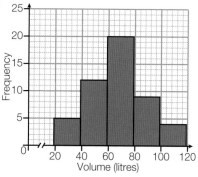

6. Answers may vary depending on how the classes were defined.
   Class boundaries: 7.05–7.45, 7.45–7.85, 7.85–8.25, 8.25–8.65, 8.65–9.05
   Frequencies: 1, 5, 10, 8, 3

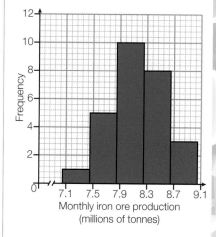

7. Class boundaries: 55.0–55.5, 55.5–56.0, 56.0–56.5, 56.5–57.0, 57.0–57.5, 57.5–58.0, 58.0–58.5, 58.5–59.0, 59.0–59.5
   Class widths: 0.5
   Mid-interval values: 55.25, 55.75, 56.25, 56.75, 57.25, 57.75, 58.25, 58.75, 59.25
   Frequencies: 2, 2, 3, 5, 4, 6, 6, 0, 2

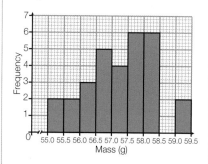

Exercise 5.7

1. 5, 12, 17, 25, 33, 42, 45

2. 1, 3, 8, 18, 30, 34, 37

3. 2, 8, 17, 32, 42, 49, 52

Exercise 5.8

1. (a) 20, 50, 62, 76, 78, 78, 79, 81

(b)

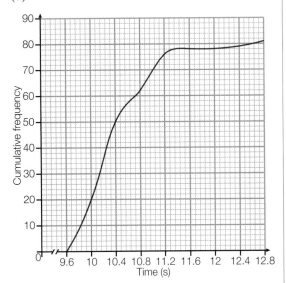

(c) 10.25 s

2. (a) 3, 4, 9, 13, 20, 31, 46, 47

(b)

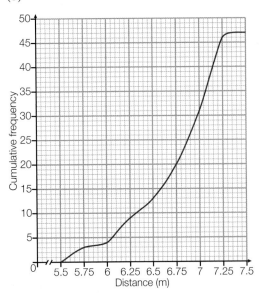

(c) 6.8 m

(d) 6.4 m, 7.1 m

3. (a) 20.2 cm   (b) 43   (c) 11.7%

Exercise 5.9

1. (a)

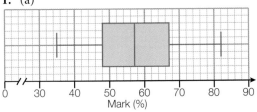

(b)

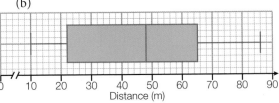

(c)

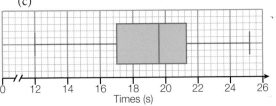

(d)

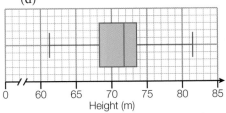

2. (Answers may vary, depending on estimates of the median and quartiles)

(a)

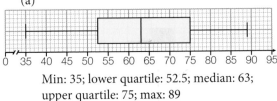

Min: 35; lower quartile: 52.5; median: 63; upper quartile: 75; max: 89

(b)

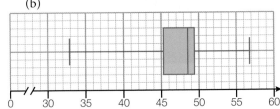

Min: 32.9; lower quartile: 45.3; median: 48.5; upper quartile: 49.4; max: 56.8

(c)

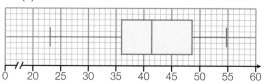

Min: 23.05; lower quartile: 36; median: 41.34; upper quartile: 48.66; max: 54.73

(d)

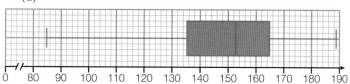

Min: 84.6; lower quartile: 135.6; median: 152.3; upper quartile: 165.3; max: 188.4

Exercise 5.10

1. (a) Min 45, max 93
    (b) 74
    (c) 58
    (d) 87

2. (a) 171 cm
    (b) Max 199 cm, min 154 cm
    (c) $Q_1 = 160$ cm, $Q_3 = 180$ cm

3. (a) Frequencies: 6, 5, 5, 4, 7, 5, 4, 6, 4, 4; total: 50
    (b)

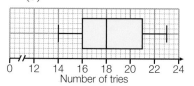

    (c) $Q_1 = 16$, median = 18, $Q_3 = 21$

Mixed examination practice 5

Exam-style questions 5

1.

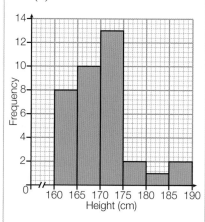

2. (a) Frequencies: 8, 10, 13, 2, 1, 2
    (b)

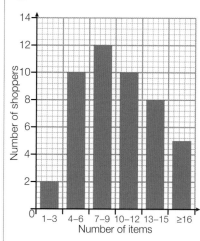

3. (a) Frequencies: 3, 7, 8, 7, 5
    (b) Cumulative frequencies: 3, 10, 18, 25, 30

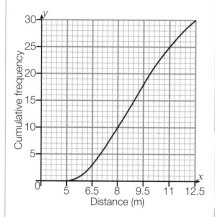

    (c)

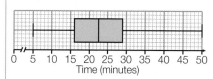

4. (a) 22.5 minutes
    (b) $Q_1 = 16$ minutes, $Q_3 = 29$ minutes
    (c) 7
    (d)

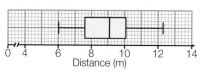

5. (a) (i)   100
        (ii) 75%
        (iii) $Q_1 = 68\%$, $Q_3 = 81\%$
    (b) 41
    (c)

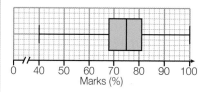

    (d) 18

6. (a) 5
(b) $Q_1 = 3$, $Q_3 = 5.5$
(c) 4
(d)

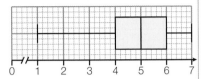

(e) Median of A2 is higher than that of A1, indicating overall better marks. Marks of A2 are slightly more consistent than those of A1, as the difference $Q_3 - Q_1$ is smaller.

7. (a)

	Year 12G	Year 12H
Median	78	73
Lower quartile	60	65
Upper quartile	85	80

(b) 12G had higher marks than 12H overall, but the test marks of 12H were more consistent, as shown by a smaller $Q_3 - Q_1$ difference.

Past paper questions 5

1. (a) 26 cm   (b) 14 cm
(c)

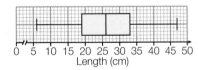

2. (a) (ii) and (iv)
(b) (i) 10   (ii) 12
(iii) 0.8

3. (a) 170 cm
(b) 163 cm
(c) 172 cm
(d)

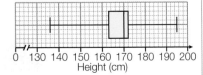

Chapter 6

Answers for comparison or discussion questions are omitted as responses may vary.

Exercise 6.1

1. 3
2. 6
3. £47

Exercise 6.2

1. £170.52
2. $79,640
3. 96.9 KB (3 s.f.)
4. (a) 4.14 years (3 s.f.)
(b) 118 lbs (3 s.f.)
5. (a) 307   (b) 12.8 (3 s.f.)
(c) 11.0 (3 s.f.)
6. (a)

	Type of car		
Average	**4-Door Sedan**	**2-Door Coupe**	**Hatchback**
Mean price($)	$12,334.08	$16,072.40	$12,270
Median price ($)	$12,295	$16,300	$12,360

(b) Mean price, because it makes use of all the data for each type of car
(c) Different sample sizes; use same/similar samples sizes

7. (a) 35   (b) 6.94 (3 s.f.)
(c) 7

8. (a) 51.5 million green tonnes
(b) 1287.5 thousand green tonnes
9. $1.22
10. 10.41 seconds

Exercise 6.3

1. (a) (i) 4   (ii) 3
(iii) 2
(b) (i) 64   (ii) 64
(iii) 57 and 70
(c) (i) 30.7 (3 s.f.)
(ii) 29
(iii) 29
(d) (i) 117.9 (ii) 110
(iii) 107 and 110
(e) (i) 42.1 (3 s.f.)
(ii) 42   (iii) 42 and 44

2. (a) 32   (b) 30.5
(c) 27
3. (a) 35   (b) 19
(c) 19
4. (a) (i) 5   (ii) 12.5
(iii) 10
(b) (i) 10.6 (ii) 19.6
(iii) 18 and 21.2
(c) (i) 5   (ii) 10.5
(iii) 7
5. (a) 25   (b) 47
(c) 1.88   (d) 0
(e) 1

6. (a)

	Round 1	Round 2	Rounds 1 and 2 combined
Mean	71.2	71.2	71.2
Mode	71 and 73	69	69 and 71
Median	71	71	71

7. (a) (i) 50.6 minutes (3 s.f.)
  (ii) 41–47 minutes
 (b) (i) 184 thousand
  (ii) 0–150 thousand

Mixed examination practice 6

Exam-style questions 6

1. (a) 308
 (b) 54
 (c) 30

2. (a) Group 1: 27; Group 2: 25
 (b) Group 1: 4.81 (3 s.f.);
  Group 2: 4
 (d) 4.42 (3 s.f.)

3. 6.70 m (3 s.f.)

4. (a) 720 million
 (b) 15 million
 (c) 17.5 million (3 s.f.)

5. (a) $x = 39$, $y = 48$
 (b) $x = 13$, $y = 18$
 (c) $x = 45$, $y = 46$

6. (a) 61   (b) 158
 (c) 2.59 (3 s.f.)   (d) 2
 (e) 2

7. (a) 3.9   (b) 3   (c) 3

Past paper questions 6

1. (a) $166 (to the nearest dollar)
 (b) $165
 (c) (i) $2430

2. (a) 10   (b) 4   (c) 6

3. (a) 51
 (b) (i) 60–70 cm
  (ii) 60–70 cm
  (iii) 69.5 cm (3 s.f.)

Chapter 7

Exercise 7.1

1. (a) (i) 6.8   (ii) 0.46
  (iii) 0.34
 (b) (i) 227   (ii) 27
  (iii) 12
 (c) (i) 72   (ii) 46
  (iii) 12
 (d) (i) 18.9   (ii) 19.2
  (iii) 7.8
 (e) (i) 330   (ii) 412
  (iii) 237
 (f) (i) 97.1   (ii) 3.5
  (iii) 1.4

2. (a) (i) 1   (ii) 5
  (iii) 2
 (b) (i) 165 cm
  (ii) 27 cm
  (iii) 18 cm
 (c) (i) 63   (ii) 6
  (iii) 2
 (d) (i) 3   (ii) 6
  (iii) 2
 (e) (i) 29 kg (ii) 7 kg
  (iii) 3 kg
 (f) (i) $1849
  (ii) $4450
  (iii) $900

3. (a) (i) 47.5 years
  (ii) 39.5 years, 51.5 years
  (iii) 12 years
 (b) (i) 438 cm
  (ii) 432 cm, 445 cm
  (iii) 13 cm
 (c) (i) 95   (ii) 86, 102
  (iii) 16

Exercise 7.2

1. (a) $\bar{x} = 2.82$ hours (3 s.f.),
  $\sigma_x = 2.08$ hours (3 s.f.)
 (b) $\bar{x} = 0.239$ inches (3 s.f.),
  $\sigma_x = 0.222$ inches (3 s.f.)
 (c) $\bar{x} = 11.5°C$, $\sigma_x = 0.782°C$
 (d) $\bar{x} = 19.2°C$, $\sigma_x = 2.55°C$

2. (a) 18°C
 (b) 1.69°C

3. (a) £2649.20
 (b) £711.91

4. (a) $\bar{x} = 47\,100$ (3 s.f.),
  $\sigma_x = 19\,300$ (3 s.f.)
 (b) $\bar{x} = 39\,600$,
  $\sigma_x = 21\,300$ (3 s.f.)

5. $\bar{x} = 39$, $\sigma_x = 9.66$ (3 s.f.)

Exercise 7.3

1. (a) (i) 2010: 649 (3 s.f.);
   2011: 662 (3 s.f.)
  (ii) 2010: 55.7 (3 s.f.);
   2011: 45.1 (3 s.f.)
 (b) On average more goals
  were scored per team in
  2011, and the number
  of goals scored was less
  varied than in 2010.

2. (a) (i) MS-A: 50; MS-B: 53
  (ii) MS-A: quartiles 33
   and 93, IQR= 60;
   MS-B: quartiles 50
   and 70, IQR = 20
 (b) MS-B performed better,
  with both higher marks
  on average and more
  consistency.

3. (a), (b)

Lab A:

Time (minutes)	Frequency	Cumulative frequency
40–42	5	5
43–45	7	12
46–48	5	17
49–51	10	27
52–54	5	32
55–57	1	33
58–60	3	36

Lab B:

Time (minutes)	Frequency	Cumulative frequency
37–39	6	6
40–42	5	11
43–45	4	15
46–48	1	16
49–51	6	22
52–54	4	26
55–57	7	33
58–60	2	35
61–63	1	36

(c)

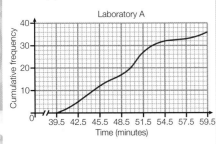

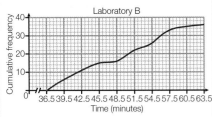

(d) Lab A: median 49.7, IQR 8; Lab B: median 49.8, IQR 14

(e) Although the two labs have approximately the same median waiting times, there is a much larger spread in waiting times at Lab B.

4. (a) 183 million
   (b) 193 million
   (c) 433 million (3 s.f.)

5. (a), (b), (c)

	M	F	M&F
$\bar{x}$	30.7	32.1	31.4
σ	20.4	21.2	20.8

(d) On average, females are older than males. The ages of males are slightly less varied than those of females.

Mixed examination practice 7

Exam-style questions 7

1. (a) $x + y = 15$
   (b) $x = 7, y = 8$
   (c) 8
   (d) 5.5 and 9
   (e) 3.5

2. (a) 25,000–30,000
   (b) 25,000–30,000
   (c) $25,500
   (d)

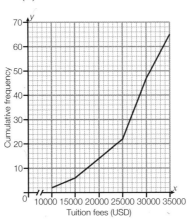

(e) (i) $27,000   (ii) $9000
   (f)

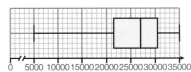

3. $x = 22, y = 2$

4. (a) 50
   (b) $c = 4, d = 8, e = 41, f = 3$

5. (a) 20.8 million barrels
   (b) 2.08 million barrels per year

6. (a) 31
   (b) 33.6

7. (a) (i) 17 million
      (ii) 46   (iii) 16%
   (b)

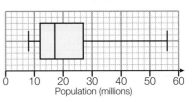

8. (a) $25 \le t < 30$
   (b) $25 \le t < 30$
   (c) $\bar{x} = 25.3$ minutes (3 s.f.), $\sigma_x = 6.11$ minutes (3 s.f.)
   (d)

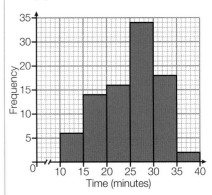

(e) The mean lies near the lower boundary of the modal class, which is also the class in which the median lies. This reflects the fact that the data leans towards the lower values, as can also be seen from the histogram.

9. (a)

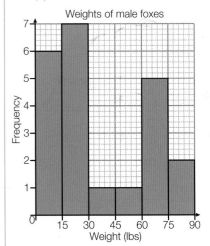

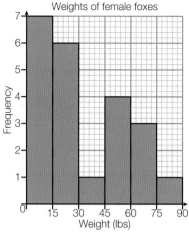

Weights of female foxes

(x-axis: Weight (lbs), y-axis: Frequency)

(b) Males: $15 \leq w < 30$; females: $0 \leq w < 15$

(c) Males: $\bar{x} = 36.1$ lbs (3 s.f.), $\sigma_x = 26.7$ lbs (3 s.f.); females: $\bar{x} = 32.7$ lbs (3 s.f.), $\sigma_x = 24.1$ lbs (3 s.f.)

(d) The male and female median weights are similar, but the weights of the males are more varied than those of the females, with greater IQR.

10. (a) 60
   (b) (i)   130–150 km
       (ii) 130–150 km
   (c) (i)   146 km (3 s.f.)
       (ii) 30.4 km (3 s.f.)
   (d) All three averages lie within the same interval, and the standard deviation is only about 1.5 times the interval width, indicating a consistency among the data values.

11. (a) (i) 152 cm (ii) 38 cm
   (b)

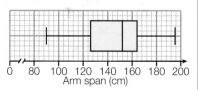

(x-axis: Arm span (cm))

   (c) $u = 10$, $v = 14$, $w = 19$
   (d) 146 cm (3 s.f.)

Chapter 8

Exercise 8.1

1. (a) $x \in A$ (b) $x \notin A$
   (c) $B \subset C$ (d) $C \cup D$
   (e) $A \cap B$

2. (a) $A = \{x, y, z\}$
   (b) $n(A \cap B) = 3$
   (c) $B = \{a, e, i, o, u\}$
   (d) $n(A) = 5$

Exercise 8.2

1. (a) $n(P) = 8$
   (b) $n(Q) = 6$
   (c) $n(R) = 10$

2. $A \cup B = \{5, 6, 7, \dots, 15\}$; $A \cap B = \{9, 10, 11\}$

3. (a)

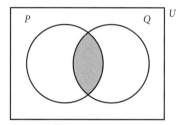

   (b)

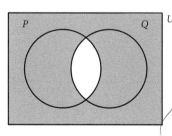

   (c)

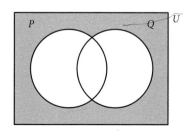

Exercise 8.3

4. (a) $A = \{1, 4, 9, 16, 25, 36, 49, 64\}$
   (b) $B = \{1, 8, 27, 64\}$
   (c) $A \cup B = \{1, 4, 8, 9, 16, 25, 27, 36, 49, 64\}$
   (d) $A \cap B' = \{4, 9, 16, 25, 36, 49\}$

Exercise 8.3

1. (a) (i)   42   (ii) 48
   (b) 9
   (c)

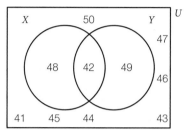

2. (a) $A = \{5, 7, 11, 13, 17, 19, 23, 29, 31, 37, 41, 43, 47, 53\}$
   (b) (i) $B \cup C = \{5, 11, 22, 33, 44, 55\}$
       (ii) $A \cap B \cup C = \{11\}$

3. (a) 8   (b) $\{12, 36\}$
   (c) $\{18\}$

4. (a) Track but not Field

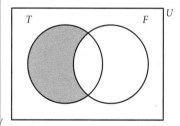

   (b) Track or Field but not both

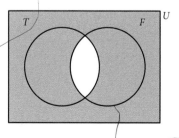

5. (a) (i)   6   (ii) 2
   (b) (i) $\{11, 12\}$
       (ii) $\{1, 8, 10\}$

Exercise 8.4

1. (a) $P \cap Q \cap R$
   (b) $P \cap R$
   (c) $(P \cup R)' \cap Q$
   (d) $R \cap (P \cup Q)$

2. (a) {g}
   (b) {a, e, f, h, j, k}
   (c) {f, h, j}
   (d) {c, f, g}

3. (a) and (b)

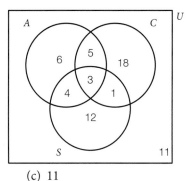

   (c) 11

4. (a)

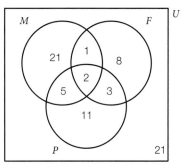

   (b) 21

Mixed examination practice 8

Exam-style questions 8

1. (a) Neither History nor Geography
   (b) 48
   (c)

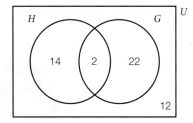

2. (a) 9
   (b) Neither F nor S. Since
   $n(F \cup S) = 40$,
   $n(F \cup S)' = 0$
   (c)

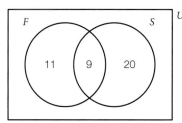

3. (a) (i) IB but not A Level
       (ii) $B \cap A'$
   (b) $x = 25$
   (c) (i) 82   (ii) 12

4. (a) Given $n(F \cap R) = 20$.
   Given that x read all 3. So,
   the region, $(F \cap R \cap N') =$
   $20 - x$
   (b) $31 - x$
   (c)

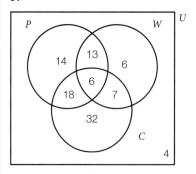

   (d) $x = 16$

5.

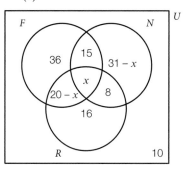

6. (a) $x = 7$
   (b) (i) 19   (ii) 144
       (iii) 23   (iv) 98

7. (a) (i) 4   (ii) 40
   (b) 42   (c) 70

8. (a)

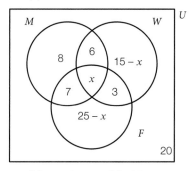

   (b) $x = 4$ (c) 80
   (d)

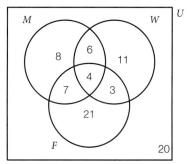

9.

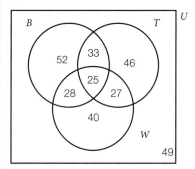

10.

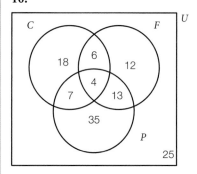

Past paper questions 8

1. (a) $20 - x$ (b) $x = 15$
   (c) 55

2. (a)

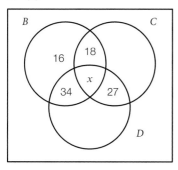

(b) $x = 31$ (c) 156

Chapter 9

Exercise 9.1

1. (a) Proposition, true
   (b) Not a proposition
   (c) Proposition, false
   (d) Proposition, true
   (e) Proposition, true
   (f) Not a proposition
   (g) Proposition, true
   (h) Not a proposition
   (i) Proposition, true
   (j) Not a proposition

Exercise 9.2

1. (a) $\neg p$ (b) $r \veebar p$
   (c) $q \wedge r$ (d) $\neg r \wedge q$

2. (a) x is not a prime number.
   (b) x is a prime number less than 100.
   (c) Either x is not a prime number or it is a 2-digit number.
   (d) Either x is not a prime number or it is not a 2-digit number.
   (e) x is not a prime number less than 100.

3. (a) Jenny hates football and she does not watch Sky Sports.
   (b) Jenny does not hate football and she watches Sky Sports.
   (c) Either Jenny watches Sky Sports or she watches the Comedy Channel, but not both.

4. (a) $q \wedge p$ (b) $\neg q \wedge \neg r$
   (c) $\neg p \vee \neg q$ (d) $\neg p \wedge \neg r$

Exercise 9.3

1. (a) Either Veejay attends football training or he passes his test, but not both.
   (b) Veejay revises for his test and he does not attend football training.
   (c) Veejay is not revising for his test and he attends football training.
   (d) If Veejay revises for his test then he does not attend football training.
   (e) If Veejay revises for his test then he passes his test.
   (f) If Veejay does not revise for his test then he does not pass his test.

2. (a) $p \Rightarrow r$ (b) $q \Rightarrow \neg r$
   (c) $\neg q \Rightarrow p$

3. (a) $p \Rightarrow q$ (b) $\neg q \Rightarrow \neg p$
   (c) $p \Leftrightarrow q$

4. (a) If x is a quadrilateral and also a 2-D shape with a pair of parallel sides then x is a parallelogram. False.
   (b) If x is a parallelogram then x is a quadrilateral. True.
   (c) If x is a parallelogram then x is a 2-D shape with a pair of parallel sides. True.
   (d) x is a quadrilateral and also a 2-D shape with a pair of parallel sides if and only if x is a parallelogram. False.

Exercise 9.4

1. (a) (i) $p \wedge q$ (ii) $\neg p \wedge \neg q$
   (b) Either Donald did not pass his driving test or Debbie passed her driving test.
   (c)

p	q	$\neg p$	$\neg p \vee q$
T	T	F	T
T	F	F	F
F	T	T	T
F	F	T	T

2. (a) (i) $\neg p \Rightarrow \neg q$
       (ii) $q \Leftrightarrow p$
   (b)

p	q	$\neg p$	$\neg q$	$\neg p \Rightarrow \neg q$
T	T	F	F	T
T	F	F	T	T
F	T	T	F	F
F	F	T	T	T

Exercise 9.5

1. (a) $m \wedge (e \veebar s)$
   (b) If a student does not choose Science then he/she chooses Economics.
   (c)

e	s	$\neg e$	$\neg e \Rightarrow s$
T	T	F	T
T	F	F	T
F	T	T	T
F	F	T	F

2. (a) If I go to the cinema then it is not the weekend.
   (b)

p	q	$\neg p$	$q \Rightarrow \neg p$
T	T	F	F
T	F	F	T
F	T	T	T
F	F	T	T

3.

p	q	r	$p \veebar q$	$r \Rightarrow (p \veebar q)$
T	T	T	F	F
T	T	F	F	T
T	F	T	T	T
T	F	F	T	T
F	T	T	T	T
F	T	F	T	T
F	F	T	F	F
F	F	F	F	T

4. (a) (i) $p \Rightarrow q$ (ii) $q \wedge \neg r$
(iii) $\neg p \Rightarrow r$

(b) If Boris does not have a football then either he is a rugby player or he has the rugby ball.

(c)

p	q	r	$\neg r$	$p \vee q$	$\neg r \Rightarrow (p \vee q)$
T	T	T	F	T	T
T	T	F	T	T	T
T	F	T	F	T	T
T	F	F	T	T	T
F	T	T	F	T	T
F	T	F	T	T	T
F	F	T	F	F	T
F	F	F	T	F	F

Exercise 9.6

1. (a) (i)

p	q	$\neg q$	$p \wedge \neg q$	$\neg(p \wedge \neg q)$
T	T	F	F	T
T	F	T	T	F
F	T	F	F	T
F	F	T	F	T

(ii) Neither

(b) (i)

p	q	$p \wedge q$	$\neg(p \wedge q)$	$p \vee \neg(p \wedge q)$
T	T	T	F	T
T	F	F	T	T
F	T	F	T	T
F	F	F	T	T

(ii) Tautology

(c) (i)

p	q	$\neg p$	$p \Rightarrow q$	$\neg p \wedge q$	$(p \Rightarrow q) \wedge (\neg p \wedge q)$
T	T	F	T	F	F
T	F	F	F	F	F
F	T	T	T	T	T
F	F	T	T	F	F

(ii) Neither

(d) (i)

p	q	$\neg p$	$p \Rightarrow q$	$\neg(p \Rightarrow q)$	$\neg p \vee q$	$\neg(p \Rightarrow q) \Leftrightarrow \neg p \vee q$
T	T	F	T	F	T	F
T	F	F	F	T	F	F
F	T	T	T	F	T	F
F	F	T	T	F	T	F

(ii) Contradiction

(e) (i)

p	q	$\neg q$	$\neg q \wedge p$	$p \wedge (\neg q \wedge p)$
T	T	F	F	F
T	F	T	T	T
F	T	F	F	F
F	F	T	F	F

(ii) Neither

2. (a) (i) Either the bad weather does not continue or this week's cricket match will be cancelled.

(ii) The bad weather does not continue and this week's cricket match is not cancelled.

(iii) This week's cricket match will not be cancelled if and only if the bad weather does not continue.

(iv) Either the bad weather continues and this week's cricket match is cancelled or the cricket match will be cancelled and the bad weather does not continue (not both).

(b) (i) Logically equivalent

p	q	$p \Rightarrow q$
T	T	T
T	F	F
F	T	T
F	F	T

p	q	$\neg p$	$\neg p \vee q$
T	T	F	T
T	F	F	F
F	T	T	T
F	F	T	T

(iii) Logically equivalent

p	q	$p \Leftrightarrow q$
T	T	T
T	F	F
F	T	F
F	F	T

p	q	$\neg p$	$\neg q$	$p \wedge q$	$\neg q \wedge \neg p$	$(p \wedge q) \vee (\neg q \wedge \neg p)$
T	T	F	F	T	F	T
T	F	F	T	F	F	F
F	T	T	F	F	F	F
F	F	T	T	F	T	T

(ii) Logically equivalent

p	q	r	$(p \wedge q)$	$(p \wedge q) \wedge r$
T	T	T	T	T
T	T	F	T	F
T	F	T	F	F
T	F	F	F	F
F	T	T	F	F
F	T	F	F	F
F	F	T	F	F
F	F	F	F	F

p	q	r	$(q \wedge r)$	$p \wedge (q \wedge r)$
T	T	T	T	T
T	T	F	F	F
T	F	T	F	F
T	F	F	F	F
F	T	T	T	F
F	T	F	F	F
F	F	T	F	F
F	F	F	F	F

(iv) Not logically equivalent

p	q	r	$p \Rightarrow q$	$(p \Rightarrow q) \Rightarrow r$
T	T	T	T	T
T	T	F	T	F
T	F	T	F	T
T	F	F	F	T
F	T	T	T	T
F	T	F	T	F
F	F	T	T	T
F	F	F	T	F

p	q	r	$q \Rightarrow r$	$q \Rightarrow (q \Rightarrow r)$
T	T	T	T	T
T	T	F	F	F
T	F	T	T	T
T	F	F	T	T
F	T	T	T	T
F	T	F	F	T
F	F	T	T	T
F	F	F	T	T

3. (a) (i) If the internet is not working then I do not check my emails.

(ii) If the internet is working then I check my emails.

(b)

p	q	$\neg p$	$\neg q$	$p \Rightarrow \neg q$	$\neg p \Rightarrow q$	$(p \Rightarrow \neg q) \vee (\neg p \Rightarrow q)$
T	T	F	F	F	T	T
T	F	F	T	T	T	T
F	T	T	F	T	T	T
F	F	T	T	T	F	T

(c) Statement is a tautology.

Exercise 9.7

1. (a) $\neg p \Rightarrow \neg r$ means: if the music is not good then I do not dance to it.
   (b) $r \Rightarrow p$ means: if I dance to the music then the music is good.
   (c) $\neg r \Rightarrow \neg q$ means: if I do not dance to the music then I do not feel like dancing.

2. (a) (i) If you do not listen attentively in class, then you do not perform well in tests.
      (ii) If you perform well in tests then you listen attentively in class.
      (iii) If you do not perform well in tests then you do not listen attentively in class.
   (b) (i) If you do not like current affairs, then you do not listen to news regularly.
      (ii) If you listen to news regularly then you like current affairs.
      (iii) If you do not listen to news regularly then you do not like current affairs.
   (c) (i) If you are not taught by Mrs Brown, then you are not brilliant at Logic.
      (ii) If you are brilliant at Logic then you are taught by Mrs Brown.
      (iii) If you are not brilliant at Logic then you are not taught by Mrs Brown.
   (d) (i) If Sandra is not unwell, then she can play in the netball match.
      (ii) If Sandra cannot play in the netball match then she is unwell.

(iii) If Sandra can play in the netball match then she is not unwell.
   (e) (i) If Andrew is not good at languages, then he cannot be a tourist guide.
      (ii) If Andrew can be a tourist guide then he is good at languages.
      (iii) If Andrew cannot be a tourist guide then he is not good at languages.

3. (a) If Grandma visits Aunt Sally then she goes to the dentist.
   (b) $\neg q \Rightarrow p$
   (c) No; it is none of these.

4. (a) (i) If a shape is a parallelogram then it is a rectangle.
      (ii) If a shape is not a rectangle then it is not a parallelogram.
      (iii) If a shape is not a parallelogram then it is not a rectangle.
   (b) Statement (iii) is true.

Mixed examination practice 9

Exam-style questions 9

1. (a) (i) My laptop is not fixed and I will not finish writing up my Portfolio task.
      (ii) If my laptop is fixed then I will finish writing up my portfolio task.
      (iii) I will finish writing up my portfolio task if and only if my laptop is fixed.
   (b) (i) $p \wedge \neg q$
      (ii) $p \wedge \neg r$

2. (a) If New Year is approaching then I will shop for presents.

(b)

p	q	$\neg p$	$\neg q$	$\neg p \Rightarrow \neg q$
T	T	F	F	T
T	F	F	T	T
F	T	T	F	F
F	F	T	T	T

3. (a) If I save enough money then I buy a new car.
   (b) $\neg p \wedge \neg q$
   (c)

p	q	$\neg p$	$\neg q$	$\neg p \Rightarrow q$	$\neg p \wedge \neg q$
T	T	F	F	T	F
T	F	F	T	T	F
F	T	T	F	T	F
F	F	T	T	F	T

4. (a) (i) If Elliot does not pass his driving test then his dad will not buy him a new car.
      (ii) If his dad buys him a new car then Elliot passes his driving test.
      (iii) If his dad does not buy him a new car then Elliot does not pass his driving test.
   (b) (i) If it does not snow heavily tonight then the roads will be busy tomorrow morning.
      (ii) If the roads are not busy tomorrow morning then it will snow heavily tonight.
      (iii) If the roads are busy tomorrow morning then it will not snow heavily tonight.
   (c) (i) If the recession does not continue then unemployment will not remain high.
      (ii) If unemployment remains high then the recession will continue.

(iii) If unemployment does not remain high then the recession will not continue.

5. (a) $p \Rightarrow \neg q$
   (b) $q \Rightarrow \neg p$

6. (a) If x has equal sides and equal angles then x is a regular polygon. False.
   (b) x is a regular polygon if and only if x is a polygon with equal sides and equal angles. True.
   (c) x is a polygon if and only if x has equal sides and equal angles. False.

7. (a) (i) If Marco is not a member of the debating society then he does not enjoy debating.

(ii) If Marco enjoys debating then he is a member of the debating society.

(b) (i)

p	q	$p \Rightarrow q$
T	T	T
T	F	F
F	T	T
F	F	T

(ii)

p	q	$\neg p$	$\neg q$	$\neg p \Rightarrow \neg q$
T	T	F	F	T
T	F	F	T	T
F	T	T	F	F
F	F	T	T	T

(iii)

p	q	$\neg q$	$p \vee \neg q$
T	T	F	T
T	F	T	T
F	T	F	F
F	F	T	T

(iv)

p	q	$\neg p$	$\neg p \wedge q$
T	T	F	F
T	F	F	F
F	T	T	T
F	F	T	F

(c) Statements (ii) and (iii) are logically equivalent.

Past paper questions 9

1.

p	q	$\neg q$	$p \wedge \neg q$	$p \vee q$	$(p \wedge \neg q) \Rightarrow (p \vee q)$
T	T	F	F	T	T
T	F	T	T	T	T
F	T	F	F	T	T
F	F	T	F	F	T

2. (a)

p	q	$p \wedge q$	$p \vee q$	$\neg p$	$(p \vee q) \wedge \neg p$	$\Rightarrow$	q
T	T	T	T	F	F	T	T
T	F	F	T	F	F	T	F
F	T	F	T	T	T	T	T
F	F	F	F	T	F	T	F

(b) Valid argument or tautology

3. (a) Both are 'p or q'; the first is 'but not both'.
   (b)

$\neg q$	$p \veebar q$	$\neg p \veebar \neg q$	$p \veebar q \Rightarrow \neg p \veebar \neg q$
F	F	F	T
T	T	T	T
F	T	T	T
T	F	F	T

(c) Tautology

p	q	$\neg p$
T	T	F
T	F	F
F	T	T
F	F	T

4. (a) (i)

p	q	$p \wedge q$	$\neg(p \wedge q)$	$\neg p$	$\neg q$	$\neg p \vee \neg q$
T	T	T	F	F	F	F
T	F	F	T	F	T	T
F	T	F	T	T	F	T
F	F	F	T	T	T	T

(ii) Yes
(b) $p \veebar q$

Chapter 10

Exercise 10.1

1. 0.01

2. (a) $\frac{5}{20}$ (b) $\frac{15}{20}$

3. (a) $\frac{3}{12}$ (b) $\frac{9}{12}$

Exercise 10.2

1.

	1	2	3	4
1	2	3	4	5
2	3	4	5	6
3	4	5	6	7
4	5	6	7	8

2.

Head	Dep. H
B	P
B	R
P	B
P	R
R	B
R	P

3.

	1	2	3	4
1	2	3	4	5
2	3	4	5	6
3	4	5	6	7
4	5	6	7	8

4. (a) 9
   (b)

1	A	A	B	B	B	C	C	C
2	B	C	B	A	C	C	A	B

   (c) 27

Exercise 10.3A

1. (a) $\frac{8}{20}$ (b) $\frac{12}{20}$ (c) $\frac{13}{20}$

2.

	1	2	3	4	5	6
Head	H1	H2	H3	H4	H5	H6
Tail	T1	T2	T3	T4	T5	T6

(a) $\frac{6}{12}$ (b) $\frac{8}{12}$
(c) $\frac{2}{12}$ (d) $\frac{9}{12}$

3. (a) $\frac{2}{11}$ (b) $\frac{2}{11}$ (c) $\frac{7}{11}$

4. (a) $\frac{2}{36}$ (b) $\frac{33}{36}$
   (c) $\frac{7}{36}$ (d) $\frac{15}{36}$

5. (a) WW, WL, WD, LW, LL,
       LD, DW, DL, DD
   (b) $\frac{4}{9}$
   (c) $\frac{4}{9}$

6. (a) $\frac{8}{30}$ (b) $\frac{17}{30}$ (c) $\frac{5}{30}$

7.

	1	2	3	4	5	6
1	1	2	3	4	5	6
2	2	4	6	8	10	12
3	3	6	9	12	15	18
4	4	8	12	16	20	24
5	5	10	15	20	25	30
6	6	12	18	24	30	36

(a) $\frac{8}{36}$ (b) $\frac{6}{36}$ (c) $\frac{3}{36}$
(d) $\frac{20}{36}$ (e) $\frac{4}{36}$

8. (a) 80
   (b) (i) $\frac{50}{80}$ (ii) $\frac{15}{80}$ (iii) $\frac{55}{80}$

9. (a)

Andrew	Fareeda	Caitlin
HL	HL	HL
HL	HL	SL
HL	SL	SL
HL	SL	HL
SL	SL	SL
SL	SL	HL
SL	HL	HL
SL	HL	SL

(b) 8   (c) $\frac{2}{8}$
(d) $\frac{3}{8}$ (e) $\frac{7}{8}$

Exercise 10.3B

1. HH, HT, TH, TT
   (a) $\frac{1}{4}$ (b) $\frac{3}{4}$ (c) 60
   (d) 30 (e) 90

2. HHH, HHT, HTH, HTT,
   THH, THT, TTH, TTT
   (a) $\frac{1}{8}$ (b) $\frac{3}{8}$ (c) $\frac{7}{8}$
   (d) $\frac{7}{8}$ (e) 12 (f) 84

3. (a) (i) $\frac{120}{300}$ (ii) $\frac{165}{300}$
   (b) (i) 52 (ii) 143

4. (a) (i) $\frac{24}{100}$ (ii) $\frac{74}{100}$
   (b) (i) 209 (ii) 814

Exercise 10.4

1. (a) $\frac{12}{32}$ (b) $\frac{20}{32}$

2. (a) $\frac{6}{16}$ (b) $\frac{3}{16}$ (c) $\frac{9}{16}$

3. (a) $\frac{6}{24}$ (b) $\frac{4}{24}$
   (c) $\frac{10}{24}$ (d) $\frac{18}{24}$

4. (a) 0.15 (b) 0.85 (c) 0.75

5. (a) $\frac{5}{28}$ (b) $\frac{19}{28}$ (c) $\frac{9}{28}$

6. (a) 1.2
   (b) (i) 0.698
       (ii) 0.151
       (iii) 0.232
   (c) (i) 464 (ii) 1396

Exercise 10.5

1. (a) 0.54
   (b) Not independent;
       $P(A) \times P(B) = 0.2706 \neq 0.54$

2. 0.83

3. (a) 0.2975
   (b) 0.9475

4. (a) (i) $\frac{174}{260}$ (0.669)
       (ii) $\frac{5}{260}$ (0.0192)
   (b) (i) 0.379
       (ii) 0.810

5. (a) 0.0125 (3 s.f.)   (b) 0.150 (3 s.f.)
    (c) 0.881 (3 s.f.)

6. (a) $\frac{3}{12}$ (b) $\frac{5}{12}$

7. (a) 0.655 (3 s.f.)   (b) 0.345 (3 s.f.)
    (c) 0.891 (3 s.f.)   (d) 0.818 (3 s.f.)

Exercise 10.6A

1. (a)

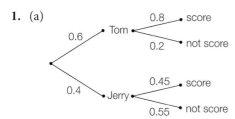

  (b) (i) 0.48   (ii) 0.66
    (iii) 0.34
  (c) (i) 0.495   (ii) 0.7975

2. (a) 0.33   (b) 0.18   (c) 0.82

3. (a)

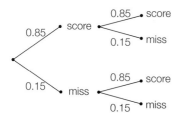

  (b) 0.18   (c) 0.81
  (d) 0.07   (e) 0.19

4. first kick   second kick

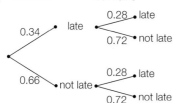

  (a) 0.0225   (b) 0.255
  (c) 0.9775

5. (a)   Carmen   Jermaine

  (b) (i) 0.475 (3 s.f.)   (ii) 0.0952 (3 s.f.)
    (iii) 0.245 (3 s.f.)   (iv) 0.430 (3 s.f.)

Exercise 10.6B

1. (a)

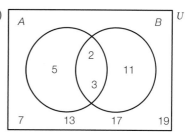

  (b) (i) $\frac{2}{8}$ (ii) $\frac{2}{8}$

2. (a)

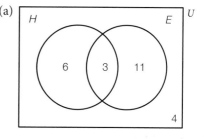

  (b) (i) $\frac{20}{24}$ (ii) $\frac{10}{24}$ (iii) $\frac{17}{24}$

3. (a) 80
  (b) (i) $\frac{37}{80}$ (ii) $\frac{23}{80}$ (iii) $\frac{39}{80}$
     (iv) $\frac{50}{80}$ (v) $\frac{30}{80}$

Exercise 10.7

1. (a) $\frac{12}{13}$ (b) $\frac{6}{13}$ (c) $\frac{6}{13}$

2. (a) $\frac{4}{25}$ (b) $\frac{12}{25}$

3. (a) $\frac{28}{153}$ (0.183)   (b) $\frac{45}{153}$ (0.294)
  (c) $\frac{125}{153}$ (0.817)

4. (a) $\frac{83}{225}$ (0.369)   (b) $\frac{142}{225}$ (0.631)
  (c) $\frac{81}{225}$ (0.36)

5. (a) $\frac{14}{95}$ (0.147)   (b) $\frac{81}{95}$ (0.853)
  (c) $\frac{48}{95}$ (0.505)

6. (a) $\frac{10}{32}$ (0.3125)   (b) $\frac{30}{32}$ (0.9375)
  (c) $\frac{3}{496}$ (0.00605)   (d) $\frac{87}{496}$ (0.175)
  (e) $\frac{90}{496}$ (0.181)

7. (a)

	R	Y	G	Br	Bl	P	Bk
R	-	3	4	5	6	7	8
Y	3	-	5	6	7	8	9
G	4	5	-	7	8	9	10
Br	5	6	7	-	9	10	11
Bl	6	7	8	9	-	11	12
P	7	8	9	10	11	-	13
Bk	8	9	10	11	12	13	-

(b) (i) $\frac{6}{42}$ (ii) $\frac{34}{42}$ (iii) $\frac{4}{42}$

8. (a) (i) $\frac{110}{140}$ (ii) $\frac{77}{140}$ (iii) $\frac{46}{140}$

(b) (i) 0.0577 (3 s.f.)
(ii) 0.412 (3 s.f.)
(iii) 0.384 (3 s.f.)

Exercise 10.8

1. (a) (i) $\frac{26}{100}$ (ii) $\frac{12}{40}$

(b) $\frac{46}{60}$

2. (a)

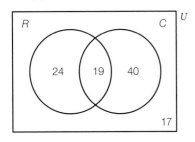

(b) 19
(c) (i) $\frac{19}{100}$ (ii) $\frac{40}{57}$ (iii) $\frac{19}{59}$

3. (a) $\frac{42}{150}$ (b) $\frac{42}{67}$ (c) $\frac{18}{43}$

Mixed examination practice 10

Exam-style questions 10

1. (a) 0.1 (b) 0.2 (c) 0.8

2. $\frac{4}{8}$

3. (a) $\frac{2}{9}$ (b) $\frac{1}{9}$ (c) $\frac{3}{9}$

4. (a) $\frac{17}{60}$ (b) $\frac{23}{60}$ (c) $\frac{40}{60}$

5. (a)

	Over 18's	18 or under	Total
Have cars	20	12	32
Do not have cars	28	20	48
Total	48	32	80

(b) $\frac{12}{80}$ (c) $\frac{48}{80}$

6. GG, GS, GB, SG, SS, SB, BG, BS, BB
(a) 9
(b) (i) $\frac{1}{9}$ (ii) $\frac{4}{9}$ (iii) $\frac{6}{9}$

7. (a)

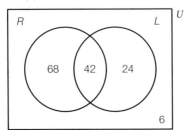

(b) (i) $\frac{66}{140}$ (ii) $\frac{68}{74}$ (iii) $\frac{24}{30}$

8. (a) 82
(b) (i) 0.179 (3 s.f.)
(ii) 0.257 (3 s.f.)
(iii) 0.459 (3 s.f.)

9. (a)

	M	F	Total
Baseball	29	10	39
Basketball	20	18	38
Hockey	14	19	33
Total	63	47	110

(b) (i) 0.424 (3 s.f.)
(ii) 0.0416 (3 s.f.)
(iii) 0.226 (3 s.f.)

10. (a) 0.702 (3 s.f.)
(b) 0.538 (3 s.f.)
(c) (i) 0.0423 (3 s.f.)
(ii) 0.605 (3 s.f.)

11. (a) (i) 0.1
(ii) 0.4
(b) (i) 0.648 (3 s.f.)
(ii) 0.133 (3 s.f.)

12. (a) (i) Walk, given that they rode to school by bike.
(ii) Travelled by car, given that they did not ride by bike.
(iii) Did not ride by bike, given that they walked and travelled by car.

(b) (i) $\frac{5}{13}$

(ii) $\frac{27}{35}$

(iii) $\frac{4}{5}$

Chapter 11

Exercise 11.1

1. (a)

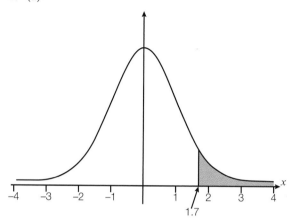

(b)

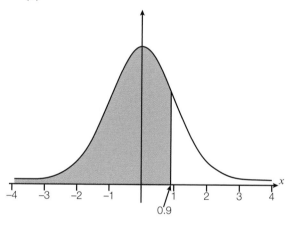

(c)

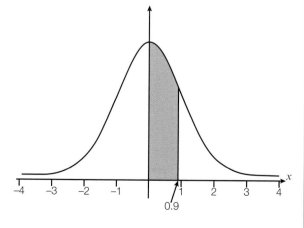

(d)

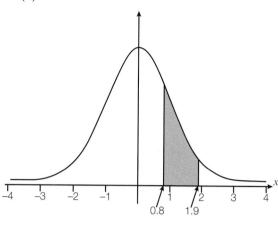

(e)

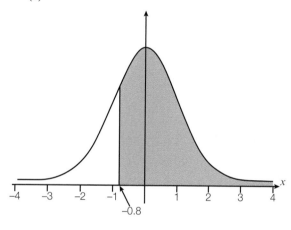

(f)

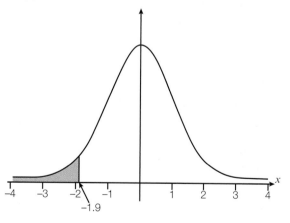

(g)

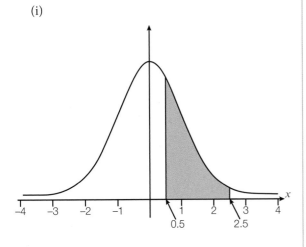

(h)

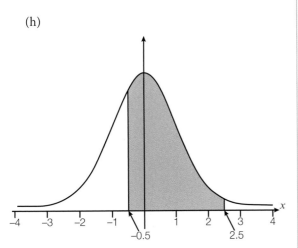

(i)

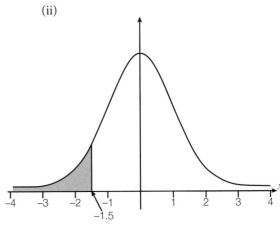

(j)

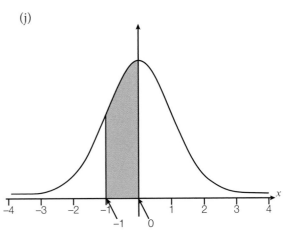

2. (a) 0.0446 (3 s.f.) (b) 0.816 (3 s.f.)
(c) 0.316 (3 s.f.) (d) 0.183 (3 s.f.)
(e) 0.788 (3 s.f.) (f) 0.0287 (3 s.f.)
(g) 0.302 (3 s.f.) (h) 0.685 (3 s.f.)
(i) 0.302 (3 s.f.) (j) 0.341 (3 s.f.)

3. (a) (i)

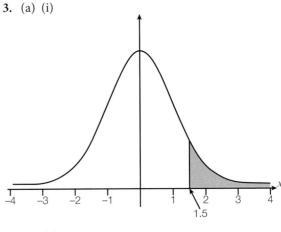

(ii)

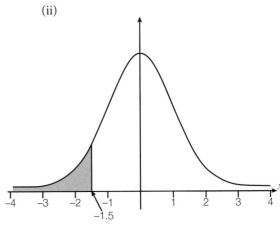

(b) Areas are equal. (c) 0.0668 (3 s.f.)

4. Their sum is equal to 1.

1. (a) (i)

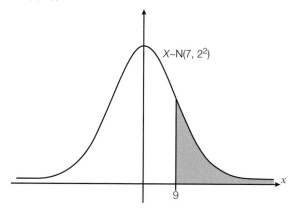

(ii)

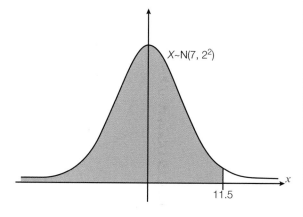

(iii)

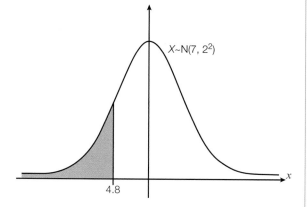

(iv)

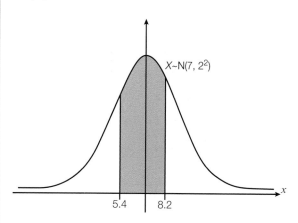

(b) (i)

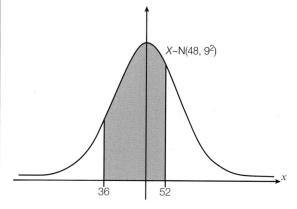

(ii)

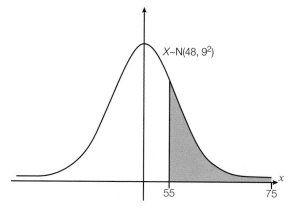

(iii)

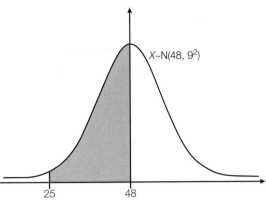

(iv)

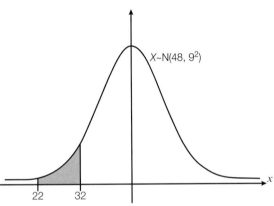

2. (a) (i) 0.159 (3 s.f.)   (ii) 0.988 (3 s.f.)
      (iii) 0.136 (3 s.f.)   (iv) 0.514 (3 s.f.)
   (b) (i) 0.580 (3 s.f.)   (ii) 0.217 (3 s.f.)
      (iii) 0.495 (3 s.f.)   (iv) 0.0358 (3 s.f.)

3. (a) 0.0712 (3 s.f.)   (b) 0.141 (3 s.f.)
   (c) 0.429 (3 s.f.)   (d) 0.791 (3 s.f.)
   (e) 0.136 (3 s.f.)

4. 0.0668 (3 s.f.)

Exercise 11.3

1. (a) 0.922 (3 s.f.)
   (b) 0.653 (3 s.f.)
   (c) 0.972 (3 s.f.)

2. (a) (i) 0.894 (3 s.f.)
      (ii) 0.994 (3 s.f.)
      (iii) 0.733 (3 s.f.)
   (b) (i) 96   (ii) all 100
   (c) No

3. (a) 0.330 (3 s.f.)   (b) 67.6% (3 s.f.)
   (c) 0.153 (3 s.f.)   (d) 92

4. (a) 97.7% (3 s.f.)   (b) 97.7% (3 s.f.)
   (c) 11.3% (3 s.f.)

5. (a) 16   (b) 3   (c) 126   (d) 5

6. (a) (i) 0.952 (3 s.f.)   (ii) 0.00621 (3 s.f.)
      (iii) 0.894 (3 s.f.)   (iv) 0.0478 (3 s.f.)
   (b) (i) 1401   (ii) 67

Exercise 11.4

1. 0.961 (3 s.f.)

2. 0.841 (3 s.f.)

3. (a) 0.141 (3 s.f.)   (b) 72.8 (3 s.f.)

4. 0.775 (3 s.f.)

5. (a) (i) 0.0668 (3 s.f.)   (ii) 0.977 (3 s.f.)
      (iii) 0.930 (3 s.f.)
   (b) (i)

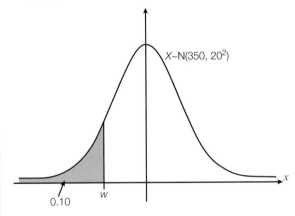

   (ii) 324 (3 s.f.)

6. $x = 141$ (3 s.f.), $y = 179$ (3 s.f.)

7. 40.6 mm to 47.7 mm

Mixed examination practice 11

Exam-style questions 11

1. (a) (i) 0.68   (ii) 0.95
   (b) (i) 0.9998 (4 s.f.)   (ii) 0.919 (3 s.f.)

2. 0.961 (3 s.f.)

3. (a) 0.150 (3 s.f.)   (b) 0.245 (3 s.f.)
   (c) 0.897 (3 s.f.)

4. (a) 0.933 (3 s.f.)   (b) 0.988 (3 s.f.)
   (c) 0.598 (3 s.f.)

5. (a) 0.141 (3 s.f.)
(b) 69.8 m (3 s.f.)
(c) 17 (not including Yurek)

6. (a) (i) 0.997 (3 s.f.)   (ii) 0.932 (3 s.f.)
(b) 76.8 (3 s.f.)

7. (a) 0.994 (3 s.f.)
(b) (i) 0.988 (3 s.f.)   (ii) 0.0124 (3 s.f.)
(c) Fewer; with smaller σ the distribution is narrower, so the area under the curve to the left of 230 will be smaller.

Past paper questions 11

1. (a) **a** = 5.1 m, **b** = 5.2 m, **c** = 4.7 m
(b) 0.933 (3 s.f.)
(c) 0.234 m (3 s.f.)

2. (a) (i) 68%   (ii) 102
(b) (i)

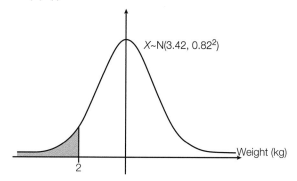

    (ii) −1.73 (3 s.f.)   (iii) 4.17% (3 s.f.)
(c) 91.2% (3 s.f.)
(d) 5.03 (3 s.f.)

Chapter 12

Exercise 12.1

1.

	Independent variable	Dependent variable	Correlation
(a)	Amount of alcohol consumed	Reaction time	Yes
(b)	Number of people in household	Monthly food expenditure	Yes
(c)	Hours of exercise per week	Body mass	Yes

(d)	Time spent exercising	Blood sugar level	Yes
(e)	Car mileage	Value of second-hand car	Yes
(f)	Length of middle finger	Sprint time	No
(g)	Screen size of TV set	Price of TV set	Yes

Exercise 12.2

1.   (i)   (ii)   (iii)

	Type of correlation	Independent variable	Dependent variable
(a)	Positive	Height of student	Arm span
(b)	Negative	Age of car	Price of car
(c)	Positive	Mock exam score	Final exam score
(d)	Positive	Hours of sunshine	Maximum temperature
(e)	Negative	Number of goals conceded	Number of points scored

Exercise 12.3

1. (a)

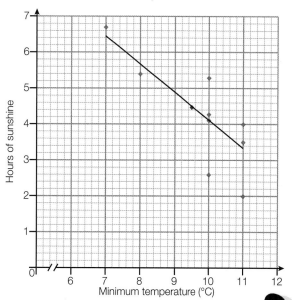

(b)

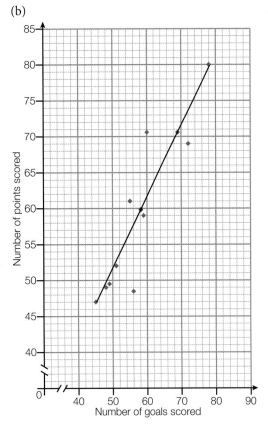

(c)

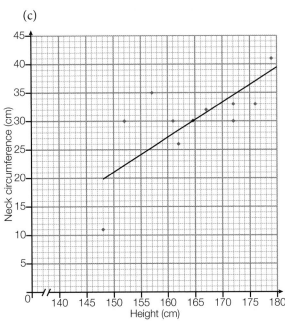

(d)

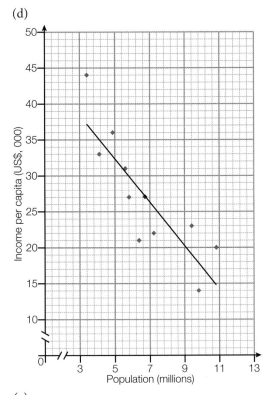

(e)

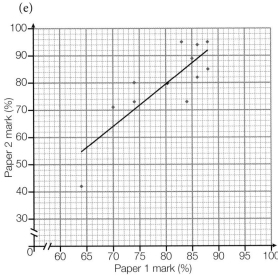

Exercise 12.4

1. (a) −0.912 (3 s.f.) (b) −0.00769 (3 s.f.)
   (c) −0.863 (3 s.f.) (d) 0.894 (3 s.f.)
   (e) 0.912 (3 s.f.)

Exercise 12.5

1. (a) $y = 1.0524x - 10.795$
   (b) 0.839 (3 s.f.)
   (c) Strong positive correlation

2. (a) $y = 0.119439x + 5.9086$
(b) 0.586
(c) Moderate positive correlation

3. (a) -0.855 (3 s.f.)
(b) Strong negative correlation
(c) $y = -57.984x + 863.72$ (d) US\$545

4. (a) $y = 0.12354x + 3.8279$ (b) 24.2 cm (3 s.f.)
(c) 0.905 (3 s.f.)
(d) Strong positive correlation

5. (a) 0.941 (3 s.f.)   (b) $m = 0.647$ (3 s.f.)
                                  $c = 1.61$ (3 s.f.)
(c) 12.0% (3 s.f.)

Exercise 12.6

1. (a) 0.708 (3 s.f.)
(b) Positive correlation (moderate)
(c) 85%   (d) 58%

2. (a) $y = -0.06706x + 11.5061$
(b) \$70,200 (3 s.f.)
(c) 9.19% (3 s.f.)
(d) -0.181 (3 s.f.)
(e) Weak negative correlation, so estimates from the regression line are unreliable.

3. (a) $r = 0.867$ (3 s.f.); Jessica's assertion is correct.
(b) $m = 0.705$ (3 s.f.), $c = 14.2$ (3 s.f.)
(c) 35 points
(d) Reliable as r is close to 1, indicating that the correlation is strong.

Mixed examination practice 12

Exam-style questions 12

1. (a) Independent variable: mileage; dependent variable: price
(b) Negative correlation (strong: $r = -0.870$)
(c) 78 400 miles, \$10,105
(d)

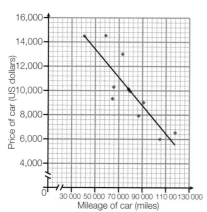

2. (a)

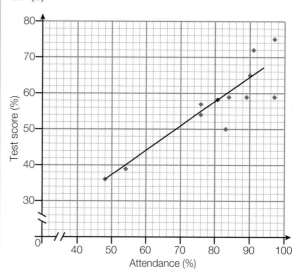

(b) Positive correlation
(c) $r = 0.887$ (3 s.f.); strong positive correlation

3. (a) $y = 1.025x - 6.912$
(b) 0.744 (3 s.f.)
(c) Positive correlation (moderate)

4. (a) 0.992 (3 s.f.)
(b) Very strong positive correlation
(c) $y = 4.592x + 14.748$
(d) 30.8 amperes (3 s.f.)
(e) Not reliable; 18.5 is outside the range of x values in the data (extrapolation).

5. (a) -0.750 (3 s.f.)
(b) $m = -0.7245$, $c = 13.9074$
(c) Unsuitable, as 15 is outside the range of x values in the data (extrapolation).
(d) 10.3°C (3 s.f.)

6. (a) $r = 0.959$ (3 s.f.), indicating very strong positive correlation, so Mr Lawrence is right.
(b) $y = 0.700x - 79.609$
(c) 1015 pence
(d) 3399 pence

7. (a) 0.820 (3 s.f.)
(b) Strong positive correlation
(c) $y = 1.844x - 0.04663$
(d) (i) 27.8 s (3 s.f.)   (ii) 14.2 s (3 s.f.)

Past paper questions 12

1. (a), (c), (f) (Here, to save space, 1 cm represents 2 kg on the horizondal axis.)

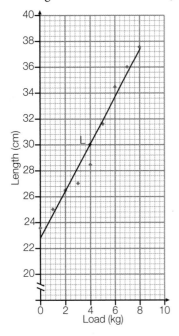

(b) (i) 4 kg (ii) 2.85 kg (3 s.f.)
   (iii) 30 cm (iv) 4.78 cm (3 s.f.)
(d) (i) 0.986 (3 s.f.)
   (ii) Very strong positive correlation
(e) $y = 1.825x + 22.7$
(g) (i) 32.6 cm (3 s.f.)
   (ii) Not reliable, as 30 lies far outside the range of x values in the data.

2. (a) $y = -0.134x + 20.9$
   (b) 17
   (c) -0.756 (3 s.f.)
   (d) Moderately strong negative correlation

Chapter 13

Exercise 13.1

1. (a) 1 (b) 2 (c) 6 (d) 3

Exercise 13.2

1. (a)

	B_1	B_2
A_1	66.3	131.7
A_2	88.7	176.3

(b)

	B_1	B_2	B_3
A_1	48.3	23.6	14.1
A_2	33.7	16.4	9.86

(c)

	B_1	B_2	B_3	B_4
A_1	38.3	88.5	78.0	26.1
A_2	33.8	78.2	68.9	23.1
A_3	37.8	87.3	77.0	25.8

(d)

	B_1	B_2
A_1	28.3	30.7
A_2	42.7	46.3
A_3	47.0	51.0

Exercise 13.3

1. (a) (i) 1 (ii) 0.207 (3 s.f.)
   (iii) 0.649 (3 s.f.)
   (b) (i) 2 (ii) 0.0277 (3 s.f.)
   (iii) 0.986 (3 s.f.)
   (c) (i) 6 (ii) 52.9 (3 s.f.)
   (iii) 1.25×10^{-9} (3 s.f.)
   (d) (i) 3 (ii) 10.1 (3 s.f.)
   (iii) 0.0177 (3 s.f.)

2. (a) 12.9 (3 s.f.) (b) 26.7 (3 s.f.)
   (c) 23.9 (3 s.f.) (d) 4.19 (3 s.f.)

3. (a) H_0: high performance at GCSE is independent of gender.
   (b) 1
   (c) 0.226 (3 s.f.)
   (d) Do not reject H_0, as $0.226 < 3.84$.

4. (a) H_0: the age of drivers involved in accidents is independent of gender.
   (b) 1
   (c) 4.69 (3 s.f.)
   (d) Reject H_0, as $4.69 > 4.61$; there is dependence between age and gender of drivers involved in accidents.

5. H_0: the genre of books borrowed by readers is independent of age. $\chi^2_{calc} = 30.0$. Reject H_0, as $30.0 > 9.49$.

Mixed examination practice 13

Exam-style questions 13

1. H_0: cell phone ownership is independent of age; H_1: cell phone ownership is dependent on age. df = 2. Expected frequencies:

	18–34	35–54	55+
Own cell phone	367.3	530.6	839.1
Do not own cell phone	100.7	145.4	229.9

$\chi^2_{calc} = 194.4$, $\chi^2_{5\%} = 5.99$; $\chi^2_{calc} > \chi^2_{5\%}$, so reject H_0.

2. (a) Voting behaviour is independent of the type of work voters do.
   (b) 2
   (c) 14.8 (3 s.f.)
   (d) Reject H_0 and conclude that voting behaviour is dependent on the type of work voters do, because $\chi^2_{calc} > \chi^2_{10\%}$.

3. (a) Low performance in GCSE Mathematics is independent of gender.
   (b) 2
   (c) 0.0903 (3 s.f.)
   (d) Mrs Elwood will not reject H_0, because $\chi^2_{calc} < \chi^2_{5\%}$.

4. (a) Ownership of smart phones is independent of age.
   (b) 2
   (c) 135 (3 s.f.)
   (d) Reject H_0, since $\chi^2_{calc} > \chi^2_{5\%}$.

5. H_0: voting behaviour is independent of the voter's age.
   $\chi^2_{calc} = 120.1 > \chi^2_{5\%}$, so reject H_0 and conclude that voting behaviour is dependent on age.

6. (a) High performance in IB Mathematics is independent of the level at which the subject is studied.
   (b) Level 5: 8.58, Level 6: 17.68, Level 7: 25.74
   (c) H_0 should not be rejected, since p-value (8.06%) > 5%.

7. H_0: involvement in accidents is independent of the driver's age.
   $p = 0.00274$, $\chi^2_{calc} = 16.2$. Reject H_0 because $p = 0.274\% < 5\%$ and, to confirm the conclusion, $\chi^2_{calc} > \chi^2_{5\%} = 7.78$.

Past paper questions 13

1. (a)

	Drama	Comedy	Film	News
Males	58	119	157	52
Females	86	98	120	61

   (b) H_0: favourite TV programme type is independent of gender; H_1: favourite TV programme type is dependent on gender.
   (c) 105
   (d) 12.6 (3 s.f.)
   (e) (i) 3
       (ii) 7.815
       (iii) Reject H_0 and conclude that favourite TV programme type is dependent on gender.

2. (a) H_0: the size of dog is independent of the time of day.
   (b) 14.9 (3 s.f.)
   (d) Reject H_0 and conclude that the size of dog present in the park is dependent on the time of day, because $\chi^2_{calc} > \chi^2_{5\%}$.

3. (a) Favourite type of music is independent of age.
   (b) 4
   (c) 51.6 (3 s.f.)
   (d) Reject H_0, because $\chi^2_{calc} > \chi^2_{5\%} = 9.488$, or $p = 1.71 \times 10^{-10} < 0.05$.

Chapter 14

Exercise 14.1

1. (a) −1 (b) 4 (c) $-\frac{11}{8}$
   (d) 3 (e) $\frac{19}{4}$

2. (a) AB: $\frac{1}{2}$ BC: $-\frac{3}{4}$ CD: $\frac{1}{2}$ AD: −2
   (b) AB and CD. They have equal gradients.
   (c) CD and AD. The product of their gradients is −1.

3. (a) AE: $-\frac{2}{3}$ CD: $\frac{1}{3}$ CE: $-\frac{2}{5}$ DE: $-\frac{3}{2}$ DF: $\frac{3}{2}$ GF: $\frac{1}{3}$
   (b) CD and GF with equal gradients.
   (c) AE and DF. Product of gradients equals −1.

4. (a) AB: $\frac{4}{5}$ CD: $-\frac{14}{5}$ EF: 4 GH: $\frac{14}{3}$ IJ: $-\frac{14}{5}$
   (b) (i) CD and IJ with equal gradients.
       (ii) None of the lines are perpendicular. No pairing has a product = −1.

Exercise 14.2

1. (a) $y = 2x$ (b) $y = 2x + 1$
   (c) $y = 3x - 1$ (d) $y = 4x - 5$
   (e) $y = -3x$ (f) $y = -3x + 1$
   (g) $y = -x + 4$

2. (a) $y = 5$ (b) $x = 7$
   (c) $y = 4x$ (d) $y = -2x + 3$
   (e) $y = 2x - 1$

3. A: $y = 3x - 1$ B: $y = -x + 5$ C: $y = \frac{1}{2}x - 3$

Exercise 14.3

1. (a) $6x - y - 11 = 0$ (b) $4x - y + 8 = 0$
   (c) $5x + y + 6 = 0$ (d) $3x + y - 3 = 0$
   (e) $4x - 2y - 9 = 0$ (f) $20x - 28y + 121 = 0$

2. (a) $2x + y - 4 = 0$ (b) $x + 5y - 22 = 0$
   (c) $x - 7y - 9 = 0$ (d) $3x - 24y - 13 = 0$
   (e) $7x - 5y + 27 = 0$ (f) $7x - 2y - 2 = 0$

3. (a) $2x - y + 1 = 0$ (b) $2x - 7y - 41 = 0$

4. (a) $7x - y - 23 = 0$ (b) $5x + 2y + 6 = 0$
   (c) $15x + 10y - 47 = 0$ (d) $5x + 8y = 0$

5. (a) $x + 3y - 3 = 0$ (b) $2x + 7y - 127 = 0$
   (c) $3x + 4y - 36 = 0$ (d) $10x - 15y + 2 = 0$

6. (a) $\frac{1}{2}$ (b) $y = \frac{1}{2}x + \frac{5}{2}$ (c) $y = -2x + 19$

7. (a) $y = 3x - 5$ (b) $y = -5x + 10$
   (c) $y = -3x + 4$ (d) $y = \frac{4}{5}x - 2$

8. (a) -1 (b) $y = -x - 1$ (c) $x + y + 1 = 0$

Exercise 14.4

1. (a)

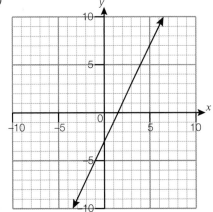

(b)

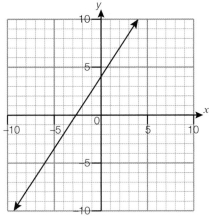

(c)

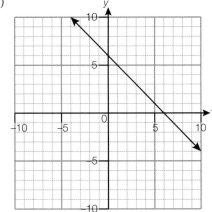

(d)

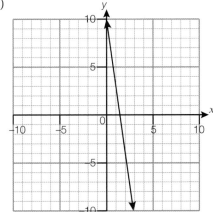

(e)

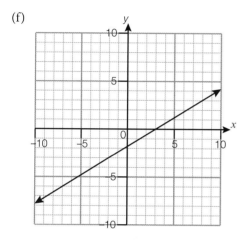

(b)

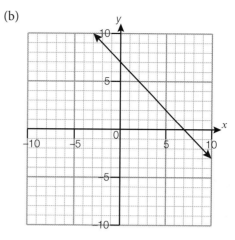

(f)

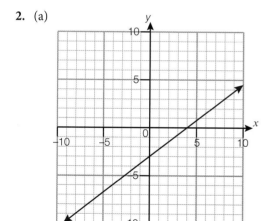

(c)

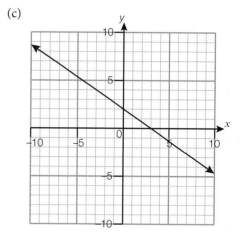

2. (a)

(d)

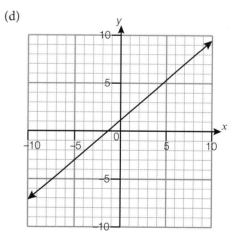

(e)

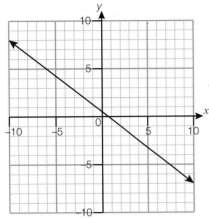

(f)

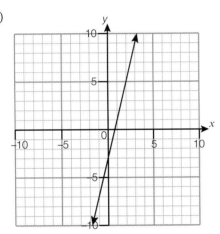

(g)

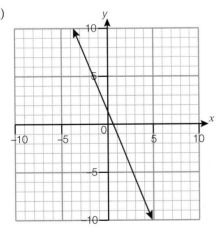

3. (a)

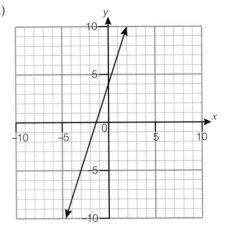

(b) $y = 3x + 1$

4. (a)

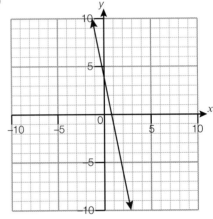

(b) $y = -5x - 3$
(c) $x - 5y + 37 = 0$

5. (a) $(1.143, 4)$ (b) $(\frac{1}{2}, 1)$
   (c) $(2, -4)$ (d) $(-2, 1)$
   (e) $(4, 1)$ (f) $(1.288, 1.475)$

Mixed examination practice 14

Exam-style questions 14

1. (a) $2x - y + 13 = 0$
   (b) $5x + y + 8 = 0$
   (c) $3x + 4y - 19 = 0$

2. Line A: $y = 3x + 8$
   Line B: $y = \frac{3}{2}x$
   Line C: $y = -5x + 6$
   Line D: $y = \frac{1}{2}x - 7$

3. (a) 5   (b) $y = 5x - 3$

4. (a)

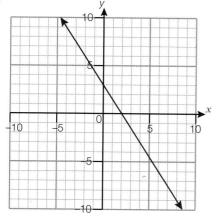

(b) $2x - 3y + 6 = 0$
(c) $3x + 2y + 2 = 0$

5. (a), (c)

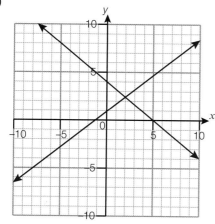

(b) (i) Any line of the form $y = -\frac{4}{5}x + c$

  (ii) any line of the form $y = \frac{5}{4}x + c$
(d) (2, 2.4)
(e) $x = 2$ and $y = 2.4$

Past paper questions 14

1. (a) 3   (b) $-\frac{1}{3}$

  (c) $y = -\frac{1}{3}x + 9$ (d) (1.5, 8.5)

2. (a) $-\frac{2}{3}$ (b) (4, 3.5)

  (c) 8.06 $(\sqrt{65})$ (d) $7x + 4y - 42 = 0$

  (e) Gradient of BC is $\frac{3}{2}$, so product of gradients is
     -1. Yes, they are perpendicular.

Chapter 15

Exercise 15.1

1. (a) 50.2 cm   (b) 64.8 cm   (c) 79.7 cm
  (d) 65.3 cm   (e) 70.9 mm   (f) 6.45 m
  (g) 10.6 m   (h) 11.50 m   (i) 67.7 m
  (j) 64.3 m   (k) 65.5 m   (l) 81.0 m

2. (a) 51.3°   (b) 47.8°   (c) 47.2°
  (d) 42.5°   (e) 57.0°   (f) 63.4°

3. 26.0 cm
4. 3.53 m
5. 38.0°
6. 49.1°

Exercise 15.2

1. 1030 m
2. 765 m
3. (a) 71.2 m   (b) 426 m

Exercise 15.3

1. (a) 40.0 cm   (b) 40.0 cm   (c) 115°
2. (a) 147 m   (b) 35.9°
3. 72.5 m
4. 28.1°
5. 132 m

Exercise 15.4

1. (a) 53.6°   (b) 35.4   (c) 51.4
  (d) 28.4°   (e) 151   (f) 52.2°

2. (a) 73.7   (b) 121   (c) 171

3. (a) 44.8°   (b) 45.5°   (c) 64.6°

4. (a) 32.0°   (b) 54.9°   (c) 43.7°
  (d) 36.9°   (e) 69.6°

5. (a) 36.4 cm   (b) 72.0 mm   (c) 53.1 m
  (d) 23.9 m   (e) 40.3 km

6. 12.2 cm
7. 32.4 m

Exercise 15.5

1. (a) 164 cm   (b) 136 cm   (c) 71.8 cm

2. (a) 55.2°   (b) 19.6°   (c) 55.0°

3. (a) 176 m; A = 43.7°; C = 31.3°
   (b) 51.7; P = 27.6°;
       Q = 128.4° (1 d.p.)
   (c) P = 52.4°; Q = 104.8°;
       R = 22.8° (1 d.p.)
   (d) A = 35°; B = 67.1°;
       C = 77.9°

4. 417 m
5. 31.1 km

Exercise 15.6

1. (a) 6470 cm²   (b) 2880 mm²
   (c) 4290 m²   (d) 1590 cm²
   (e) 490 m²

Exercise 15.7

1. (a) 396 m   (b) 34 200 m²
   (c) 45 800 m²   (d) 1160 m

2. 3570 m
3. 64.2 m
4. A = 39.9°; B = 105.3°;
   C = 34.8° (1 d.p.)
5. 331 km
6. 17.4 km

Mixed examination practice 15

Exam-style questions 15

1. 104 m
2. 180 m and 73.7 m

3. (a) 2510 m
   (b) 157° anticlockwise

4. 199 m
5. 56.6°
6. 319°
7. 47.9 m²

8. (a) 181 m   (b) 75.3°
   (c) 86.5 m, 477 m
   (d) 11 600 m²

9. 15.6 m
10. 25.7 m

Past paper questions 15

1.

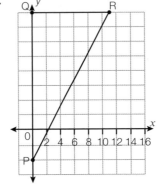

   (a) Point R on diagram
   (b) 28.8° (28° 49′)
   (c) 43.4 square units

2. (a) (i)

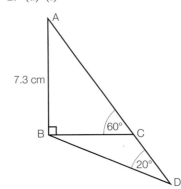

   (ii) 4.21 cm
   (b) (i) ACD is a straight line.
       B joins D at 20° to
       ACD. D must be on
       AC extended.

   (ii) CB̂D = 40°

3. (a) (i) 73.5°   (ii) 55.8 m
   (b) 55.0 m
   (c) 217 m

Chapter 16

Exercise 16.1

1. 56.6 cm

2. (a) 4.72 m   (b) 5.49 m

3. 28.3 cm

---

4. (a) 15 cm
   (b) 7 cm
   (c) 13.3 cm

5. (a) 28.3 cm   (b) 26.5 cm

6. 41.6 cm

7. (a) 5.83 m
   (b) 5.22 m
   (c) AH by 0.728 m
       (AH = 6.892, AG = 6.164)

Exercise 16.2

1. (a) 56.6 cm   (b) 38.9°

2. (a) 14.4 cm   (b) 16.5 cm
   (c) 29.0°

3. 61.1°

4. (a) 85.4 cm   (b) 89.0 cm
   (c) 16.3°

5. x = 19.4°   y = 127°

6. (a) (i)   17.3 cm
       (ii) 7.07 cm
   (b) 78.2°

7. (a) ME = MF = 87.7 cm
   (b) 54.3°

8. (a) 107 cm   (b) 20.3°
   (c) 20.1°

Exercise 16.3

1.

	(a) Total surface area	(b) Volume
1	5027 cm²	23695 cm³
2	56 m²	28 m³
3	1504 cm²	3840 cm³
4	1414 cm²	7069 cm³
5	1531 cm²	3528 cm³
6	6082 cm²	44602 cm³

2. (a) 33 510 cm³
   (b) 28 953 cm³
   (c) 386 039 cm³
   (d) 157 080 cm³
   (e) 837 758 cm³

3. (a) 5027 cm²   (b) 5429 cm²
   (c) 30 561 cm²   (d) 16 493 cm²
   (e) 50 265 cm²

4. (a) $r = 6.20$ cm (b) $x = 10$ cm

5. (a) 29.4 m³   (b) 16 m²

6. (a) radius = 3.2 cm, length = 25.6 cm
   (b) 275 cm³

Mixed examination practice 16

Exam-style questions 16

1. (a) 11.3 cm   (b) 13.9 cm

2. (a) 71.1°   (b) 17.7°

3. 5.10 m

4. (a) 115 000 cm³   (b) 12 700 cm²

5. 2090 cm³

6. 25.5 cm and 76.4 cm

7. (a) (i) 7240 cm³
      (ii) 1810 cm²
   (b) 1810 cm³
   (c) 7.56 cm
   (d) No, total surface area of 4 smaller spheres
      (2872 cm²) is more than the surface area of
      original sphere.

Past paper questions 16

1. (a) 1294.14 cm³ (2 d.p.)
   (b) 6
   (c) (i) 431 cm³
      (ii) 0.000431 m³ or 4.31×10^{-4} m³

2. (a)

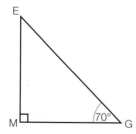

   (c) (i) EG = 14.6 cm
      (ii) = 37.8°
   (d) 392 cm²
   (e) 458 cm³

Chapter 17

Exercise 17.1

1. (a) No   (b) Yes   (c) Yes
   (d) No   (e) Yes   (f) Yes

Exercise 17.2

1. (a) 4   (b) −11
   (c) −7   (d) $3a - 8$

2. (a) −19   (b) 12
   (c) −11   (d) $11 - 10a$

3. (a) 27   (b) 5
   (c) −3   (d) $2c^2 - 7c + 5$

4. (a) −147   (b) −15   (c) 429

5. (a) 9.1   (b) 1.9
   (c) −10.5   (d) −1550

6. (a) $\frac{5}{9}$ (b) $-\frac{11}{5} = -2.2$
   (c) 3   (d) $\frac{3+x}{x-1}$

Exercise 17.3

1. (a) $-4 < x \le 4, -5 \le y < 11$
   (b) $x > -4, y \ge -2$
   (c) $x \ge -5, y \ge -80$
   (d) $-3 < x \le 6, 3 < y \le 15$
   (e) $x \ge -3, y \le 12.8$
   (f) $-6 \le x \le 4, -5.125 \le y \le 50$

2. (a)

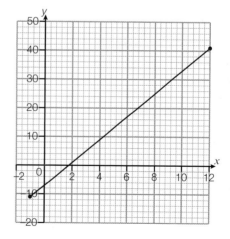

   $-11 \le y \le 41$

(b)

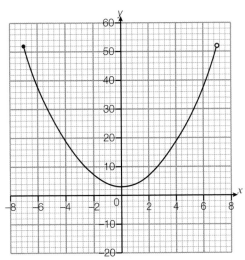

$3 \leq y < 52$

(c)

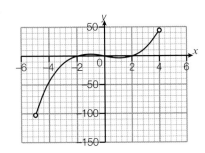

$-105 \leq y \leq 48$

(d)

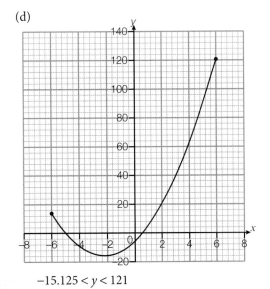

$-15.125 < y < 121$

Exercise 17.4

1. (a) (i) $x = 0$ (ii) $y = 0$
    (b) (i) $x = 0$ (ii) $y = 0$
    (c) (i) $x = -1$ (ii) $y = 0$
    (d) (i) $x = -1$ (ii) $y = 0$
    (e) (i) $x = -0.5$ (ii) $y = 0$
    (f) (i) $x = 1.5$ (ii) $y = 0$
    (g) (i) $x = 1.5$ (ii) $y = 5$
    (h) (i) $x = \frac{2}{3}$ (ii) $y = 4$

Exercise 17.5

1. (a)

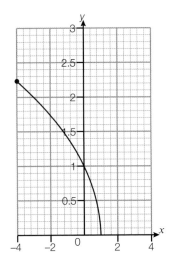

    (b) $0 \leq f(x) \leq 2.24$; the curve does not exist beyond $x = 1$, and lies above the x-axis for all values of $x < 1$.
    (c) $5 \leq g(x) \leq 7.24$; the graph of $g(x)$ is obtained by shifting the graph of $f(x)$ up by 5 units.

2. (a)

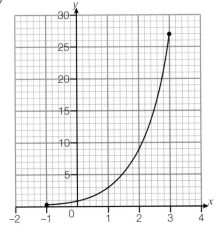

    $\frac{1}{3} \leq f(x) \leq 27$

(b)

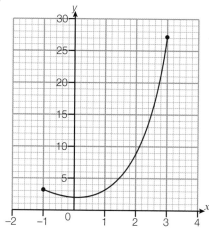

$2 \leq g(x) \leq 27.0$

(c)

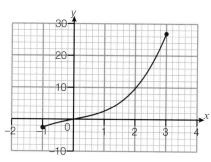

$-2\frac{2}{3} \leq h(x) \leq 27.0$

(d) $g(x) + h(x) = 2f(x)$, so the range is $\frac{2}{3} \leq y \leq 54$

3. (a)

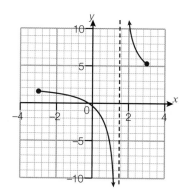

(b)

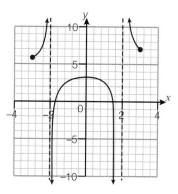

(c)

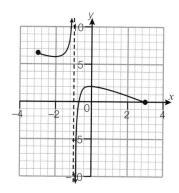

(d)

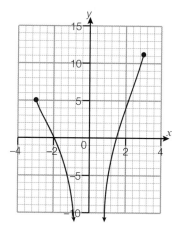

4. (a)

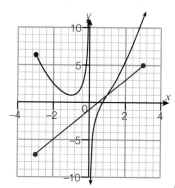

Point of intersection: $(1, 1)$

(b)

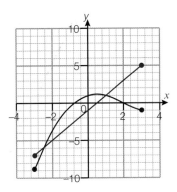

Points of intersection: $(-2.48, -5.95)$ and $(1, 1)$

(c)

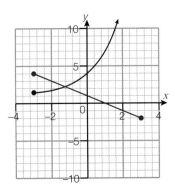

Point of intersection: $(-1.26, 2.26)$

(d)

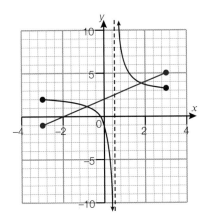

Points of intersection: $(-0.82, 1.18)$ and $(1.82, 3.82)$

Exercise 17.6

1. (a)

x	-2	-1	0	1	2	3	4
$f(x)$	8	3	0	-1	0	3	8
$g(x)$	4	3	2	1	0	-1	-2

(b)

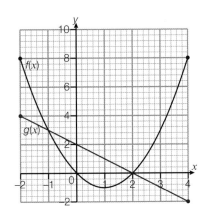

(c) $-1, 2$

2. (a)

x	-2	-1	0	1	2
$f(x)$	-17	-3	-1	1	15
$g(x)$	-10	-5	0	5	10

(b)

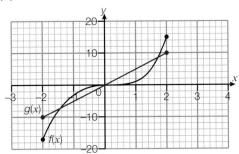

(c) $-1.5, -0.2, 1.7$

3. (a)

x	-4	-3	-2	-1	0	1	2
$f(x)$	-1.99	-1.96	-1.89	-1.67	-1	1	7
$g(x)$	-7	-2	1	2	1	-2	-7

(b)

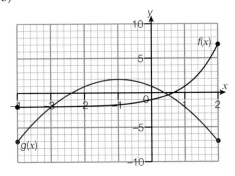

(c) $-3.0, 0.5$

4. (a)

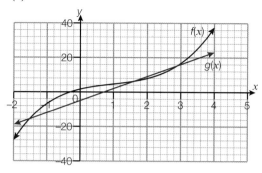

(b) 3   (c) −1.5, 1.7, 2.8

5. (a) (i) 3   (ii) −1.03, −0.207, 1.01
    (b) (i) 1   (ii) 1.71
    (c) (i) 1   (ii) 0.330
    (d) (i) 2   (ii) 0.847, 3.47
    (e) (i) 3   (ii) −1.73, −1.29, 1.64
    (f) (i) 3   (ii) −1.79, 1.54, 2

6. (a) −1.37, 4.37   (b) −2.93, −0.363, 0.627
    (c) −3.25, −1.62, 0.878   (d) −2.24, 2.24
    (e) 1.17, 2.29   (f) −2.96, −0.633
    (g) −4.06, −1.12, 2.18

7. (a) $t = 81.3$ (b) $x = 0$
    (c) $t = 0.928$ (d) $x = -0.0692$
    (e) $x = -3.06, 0.969$ (f) $x = -2.29, -0.671$
    (g) $x = -2.71, -1.06$ (h) $x = 1.45$

Mixed examination practice 17

Exam-style questions 17

1. (a) −13   (b) 8
    (c) (i) $7a - 13$
        (ii) $7a - 27$

2. (a) $x \geq -3$ (b) $y \leq 13$ (c) −3, 0.25, 2

3. (a)

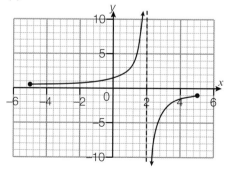

    (i) $x = 2$ (ii) $y = 0$

(b)

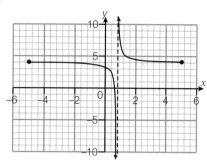

    (i) $x = \frac{7}{9}$ (ii) $y = 4$

4.

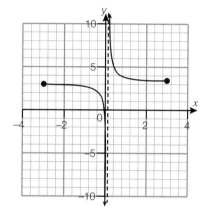

5. (a)

x	−3	−2	−1	0	1	2	3
$f(x)$	40	17	6	1	−4	−15	−38
$g(x)$	13	11	9	7	5	3	1

(b)

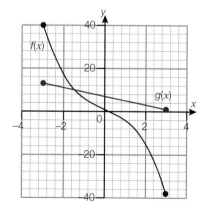

(c) −1.5

6. (a)

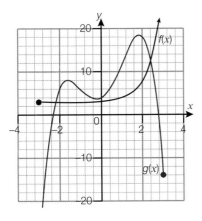

(b) 2   (c) -2.2, 2.4

Chapter 18

Exercise 18.1

1. (a) $D = 50 + 0.15m$
(b) 400
(c) Safe Ride: it costs less (has a lower graph) for $m > 400$

2. (a) $C(n) = 6.50 + 0.035n$
(b) £52
(c) 1840 units

3. (a) $C(n) = 5.18 + 0.13n$
(b) £70.18
(c) 650 units

4. (a) 60 visits
(b) (i) Gym Buddies
    (ii) Fit Mates
(c) (i) At least £24
    (ii) At least £30

5. (a) (i) 150   (ii) 120   (iii) 100
(b) £180
(c) £200
(d) £160

Exercise 18.2A

1. (a) (i) $(-1.5, -2.25)$
    (ii) $x = -1.5$
    (iii) $f(x) \geq -2.25$

(b) (i) $(3.5, -10.25)$
    (ii) $x = 3.5$
    (iii) $f(x) \geq -10.25$
(c) (i) $(0.25, -5.875)$
    (ii) $x = 0.25$
    (iii) $f(x) \leq -5.875$
(d) (i) $(0.667, 7.67)$
    (ii) $x = 0.667$
    (iii) $g(x) \geq 7.67$
(e) (i) $(-1, -16)$
    (ii) $x = -1$
    (iii) $g(x) \geq -16$
(f) (i) $(0.5, -1.25)$
    (ii) $x = 0.5$
    (iii) $g(x) \geq -1.25$
(g) (i) $(0.75, 2.22)$
    (ii) $x = 0.75$
    (iii) $h(x) \geq 2.22$
(h) (i) $(3.5, 13.9)$
    (ii) $x = 3.5$
    (iii) $f(x) \leq 13.9$

2. (a) $(0, 1.44)$
    (i) Max 1.44   (ii) $x = 0$ (iii) $f(x) \leq 1.44$
(b) $(2.5, 10)$
    (i) Max 10   (ii) $x = 2.5$ (iii) $g(x) \leq 10$
(c) $(-1.7, 8)$
    (i) Min 8   (ii) $x = -1.7$ (iii) $h(x) \geq 8$

Exercise 18.2B

1. $(-1.83, 0)$ and $(3.83, 0)$

2. (a) (i) $f(x)$ (ii) $g(x)$ (iii) $h(x)$

(b) $f(x)$: $(0, -5)$; $g(x)$: $(0, 5)$; $h(x)$: $(0, \frac{25}{4})$

3. (a) (i) $(-2, 0)$ and $(2, 0)$ (ii) $(0, -12)$
(b) (i) $(-1.33, 0)$ and $(1.33, 0)$ (ii) $(0, 16)$
(c) (i) $(-1.27, 0)$ and $(6.27, 0)$ (ii) $(0, 8)$
(d) (i) $(-2, 0)$ and $(1.33, 0)$ (ii) $(0, 8)$
(e) (i) $(-2.92, 0)$ and $(3.42, 0)$ (ii) $(0, -20)$
(f) (i) $(1.64, 0)$ and $(3.36, 0)$ (ii) $(0, -23.6)$

4. (a) $(0, 0)$ and $(5, 0)$
(b) $x = 2.5$
(c) $-8.4 \leq f(x) \leq 8.75$

5. (a) P$(-6.82, 0)$, Q$(-2.75, 33.1)$, R$(0, 18)$, S$(1.32, 0)$
(b) $f(x) \leq 33.1$
(c) $x = -2.75$

Exercise 18.3

1. (a) 20.4 m (b) 21.8 m (c) 4.08 s

2. 43.8, 82.7, 132.6, 193.7, 265.9, 349.1

3. (a)

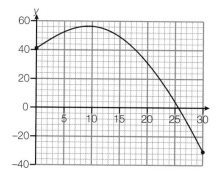

(b) €9 million
(c) €53.8 million

4. (a) 12 m (b) 2 s
   (c) 12.25 m (d) 4.12 s

5. (a) (i) 15.3 m (ii) 35.3 m
   (b) (i) 13.7 m (ii) 15.0 m
   (c) 10.8 m

Mixed examination practice 18

Exam-style questions 18

1. (a) (i) $(0.9, -4.05)$ (ii) $x = 0.9$ (iii) $y \geq -4.05$
   (b) (i) $(0, 7)$ (ii) $x = 0$ (iii) $y \leq 7$
   (c) (i) $(1.5, -30.25)$ (ii) $x = 1.5$ (iii) $y \geq -30.25$

2. (a) Max $(-0.333, 11.7)$
   (b) $x = -0.333$
   (c) $f(x) \leq 11.7$

3. (a) $a = 140, b = 98$ (b) \$630 (c) 7 hours

4. (a) $135 - x$ (c) 45 m by 90 m

5. (a) 34.2 m (b) 240 m (c) 40 m or 200 m

6. (a) (i) £11.60 (ii) £29.00
   (b) Saif: £10.35; Jeevan: £29.20
   (c) (i) MATHSMANAGER
       (ii) At least £3.20

Past paper questions 18

1. (a) 25 (b) 13.7
   (c) 0.535 (d) 54.0

Chapter 19

Exercise 19.1

1. (a) $y = 0$ (b) $y = 0$ (c) $y = 5$
   (d) $y = -4$ (e) $y = -4$

2. (a) $(0, 1); 0.008 \leq g(x) \leq 15625$
   (b) $(0, 1); 4.096 \times 10^{-9} \leq g(x) \leq 2.44 \times 10^{8}$
   (c) $(0, 25); 0.0016 \leq g(x) \leq 7.63 \times 10^{11}$
   (d) $(0, 78125); 0.008 \leq g(x) \leq 78125$
   (e) $(0, 0.0016); 0.0016 \leq g(x) \leq 3125$

3. (a) (i) $y = 0$ (ii) $(0, 1)$
       (iii) $0 < f(x) \leq 16$
   (b) (i) $y = 0$ (ii) $(0, 1)$
       (iii) $0 < f(x) \leq 64$
   (c) (i) $y = 0$ (ii) $(0, 1)$
       (iii) $0 < f(x) \leq 256$
   (d) (i) $y = 0$ (ii) $(0, 1)$
       (iii) $0 < f(x) \leq 8$
   (e) (i) $y = 5$ (ii) $(0, 6)$
       (iii) $5 < f(x) \leq 7781$
   (f) (i) $y = -4$ (ii) $(0, -3)$
       (iii) $-4 < f(x) \leq -3$
   (g) (i) $y = 0$ (ii) $(0, 2)$
       (iii) $0 < f(x) \leq 31250$
   (h) (i) $y = 0$ (ii) $(0, 4)$
       (iii) $0 < f(x) \leq 3.91 \times 10^{7}$

4. (a) (i) 1 (ii) 125
       (iii) 0.2 (iv) 2.24
   (b) (i) 1 (ii) 15625
       (iii) 0.04 (iv) 5
   (c) (i) 125 (ii) 1.95×10^{6}
       (iii) 5 (iv) 625
   (d) (i) 1.28×10^{-5} (ii) 0.2
       (iii) 5.12×10^{-7} (iv) 6.4×10^{-5}
   (e) (i) 1.608 (ii) 201
       (iii) 0.3216 (iv) 3.60
   (f) (i) 32640 (ii) 3.264×10^{10}
       (iii) 326.4 (iv) 3.264×10^{5}
   (g) (i) 5.27×10^{-8} (ii) 52.7
       (iii) 5.27×10^{-11} (iv) 1.67×10^{-6}
   (h) (i) 1 (ii) 83.8
       (iii) 0.229 (iv) 2.09
   (i) (i) 34 (ii) 693
       (iii) 12.4 (iv) 56.2
   (j) (i) 0.0238 (ii) 134
       (iii) 0.00134 (iv) 0.100

Exercise 19.2

1. (a) (i) 52 996   (ii) 60 876   (iii) 63 965
   (b) (i) 11.3 years   (ii) 37.1 years
   (c) (i) 35.0 years   (ii) 55.5 years

2. (a) (i) 6.87 million (ii) 8.21 million
   (b) 2031
   (c) 2007

3. (a) 200 mg
   (b) (i) 117 mg   (ii) 68.7 mg
   (c) 12.1 hours

4. (a) 420   (b) 488
   (c) 2540   (d) 6250
   (e) 23.1 hours   (f) 29.3 hours

5. (a) (i) 95.3°C   (ii) 88.7°C   (iii) 75.0°C
   (b) 93.0 minutes
   (c) 382 minutes

Exercise 19.3

1. (a) (i) (0, 6)   (ii) (−3, 0), (1, 0), (2, 0)
   (b) (i) (0, 3)   (ii) (−3, 0), (1, 0)
   (c) (i) (0, 8)   (ii) (−4, 0), (−2, 0), (1, 0)
   (d) (i) (0, 6)   (ii) (−3, 0), (−1, 0), (0.4 , 0)
   (e) (i) (0, −4)   (ii) (−2, 0), (1, 0)
   (f) (i) (0, 0)   (ii) (−6, 0), (0, 0), (1, 0)
   (g) (i) (0, 6)   (ii) (−3, 0), (0.5, 0), (2, 0)
   (h) (i) (0, −8)   (ii) (−2.67, 0), (2.67, 0)
   (i) (i) (0, 4)   (ii) (−4, 0), (−1, 0), (0.5, 0), (1, 0)
   (j) (i) (0, −9)   (ii) (−3, 0), (−1, 0), (3, 0)

2. (a) (i) (0, −12); (−3, 0), (4, 0)
       (ii) $-12.25 \leq f(x) \leq 8$
   (b) (i) (0, 1); (−0.140, 0), (7.14, 0)
       (ii) $-7 \leq f(x) \leq 13.25$
   (c) (i) (0, 0); (−2, 0), (0, 0), (4, 0)
       (ii) $-96 \leq f(x) \leq 64$
   (d) (i) (0, 6); (−2, 0), (1, 0), (3, 0)
       (ii) $-4.06 \leq f(x) \leq 18$
   (e) (i) (0, 3); (−0.538, 0), (2.33, 0)
       (ii) $-24 \leq g(x) \leq 3.39$
   (f) (i) (0, 4); (−3.06, 0)
       (ii) $-24 \leq g(x) \leq 226$

(g) (i) (0, 10); (−1.19, 0), (1.20, 0)
    (ii) $-19.3 \leq f(x) \leq 10.0$
(h) (i) (0, 6)   (ii) $5.75 \leq f(x) \leq 20$

Exercise 19.4

1. (a) (i) 1.4115   (ii) 1.4535   (iii) 1.4262
   (b) 1.46

2. (a)

Decade		1970	1990	2010
Population (billions)	Actual	3.706618	5.278640	6.848933
	Estimated from model	3.702066	5.272624	6.854624
Percentage error		0.123%	0.114%	0.0831%

   (b) (i) 7.58 billion   (ii) 8.25 billion
       (iii) 8.85 billion

3. (a)

Year	2000	2002	2004	2006
Price of silver on 1 January	$15.78	$4.68	$9.09	$18.57

   (b) US$15.34 per ounce   (c) 0.11%

4. (a)

Year	2002	2004	2006	2008	2010	2012
Price of gold on 1 January	$278	$293.24	$387.29	538.58	$768.80	$1116.07

   (b) US$925.52 per ounce   (c) 8.43%

Mixed examination practice 19

Exam-style questions 19

1. (a) (0, −4)
   (b) (−1.22, 0), (−0.47, 0), (1.15, 0), (3.04, 0)
   (c) $-128 \leq g(x) \leq 16.6$

2. (a) (0, 1)   (b) $y = 0$ (c) $f(x) > 0$

3. (a) $A = 3$ (b) $y = 5$

4. (a) (i) 47.3°C   (ii) 37.8°C
       (iii) 25.7°C   (iv) 24.6°C
   (b) (i) 0.112 h (6.73 min)
       (ii) 0.982 h (58.9 min)
       (iii) 1.50 h

5.

Year	2000	2002	2004	2006	2008	2010
Debt (% of GDP)	30.8	28.1	31.4	34.5	37.8	48.1

6. $C_0 = 8$ mg/ml and $k = -0.0851$

7. (a) (i) 28 040 MW
    (ii) 46 680 MW
    (iii) 47 340 MW
    (iv) 40 090 MW
  (b) (i) 8.58 a.m. and 9.37 p.m.
    (ii) 10.32 a.m. and 8 p.m

Past paper questions 19

1. (a)

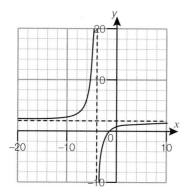

  (b) $x = -4$
  (c)

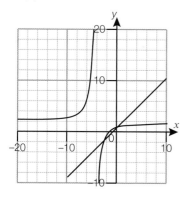

  (d) $(-2.85078, -2.35078)$ or
    $(0.35078, 0.85078)$
  (e) 1
  (f) $y = -x - 5$

2. (a) 1800
  (b) 145 800
  (c) 33.5 hours

3. (a) 90°C   (b) $y = 16$
  (c) 16°C   (d) 25.4°C
  (e) 42.8°C
  (f) 1.55 minutes or 93 seconds

Chapter 20

Learning links 20A

1. 15.25, 13.89, 12.61, 12.0601,
  12.006001, 12.00060001
  (a) 12   (b) 12

2. (a)

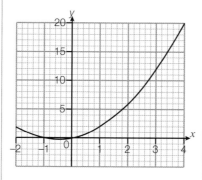

  (b) 7.2, 7.1, 7.01, 7.001, 7.0001
  (c) 7   (d) 7

Exercise 20.1

1. (a) $5x^4$ (b) $18x^2$
  (c) $-28x^3$ (d) $8x^5$
  (e) $2x - 4$ (f) $72x^8 - 30x$
  (g) $19 + 22x$ (h) $6x + 5 - 21x^2$

2. (a) $1 - 7x^6$
  (b) $40x - 9x^8$
  (c) $33x^2 - 18x - 7$
  (d) $30x^4 - 3x^2 - 13$
  (e) $10 - 18x - 4x^3$
  (f) $32x^3 - 15x^2 + 4x + 7$
  (g) $x + 3x^2 - \frac{10}{3}x^4$
  (h) $0.9x^2 + 0.24x - 1$

Exercise 20.2

1. (a) $-\frac{5}{7x^2}$
  (b) $10x^4 + 2x^{-3}$
  (c) $3x^2 + \frac{9}{4x^3}$
  (d) $1 + \frac{3}{2x^3}$
  (e) $-15x^{-6} - 22x$

2. (a) $8x^7 - 5x^{-6}$
  (b) $32x^3 - 6x^2 - 4x^{-5} + 13$
  (c) $-\frac{3}{x^4} - 10$
  (d) $-\frac{35}{x^8} + 4$
  (e) $9 + \frac{3}{5x^2}$

3. (a) $1 - 9x^2 + 25x^4 - 49x^6$
  (b) $8x^{-3}$
  (c) $10 - 27x^{-4} - 2x^{-2}$
  (d) $\frac{6}{7}x - \frac{10}{x^3}$
  (e) $-\frac{3}{x^4} + \frac{20}{x^6}$

4. (a) $6x^2 - 14x - 4$
  (b) (i) -12
    (ii) 48
    (iii) -4
  (c) 16; gradient of the $f(x)$
    curve at the point
    where $x = -1$

5. (a) $8 - 6x^2$
  (b) (i) 8
    (ii) -16
    (iii) -46

Exercise 20.3

1. (a) $10\,\text{m s}^{-1}$
  (b) $25\,\text{m s}^{-1}$
  (c) $13\,\text{m s}^{-1}$; velocity of the
    particle at $t = 3$

2. (a) $14 - 20t$
  (b) (i) 4   (ii) 0

3. (a) $6\pi = 18.8$
  (b) $10\pi = 31.4$

Exercise 20.4

1. (a) 1500   (b) −36   (c) −13
   (d) 18   (e) −4   (f) −42
   (g) 10   (h) −0.5   (i) −32
   (j) −10   (k) 3.20   (l) −1

2. (a) (i) $16q$ (ii) 160
   (b) (i) $10q$ (ii) 1200
   (c) (i) $5 + 6q$ (ii) 485
   (d) (i) $6q - 10$ (ii) 74
   (e) (i) $6q^2 - 18q + 45$ (ii) 236445

3. (a) $2x - 4$ (b) 2   (c) 6

4. (a) $3x^2 - 8x$
   (b) 28
   (c) (0.667, 6.52) and (2, 0)

5. (a) $2 - \frac{1}{x^2}$
   (b) 1
   (c) (−0.333, −3.67) and (0.333, 3.67)

6. (a) \$115   (b) 45
7. (a) $28 - 20t$ (b) −20

Exercise 20.5

1. (a) $y = 24x - 58$ (b) $y = 6x + 13$
   (c) $y = 4x + 12$ (d) $y = 0.25x + 0.25$
   (e) $y = 17x - 7$ (f) $y = -0.25x + 1$
   (g) $y = 0.75x + 5.75$ (h) $y = -3.56x + 6.96$

2. (a) $y = -7x - 21$ (b) $y = 13x - 56$
   (c) $y = 42.5x + 0.25$ (d) $y = -12x + 29$
   (e) $y = -49x + 36$ (f) $y = 5$

3. (a) $6x^2 - 2x + 4$ (b) 24
   (c) 21   (d) $y = 24x - 27$

4. (a) $-\frac{x}{8}$ (b) $\frac{1}{8} = 0.125$
   (c) $\frac{143}{16} = 8.94$ (d) $2x - 16y + 145 = 0$

Exercise 20.6

1. (a) $y = -0.0417x + 38.2$
   (b) $y = -0.167x - 5.5$
   (c) $y = -0.25x + 7.75$
   (d) $y = -4x + 2.375$
   (e) $y = -0.0588x + 10.1$
   (f) $y = 4x + 9.5$
   (g) $y = -1.33x + 9.92$
   (h) $y = 0.281x + 1.21$

2. (a) $y = 0.143x + 0.429$
   (b) $y = -0.0769x - 29.8$
   (c) $y = -0.0235x - 21.0$
   (d) $y = 0.0833x - 7.25$
   (e) $y = 0.0204x + 11.5$
   (f) $x = -1$

3. $y = -\frac{1}{3}x - \frac{4}{3}$ or $y = -0.333x - 1.33$

4. $y = -0.125x + 13.5$

Mixed examination practice 20

Exam-style questions 20

1. $4x^3 - 21x^2 - 9$

2. (a) $2x - 8$ (b) −2
   (c) 7

3. (a) $\frac{dC_T}{dq} = 120 - 2q - 0.015q^2$
   (b) 16

4. (a) $-2\,\text{m s}^{-1}$ (b) $-5\,\text{m s}^{-1}$
   (c) $-6\,\text{m s}^{-1}$; velocity of the particle at $t = 3.5$

5. (a) (i) $6t^2 - 8t + 4$
   (ii) $12t - 8$
   (b) (i) $12\,\text{m s}^{-1}$
   (ii) $68\,\text{m s}^{-1}$
   (c) (i) $4\,\text{m s}^{-2}$
   (ii) $40\,\text{m s}^{-2}$
   (d) $\frac{2}{3}$ s

6. (a) −2; the y-coordinate of the point on the curve where $x = 1$
   (b) 9; the gradient of the curve at the point where $x = 1$
   (c) $y = 9x - 11$

7. (a) −6   (b) $\frac{1}{6}$
   (c) 1   (d) $y = -6x + 7$
   (e) $y = \frac{1}{6}x + \frac{5}{6}$

8. (a) $3x^3 - 5x^2$ (b) $9x^2 - 10x$
   (c) (i) 56   (ii) $-\frac{1}{56}$
   (d) (i) $y = 56x + 68$
   (ii) $y = -\frac{1}{56}x - \frac{1233}{28} = -0.0179x - 44.0$

1. (a) (i) $f_1'(x) = 1$
       (ii) $f_2'(x) = -2x$

    (b) $x = -\frac{1}{2}$

    (c)

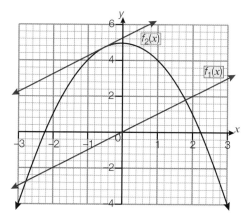

2. (a) $6x^2 - 10x + 3$
    (b) 7
    (c) $y = 7x - 11$

3. (a) 2
    (b) $f'(x) = 2x - 3$
    (c) $(2.5, -5.25)$
    (d) $(1.25, -6.1875)$
    (e) (i) 1   (ii) $y = x - 8$
    (f) $x = 1.5$
    (g) $(1.5, -6.25)$; gradient 0

Chapter 21

Exercise 21.1

1. Increasing for $0 < x < 2$;
    decreasing for $x < 0$ and $x > 2$

2. (a) $x < -1.94$ and $x > 0.943$
    (b) $-1.94 < x < 0.943$

3. (a) (i) $x > 4$
       (ii) $x < 4$
    (b) (i) $x > -2.25$
       (ii) $x < -2.25$
    (c) (i) $x > 0.500$
       (ii) $x < 0.500$
    (d) (i) $x \in \mathbb{R}$
       (ii) None

    (e) (i) $x < -2$ and $x > 2$
       (ii) $-2 < x < 2$
    (f) (i) $x < -1$ and $x > 2$
       (ii) $-1 < x < 2$
    (g) (i) $x < 0$ and $x > 6$
       (ii) $0 < x < 6$
    (h) (i) $x < -2.56$ and $x > 1.56$
       (ii) $-2.56 < x < 1.56$

4. $x < 0.268$ and $x > 3.73$

5. (a) $9 + 6x - 3x^2$
    (b) -15
    (c) Decreasing

6. (a) $x^2 - 2x - 3$
    (b) (i) 21
       (ii) -4
    (c) (i) Increasing
       (ii) Decreasing

Exercise 21.2

1. (a) Min $(-2, -4)$
    (b) Max $(4, 16)$
    (c) Min $(3, -4)$
    (d) Max $(1.5, 6.25)$
    (e) Max $(-0.333, 0.185)$;
       min $(1, -1)$
    (f) Max $(-1, 1)$; min $(1, -3)$
    (g) Min $(-1, 2)$; max $(1, 6)$
    (h) Max $(-0.5, 6)$; min $(0.5, 4)$
    (i) Max $(0.667, 4.19)$;
       min $(2, 3)$
    (j) Max $(-1, 3)$; min $(1, -5)$

2. Stationary points and classification as in 1.
    Gradient functions:
    (a) $2x + 4$ (b) $8 - 2x$
    (c) $2x - 6$ (d) $3 - 2x$
    (e) $3x^2 - 2x - 1$ (f) $3x^2 - 3$
    (g) $3 - 3x^2$ (h) $12x^2 - 3$
    (i) $3x^2 - 8x + 4$ (j) $5x^4 - 5$

3. (a) $\frac{dy}{dx} = 3x^2 - 6x - 8$

    (b) P$(-0.915, -6.96)$ and Q$(2.92, -35.0)$
    (c) P - point ; Q - min point

4. (b) R: max; S: min

5. (a) $3x^2 - 4$ (b) ± 1.15
    (c), (d) Max $(-1.15, 3.08)$;
           min $(1.15, -3.08)$

6. Max $(0, 0)$; min $(4, -32)$
7. Max $(-1, 2)$; min $(1, -2)$

Exercise 21.3

1. Length = width =

   $\frac{40}{3} = 13\frac{1}{3} = 13.3$ cm;

   height = $\frac{10}{3} = 3\frac{1}{3} = 3.33$ cm

2. $6 \times 7 = 42$
3. 6 cm by 6 cm
4. 3 cm by 6 cm

Exercise 21.4

1. (a) $120 - 8q$ (b) 15
   (c) £925,000

2. (a) 80
   (b) $\frac{dC}{dn}$ is negative to the left
       of $n = 80$ and positive
       to the right of $n = 80$; or
       $\frac{d^2C}{dn^2} > 0$ at $n = 80$; or the
       graph is a parabola that
       opens upward and so has a
       unique minimum point.

3. (b) $12x^2 - 160x + 400$
   (c) $\frac{10}{3} = 3.33$ cm
   (d) Length = width =
       $\frac{40}{3} = 13.3$ cm;
       height = $\frac{10}{3} = 3.33$ cm;
       volume = 593 cm³

4. (c) $2808 - \frac{27}{8}x^2$
   (d) 28.84
   (e) Length = 86.5 cm;
       width = 28.8 cm;
       height = 21.6 cm
   (f) 53 997 cm³

5. (a) $320 - 8n$
   (b) 40; $\frac{dR}{dn}$ is positive to the
       left of $n = 40$ and negative
       to the right of $n = 40$; or
       $\frac{d^2R}{dn^2} > 0$ at $n = 40$; or the
       graph is a parabola that
       opens downward and so
       has a unique maximum
       point.
   (c) $6,400,000

6. (c) $120\pi r - 6\pi^2 r^2$
   (d) 6.37   (e) 2546 cm³

Mixed examination practice 21

Exam-style questions 21

1. (a) $x < 0.268, x > 3.73$
   (b) $0.268 < x < 3.73$

2. (a) $21x^2 - 12$
   (b) 324
   (c) Increasing

3. (a) $12x - 12x^2$
   (c) Min (0, 3); max (1, 5)

4. (a) $6x^2 - 18x - 24$
   (b) −1 and 4
   (c), (d) Max (−1, 16);
            min (4, −109)

5. R(0, 5) and S(4, 37)

6. 5000 m²; 50 m × 100 m

7. $r = 3.74, h = 7.49$

8. 200 m × 200 m = 40 000 m²

9. Length = width = height
   = 20 cm; area = 2400 cm²

10. Length = width = 25.2 cm;
    height = 12.6 cm;
    area = 1900 cm²

Past paper questions 21

1. (a) $f'(x) = 2ax - 4x^{-2} = 2ax - \frac{4}{x^2}$
   (b) −2

2. (a) 5.30
   (b) $-0.042x + 1.245$
   (c) (i) 24.3 m   (ii) 12.4 m
   (d)

   (e) 10.1 m

3. (b) $1 - \frac{324}{x^2}$ (c) 18
   (d) 36   (e) $a = 36, b = 39$
   (f)

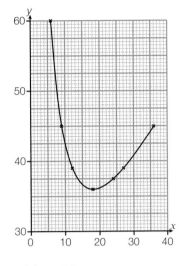

   (g) $x > 18$

4. (b) $y = \frac{300 - 4x^2}{6x} = \frac{150 - 2x^2}{3x}$
   (d) $100 - 4x^2$
   (e) (i) $x = 5, y = \frac{20}{3}$
       (ii) $333\frac{1}{3}$ cm³

5. (a) $y = 2$
   (b) Less than
   (c) P is a local minimum

Glossary

A

acceleration the rate of change of velocity in relation to time

algebra a method of generalising problems in arithmetic

algorithm a systematic step-by-step process (a set of instructions) leading to a result

angle of depression angle between the horizontal and a lower line-of-sight line

angle of elevation angle between the horizontal and a higher line-of-sight line

arithmetic progression/sequence a list of numbers where the difference between consecutive numbers is constant

arithmetic series the sum of terms in an arithmetic sequence

asymptote a line approached by a curve but never reached

axis (pl. axes) a line which is used as a reference, e.g. on a graph

B

bar chart diagram in which information is arranged into vertical or horizontal blocks

bias influence within a sample of data that favours a particular member(s) of a population

biased sample a sample which is limited to a particular, possibly unrepresentative group

BIDMAS the order of operations in working out an arithmetical expression (Brackets, Indices, Division, Multiplication, Addition, Subtraction)

bivariate data data showing the relationship between two variables

boundary used in a grouped frequency table, to describe the top or bottom values of one class

box and whisker diagram statistical diagram to display a five-figure summary

break-even point the point at which the cost of production and income are the same

C

chi-squared statistic (χ^2) used in a two-way table to test observed values against expected values

chord a straight line which joins two points on a curve

coefficient a number which is used to multiply a variable

commission amount (usually a percentage) charged by a financial institution for handling money

common difference the fixed difference between consecutive terms in an arithmetic sequence

common ratio the fixed multiplier from each term to the next in a geometric sequence

complement of a set element(s) which are not included in the set

compound interest a system in which interest is recalculated at regular intervals to include previous interest accumulated

compound statement a logical statement containing two or more propositions

conditional probability probability based on the assumption that an event has already occurred

cone a solid with one vertex and a circular base

conjunction a compound statement where two propositions are connected by 'and'

connective a symbol that links two propositions

constant a quantity with a fixed value

continuous data data that can be measured

contradiction a compound statement that is always logically false

contrapositive a new statement that combines the converse and inverse of an original logical statement

converse the reversal of two propositions in a logical statement

coordinates pairs of numbers which are used to uniquely locate a point on a graph

correlation the degree of association between two variables (can be positive or negative)

cosine a trigonometric ratio (usually abbreviated to 'cos'); $\frac{\text{adjacent}}{\text{hypotenuse}}$

covariance a measure of the connection between two variables

cube a solid in which the six faces are all squares

cuboid a solid in which the six faces are all rectangles

cumulative frequency the total frequency up to a certain data value

cylinder a solid prism with straight, parallel sides and a circular base

D

decimal places (d.p.) the number of digits after the decimal point

decreasing function the section of the function where the gradient is always negative

deflation a progressive decrease in consumer prices

degrees of freedom in the chi-squared test, the number of pieces of independent data

denominator the bottom part of a fraction

depreciation a decrease in value due to age or other factors

derived unit a unit defined in terms of another unit

difference the result of subtracting a smaller number from a larger number

differentiation the process of finding the gradient function for any given function

discrete data data that can be counted

disjunction a compound statement where two propositions are connected by 'or'

dispersion the spread in a set of values

displacement the amount of movement of an object measured in a particular direction

domain the set of inputs into a function

E

empty (null) set a set containing no elements

equilateral triangle a triangle in which all sides are the same length

equivalence a compound statement where two propositions are connected by 'if and only if'. Do not confuse this with **logical equivalence**

estimate to make a preliminary approximation

event in probability, an individual outcome or combination of outcomes being investigated, such as a particular result of rolling a die or choosing an object from a bag

exchange rate the relationship between the values of two different currencies

exclusive disjunction a compound statement where two propositions are connected by 'or ... , but not both'

exponent small number to the upper right of a number/letter (also called index or power)

exponential function a function of the form $y = ka^n$

exponential growth growth in the form $y = a^n$

F

factorise to resolve an expression into a product of two or more factors, e.g. $12 = 2 \times 6$; $15x + 12y = 3(5x + 4y)$

frequency table a table that records the number of occurrences of an item or group of data

function the one-to-one, or many-to-one, relationship between two variables

future value a quantity used in financial calculations: the value of an investment after a certain number of years

G

general form the most commonly written form of a formula

geometric sequence a sequence created by multiplying by the same value each time

geometric series the sum of terms in a geometric sequence

gradient the measure of the steepness of a slope

grouped data statistical data that has been put into groups, not listed individually

H

hemisphere half of a sphere

histogram a diagram with the appearance of a bar chart in which the area of each bar (not the height) represents the frequency of the group of data

hypotenuse the side opposite the right angle in a right-angled triangle

I

implication where two logical statements are connected by the words 'if ... then'

improper fraction a fraction in which the numerator is greater than the denominator

included angle angle between two given sides

increasing function the section of the function where the gradient is always positive

index (indices) small number to the upper right of a number/letter

infinity the concept of having no end

inflation a general increase in prices, and the corresponding decrease in purchasing power, over time

integer a whole number, which may be positive, negative, or zero

intercept point at which a line or curve crosses an axis; may be specifically referred to as x-intercept or y-intercept

interest rate percentage charged by a financial institution on a borrowed sum

interquartile range the value obtained by subtracting the lower quartile from the upper quartile

intersection (geometry) the point where two lines cross

intersection (set theory) the overlap of two or more sets

interval the space between two numbers or between two boundaries

inverse an opposite operation, e.g. adding and subtracting are inverse operations

irrational number a real number that cannot be written as a fraction, e.g. π, $\sqrt{2}$

isosceles triangle a triangle with two sides of equal length

K

kelvin the SI unit of temperature; $0°C = 273.16\,K$

L

limit a value that is approached but not reached

line of best fit a line on a graph which shows a general trend

line of symmetry a line that cuts a figure into two parts that are mirror images of each other

line segment a line which has fixed end points

linear equation an equation with two variables which gives a straight line when plotted on a graph

logical equivalence is when two compound statements mean the same thing; the compound statements will have exactly the same final column in their truth tables. (Also known as 'logically equivalent'.) Do not confuse this with **equivalence**

lump sum in finance, money paid in a single payment, not in instalments

M

mapping a relationship between two sets of numbers

maximum (pl. maxima) a stationary point where the gradient changes from positive to zero to negative

mean the sum of data values divided by the number of data values, usually denoted by the Greek letter μ (population) or $\bar{x}$ (sample)

measure of central tendency the mean, the median or the mode

median the middle number of a set of ordered data values

midpoint the halfway mark between two points

minimum (pl. minima) a stationary point where the gradient changes from negative to zero to positive

mode (modal) the most frequently occurring value (group) in a set of statistical data

mutually exclusive describes events that cannot happen at the same time

N

natural number a number from the set of counting numbers: a whole number that is greater than or equal to zero

negation a statement of denial or contradiction, the assertion that a particular proposition is false

normal a line at right angles to the tangent of a curve

null hypothesis a statement asserting that there is no relationship between two variables

number line a line drawn to illustrate the order of real numbers

numerator the top part of a fraction

O

ogive a distribution curve where the frequencies are cumulative

optimisation using calculus to find the best solution to a problem

outcome the result(s) of a probability experiment, such as obtaining a tail from one throw of a coin

outlier a value that lies a long way outside the general range of data

P

parabola a $\cup$ or $\cap$-shaped curve demonstrating a quadratic equation

per annum for each year, e.g. 5% interest per annum

percentage error the difference between an estimated value and the exact value, calculated as a percentage relative to the exact value

perimeter the length of the outline of a closed figure

perpendicular at right angles to a line or plane

pie chart diagram in which data is arranged as sectors of a circle, the angles of the sectors representing the frequency of the data

polynomial a sum of two or more terms in the form $y = a + bx + cx^2 + \ldots$

population the whole group that is being studied

power small number to the upper right of a number/letter (also called exponent or index)

prime number a number that has exactly two different factors, itself and 1

prism a solid whose cross-sections parallel to an end are all identical

probability the chance that an event will occur

proportion the relationship between two or more numbers, or between the parts of a whole

proposition a basic statement in logic; it can be true, false or indeterminate

present value a quantity used in financial calculations: the initial amount of an investment

***p*-value** a measure of evidence against the null hypothesis

pyramid a solid with a polygonal base and an apex above the base. This is only correct for a right pyramid

Pythagoras' theorem the theorem for a right-angled triangle that links the length of the hypotenuse with the lengths of the other two sides

Pythagorean triples sets of three numbers that fit Pythagoras' theorem, e.g. 5, 12, 13

Q

quadratic equation an equation in which the highest exponent of the variable is 2, i.e. it contains a square term: $ax^2 + bx + c = 0$

qualitative data data that is neither counted nor measured

quantitative data data that is counted or measured

quartile the values that divide a set of data into four equal parts

quotient The 'whole-number' part of the result of dividing one number (or expression) by another

R

radius the distance from the centre of a circle to the circumference

random sample a sample of subjects that is randomly selected from a group

range (function) the set of output values of a function

range (statistics) the difference between the highest and lowest values of a set of data

ratio the relationship between two different numbers or quantities, e.g. 5 : 6

rational number a number that may be expressed as a fraction, e.g. $\frac{a}{b}$

real number any number that can be placed on the number line

regression line used to analyse information on a scatter diagram

representative sample a statistical sample that fairly represents all the data collected

right cone/prism/pyramid a figure where the apex is directly above the centre of its base

right-angled triangle a triangle with one right angle (90°)

root of an equation the solution to a polynomial equation of any degree

rounding the approximation of a number to a given degree of accuracy

S

sample a subset of a larger group

sample space the complete set of possible outcomes from an experiment

sample space diagram a diagram listing every result of a probability experiment

scatter diagram a graph which uses paired data to analyse the correlation between two variables

scientific notation writing very large or very small numbers in standard form

sequence an ordered list of numbers (that follow a 'rule')

series sum of a sequence

set a group of numbers or objects with a common characteristic

SI unit the international system of units; there are seven base units of measurement

significant figures (s.f.) the number of digits used to specify how precisely a value is expressed

simple interest a system where interest calculations are based only the original amount deposited or borrowed

simultaneous equations a set of equations for which a common solution is sought

sine a trigonometric ratio (usually abbreviated to 'sin'); $\frac{\text{opposite}}{\text{hypotenuse}}$

skewed slanted to one side

slant height distance from the apex of a cone or pyramid to a point on the perimeter of its base

solid three-dimensional figure

solution the answer to a problem; a value which, when substituted for the variable, makes the equation true

sphere solid on which all points on the surface are equidistant from the centre (a ball)

standard deviation the measure of the amount by which a set of values differs from the arithmetical mean

standard form a method of writing very large or very small numbers in a compact form, e.g. $25\,000\,000$ in standard form is 2.5×10^7 (also called scientific notation)

statement a proposition in logic

stationary point a point on a curve where the gradient of the curve is zero

subset a set contained within a larger set

T

tangent (graph) a line which touches (but does not cross) a curve

tangent (trigonometry) a trigonometric ratio (usually abbreviated to 'tan'); $\frac{\text{opposite}}{\text{adjacent}}$

tautology a compound statement that is always true

term a number in a sequence, or an element of an algebraic expression that is separated from other elements by a $+$ or $-$ sign

tree diagram a branched diagram used to illustrate probabilities

trend line a line on a graph which shows a general trend

trial and improvement improving accuracy through repeated calculations

trigonometric ratio the ratio of two sides in any right-angled triangle

trigonometry In triangles, the study of angles and lines and their relationships

truth table a table for the study of logic that lists all possible combinations of True and False

turning point a point where a curve changes direction

U

union contains all elements of two or more sets without repeats

universal set the set that includes all the elements that are under consideration

unknown a value represented by a letter

V

variable a quantity that can change

variance the square of the standard deviation

velocity the rate of change of the displacement (distance) of an object as it moves in a particular direction

Venn diagram a diagram that uses circles to demonstrate the relationships between sets

Index